Ancient Mediterranean Sacrifice

Ancient Mediterranean Sacrifice

Edited by Jennifer Wright Knust
and Zsuzsanna Várhelyi

OXFORD
UNIVERSITY PRESS

OXFORD
UNIVERSITY PRESS

Oxford University Press, Inc., publishes works that further
Oxford University's objective of excellence
in research, scholarship, and education.

Oxford   New York
Auckland   Cape Town   Dar es Salaam   Hong Kong   Karachi
Kuala Lumpur   Madrid   Melbourne   Mexico City   Nairobi
New Delhi   Shanghai   Taipei   Toronto

With offices in
Argentina   Austria   Brazil   Chile   Czech Republic   France   Greece
Guatemala   Hungary   Italy   Japan   Poland   Portugal   Singapore
South Korea   Switzerland   Thailand   Turkey   Ukraine   Vietnam

Published by Oxford University Press, Inc.
198 Madison Avenue, New York, New York 10016

www.oup.com

Oxford is a registered trademark of Oxford University Press

Library of Congress Cataloging-in-Publication Data
Ancient Mediterranean sacrifice / edited by Jennifer Wright Knust and Zsuzsanna Várhelyi.
p.   cm.
Includes bibliographical references.
ISBN 978-0-19-973896-0 (hardcover : alk. paper) 1. Sacrifice—Mediterranean Region.
2. Mediterranean Region—Religion. I. Knust, Jennifer Wright, 1966- II. Várhelyi, Zsuzsanna.
BL687.A53   2011
203'.4—dc22   2010041715

{ CONTENTS }

PART III: **Toward a Theology of Sacrifice**

PART IV: **Imaginary Sacrifice**

    KATHRYN MCCLYMOND

13. **Passing: Jesus' Circumcision and Strategic Self-Sacrifice**   251
    ANDREW S. JACOBS

14. **Confounding Blood: Jewish Narratives of Sacrifice and Violence in Late Antiquity**   265
    RA'ANAN S. BOUSTAN

    Bibliography   287
    Index   325

{ ACKNOWLEDGMENTS }

This volume originated in the conference "What the Gods Demand: Blood Sacrifice in Mediterranean Antiquity," held at Boston University (BU) in November 2008, and as editors we owe sincere gratitude to all those who have supported this project. Our goal in gathering a group of scholars from the United States, Europe, and Israel was to engage in a lively discussion about the multiple meanings and functions of sacrifice across the Greek, Roman, Jewish, and Christian traditions. We wish to thank all those who attended and contributed to the many spirited exchanges that took place both before and after the stimulating presentations of panelists. We are especially grateful to conference presenters and respondents; their steady alacrity and insightful engagement with each other's arguments made our organizational and then editorial tasks easy.

The conference would not have been possible without the generous support of Boston University, especially our home departments of Classical Studies and Religion and the School of Theology. Key support was also provided by the Brown Lecture Series (School of Theology), the Center for Philosophy and History of Science, the College of Arts and Sciences, the Development and Alumni Relations Office at the School of Theology, the Boston University School of Theology Student Association, the Elie Wiesel Center for Judaic Studies, the Florence Chavetz Hillel House, the Humanities Foundation at Boston University, the Luce Program in Scripture and Literary Arts, and the William Goodwin Aurelio Endowment. We are also grateful to the American Academy of Religion's New England Maritimes Region for their important sponsorship.

The organizational work of the conference could not possibly have been completed without the invaluable assistance of Krista Millay, an outstanding doctoral student at the School of Theology, as well as Stacy Fox and Melissa Joseph in the Department of Classical Studies. Many students from the Departments of Classics and Religion as well as the School of Theology volunteered to help with registration and other tasks throughout the conference, reminding us once again of just how lucky we are to work with such dedicated young scholars. We are further indebted to Krista Millay for her continued participation throughout the editing process; her careful work has been much appreciated.

We wish to express our deep appreciation to many colleagues in the Boston area and beyond who agreed to respond to the papers presented at the conference: Oded Irshai (The Hebrew University), Thomas Kazen (Stockholm School of Theology), Jonathan Klawans (BU), Ross Kraemer (Brown University), Larry Myer and Kimberly Patton (Harvard University), Stephen Scully (BU), James Walters (BU), and Lawrence Wills (Episcopal Divinity School). Their astute comments enriched both the conference and this volume. Others colleagues chaired sessions, including Mark Alonge, Katheryn Pfisterer Darr, Jeffrey Henderson, Deeana Klepper, Loren J. Samons II, Courtney Wilson VanVeller, Michael Zank, all from Boston University, as well as Peter Hawkins from Yale University and Kimberly B. Stratton from Carlton University. Prior publishing commitments kept some of the original essays from inclusion in the current volume, but we remain grateful to these participants for their significant contributions. A heartfelt thank you to Joan Branham (Providence College), Jan Bremmer (University of Groningen), Paula Fredriksen (Boston University), J. Albert Harrill (Indiana University), and Sarah Iles Johnston (Ohio State University) for presenting papers and making our discussions all the more comprehensive.

Acknowledgement is also gratefully made to Theo Calderara and the staff at Oxford University Press for offering such a welcoming home for our volume. We are indebted to the anonymous referees for their crucial suggestions and to all of those who played a part in the production of this volume.

Boston University, 2010

{ CONTRIBUTORS }

Ra'anan Boustan, Assistant Professor in the Departments of History and Near Eastern Languages and Cultures at UCLA and Director of the UCLA Center for the Study of Religion, is a scholar of Jewish culture, literature, and society in late antiquity. Author of *From Martyr to Mystic: Martyrology and the Making of Merkavah Mysticism* (2005) and coeditor of *Heavenly Realms and Earthly Realities in Late Antique Religions* (2004) and of *Violence, Scripture, and Textual Practice in Early Judaism and Christianity* (2010), he was a recent fellow of the University of Pennsylvania's Center for Advanced Judaic Studies.

David Frankfurter, Aurelio Professor for the Appreciation of Scripture at Boston University and formerly Professor of Religious Studies and History at the University of New Hampshire, is a comparative scholar of ancient religions, specializing in Roman and late-antique Egypt. Author of the award-winning books *Religion in Roman Egypt* (1998) and *Evil Incarnate: Rumors of Demonic Conspiracy and Satanic Abuse in History* (2006), as well as many articles and essays on such topics as magic and Christianization, he has held fellowships with the Institute for Advanced Study (Princeton University), the Guggenheim Foundation, and the Radcliffe Institute for Advanced Study.

William K. Gilders, Associate Professor and Associate Director of the Graduate Division in Religion at Emory University, is a professor of Hebrew Bible with interests in literary criticism, ritual theory, and gender. Author of *Blood Ritual in the Hebrew Bible: Meaning and Power* (2004), he has written extensively on ritual and sacrifice in ancient Israel and early Judaism.

Fritz Graf, Professor and Chair of the Department of Greek and Latin at the Ohio State University, is an internationally known scholar and author with publications in German, French, Italian, and English. An expert on Greek and Roman religions, he is author or editor of more than a dozen books, including the recent *Apollo* (2008), as well as *Ritual Texts for the Afterlife: The Bacchic Gold Tablets* (2007), which is coauthored with Sarah Iles Johnston.

Andrew S. Jacobs, Associate Professor of Religious Studies at Scripps College, is author of *Remains of the Jews: The Holy Land and Christian Empire in Late Antiquity* (2004) and the forthcoming book *Christ Circumcised: A Study in Early Christian History and Difference*. An expert on late-antique Jewish-Christian interface, he serves on the editorial board of the *Journal of Christian Studies* and on the council of the American Society of Church History.

Jonathan Klawans, Associate Professor of Religious Studies and Director of the Division of Religious and Theological Studies at Boston University, is a specialist in the religion and religious literature of ancient Judaism. Author of the award-winning and highly regarded books *Impurity and Sin in Ancient Judaism* and *Purity* (2000), *Sacrifice and the Temple* (2006), he has also published a number of articles in the *AJS Review, Harvard Theological Review, Journal of Jewish Studies, New Testament Studies, Numen,* and *Religious Studies Review.*

Jennifer Wright Knust, Associate Professor of New Testament and Christian Origins at Boston University, is author of *Abandoned to Lust: Sexual Slander and Ancient Christianity* (2005). Currently completing a book on the transmission of the story of the woman taken in adultery (John 8:1–11), she has held recent fellowships from the Henry Luce III Foundation/Association of Theological Schools and the Humanities Foundation at Boston University.

Kathryn McClymond, Associate Professor and Chair of the Department of Religious Studies, Georgia State University, is a professor of the comparative history of religions, with a particular focus on Judaism, Hinduism and ritual theory. Author of the recent book, *Beyond Sacred Violence: A Comparative Study of Sacrifice* (2008), as well as several other essays, she is a steering committee member for the Comparative Studies in Religion Section of the American Academy of Religion.

Laura Nasrallah, Associate Professor of New Testament and Christian Origins at Harvard Divinity School, is author of *An Ecstasy of Folly: Prophecy and Authority in Early Christianity* (2003) and *Christian Responses to Roman Art and Architecture: The Second-Century Church Amid the Spaces of Empire* (2010). She is coeditor of *Prejudice and Christian Beginnings: Investigating Race, Gender, and Ethnicity in Early Christian Studies* (2009). Her work is informed by feminist and postcolonial criticisms and focuses on New Testament and Early Christian literature in the context of the archaeological remains of the Roman world.

James Rives, Kenan Eminent Professor of Classics at the University of North Carolina at Chapel Hill, is author of *Religion and Authority in Roman Carthage* (1995), a commentary on Tacitus's *Germania* (1999) and the highly acclaimed *Religion in the Roman Empire* (2007). An expert in the religions of the Roman imperial period, he is particularly interested in the interrelation of religion with sociopolitical power and the nature of religious change between the first century BCE and the fourth century CE.

Michele R. Salzman, Professor of History at the University of California, Riverside, is author of *On Roman Time: The Codex-Calendar of 354 and the Rhythms of Urban Life in Late Antiquity* (1990) and *The Making of a Christian Aristocracy* (2002) as well as several other studies of religion in late antiquity. Currently completing a commentary and translation of the letters of Symmachus, she is on the editorial board of the *American Journal of Archaeology*.

Stanley K. Stowers, Professor of Religious Studies at Brown University, is author of the ground-breaking study *A Rereading Romans: Justice, Jews and the Gentiles* (1994). A scholar of early Christian history and literature, ancient philosophy, and Greek religion, he has also published several articles on Greek sacrifice, religion and the Greco-Roman household, and theoretical approaches to the study of religion.

Philippa Townsend, Assistant Professor at Ursinus College, currently holds a National Endowment for the Humanities Fellowship at the W. F. Albright Institute for Archaeological Research in Jerusalem. She earned her Ph.D. in Religion at Princeton University in 2009, and is reworking her dissertation, *Another Race? Ethnicity, Universalism, and the Emergence of Christianity*, into a monograph. She has written articles on first-century Christianity and the Gospel of Judas, and has an edited volume forthcoming, with Moulie Vidas, entitled *Revelation, Literature, and Society in Late Antiquity*.

Daniel Ullucci, Visiting Assistant Professor at Bowdoin College, earned his Ph.D. at Brown University in 2009 and is currently reworking his dissertation, *The End of Animal Sacrifice*, into a monograph.

Zsuzsanna Várhelyi, Associate Professor of Classical Studies at Boston University, works primarily on Roman social, cultural, and religious history. She is author of essays on Roman religion, sacrifice, and ancient society. Her monograph, *The Religion of Senators in the Roman Empire: Power and the Beyond*, appeared with Cambridge University Press in 2010.

{ ABBREVIATIONS }

1 Clem	1 Clement
1QS	*Rule of the Community*
Aesch.	Aeschines
In Ctes.	*Against Ctesiphon*
AJA	*American Journal of Archaeology*
AJAH	*American Journal of Ancient History*
Ambrose	
Ep.	*Epistles*
AB	Anchor Bible Series
ACW	Ancient Christian Writers
Andoc.	Andocides
ANF	*Ante-Nicene Fathers*
ANRW	*Aufstieg und Niedergang der römischen Welt*
AnTard	Antiquité Tardive
Anth. Lat.	*Anthologia Latina*
App.	Appian
BC	*Bellum civile*
Ar.	Aristophanes
Av.	*Aves*
Nub.	*Nubes*
Ran.	*Ranae*
Arist.	Aristotle
AS	*Annali di storia dell'esegesi*
Ath.	Athenaeus
Athenagoras	
Leg.	*Legatio pro Christianis*
August.	Augustine
De civ. D.	*De civitatae Dei*
Ep.	*Epistles*
Aulus Gell.	Aulus Gellius
NA	*Noctes Atticae*
b. Metzi'a	Babylonian Talmud, Tractate Bava Metzi'a
Barn	*Epistle of Barnabas*
b'Arak	Babylonian Talmud, Tractate 'Arakhin
BEHE SR	Bibliothèque de l'École des Hautes Études Sciences religieuses
Bernabé	A. Bernabé
PEG	*Poetarum epicorum Graecorum*
bGit	Babylonian Talmud, Tractate Gittin
Bib	*Biblica*

BICS	*Bulletin of the Institute of Classical Studies*
BIFAO	Bulletin de l'Institut Français d'Archéologie Orientale
bSan	Babylonian Talmud, Tractate Sanhedrin
BT	Bibliotheca Scriptorum Graecorum et Romanorum Teubneriana
BTEL	Bibliotheca Ephemeridum Theologicarum Lovaniensium
bZev	Babylonian Talmud, Tractate Zevahim
BZNW	*Beihefte zur Zeitschrift für die neutestamentliche Wissenschaft und die Kunde der älteren Kirche*
C. Th.	*Codex Theodosianus*
CAH	Cambridge Ancient History
Cass. Dio	Cassius Dio, *Roman History*
CCL	Corpus Christianorum series Latina
CD	Cairo Genizah copy of the *Damascus Document*
CEFR	Common European Framework for References
Cic.	Cicero
De off.	*De officiis*
Fam.	*Epistulae ad familiares*
Leg.	*De legibus*
Nat. D.	*De natura deorum*
Tusc. Disp.	*Tusculanae disputationes*
CIL	*Corpus Inscriptionum Latinarium*
Clem. Al.	Clement of Alexandria
Protr.	*Protrepticus*
Strom.	*Stromateis*
Cod. Iust.	*Codex Iustinianus*
CSEL	Corpus Scriptorum Ecclesiasticorum Latinorum
Cyprian	
Ep.	*Epistles*
DAIR	Deutsches Archäologisches Institut, Rome
Dem.	Demosthenes
54	Oration 54, *Against Conon*
Dio of Prusa	Dio Chrysostom
Or.	*Rhodian Oration* (31)
Diod.	Diodorus Siculus
Diog.	*Epistle to Diognetus*
Diog. Laert.	Diogenes Laertius
EcclR	Ecclesiastes Rabbah
EE	*Ephemeris epigraphica. Corporis inscriptionum Latinarum supplementum.* Rome and Berlin: Georgium Reimerum, 1872–1913.
Epiph.	Epiphanius
Eur.	Euripides
Hipp.	*Hippolytus*
Euseb.	Eusebius
Praep. evang.	*Praeparatio evangelica*
FC	Fathers of the Church

Festus *L*	Festus, *Glossaria*
FGrHist	*Die Fragmente der griechischen Historiker*
GCS	Die Griechischen Christlichen Schriftsteller der ersten drei Jahrhunderte
Gelasius	
Ep.	*Epistles*
Hdt.	Herodotus
Heliod	Heliodorus
Aeth.	*Aethiopica*
Hesiod	
Th.	*Theogony*
Hom.	Homer
Il.	*Iliad*
Hor.	Horace
HSCP	*Harvard Studies in Classical Philology*
HTR	*Harvard Theological Review*
HUCA	*Hebrew Union College Annual*
Iambl.	Iamblichus
Myst.	*De Mysteriis*
VP	*Vita Pythagorae*
IG	*Inscriptiones Graecae*, Berlin, 1873–
JAAR	*Journal of the American Academy of Religion*
JANER	*Journal of Ancient Near Eastern Religions*
JBL	*Journal of Biblical Literature*
JECS	*Journal of Early Christian Studies*
JHS	*Journal of Hellenic Studies*
Joseph.	Josephus
Ant.	*Jewish Antiquities*
C. Ap.	*Contra Apionem*
JQR	*Jewish Quarterly Review*
JRS	*Journal of Roman Studies*
JSNT	*Journal of the Study of the New Testament*
JSNTSup	Journal for the Study of the New Testament Supplement
JSOTSup	Journal for the Study of the Old Testament Supplement
Justin Martyr	
Apol.	*Apologia*
Dial.	*Dialogus cum Tryphone*
Justinian	
CJ	*Corpus Iuris Civilis*
Lactant.	Lactantius
Div. inst.	*Divinae institutions*
LamR	Lamentations Rabbah
LCL	Loeb Classical Library
LevR	Leviticus Rabbah
Lib.	Libanius
Livy	

AUC	*Ab urbe condita libri*
Per.	*Periochae*
LSJ	H.G. Liddell, R. Scott, and H. Jones, *A Greek-English Lexicon with Revised Supplement* (Oxford: Oxford University Press, 1996).
Lucian	
Icar.	*Icaromenippus*
Iupp. conf.	*Iuppiter confutatus*
Iupp. trag.	*Iuppiter tragoedus*
De sacr.	*On Sacrifices*
Lucr.	Lucretius
Lys.	Lysias
M. Ber.	*Mishnah Berakot*
M. Ker	*Mishnah Keritot*
M. Meg.	*Mishnah Megillah*
M. Pesachim	*Mishnah Pesachim*
M. Shab.	*Mishnah Shabbat*
M. Zev.	*Mishnah Zevachim*
Macrob.	Macrobius
Sat.	*Saturnalia*
Migne	J.-P. Migne
PG	*Patrologiae cursus completus: series Graeca*
PL	*Patrologiae cursus completus: series Latina*
Min. Fel.	Minucius Felix
Oct.	*Octavius*
NICC	New International Critical Commentary
NPNF	*Nicene and Post-Nicene Fathers*
NT	New Testament
OBT	Overtures to Biblical Theology
OGI	Orientis Graeci Inscriptiones Selectae
Origen	
C. Cels.	*Contra Celsum*
Ov.	Ovid
Fast.	*Fasti*
Met.	*Metamorphoses*
P. Genève	Geneva Papyri
P. Oxy	Oxyrhynchus Papyri (1898–)
PGM	K. Preisendanz and others (eds.), *Papyri Graecae Magicae: Die griechischen Zauberpapyri*, 2 vols. 2nd ed. (1973–74).
Philo	
Spec. Laws	*On the Special Laws*
Philostr.	Philostratus
VA	*Vita Apollonii*
Pind.	Pindar
Ol.	*Olympian Odes*
Pl.	Plato

Criti.	*Critias*
Euthphr.	*Euthyphro*
Leg.	*Leges*
Resp.	*Respublica*
Plaut.	Plautus
Rud.	*Rudens*
Plin. (E)	Pliny (the Elder)
NH	*Naturalis historia*
Plin. (Y)	Pliny (the Younger)
Ep.	*Epistulae*
Pan.	*Panegyricus*
PLRE	*Prosopography of the Later Roman Empire*
Plut.	Plutarch
Mor.	*Moralia*
Conv. sept. sap.	*Convivium septem sapientium*
De def. or.	*De defectu oraculorum*
De esu	*De esu*
De. Is. et Os.	*De Iside et Osiride*
De soll. an.	*De sollertia animalium*
De superst.	*De superstitione*
Quaest. Rom	*Quaestiones Romanae*
Vit.	*Vitae Parallelae*
Arist.	*Aristides*
G. Gracch.	*Gaius Gracchus*
Phil.	*Philopoemen*
Sol.	*Solon*
Ti. Gracch	*Tiberius Gracchus*
Porph.	Porphyry
Abst.	*De Abstinentia*
Plot.	*Via Plotini*
Vit. Pyth.	*Vita Pythogorae*
Prudent.	Prudentius
Apoth.	*Apotheosis*
RE	A. Pauly, G. Wissowa, and W. Kroll, Real-Encyclopädie der klassischen Altertumswissenschaft (1893–)
REA	*Revue des études anciennes*
RRC	*Roman Republican Coinage.* Michael H. Crawford (Cambridge: Cambridge University Press, 1974; repr. 2001).
SBLDS	Society of Biblical Literature Dissertation Series
SBLSMS	Society of Biblical Literature Monograph Series
SC	Sources chrétiennes
Sen.	Seneca
Ep.	*Epistulae*
Servius	
Comm. Ad Aen.	*Commentary to the Aeneid*
SongR	Song of Songs Rabbah

Sozom.	Sozomen
Hist. eccl.	*Historia ecclesiastica*
STDJ	Studies on the Texts of the Desert of Judah
StPatr	Studia Patristica
Strabo	
Geog.	*Geography*
Suda	Suidae Lexicon
Suet.	Suetonius
Aug.	*Divus Agustus*
Syll.3	W. Dittenberger, *Sylloge Inscriptionum Graecarum*, 3rd ed. (1915–24).
Tac.	Tacitus
Ann.	*Annales*
Hist.	*Historiae*
TAPA	*Transactions of the American Philological Association*
Tatian	
Ad Gr.	*Oratio ad Graecos*
Ter.	Terence
Phorm.	*Phormio*
Tert.	Tertullian
Adv. Marcionmen	*Adversus Marcionem*
De idol.	*De idololatria*
TGI	Theologie und Glaube
ThesCRA	Thesaurus Cultus et Rituum Antiquorum
TSAJ	Text und Studien zum antiken Judentum
TLG	Thesaurus Linguae Graecae
TU	Texte und Untersuchungen zur Geschichte der altchristlichen Literatur
UF	*Ugarit-Forschungen*
Val. Max.	Valerius Maximus
Varro	
Ant. div.	*Antiquitates rerum divinarum*
VC	*Vigiliae Christianae*
Vell. Pat.	Velleius Paterculus
Vet. Val.	Vettius Valens, *Anthologies* 7.1
Xen.	Xenophon
Eg. mag.	*De equitum magistro*
Mem.	*Memorabilia*
Symp.	*Symposium*
VTSup	Supplements to Vetus Testamentum
yTa'an	Jerusalem/Palestinian Talmud, Tractate Ta'anit
yYom	Jerusalem/Palestinian Talmud, Tractate Yoma'
Zachariah of Mytilene	
V. Severi	*Life of Severus*
ZAW	*Zeitschrift für die alttestamentliche Wissenschaft*

Ancient Mediterranean Sacrifice

{ Introduction }

IMAGES, ACTS, MEANINGS AND ANCIENT
MEDITERRANEAN SACRIFICE
Jennifer Wright Knust and Zsuzsanna Várhelyi

The chapters in this volume reconsider ancient sacrifice as interpreted and practiced in multiple contexts across the ancient Mediterranean world during the late Hellenistic and Roman periods. By considering sacrifice within diverse religious texts and practices, but within a shared geographical region and limited chronological frame, our goal has been to illuminate both the connections between—and the disjunctures among—ancient religions and, in the process, to investigate the very category of "sacrifice" (θυσία, *sacrificium*). As a number of our contributors demonstrate, it is becoming apparent that searching for a single definition of sacrifice capable of encapsulating such diverse practices and discourses is fruitless, even as the meanings ascribed to sacrifice and the proper ways of relating to it were brought into new focus as the cultures of the ancient Mediterranean encountered one another, under Greek and then Roman rule. By gathering together essays that address a diverse set of sacrificial acts, theories, and points of view, this volume engages both the conceptualizations of sacrifice implied within ancient discourses and also the practices that undergirded these discourses.

In recent decades, there have been important reassessments of the multiple meanings and functions of sacrifice in the ancient world. What we learned is that whether understood as an act of *imitatio Dei*, a ritual designed to appease a deity, or as a substitutionary offering intended to ward off danger, it seems increasingly futile to explain sacrifices solely in terms of surrogate victims or a need for a blood-letting that atones. Reconsiderations of human sacrifice have added a further point connecting the practice of sacrifice to the rhetorical function of charges of ritual murder in literary sources and to ceremonial death in numerous cultural settings.[1] The essays in this volume contribute to these theoretical advances, particularly those that challenge the metonymical equation of sacrifice-religion and sacrifice-violence. Inviting careful analysis and comparison of practices, ideologies, and acts, our essays demonstrate that it is time to move beyond the exclusive identification of ancient sacrifice with aggression or a "primitive" impulse.

Approaching ancient sacrifice in a new way requires attention to the particular and local character of both practices and meanings as well as a recognition that sacrifice is often a contested, fluid category. As Folkert Van Straten has argued, sacrifice is better understood if we think of it as "a continuous field of overlapping shades of meaning or potential meaning" rather than as a single, static category.[2] Participants at the very same ritual performance may not share the same set of assumptions or symbolic associations, even when taking part in shared ritual acts. Thus varied meanings, functions, and symbols can coexist simultaneously—not only among distinct religious groups, but even within a shared interpretative circle. Despite this variety, sacrifice remained both a dominant metaphor and a wide-spread practice in antiquity; more often than not, the importance of sacrificial rit-uals could simply be assumed. Even in late antiquity, after pagan sacrifices had been banned and temples refounded as Christian churches, sacrificial images, acts, and meanings did not so much end as change. Christianity positioned itself in contrast to Roman imperial sacrifice, yet, as Guy G. Stroumsa has insisted, "Christianity defined itself precisely as a religion centered on sacrifice." Even with the Jerusa-lem Temple destroyed, Judaism and Christianity both became "sacrificial religions without blood sacrifice," not nonsacrificial religions.[3] At the same time, elite pagans displayed some flexibility in the face of imperially sponsored Christian aggression that enabled some forms of ancient paganisms to survive, albeit in altered forms. Sacrifice as a practice and a symbol, then, endured as a key site upon which iden-tities, relationships, and difference were both theorized and performed long after sacrifice had been formally brought to an end.

Sacrifice, Violence, and the "Primitive"

The effort to define sacrifice across the multiple cultures of the ancient Mediterra-nean has been foundational to debates concerning the meaning and significance of modernity itself.[4] Defining the abandonment of blood sacrifice as a central sign of European civilization, nineteenth-century scholars argued that modernity was a "natural" development produced at the intersections of the very pagan, Jewish, and Christian practices and discourses we investigate in this volume. Sacrifice was clas-sified as a principal sign of the "primitive," necessarily antithetical to the "modern" achievement toward which civilized Europe was (inevitably) heading.[5] Civilization could therefore be measured, charted, and assessed, according to the degree to which sacrifice had been successfully overcome.

Placing sacrificial ritual within such an evolutionary scheme, Edward Burnett Tylor suggested in 1871 that the most primitive form of sacrifice involved sacrifice as a gift, given by primitive peoples to a deity "as if he were a man" with the hope that the divine favor would be bestowed in return.[6] This form of sacrifice, he argued, is naturally overturned by historical progress: as human cultures develop, both the meanings ascribed to sacrifice and the intentions of the sacrificer become increasingly complex, culminating finally in the Christian (Catholic) view of sacrifice as substitutionary atonement. But even this form of sacrifice is primitive, he insisted. With the advancement of (European) civilization, the gods grow more distant and finally recede altogether, making sacrifice obsolete. Rooted in error, sacrifice and its vestiges survive only within the "lesser" civilizations, whether in Mediterranean antiquity or among the less developed peoples of the world of Tylor's contemporaries.[7]

Theorists of the following generation modified Tylor's approach, but retained his evolutionary framework. In 1890 James George Frazer published the first edition of his highly influential study, *The Golden Bough*, a work he continued to revise and expand throughout his long career. Though widely criticized today, Frazer's project was essential to the establishment of the myth-and-ritual school in the study of ancient religion.[8] While working to develop a theory of myth, he came to understand ritual, and not myth, as primary in the development of religion, a conclusion he reached on the basis of his study of the ancient cult of Diana at Aricia.[9] The primeval cycle of the symbolic death and then revival of the priest enacted in the context of this cult marked for Frazer the pattern underlying all ritual activity:[10] a ritual murder capable of guaranteeing fertility and well-being was therefore at the heart of sacrifice.[11] To mention a few representative examples, from his perspective, myths and practices associated with the death and resurrection of the god Adonis dramatized the cycle of the seasons from fall to winter to spring;[12] bull testicles sacrificed and blood shed in the cult of Attis offered "a powerful charm to promote fertility and hasten new birth";[13] and the rites of Osiris magically ensured the regeneration of plants and the multiplication of animals.[14] Under the influence of Christianity, however, such superstitious "magic" eventually gave way to "religion," which led to the retreat and reconfiguration of sacrifice, if not its underlying principles. The desire for fertility and the wish that nature could be controlled linger on, he argued, looking forward to a better day when religion would finally be superseded by science altogether, and thus both sacrifice and religion would cease.[15]

Sacrifice and the Social

A different approach to sacrifice was taken by William Robertson Smith's *The Religion of the Semites* (1889), which sought an explanation for sacrifice in social relationships rather than primitive impulses. A professor of Arabic at Cambridge, he selected the cult of ancient Israel as his particular example, situating Israel's sacrificial practices within a larger historical frame of progress and development.[16] Emphasizing the communal aspects of the sacrificial meal, he suggested that the rite of sacrifice produces groups of kin bound together by both common ancestry and ritual practice.[17] Since the "fundamental ideal of ancient sacrifice is sacramental communion," he pointed out, Christian or Israelite sacrifices "owe their efficacy to a communication of divine life to the worshippers." To Robertson Smith, sacrifice, growing out of a community meal, preceded any ethical interpretation of the practice by biblical writers, and the ideals affixed to early Israelite sacrificial practice by biblical writers represent a later time in Israel's historical development. Yet he also argued that the original context of sacrifice had staying power and that "Hebrew religion" remained troubled by savage desires and impulses, especially those expressed in the purity regulations of Leviticus.[18]

The end of the nineteenth century brought both a rethinking of evolutionary models and a more decisive turn toward the kind of sociological and psychological explanations of sacrifice that were anticipated in Robertson Smith's work, even as the quest for sacrifice's true origin—and therefore its essential meaning—endured. In 1898, Henri Hubert and Marcel Mauss published their renowned "Essai sur la Nature et la Fonction du Sacrifice," followed soon after by Émile Durkheim's *Les formes élementaires de la vie religieuse* and Sigmund Freud's *Über einige Übereinstimmungen im Seelenleben der Wilden und der Neurotiker*, later known as *Totem und Tabu* (1912–13).[19] All three works were influenced by Tylor, Frazer, and, above all, Robertson Smith, and all three sought to explain the origins and modern remains of sacrificial practice emphasizing a social perspective, even if they retained some evolutionary interests.

According to Hubert and Mauss, earlier interpreters had failed to uncover the essential unity that undergirds the multiplicity of sacrificial forms: the necessity that the sacrificial victim (animal, vegetable, or human) be destroyed.[20] Against Robertson Smith, they argued that the "totem"—a symbol of communal identity and survival—is not the appropriate place to locate sacrificial meaning. Not every tribe has a totem that is sacrificed and then eaten for the sake of community preservation. Rather, sacrificial expiation is not a secondary stage in the evolution of sacrifice but its primary function.[21] "The expulsion of a sacred spirit" by means of sacrificial killing is, according to Hubert and Mauss, the "primordial component" of the practice, not a secondary accretion gained only after the original purpose of sacrifice has been forgotten.[22] The essential meaning of sacrifice was therefore to be found not in a scheme of historical progress, but in sacrifice's primordial mediating function. Every sacrifice establishes "a means of communication between the sacred and the profane worlds through the mediation of a victim, that is, of a thing that in the course of the ceremony is destroyed."[23] To Hubert and Mauss, violence against the sacrificial victim provided an indispensable, unifying significance to the sacrificial act, which led to community integration.

Inspired, in part, by the challenge of Hubert and Mauss to more fully account for the social function of sacrifice, and also by Robertson Smith's earlier observation that sacrifice is an act of "alimentary communion," Durkheim connected his study of sacrifice to a much larger claim: religion is uniformly the product of human societies. Sacrifice, he argued, keeps the gods of the group alive. Were it not for the repeated performance of a cult to honor these gods, they would cease to exist, as would the sense of cohesion produced for the group assembled to worship them.[24] Everywhere and in every epoch, he argued, human beings will seek to uphold and reaffirm their identity as a collectivity; thus, as long as there are common sentiments, there will be religion, for science cannot fulfill this function.[25] Nevertheless, on Durkheim's reading, the actual performance of sacrifice remains an activity largely limited to primitives, convinced as they are that the benefits they seek for their clan cannot be obtained apart from a ceremonial spilling of blood and the ritual re-enlivening of the life they seek to control.

The Psychology of Sacrifice

Hubert and Mauss's emphasis on sacrifice as a substitution and Roberson Smith's claim that sacrifice is a communal rite received further elaboration in the work of Sigmund Freud. Freud connected his work on neuroses, which he understood to be rooted in the repression of incestuous desires, to the repressed desire to kill the totem animal. According to Freud, the murder of the sacrificial victim recalled and repeated the primal murder of the father, with the victim serving as the substitute for the all-powerful father figure, murdered and consumed by his sons at some distant point in the history of primitive man.[26] Sacrifice from this perspective fulfills two needs: it expresses a violent desire, while, at the same time, it works to alleviate the guilt associated with the murder. As Freud explained, following the primordial murder of the father, the sons were consumed by remorse at what they had done, and so formulated religion to assuage their guilt. This guilt continues to serve as the primary—though unconscious—motivation for religion to this day. "Society," he explained, "is now based on complicity in the common crime," and "religion on the sense of guilt and the consequent remorse," a pattern that is repeated, over and over, in the sacrificial rite. Though the solemn killing of the father was soon replaced by the solemn execution of an animal substitute, this animal nevertheless bears the "sin" of the primeval execution.[27] Applying this same insight to Christianity, Freud observed: "the Christian communion is a new setting aside of the father, a repetition of the crime that must be expiated."[28] Sacrifice, on this account, retained an original element, hidden in the unconscious desires and irrational practices of civilized man.[29]

The Violence at the Heart of Sacrifice

In the 1920s and 1930s, the claim that primal violence lies at the heart of sacrifice was given renewed emphasis by Karl Meuli, who argued this view on the basis of Greek religion. Connecting Greek practices to the rituals of prehistoric hunters, Meuli posited a continuity between rituals associated with hunting and those described in Greek myth, arguing that sacrifice alleviates the guilt associated with the murder of the hunted animal. Gathering bones, raising the skull of the victim, and honoring the animal's carcass, the tribe attempts to relieve anxiety about the cost of killing for the sake of the life of the community by inventing ritual "comedies of innocence" in which the blame for the murder is displaced.[30] Olympic sacrifice follows a similar pattern, he argued, which is why the participants in the events ate the meat but left the bones to the gods. Just as hunters once reassembled the bones in a primitive attempt to "resurrect" the animal and thereby ward off the guilt of the murder, the Greeks offered bones to the gods even as they consumed the choice portions of the animal themselves.

Building on Meuli's influential thesis, in his *Homo Necans* (1972), Walter Burkert developed a similarly substitutionary theory, which suggested that sacrifice is ritual killing formulated as a response to the violent experiences of Paleolithic hunters.[31] Caught in the demand that they must kill to live, hunters relieved their anxieties by sanctifying violence against some, whether animal or human, in order to contain violence against others, most crucially, against members of their own community.[32] As he explained, "Civilized life endures only by giving a ritual form to the brute force that still lurks in men."[33] He then applied this theory to the Panathenaic festival in Athens, the sacrificial processions in Sparta, the sacrifices associated with the Eleusinian mysteries, the cult of Dionysus, and other Greek practices—all of which, on his reading, recall the primitive hunt. In every one of these cases, he argued, communal feasting and ritual killing offered the necessary solution to the paradox of maintaining life at the cost of death.[34]

René Girard's influential monograph *La violence et le sacré* (1972) has done the most to popularize the notion that violence is the very heart of sacrifice. Sacrifice protects the community from its own violence, he claimed, by drawing that violence toward a single victim whose death "stems this rising tide of indiscriminate substitutions" and redirects it "into 'proper' channels."[35] In contrast to Freud, Girard found the origin of violence not in the desire for the death of the father—and the concomitant consumption of his power—but in a "mimetic desire," which he defined as the desire to imitate a rival with whom one is competing for a desired object.[36] Since both competitors cannot actually share the desired object, full imitation would necessarily lead to social chaos: thus a mechanism to displace violence is fundamental to civilization. Sacrificial cult offers the solution to this dilemma: by projecting the violence of the group onto a scapegoat, a surrogate victim is found and violence is displaced onto him alone. In this way, the competitor is replaced by a ritual substitute (an animal, an alternative human victim) capable of receiving and alleviating the violent mimetic desires of the members of the group.[37] It is true that modern society appears to have overcome sacrifice, but this apparent progress has been made possible only through the development of a judicial system that shifts the sacrificial act onto a juridical, rationalized process, but without ending it; to Girard, the murderous wish for common desired objects and the violent mechanism of the surrogate victim pervade all human institutions and rituals.[38]

The names of Meuli, Burkert and Girard and the notion that sacrifice is, above all, a mechanism for mediating humankind's primeval violence have dominated studies of sacrifice for more than a century.[39] They emphasize that motivated by guilt, aggression or desire, sacrifice requires blood, killing, and the destruction of a victim. Distracted by "comedies of innocence" (Meuli-Burkert), the brute force of human desire has called forth a ritual capable of channeling the violent fantasies that would lead to social chaos, while also alleviating the remorse associated with the murder of either animal or human victims. Or, as Girard put it, "*Religion*, in its broadest sense, then must be another term for that obscurity that surrounds man's efforts to defend himself by curative or preventative means against his own violence" (emphasis in the original).[40] These readings suggest that sacrifice and violence have been inextricably linked, almost as if they were one phenomenon, which must be solved by modernity, civilization, or a better, "true religion."[41]

Sacrifice as Cuisine

Over the last several decades, however, this primeval connection between sacrifice and violence has also been increasingly challenged, particularly by scholars of antiquity. The ancient myths, practices, beliefs, and texts mined to develop these theories have been thoroughly reevaluated, and the view that sacrifice is essentially, or even primarily, about killing can no longer be maintained. Already in 1979, the volume *La cuisine du sacrifice en pays grec*, a product of the Center for Comparative Studies of Ancient Societies (Paris), edited by Marcel Detienne and Jean-Pierre Vernant, offered a serious challenge to the view that sacrifice is essentially a violent act, even if the "Paris school" did accept the notion that sacrifice seeks, in part, to handle the guilt of killing.[42] As Detienne pointed out, sacrifice in ancient Greek settings is always associated with meat eating, not with killing per se: "All consumable meat comes from ritually slaughtered animals, and the butcher who sheds the animal's blood bears the same functional name as the sacrificer posted next to the bloody altar."[43] Thus, to the Greeks, sacrifice had to do with the consumption of food. At the same time, sacrifice was also highly political: citizens of the polis were expected to participate in sacrifices, all political activities included a sacrifice followed by a meal, and filial relationships were established with colonies by means of such ritual meals.[44] Jean-Louis Durand expanded this point of view, arguing that the politics of sacrifice were expressed through the distribution of the meat, with the divisions of animal portions reflecting and upholding the social order among the divine and human participants.[45] The distribution of the meat divides the animal in order to knit together the community, including humans and gods, affirming particular social structures that then appear to be eternal and unquestionable. As these authors point out, the violence of sacrifice was never emphasized in Greek sources; instead, violent sacrificial killing was projected onto non-Greeks, who, at least according to Greek sources, kill their victims cruelly, without asking for permission from those about to be sacrificed.[46]

Attacking the primeval link between violence and sacrifice from a different angle,[47] Jonathan Z. Smith has also noted the importance of food to many forms of sacrificial practice. As he pointed out, there is significant distance between sacrificial rites, hunting, and ritualized violence. "*Animal sacrifice*," he argued, "*appears to *be, universally, the ritual killing of a domesticated animal by agrarian or pastoralist societies*" (emphasis in the original).[48] If sacrifice is intended to overcome some sort of guilt about hunting or killing, then known sacrificial systems hide this "fact" very well. Sacrifice kills domesticated, carefully managed animals, not wild animals captured in the context of a hunt. Sacrifice is therefore inextricably related to alimentation, not to violence, and is fundamental to the "basic cultural process of reduction and ingenuity, of food and cuisine;"[49] interpreting it as a "primitive" rite is mistaken—if by "primitive" we mean characteristic of hunter-gatherer societies. In cultures where sacrifice is theorized in terms of gift giving or offering, a developed notion of property must also be in place, so once again "civilization" is in view.[50] Sacrifice may involve killing, but it is not characteristic of "the primitive," nor is violence the focus of its procedures.

This emphasis on the alimentary aspect of sacrifice, particularly in Greek contexts, has received further support in the work of several classicists. Sarah Pierce, for example, notes that Attic vase paintings do not emphasize killing when depicting *thysia* (sacrifice): the moment of slaughter—the *sphagê*—is only rarely depicted; when it is shown, that moment is only a minor feature within a much larger visual program focusing on the gods' joyous reception of the dedication, the elements of the feast, and the pleasure of those present at the festival. Thus, vase imagery depicts *thysia* as "a visual metaphor for ideas of festivity, celebrations, and blessings," and does not seek to address or explain away an act experienced as "awesome, fearsome or guilty."[51] Vase iconography offers no support to the assumption that ancient Greeks were troubled by the slaughter of animals, and therefore in need of a ritual to alleviate guilt,[52] an observation that has received further confirmation in the work of Stella Georgoudi, who studied the concealment of sacrificial violence in Greek ritual.[53]

Folkert van Straten pointed to further difficulties with the earlier tendency to draw general theories from ancient Greek examples: terminology and variety. The Greek verb *thyein* may come close to the English word "sacrifice," but what about votive offerings of noncomestible objects or offerings of fruits, cakes, or grains? Are these "sacrifices" as well?[54] Robert Parker further noted that the notion that sacrifice involves consecration of a sacrificial victim to a god in the form of a gift makes sense in a Latin context—after all, the term *sacrifice* is drawn from the Latin *sacrificum*— but is ill suited to Greek contexts: the emphasis in *thyein* is on the offering, not on the consecration of the victim.[55] Moreover, as Jesper Svenbro added, *thysia* does not refer to sacrificial destruction but to the burning of the sacrificial shares intended for the gods.[56] Once again, the Greek emphasis is on communion, both with the gods and with one another, not on death or destruction. Burning the designated portions of the sacrifice, the worshipper and the gods communicate regard for one another; they do not negotiate an exchange by means of a violent ritual killing. Most recently, a volume edited by Sarah Hitch and Ian Rutherford has demonstrated the importance of considering the widest possible variety of evidence when evaluating Greek sacrifice; as is so often the case, a close analysis of particular examples complicates the facility of universalizing claims, including those put forward by Burkert and the "Paris school."[57]

Sacrifice and Kinship

Following up on studies of Greek sacrificial ritual that emphasized aspects other than killing, Nancy Jay brought a new element into the discussion in 1991—namely, that, even if sacrifice does not emphasize violence, it enforces gendered hierarchies. Offering Greek practices as a prominent example, Jay argued that sacrificial practice organizes kinship groups, and it does so in such a way that male dominance is promoted. "It is a common feature of unrelated traditions that only adult males—fathers, real and metaphorical—may perform sacrifice," she observed. "Where women are reported as performing sacrifice it is never as mothers, but almost always in some specifically non-childbearing role: as virgins . . ., as consecrated unmarried women, or as post-menopausal women."[58] Animal sacrifice is nearly always related to procreation, producing, and reproducing "forms of intergenerational continuity generated by males, transmitted through males, and transcending continuity through women."[59] In other words, sacrifice manufactures patrilineal lines of kinship at the expense of women, instituting social relations of reproduction in such a way that the ties between fathers and sons are cemented, apart from biological ties with particular mothers.[60]

In 1995, influenced by Jay, Stanley Stowers emphasized both the alimentary setting of Greek sacrifice and its consequences for kinship. Greeks may have attached little significance to the animal's death in their diverse sacrificial practices, he argued, but these functioned to produce and maintain social difference. Largely excluding women, foreigners, and noncitizens, sacrifice bound groups of men together as citizens, and it did so in opposition to others.[61] When it comes to the ancient Greeks, "the significant forms of Greek life were always organized by agnation and the criterion for membership was not birth but sacrifice."[62] Sacrifice organizes society by placing human beings within a cosmic hierarchy in which male citizens, often male citizen-priests, are at the center, but childbearing women, foreigners, noncitizen residents of the city, and illegitimate children are pushed to the periphery. Contrary to Jay, however, Stowers also asserted that Greek sacrifice cannot and should not serve as a stand-in for all sacrifice. Parting company with Durkheim, Hubert and Mauss, Girard, and others, Stowers has insisted that sacrificial practice is local, not universal, and historical, not an abstract essence. One can compare sacrificial practice and function, but without insisting that universal psychological, social, or epistemological traits are to be extracted from the objects of comparison.[63]

Israelite Sacrifice

As we have seen, Greek religion has served as an important object of study on which to debate the nuances of sacrificial practice. Reappraisals of the religious practices of Jews have been equally important. From Robertson Smith's groundbreaking *Lectures on the Religion of the Semites* (1927) to Mary Douglas's influential *Purity and Danger* (1966), a study of the purity regulations in Leviticus,[64]

Israelite and later Jewish forms of sacrifice have been a regular subject of analysis and critique, and, as in the case of Greek religion, earlier arguments regarding the close association between sacrifice and violence have now been roundly challenged. Already in 1966, Mary Douglas resisted the violence hypothesis: her *Purity and Danger*, while interested primarily in pollution, invested sacrifice with profound symbolic significance. Pollution beliefs, including those pertaining to sacrifice, carry a "symbolic load," and, as such, they serve to separate, purify, and demarcate, imposing a system on our "inherently untidy experience."[65] Sacrificial systems, then, do not so much relate to violence as address untidiness, impressing order by means of categorization, taxonomy, and the avoidance of anomalous events and things, which are characterized as dangerous and off limits.[66]

Douglas applied these principles to biblical purity codes, which were taken as highly symbolic and sophisticated interpretations of Israel's natural surroundings. In Douglas's account, Hebrew dietary laws were no longer a sign of "the primitive," but "inspired meditation on the oneness, purity and completeness of God,"[67] an insight she further expanded in *Leviticus as Literature* (1999). In this later interpretation of the same biblical material, Douglas emphasized the culinary aspects of Israelite sacrifice, noting that, as in Greek religion, Hebrew laws were concerned with matters of distribution, cooking, and the allocation of meat to different groups, not with the violence of the slaughter. These concerns, she argued, reflect an underlying logic with both cosmic and social significance: the body of the animal, devoted to different recipients, maps the universe as Leviticus sought to explain it, with God at the summit, Moses in the middle, and the priests and the congregation awaiting God's directives.[68]

Following up on Douglas's studies, Jonathan Klawans has further debunked the conflation of religion, sacrifice, and "the primitive" in studies of Israelite culture.[69] Adopting Douglas's insistence that sacrifice can be both meaningful and highly symbolic, as well as the assertion of Detienne, Vernant, Stowers, and others that sacrificial systems are historically and culturally specific rather than universalizable, Klawans has argued that Hebrew sacrifice was governed, at least in part, by the organizing principle of *imitatio Dei*.[70] In Israelite contexts, on his reading, sacrifice involved controlled killing and eating, behaviors also associated with God—"God, too, selects, kills, looks inside things, and appears on earth as a consuming fire."[71] As imitators of God, Israelite priests did not feel guilty about slaughtering animals, nor did they see themselves as participants in violence that is somehow illegitimate or suspect—quite the opposite. Resisting evolutionary approaches to Israelite practices and texts, Klawans has argued that the sacrificial cult and purity regulations of Israel were complex, diverse, and symbolically significant. They were not simply one step on the road from "the primitive" to "the modern"—an argument that is both specious and supersessionist, charting as it does historical progress from the Greeks through the Jews and finally to the Christians, who, of all religions, are closest to getting symbol and theology "right."

Other scholars have also sought to decouple killing from sacrifice in Israelite practice. Kathryn McClymond has observed that blood manipulation, not the slaughter of the animal, "signals the purpose and personality of each sacrifice."[72] Encouraging scholars of religion to adopt a "polythetic" approach to sacrifice, she has suggested that human activities become sacrificial in character only when formally or intimately connected with other activities. Killing alone is not sacrifice, neither is eating, but "the killing of a preselected animal victim, which is subsequently divided according to traditional guidelines by ritual experts and apportioned to individual participants according to social and religious ranking, is highly sacrificial."[73] Turning this insight to biblical and rabbinic literature, she has noted that killing procedures are only important insofar as they are performed in conjunction with other procedures of distribution. In the case of cereal offerings, no death or destruction takes place. In fact, the goat led into the wilderness as a "sacrificial" expiation for the people on Yom Kippur is not killed at all, but set free. She concluded, "A theoretical approach that views killing as only one of many possible sacrificial manipulations allows us to consider other ways of understanding this act as 'sacrificial.'"[74] In other words, discussions of sacrifice need to attend to the variety of elements that go into particular sacrificial practices, without normalizing any one specific procedure, such as killing, at the expense of others.

William K. Gilders has recommended yet another approach, also resisting the notion that blood manipulation would necessarily involve anxiety about killing. Addressing the peculiarly Israelite ban on the consumption of blood, he has located the meanings of the sacrificial bloodletting not in violence, but in the Israelite observation that blood is life. Without blood, ancient Israelites observed, living creatures cannot live. In the context of Leviticus, then, "the fact that blood is identified with the animation of the body provides the basis for rules governing its treatment."[75] As he was careful to note, texts specifying the ban on eating blood offer no interpretive rationale: rituals are specified, but not their theological or functional significance. Still, limited as it was to priests, blood manipulation did serve to order social-cultural relationships, status, and identity in ancient Israelite society. Thus, whatever biblical texts may or may not say, a possible function of their recommended ritual procedures can be discerned.[76]

David Biale concurs with these assessments: the biblical discourse of blood is a discourse of priestly power, and not a response to violence.[77] Arguing against Jacob Milgrom's magisterial, three-volume work on Leviticus (1992),[78] Biale resisted the notion that the Bible connects homicide, blood, and animal slaughter. He explained:

[I]f the killing of a sacrificial animal had been a capital crime, then only the death of the sacrificer would have atoned for it—clearly an absurdity in any sacrificial religion. Or, conversely, if the blood of the victim could atone for its death, why couldn't some ritual of purification using the blood of the victim suffice for homicide? Since both of these suggestions are patently absurd, it is hard to imagine that biblical culture really thought that the killing of animals for food or sacrifice was a form of murder.[79]

Thus, as in the case of Greek religion, the sacrificial practices of ancient Israel cannot easily be simply reduced to sociological or psychological explanations of violence, murder, and the guilt brought on by killing.

Sacrifice and Empire

While few have sought the origins of ancient sacrificial practices in Roman ritual, recent studies of Roman religion have also challenged earlier general models of sacrifice, noting that, like Greek and Israelite practices, Roman sacrifice was both complex and distinctive. Latin evidence is significantly less focused on the connection between sacrificial killing and the imaginary shared meal between humans and gods, though the ritual meal remained a feature of Roman sacrifice as well. A careful analysis of the distribution of sacrificial meat by John Scheid has demonstrated that, as in the Greek case, the divine-human meal was a key factor in Roman sacrifice, even if Romans were not likely to reference sacrifice as "cuisine."[80] Yet the connection between sacrifice and feasting in Roman culture has also been challenged of late. Among others, Nicole Belayche studied Roman practices of acquiring and consuming meat, which largely depended on the purchase of both sacrificial and nonsacrificial portions.[81] Jörg Rüpke has also emphasized the significant disjunctions between the ritual meal held at occasions of public sacrifice and the regular dining customs in Rome.[82] As Mary Beard, John North, and Simon Price have further asserted, the emphasis in Roman religion, at least in the republican era, was on the priestly skill and wisdom of Roman senators in maintaining order and coping with crises.[83] Feasting seems to have played a less critical role in this conceptualization, with sacrifice more often serving to perform and consecrate various forms of power. The relatively archaic "Plebeian Games" with their feast of Jupiter (*epulum Jovis*) offers an interesting example in this regard: the senatorial priests responsible for this ritual, the *triumviri* (later *septemviri*) *epulones* were first appointed only in the early second century BCE.[84] Further, Roman tradition preserved the introduction of the *lectisternium* ritual, a feast that involved sharing a meal with statues of gods, as an innovation engaging Greek, not Roman gods, suggesting again that the sacrificial feast shared between humans and gods may not have been a central element in Roman ritual practice.[85]

Roman sacrificial customs, then, appear tightly embedded within a complex system of social and political hierarchies, in which public festivals were largely controlled by members of the elite and religion itself was subject to various disciplinary interventions. This was certainly the case with the relatively harsh limitations set by the Roman senate on the popular rituals associated with Dionysus/ Bacchus in 186 BCE. Given the primary role the elite played in facilitating rituals, it seems fitting that the emphasis in Roman depictions of sacrifice was on ritual action over language, and John Scheid has accordingly called Roman sacrifice "a 'credo' expressed by action."[86] The same emphasis on sacrificial action within the larger interpretation of religious piety is further demonstrated by the popularity of representations of sacrifice; these, as James Rives has shown, were among the most frequently employed symbols of piety in Roman visual art.[87]

Under Hellenistic influence, Roman discourse in the late republic increasingly came to identify violent sacrifice as something other people do. Just as classical Greek writers (mis)characterized Scythian, Persian, and Egyptian sacrifice as improper and devoid of any real sacrificial significance,[88] Romans (mis)characterized human sacrifice as a particularly barbarian trait. Thus descriptions of the three instances of Roman "human sacrifice," in 228, 216, and 114/113 BCE, respectively, survive only in sources from the late republic or later—that is, after the middle of the second century BCE—and they offer only hostile interpretations.[89] As time went on, the charge of human sacrifice was in particular employed to identify the "enemy within," a group so distant from truly Roman practice and piety that they were wholly other, even when the group or individual was, for all practical purposes, "Roman," as James Rives has argued.[90] This same phenomenon, when later turned back on Romans by Christians, went on to influence the historiography of Roman religion for centuries. Yet, just as Roman descriptions of Christian ritual ought to be disregarded as evidence of "what Christians were doing," so too ought Christian depictions of Roman sacrifice be considered unreliable glimpses into Roman ritual practice.[91]

Within the history of Roman religion, the late republic also meant that limitations on religion became increasingly less effective under the intense pressure of civil wars and social upheavals. In the final pre-Christian century, political allegations often took the form of accusations regarding religious improprieties, as when Cicero famously claimed that Catiline and his fellow conspirators shared a drink of blood following their participation in human sacrifice.[92] Latin literature from this period regularly offers symbolic interpretations of sacrifice,[93] providing a discursive counterpart to the contentions over practice that were taking place in the civil infighting of the late republic.[94]

From a Roman perspective, peace was finally brought about by the imperial rule of Augustus, which also brought with it a comprehensive religious reorganization that would impact religion in the Roman empire for centuries. As Richard Gordon has convincingly argued, Augustan rule connected the exercise of political power to the primacy of the emperor in such a way that the imperial performance of sacrifice established a firm relationship between religion and the newly enforced social order.[95] Coining the phrase "civic compromise," Gordon suggested that a nexus developed "between (a) the political structure of the empire (summarized in the emperor's relations with both centre and periphery), (b) the use of inequality of wealth to perpetuate structures of dependence more effective than those based on mere violence, and (c) the sacrificial system."[96] While the strong association Gordon makes between public religion and civic life in this model has been criticized,[97] his contribution has been accepted inasmuch as he confirms that imperial rule led to a new association of the larger social order with a sacrificial system, in which the emperor played the prime role.[98] The religious variety and creativity characteristic

of the imperial period suggests that dominance was only one aspect of Roman imperial religion. As John North and others have shown, a "marketplace of religions"
made individual religious choice possible in this period, and, as Gregory Woolf
has suggested, religious variety limited the extent to which the polis religion of
Rome could be exported outside the city walls.[99] Yet, the widespread presence of
the Roman emperor as the model sacrificer shaped the understanding and practice
of sacrifice by Romans, Jews, and Christians alike.

Christian Sacrifice

Christianity developed within this complex mix of Roman, Greek, and Jewish sacrificial practices and concepts; and, as a number of studies have shown, Christians
were just as invested in sacrifice as their neighbors. For example, we can no longer
presume that the Jesus movement hoped to replace sacrificial practice with sacrificial theology, especially while the Jerusalem Temple was still standing. As Paula
Fredriksen has pointed out, the Gospel authors depict Jesus visiting the Temple,
attending Jewish cult festivals, and recommending sacrifice both to his followers
and to those whom he heals. Writing before the destruction of the Temple, the
apostle Paul simply assumed the basic validity of the Jerusalem cult.[100] Reinterpret-
ing the Gospels' Last Supper narratives, Jonathan Klawans has also revised earlier
thinking regarding Jesus' relationship to the Jerusalem cult. These and other Gospel stories do not prove that Jesus positioned himself against the Temple's institutions and practices, despite the views of later Christians, but present Jesus and his
disciples as visiting the Temple regularly, both before and after Jesus' death; moreover, the earliest description of the Last Supper, found in a letter of Paul to the
Corinthian *ekklesia*, emphasizes the seriousness and efficacy of Israel's sacrificial
practice, not its irrelevance in light of Christ.[101] In fact, Paul reserves his critique of
sacrifice for gentile practices alone. Having shared the "cup of the Lord," gentile
followers of Jesus must not share in a "cup of demons" (1 Cor 10:21), a reference to
the widespread practice of eating a common meal in the presence of a patron god.
According to Paul, participating in a communal meal that memorializes Christ,
then, Jesus' gentile followers became the children of a different patron god and were
sealed with the blood of this God's Messiah, a conviction that grants sacrificial and
memorial meaning to their activities.[102] Prior to its destruction, the Temple cult
appears to have been prized as efficacious by Jesus, Paul, and other Messianic Jews,
even among those who viewed Jesus' death as sacrificial.[103]

As Lawrence Wills has shown, by claiming that Jesus' death was both sacrificial
and noble, Christian writers participated in a wider discourse of heroic self-sacrifice
familiar to the pagan texts of the Roman era.[104] Shaping their portraits of Jesus
on the basis of shared traditions regarding endurance during suffering, Christians
also adapted a discursive model already developed among Greek-speaking Jews:
that of the martyr who dies for the law.[105] As Jan Willem van Henten, Tessa Rajak,

and Daniel Boyarin have demonstrated, stories about righteous Jews who died as a result of persecution were popular among Jews long before Christians began to write their own martyrologies.[106] Refusing to compromise with unjust rulers, Jewish martyrs were depicted as gladly welcoming death over the violation of God's covenantal provisions. So, for example, in 2 Maccabees, the death of the martyr Eleazar was presented as "an example of nobility and a memorial of courage, not only to the young but to the great body of his nation" (2 Macc 6:31). Pre-Christian Jewish martyrs "served to encapsulate statements about national identity, to define the nation's relation to outsiders and to explore potential political crises,"[107] a strategy that Christian writers shared. The Gospel of John, for example, emphasized Jesus' exceptional courage throughout his ordeal in such a way that Christian identity and the nobility of Jesus could be defended, as Jennifer Glancy has argued. Rethinking sacrifice, this Gospel works to shift blame away from the tortured victim, Jesus, and toward the torturer, Pilate, interpreting Jesus' marked flesh as a sign of the dominion of God and therefore of Jesus himself.[108]

With the destruction of the Temple, new ways of theorizing martyrdom emerged among Christians and Jews alike. As Stroumsa suggests, the full identification of the martyr with sacrifice could emerge only after sacrifice in the Temple could no longer take place; only then could "such a metaphoric acceptance" be developed.[109] Following the Temple's violent demise, the notion that Jesus' death was a once-and-for-all sacrifice received ever-greater elaboration: Jesus became the Passover lamb, or the immolated goat of Yom Kippur, or a high priest who paradoxically sacrifices himself to establish a new covenant.[110] Still, all of these images of Jesus' death operate within a sacrificial logic, in which the spilling of blood seals the divine-human relationship. In this way, sacrifice was not overturned so much as transformed to a different purpose. As George Heyman suggests, Christians "did not abandon the concept [of sacrifice] or its ritual interpretation"; instead, they "fashioned their discourse of sacrifice . . . in order to oppose the religious and political hegemony of the Roman state."[111] Transferring notions of Jesus as sacrifice, martyr, and innocent victim to representations of Christian martyrs, sacrifice became both the central provocation for martyrdom and also as the central purpose of the martyr's death. Elizabeth Castelli explains: "In refusing to perform sacrifice, Christians removed themselves from the position of agent (sacrificer) to the position of victim (sacrificed)."[112] In this way, the blood of the martyrs was given cultic significance, likened to the animal blood sprinkled on the altar of the Jerusalem Temple by the priests prior to the fulfillment—and replacement—of these sacrifices by Jesus. The martyrs, then, imitate their hero by spilling their blood for the sake of the continuing forgiveness of Christian sin.[113]

Arguably, then, it is the Christians who bequeathed to future generations the metonymic equivalence of sacrifice and violence: envisioning the deaths of Jesus and the martyrs as the only truly efficacious sacrifices, second-century Christians demoted Israelite animal sacrifice to the role of either allegorical precursor or divine concession. Pagan sacrifice, however, was interpreted as demon-inspired violence.

Jesus and the martyrs were portrayed as innocent and willing sacrificial victims who nobly offer themselves for others, while the sacrificers—variously depicted as corrupt representatives of the Roman government or mobs of bloodthirsty Jews—were represented as inherently and wickedly violent. According to this logic, the victim is by definition innocent while the sacrificer is necessarily guilty, even if it is God who is honored by the sacrifice, a logic that went on to inform the theories of violent sacrifice discussed at the start of this essay. Sacrifice, then, is a site of violence, but not of "the primitive." Yet the sacrificers are, Christian writers suggest, entirely savage.

Plan of the Volume

PART I: THEORIZING SACRIFICE

The essays gathered in the first section of the volume offer important reappraisals of contemporary approaches to sacrifice by examining ancient practices and texts. As Stanley Stowers argues in his paper, "The Religion of Plant and Animal Offerings Versus the Religion of Meanings, Essences, and Textual Mysteries," the "religion of everyday social exchange" focused on plant and animal offerings, not on interpretations, which remained the purview of "literate specialists." Textualizing practice, these experts turned sacrifice into a matter of truths and meanings, instead of what Stowers sees as primary: a strategic, practical system of reciprocity between gods and humans.

Daniel Ullucci's contribution, "Contesting the Meaning of Animal Sacrifice," agrees with Stowers's assessment, noting that ancient literary critiques of practice did not so much describe what sacrifice meant as engage in an ongoing competition for legitimacy. Sacrificial practice serves as a backdrop against which the competitive machinations of literate elites could take place.

Turning to Egypt, David Frankfurter's chapter "Egyptian Religion and the Problem of the Category 'Sacrifice'" takes aim at the focus on blood and killing in the notion of sacrifice as popularized by Girard and Burkert. Adapting Katherine McClymond's method of breaking down sacrifice into a series of ritual stages, Frankfurter argues that, in the case of Egypt, elements and procedures other than killing were much more important to religious practice. He wonders, then, if sacrifice (*thysia* or *sacrificium*) was as universally present and important as it is generally presumed in modern scholarly studies. Animal killing was simply not central to Egyptian cult; instead, the manifestation and procession of the divine image served as the central ritual and any killing that did take place occurred off stage, away from the zone of pilgrims and worshipers. Even within a single geographical and chronological milieu, then, no single backdrop of practice can be assumed.

As William Gilders points out in "Jewish Sacrifice: Its Nature and Function (According to Philo)," however, ancient writers such as Philo of Alexandria did assume that sacrifice was a universal practice. Philo applied the Greek term *thysia* to Jewish sacrifices and suggested that Greeks, Romans, and Jews pursued similar goals when presenting their offerings to the Divine. Still, he suggests, Philo's interpretation can only be decoded using the cultural lexicon of his context, suggesting that symbolism is always historically and culturally bound. Gilders therefore resists symbolic interpretations of religion in his chapter, arguing that indigenous interpreters and scholars alike extract meanings—symbolic, instrumental, and otherwise—that are culturally and historically contingent. They do not explain sacrifice—or any other ritual—once and for all. To Jonathan Klawans, however, symbolic interpretations remain important, especially in contexts like ancient Israel, where symbolism was dense, intentional, and significant for both biblical writers and their audiences. As he argues in his essay, "Symbol, Function, Theology, and Morality in the Study of Priestly Ritual," tensions between meaning claims, symbolic acts, and practices among diverse ancient groups suggest that the category "sacrifice" is much more complicated than is often thought.

PART II: NEGOTIATING POWER THROUGH SACRIFICE

The essays gather in the second section of the volume examine how sacrifice carried potentially dangerous associations in antiquity, and was therefore a useful category for negotiating the boundaries of acceptable and unacceptable religion. In her chapter "Political Murder and Sacrifice: From Roman Republic to Empire," Zsuzsanna Várhelyi studies politically high-stake murders in late-republican Rome that were tentatively interpreted in sacrificial terms. Opening the essay with a description of the killing of Tiberius Gracchus at the hands of Scipio Nasica, the pontifex maximus in Rome, she traces how the political debates of the period incorporated assumptions about rightful religious acts. Reading through a number of Roman arguments regarding proper political and religious conduct, Várhelyi shows how closely the proper execution of power and the proper performance of sacrifice came to touch upon one another, leading to a combination of political and religious authority—and primacy in performing sacrifice—in the hands of the first emperor, Augustus.

In her chapter "The Embarrassment of Blood: Early Christians and Others on Sacrifice, War, and Rational Worship," Laura Nasrallah analyzes first- and second-century discourses concerning human sacrifice, as put forward in Roman art and Roman and Christian literature. She distinguishes four major discursive sites through which sacrifice was thematized: (1) in polemical accusations of human sacrifice; (2) in discussions of humans as appropriate living, rational sacrifices to the gods, if those humans are philosophically and theologically trained; (3) in the context of interpretations of Christ's death; and (4) in the rarely discussed theological realm of Roman political-religious life. Nasrallah points to the juxtaposition of warfare and human sacrifice in this final context. She reveals the ideological interconnections of war and human sacrifice, connections that haunt the literary and sculptural imagery of this period—specifically, on the altar of the Temple of the Flavian Sebastoi at Ephesos, and on the Column of Trajan at Rome—as well as the literary texts of Tatian and Plutarch, among others. Sacrifice may not have been *about* violence, but it could be put into conversation with violence, especially in the context of warfare.

In her essay "The End of Public Sacrifice: Changing Definitions of Sacrifice in Post-Constantinian Rome and Italy," Michele Renee Salzman reconsiders the pagan response to the heightened contestation of animal sacrifice in fourth-century Rome. She analyzes the writings of Symmachus, noting how he creatively redefined the tradition of sacrifice in light of the strong Christian opposition to it. Salzman identifies two main ways in which Symmachus tried to keep Roman sacrifices alive: through allowing private individuals to fund and perform these rites, and by expanding the scope of the ritual so that it could be fulfilled in ways other than by animal killing. Salzman concludes that the absence of a communal, public aspect in this reinvented version of sacrifice led to its inevitable demise; yet the evidence of Symmachus allows us to see the creative engagement with this problem by late-ancient Romans committed to earlier forms of sacrificial practice.

PART III: TOWARDS A THEOLOGY OF SACRIFICE

The third section of the volume focuses on the interrelationships among ancient sacrificial theories, noting the importance of these interactions to the approaches to sacrifice taken by Greek, Roman, Jewish, and Christian intellectuals alike. Contesting in the interest of their privilege, literate elites developed new theologies of sacrifice—rejecting not practice per se, but particular meanings ascribed to practice. In his contribution, "The Theology of Animal Sacrifice in the Ancient Greek World: Origins and Developments," James B. Rives questions the monolithic place of animal sacrifice in accounts of ancient Greek religion. His reading reintroduces a chronological perspective, suggesting that the philosophers of the imperial era were the first to develop a pagan theology of sacrifice, likely in the Neo-Pythagorean circles of the first century CE. In Rives's estimation, the new importance of animal sacrifice in the imperial cult and in the rituals associated with euergetism required those who did not wish to participate in civic worship to develop a more sophisticated reasoning for their rejection. Tracing this theology in the works of Porphyry of Tyre (third century CE), Rives points at the parallel associations of certain kinds of sacrifices to certain kinds of divinities.

Fritz Graf's chapter, "A Satirist's Sacrifices: Lucian's *On Sacrifices* and the Contestation of Religious Traditions," considers the criticism of sacrifice by the Syrian Greek satirist Lucian of Samosata. Graf argues that sacrifice, in Lucian as in other writers, is never contested by itself; rather, these discussions are always developed as part of a larger rethinking of religious traditions, in which sacrifice is intentionally misinterpreted as a form of *do ut des* logic and divine-human violence—just as myth and visual representations fail to capture what a philosopher understands about the gods, so, too, do philosophers misunderstand sacrificial practice. While satire, as it is typical of the genre, does not aim at providing a positive theological alternative to imperial Greek sacrificial practice, its overall tone fits well with other second-century ethical discussions about the subject, such as those of Philostratus or Maximus of Tyre. Graf concludes by suggesting that there was an increased interest in theological discussion among the educated elite of the empire in the second century. Lucian's diatribe, just as those other writings, did not aspire to intercept current sacrificial practices; instead they sought to articulate and spread a view of higher philosophical theology, which nevertheless allowed them to participate in sacrifice, along with other ritual practices, through distinctive and "higher" standards of their own.

Philippa Townsend's chapter, "Bonds of Flesh and Blood: Porphyry, Animal Sacrifice, and Empire," addresses the criticism of sacrifice offered by the third-century Porphyry in his treatise *On Abstinence from Killing Animals*. Building on the insights of Nancy Jay and Stanley Stowers regarding the role of sacrifice in the constitution of gender and of social hierarchies, Townsend examines the connection of sacrifice to kinship relations. In the second century, Christians claimed to have established a "new race" with its own sacrificial logic. Similarly, Porphyry's criticism of animal sacrifice went hand in hand with a devaluation of established ethnic divisions. Associating animal sacrifice with imperial violence, Porphyry advocates minimal participation among those interested in a universal kinship based in forms' inner virtue.

PART IV: IMAGINARY SACRIFICE

The final section of the volume focuses on ancient engagements with sacrifice in contexts in which sacrificial practices were no longer available, yet continued to shape notions of religious propriety and group identity nonetheless. Kathryn McClymond, in her chapter "Don't Cry Over Spilled Blood," turns to rabbinic discussions of ritual mistakes. Writing long after the destruction of the Jerusalem Temple, the compilers of the Mishnah (ca. 220 CE) nevertheless include several instructions regarding the remedies appropriate to various sacrificial mistakes. Focusing on Mishnah tractate Zevachim, McClymond considers rabbinic advice about the mishandling of blood—despite the fact that this discussion of blood manipulation had no practical application whatsoever. Yet, whereas the biblical material only rarely discusses mistakes, the Mishnah considers the problem at great length, seeking to ensure that priestly intention is correct and also that blood is manipulated at the right time and in the right place. In the process, a new intellectual system is developed in which priestly authority and ritual practice are replaced by rabbinic authority and ritual argument. The discussions of ritual error, then, reinforce the shift from a priestly-cultic matrix to a rabbinic-textual matrix, presenting a system in which ritual errors can be both addressed and nullified by rabbinic mastery. McClymond's original and striking approach to (imagined) ritual errors encourages comparison with other ritual systems and their attempts at dealing with human error, real or imagined.

Considering Christian applications of the Roman concept of self-sacrifice, Andrew S. Jacobs' chapter "Passing: Jesus' Circumcision and Strategic Self-Sacrifice" discusses late-ancient representations of Jesus' circumcision, which, he demonstrates, was reinterpreted as a form of strategic sacrificial giving. Assuming that Jesus' Jewish identity was demeaning, Christians like Tertullian and Ambrose argued that Jesus only seemed to take on a Jewish guise: As they argued, circumcision enabled Jesus' initially Jewish mission, but his submission to the practice was intended to fool Jews so that their future critique would have no merit. Employing contemporary discussions of "passing" as a phenomenon and practice, Jacobs suggests that, from the late-ancient Christian point of view, Jesus "passed" as Jewish, but was not, in fact Jewish at all. Depending upon and yet challenging Roman sacrificial economies, Christians rearranged sacrificial politics, making the subject of sacrifice (God) the sacrificial victim. Their depictions of Jesus' circumcision fit into this larger argument, claiming that, just as Jesus sacrificed his body for all during the crucifixion, he also sacrificed his foreskin, thereby sacrificing himself to Judaism as well. In the process, the discussion of Jesus' circumcision reified Judaism as a thing to be conquered and repudiated.

As Ra'anan S. Boustan observes in "Confounding Blood: Jewish Narratives of Sacrifice and Violence in Late Antiquity," sacrificial cult remained the dominant paradigm for ritual action and religious piety among Jews and Christians alike, despite the absence of sacrificial practice in both contexts. Reinvigorated in the context of discourses of martyrdom, blood remained a charged site of discursive contact, ritual contestation, and exegetical competition. In this case, then, Girard's notion of sacrifice as sublimated violence can actually be illuminating, even as his overarching claims obfuscate the diversity of late-ancient Jewish narratives. Comparing accounts of the murder of Zechariah to the *Story of the Ten Martyrs*, Boustan notes that, according to *Lamentations Rabbah,* human and animal victims fail to provide the redemption Israel needs. By contrast, in the *Story of the Ten Martyrs,* heroic rabbis are represented as sacrificial victims who willingly lay down their lives to atone for Israel's sin. Though their approaches to sacrificial death are quite different, both of these texts nevertheless participate in a common project of wresting control over the meaning and function of righteous human blood from an increasingly hegemonic Roman-Christian culture. As such, they resist the violence of Roman-Christian domination even as they sanction divine vengeance on Israel's behalf.

Ancient Mediterranean Sacrifice, Reconsidered

As we have seen, the accusation that improper, violent sacrifice is something that other people do is as old as accusations lodged against Scythians by Greeks, against Canaanites by Israelites, and against the barbarians by Romans; in this regard, Christian condemnation of pagan or Israelite sacrifice followed an established script. Yet, the essays in this volume suggest that in the ancient world the accusation that certain sacrificial rites are objectionable did not imply a rejection of the sacrificial practice in general, an insight that can be applied across the board. As participants in sacrificial religions without sacrifice, Christians and Jews made metaphorical or imaginary sacrifice key to both their discourses and their practices, as Boustan, Jacobs, and McClymond demonstrate. As participants in a wider competitive discourse, they, too, engaged in a process of contestation and identity formulation, as Ullucci shows. But, as the essays by Stowers and Frankfurter caution, blanket claims about sacrifice, even within this limited geographical and chronological frame, remain problematic. Frankfurter's discussion of Egyptian religion makes the point in a particularly striking way: in Egypt, animal killing was a side practice, not the main event. In this instance at least, the obsession with sacrifice on the part of modern interpreters is misplaced.

Nevertheless, the juxtaposition of sacrifice and violence can be found in antiquity as well, as Nasrallah's essay reminds us. Thinking with and through first- and second-century discussions of human sacrifice, Nasrallah points to the lingering associations of warfare and sacrifice, despite sanitized images of the emperor at sacrifice. Surely, thematized violence was in view, both in Christian and Roman contexts. Boustan's consideration of late-ancient Jewish martyrological literature is also helpful in this regard. Though the argument that sacrifice *is*—essentially and undeniably—about violence should be resisted, the insight that discourses of sacrifice can serve to sublimate and displace violence from one arena onto another does illuminate Jewish martyrological texts. Competing with Roman-Christian notions of sublimated violence in the form of Jesus' death on a cross, late-ancient Jews offered their own versions of the meaning and function of righteous human blood—and did so to deflect the actual violence of an increasingly consolidated Roman-Christian empire.

But sacrificial discourse, if not sacrificial practice, was in the air, as it had been for centuries. Negotiations over the "true" meaning of sacrifice occupied such Roman-era thinkers as Porphyry, Lucian, and Philostratus, each of whom belittled sacrificial practice in various ways, as Rives, Graf, and Townsend explain. Sophisticated theological arguments regarding sacrifice produced universalizing theories of meaning and kinship that undermined practice, but without any desire for the actual cessation of sacrifice. When animal sacrifice was suppressed by newly Christian emperors, eager to display their loyalty to Christian sacrificial systems, highly educated pagans like Symmachus could then turn these arguments around to defend traditional Roman practice, as Salzman demonstrates.

Historical circumstances and interactions therefore matter a great deal, as essays by Rives, Salzman, and Várhelyi propose. The emerging role of euergetism in the imperial context required those who rejected Roman sacrifice to explain their rejections, as Rives suggests, leading to new theological theories. The crises brought on by late-republican political murders enabled new ways of thinking about—and deploying—religious arguments, as Várhelyi observes. Finally, the actions of Christian emperors transformed Roman sacrifice from public to a private settings, contributing to their eventual demise. Ancient sacrifice—images, texts, and meanings—was highly contested and yet central to identities and discourses across the Mediterranean world.[114]

Notes

1. See esp. James Rives, "Human Sacrifice among Pagans and Christians," *JRS* 85 (1995): 65–85; Andrew McGowan, "Eating People: Accusations of Cannibalism against Christians in the Second Century," *JECS* 2.3 (1994): 413–42; Jan N. Bremmer, "Human Sacrifice: A Brief Introduction," in *The Strange World of Human Sacrifice*, edited by Jan N. Bremmer (Leuven: Peeters, 2007), 1–8; Lautaro Roig Lanzilotta, "The Early Christians and Human Sacrifice," in *Strange World of Human Sacrifice*, 81–102; Ed Noort, "Child Sacrifice in Ancient Israel: The *Status Quaestionis*," in *Strange World of Human Sacrifice*, 103–25; Katell Berthelot, "Jewish Views of Human Sacrifice in the Hellenistic and Roman Period," in *Human Sacrifice in Jewish and Christian Tradition*, edited by Karin Finsterbusch, Armin Lange, and K. F. Deithard Römheld, Numen 112 (Leiden: Brill, 2007), 151–73; Peter Lampe, "Human Sacrifice and Pauline Christology," in *Human Sacrifice in Jewish and Christian Tradition*, 191–209; Zsuzsanna Várhelyi, "The Specters of Roman Imperialism: The Live Burials of Gauls and Greeks in Rome," *Classical Antiquity* 26 (2007): 277–304.

2. Folkert van Straten, "Ancient Greek Animal Sacrifice: Gift, Ritual Slaughter, Communion, Food Supply, or What? Some Thoughts on Simple Explanations of a Complex Ritual," in *La cuisine et l'autel: Les sacrifices en questions dans les sociétés de la Méditerranée ancienne*, edited by Stella Georgoudi, Renée Piettre, and Francis Schmidt, Bibliothèque de l'École des Hautes Études Sciences Religieuses 124 (Turnhout: Brepols, 2005), 15–29.

3. Guy G. Stroumsa, *The End of Sacrifice: Religious Transformations in Late Antiquity*, translated by Susan Emmanuel (Chicago: University of Chicago Press, 2009), 72–78, at 72. Also see Guy G. Stroumsa, "The End of Sacrifice. Religious Mutations of Late Antiquity," in *Empsychoi logoi—Religious Innovations in Antiquity: Studies in Honour of Pieter Willem van der Horst*, edited by Alberdina Houtman, Albert de Jong, and Magda Misset-van de Weg (Leiden: Brill, 2008), 30–46, at 42: "Transformed, reinterpreted, metaphorized, memorized," Stroumsa observes, sacrifice "seems never to have died out completely."

4. Susan Laura Mizruchi, *The Science of Sacrifice: American Literature and Modern Social Theory* (Princeton: Princeton University Press, 1998), 369.

5. Mark C. Taylor, "The Politics of Theo-ry," *JAAR* 59.1 (1991): 1–37, at 6.

6. E. G. Tylor, *Primitive Culture* (London: John Murray; New York: Putnam, 1920), 2: 375.

7. On the ideological work performed by this version of world history, see Dipesh Chakrabarty, *Provincializing Europe: Postcolonial Thought and Historical Difference* (Princeton: Princeton University Press, 2000).

8. Robert Ackerman has traced the intellectual and personal relationship of William Robertson Smith and J. G. Frazer in his work, *The Myth and Ritual School: J. G. Frazer and the Cambridge Ritualists* (London: Routledge, 2002), 45–49. As Ackerman points out, in successive editions of *The Golden Bough* Frazer sought to distance himself from Smith's theories (54–57). Jonathan Z. Smith has discussed the successive editions of *The Golden Bough*, noting the transformation of Frazer's initially modest goal (an explanation of the cult of Diana at Aricia) to a full-scale theory of myth and religion, an effort that largely ended in defeat ("When the Bough Breaks," *History of Religions* 12.4 [1973]: 342–71). But also see Smith's positive evaluation of Frazer's methodological advances in *Drudgery Divine: On the Comparison of Early Christianities and the Religions of Late Antiquity* (Chicago: University of Chicago Press, 1990), 99.

9. Frazer built his analysis on a brief mention of this cult in Strabo, *Geog.* 5.3.12: τῆς δ᾽ Ἀρικίνης τὸ ἱερὸν λέγουσιν ἀφίδρυμά τι τῆς Ταυροπόλου· καὶ γάρ τι βαρβαρικὸν κρατεῖ καὶ Σκυθικὸν περὶ τὸ ἱερὸν ἔθος. καθίσταται γὰρ ἱερεὺς ὁ γενηθεὶς αὐτόχειρ τοῦ ἱερωμένου πρότερον δραπέτης ἀνήρ· ξιφήρης οὖν ἐστιν ἀεὶ περισκοπῶν τὰς ἐπιθέσεις, ἕτοιμος ἀμύνεσθαι. A. Meineke, *Strabonis geographica*, 3 vols. (Leipzig: Teubner, 1877; repr., 1969). For further discussion, see Smith, "When the Bough Breaks," 347–48.

10. Catherine M. Bell, *Ritual: Perspectives and Dimensions* (New York: Oxford University Press, 1997), 5. For a bibliography on more recent appraisals of this cult, and a perspective that connects Frazer's insights with those of Burkert, see C. M. C. Green, *Roman Religion and the Cult of Diana Aricia* (Cambridge: Cambridge University Press, 2007), esp. 147–83.

11. James G. Frazer, *The Golden Bough*, 2 vols. (London: Macmillan, 1890); revised in 3 vols. (London: MacMillan, 1900); revised in 12 vols. (London: Macmillan, 1911–1915); revised and abridged in 1 vol. (London: Macmillan, 1927).

12. Frazer, *Golden Bough*, 1927 edition, 337–39.

13. Frazer, *Golden Bough*, 1927 edition, 352.

14. Frazer, *Golden Bough*, 1927 edition, 384–85.

15. "Thus in the acuter minds magic is gradually superseded by religion, which explains the succession of natural phenomena as regulated by the will, the passion, or the caprice of spiritual beings like man in kind, though vastly superior to him in power. But as time goes on this explanation in its turn proves to be unsatisfactory. . . . Thus the keener minds, still pressing forward to a deeper solution of the mysteries of the universe come to reject the religious theory of nature as inadequate. . . . In short, religion, regarded as an explanation of nature, is displaced by science" (Frazer, *Golden Bough*, 1927 edition, 711–12).

16. Robertson Smith announces his apologetic intent at the start of the lectures: "Judaism, Christianity and Islam are *positive* religions, that is, they did not grow up like the systems of ancient heathenism, under the action of unconscious forces operating silently from age to age, but trace their origin to the teaching of great religious innovators, who spoke as the organs of divine revelation." They, too, suffered from the residues of past primitivism, but they "displaced what they could not assimilate." William Robertson Smith, *The Religion of the Semites: The Fundamental Institutions* (New York: Meridian, 1956), 1–2.

17. Smith, *Religion of the Semites*, 439.

18. Smith, *Religion of the Semites*, 446–54. For further discussion, see Maria-Zoe Petropoulou, *Animal Sacrifice in Ancient Greek Religion, Judaism, and Christianity, 100 BC–AD 200* (Oxford: Oxford University Press, 2008), 1–4; Jonathan Klawans, *Purity, Sacrifice, and the Temple: Symbolism and Supersessionism in the Study of Ancient Judaism* (New York: Oxford University Press, 2006), 18–19.

19. Henri Hubert and Marcel Mauss, "Essai sur la nature et la fonction du sacrifice," *L'Année sociologique* 2 (Paris, 1898): 29–138; Émile Durkhiem, *Les formes élementaires de la vie religieuse, le système totémique en Australie* (Paris: Presses Universitaires de France, 1912); Sigmund Freud, *Über einige Übereinstimmungen im Seelenleben der Wilden und der Neurotiker*, 2 vols. (1912–13), republished as *Totem und Tabu: Übereinstimmungen im Seelenleben der Wilden und der Neurotiker* (Leipzig: H. Heller, 1913).

20. Henri Hubert and Marcel Mauss, *Sacrifice: Its Nature and Function*, translated by W. D. Halls (Chicago: University of Chicago Press, 1964), 7.

21. For a similar critique of Robertson Smith, see E. E. Evans-Pritchard, *Theories of Primitive Religion* (Oxford: Clarendon, 1965), 51–52.

22. Hubert and Mauss, *Sacrifice*, 6.

23. Hubert and Mauss, *Sacrifice*, 97.

24. Durkheim, *Formes élémentaires de la vie religieuse* (1912), translated by Joseph Ward Swain, *The Elementary Forms of Religious Life* (New York: Free Press, 1965), 377–92. See further Taylor, "Politics of Theo-ry," 7–12, and David Frankfurter, "Ritual as Accusation and Atrocity: Satanic Ritual Abuse, Gnostic Libertinism, and Primal Murders," *History of Religions* 40.4 (2001): 352–80. As Frankfurter points out, Durkheim depicted primitive ritual as representative of the "orgiastic and sexually amoral degrees to which human groups in their primal state might bring themselves during ritual events" (367).

25. Durkheim, *Elementary Forms*, 462–96.

26. Sigmund Freud, *Totem and Taboo: Resemblances between the Psychic Lives of Savages and Neurotics*, translated by A. A. Brill (London: Routledge, 1919), esp. 235–37.

27. Freud, *Totem and Taboo*, 243, 251.

28. Freud, *Totem and Taboo*, 257. For a contemporary application of Freud's theory, see, e.g., Brian K. Smith and Wendy Doniger, "Sacrifice and Substitution: Ritual Mystification and Mythical Demystification," *Numen* 36.2 (1989): 189–224. As we will see, René Girard was also heavily dependent on Freud: *La violence et le sacré* (Paris: Editions Bernard Grasset, 1972), translated by Patrick Gregory, *Violence and the Sacred* (Baltimore: Johns Hopkins University Press, 1977).

29. Taylor, "The Politics of Theo-ry," 16–18.

30. Karl Meuli, "Griechische Opferbräuche," in *Phyllobolia, für Peter von Muhll zum 60. Geburtstag am 1 August 1945*, edited by Olaf Gigon (Basel: Schwabe, 1946), 185–288, reprinted in *Gesammelte Schriften*, edited by Thomas Gelzer (Basel: Schwabe, 1975), 2: 907–1021. For further evaluation of Meuli's theories, see the essays in Fritz Graf, ed., *Klassische Antike und neue Wege der Kulturwissenshaften: Symposium Karl Meuli (Basel, 11–13 September 1991)*, Beiträge zur Volkskunde 11 (Basel: Schweizerische Gesellschaft für Volkskunde, 1992), and Jan Bremmer, *Greek Religion*, Greece and Rome: New Surveys in the Classics 24 (Oxford: Oxford University Press, 2003), 41–43.

31. Walter Burkert, *Homo Necans: Interpretationen Altgrichische Opferriten und Mythen*, Religionsgeschichtliche Versuche und Vorarbeiten 32 (Berlin: Walter de Gruyter, 1972), translated by Peter Bing, *Homo Necans: The Anthropology of Ancient Greek Sacrificial Ritual and Myth* (Berkeley: University of California Press, 1983).

32. Burkert, *Homo Necans*, esp. 35–48.

33. Burkert, *Homo Necans*, 45.

34. See also Walter Burkert, *Ancient Mystery Cults* (Cambridge: Harvard University Press, 1987).

35. Girard, *Violence and the Sacred*, 10.

36. Girard, *Violence and the Sacred*, esp. 143–62.

37. Girard, *Violence and the Sacred*, 11.

38. Girard, *Violence and the Sacred*, 297–99, 306, 309–12.

39. On the popular reception of this approach in contemporary contexts, see Frankfurter, "Ritual as Accusation and Atrocity," 352–80.

40. Girard, *Violence and the Sacred*, 23. For an important overview of these theories, see Fritz Graf, "One Generation after Burkert and Girard: Where Are the Great Theories?" in *Ancient*

Victims, Modern Observers: Reflections on Greek and Animal Sacrifice, edited by Christopher A. Faraone and F. S. Naiden (Cambridge: Cambridge University Press, 2011), forthcoming.

41. Recent interpretations along these lines include Mark Juergensmeyer's influential *Terror in the Mind of God: The Global Rise of Religious Violence* (Berkeley: University of California Press, 2000), and Regina M. Schwartz, *The Curse of Cain: The Violent Legacy of Monotheism* (Chicago: University of Chicago Press, 1997). According to Juergensmeyer, religions are inherently absolutist and prone to violence. Still, the solution to this problem is not secularism or science, but a more loving and pluralistic religion. Schwartz also views religion as a troubling phenomenon. Religion offers a strong theory of group identity and collective memory that enables violence against others, parasitically and agonistically, she argues. Again, however, the proposed solution is better religion. For important counterarguments to these works, see Terry Nardin, review of *Terror in the Mind of God: The Global Rise of Religious Violence*, *Journal of Politics* 63.2 (2001): 683–84; Brian K. Smith, "Monotheism and Its Discontents: Religious Violence and the Bible," *JAAR* 66.2 (1998): 403–11; Talal Asad, "Religion, Nation-State, Secularism," in *Nation and Religion: Perspectives on Europe and Asia*, edited by Peter van der Veer and Hartmut Lehman (Princeton: Princeton University Press, 1999), 178–96; Ananda Abeysekara, "The Saffron Army, Violence, Terror(ism): Buddhism, Identity, and Difference in Sri Lanka," *Numen* 48.1 (2001): 1–46, and *Colors of the Robe: Religion, Identity, and Difference* (Columbia: University of South Carolina Press, 2002).

42. Marcel Detienne and Jean-Pierre Vernant, eds., *La cuisine du sacrifice en pays grec* (Paris: Editions Gallimard, 1979), English translation by Paula Wissing, *The Cuisine of Sacrifice among the Greeks* (Chicago: University of Chicago Press, 1989). For a review of the approach of the Paris school, see Petropoulou, *Animal Sacrifice*, 13–14. Over the past few years, several symposia have been organized to assess the Detienne-Vernant-Durand hypothesis. See, for example, Stella Georgoudi, Renée Piettre, and Francis Schmidt, eds., *La cuisine et l'autel: Les sacrifices en questions dans les sociétés de la Méditerranée ancienne*, Bibliothèque de l'École des Hautes Études Sciences Religieuses 124 (Turnhout: Brepols, 2005), and Véronique Mehl and Pierre Brulé, *Le sacrifice antique: Vestiges, procedures et strategies*, Collection "Histoire" (Rennes: Presses Universitaires de Rennes, 2008).

43. Detienne, "Culinary Practices and the Spirit of Sacrifice," in *Cuisine of Sacrifice*, 3.

44. Detienne, "Culinary Practices and the Spirit of Sacrifice," in *Cuisine of Sacrifice*, 4–5.

45. Jean-Louis Durand, "Greek Animals: Toward a Topology of Edible Bodies," in *Cuisine of Sacrifice*, 87–118.

46. As Durand points out, Greek vase paintings never depict sacrifice as a violent act ("Greek Animals"). Scythians, however, are accused of violent sacrifice. Wringing the necks of their victims, they sacrifice inappropriately, and violently, including humans among their victims, or so Herodotus suggests (François Hartog, "Self-Cooking Beef and the Drinks of Ares," in *Cuisine of Sacrifice*, 173–82).

47. Robert G. Hammerton-Kelly, ed., *Violent Origins: Walter Burkert, René Girard and Jonathan Z. Smith on Ritual Killing and Cultural Formation* (Stanford: Stanford University Press, 1987).

48. Jonathan Z. Smith, "The Domestication of Sacrifice," in Hammerton-Kelly, *Violent Origins*, 191–205; reprinted in Jonathan Z. Smith, *Relating Religion: Essays in the Study of Religion* (Chicago: University of Chicago Press, 2004), 145–59, at 149.

49. Smith, "Domestication of Sacrifice," 152.

50. Smith, "Domestication of Sacrifice," 150.

51. Sarah Pierce, "Death, Revelry, and *Thysia*," *Classical Antiquity* 12.2 (1993): 219–60, at 260.

52. Pierce, "Death, Revelry, and *Thysia*."

53. Stella Georgoudi, "L' 'occultation de la violence' dans le sacrifice grec," in Georgoudi, et al., *La cuisine et l'autel* (Turnhout: Brepols), 115–41.

54. Van Straten, "Ancient Greek Animal Sacrifice," 15–29.

55. Robert Parker, Preface to Mehl and Brulé, *Le sacrifice antique*, i–ii.

56. Jesper Svenbro, "La *thusia et le partage*. Remarques sur la 'destruction' par le feu dans le sacrifice grec," in *La cuisine et l'autel*, 217–25. Here Svenbro parts company with Gunnel Ekroth, who has persuasively linked Greek sacrifices to the gods with sacrifices to heroes. See Ekroth, *The Sacrificial Rituals of Greek Hero-Cults in the Archaic to Early Hellenistic Periods* (Liege: Centre International d'Étude de la Religion Grecque Antique, 2002). In a recent essay, Ekroth considers the distance between gods and humans as negotiated, in part, on the basis of cooking methods and animal parts; "Burnt, Cooked or Raw? Divine and Human Culinary Desires at Greek Animal Sacrifice," in *Transformations in Sacrificial Practices from Antiquity to Modern Times*, edited by Eftychia Stavrianopoulou, Axel Michaels, and Claus Ambos (Berlin: Lit, 2008), 87–111.

57. Sarah Hitch and Ian P. Rutherford, eds., *Animal Sacrifice in the Ancient Greek World* (Cambridge: Cambridge University Press, 2011).

58. Nancy Jay, *Throughout Your Generations Forever: Sacrifice, Religion and Paternity* (Chicago: University of Chicago Press, 1991), xxiii.

59. Jay, *Throughout Your Generations*, 32.

60. Robyn Osborne has critiqued the specifics of Jay's analysis of Greek sacrifice, and at length. See her essay, "Women and Sacrifice in Classical Greece," *Classical Quarterly* 43 (1993): 392–405.

61. Stanley K. Stowers, "Greeks Who Sacrifice and Those Who Do Not: Toward an Anthropology of Greek Religion," in *The Social World of the First Christians: Essays in Honor of Wayne A. Meeks*, edited by L. Michael White and O. Larry Yarbrough (Minneapolis: Fortress, 1995), 293–333, at 298.

62. Stowers, "Greeks Who Sacrifice," 311.

63. Stowers, "Greeks Who Sacrifice," 331–32.

64. Mary Douglas, *Purity and Danger: An Analysis of the Concepts of Pollution and Taboo* (London: Routledge, 1966; repr., London: Routledge, 1991), 41–57; "Atonement in Leviticus," *Jewish Studies Quarterly* 1.2 (1993–1994): 109–30; *Leviticus as Literature* (Oxford: Oxford University Press, 1999).

65. Douglas, *Purity and Danger*, 3–4.

66. Douglas, *Purity and Danger*, 29–40.

67. Douglas, *Purity and Danger*, 57.

68. Douglas, *Leviticus as Literature*, 66–86. For an alternative and yet related point of view, see Naphtali S. Meschel, "Pure, Impure, Permitted, Prohibited: A Study of Classification Systems in P," in *Perspectives on Purity and Purification in the Bible*, edited by Baruch Schwartz and David P. Wright (London: T. & T. Clark International, 2008), 32–42. Meschel applies Levì-Strauss's analysis of taboo to biblical sources, concluding that, as in other "primitive societies," a homologous link between the classification of animals and of human groups was in play. Leviticus 11 sought to address the relationship of human to animal and culture to nature.

69. Among other studies, see Jonathan Klawans, *Impurity and Sin in Ancient Judaism* (New York: Oxford University Press, 2000); "Pure Violence: Sacrifice and Defilement in Ancient Israel," *Harvard Theological Review* 94.2 (2001): 135–57; "Ritual Purity, Moral Purity, and Sacrifice in Jacob Milgrom's *Leviticus*," *Religious Studies Review* 29.1 (2003): 19–28; *Purity, Sacrifice, and the Temple*; "Introduction: Religion, Violence and the Bible," with contributions by David Bernat, in *Religion and Violence: The Biblical Heritage* (Sheffield: Sheffield Phoenix, 2007), 1–15.

70. Klawans, "Pure Violence," esp. 151–53; *Purity, Sacrifice, and the Temple*, 55–72, 112–17.

71. Klawans, "Pure Violence," 151; cf. *Purity, Sacrifice, and the Temple*, 65.

72. Kathryn McClymond, *Beyond Sacred Violence: A Comparative Study of Sacrifice* (Baltimore: Johns Hopkins University Press, 2008), 58.

73. McClymond, *Beyond Sacred Violence*, 33.

74. McClymond, *Beyond Sacred Violence*, 44–64, at 64.

75. William K. Gilders, *Blood Ritual in the Hebrew Bible: Meaning and Power* (Baltimore: Johns Hopkins University Press, 2004), 24.

76. Gilders, *Blood Ritual in the Hebrew Bible*, 186–91.

77. David Biale, *Blood and Belief: The Circulation of a Symbol between Jews and Christians* (Berkeley: University of California Press, 2007), 9–14. Though deeply appreciative of Klawans's work, Gilders has nevertheless expressed objections to Klawans's focus on the symbolic or metaphorical meaning of Israelite sacrifice. See his review of *Purity, Sacrifice, and the Temple* in *Catholic Biblical Quarterly* 69 (2007): 784–85.

78. Jacob Milgrom, *Leviticus: A New Translation and Commentary*, 3 vols., Anchor Bible 3–3b (New York: Doubleday, 1992–2001).

79. Biale, *Blood and Belief*, 18–19. Also see Klawans, "Ritual Purity, Moral Purity, and Sacrifice," and Gilders, *Blood Ritual*, 3–4, 31, 91–94.

80. John Scheid, "La spartizione sacrificale a Roma," in *Sacrificio e società nel mondo antico*, edited by C. Grottanelli and N. Parise (Rome: Laterza, 1988), 267–92.

81. Nicole Belayche, "Religion et consummation de la viande dans le monde romaine: Des réalités voilées," *Food and History* 5.1 (2007): 29–43.

82. Jörg Rüpke, *Die Religion der Römer*, 2nd ed. (Munich: Beck, 2006).

83. Mary Beard, John North, and Simon Price, *Religions of Rome* (Cambridge: Cambridge University Press, 1998), 1:36–38.

84. Beard, North, and Price, *Religions of Rome*, 66–67.

85. Livy, *Ab urbe condita* 5.13.

86. John Scheid, *An Introduction to Roman Religion*, translated by J. Lloyd (Bloomington: Indiana University Press, 2003), 95–96. Also see his essay, "Roman Sacrifice and the System of Being," in Faraone and Naiden, *Ancient Victims, Modern Observers*, Cambridge: Cambridge, forthcoming.

87. James B. Rives, *Religion in the Roman Empire* (Malden, Mass.: Blackwell 2007), 25.

88. Hartog, "Self-Cooking Beef."

89. Várhelyi, "Spectres of Roman Imperialism," 283–85.

90. Rives, "Human Sacrifice."

91. Rives, "Human Sacrifice"; Várhelyi, "Spectres of Roman Imperialism," 278–79. As to ridiculing depictions, see the famous passage in Arnobius, *Against Gentiles* 7.24.

92. Rives, "Human Sacrifice," 73.

93. Denis Feeney, *Literature and Religion at Rome: Cultures, Contexts and Beliefs* (Cambridge: Cambridge University Press, 1988), 118.

94. Also see the famous debate between Thomas Habinek and Richard Thomas, with regard to the *Georgics* of Vergil (29 BCE): T. N. Habinek, "Sacrifice, Society, and Vergil's Ox-Born Bees," in *Cabinet of the Muses: Essays on Classical and Comparative Literature in Honor of Thomas G. Rosenmeyer*, edited by M. Griffith and D. J. Mastronarde (Atlanta: Scholars Press, 1990), 209–223; R. F. Thomas, "The 'Sacrifice' at the End of the Georgics, Aristaeus, and Vergilian Closure," *CP* 86 (1991): 211–18.

95. Richard Gordon, "The Veil of Power: Emperors, Sacrificers and Benefactors," in *Pagan Priests: Religion and Power in the Ancient World*, edited by Mary Beard and John North (Ithaca: Cornell University Press, 1990), 199–232, at 206.

96. Gordon, "Veil of Power," 219.

97. Andreas Bendlin, "Looking beyond the Civic Compromise: Religious Pluralism in Late Republican Rome," in *Religion in Archaic and Republican Rome and Italy: Evidence and Experience*, edited by Edward Bispham and Christopher Smith (Edinburgh: University of Edinburgh Press, 2000), 115–35.

98. See further Zsuzsanna Várhelyi, *The Religion of Senators in the Roman Empire* (Cambridge: Cambridge University Press, 2010).

99. For the marketplace of religions, see J. A. North, "The Development of Religious Pluralism," in *The Jews among Pagans and Christians in the Roman Empire*, edited by Judith Lieu, John North, and Tessa Rajak (London: Routledge, 1992), 174–193. For a critical review of considering Rome's religion as a polis religion, see Gregory Woolf, "*Polis*-religion and Its Alternatives in the Roman Provinces," in *Römische Reichsreligion und Provinzialreligion*, edited by Hubert Canick Jörge Rüpke (Tübingen: Mohr Siebeck, 1997), 71–84.

100. Paula Fredriksen, *From Jesus to Christ: The Origins of the New Testament Images of Jesus* (New Haven: Yale University Press, 1988); "Did Jesus Oppose the Purity Laws?" *Bible Review* 11.3 (1995): 20–25, 42–47; *Jesus of Nazareth: King of the Jews* (New York: Vintage, 1999); "Mandatory Retirement: Ideas in the Study of Christian Origins Whose Time Has Come to Go," *Studies in Religion/Sciences Religieuses* 35.2 (2006): 231–46.

101. Klawans, *Purity, Sacrifice and the Temple*, 213–245, at 219. For an alternative point of view that is nevertheless sympathetic to Jesus' Jewish identity, see Bruce Chilton, *Rabbi Jesus: An Intimate Biography* (New York: Doubleday, 2000), 249–68.

102. See further Peter Lampe, "Human Sacrifice and Pauline Christology," esp. 206–209; Jorunn Økland, *Women in Their Place: Paul and the Corinthian Discourse of Gender and Sanctuary Space*, JSNT Supplement Series 269 (Sheffield: T. & T. Clark, 2004), 134–147; Andrew McGowan, "'Is there a Liturgical Text in this Gospel?' The Institution Narratives and Their Early Interpretive Communities," *JBL* 118.1 (1999): 73–87; Andrew McGowan, *Ascetic Eucharists: Food and Drink in Early Christian Ritual Meals* (New York: Oxford University Press, 1999); Ellen Bradshaw Aitken, "τὰ δρώμενα καὶ τὰ λεγόμενα: The Eucharistic Memory of Jesus' Words in First Corinthians," *HTR* 90.4 (1997): 359–70.

103. See, for example, the concerns for purity in the book of Revelation, which entitles Jesus "Lamb of God." As David Frankfurter has shown, the author assumes that his coreligionists participate in a movement that "rests entirely on proper Jewish observance"; "Jews or Not? Reconstructing the 'Other' in Rev 2:9 and 3:9," *HTR* 94.4 (2001): 403–25, at 416. Jennifer Maclean's analysis of the Barrabas traditions in Mark and Matthew offer another cogent example. As she observes, typologically interpreting Barrabas as the

scapegoat and Jesus as the immolated goat of the Yom Kippur festival, Mark and Matthew defended the sanctity of the Temple; they did not argue for its inherent injustice and impurity; "Barrabas, the Scapegoat Ritual, and the Development of the Passion Narrative," *HTR* 100.3 (2007): 309–34.

104. Lawrence M. Wills, *The Quest of the Historical Gospel: Mark, John and the Origins of the Gospel Genre* (London: Routledge, 1997), and "The Death of the Hero and the Violent Death of Jesus," in *Religion and Violence: The Biblical Heritage*, edited by David A. Bernat and Jonathan Klawans (Sheffield: Sheffield Phoenix, 2007), 79–99. See also Jennifer Maclean, "Jesus as Cult Hero in the Fourth Gospel," in *Philostratus's Heroikos: Religion and Cultural Identity in the Third Century C.E.*, edited by Ellen Aitken and Jennifer Maclean (Atlanta: Society of Biblical Literature, 2004), 195–218. On the noble deaths of the Romans, see Carlin Barton, "Honor and Sacredness in the Roman and Christian Worlds," in *Sacrificing the Self: Perspectives on Martyrdom and Religion*, edited by Margaret Cormack (New York: Oxford University Press, 2001), 23–38, and *Roman Honor: The Fire in the Bones* (Berkeley: University of California Press, 2001).

105. For a different point of view, see Glen Bowerstock, *Martyrdom and Rome* (Cambridge: Cambridge University Press, 1995).

106. Jan Willem van Henten, *The Maccabean Martyrs as Saviors of the Jewish People: A Study of 2 and 4 Maccabees* (Leiden: Brill, 1997); Tessa Rajak, "Dying for the Law: The Martyr's Portrait in Jewish-Greek Literature," in *The Jewish Dialogue with Greece and Rome: Studies in Cultural and Social Interaction* (Leiden: Brill, 2002), 99–133; Daniel Boyarin, *Dying for God: Martyrdom and the Making of Christianity and Judaism,* Figurae: Reading Medieval Culture (Stanford: Stanford University Press, 1999).

107. Rajak, "Dying for the Law," 129–30.

108. Jennifer Glancy, "Flesh, Truth and the Fourth Gospel," *Biblical Interpretation* 13.2 (2005): 107–36.

109. Stroumsa, "End of Sacrifice," 75.

110. See further David Biale, *Blood and Belief: The Circulation of a Symbol between Jews and Christians* (Berkeley: University of California Press, 2007), 55–57; Maclean, "Barrabas, the Scapegoat Ritual, and the Development of the Passion Narrative," 309–34; Jennifer Wright Knust, "Roasting the Lamb: Sacrifice and Sacred Text in Justin's *Dialogue with Trypho*," in Bernat and Klawans, *Religion and Violence*, 100–113.

111. George Heyman, *The Power of Sacrifice: Roman and Christian Discourses in Conflict* (Washington, D.C.: Catholic University of America Press, 2007), xv.

112. Elizabeth A. Castelli, *Martyrdom and Memory: Early Christian Culture Making, Gender, Theory, Religion* (New York: Columbia University Press, 2004), 51.

113. Castelli, *Martyrdom and Memory*, 51–55; Biale, *Circulation of Blood*, 74–76.

114. For further discussion of theoretical advances in the study of Greek and Roman animal sacrifice, also see the excellent collection of essays in *Ancient Victims, Modern Observers*, edited by Christopher Faraone and F. S. Naiden, forthcoming.

PART I

Theorizing Sacrifice

The Religion of Plant and Animal Offerings Versus the Religion of Meanings, Essences, and Textual Mysteries

Stanley Stowers

The program of this chapter springs from the intuition that much of both ancient and modern writing about animal sacrifice wrongly assumes some sort of essence that ties the practice intrinsically to an idea or symbol through time and across cultural areas. I wish to explore a hypothesis, namely, that it might illuminate this assumption about the relations of the relevant practices and ideas to think in terms of different modes of religiosity. Can it be useful, instead of thinking of religion as one thing, to think of different ancient Mediterranean modes of religion through which to make sense of sacrificial activities and concepts of sacrifice?[1] I can only suggest the bare outlines of this analytical exercise here.

Like all worthwhile intellectual enterprises, typology and classification in the study of religion is fraught with difficulty. I find the following past attempts both suggestive of helpful intuitions and full of unworkable difficulties: routinized and charismatic, great and little traditions, urban and rural, private and public, literate and nonliterate, elite and mass. As I have advocated elsewhere, instead of focusing on institutions, supposed social wholes, or individuals and their minds, as the dualities above variously do, I want to focus upon practices and the ways that they link together.[2] But in order to make this an exploration about religion and not just human sociality more generally, I will have to ask how these patterns of human activity involve beliefs and inferences about gods and similar beings.[3] I will focus on Greek examples because the evidence is so rich; but I believe that the patterns are much broader.

I want to talk about two modes and then offer a modification and overlay of each mode so that one might think perhaps of four modes. These modes are ways of organizing activities that involve beliefs and inferences about gods and similar beings in the organization of those activities. This approach denies that one can understand animal sacrifice by isolating that practice and asking about its "meaning" across the temporal and cultural areas that I have mentioned. I also do not want to talk about religious or social "systems." That language misses the unbounded and open-ended quality of the social, of human activities.[4] Instead, there are advantages to thinking of the social in terms of inherited activities that are partly constituted by goals, skills, and mostly implicit norms and that link in myriads of ways to other practices to make up larger social formations.

Thus I can make the analytically crucial distinction between religion and a religion or religions as in "Greek religion" or "Christianity and Buddhism are religions."[5] I am interested in all activities connected with beliefs about gods, ancestors, and so on—not just those that can be thought of as sanctioned by the kinds of complex social formations that we call religions. "Religion" is simply a class of human activity; but "a religion" is typically a set of social formations in which some elite group, through their political formations, their writings and iconic art, claims that a certain population forms some kind of social unity.[6] Among other problems, the failure to distinguish between religion as a human cognitive-practical phenomenon and "religions" has led to the minimization or exclusion by scholars of family and household religion; the religion of women, children, and slaves; so-called magic and sorcery; and any religious behavior that did not fit the legitimized descriptions and prescriptions of social formations called "religions."[7] My distinction would require that the actual social and mental cohesion of claimed groups become variables that must be proven by the scholar rather than postulates from which the reality of religion is deduced. In particular historical contexts, various combinations of the types of religion that I propose might meld seamlessly together for a particular individual and might only be theoretically and hypothetically analyzed. But at times and in some places, they also form rather distinct sets of linked practices, especially the first two types on which I will focus.

I will call the first mode the religion of everyday social exchange. For convenience, I will call the third mode civic religion, although examples range from forms of the Greek polis and Roman cities to domains ruled by kings or kings and priesthoods. The religious practices of the family and household are central to the religion of everyday social exchange, but are by no means the only practices that characterize it.[8] Participants understand gods and similar beings as agents who impinge upon and participate in quite specific and local ways in their activities of everyday life. People everywhere in the various cultural areas of the Mediterranean and West Asia practiced this kind of religion. It was in some sense, as I shall argue, basic. Animal and plant offerings have a central place here, but only make sense as activities linked to certain other practices that involve inferences about a host of beings that share certain characteristics: gods, heroes, and heroines; ancestors; ghosts, spirits, and unknown or unidentified agents of this class; and many others.[9] Now it would be a complete misunderstanding of these practices to construe these inferences as theologies, as rationalized systematic thought, that are supposed to provide the meaning for the practices. Greeks normally did not, for instance, rationalize and theorize the relations of the supremely local Zeus of the Possessions— sometimes translated as Zeus of the Pantry or Zeus of the Household Fence—and the cosmic Zeus of Olympus.[10] They did not need to because they knew what to do in contexts relevant to each of these in order to achieve their goals.[11] All Greeks seem to have known that Zeus was responsible for the weather. If rain was needed, an appeal to the heavenly or cosmic Zeus was in order. Zeus of the Possessions was represented by a jar, perhaps placed in a storeroom. Presumably one would appeal to him in order to protect the grain from mice. Scholars cannot agree on whether Greeks thought of these and numerous other Zeuses as manifestations of the same god or different gods.[12] This disagreement, I suggest, is because Greeks normally related to their deities in locally particular ways organized by what I am calling everyday social exchange. Civic religion built upon this practical sense, but modified it according to its own principles and interests. Few Greeks cared about the theoretical question regarding the nature of Zeus. As strange as it might seem to us academics, especially after centuries of Christianity, Islam, and Buddhism, there are social conditions necessary for having an interest in such questions.

Rather than imagining people carrying around highly organized and complete systems of belief that then generate actions, we should imagine that religious inferences and beliefs were evoked as aspects of their practical skills for living life day to day and were dispersed in their practices. Thus thinkings, believings, and inferrings about the gods are to be themselves understood as human activities that make sense in the context of the locally specific unfolding practices of which they are a part. Practices take place at specific places in time and space. As I will suggest below, one important set of practices for my account—reading and writing practices—by contrast tend to hide their location in time and place.

In this religion of mundane social exchange, gods and similar beings were conceived not primarily as relating to humans as dedicated patrons (e.g., Athena to Athens, Yahweh to Judeans), cosmic principles, legislators, or moral exemplars, but as interested parties.[13] Thus a deity might be willing to guarantee an oath when two people call upon it. A goddess might champion a heroic warrior. A daimon might lend the power to cast a spell. Four characteristics of conceiving gods and similar beings in this mode of religiosity stand out: People interact with them as if they were persons; they are local in ways that are significant for humans; one maintains a relationship to them with practices of generalized reciprocity; and humans have a particular epistemological stance toward them. Religious social formations with gods who are legislators, cosmic principles, or moral exemplars, I would argue, require or usually require an institutionalized, literate elite. The default position found very widely around the globe is types of religiosity with gods and similar beings who are conceived as interested parties with whom people carry on mundane social exchange.

The practices that involve inferences about and representations of gods, ancestors, unknown beings, and so on construe them as being like persons, but persons with some very special and powerful abilities.[14] These beings have human-like minds in that they think, believe, and have desires, emotions, personalities, and preferences of various sorts. In the ancient Mediterranean and West Asia, they were often conceived as immortal, although this might not be so for ghosts or the most local of beings. Even with all of their often great and diverse powers, these beings are not unlimited. Indeed, they are limited by space and time. They, for example, are conceived as being in specific places and as sometimes needing to use messengers for communication. Now, we might be tempted to say that I am making these ancient beliefs literal when they are actually only symbolic and metaphorical.[15] But while symbol and metaphor are certainly involved in this kind of religiosity, I want to argue that this global move of claiming that these beliefs are essentially symbolic and metaphorical is precisely a move that belongs to the second kind of religiosity of the literate specialist and to modernist thought. Conceiving gods and so on as possessing spatial limitations is a condition for the second characteristic of local relevance.

These practices that involve contact with the gods, heroes, and ancestors typically take place at sites with special significance. This is partly related to the idea that these beings have a history, even before human history, connected to the land and the landscape.[16] Moreover, some of these beings are responsible for the plant and animal life that belongs to the land. When Greeks laid out new cities, they first decided which deities belonged to the area and set off places for temples.[17] Yet more locally, the Greek house also had its sites for Zeus of the Possessions, Zeus of the Fence, Apollo, Hecate, Hestia, and Hermes.[18] For all of their difference from mortal humans and their powers, such beings were natural inhabitants of the specific environment just as much as were eagles, olive trees, and butterflies.

The persistent central practices in the religion of everyday social exchange follow from the very particular assumptions about the class of gods and related beings. Animal sacrifice makes sense in this context. Three families of practices have their sense in light of these assumptions: divinatory practices; "speaking" practices, including prayer, promising, blessing, cursing, and other social transactions; and practices of social reciprocity more narrowly, including sacrificial gifts (drink offerings, plant and grain offerings, meat offerings). To these three one should add a more ambiguous, but important class of meals and offerings for the dead. These are not the only practices in this mode of religiosity, but they are the most important.

What knowledge was most important to this kind of religion? The answer, I believe, is not myth or theological concepts—these were often sketchy at best. Rather, it was a matching-up of the how-to knowledge of common social practices with lore and stock inferences about how gods and such beings would behave as kinds of persons. Who in the ancient Mediterranean did not know how to give gifts, prepare food for others, share in celebratory meals, clean up a place for others, talk to others, request from others, ask for help, get someone powerful to help you, appease the hostile, make promises, honor and praise, sing for someone, seek information about another's disposition, whether kindly or hostile, and seek expert or insider advice? Simply add the idea that the other person involved was a god, ancestor, hero, angel, dead martyr, or other such being who might be a willing participant, and one has a list of the religious practices of this mundane religiosity. Modifications of everyday practices were the most important religious practices. Of course, such beings had special qualities, and so there was a certain logic to the way that everyday practices of social exchange got modified. Gods, for instance, did not often directly show themselves or talk back directly like humans or consume food like humans; in this sense, they were "nonobvious." They had their own ways to participate, communicate, and appear, even if they were ordinarily excellent partners in generalized reciprocity. An adequate theory of sacrifice requires an account of common human practices and the kinds of basic beliefs and inferences about gods and similar beings that provided the practical logic and skills for the religious modifications of the common practices.

The dominant epistemological mood in the religion of everyday social exchange was uncertainty—not uncertainty about the existence of the gods and similar beings or about the gods as the source of goods from the land and aid for human activities, but uncertainty about how and when the gods act and about their moods and desires. Humans know very little about how the gods are feeling and what they are doing; but they know that the gods know much or all of what humans think, feel, and do.[19] This epistemological imbalance produces a situation for humans that is similar to being in a many-windowed house with curtains up after dark. Those inside have a feeling that they are being watched, which may be likely in the busy neighborhood, but they do not know who the watchers are, when they are watching, or what their intentions are. The situation makes the gods excellent guarantors of human social transactions—for example, of oaths and vows. The gods can also be a uniquely valuable source for information about what humans are doing, whether the machinations of an enemy or the true feelings of a love interest. Thus the enormous importance of divinatory practices both for this sort of information and for detecting the dispositions of the gods and what they foresee. The dispositions and advice of the gods was seen primarily in signs and traces, and frequently took the form of yes or no, well disposed or not. Pindar expresses the typical epistemological uncertainty that should be contrasted with the certainty in the second mode of religiosity: "Never yet has anyone who walks upon the earth found a reliable symbol from the gods concerning a future matter" (*Ol.* 12.7–12). Xenophon can both write, "The gods know everything and in sacrifices, omens, voices, and dreams they give forewarnings to whomever they want" (*Eq. mag.* 9.7–9), and point out that people were also skeptical of divine omniscience (*Symp.* 4.47–49; *Mem.* 1.1.19).[20] The gods at least knew a great deal, perhaps everything.

There is one activity of the gods that humans in this mode of religiosity know most clearly and feel as immanent. The gods regularly give the fruit of the land— the grain, the oil, the offspring of animals, and the children of humans. These new products mysteriously come from somewhere. Why not from someone? This assumption, together with the default intuition that the gods are persons, forms the context for practices of social reciprocity with the gods. Market exchange creates a relationship between commodities by way of money and price equivalences.[21] Such an exchange comes to an end with the end of the transaction. Reciprocity is exactly the opposite. Exchanged commodities have no exact equivalence or exact value. Rather, reciprocal exchange furthers an unending (in principle) relationship between persons. Mutual gift giving across time maintains the relationship because there is always something left over that calls for another exchange. One never achieves a balance, an equivalence, that would call for the end of gift giving. These practices worked well even for quite unequal relationships, say between the wealthy or powerful and the poor, because the point (at least in theory) is not the value of the gifts, but the relationship based on honor and mutual respect.

Greek and ancient Mediterranean religious practices acted out such reciprocity with the gods. At center were gifts of food from plants and animals in return for the gift of those very goods from the gods. The overwhelmingly dominant forms of sacrifice were ritualized versions of festive food preparation and eating practices with very special guests. If the gods had demanded sacrifice, it would not have been a matter of giving or reciprocity. How did the death of the animal fit these activities? If you have ever tried to eat a live and uncooked animal, then you know the answer. Were it not for the later Christian theologizing of Christ's death as a sacrifice, we would not even be asking this question. In the religion of everyday social exchange, animal sacrifice was not a dramatic action, but a relatively mundane occasion in which meat was shared with the gods as it was eaten.

Because of Christian theology, scholarly attention has focused on so-called expiatory and apotropaic sacrifices, what the Greeks often called *enagismos*.[22] It is important to understand how these sorts of practices do not negate the generalizations about gift giving and reciprocity. Although I have focused upon "the gods," these religions contained both a range of nonobvious beings and a range of personality with and among particular gods. "The gods" were the public, most powerful, and well disposed of these beings with whom the various ethnic populations had had long and regular relations. But there were other sorts of beings. Beings that we call spirits, demons, the restless dead, angels, ancestors, daimones, nymphs, and satyrs (shading off into anthropomorphisms such as the evil eye) are typically found in very specific local contexts, where they have a variety of temperaments. One might encounter these beings in specific contexts or seek them out for specific purposes, without doing much if anything to maintain a steady reciprocal relationship with them. Even the Olympian deities have differing moods and contextual manifestations. As in reciprocity among humans, relations of reciprocity with nonobvious beings are complex and may become strained or broken or difficult. A gift/sacrifice can even be rejected.[23] As personalities vary, such relations are more difficult with some beings than with others. Sometimes normal gift giving is the wrong thing to do, and gifts that represent appeasement, conciliation, or caution about the relationship make sense. Thus a whole range of plant, drink, and animal offerings, which did not show the presumption of festive *thusia*, gave people options for special occasions or for difficult gods and daimones.

So-called magical practices were important in the religion of everyday social exchange and made sense there, but often ran against the larger communitarian norms of civic religion. The more than three hundred curse tablets just from Attica show us that the same people who were paragons of civic religion also secretly employed the curses aimed at people in civic contexts (e.g., court cases).[24] The religion of everyday social exchange often supported civic religion, but also was often at cross-purposes with it.

The second mode is the religion of the literate cultural producer, together with people who clustered around more entrepreneurial versions of this specialist. These people were specialists by virtue of the skills, prestige, and legitimacy derived from their belonging to the perhaps 2 percent or less of people who were literate enough to produce and authoritatively interpret complex, written texts.[25] Although small in number in any one location, they formed a large network due to the mobility and endurance of written texts across time and place. These networks—or fields, to vary the metaphor—were united by a set of common literate practices that allowed skills, writings, ideas, motifs, and so on to cross ethnic, linguistic, and status boundaries. The point of view of these specialists has dominated scholarship on animal sacrifice. It has been difficult for scholars to notice that writing a text or taking an interpretive position as a literate specialist are different practices, with different socio-cultural locations, than killing, cutting up, and cooking an animal to honor a god. This, I believe, is because scholars on religion have continued in modernist forms to reproduce the discourse and to inhabit the practices of the ancient specialists. It is a case of being able to see around oneself, but not oneself. To my claims, I suspect that the scholar wants to reply: "The sacrificer may not have been literate, but it is all about meaning; one writes it down and finds it in a writing, but the other possesses the meanings in his head. What is the difference?" Precisely this move of assimilation, which denies different modes of religiosity, gives the specialist his or her unacknowledged assumption of an Archimedian point of view and God's eye vantage.

The person who offered a sacrificial animal did not need to be literate, and the practice did not depend upon writings and their interpretation. Any Greek, Italian, Judean, or other culturally similar illiterate farmer could offer cakes or sacrifice an animal. And while the religion of the specialist producer might include the practices of everyday social exchange, even be parasitic upon them, the religion of the specialist could not exist without writings, high literacy, networks of literate exchange, and various textually oriented interpretive practices. It is important to stress that I am not drawing a contrast between intelligent, knowledgeable people with skilled interpretive practices and those who do not possess these qualities. The illiterate farmer might be highly intelligent and a skillful interpreter of a vast amount of religious knowledge and be a skilled interpreter of the relevant signs, but his offerings and knowledge do not make him part of a distinctive arena of competing producers of writings and interpretive practices based upon the translocal circulation of these products.[26]

Two things must be kept in mind in order to understand the effects of literate specialists on religion. First, any literate textual practice, including writing, reading, and interpretive practices, introduces modifications into, or overlaid against, the religion of everyday social exchange and civic religion. Second, the degrees of novelty and difference that separated the religion of the literate specialist from the religion of everyday social exchange and civic religion varied greatly among different kinds of specialists in the field. This field of literate exchange had many subfields, organized by ethnicity, social rank, educational opportunity, etc. It also had two poles that were in creative tension.[27] On one end of the spectrum, specialists were not very entrepreneurial and depended upon kings, patrons, the scribal needs of aristocrats, and even public patronage. Although literate specialists on this pole tended to intellectualize and textualize sacrifice, they took a much less radical position than those on the other pole. By the second century CE, for example, this pole was represented by the dominant Greek and Latin rhetorical education and by the orators and writers of the so-called Second Sophistic. But there was an opposing pole made up of certain sorts of philosophers, Christian teachers, and many sorts of independent operators who defined themselves in opposition to the dominant pole. The traditionally legitimized specialists, in their view, had been corrupted by depending upon the money, power, and prestige that belonged to the dominant pole. Truth and morals could only come from those who had not sold out, those who showed disinterest in money, wealth, and power. Specialists on this dominated side had no position by inheritance or bestowal and could only gain legitimacy by outdoing other specialists in displaying disinterest and novelty. Unsurprisingly, these entrepreneurs criticized reciprocity as a mode of relating to the gods.[28] The gods could not be bribed, bargained with, or honored with petty offerings. The gods wanted true beliefs and the right inner formation of individuals.

In the case of classical Athens, the poets were the literate specialists who stood closest to the everyday religion and the religion of the polis (i. e., civic religion). Epic, tragedy, and comedy were in many ways conservative, but literate specialists by definition followed norms inherited from other specialists in the field that operated by literary, interpretive, and textual principles that were semiautonomous in relation to everyday religion and civic religion. Thus, Zeus in epic poetry and comedy was often lusty, adulterous, and in a troubled marriage with Hera. This Zeus fit ancient storytelling conventions of the relevant genres and their entertainment values. In the religion of everyday social exchange, by contrast, and in the religion of the polis, Zeus and Hera were most sober models of marital propriety.[29] Zeus in Homer or Aeschylus is remote from Zeus of the Possessions, who had little or no myth and did not need personality. Yet poetry was performed publicly, and poets lived by public patronage. The underlying conservatism of the poets allowed their textual innovations on religion to exist in semiautonomy alongside the religion of everyday social exchange in civic religion. If the Homeric epics or Athenian drama had disappeared, the religion of everyday social exchange would have been little affected.[30]

The oppositional pole of the field of literate specialists in Athens was occupied by philosophers of various sorts, certain so-called sophists, independent religious entrepreneurs, and traditions such as Orphism.[31] This pole was important for the future because it was necessary to the formation of Christianity. Many of these literate specialists centrally criticized both poetry and the religion of everyday social exchange. The opposition of philosophy to poetry is too well known to us. For all of the differences that separated the legitimized poets from the religious entrepreneurs and philosophers, it is important to recognize that they were—excuse the metaphor—playing versions of the same game on a common field. This shared game can be seen—among other ways—in their sense of opposition to one another, one pole of the field to the other. One side guarded traditional religious sensibilities, and the other attacked these as false religion. Their reading, writing, interpretive practices, and generalizing, even universalizing, points of view allowed both sides to take intellectualist positions on religious matters. The Greek farmer in the religion of everyday social exchange did not take competing positions on the true nature of Demeter or Zeus of the Possessions or on the origins and meaning of some civic cult as an essential part of his religiosity.

Drama, in virtue of its proximity to the less independent side of the field, only took positions in indirect ways, often by voicing difficult theological questions and providing kinds of explanations, including the invention of memorable foundation stories for established civic cults.[32] The questioning and explaining took place safely inside the different world and time of heroic myth. In this mythic time and world, gods could be imagined as demanding human sacrifice by a writer who inhabited this literary world. But such imagining was utterly remote from everyday sacrificial practices and not the perception of some essence or origin to sacrifice. The literate products of drama also created other novelties for both civic religion and the religion of everyday social exchange. In the world of myth, the gods were often irrationally angry, vengeful, seemingly unjust, and undependable. Athenians in their civic religion never spoke of the gods in this way.[33] In the public religion of the city, the gods were always good, gracious, and trustworthy. Furthermore, the gods loved Athens in a way that gods did not love individuals in the religion of everyday social exchange.

Robert Parker makes yet another point about drama's difference from everyday religion. In contrast to the rich divine and heroic personalities of drama, "In daily life the experience of the gods was muted and anonymous. One might suspect a divine element in many aspects of life, but one never or hardly ever saw an identifiable god at work. In ordinary speech accordingly one normally spoke of 'the divine' or 'the gods' or an unspecified 'god/the god/some god,' not of named Olympians."[34] These speech practices that Parker describes, with their implied modest epistemology, comes from what I have argued is the religion of everyday social exchange, a default basic religiosity that was built upon and modified in the religion of literate specialists and in civic religion. Fitting with drama's location toward the dominant pole of literate specialty, which is most closely connected to civic and everyday religion, its position-takings about religion took place in the bracketed arena of fictionality and of a fabulous yonder-world of myth. Here knowledge about the gods presented itself as story told by someone from some place. This approach connected with the often-richer divine personalities and language of secure knowledge favored in civic cult, but in terms of the semiautonomous literate practices of this kind of specialist.[35]

By contrast, speaking from the oppositional pole, Zeno of Citium *knew* that Zeus was the one deity who had created this cycle of the cosmos and who pervaded the world as the structuring *pneuma*, and he explicitly argued that other positions were quite wrong.[36] Moreover, he knew that Homer had craftily presented his gods as symbols for this underlying reality. The popular and civic understanding of the poets was theologically wrong and immoral. Proper interpretation was required. The priest who wrote the Derveni papyrus laments the ignorant literalist views that most people have.[37] Just as one might expect, Aristophanes in turn ridicules such literate specialists who come from the independent and nonlegitimized side of the field. On this kind of analysis, his famous criticisms of Socrates are predictable. In *Peace* (38–49), a slave who has to tend the disgusting dung beetle wonders if some angry god has given him the job as a punishment. Then his fellow servant says, "But perhaps now some spectator, some beardless youth who thinks himself a sage, will say, What is this? What does the beetle *mean*? And then an Ionian, sitting next to him, will add, I think he refers this *enigmatically* to Cleon, who so shamelessly feeds on filth all by himself."[38] Of interest here, are the student sage-want-to-be, the Ionian next to him, and the practice of seeking the meaning of enigmas. The second is surely a reference to the many Ionian philosophers and similar intellectuals who came to Athens in the fifth century or perhaps especially to one of them. Many of these operated by the allegorical or symbolic interpretation of texts, finding deep meanings not found in civic religion and the religion of everyday social exchange. To use Gregory Nagy's language, such practices often participated in an "ideology of exclusiveness."[39]

The tension between traditional religion and the claimed authority of the specialist with his books and interpretive practices is wonderfully captured in the *Birds* of Aristophanes (959–90). Pisthetaerus is about to sacrifice a goat for the founding of the new city in the sky when an oracle-speaker (*chresmologos*) appears:

> Oracle-Speaker: Let not the goat be sacrificed.
> Pisthetaerus: Who are you?
> Oracle-Speaker: Who am I? An Oracle-Speaker.
> Pisthetaerus: Get out!
> Oracle-Speaker: Wretched man, insult not sacred things. For there is an
>   oracle of Bacis which exactly applies to Cloudcuckooland. . . .
> Oracle-Speaker: *But when the wolves and the white crows shall dwell together*
>   *between Corinth and Sicyon . . .*
> Pisthetaerus: What do the Corinthians have to do with me?
> Oracle-Speaker: Bacis enigmatizes this to the air [*aer*].
> *They must first sacrifice a white-fleeced goat to Pandora, and give the prophet*
>   *who first reveals my words a good cloak and new sandals.*
> Pisthetaerus: Does it say sandals there?
> Oracle-Speaker: Look at the book.[40]

Beyond the standard joke about the greedy motives of seers in this exchange, Aristophanes gives some interesting details about this particular oracle-speaker.

The latter interprets a book of oracles by Bacis, the famous oracle-speaker of the fifth century from Boeotia who was credited with important prophecies about the Persian War; prophecies under his name were important during the Peloponnesian War. Books of his oracles circulated widely and were used at least as late as the second century CE. The figure in the *Birds* is an expert interpreter of a book that is an accumulation of literate knowledge-practices. Whether these are supposed to be ecstatic prophecies of Bacis committed to writing or prophecies from elsewhere that Bacis collected is not clear. But the specialist in the *Birds* applies to the situation of Cloudcuckooland an interpretation that Bacis gave to an oracle in another context. Peter Struck has pointed out that Aristophanes uses the same technical language for interpretation here as he does of the Ionian philosopher in *Peace*: "Bacis enigmatizes this to *aer*."[41] The language comes from the symbolic interpretation of texts. We should not universalize and naturalize symbolic interpretation, as has been done in much literary and anthropological theory. The symbolic interpretation of writings has a beginning and a history. Its modern practitioners have bedeviled the study of sacrifice. In the *Birds, aer* is, of course, the lower atmosphere where Cloudcuckooland was to be. But what symbolic interpreters of Homer and other writings had found, at least as far back as the sixth century, was that the ancient writers had left enigmas in the text with symbolic meanings. The real meanings of these enigmas were often physical and cosmological truths, such as the idea popular from Empedocles to the Stoics that Hera represented *aer*, both the element and the heavenly realm.[42] In the examples from *Peace* and the *Birds*, Aristophanes makes light of a kind of claim to literate interpretive knowledge that is particularly annoying to him; that of the annoyingly independent and unsanctioned fellow specialists in texts, literature, and opinions about what is right and true.

Such specialists often criticized the religion of everyday social exchange by claiming that their textually based knowledge disclosed the true and deeper meaning of everyday practices. Rather than the mundane local perspectives and interests of the first mode of religiosity, the literate specialist, especially those of the more entrepreneurial kind, sought to discover the deep meanings and hidden wisdom about the gods, the cosmos, the structure of the world and human nature. Paul's words in Romans 12:1–2 provide an example: "[P]resent your bodies as a living sacrifice [*thusia*], holy and well-pleasing to God which is your rational worship. And do not be structured by this age, but be transformed by the renewal of your mind so that you might test for what is the will of God. . . ." The "rational worship" of the exhortation implies a contrast with the non-Judean ritual practices that Paul excoriates earlier in Romans 1:21–25. Specifically, he claims that practices, surely involving animal sacrifice, that employ carved and variously formed representations of gods in anthropomorphic, theriomorphic, and other iconic forms are foolish, dishonor God, represent a corruption of rationality, and lead to gross immorality. From the perspective of this specialist producer, a self-proclaimed expert interpreter of Judean writings, these common practices featuring gods of many locales miss the truth of one transcendent universal god who should be worshipped with the right conceptions, a mind in the proper disposition, and the right moral character. Religion here is not about the everyday interests of family, clan, friends, and neighbors; good crops; the health of a child; the powers of revenge for a perceived injustice; and so on. Rather it concerns products of mind, right belief about the divine, the true nature of the self, and discernment of one's place in the drama of world history. This intellectualist origin of Christian religion is why it took centuries for Christians to develop distinctive life-course rituals, such as for weddings, funerals, and local agricultural festivals. In the religion of literate specialists, sacrifice is often not festively eating an animal in the presence of the gods. It is a cipher for supposedly deeper meanings.

Of course, all of these deeper truths required the interpretive skills of the specialist who alone could decipher the meaning of things by means of their literate abilities. One could include Zeno of Citium, who thought that there was no need for temples at all, and Chrysippus, who read traditional Greek representations of the gods as symbols that pointed to the one theistic-pantheistic god. Plutarch used similar methods to find a different sort of god in a vastly more hierarchical universe. Or it could be Lucian of Samosata, who ridiculed animal sacrifice and ordinary religious practices. The list is very large. The important thing is to see that Paul, Zeno, Plutarch, and Lucian—in spite of the competitive opposition that they would have had toward each other by virtue of being specialists whose raison d'etre was staking positions about what is true, right, and good—shared more with each other than they did with the Greek farmer or Egyptian Jewish weaver. Above all, the practices about the gods that they valued most highly and upon which their power depended were their competitive literate skills.[43]

Plato takes the literate specialist's point of view on the religion of everyday social exchange when, in the *Laws*, he proposes to do away with practices that he sees as too private, local and reflective of misunderstandings about the nature of the gods:

> It is not easy to establish temples and gods, and to do this properly requires great intelligence [*dianoia*], but it is customary for all women especially, and for people who are sick everywhere, and people in danger or trouble—no matter what kind of trouble—and conversely, when people have some good fortune, to consecrate whatever happens to be at hand right then, and to vow sacrifices and promise the building of sacred places or objects for gods, daemons and children of the gods: and because of fears caused by apparitions while awake or dreams . . . they chance to found altars and sacred sites, filling every house and every village with them, and open spaces too, and every spot that was the place of such experiences. [*Leg.* 909e–910b][44]

True religion must show a disinterest in the private and local and show an interest in the city as a whole, the universal and the true nature of the gods.

The specialist thinks that what is essential to a practice is its meaning. Meaning here is some determinate proposition or set of propositions about the practice that usually derives from the specialist's textual activities.[45] Such propositions often come with criticisms about sacrificial practices being too local, too interested, and too literal. "Literal" means supposedly ranking the traditional activity, understood as mundane interaction with the gods, over meaning. The most important practices of the literate specialist were acts of translation. Even their writings depended upon interpretive reading activities involving books deemed to have authority of various types. The earliest known Greek example involving such translation is Pherekydes of Syron, who wrote about 544 BCE. Fragments of Pherekydes show him interpreting passages from Homer as truly about the fundamental nature of the cosmos. From Pherekydes to Aristotle, one finds Metrodorus of Lampascus, Theagones of Rhegium, Anaxagoras, and Stesimbrotus of Thasos treating Homer in similar ways.[46] The act of translation works like this: The shallow person, probably the average participant in the religion of social exchange, understands Homer, and presumably rituals, at the surface level. But these literate specialists know that "difficult" passages in Homer are "enigmas" and "symbols" that reveal truths about the nature of the soul, the cosmos, and other wisdom. So Aristobulus, Philo of Alexandria, and numerous other Jewish specialists treated the Books of Moses. Christians would likewise translate from Judean scripture into truths about the true nature of the world order, its future, true worship, and a particular figure from recent history. In each case, what ordinary people practiced as local, particular, and unsystematic, the specialist translates into another idiom that tends toward the universal, the nonlocal, and harmonized knowledge.

The writers of the rabbinic literature produced another translation that can be used to illustrate the range of creative possibility available to the specialists. They imaginatively "replaced" a Temple-centered religion of plant and animal offerings with a nonlocative, highly portable religion that ingeniously featured not the meanings of the literate specialists, but their practices. The study and legal discussions themselves of written and oral divine revelations became the central religious practices. Performance of acts with textualized significance became central. Jonathan Z. Smith gives one way of doing this: "[A]ttributed to Rabbi Gamaliel: 'Whoever does not say these three things on Passover has not fulfilled his obligations,' with the first of these being the sacrifice of the Paschal lamb (*M.* Pesachim 10.5). This is a sentence about ritual speech that, by virtue of its inclusion in the later *Passover Haggadah*, has itself become ritual speech."[47] Moreover, this latter move makes the ritual speech into a substitute for animal sacrifice. In some ways reminding me of the Attic tragedians, these central practices that connected with everyday practices of the household, like prayer and meals, were set in an epic, mythic framework that intertwined the mythic world with contemporary interpretation and practice. So with sacrifice, the myth of a portable temple in a wilderness and its ritual laws from the Hebrew Bible was projected onto the imagination of two temples built and destroyed before any of the "rabbis" lived. The Mishna and Talmuds discuss and encourage study and discussion of laws imagined for a conflation of these mythic temples as if they were laws for the present. The bloody contingency, mind-numbing repetition, and fatigue of priests slaughtering, dismembering, and reducing hundreds and even many thousands of animals a day in a historical "second" Judean Temple must not be confused with learned imaginative study and the invention of regulations that circumscribe imagined priestly activity with practices that are in the rethinking of epic myth written small to theoretically avoid ritual error.

Another early Greek example of such specialists comes from the Derveni Papyrus.[48] The fourth-century author of this commentary on an Orphic cosmological poem was a divinatory priest, who mentions his oracle-reading activity (cols. V, XI) and alludes to other divinatory practices. In the manner of the literate specialist, he has textualized ritual. He expresses unhappiness with the people who come to him for rituals. The truly pious have a full understanding of the rituals through the proper interpretation of the texts, while others perform the rituals without the right thoughts (col. XX). The author harshly criticizes the normal person's participation in ritual as ignorant and impious. What they must have for the proper rituals, which include animal sacrifice (cols. II, IV—to the Erinyes; col. VI—preliminary sacrifice to the Eumenides, bird to the gods), is a proper allegorical understanding of meaning. The author-priest interprets the writings of Orpheus as oracular and full of enigmas, riddles to be translated into cosmogonic and cosmological truths. Important work by David Konstan has convincingly argued that ancient reading practices in general, not just the work of allegorists and the like, featured the search for riddles, problems to be solved, and the underlying meanings in the text.[49] High literacy in general then fostered the kind of outlook on the world featured in the religion of literate specialists.

A more general tendency for the religion of literate specialists entails not only claiming that rituals are about meanings revealed by translation, but also textualizing the rituals. Practices of claiming a fixed text as the truth of a ritual introduce a far different dynamic than the mythic fragments to which the practices of everyday religion allude or the endless strategic variations of oral mythic storytellers. To say that a text—from Hesiod, Paul's institution text for the Lord's supper, or a liturgy—is the privileged meaning not only aims to limit interpretation, but also tends to move the emphasis from everyday local goals to truths and ritual actions that concern supposedly deeper universal human and cosmic issues.

I believe that modern scholarship on animal sacrifice has been too close to the habits of the ancient literate specialists. Meanings of guilt and atonement, the sacredness of life, sacred violence, the scapegoat mentality, the idea of the sacred and the profane—these are among the very large number of such translations.[50] But are meanings the essential or important thing about social practices that are not themselves literate textual practices? What is the meaning of lunch? Lunch has as many meanings as it does diners, and those meanings are secondary to the everyday goals of acquiring nutrition and enjoying pleasure in eating and in sharing these ends with others. Of course, someone can always say that lunch on a certain day will be eaten so as to commemorate a certain story. The problem would come from claiming that the essential, basic, or important thing about the everyday practice of eating lunch was that story or its meaning. The Greek gods were participants in the everyday social world of the Greeks. The activities of living with the gods, including cooking and eating animals, did not need the texts and the meanings of the specialists in order for Greeks to carry on that imagined divine-human sociality. This is not to say that sacrificial practices did not do social work by indexing types of participants (e.g., men/women, young/mature, Greek citizens/noncitizens). Nor does my approach deny that individuals might sometimes have various symbolic or propositional associations and symbolic intuitions. But these will be too indeterminate, varied, and changing to be the "meaning" of sacrificial practice or what is important about it for participants. Sacrifice like lunch did not encode its own interpretation apart from the implicit practical understandings that constituted it as an act of cooking, eating, giving, and honoring. For Greeks, Romans, and others it was interpretive because it involved divinatory practices: reading the inner organs of the animal, watching the burning and the movements of the fire, and watching the tail, bladder, and behavior of the animal as it processed to the altar. All of these and more might indicate messages from the gods, but in the form of signs and traces, not the certain propositions or legal opinions of privileged texts and interpreters.

Finally, I can only in the briefest way suggest the two additional modes of the analytical typology. These are both something like overlays upon the religion of everyday social exchange and the religion of literate specialists. Both involve the larger scale political and institutional development of one or both of the other modes. One thinks about these by noting that they both require the religion of everyday social exchange for their existence, but not vice versa. Then one can inquire (e.g., in the case of civic religion, which I term the third mode) about what was added to the religion of everyday social exchange by the development of the Mediterranean city and civic culture and how did the civic culture modify and interact with everyday religion. This third mode is the religion of political power and civic ideology, to which I have already alluded in my Greek examples. The most important practices of this mode are elaborations of the religion of everyday social exchange according to political and civic interests and principles. This mode of religion does not require literate specialists. So, for example, the religion of the Greek city presupposed, built upon, and extended the religion of everyday social exchange. It incorporated almost all of the latter's practices. When temples moved from the houses and lands of kings and aristocrats to the emerging polis, they became places where all families could practice.[51] Practices of households and very local shrines developed into carriers of the ideology of the city and mirrored its social organization with developing phratries, demes, tribes, and centralized civic institutions, all with their own versions of sacrificial practices. The main social figure here is the local landowner, forming a hierarchical alliance with the aristocratic landowner; the main practice consists of offerings from such landowners sacrificed at temples, which are centralized to varying degrees. Rituals that involve bounded groups defined as citizens or descendants of common ancestors coming together in centralizing activities orchestrated with calendars are perhaps the most important

modification of practices from the religion of everyday social exchange. My hunch
is that the further away (in physical distance, as well as socially and culturally) cel-
ebrants were from the very small number of elites who could be accommodated at
civic temples and shrines, the more their religion would look like everyday religion,
even on civic holidays. I would argue that non-Greek cities in Italy and the Judean
temple state were different versions of this same overlay. I call it an overlay because
one could have the religion of everyday social exchange, including animal sacrifice,
without these political-cultural-institutional elaborations. The proverbial Arcadian
village or Euboean farmer practiced in this mode perfectly well without such developments. History, ethnography, and perhaps cognitive science has shown that the
everyday religion is the default mode.[52]

The fourth mode based itself upon the religion of literate specialists that itself
presupposed the religion of everyday social exchange, but with political and institutional developments based upon literate specialists rather than the nonspecialist
political elaboration of the third mode based on the landowners. I will call this the
religion of literate specialists and political power. The Christian churches are the
most obvious ancient Mediterranean examples, a religion distant from the agricultural life and economy and requiring specialists with books. Here the religion
of entrepreneurial specialists like Paul, Valentinus, Tatian, Justin, and numerous
others received institutionalized forms and political organization that also changed
the mode of the religiosity. This mode of politically and institutionally organized
literate specialists did not completely leave behind the religion of everyday social
exchange, but intellectualized it and tried to subordinate it to the control of the polit-
ical-institutional literate specialists like priests and bishops. Thus it reintroduced a
dominated version of everyday religion "reformed" by the teachings of the more
entrepreneurial specialists. In a great reversal, literate specialists (e.g., textualized
ritual expertise) came to perform their powers on stages before audiences of landowners. Ramsey MacMullen's brilliantly documented "first and second churches"
illustrate my theorization.[53] The first church of clergy, other literate elite, and well-
to-do property owners worshipped in the rather small spaces of the church edifices
and claimed to represent and control the whole Christian population. Here the
divine was conceived as remote and hierarchically mediated, as in Trinitarian theology. The masses of Christians, including those only ambiguously so, celebrated in
cemeteries with familial dead, in martyr-hero shrines, and in other settings of the
religion of everyday social exchange. By the fifth century, those in power were developing or at least allowing a religion that would mediate between the religion of
the literate specialist and a religion of everyday social exchange, with the places of
saints, martyrs, miracles, and other holy sites spreading across the urban and rural
landscape; but ultimate authority rested in the interpreters of books. As this fourth
mode emerged from the late second century on, it became important, if difficult, to
enforce the right meanings of rituals and to control the entrepreneurial activities
of the literate producers. At the same time, the mode organized institutions for
education in the right meanings by the constant repetition of approved teachings

and through rituals that featured approved meanings connected to authoritative, written texts. Now the butchering, cooking, and eating of animals came to seem like a crude gesture that had failed to grasp some deeper proposition or symbols revealed in texts that had been the true essence of the practice all along.

Notes

1. David Frankfurter in this volume (chapter 3) argues that the category represented by the word *sacrifice* has no descriptive utility and that its absence from Egyptian religion should cause scholars to "decentralize" sacrifice as a "characteristic rite in Near Eastern and Greco-Roman religions." The concept has no utility because it carries theological and theoretical baggage. I agree about the baggage, but not about the conclusions regarding the concept(s). I find it a false dichotomy that one must choose between accepting conceptions of sacrifice that define it as a kind of killing, destruction, and violence and abandoning the category. The word carries baggage, but no act of language purification could solve the problem, partly because the problem inheres in the history of antiquity itself. Christianity mythically "changed" the practice of an animal food offering into the idea of the death and suffering of Christ as a sacrifice using ubiquitous Greek and Latin concepts. The arguments against those who would similarly eliminate the concept of "religion" as too problematic also apply to Frankfurter's case and have been powerfully made by Kevin Schilbrack ("Religions: Are There Any?" *JAAR* forthcoming; "The Social Construction of 'Religion' and Its Limits: A Critical Reading of Timothy Fitzgerald," *Method and Theory in the Study of Religion*, forthcoming). It is indeed helpful to show that the typical modes of Mediterranean sacrifice were not important to native Egyptian religion, but I do not understand how this makes the former phenomena less important. I also believe that Frankfurter has minimized the evidence for sacrificial practices in Greek, Roman, and Hellenized Egyptian contexts.

2. See my "The Ontology of Religion," in *Introducing Religion: Essays in Honor of Jonathan Z. Smith*, edited by Willi Braun and Russell T. McCutcheon (London: Equinox, 2008), 434–49. Practices are socially organized doings and saying. Thus they are mostly inherited by participants in particular societies and involve implicit norms, that is, they can be done in right and wrong ways.

3. Stowers, "Ontology of Religion," 442–47.

4. Theodore Schatzki, *The Site of the Social: A Philosophical Account of the Constitution of Social Life and Social Change* (University Park: Pennsylvania State University Press, 2002).

5. This distinction is outlined theoretically in my "Ontology of Religion." As I hint in that article, I need an account of the cognitive structures of the evolved human mind in order to complete the account. I am currently working on a second part that attempts to provide the psychological component necessary to a theory of practices.

6. The elite group not only consists of those who claim to represent the religion, but might also be modern scholars (e.g., who describe Hinduism as the ancient religion of India).

7. For classical Athens, one might add to this list many sorts of intellectuals, much religious practice in connection with the dead and heroes, many local and ad hoc rites of

individuals and groups (e.g., Plato, *Resp.*, 909e–910b), and foreign and mixed practices. All of these on both lists are often marginalized or excluded in the polis-religion model.

8. It is extremely important not to read the conventional private/public distinction into my modes. My modes are extremely relational and interactive when they exist together and on a continuum of more and less. See my "Theorizing the Religion of the Ancient Household and Family" and the other essays in *Household and Family Religion in Antiquity*, edited by John Bodel and Saul M. Olyan (Oxford: Blackwell, 2008). The chapters by Faraone and Boedeker join a mounting chorus of protest against the tendency to claim that all religion in the classical Greek city (sometimes meaning Athens) was "polis religion," as defined in the brilliant and influential articles by Sourvinou-Inwood: "What is Polis Religion?" in *The Greek City from Homer to Alexander*, edited by Oswyn Murray and S.R.F. Price (Oxford: Clarendon, 1990), 295–322; "Further Aspects of Polis Religion," *Annali Instituto Orientale di Napoli: Archaeologia e Storia* 10 (1988): 259–74.

9. I agree with cognitivist theories of religion that require such beings or other anthropomorphizing interpretations of the world to have religion (Stowers, "Ontology of Religion," 443–47). Thus I think that older cognitivist approaches, such as those of Robin Horton, Melford Spiro, Ernest Gellner, and Stewart Guthrie, and the recent cognitive science approaches are on the right track. For the former, see Robin Horton, *Patterns of Thought in Africa and the West* (New York: Cambridge University Press, 1993); Melford E. Spiro, "Religion: Some Problems of Definition and Explanation," in *Anthropological Approaches to the Study of Religion*, edited by Michael Banton (New York: Praeger, 1966); Stewart Guthrie, *Faces in the Clouds* (New York: Oxford University Press, 1993). On the latter, see notes 13, 14, 19, and 52 below.

10. By my count, in classical Athens, Zeus went by at least twenty-eight different names or titles. On Zeus, see Hans Schwabl and Erika Simon, "Zeus," *RE* 10A (1927): 253–376, and supplement 15: 993–1481; Karim Arafat, *Classical Zeus: A Study in Art and Literature* (Oxford: Oxford University Press, 1990).

11. My statement should not be taken in an overly instrumental way. Goals might include attempts to understand the world and the course of events and to interpret one's life, but such local and dispersed understandings should not be segregated and made central.

12. The two sides can be represented by Jon D. Mikalson, *Honor thy Gods: Popular Religion in Greek Tragedy* (Chapel Hill: University of North Carolina Press, 1991), and Christine Sourvinou-Inwood, "Tragedy and Religion: Constructs and Readings," in *Greek Tragedy and the Historian*, edited by Christopher Pelling (Oxford: Clarendon, 1997), 161–85; *Tragedy and Athenian Religion* (Lanham, Md.: Lexington Books, 2003). Mikalson argues that Athenians did not have one unified Zeus in all of their cults, and he also emphasizes the distance between the gods of everyday cult and of the poets. Sourvinou-Inwood developed the extremely influential idea of "polis religion" (see note 8 above). My approach undermines this idea of a totalizing official religion of the Greek city that formed a kind of systemic symbolic order. In my estimation, the idea of polis religion came about from a scholarship deeply influenced by structuralism, the ideology of the European nation-state, and from viewing Greek religion through the lens of the civic and official sources—literary, iconic, and epigraphical. If true, the polis-religion interpretation would rival or surpass all published examples for the totalizing orchestration of religion in a significant population and should be compared to John Calvin's Geneva and certain Roman Catholic cities in the

century after the council of Trent. For approaches that recognize more to Greek religion than "the religion of the polis," see Christopher Faraone, "Household Religion in Ancient Greece," and Deborah Boedeker, "Domestic Religion in Classical Greece," in *Household and Family Religion in Antiquity*, 210–28 and 29–47. Robert Parker's masterful account follows a somewhat moderated polis-religion model (see note 19 below).

13. For a summary account of three of these models, see Pascal Boyer, "Why Do Gods and Spirits Matter at All?" in *Current Approaches in the Cognitive Science of Religion*, edited by Ilkka Pyysiäinen and Veikko Anttonen (London: Contiuum, 2002), 81–82. I have been influenced at several points by Boyer's account.

14. This is a basic premise of the recent cognitive psychology of religion, but was already a central assumption of older cognitivist or so-called intellectualist approaches. The former have tried to show that the brain's agent-detecting system and innate theory of mind are basic to religious concepts and religious activity. A useful introduction to the cognitive science approach is Tod Tremlin, *Minds and Gods: The Cognitive Foundations of Religion* (Oxford: Oxford University Press, 2006).

15. The groundbreaking book that definitively undermined symbolic interpretation is Dan Sperber, *Rethinking Symbolism* (Cambridge: Cambridge University Press, 1975). For an excellent treatment of some issues regarding symbolism, see the chapter by William Gilders in this volume.

16. The best discussion of the locative nature of Greek religion is Susan Guettel Cole, *Landscapes, Gender, and Ritual Space: The Ancient Greek Experience* (Berkeley: University of California Press, 2004), and *Placing the Gods: Sanctuaries and Sacred Space in Ancient Greece* (Oxford: Clarendon Press, 1994).

17. A decree of fourth-century BCE colophon gives a plan to restore the neglected or abandoned old city and speaks of the gods and heroes "who occupy our city and territory," in Franz G. Maier, *Griechische Mauerbauinschriften* (Heidelberg: Quelle & Meyer, 1959), no. 69, lines 9–21.

18. Again, at least in classical Athens.

19. On this point and the following discussion, recent work in cognitive science of religion matches well with the Greek and Roman evidence (e.g., Boyer, "Why Do Gods and Spirits Matter," 76–81) and with what the best scholarship on these cultures has concluded. On the latter, for instance, see Robert Parker, *Polytheism and Society at Athens* (Oxford: Oxford University Press, 2005), 105, 140. There is much important ferment and renewal in the study of Roman religion, generating insightful and work that implicates extremely challenging problems (e.g., the inability to sort out the various meanings and mental states of believe/belief and of literate from nonliterate religion; misunderstandings of ancient—including folk, philosophical, and Christian—epistemologies and ontologies; the assumption that civic/state religion is totalizing), helpful at many points. See Clifford Ando, *The Matter of the Gods: Religion and the Roman Empire* (Berkeley: University of California Press, 2008), 13–18, 43–56; Denis Feeney, *Literature and Religion at Rome: Cultures, Contexts and Beliefs* (Cambridge: Cambridge University Press, 1988), 12–28, 137–43.

20. My translations.

21. See the excellent discussion of reciprocity, with bibliography, in Daniel Ullucci, "The End of Sacrifice" (Ph.D. diss., Brown University, 2008) and in his chapter in this volume; Hans van Wees, "The Law of Gratitude: Reciprocity in Anthropological Theory,"

in *Reciprocity in Ancient Greece*, edited by Christopher Gill, Norman Postlethwaite, and Richard Seaford (New York: Oxford University Press, 1998), 13–50.

22. The old distinction between Olympian and Chthonian rites should be completely abandoned. For a recent discussion, see Maria-Zoe Petropoulou, *Animal Sacrifice in Ancient Greek Religion, Judaism, and Christianity, 100 BC–AD 200* (Oxford: Oxford University Press, 2008), 34–37. See Ullucci, "End of Animal Sacrifice," for an important correction of Petropoulou's claims about Jews and Christians. The Christian influence can be seen in the numerous theories of sacrifice that construe it as ritual violence and focus on the death of the animal and on some sort of transformation of the sacrificer.

23. F. S. Naiden, "Rejected Sacrifice in Greek and Hebrew Religion," *JANER* 6 (2006): 186–223.

24. Fritz Graf, *Magic in the Ancient World* (Cambridge: Harvard University Press, 1997); Christopher A. Faraone and Dirk Obbink, eds., *Magika Hiera: Ancient Greek Magic and Religion* (New York: Oxford University Press, 1991), especially the chapter by Faraone; John Gager, *Curse Tablets and Binding Spells from the Ancient World* (New York: Oxford University Press, 1992). The tendency of scholars to separate magic from religion is still an enormous impediment to understanding ancient religion.

25. For an application of this insight to some ancient instances, see my "Types of Meals, Myths, and Power: Paul and the Corinthians," in *Redescribing Christian Origins,* vol. 2, edited by Ron Cameron and Merrill P. Miller (Atlanta: Society of Biblical Literature, forthcoming).

26. It is also important not to confuse my types with the distinction between popular and elite religion. The civic religion dominated by aristocratic classes did not require literate practices; religious specialists and elites themselves might not even be highly literate.

27. My account is clearly indebted to Pierre Bourdieu's demystified reformulation of Max Weber: "Genesis and Structure of the Religious Field," *Comparative Social Research*, edited by C. Calhoun 13 (1991): 1–44; "Legitimation and Structured Interests in Weber's Sociology of Religion," in *Max Weber: Rationality and Modernity*, edited by Scott Lash and Sam Whimster (London: Allen and Unwin, 1987), 119–36; *The Rules of Art: Genesis and Structure of the Literary Field* (Cambridge: Polity, 1996); *The Field of Cultural Production* (New York: Columbia University Press, 1993).

28. Ullucci, "End of Animal Sacrifice."

29. Parker, *Polytheism and Society,* 393, 441.

30. Which is not to say that practitioners would have been little affected.

31. Documenting the category would require a book. The unfortunate tendency of many classicists not only to describe (admirably and fully), but also to use categories internal to the traditions instead of analytical categories (i.e., those designed to add knowledge to the disciplines of the modern university) means that the necessary work has not been done on this Weberian-like category. For religion, Robert Parker has discussed some appropriate evidence under the category of "Unlicensed Religion and Magic" (*Polytheism and Society*, 116–52). From the perspective of this chapter, his categories are heterogeneous and represent the internal perspectives of civic religion ("polis religion"). An important discussion of Orphism and related movements and of entrepreneurial specialist can be found in Fritz Graf and Sarah Iles Johnston, *Ritual Texts for the Afterlife: Orpheus and the Bacchic Gold Tablets* (London: Routledge, 2007).

32. Mikalson, *Honor Thy Gods*; Sourvinou-Inwood, *Tragedy and Athenian Religion.*

33. Parker, *Polytheism and Society*, 146.

34. Parker, *Polytheism and Society*, 140.

35. I do not mean that in civic cults people knew what the gods were up to or thought, but that they spoke confidently of particular deities, of what they had done in the past, and of their benevolent disposition toward Athens. Such knowledge was a requirement of civic cults where particular temples and festivals belonged to particular gods.

36. Keimpe Algra, "Stoic Theology," in *The Cambridge Companion to the Stoics*, edited by Brad Inwood (Cambridge: Cambridge University Press, 2003), 153–78.

37. See note 48 below and the associated text.

38. For the example and translation, see Peter T. Struck, *Birth of the Symbol: Ancient Readers at the Limits of Their Texts* (Princeton: Princeton University Press, 2004), 39–41.

39. Gregory Nagy, *The Best of the Achaeans: Concepts of the Hero in Archaic Greek Poetry*, rev. ed. (Baltimore: Johns Hopkins University Press, 1999), 239; Struck, *Birth of the Symbol*, 41. On such allegorical and symbolic interpretation, in addition to Struck, see *Heraclitus: Homeric Problems*, edited and translated by Donald A. Russell and David Konstan (Atlanta: Society of Biblical Literature, 2005), xi–xxx; G. R. Boys-Stones, *Metaphor Alleàgory and the Classical Tradition* (Oxford: Oxford University Press, 2003); Wolfgang Bernard, *Spätantike Dichtungs-theorien: Untersuchungen zu Proklos, Herakleitos und Plutarch* (Stuttgart: Teubner, 1990).

40. The translation is adapted from Eugene O'Neill, *The Complete Greek Dramas* (New York: Random House, 1938), and Struck, *Birth of the Symbol*, 175–76.

41. Struck, *Birth of the Symbol*, 176.

42. Peter Kingsley, *Ancient Philosophy, Mystery, and Magic: Empedocles and the Pythagorean Tradition* (Oxford: Clarendon, 1995), 24–35.

43. By contrast, the practices of animal sacrifice, as I have argued, were related to agriculture, animal husbandry, and the land. Not writing, reading, interpretive techniques, oratory, position-taking about truth, but special versions of butchering, cooking, and eating what came from the land and watching for signs were the central religious skills of the sacrificer.

44. My translation.

45. Ullucci, "End of Animal Sacrifice."

46. Struck, *Birth of the Symbol*, 26–29.

47. Jonathan Z. Smith, *Relating Religion: Essays on the Study of Religion* (Chicago: University of Chicago Press, 204), 223.

48. The critical text is still unpublished. I am following the textual numbering of André Laks and Glenn Most, *Studies in the Derveni Papyrus* (New York: Oxford University Press, 1997).

49. David Konstan, "The Active Reader in Classical Antiquity," unpublished paper.

50. See, for instance, most of the approaches in Jeffrey Carter, ed., *Understanding Religious Sacrifice: A Reader* (New York: Continuum, 2003).

51. Stowers, "Religion of the Ancient Household," 14–16.

52. The very young, but highly promising field of the cognitive psychology of religion tries to show that certain concepts and practices are more easily remembered and transmitted and more intuitive than others due to the structures of the evolved human brain/mind. They have developed the concept of the "cognitive optimal" that can be contrasted

with cognitive processes that require more cognitive and cultural labor that may even work against what is optimal. For a brief discussion of the concept, see Harvey Whitehouse and James Laidlaw, eds., *Ritual and Memory: Toward a Comparative Anthropology of Religion* (Walnut Creek, Calif.: AltaMira, 2004), 189–203, and Pascal Boyer, who has developed the idea—not without its paradoxes—of the minimally counterintuitive as optimal, for example, *Religion Explained: The Evolutionary Origins of Religious Thought* (New York: Basic Books, 2001).

53. *The Second Church: Popular Christianity A.D. 200–400* (Atlanta: Society of Biblical Literature, 2009).

2

Contesting the Meaning of Animal Sacrifice
Daniel Ullucci

Do the gods truly want animal sacrifice? Do they need it?[1] For many ancient Mediterranean authors, the answer to these questions was no, the gods do not need burned animal parts; in fact, they do not need anything. It is humans, these ancient texts claim, who stand in need of things from the gods, things like fertility, protection, and general good will. So what of sacrifice? Is it useless, incoherent, or even offensive to the gods? Many of these ancient authors respond with the same resounding no. That is, the same authors who claim that the gods do not need sacrifice also argue for continued participation in sacrifice. The group of ancient authors whose texts contain such seemingly paradoxical positions is large and varied, ranging from Greek, Roman, and Jewish philosophers to Hebrew Bible authors, Roman satirists like Lucian, and Christian authors like Paul—just to name a few. This apparent paradox serves as the focal point of this chapter. The fact that these positions appear paradoxical to us is, I argue, evidence that current models for understanding ancient discussions of animal sacrifice are flawed.

This chapter attempts to reposition the views of such ancient authors and to offer a new model for understanding their texts. Currently, texts of this type are often grouped together under the rubric "critiques of sacrifice." I hope to show that this current interpretive model, which I call the "critique model," is theoretically inadequate and fundamentally incorrect in two main ways. First, the critique model ignores the complexity of the ancient debate over animal sacrifice by collapsing a diverse range of positions into the single, ill-defined category of critique. Second, the present model serves to inscribe a modern, largely Christian narrative onto the history of animal sacrifice. This narrative presents the debate over animal sacrifice as an evolution from primitive barbaric practice to pure enlightened religion.

The first part of this chapter lays bare the faults of the critique model. I argue that texts that have traditionally been interpreted as critiques of sacrifice must be seen not as critiques, but as part of an ongoing competition over the meaning and purpose of animal sacrifice. The authors of the texts in question were elite, educated textual specialists—persons that Pierre Bourdieu refers to as cultural producers.[2] These cultural producers tended to focus their literary production on what we might call "life's big questions": What is the true nature of the divine? What is the relationship between humans and the divine? And how should one live in light of all this? One part of this larger struggle involved parsing the act of animal sacrifice, that is, explicating how sacrifice works and how it should be done.[3] The key to understanding these texts is to see that their authors are attempting to provide a singular, definitive interpretation for a ritual practice that does not intrinsically have one. Rather than critiquing some intrinsic meaning or interpretation of sacrifice, they are competing with each other, through the medium of textual production, to define that very meaning.

The model that I propose involves a transition to new terms and new concepts; that is, it involves a rectification of categories (specifically three categories). The category "meanings of sacrifice," I argue, should be replaced by the category (1) "interpretations of sacrifice." The category "critique of sacrifice" should be replaced by (2) "debate" over these interpretations. The category "critics" should be replaced by the concept of (3) "cultural producers engaged in debate." These terms and this model are, I argue, much more useful for understanding the ancient data. I will begin by discussing the critique model and then move on to a number of texts that illustrate my approach.

Deficiencies of the Critique Model

The main defect of the critique model is the use of the conceptual category "critique" itself. In this view, ancient authors found something endemic to the practice of animal sacrifice that was fundamentally wrong, be it corruption, amorality, economic exploitation, incoherence, or some other purported flaw. These forward-thinking religious critics and reformers identified the failures of sacrifice and rejected it as an appropriate religious activity or attempted to improve the ritual through "spiritualization." This interpretation has two main faults: (1) it fails to recognize the complexity of the data, and (2) it assumes that these so-called critics are motivated solely by an altruistic quest for pure and true religion, not by competition for their own legitimacy, struggles for power, or similar social factors.

Indeed, individual passages, when removed from any social context (and often from their own literary context), can appear to be biting condemnations of sacrifice. For example, Epicurus, the founder of the eponymous philosophy, argued that the gods do not need sacrifice, nor can they receive sacrifice (living as they do in a separate realm from earthbound humans), nor can they respond to sacrifice since, in the Epicurean view of the cosmos, the gods have no agency in the human world.[4] In short, Epicurus argued, the gods do not want sacrifice, the gods cannot receive sacrifice, and the gods do not respond to sacrifice. One might conclude from this that Epicurus would reject the practice of sacrifice, but, in fact, our sources suggest the opposite: Epicurus and his school taught that sacrifice was a good and proper religious act. He practiced sacrifice himself and instructed his followers to do the same.[5] Under the critique model, Epicurus's position is completely incoherent.

Epicurus, of course, would disagree. His seemingly contradictory position was possible because he had his own ideas of what sacrifice did and how it worked, which were fully compatible with his understanding of the nature of the gods and the workings of cosmos.[6] His comments can only be construed as a critique of sacrifice if one brings to them a priori assumptions about what sacrifice means and what it does, assumptions that Epicurus did not hold. He does not critique the practice of sacrifice itself. Rather, he critiques only a *rival interpretation* of the practice.

Thus, the critique model appears to produce strange inconsistencies in the data: texts condemn sacrifice but then just as quickly praise it; philosophers critique sacrifice but then continue to participate and encourage their followers to do the same. A similar paradox is visible within Judean tradition. The Hebrew Bible appears to contain texts that reject sacrifice, but Judean tradition seemingly ignores these texts and continues to sacrifice in spite of them. All of this creates a sense of incompleteness—that the texts are driving towards some goal they do not quite reach. Scholars have at times reinforced this trend by suggesting that figures like the classical philosophers or the Hebrew Bible prophets wanted to change or abolish the practice of animal sacrifice but were forced to acquiesce to popular opinion and the power of traditional religion.[7] I think this an unfair reading of our sources. It turns ancient authors into people with remarkably modern concerns and assumptions. Certainly there is nothing in the texts themselves to indicate acquiescence. The Greek and Roman philosophers, for example, show little squeamishness when attacking other aspects of popular religion. I think we must conclude that if these authors wanted to attack and reject sacrifice they would have. Indeed, other ancient authors do just that. These include some Pythagoreans, Cynics, Orphics, and others to whom I will return later. In sum, the critique model cannot explain why so many ancient authors supposedly critiqued sacrifice but still genuinely supported the continuation of the practice.

The tendency to see these texts as preliminary or incomplete attempts to change the practice of animal sacrifice feeds directly into a second trend in scholarship on sacrifice, evolutionary interpretations.[8] Evolutionary interpretations see the history of religion, in its entirety, as a progression from simplistic beliefs towards a fully developed theology. In the realm of practice, this interpretation often takes the form of a progression from crude ritual to some model of pure or spiritual worship. The paradigm of "pure religion" in such a view is, almost invariably, Protestant Christianity. This tendency within religious studies is well known, and its impact on the issue of sacrifice has been recently addressed well by Jonathan Klawans.[9]

Evolutionary, or what Klawans usefully terms "supersessionist," interpretations of sacrifice see it as an essentially base act, a throwback to our more savage ancestors, and an act *destined* for replacement.[10] In this interpretation, the human race slowly outgrows animal sacrifice through a series of steps. It begins with enlightened voices like the classical philosophers and the Judean prophets, who critique the act and pave the way for its demise. These preliminary critiques lead directly to Jesus, the so-called cleansing of the Temple, and the rightful abolishment of all sacrifice under the aegis of a Christian empire.

The critique model thus reinforces modern misinterpretations of the practice of animal sacrifice and the supersessionist view that sees Christianity, with its rejection of animal sacrifice, as the pinnacle of true religion. In some ways this is not surprising as, I will argue, the critique model itself has its roots in early Christian theologizing about the relationship between Christianity, on the one hand, and Judaism and Greek and Roman religion, on the other. It was Christian authors who first defended Christian nonparticipation in sacrifice through an appeal to what they argued were critiques of sacrifice within the Hebrew Bible and Greek philosophers. It was these Christian authors who first turned *debate* over the meaning of sacrifice into *critique* of sacrifice.

Discursive Versus Nondiscursive Practices

I argue that we must understand the ancient evidence in a very different way. The orienting point for my approach is the concept of practices.[11] In examining these texts, we are looking at practice on two levels: First, the authors' own text-writing practices and, second, the practices discussed by the author in the text. A distinction between these two types of practice is crucial for coherent social analysis to take place. To give an example, a book about carpentry will discuss various carpentry practices, but *writing* a book about carpentry does not involve any carpentry practices. The writers of such books may, in fact, be carpenters, but they are not being carpenters when they write books; they are being authors. A blurring of the line between these two levels of analysis has caused a great deal of confusion in present scholarship. A clear distinction between them is crucial to moving beyond the critique model.

In short, writing a text about sacrifice is a completely different practice from actually participating in sacrifice.[12] Likewise, writing a text that raises concern over sacrifice is a completely different social practice than refusing to participate in an actual sacrificial ritual.

The key difference between animal sacrifice itself and texts about sacrifice is the difference between discursive and nondiscursive action. In analysis of sacrifice, this issue most often comes to the fore in debate over the meaning, origin, or essence of sacrifice. Numerous thinkers such as Sigmund Freud, Émile Durkheim, Walter Burkert, René Girard, and others claimed to have discovered some essential deep meaning that is universal to all sacrificial practice.[13] These efforts have not proved convincing. In each case, the author focuses on one aspect of animal sacrifice in a particular tradition, turning it into the essence of sacrifice generally, while ignoring other key elements of sacrificial practice both within the subject culture and cross-culturally. Improved social and cognitive theory, from scholars such as Catherine Bell[14], Theodore Schatzki[15], Jonathan Z. Smith[16], and Harvey Whitehouse[17], shows that the search for the origin or essence of sacrifice is a misguided pursuit. Sacrifice, like many religious practices, is a nondiscursive action.

Nondiscursive actions, including most religious rituals,[18] do not, and cannot, encode their own deep meaning or essence. Participants in nondiscursive practices operate on what Schatzki calls "practical understandings" of how to do various tasks.[19] For example, in order for a car to function, there must be gas in the tank. Getting gas into the tank requires a series of nondiscursive tasks for which many people have practical understandings. These practical understandings are not *meanings*, at least not in our normal understanding of the term.

In fact, discussion of meanings is often foreign to nondiscursive practices. Questioning the *meaning* of a nondiscursive action is often very puzzling for practitioners. For example, what is the meaning of removing the filler cap on your car? This crucial aspect of ritual has been shown time and time again when ethnographers analyze indigenous religious groups. Upon singling out some aspect of their ritual that seems particularly momentous, researchers are often baffled to find that practitioners do not have a satisfying or consistent explanation for what such an action means.[20] This is because participants in these practices rely on practical understandings; they do not need an explicit or conscious meaning to do the task.

This is not to say that actions do not have meanings. Nondiscursive actions can, and very often do, have discursive meanings attached to them. However, these discursive meanings are not *necessary* for the practice to be done.[21] More importantly, different participants in the same practice can, and often do, attach different discursive meanings to the same practice.[22] The notion that religious rituals must have a singular, clear, authoritative meaning that all participants understand and agree to is simply not a universal feature of religious practice.[23]

A limitless array of discursive meanings could be attached to the practice of animal sacrifice, but they are not necessary for the doing of the action. Likewise, unity of discursive meaning is not necessary for the doing of the action. An Epicurean philosopher who denied any interaction by the gods in the human world could stand shoulder to shoulder at a sacrifice with a farmer begging for rain.

The fundamental nature of nondiscursive practices meant that there could be a multitude of different positions on the meaning and purpose of sacrifice. This fact made an entire arena of cultural competition possible.[24] There is nothing inherent in the act of sacrificing an animal that tells you what it means, exactly what it does, or what moods or mental states ought to accompany it. All these things are open for debate. Where there is the possibility of debate, there will be competition among debaters.[25] This competition was alive and well among Greek, Roman, and Judean authors. Debate over the meaning of sacrifice must be understood as part of this ongoing competition between cultural producers, not as critiques of some essential or universal meaning or purpose of animal sacrifice.

Reciprocity and Sacrifice

One more element of the practice of sacrifice must be discussed before analyzing the primary texts. To appreciate these authors' various positions on sacrifice, it is crucial to understand the basic logic on which the practice rests. Insights from cognitive science of religion shed light on this subject by suggesting that rituals such as sacrifice take their logical cue from human social patterns. If gods are a projection of human-like agency, then one can interact with gods just like one would interact with a human.[26] For sacrifice in the ancient Mediterranean, I argue, the social logic at work is the logic of reciprocity. The assumption that one can have a human-like reciprocal relationship with a god follows intuitively from the belief that gods are human-like agents.[27] This is a critical point for understanding ancient debate over sacrifice. Modern misrepresentations of the logic of reciprocity are partly responsible for the success of the critique model.

Sacrifice is a practice based on the logic of reciprocity as a mode of exchange. To understand this logic, it is necessary to divorce ourselves from the most pervasive modern mode of exchange, economic exchange. It is also necessary to divorce ourselves from notions of altruism, egoism, and *do ut des* relationships. These categories are elements of a particular discourse about action. They are neither objective nor analytical and serve only to confuse discussion of sacrifice by imposing a secondary discourse upon it.

All of these elements introduce categories and relationships that are foreign to the logic of reciprocity. Reciprocity, simply put, is a system of *different and differed return*.[28] It is a system in which humans give *things,* in the broadest sense (goods, services, influence, etc.) and subsequently get things back. Because the things exchanged in reciprocity have no definite value (or, if they do, this fact is ignored for the purposes of exchange), balance between parties can never be achieved, nor is it sought. As a result, reciprocity creates a relationship *between the people making the exchange*, not the commodities exchanged. This is the opposite of economic exchange, in which goods or services have finite value, and the relationship created exists between the things exchanged, not the persons exchanging them.[29]

Because reciprocity creates relationships between people, it tends to index and reinforce power hierarchies. In any given instance of reciprocity, there will usually be one party able to give more and one able to give less. This situation, repeated again and again, over a broad range of reciprocal exchanges, creates complex social networks of nested superiorities and dependencies.

A key component of the social workings of reciprocity is what Bourdieu calls misrecognition.[30] Within reciprocal exchange, the social consequences of the reciprocal relationship (that is, power hierarchies) are often consciously or unconsciously ignored (misrecognized) by both parties. This allows both parties to view the objects of exchange as free gifts, although each party understands the social realities involved. In our own society, economic exchange is the most prevalent mode; however, reciprocity, in the form of gift giving, still plays an important role in the formation of social relationships.

From the time we are children, we all learn the etiquette of gift giving and re-ceiving—the rules of the game. For example, one always removes the price tag before giving a gift. One does not give someone the exact same gift they previously gave you. These rules do not make practical sense, but they make perfect sense within the logic of reciprocity. The actions just mentioned are too close to economic exchange, which we see as antithetical to gift giving. The very language used for reciprocal exchange highlights the misrecognition involved. In gift giving, we use terms like *favor, reward,* or *token of appreciation.* We avoid words that would hint at economic exchange, such as *return, repayment, debt,* etc. Ancient Greek, Latin, and Hebrew had similarly subtle vocabulary.[31]

Despite the phenomenon of misrecognition, we all learn how to recognize the social hierarchies involved in reciprocal exchange and how to manipulate these hier-archies.[32] We are all aware that different social situations demand different gifts and that the wrong gift can have serious consequences. Navigating this social minefield takes a fair amount of effort, but it is something that most of us master at a young age. Ancient participants in animal sacrifice had similar mastery in the arts of reci-procity. Different gods and different circumstances demanded different sacrifices. The ritual must fit the occasion, and the offering must fit both the giver and the deity. For example, the various gods of the ancient Mediterranean household generally received different sacrifices, in different locations, and for difference reasons as compared to the gods of the city.[33] The basic reciprocal logic, however, is the same in both cases.

Even considering the modern parallel of gift giving, reciprocity played a much larger role in ancient Mediterranean society than it does in our own. Thus, it was natural that when these people imagined superhuman beings, or gods, they modeled their relationships with these beings on their relationships with each other. That is, they imagined a system of reciprocity with the gods that mirrored the system of reciprocity that governed their everyday life.[34] Sacrifice was one key practice of this relationship.[35]

Understanding the logic of reciprocity is crucial to dispelling the most prevalent modern misunderstanding of sacrifice, the notion that the gods needed sacrifice. For most in the ancient Mediterranean, the statement "the gods do not need sac-rifice" was a simple truism that derived from the nature of the universe. It was not a reason to abstain from sacrifice. Sacrifice was not an indication that the gods were beholden to humans for food, attention, or praise. Such conclusions are a misunderstanding of the logic of reciprocity. To cite a modern (albeit potentially apocryphal) parallel, students give apples to teachers. We do not conclude from this that teachers are too poor to buy their own apples, or that they subsist solely on apples, or that they are dependant on student-brought apples in order to survive. Rather, we parse this action for what it is, an attempt to foster a relationship of reciprocity. Sacrifice is no different. In each situation, the reciprocal relationship is paramount, while the actual items exchanged are secondary.

Fully appreciating that sacrifice is a nondiscursive practice that relies on the logic of reciprocity allows us to move beyond the critique model. Ancient authors who discuss sacrifice are not critiquing some universal essential meaning of the act. Rather, they are themselves attempting to argue for one particular interpretation. They are attempting to impose their own discursive parsing of sacrifice upon the practice; they are trying to say definitively what sacrifice does, how it works, and how it should be done. These authors are not typical or average sacrificial participants. They are members of an elite, literate, educated class that comprised a very small percentage of ancient society. Their explication of the meaning and purpose of sacrifice was part of their participation in a larger field of cultural production that brought them power, authority, and prestige through textual expertise.

Exempla

I will discuss three examples to illustrate the approach outlined above.[36] These texts span several cultural contexts and several centuries, yet each author is trying to accomplish the same thing: the imposition of a singular interpretation on the practice of sacrifice.

One of the early commentators on sacrifice is Plato. Plato identifies what he takes to be two areas of potential problem with sacrificial practice: (1) the moral condition of the sacrificer, and (2) the conception of the gods that the sacrificer holds in his or her head.

Plato is concerned that people think morality does not matter in sacrifice. He is one of the first philosophers to voice this concern, which is echoed by almost every other writer on the topic. He writes in *Laws*:

> For the wicked man is unclean of soul, whereas the good man is clean; and from him that is defiled no good man, nor god, can ever rightly receive gifts [δῶρα]. Therefore all the great labor that impious men spend upon the gods is in vain, but that of the pious is most profitable to them all.[37]

A few simple but often overlooked points can be made about this passage. First, the passage is not a critique of sacrifice itself, only a critique of a particular view of the conditions necessary for the ritual to be efficacious. The view of sacrifice Plato rails against relates directly back to my earlier discussion of reciprocity. It is one that sees sacrifice as *automatic* reciprocity. Plato argues that, just as a good man would not accept gifts from a wicked man (and thereby enter into a reciprocal relationship with him), the gods will not accept sacrifices from a wicked man. Thus, sacrifices made by immoral individuals are useless because they will not produce the desired reciprocal relationship. The gods cannot be bribed with sacrifices to overlook wrongdoing. On the other hand, the sacrifices of good people will be accepted and will bring the favor of the gods. In other words, sacrifice does not automatically put the gods in debt; other factors are in play, just as in human relationships.

A full analysis Plato's comments on sacrifice reveal that his view of sacrifice is, predictably, a Platonic view of sacrifice.[38] That is, it is a parsing of the practice through the lens of Platonic thinking on the nature of the divine and the cosmos.[39]

This analysis can be repeated for all the classical schools of philosophy with similar results. In each case, philosophers attempted to interpret the practice of animal sacrifice, what it means and what it does, according to their own understanding of the gods and the cosmos.[40] The Stoics, for example, argue against popular anthropomorphic conceptions of the gods; however, their support of sacrifice is well known.[41] There is nothing wrong with animal sacrifice in the Stoic view, so long as correct (i.e., Stoic) interpretations were maintained. The Stoics argued that the divine was a power that pervaded all matter. Humans, for their part, must understand this and act in accordance with nature. Animal sacrifice was an opportunity to reinforce these Stoic interpretations and ideals.[42] Epicureans, as I mentioned above, saw sacrifice as an opportunity to contemplate Epicurean beliefs, despite their assertion that the gods are not active in the human world.[43]

To describe these comments as critiques of sacrifice is misleading and inaccurate. Most importantly, this interpretation masks the reality of what these writers (be they Platonists, Stoics, or Epicureans) are attempting to do—that is, impose their own interpretation on a key religious ritual.

Similar conclusions can be derived from the analysis of Hebrew Bible texts, of which I will give two examples. Hebrew Bible statements on sacrifice are some of the most well known of the so-called critiques. This is the case because the Hebrew Bible served as rich source material for later Christian authors, who took these passages out of context and presented them *as if they were critiques*—that is, they used them as proof texts for their own positions against animal sacrifice. In their original context, however, these passages are not critiques. In fact, I argue that these texts are an excellent example of the alternate model I am proposing. The first text I would like to discuss is Psalm 51:15–19:

> O Lord, open my lips, and my mouth will declare your praise. For you have no delight in sacrifice; if I were to give a burnt offering, you would not be pleased. The sacrifice acceptable to God is a broken spirit; a broken and contrite heart, O God, you will not despise. Do good to Zion in your good pleasure; rebuild the walls of Jerusalem, then you will delight in right sacrifices, in burnt offerings and whole burnt offerings; then bulls will be offered on your altar.

It is clear in this example that the first part of this passage, if taken out of context, could appear to be a biting critique of animal sacrifice; and, in fact, this is exactly how later Christian authors used it.[44] However, when the passage is seen in the context of the psalm as a whole—or even, as here, in the context of the next few lines—a different picture emerges. The psalmist is playing on the theme of God's chastisement but continued love for Israel. Burnt offerings are unacceptable given the current state of estrangement from God, but contrition will lead to reconciliation.

God will restore Jerusalem and its ruined temple; proper sacrifices will resume. For the psalmist, ideal sacrifice requires a restored Jerusalem and a restored relationship between God and Israel.

The Hebrew Bible prophets provide a similar example. Despite the remarkable endurance of Weber's priest-versus-prophet model, it has been shown time and again that the Hebrew Bible prophets were not outside critics attacking Judean cult.[45] Many of the prophets were themselves priests or other cultic functionaries.[46] They do not reject the practice of animal sacrifice to Yahweh, nor do they critique the basic logic of this act. Rather, just like the texts above, they provide an interpretation of the act of sacrifice in light of their understanding of Yahweh and the cosmos. The main feature of this interpretation is the assertion that the relationship between Yahweh and Israel is more important that the amount of stuff sacrificed. An example of this is a passage from Isaiah:

> What to me is the multitude of your sacrifices? Says the Lord; I have had enough of burnt offerings of rams and the fat of fed beasts; I do not delight in the blood of bulls, or lambs, or of goats. (Isa 1:11–12)

Once again this isolated passage appears to condemn sacrifice, but when the book of Isaiah is considered as a whole a different picture emerges. There is no suggestion in Isaiah that the temple cult with its animal sacrifices should be abolished. Rather, the text dwells on the notion that Israel must repent, reform, and return to God. Only then will their sacrifices be appropriate. Again, the logic of reciprocity is foremost. Yahweh's good will cannot be bought. Lavish sacrifices are not necessarily more efficacious sacrifices, nor are they automatic. In other words, the author of Isaiah is arguing that specific moral states must accompany animal sacrifice; endless sacrifice without the correct moral state is useless and is actually offensive to God. None of this is a critique of sacrifice itself, only a critique of what the author of Isaiah sees as an incorrect interpretation of Yahweh and his relationship with his people. Exactly the same conclusions hold for the other Hebrew Bible prophets.[47]

To summarize my argument thus far, all of these authors—both Greek philosophers and Hebrew Bible prophets—wanted to continue the practice of animal sacrifice, *but under their own terms and with their own interpretation.* For these authors, sacrifice was an appropriate and efficacious action only if understood through their discursive parsing, informed by their understanding of the gods/god and the workings of the universe.

This is not to say that *no* ancient authors critiqued or rejected the practice of animal sacrifice. There is evidence for a small number of groups throughout the Greek and Roman periods who reject the practice of animal sacrifice and abstained from it. These include some Pythagorean, Cynic, and Orphic groups.[48]

I do not wish to discount the importance of these groups to understanding ancient positions on sacrifice. Rather, I wish to stress the need to separate this data from the texts and authors discussed above. *Some* Greek and Latin cultural producers did in fact critique and reject animal sacrifice as a religious practice, but they are a minority. Many other producers debated the meaning and purpose of sacrifice *without* questioning the actual practice itself.

In short, not every discussion of the meaning and purpose of sacrifice in ancient texts is a critique. The critique model is the result of the imposition of essentialist interpretations of sacrifice on ancient thinkers, interpretations that these people did not hold (i.e., sacrifice feeds the gods or sacrifice bribes the gods). Once the critique model is rejected, it is possible to appreciate the complexity and sophistication of ancient debates over this practice. It is also clear that this debate is taking place among a small number of elite, literate cultural producers, each vying to impose their own interpretation on the practice of sacrifice. Christian texts must be seen as part of this ongoing competition.

Christian Data

In the remaining space, I would like to highlight the ways in which the previous discussion forces a reevaluation of the early Christian data. How do Christian authors fit into the ongoing cultural competition we have sketched? If early Christian authors were not "spiritualizing" sacrifice or critiquing some essential meaning of sacrifice, what were they doing? A final benefit of this brief foray into Christian positions is that it illustrates the historical origins of the critique model I have argued against, and it begins to explain the pervasiveness of this model.

I begin with two key observations on the early Christian data. First, positions on sacrifice within Christian authors are highly dependent on chronology. This is a simple observation, but it has been argued against so frequently that it bears highlighting. In short, the finely articulated positions on animal sacrifice found in later Christian authors (from the second century onwards) are not present in the earliest Christian texts. This change, therefore, demands explanation. Second, Christian positions on sacrifice do not show smooth progression or linear development. Rather, early Christian texts contain numerous independent, often contradictory responses to animal sacrifice.

The earliest sources (Paul and the New Testament Gospels) show no rejection of animal sacrifice. Paul, as a Judean, rejects Greco-Roman animal sacrifice. He does this on the grounds that Greek and Roman gods are not real gods, only the Judean god is a real god and only he is worthy of sacrifice.[49] Paul fully supports the Jerusalem temple cult and never suggests that anything replaces or supercedes it. The New Testament Gospels take a similar position. They say nothing against animal sacrifice. In fact, they imagine Jesus and his followers participating in animal sacrifice. The so-called Last Supper in the synoptic Gospels is, after all, a dinner of sacrificial meat.[50] The book of Acts even portrays the disciples frequenting the temple after Jesus' death and resurrection.[51]

The gospel texts are particularly important because of their dates. With the possible, but in my view unlikely, exception of Mark, all of the Gospels were written after the destruction of the Jerusalem temple in 70 CE. This means that they were written *after* many Christians had become de facto nonparticipants in sacrifice. But the texts themselves do not give any reflection of this fact. This is a key piece of evidence; it shows that historical circumstances (distance from Jerusalem for many Christians before 70 CE and the nonexistence of the temple after this date) made Christians nonsacrificers *first*. It was left to later Christian writers to theologize this situation and provide an explanation for Christian nonparticipation.

The Christian group that ultimately won the historical battle (Burton Mack calls them the "centrist Christians")[52] had a particular problem to deal with. The centrist Christians, in contrast to other Christian groups (e.g., the Marcionites and Valentinians), believed that the Jewish god was also the Christian god and that the Jewish scriptures were also Christian scriptures. This meant that they had to explain why so much of their own sacred writings were rules and regulations for animal sacrifice.[53] According to the centrists' own scriptures, God wanted animal sacrifice. Why then did the Christians not do it? Moreover, if God wanted a sacrificial cult in Jerusalem, and the Hebrew Bible clearly indicates that he does, why did he allow the Romans to destroy his temple? These were major problems for the centrists and vulnerable points in their battles with other Christian groups.[54]

Cultural producers of the centrist camp devised various creative solutions to these problems. For example, the author of the Epistle of Barnabas argued that God never really wanted sacrifice. All of the passages in the Hebrew Bible that appear to mandate animal sacrifice were actually, according to this author, allegories for Jesus and the Christian church. Thus, according to Barnabas, the whole edifice of the Jerusalem Temple was an unfortunate case of overly literal reading.[55] God had tried to make this clear through the prophets, but was ignored.[56] Here, one sees a Christian author in the process of creating the critique model. The author of Barnabas claims that the Hebrew Bible prophets critiqued sacrifice and tried to put a stop to it. He does so by taking Hebrew Bible passages (including the two presented above) out of context and presenting them *as critiques*.[57] Christianity, in this author's view, enacts these critiques and performs the correct, nonsacrificial, worship that God had always intended.

Other early Christian authors fashioned other positions. For example, Justin Martyr (d. ca. 165) argued that God had created sacrifice as a stopgap measure to cover the interim before Jesus came. He claimed that God gave the Judeans their sacrificial cult in an attempt to prevent their habitual apostasy and idol worship (the logic apparently being that worshiping the right god in the wrong way is better than worshiping the wrong god altogether, *Dial.* 22.11). Once Jesus had come, however, sacrifice's raison d'être vanished, and Judeans, in Justin's mind, were supposed to become Christians.

Here one sees the supersessionist model being formed. Justin argues that Christianity is the *replacement* for animal sacrifice, which was always meant to be temporary. Other Christian authors formulate still more positions, which cannot be elaborated here. These included the ideas that Jesus' death was a replacement for sacrifice, that Christian prayers are superior to sacrifice, and, ultimately, that Christian practices like the Eucharist are equivalent to sacrifice.[58]

The key thing to notice about these positions is that they do not cohere well. Did God never want animal sacrifice? Or is Jesus an animal sacrifice? Or are prayers better than sacrifice anyway?[59] The centrist position is not one position; it is not even a logical chain of positions. It is a collection of different arguments from different periods and different authors all useful against different opponents (Romans, Judeans, other Christians, etc.). This process of agglomeration is characteristic of the centrist group and is one of its keys to success. As Christianity evolved and different opponents arose, the centrists could almost always find a solution in one of their vetted texts or, more commonly, in a recombination of passages from several texts.

To conclude, it is critical to see early Christian authors as elite producers engaged in a competition to define the true nature of sacrifice against various opponents. Such a model is far more illuminative to the Christian data than notions of spiritualization or critique. Many Christian authors of the second century onward do, in fact, reject the practice of animal sacrifice as a useful religious ritual. However, the proper context for understanding such texts is not some imagined tradition of critique. Instead, it is a field of cultural competition in which textual producers vied with each other to define the meaning and purpose of a nondiscursive ritual.

The competitive success of particular positions within this arena was contingent, as always, on a complex matrix of historical events, including the destruction of the Jerusalem temple and the success of one particular group of Christian elite (the centrists) with its own collection of consecrated texts. This context, I hope, begins to remove the lens of Christian theology through which so much of the history of the practice of animal sacrifice has been viewed.

Notes

This chapter is a distillation of some of the key points of my dissertation. For a full discussion, see Daniel Ullucci, "The End of Animal Sacrifice" (Brown University, 2009).

1. I lay aside for the moment the question of whether sacrifice pleases the gods. The majority of the texts discussed below assume that sacrifice pleases the gods, but this is very different from saying that the gods *need* sacrifice. A key goal of this chapter is to explicate these crucial differences.

2. The two main models I employ from Bourdieu are 1) the extension of the concept of "capital" to noneconomic systems (such as culture) and 2) the assertion that much of social life consists of competition for various types of capital. Bourdieu's theories of capital and social competition are spread out across many of his writings; for a concise summary and discussion, see David Swartz, *Culture and Power: The Sociology of Pierre Bourdieu* (Chicago: University of Chicago Press, 1997), 73–82.

3. For a full discussion of cultural producers and their interest in broad questions of meaning, see Stanley Stowers, "The Religion of Plant and Animal Offerings versus the Religion of Meanings, Essences, and Textual Mysteries," chapter 1 in this volume.

4. See Diog. Laert. 10.123; Lucr., *De rerum natura* 5.146–94. See also A. A. Long and D. N. Sedley, *The Hellenistic Philosophers*, 2 vols. (Cambridge: Cambridge University Press, 1987), 1:139–49.

5. The most direct statement of Epicurus's support of sacrifice comes from a very late source, *On Piety*, 873–95, attributed to Philodemus. However, earlier sources provide evidence of Epicurean participation in traditional religious practice. See Cic., *Nat. D.* 1.17.45; Diog. Laert., 10.120. See also Harold W. Attridge, "The Philosophical Critique of Religion under the Early Empire," *ANRW* 2.16.1 (1978), 51–53.

6. Traditional religious practices could provide an opportunity for the Epicurean to contemplate the *true*, that is Epicurean, understanding of the gods. See Attridge, "Philosophical Critique," 52–53.

7. This interpretive tendency can even be seen in so careful a scholar as Simon Price. He writes in regard to Greek and Roman philosophical "critiques": "The crucial point is that the criticisms of the philosophers, though searching, were not innovative in the field of ritual and that as a result traditions were upheld"; Simon Price, *Rituals and Power: The Roman Imperial Cult in Asia Minor* (Cambridge: Cambridge University Press, 1984), 228. I take this to mean that some Greek and Roman philosophers, in Price's view, *wanted* to change religious practice but were constrained by the inertia of traditional religious practices. Price's discussion of imperial sacrifice is excellent, and he is a rare example of a scholar who does not view sacrifice through a modern lens. This fact makes the above quote all the more surprising and highlights the need for a full exploration of the issue of "critique."

8. I take this term from Jonathan Klawans. Klawans argues that evolutionist and supersessionist theories (whether implicit or explicit) have deeply colored much scholarly discussion of the practice of sacrifice. See Jonathan Klawans, *Purity, Sacrifice, and the Temple: Symbolism and Supersessionism in the Study of Ancient Judaism* (New York: Oxford University Press, 2006), 6–8.

9. For a discussion of evolutionary and supersessionist tendencies in the history of religious studies, including the influential work of Edward B. Tylor, James Frazer, and Émile Durkheim, see Klawans, *Purity, Sacrifice, and the Temple*, 6–8.

10. Klawans, *Purity, Sacrifice, and the Temple*, 6–10.

11. Following Theodore Schatzki, I define practice as an open-ended bundle of doings or sayings. The distinctiveness of a particular practice (what makes it X and not Y) is a function of the distinctiveness of its package of doings and sayings. See Theodore Schatzki, *The Site of the Social* (University Park: Pennsylvania State University Press, 2002), 70–72.

12. This key point is already made by Price; however, Price employs the term *discourse*. Following Schatzki, I use the more concrete concept of *practice*. Price argues, "To write a literary work is to engage in a different type of discourse from that involved in the ritual itself" (*Rituals and Power*, 115).

13. These theorists argued that the essence of sacrifice was, respectively: Oedipal slaughter and an attempt to protect the father figure; communal gift giving and the experience of "collective effervesces"; the communal spirit of the hunt; and the necessary redirection of communal violence. See Sigmund Freud, *Totem and Taboo: Some Points of Agreement between the Mental Lives of Savages and Neurotics*, translated by James Strachey (New York: W. W. Norton, 1950), 146–55; Émile Durkheim, *The Elementary Forms of Religious Life*, translated by Joseph Ward Swain (New York: Free Press, 1965), 381–92; Walter

Burkert, *Homo Necans: The Anthropology of Ancient Greek Sacrificial Ritual and Myth,* translated by Peter Bing (Berkeley: University of California Press, 1983); and René Girard, *Violence and the Sacred,* translated by Patrick Gregory (Baltimore: Johns Hopkins University Press, 1977).

14. See Catherine Bell, *Ritual Theory, Ritual Practice* (New York: Oxford University Press, 1992), 90. The same position is echoed by Nancy Jay, who argues: "The meaning of any action not only varies with the way in which it is interpreted, it *is* the way it is interpreted. The meaning is not already there in the action, like the gin is in the bottle, in such a way that you can get it out, unadulterated, by performing certain operations on the action"; Nancy Jay, *Throughout Your Generations Forever: Sacrifice, Religion, and Paternity* (Chicago: University of Chicago Press, 1992), 8.

15. Schatzki, *Site of the Social,* 76–77.

16. The strongest critic of quests for the essence of sacrifice is Jonathan Z. Smith. See Jonathan Z. Smith, "The Domestication of Sacrifice," in *Violent Origins: Walter Burkert, René Girard, and Jonathan Z. Smith on Ritual Killing and Cultural Formation,* edited by Robert G. Hamerton-Kelly (Stanford: Stanford University Press, 1987), 191–238.

17. Harvey Whitehouse, *Modes of Religiosity: A Cognitive Theory of Religious Transmission* (Walnut Creek, Calif.: AltaMira, 2004), 4.

18. Following Catherine Bell, I define "ritual" as an action that is strategically separated from normal, everyday, action. As Bell argues, it is more useful to speak not of "ritual" but of "ritualization": "a way of acting that is designed and orchestrated to distinguish and privilege what is being done in comparison to other, usually more quotidian, activities." See Catherine Bell, *Ritual Theory, Ritual Practice* (New York: Oxford University Press, 1992), 74.

19. Schatzki defines practical understandings as ability with or mastery of acts that form part of a practice. He argues: "Above all, three such abilities are germane to practices: knowing how to X, knowing how to identify X-ings, and knowing how to prompt and respond to X-ings. All participants in a practice are able to perform, identify, and prompt some subset of the practice's doings, sayings, tasks, and projects" (Schatzki, *Site of the Social,* 77–78).

20. For a discussion of this key cognitive feature of ritual and for ethnographic examples, see Whitehouse, *Modes of Religiosity,* 95–96.

21. By "not necessary" I mean that participants in an action often do not consciously rehearse the meanings of every action they do. Upon *post facto* reflection, participants often ascribe meanings to various actions, but these are second-order reflections. They do not guide everyday action in the moment.

22. See Whitehouse, *Modes of Religiosity,* 95–96.

23. The desire to affirm one particular interpretation of the meaning of sacrifice arises in particular groups at particular times. For a discussion of this trend in the ancient Mediterranean, see J. B. Rives's excellent article "The Theology of Animal Sacrifice in the Ancient Greek World," chapter 9 in this volume.

24. Whitehouse argues that the nondiscursive nature of religious rituals does not simply *allow* for multiple interpretations. Rather, certain types of religious rituals (I would include sacrifice in this group) actually *encourage* spontaneous exegesis. See Whitehouse, *Modes of Religiosity,* 4–6, 72–73.

25. This is a corollary to Jay's observation that "wherever there is ritual there is always a politics of its interpretation, because ritual action can always transcend any final perfect

interpretation of it. . . . The question inevitably arises as to who is socially entitled to a position (perhaps *the* position) from which it is legitimate to interpret ritual. What is being defended in accusations of heresy is not just specific interpretations of texts or actions, but the position of the only true point of perspective and also the principle that there is such a point" (*Throughout Your Generations*, 11).

26. Gods are essentially human-like agents presumed to exist *out there*. Gods have certain characteristics that make them superhuman (they have special powers, they never die, they can read your mind, etc.), but, in the main, they are human-like. One could refer to them as cognitively anthropomorphic. Whatever gods may look like, or whatever special powers they may have, they *think* like humans. This is an obvious consequence of what gods are, that is, projections of human-like agency. For an excellent summary discussion of current cognitive science theory of gods as projections of human-like agency see Justin Barrett, "Gods," in *Religion, Anthropology, and Cognitive Science*, edited by Harvey Whitehouse and James Laidlaw (Durham: Carolina Academic Press, 2007), 179–207.

27. See Barrett, "Gods," 193–94.

28. Hans van Wees, "The Law of Gratitude: Reciprocity in Anthropological Theory," in *Reciprocity in Ancient Greece*, edited by Christopher Gill, Norman Postlethwaite, and Richard Seaford (New York: Oxford University Press, 1998), 25–26.

29. Richard Seaford, introduction to *Reciprocity in Ancient Greece*, edited by Christopher Gill, Norman Postlethwaite, and Richard Seaford (New York: Oxford University Press, 1998); J. van Baal, "Offering, Sacrifice and Gift," *Numen* 23.3 (December 1976): 165–66.

30. See Bourdieu, *Outline of a Theory of Practice* (Cambridge: Cambridge University Press, 1977), 5–6.

31. An excellent example of this is Robert Parker's discussion of the Greek term χάρις, a word ubiquitous in Greek texts on sacrifice, which is best translated as "favor" or "pleasure." See Robert Parker, "Pleasing Thighs: Reciprocity in Greek Religion," in *Reciprocity in Ancient Greece*, edited by Christopher Gill, Norman Postlethwaite, and Richard Seaford (New York: Oxford University Press, 1998), 105–126.

32. In Schatzki's terms, we have practical understandings in regard to gift giving. We know how to give gifts, recognize when a gift has been given, and respond to gifts.

33. For an excellent theoretical discussion of household religion in the ancient Mediterranean, see Stanley Stowers, "Theorizing Religion of the Ancient Household and Family," in *Household and Family Religion in Antiquity*, edited by Saul Olyan and John Bodel (Malden, Mass.: Blackwell, 2008), 5–19.

34. This is a cornerstone of cognitive science of religion. Ongoing research in this new field has shown convincingly that religious practices and beliefs employ the same cognitive patterns as everyday action. The key distinction (and I take this as my definition of religion) is that religious beliefs and practices assume the existence of superhuman agents. For a general introduction to cognitive science of religion, see Pascal Boyer, *Religion Explained* (New York: Basic Books, 2001).

35. Despite the undeniable importance of animal sacrifice in ancient Mediterranean religion, it is important to point out that animal sacrifice was only one practice in the range of imagined interactions between humans and superhuman agents. Nonanimal offerings and prayers could be just as important and were very likely more common experiences for most ancient Mediterraneans.

36. For a more complete discussion of the Greek, Roman, Judean, and early Christian data, see Ullucci, "End of Animal Sacrifice."

37. Pl., *Leg.* 4.716e–4.717a.

38. Other key passages include *Euthphr.* 14–15; *Resp.* 2.364b–e; *Leg.* 10.885b and 906b–c. In each of these passages, Plato is concerned with reciprocal logic of sacrifice. Particularly he is concerned, as discussed above, with the moral status of the sacrificer and human conceptions of the divine. For a full discussion, see Ullucci, "End of Animal Sacrifice," 92–97.

39. I think it is appropriate to call such a position a theology of sacrifice. I therefore differ with J. B. Rives's argument that theologies of sacrifice only arise in the imperial period. I agree that philosophers of the imperial period (Porphyry being the main example) develop much more complex explanations of the role of sacrifice. However, numerous religious experts before the imperial period (Epicurus, Plato, Hebrew Bible authors, et al.) had positions on the nature of the gods that influenced their positions on the practice of animal sacrifice. The key distinction, I believe, is not chronological but social. Theologies of sacrifice do not arise at one particular time; rather, they arise among a particular group of people, religious experts. Religious experts create theologies of sacrifice, and they are present throughout the time period in question.

40. See Ullucci, "End of Animal Sacrifice," 92–107.

41. The main Stoic strategy was to allegorize traditional religious myths and rituals. See Malcolm Schofield, "Cicero For and Against Divination," *JRS* 76 (1986): 47–65; Charles Manning, "Seneca and Roman Religious Practice," in *Religion in the Ancient World*, edited by Matthew Dillon (Amsterdam: Adolph M. Hakkert, 1996), 311–12; P. A. Brunt, "Philosophy and Religion in the Late Republic," in *Philosophia Togata: Essays on Philosophy and Roman Society*, edited by Miriam Griffin and Jonathan Barnes, 2 vols. (Oxford: Clarendon, 1989), 187–89.

42. See, for example, Epictetus, *Enchiridion* 31.1 and 31.5; Sen., *de Superstitione*, fr. 38 (= August., *De civ. D.* 6.10). This is also the conclusion of Attridge, who sees the Stoic position as one of accommodation. See Attridge, "Philosophical Critique," 66–69. I think it best to avoid the term *accommodation,* since its English usage has such as strong connotation of reticence or unwillingness. To suggest that the Stoic position on sacrifice is a half-willing compromise or acquiescence is to read the modern position on sacrifice back into these texts.

43. For a discussion of Epicurean positions, see Attridge, "Philosophical Critique," 52–53. Attridge ultimately concludes: "Epicureanism maintained a fairly constant position on religious questions. In its eyes the defects of popular piety were significant, but for the most part were defects of attitude among those who worshiped. If those attitudes and ideas about the gods were fundamentally altered, legitimate piety could flourish" (55).

44. See Barn 2:10; 1 Clem 18.

45. For an excellent summary discussion, see Klawans, *Purity, Sacrifice, and the Temple,* 75–100.

46. Peter Berger, "Charisma and Religious Innovation: The Social Location of Israelite Prophecy," *American Sociological Review* 28.6 (1963): 942.

47. For a discussion of the Hebrew Bible data, see Ullucci, "End of Animal Sacrifice," 109–20.

48. Evidence for these groups and their positions on sacrifice is limited. However, the available data supports the conclusion that some individuals who claimed to represent these

groups rejected animal sacrifice and that antisacrificial positions were commonly associated with these group labels. Crucially, the antisacrificial positions of these groups are often part of broader attacks on popular religion and society in general. Nonparticipation in sacrifice, for some of these groups, however, did not actually stem from a rejection of the practice of sacrifice itself. J. B. Rives argues that Pythagorean and Orphic groups abstained from sacrifice because of their rejection of ensouled food. Their rejection of sacrifice, therefore, is indirect. Their main concern is ensouled food, and animal sacrifice just happens to involve one in the eating of such food. See Rives, "The Theology of Animal Sacrifice in the Ancient Greek World" in this volume.

49. Paul supports the assertion made by the Corinthians that "no idol in the world really exists" (1 Cor 8:4). He later asserts that "there may be many so-called gods" and states that non-Judean sacrifices are offered to demons (1 Cor 8:5, 10:19–20). Paul's position on the exact nature of non-Judean deities is an interesting question, but cannot be addressed here. Who or whatever these beings are for Paul, they are clearly not the one true god and are therefore not worthy of sacrifice.

50. Mk 14:12–15.

51. Acts 3:1. I do not take any of the events described in the Gospels or Acts as necessarily historical. My only concern here is that these events were *historically plausible* to the Gospel writers. This is crucial evidence for their positions on sacrifice.

52. Burton Mack, *Who Wrote the New Testament?* (New York: HarperOne, 1995), 6.

53. This tension is particularly evident in the different ways centrist Christian authors treat Greco-Roman animal sacrifice versus Judean animal sacrifice. Greco-Roman sacrifice can be rejected offhand; Judean animal sacrifice, however, requires special explanation. It cannot be attacked directly without threatening the truth of the Hebrew Bible. Justin Martyr is an excellent example of this. See Ullucci, "End of Animal Sacrifice," 210–14.

54. These problems were equally momentous for Judean groups. For a discussion of Judean responses to the destruction of the temple see, Klawans, *Purity, Sacrifice, and the Temple,* 175–211.

55. Barnabas equates the Jerusalem temple to pagan temples and mocks the notion that a god could live in a structure. Barnabas also claims that Hebrew Bible authors such as Isaiah, Daniel, and Enoch had spoken of a "pneumatic" temple, but this was misunderstood. See Barn 16.

56. Barn 2:4.

57. See, for example, Barn 2, in which passages from Isaiah, Jeremian, Zechariah, and Psalm 51 are put forward as proof texts.

58. See Ullucci, "End of Animal Sacrifice," 262–68.

59. Much attention has been paid to Christian texts that redefine animal sacrifice in order to give it a Christian meaning (the sacrifice of Jesus, the sacrifice of the Eucharist, etc.). It is equally important to notice that some early Christian texts reject animal sacrifice outright and never attempt to give it any positive reformulation (e.g., Barn).

3

Egyptian Religion and the Problem
of the Category "Sacrifice"
David Frankfurter

For some time now I have been worried that the category "sacrifice" is both too vague and too theological to have any descriptive utility and, at the same time, is too beholden to Girard and Burkert in their focus on blood and killing to allow any real comparative flexibility. If the archetypal sacrifice is to be the killing of an animal, with all its latent violence, then every other offering or ritualized food preparation must be either a substitution or a pale imitation. If ritual killing lies at the very core of religion, as Girard and Burkert suggest, then it becomes difficult to conceptualize religious traditions that neither perpetuate public sacrifices nor sublimate them with Christ. And when some form of ritual slaughter *does* hold a prominent place in a religion, as in Rome or ancient Israel, it has been difficult to read it *except* as the perpetuation of some archetypal, primal act. Ancient religion and sacrifice— blood sacrifice—have been for many scholars inextricable cultural formations.

Of course, there have been many historians of religions who have tried to chip away at the Girardian legacy in the interpretation of, say, Israelite religion or Roman religion.[1] But in theorizing ancient sacrifice as a general category, we are still left with a theologically laden term that inevitably demands center stage yet also challenges us in its bloodier forms to accept the sacredness of a violent act.[2]

I would credit Katherine McClymond for breaking down the category into a *series* of key ritual stages, only a *secondary* component of which in most cultures was killing. Ritual dedication of animals, she shows, included their selection, their declarative association with a deity, the heating of their carcasses to various degrees, and their consumption by select individuals. The killing itself was often the least deliberate part of the process. When the ceremonial goal was the acquisition of fresh blood or the complete incineration of a carcass, *killing* constituted merely a means to an end, not an end in itself.[3] This relative marginalization of slaughter rather offsets the relevance of hunting or primal violence for the understanding of sacrifice, as well as complicating constructions of "sacrifice" in terms of gift or reciprocity, which unnecessarily limit the ritual contexts in which animals might be slaughtered.[4]

But McClymond's work has also led me to view "sacrifice" as an inappropriate term to use to cover so many stages or discrete acts—or to translate indigenous terms for such different ritual sequences, in which killing was so often *not* the central act—where the point was to incinerate the flesh or to examine the entrails or to process to the shrine or simply to feast.[5] Some might endeavor to rectify the term—to preserve it with a nuanced, flexible sense. But given the bloody, Girardian connotations the category evokes in the study of ancient religions, from Bacchantic *sparagmos* to Christian martyrs, from *taurobolia* to Moloch baby-slaughter, can we really hope to nuance "sacrifice" to accommodate such a diversity of ritual sequences and apexes?[6] Would it not be better to describe ritual systems in which animals are killed on their own terms—e.g., as forms of offering or social contract making—rather than as "sacrifices" that simply revolved around slaughter?[7]

This chapter will explore the utility of the category "sacrifice" through a review of the multiple ritual contexts for animal slaughter in classical and Greco-Roman Egypt. These materials, I will argue, complicate not only the definition of sacrifice but also the centrality of sacrifice in the history of religions.

I

Egypt offers a host of examples of the ritual killing of animals and their dedication in some form to gods. However, the actual slaughter is so peripheral, and the forms of dedication so different, that the term *sacrifice* and all it conveys does *not* effectively capture the rites or frame their effective comparison with other historical rituals.

The first context for the ritual killing of animals is exemplified in the offering tablets used from about 1900 to 500 BCE and now found in many museums' Egyptian collections (figs. 3.1, 3.2). The flat tablet, often with a spout for the draining of milk or wine offerings, depicts the various substances that priests would present to particular gods (or ancestors as gods). One can invariably make out, in shallow relief, bread loaves, fruit, lotus flowers, jugs and vases, and cuts of prebutchered meat. This assortment on offering tablets matches what pharaohs and supplicants present to gods on wall-reliefs, stelae, and papyri, although the offering tablets actually served as ritual spaces, located near tombs, so I focus on them here.

This particular assortment of dedicatory substances represents the areas of production and vitality that the god or ancestor is meant to augment. They signify both food and ordered life in the terrestrial world; through the *act* of presenting these fresh vital substances, representative of what refreshes us humans, life itself is refreshed and maintained.[8] What is most crucial for testing the category of sacrifice, however, is what is *not* depicted: on the one hand, any physical transformation of these substances to remove them to a divine realm and, on the other hand, the actual slaughter and butchery that would have to occur to produce the cuts of meat or dressed poultry for the presentation table. Indeed, in many cases it seems that the

FIGURE 3.1 *Offering table depicting dressed poultry among breadloaves and vases. The spout at the front channeled liquids poured over the offering images to convey their essence. W: 83 cm.; L: 73cm.; H: 20 cm. 26th dynasty (664–525 BCE). Granite.*

depiction itself represents the offering, rather than merely recording the offering, and that the actual substance presented to the god or ancestor is the milk, wine, or other liquids represented in the vases and implied in the very spouts of the offering tablets.[9] In one rare case where we know animals were killed for such offering scenes, they—or, rather, their cutlets—were packed inside wooden containers in the shape of the idealized meats—again, image taking priority over actual meat, with the slaughter again removed to a peripheral, even nonritualized preparatory stage.[10]

The second principal context in—or for—which animals were killed for religious purposes appears at certain pilgrimage cults around Egypt flourishing in the Ptolemaic and Roman periods.[11] Dogs, cats, ibises, and other animals would be killed on demand, mummified, and deposited for the god as a votive sign, allowing the pilgrim's participation in the mythical transformation of the god into a potent Osiris being (figs. 3.3, 3.4). While there were also cults that mummified animals that died

FIGURE 3.2 *Offering table depicting steer's head and haunch among breadloaves and vases, with two wells and spout for liquids. L: 27 cm.; W: 19 cm. Middle Kingdom (2040–1640 BCE), limestone.*

naturally in their capacity as divine avatars, the clear evidence of strangling or skull crushing in the many thousands of animal mummies deposited at Saqqara (and the oasis site of El-Deir) show that the animals were raised to be killed and mummified (fig. 3.5). Through the mummification, interment, and presumably some verbal rites over the carcass, the once-neutral dog or cat became sacralized as an Osiris.[12]

The killing itself seems to have been *so* peripheral to the ritual presentation of the corpses that it took place at some site entirely outside the zone of the pilgrims, who sought only the mummy itself and had no interest in the manner of death.[13] Presumably, in sponsoring the transformation of a representative of the cult god into an Osiris, the devotee could participate personally in a dynamic area of temple ritual. We see, then, another type of "offering" of a living being in which killing was peripheral to the main pilgrim's rituals—where, indeed, the value lay in its deceased form.

A third context, somewhat closer to the popular conception of sacrifice, is the ritual incineration of certain animals. These rites were meant in one capacity to please the gods with the aroma of barbecue, but also, more importantly, to ward off chaos through the ritual destruction of cosmic enemies. The animal carcasses

FIGURE 3.3 *Case for Ibis mummy, gilded, with bronze head and feet. H.: 34 cm. Roman period. Wood/bronze/gold.*

are presented as images or incarnations (*iḥryt*) of divine enemies, and the grilling process is declared to be the vanquishing of those enemies. Across the various temple inscriptions that record these rites through the Roman period, it is entirely ambiguous whether the gods actually are meant to gain food through this incineration and whether some meat grilled for such apotropaic purposes might have fed priests or festival participants.[14] But the animals in the case of these ritual incinerations are quite specific: antelopes, certain fowl, reddish bovines, and crocodiles. These representatives of the chaos god Seth-Typhon have a predominantly wild character, and even those from domestic sources are specially marked for this ritual destruction, as we see recorded in a papyrus of 148 CE.[15] In this way the Egyptian rites of apotropaic incineration resist interpretations either in terms of hunting or in terms of domesticized "selective kill."[16] On the other hand, in their combination of combustion and divine consumption, these incineration rites do evoke Hubert and Mauss: "The complete elimination from temporal surroundings of the parts of the animal thus destroyed or eaten."[17] The important difference here would lie in the *sense* of destruction: not so much to feed the gods with physically transformed meat as to vanquish cosmic enemies through their animal representatives. But even more importantly, the *ritual* destruction takes place on the fire, not by the knife.[18]

FIGURE 3.4 *Case for cat mummy, with green-painted head. H.: 70 cm. Greco-Roman period.*
Painted wood.

That is, the killing itself is peripheral to the rite, which revolves around burning and aroma, not killing or blood.

There were certainly regional variations in the animal incineration rites, some perhaps providing food for festivals (as Derchain has argued for the temple of Denderah), while others, as Plutarch depicted in Apollinopolis, beginning with a mass, popular animal slaughter: "After hunting as many [crocodiles] as they can and killing them, [the villagers] throw them out opposite the temple"—presumably then to be ritually burned by priests.[19] This is a rare reference to the act of killing

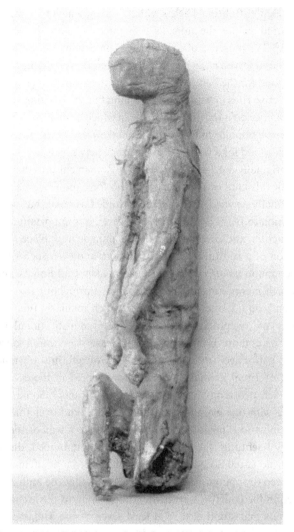

FIGURE 3.5 *Dog mummy. H.: 13.4 cm.; L: 18.7 cm.; W: 9.6 cm. Roman period. Wrappings and canine tissue.*

for such ritual purposes; even in this particular case of collective enthusiasm, the slaughter is fundamentally set off from the official ceremony. Indeed, to the extent that "sacrifice" as a form of ritual should intrinsically *obscure* its underlying events, whether hunting or butchery, this crocodile hunt would not be considered sacrifice.[20]

It is interesting to note that this same kind of apotropaic use of an animal's carcass is attested in a series of graffiti over a period of the fourth century CE by a society of ironworkers. They would annually come to the dilapidated shrine of

Amenhotep at Deir el-Bahri in Thebes with a donkey, which they would consign to a *thusia* that would include the animal's "slaughtering before the god," before they held a banquet.[21] The presence of the donkey, iconic animal of Seth-Typhon, indicates that this *thusia* served as an apotropaic incineration of divine enemies, not the preparation of food for the banquet. By this time the term *thusia* had come to cover even such distinctive rites in which not the killing but the roasting was the point.[22]

By the Roman period a fourth type of rite in which animal slaughter was a component had become popular in Egypt: the animal offered to the god and then killed *in order* to provide food for a festival or religious society's banquet—the classic form of "sacrifice," originally more at home in Greco-Roman cultures than Egyptian. We find evidence for this kind of ritualized butchery for banquets especially in the use of *pigs*, traditionally deemed "Sethian" and avoided as meat, but which became a popular dedication to Isis.[23] In these cases, however, it is important to note that the dedication, slaughter, and consumption of the animals took place *outside* temples, not as a function of a central *religious* institution; and even such ritual pig-roasts were far less common as *offerings* than breads, cakes, and liquids. Indeed, in this regard it is worth mentioning the predominance, throughout the Mediterranean world, of vegetal, liquid, and cake offerings, which regularly functioned as signs of propitiation, vow, reciprocity, celebration, and even institutional authority. The use of animals serves more as an elaboration of feast—and thus a social gesture, an opportunity for patronage—than as the archetype of offering-substance.[24]

A fifth type of ritual animal slaughter has emerged in the excavations of an esplanade between two temples in early Roman Tebtunis.[25] Some sixty skeletons of sheep (along with one cat and three dogs) were found over three first-century CE layers, lying in various positions near the northeastern wall of the temple of the crocodile god Soknebtunis, their bodies intact (not mummified, dismembered, or cremated), with no ritual accoutrements and no indications of manner of death. Evidence of sheep droppings in the vicinity suggests that the animals, singly or in groups, arrived in the courtyard alive. Most interesting to the archaeologists were the crude markers that stood next to at least seven of the carcasses: stone blocks or piles of bricks or potsherds. Presumably the site or placement of each body, although ostensibly random in arrangement, had some importance.[26] Could these remains be "sacrifices," even with their bodies intact and so randomly interred?[27]

The most likely explanation for this kind of animal slaughter would be some type of public divination practice linked spatially to the temples, but not as an extension of its cult, in which the sheep were stabbed or slit and then observed as they moved about the courtyard in their death throes—much as in other places priests were said to observe the (living) movements of birds or children.[28] This kind of process would explain their haphazard burial near a wall (where sheep in panic would tend to cluster), the attention to the site of the body, and the otherwise unprocessed state of the carcasses. Such a hypothetical oracular practice (otherwise unattested in Egypt) might have constituted a local interpretation of Roman extispicy (in which the internal features of a consecrated animal served as divinatory palette) or might simply have represented one more innovation in this town's diverse array of divination procedures. In either case, it would have turned the *dying* of the animal into the focal point, rather than the preparation, killing, corpse, meat, or residues. It might have taken place as a popular, extramural devotion to one or both gods, as one occasionally finds at Egyptian temples (perhaps, one may further speculate, as a votive offering).[29] As a divination rite the cutting—the bloodletting—of the sheep in the esplanade would have initiated the mantic palette, the array of possible events, whose expert interpretation produced an oracle. The death itself would have been incidental to the oracle.

While it may be impossible to offer more than speculation on these animal remains, the state of the remains do present the historian of religions with another type of animal slaughter, ostensibly ritualized (in its perpetuation over three archaeological layers and its contiguity to sacred precincts), that defies the category "sacrifice" in its traditional sense.

II

We have so far seen four ritual contexts in which animal slaughter was involved as a preparatory (although never central) stage and a fifth context (hypothetically) in which cutting and actual death were both separated and incidental to the animal's dying movements. What should strike us at this point is the considerable diversity of these rites. While all held some central significance *as* ceremony, whether conducted in a temple or designated as *thusia* among people outside, the animal's killing assumed a quite different status in each case. What is important to note now is that none of these ceremonies that involved animal slaughter at some stage could be regarded either as ultimate forms of offering or as the central rites in Egyptian religion as understood by priests or laity.[30] What ritual occasions, then, *did* function as central rites? The emergence and procession of the deity's image from its shrine: the *appearance* of the god.

Within the temple, the key moments of ritual precision—gestural, verbal, choreographical—took place at the awakening of an image, its emergence from an inner shrine, and its perambulations among other shrines within, or even beyond, the temple precinct. Inscriptions celebrate the god's appearance—often in solar terms, like the sun's emergence from the night. At Dendarah, for example, the solar imagery would pertain to the images' procession to shrines on the temple roof to unite with the sun each morning. It was at these moments that all manner of ritual elements—music, incense, dance—coalesced around the central acts of emergence and procession.[31]

If so great a degree of priestly scripting surrounded procession within the temple, how much more acclamation greeted processions that departed the temple during festivals? From all we can reconstruct from temple inscriptions, relief images, and even popular terra-cotta figurines, the emergence of the god on his processional bark was the key moment of any festival, whether the divine image was hidden or visible.[32] Such processions signified the god's visit to other regional shrines to reaffirm certain mythic connections; in the course of such visits, the procession would revitalize landscape and cosmos. "Welcome, child great of power, son of Menhyt," the song greeted the Heqa procession as it arrived at the temple of Khnum at Roman Esna:

> You reunite with your father Khnum, and his heart rejoices to see you. How beautiful is your arrival after you have traversed country and desert in [your] bark! You are the vital infusion that makes verdant the nourishing earth, that makes vegetation flourish, that creates grain and barley, that swells the corn— master of the fields![33]

It was at such processions also, both within and beyond the inner precincts, that *divination* would take place. The procession would stop, and a priest would ask questions of the god in his bark, which was carried on the shoulders of other priests. The god would be felt and seen to answer in the movements of the bark on the shoulders of the priests. The movements would be interpreted as oracles, and so the procession brought more than religious spectacle and divine presence to participants; it brought justice and social direction.[34]

It is important to take seriously this *mantic* capacity of processions at Egyptian temples, because the oracle application shows how centrally processions themselves functioned in public religion in ancient Egypt. It was the moment of greatest attention for all participants and epitomizes for Egypt what J. Z. Smith would call "the religion of 'there'"—of civic or state cult. In his 2003 essay Smith actually proposed animal sacrifice to be "the central ritual of the religion of 'there,'" insofar as it mediates society with its chief gods and establishes "complex systems of sacred/profane, purity/impurity, permitted/ forbidden."[35] While this generalization doubtless holds true for Roman religion, whose ritual animal slaughter notably also culminated in divination (extispicy), and to some extent for Roman civic religion in the broader empire, for Egypt and many other Near Eastern cultures it was the procession itself that served as the axial, integrating moment of civic religion. It articulated the god's relationship to a regional theology, to powers of agriculture and generation, and to protection from enemies; it dramatized hierarchy and affirmed boundaries between sacred and neutral; and it mediated divine presence through a visual spectacle with the capacity to "speak."

All this is to say that animal slaughter of any kind stood at the periphery of the ceremonial world of traditional Egyptian religion through the Roman period, while the emergence and the procession of the images of gods held a vividly central place.[36] Of course, as we saw in connection with the fourth context of ritual animal slaughter, for ceremonial feasting, most towns in Egypt would by the Roman empire have assimilated a Greco-Roman discourse of *thusia*, such that ritual animal slaughter came to punctuate most civic events, provided local elite opportunities for euergetism, and signified imperial authority over events and religious displays.

But even in this larger, multicultural context in which animal slaughter might complement festivals and civic religious events, *thusia* as a concept and a public act could be epitomized in the smaller-scale libation, the wine or milk offering, such as we see the deceased performing in representations on stelae from the town of Terenouthis.[37] Thus to the extent that—and in the towns where—Egyptian public religion by Roman times was Hellenized, we can say that animal slaughter had gained a central place in public ritual, while *thusia* was probably more regularly imagined in simpler forms of offering. But the priestly performances of Egyptian temples, which did continue to inform Egyptian religious life in many areas through the fourth century, revolved around manifestation and procession, *not* animal slaughter.

It is remarkable, then, to see the problematic influence that "sacrifice"-centered theory has exerted on Egyptology as well. In her striking contribution to the 2001 Paris conference on ancient sacrifice, Catherine Graindorge critiqued the various modern interpretations surrounding a particular Egyptian procession of the god Min that included a white bull, to which would be offered a sheaf of wheat at a certain point in the procession.[38] This white bull served as the processional manifestation of Kamoutef, an aspect of Min that both fructifies the land and vanquishes cosmic enemies, and so was quite the opposite in function from those *red* bulls that might be incinerated to vanquish enemies.[39] The efficacy of the god Kamoutef in his bull manifestation would be dramatized through the bull's eating of the wheat stalks. The bull itself would have lived to a ripe old age in his capacity as divine animal. Yet to some authoritative interpreters the mere *notion* of a bull in a religious procession with the function of bringing agricultural fertility implied its bloody slaughter at some key point in the ritual. This presumption turns out to be quite wrong, and Graindorge wisely showed the errors that arise when we generalize sacrifice as the central religious rite, such that even processions get assimilated to this model.[40]

III

Of course, many processions (as in ancient Rome) did precede and even frame ritual animal slaughter, so the question arises: Can the case of Egypt be considered as anything more than an outlying example compared to those ancient cultures—Rome, Greece, and Israel, for example—in which animal slaughter did play a major role?[41] Can the peripheral place of animal slaughter in *Egyptian* religion actually serve the rectification, or even abandonment, of the *general* category "sacrifice," as it has been used and elevated in the history of religions?

This is the contention of this chapter. At the very least, Egyptian religion confirms McClymond's crucial observation about the preliminary, secondary, even peripheral status of killing in most rites of blood sacrifice and alerts us to the many *different* rituals that might involve or simply presume the dedication and killing of animals.[42] But do all rituals that involve animal carcasses amount to a heuristically meaningful cluster—a pattern we can designate "sacrifice"? Does not a term that *focuses* on the act of slaughter rather obliterate the sheer diversity of ritual contexts in which animal slaughter may have played some role? Even allowing for the historical uniqueness of Egypt's votive animal mummies, I suspect that *any* ceremony in the ancient world in which animals in some form are ritually dedicated would be better understood *without* a category that revolves around animal slaughter.[43]

But even more, Egypt's religious forms might prompt us to remove sacrifice in general from the kind of monolithic center stage it has acquired in the history of Near Eastern, Greco-Roman, or so-called pagan religions. We have long entertained the generalization that "paganism" revolved around sacrifice *by definition*: in the words of Robin Lane Fox, "Animal bloodshed remained central to pagan cult."[44] As it has been repeated, however, the generalization has served more to demonstrate "pagan" religions' primitivity and anticipation of Christ's sacrifice than to capture the nuances of civic or temple ritual in the ancient world. To be sure, the imperial edicts of the third century CE have contributed to this scholarly impression, demanding as they did a consistency in public ritual practice across the empire—although what was enjoined on citizens was libations and sharing in consecrated meat, not animal slaughter itself.[45] It is also true that, by the mid-fourth century, both intellectual Hellenists and Christian hagiographers were *mutually* constructing a simplified or caricatured "paganism" that revolved around animal sacrifice—or human sacrifice, in many Christians' view.[46] So it can hardly be denied that many late-antique writers *did* see "sacrifice"—or, more properly, *thusia*—as a sine qua non of traditional religion, even if its official proscription may not have had the devastating effect on local religion that bishops hoped (or modern scholars assume).[47]

Yet modern scholarship on ancient religion need not itself kneel in thrall to the hybrid images of sacrifice of Decius and Julian. The religions of the ancient world in their local or regional contexts were about much more than sacrifice (as this term is generally conceived). Processions and the public beholding of images, official divination, feasts, and spectacles—any of these expressions might function as the ceremonial center of religion in antiquity; and it seems the height of simplification to put sacrifice at the center, however we define it.[48] *Thusia* itself was a shifting category in the Roman empire—a "vacant sign," as Richard Gordon puts it—that enveloped many possible acts, ceremonies, and offerings and that often endowed them with an imperial aura.[49] Furthermore, when the dedication and slaughter of animals do constitute *some* part of an authentic ritual sequence, as in the case of votive cat mummies, our interpretation of that ritual is ill-served by a category inextricably bound up with a bloody practice stereotypically associated with heathens. An important case in point appears in the florid exhortations of the fifth-century Christian priest Paulinus of Nola to villagers to dedicate animals to the cult of St. Felix for ritual slaughter on the saint's behalf (and to feed festival participants). Could Paulinus be demanding a return to animal sacrifice? Church historians' own apprehension in answering this question derives from the very ambiguity of the term *sacrifice,* which in this case carries overtones of "pagan survival" that clash with our historical sense of Paulinus's Christian worldview. But the real theoretical challenge here revolves around how to describe a fifth-century Italian festival practice associated with a Christian saint's shrine. For this purpose a more nuanced approach to the language and ritual contexts of animal slaughter, unmoored from the Christian/Roman theological polarity inevitably tied to "sacrifice," offers a more profitable means of understanding these late-antique Christian ritual innovations. Indeed, it makes more sense to speak of animal slaughter as a continuing medium for festival conviviality and patronage than of "sacrifice," a needlessly confusing and theologically laden category.[50]

In the end, the Egyptian examples of animal slaughter for ritual purposes should certainly challenge us (1) to decentralize *killing* in our conception of sacrifice as a category, (2) to decentralize *sacrifice* as the focal or characteristic rite in Near Eastern and Greco-Roman religions, and (3) to question the capacity of the *category sacrifice*, so loaded with Frazerian, Girardian, and theological baggage, to describe effectively the slaughter of animals in religious ceremonies. To quote Marcel Détienne,

> Sacrifice is indeed a category of the thought of yesterday, conceived of as arbitrarily as totemism . . . both because it gathers into one artificial type elements taken from here and there in the symbolic fabric of societies and because it reveals the surprising power of annexation that Christianity still subtly exercises on scholars.[51]

Notes

1. On Israel, see Jonathan Klawans, *Purity, Sacrifice, and the Temple: Symbolism and Supersessionism in the Study of Ancient Judaism* (New York: Oxford University Press, 2006). On Rome, see Richard Gordon, "The Veil of Power: Emperors, Sacrificers, and Benefactors," *Pagan Priests*, edited by Mary Beard and John North (Ithaca: Cornell University Press, 1990), 202–19; Mary Beard, John North, and Simon Price, *Religions of Rome* (Cambridge: Cambridge University Press, 1998), 1: 36–37. See also Beate Pongratz-Leisten, "Ritual Killing and Sacrifice in the Ancient Near East," *Human Sacrifice in Jewish and Christian Tradition*, Numen Supplement 112, edited by Karin Finsterbusch, Armin Lange, and K. F. Diethard Römheld (Leiden: Brill, 2007), 3–33.

2. See Jill Robbins, "Sacrifice," in *Critical Terms for Religious Studies*, edited by Mark C. Taylor (Chicago: University of Chicago Press, 1998), 285–97.

3. Kathryn McClymond, "The Nature and Elements of Sacrificial Ritual," *Method and Theory in the Study of Religion* 16 (2004): 337–66; *Beyond Sacred Violence: A Comparative Study of Sacrifice* (Baltimore: Johns Hopkins University Press, 2008). See also Caroline Humphrey and James Laidlaw, "Sacrifice and Ritualization," in *The Archaeology of Ritual*, edited by Evangelos Kyriakidis (Los Angeles: Cotsen Institute of Archaeology, 2007), 255–76, esp. 265–71.

4. Cf. Stowers, "The Religion of Plant and Animal Offerings versus the Religion of Meanings, Essences, and Textual Mysteries," chapter 1 in this volume.

5. See also James W. Watts, review of McClymond, *Beyond Sacred Violence, Religion* 39 (2009): 300–302, esp. 301–302. On the diverse ritual locations and functions of animal slaughter, see esp. M. P. J. Dillon, "'Xenophon Sacrificed on Account of an Expedition': Divination and the *sphagia* before Ancient Greek Battles," in *Le sacrifice antique: Vestiges, procédures et stratégies*, edited by Véronique Mehl and Pierre Brulé (Rennes: Presses Universitaires de Rennes, 2008), 235–51. See also Sarah Peirce, "Death, Revelry, and 'Thysia'," *Classical Antiquity* 12.2 (1993): 219–66.

6. The diverse materials in Laura Nasrallah's contribution to this volume, "The Embarrassment of Blood: Early Christians and Others on Sacrifice, War, and Rational Worship" (chapter 7), illustrate the problem.

7. Here I follow the general observations of Stanley Stowers ("The Religion of Plant and Animal Offerings versus the Religion of Meanings, Essences and Textual Mysteries," in this volume) and Daniel Ullucci ("Contesting the Meaning of Animal Sacrifice," chapter 2 in this volume) on the *function* of animal slaughter in the Greco-Roman world, although not their persistent use of the label "sacrifice."

8. Byron E. Shafer, "Temples, Priests, and Rituals: An Overview," in *Temples of Ancient Egypt*, edited by Byron E. Shafer (Ithaca: Cornell University Press, 1997), 23–25.

9. For example, Chicago, Oriental Institute Museum, 10578, 1351, 1394–95; and Marco Zecchi, "On the Offering of Honey in the Graeco-Roman Temples," *Aegyptus* 77 (1997): 71–83. Similarly, Emma Stafford discusses the relatively minor role of animal offerings *ex voto* at the Greek Asclepius shrines, as represented in votive stelae: "Cocks to Asclepios: Sacrificial Practice and Healing Cult," in Mehl and Brulé, *Le sacrifice antique*, 205–21.

10. Salima Ikram, "Divine Creatures: Animal Mummies," in *Divine Creatures: Animal Mummies in Ancient Egypt*, edited by Salima Ikram (Cairo: American University in Cairo Press, 2005), 4–5.

11. On the problem of the category "pilgrimage" as applied to classical and Greco-Roman Egypt, see Youri Volokhine, "Les déplacements pieux en Égypte pharaonique: Sites et pratiques cultuelles," in *Pilgrimage and Holy Space in Late Antique Egypt*, edited by David Frankfurter, RGRW 134 (Leiden: Brill, 1998), 51–97; and Rutherford, "Down-Stream to the Cat-Goddess: Herodotus on Egyptian Pilgrimage," in *Pilgrimage in Graeco-Roman and Early Christian Antiquity: Seeing the Gods*, edited by Jaś Elsner and Ian Rutherford (Oxford: Oxford University Press, 2005), 135–40.

12. Alain Zivie and Roger Lichtenberg, "Les momies d'animaux," *Dossiers d'archéologie* 252 (2000): 52–55; Catidem, "Les chats du Bubasteion de Saqqâra: État de la question et perspectives," *Egyptology at the Dawn of the Twenty-First Century: Proceedings of the 8th Inernational Congress of Egyptologists*, vol. 2, edited by Zahi Hawass (Cairo: American University in Cairo Press, 2003), 605–11; idem, "The Cats of the Goddess Bastet," in Ikram, *Divine Creatures*, 117–18; Françoise Dunand and Roger Lichtenberg, "Des chiens momifiés à El-Deir Oasis de Kharga," *BIFAO* 105 (2005): 77. On the mummification of animal avatars, see Dieter Kessler and Abd el Halim Nur el-Din, "Tuna al-Gebel: Millions of Ibises and Other Animals," in Ikram, *Divine Creatures*, 120–63.

13. Alain Charron, "Massacres d'animaux à la Basse Époque," *Revue d'Égyptologie* 41 (1990): 209–13. See also Rutherford, "Herodotus on Egyptian Pilgrimage," 144–46, on Herodotus's vague account of Egyptian animal interment (*Histories* 2.65–67). A Greek ritual spell from third/fourth-century Egypt transforms the pilgrims' devotional rite for Bastet into one that revolves around the cat's slaughter, reconfiguring this act as the "mistreatment

[*adikoumenēn*]" of Bastet's image, declaratively attributed to the goddess's opponents (so that she might afflict them in turn; PGM III.1–14). Subsequently, the slaughtered cat is ritually prepared and entombed (III.15–29). This hybrid form of the traditional cat slaughter reflects the versatility of ritual forms in antiquity, especially to address the exigencies of aggressive magic.

14. In general on apotropaic incineration of animals, see Jean Yoyotte, "Héra d'Héliopolis et le sacrifice humain," *Annuaire de l'École pratique des hautes-études, 5è section—sciences religieuses* 89 (1980–81): 31–102; Christiane Zivie-Coche, "Pharaonic Egypt," *Gods and Men in Egypt*, translated by David Lorton (Ithaca: Cornell University Press, 2004), 90–91; Catherine Bouanich, "Mise à mort rituelle de l'animal. Offrande carnée dans le temple égyptien," in *La cuisine et l'autel: Les sacrifices en questions dans les sociétés de la méditerranée ancienne*, edited by Stella Georgoudi, Renée Koch Piettre, and Francis Schmidt, BEHE SR 124 (Turnhout: Brepols, 2005), 149–62. On the ambiguity of "alimentary" symbolism, see Jan Quaegebeur, "L'autel-à-feu et l'abattoir en Égypte tardive," in *Ritual and Sacrifice in the Ancient Near East*, edited by J. Quaegebeur, OLA 55 (Leuven: Peeters, 1993), 329–53, and Philippe Derchain, "De l'holocauste au barbecue: Les avatars d'un sacrifice," *Göttinger Miszellen* 213 (2007): 19–22.

15. P. Geneva I.32, in P. Schubert, "Continuité et changement des cultes locaux en Égypte romaine: À travers trois documents de la collection papyrologique de Genève," in *Les cultes locaux dans les mondes grec et romain*, edited by G. Labarre (Paris: Boccard, 2004), 295–303. On animals consigned to apotropaic incineration, see Yoyotte, "Héra d'Héliopolis," 43–44; Plut., *De Is. et Os.* 31. On sealing animals for apotropaeic destruction, see Yoyotte, "Héra d'Héliopolis," 52–55. The first-century CE Egyptian priest Apion criticized Jews for ritually slaughtering domestic animals, implying Egyptian ritual preference for wild animals: Josephus, *C. Ap.* 2.137–38.

16. On hunting, see Walter Burkert, *Homo Necans: The Anthropology of Ancient Greek Sacrificial Ritual and Myth*, translated by Peter Bing (Berkeley: University of California Press, 1983), 12–22, 42–46. On selective kill, see Jonathan Z. Smith, "The Domestication of Sacrifice," in *Violent Origins: Ritual Killing and Cultural Formation*, edited by Robert G. Hamerton-Kelly (Stanford: Stanford University Press, 1987), 199–202.

17. Henri Hubert and Marcel Mauss, *Sacrifice: Its Nature and Functions*, translated by W. D. Halls (Chicago: University of Chicago Press, 1964; repr., 1981), 38.

18. As noted by Zivie-Coche, "Pharaonic Egypt," 91. Cf. Yoyotte, "Hiéra d'Héliopolis," 46–47, suggesting an apotropaic sense to the slaughter as well.

19. On Denderah, see Derchain, "De l'holocauste au barbecue." On Apollinopolis (Edfu), see Plut., *De Is. et Os.* 50, on which see J. G. Griffiths in his edition *De Iside et Osiride* (Cardiff: University of Wales Press, 1970), 492–93.

20. On the relationship of sacrifice to "underlying events," see Humphrey and Laidlaw, "Sacrifice and Ritualization," 262.

21. Adam Łajtar, *Deir el-Bahari in the Hellenistic and Roman Periods: A Study of an Egyptian Temple Based on Greek Sources*, Journal of Juristic Papyrology Supplement 4 (Warsaw: Institute of Archaeology, 2006), 163, 168, 172.

22. See Łajtar, *Deir el-Bahari in the Hellenistic and Roman Periods*, 96–99. Porphyry notes that donkeys, being inedible, were not customarily slaughtered as ritual offering in Greco-Roman culture (*Abst.* 2.25.6).

23. On Egyptian priests' abstinence from pork, see Joseph., *C. Ap.* 2.141; cf. Hdt., 2.47.

24. See Françoise Perpillou-Thomas, *Fêtes d'Égypte ptolémaïque et romaine d'après la documentation papyrologique grecque*, Studia Hellenistica 31 (Leuven: Studia Hellenistica, 1993), 204–8; Georges Nachtergael, "Un sacrifice en l'honneur de 'Baubo': Scènes figurées sur un moule cubique de l'Égypte romaine," *Egyptian Religion: The Last Thousand Years*, edited by Willy Clarysse, Antoon Schoors, and Harco Willems OLA 84 (Leuven: Peeters, 1998), 159–77. A fourth-century CE letter still refers to the ritual slaughter of a pig as *thusia*: P.Oxy 10.1299, 7, with Malcolm Choat, *Belief and Cult in Fourth-Century Papyri* (Turnhout: Brepols, 2006), 99. On the offering of cakes and breads, see Ladislas Castiglione, "Greichisch-ägyptische Studien: Beitrag zu dem griechisch-ägyptischen Privatkult," *Acta antiqua hungaricae* 5 (1957): 220–27; S. Hirsch, "Spätantike Brotstempel mit der Maske des ägyptischen Gottes Bes," *Coptic Studies on the Threshold of a New Millennium*, edited by M. Immerzeel and J. van der Vliet OLA 133 (Leuven: Peeters, 2004) 1259–72; and the remarks on baked goods as sacrifice in McClymond, *Beyond Sacred Violence*, 78–80. Cf. Gordon, "Veil of Power," 217–18, on the use of stamped cakes to commemorate official *thusia* in particular locales in the Roman empire. Porphyry describes in detail the predominance of vegetal offerings: *Abst.* 2.14–16, 19.1, 20. See also Véronique Mehl, "Parfums de fêtes: Usage de parfums et sacrifices sanglants," in Mehl and Brulé, *Le sacrifice antique*, 167–86, on the efficacy and central function of incense in festivals that included animal slaughter.

25. The esplanade lies to the east of the vestibule of the temple of Soknebtunis and south of the chapel of Isis-Thermouthis, and abuts the northeastern wall of the second courtyard of the Soknebtunis temple.

26. Claudio Gallazzi and Gisèle Hadji-Minaglou, *Tebtynis I: La reprise des fouilles et le quartier de la chapelle d'Isis-Thermouthis* (Cairo:Institut Français d'Archéologie Orientale, 2000), 109–16, 154–59 (photos). I am indebted to both Claudio Gallazzi and Gisèle Hadji-Minaglou for discussion of these remains.

27. Contrast the typical archaeology of animal offerings in the Roman world, discussed in Sébastien Lepetz and William Van Andringa, "Pour une archéologie du sacrifice à l'époque romaine," in Mehl and Brulé, *Le sacrifice antique*, 39–58.

28. On divination at Tebtunis and elsewhere in Fayyum, see David Frankfurter, *Religion in Roman Egypt: Assimilation and Resistance* (Princeton: Princeton University Press, 1998), 153–61, esp. 159–60.

29. On forms of extramural devotion at Egyptian temples, see Frankfurter, *Religion in Roman Egypt*, 46–58.

30. As noted by Zivie-Coche, "Pharaonic Egypt," 91.

31. See esp. Ragnhild Bjerre Finnestad, "Temples of the Ptolemaic and Roman Periods: Ancient Traditions in New Contexts," in Schafer, *Temples of Ancient Egypt*, 207–17.

32. Françoise Dunand, *Religion populaire en Égypte romaine*, Études preliminaries aux religions orientales dans l'empire 77 (Leiden: Brill, 1979), 93; Finnestad, "Temples of the Ptolemaic and Roman Periods," 220–21; Katherine Eaton, "Types of Cult-Image Carried in Divine Barques and the Logistics of Performing Temple Ritual in the New Kingdom," *Zeitschrift für ägyptische Sprache und Altertumskunde* 134 (2007): 15–25; and esp. Serge Sauneron, *Les fêtes religieuses d'Esna aux derniers siècles du paganisme*, Esna 5 (Cairo: Institut Français d'Archéologie Orientale, 1962).

33. Esna 341, 8, translated by Sauneron, *Les fêtes religieuses d'Esna*, 35.

34. See Frankfurter, *Religion in Roman Egypt*, 145–61.

35. Jonathan Z. Smith, "Here, There, and Anywhere," in *Relating Religion: Essays in the Study of Religion* (2003; repr, Chicago: University of Chicago Press, 2004), 329. See also Gordon, "Veil of Power," 202–19.

36. In characterizing traditional Egyptian religion as it existed throughout Egypt in relationship to temples, I do not deny that many cities came to be dominated by a Roman imperial sensibility that put *thusia*—with animal slaughter and festival consumption—at the center of civic religious expression, capturing both popular ambitions for Roman identity and elite ambitions for prestige through euergetism, donating materials for processions, games, and ritual animal slaughter.

37. See S.A.A. El-Nassery and Guy Wagner, "Nouvelles stèles de Kom Abu Bellou," *BIFAO* 78 (1978): 24–29.

38. Catherine Graindorge, "Le taureau blanc du dieu Min et l'offrande de la gerbe de blé," in Georgoudi, Koch Piettre, and Schmidt, *La cuisine et l'autel*, 47–76.

39. Cf. Plut., *De Is. et Os.* 31.

40. Graindorge, "Le taureau blanc," esp. 49–51. Cf. Porphyry's description of a legendary bull-slaughter rite in which the bull *was* slaughtered after eating special grain: *Abst.* 2.30.4.

41. See, for example, Fritz Graf, "What Is New about Greek Sacrifice?" in *Kykeon: Studies in Honour of H. S. Versnel*, edited by H.F.J. Horstmanshoff, H. W. Singor, F. T. Van Straten, and J. H. M. Strubbe RGRW 142 (Leiden: Brill, 2002), 113–25.

42. Many *thusia* rites described in the PGM make killing a preparatory, or simply presumed, stage in creating efficacious substances—for example, PGM IV.26–51, 1390–1495, 2891–2942, on which see Sarah Iles Johnston, "Sacrifice in the Greek Magical Papyri," in *Magic and Ritual in the Ancient World*, edited by Paul Mirecki and Marvin Meyer RGRW 141 (Leiden: Brill, 2002), 344–58. Cf. PGM XII.36ff, 205ff.

43. I am grateful to Larry Myers's challenge in his session response (11/1912008) to devise a better means for constructively comparing ritual animal slaughter; but it is questionable whether animal slaughter *per se* should be the basis for the comparison of rituals. In fact, the model for sacrifice proposed by Hubert and Mauss allows much more comparative flexibility, as I have shown with cases of ritual destruction of human bodies: "On Sacrifice and Residues: Processing the Potent Body," in *Religion in Cultural Discourse*, edited by Brigitte Luchesi and Kocku von Stuckrad, Religionsgeschichtliche Versuche und Vorarbeiten 52, (Berlin: De Gruyter, 2004), 511–33.

44. *Pagans and Christians* (New York: Knopf, 1987), 72. See also Scott Bradbury, "Julian's Pagan Revival and the Decline of Blood Sacrifice," *Phoenix* 49 (1995): 332–41; H.-J. Klauck, *The Religious Context of Early Christianity* (Edinburgh: T. & T. Clark, 2000), 12–19; and cf. the more nuanced discussion by S.R.F. Price, *Rituals and Power: The Roman Imperial Cult in Asia Minor* (Cambridge: Cambridge University Press, 1984), 207–33.

45. Plin., *Ep.* 10.96.5; P. Oxy 58.3929, 1.9–10, with further sources in John R. Knipfing, "The Libelli of the Decian Persecution," *HTR* 16 (1923): 345–90; W. L. Leadbetter, "A *libelllus* of the Decian Persecution," *New Documents Illustrating Early Christianity* 2 (1982): 180–85; and historical comments by Ewa Wipszycka, "Considérations sur les persécutions contre les Chrétiens: Qui frappaient-elles?" *Poikilia: Études offertes à Jean-Pierre Vernant* (Paris: Éditions de l'École des Hautes-Études en Sciences Sociales, 1987), 397–405, and James Rives, "The Decree of Decius and the Religion of Empire," *JRS* 89

(1999): 135–154. H. A. Drake has convincingly proposed that the actual rites required
under the edicts had, by the late fourth century, merged with images of martyrdom *and*
with fears of Julian's revival in Christian memory to create a general image of "blood-
drenched heathen altars" that motivated an upsurge in Christian violence: H. A. Drake,
"Lambs into Lions: Explaining Early Christian Intolerance," *Past and Present* 153
(1996): 33–36.

46. This debate and the larger discourse of thusia are incisively analyzed in the chapters in this volume by Daniel Ullucci ("Contesting the Meaning of Animal Sacrifice"),
Laura Nasrallah ("The Embarrassment of Blood"), and Michele Salzman ("The End of
Public Sacrifice"). Further on the image of sacrifice promoted by intellectual Hellenists,
see Nicole Belayche, "Sacrifice and Theory of Sacrifice during the 'Pagan Reaction':
Julian the Emperor," in *Sacrifice in Religious Experience*, edited by Albert I. Baumgar-
ten, Numen Supplements 93 (Leiden: Brill, 2002), 101–26. Others in the same milieux
criticized blood sacrifice: Scott Bradbury, "Julian's Pagan Revival," Guy Stroumsa,
The End of Sacrifice: Religious Transformations in Late Antiquity, translated by Susan
Emanuel (Chicago: University of Chicago Press, 2009), 58–62; and, of course, Porph.,
Abst. 2. Christian constructions of heathenism in proscriptions of sacrifices: *C. Th.*
16; Zachariah of Mytilene, *V. Severi*. For Christian authors imputing human sacrifice
to heathens, see James B. Rives, "Human Sacrifice among Pagans and Christians," *JRS*
85 (1995): 65–85, and David Frankfurter, "Illuminating the Cult of Kothos: The *Pane-
gryic on Macarius* and Local Religion in Fifth-Century Egypt," *InThe World of Early
Egyptian Christianity: Language, Literature, and Social Context*, edited by James E.
Goehring and Janet A. Timbie (Washington D.C.: Catholic University of America
Press, 2007), 184–87.

47. Peter Brown observes trenchantly that "though essential to the Christian representation of the end of polytheism, and deeply resented, laws against sacrifice may have been less
disruptive to traditional piety than we might suppose," "in Christianization and Religious
Conflict," *Cambridge Ancient History* 13 (Cambridge: Cambridge University Press, 1998),
645. Cf. Frankfurter, *Religion in Roman Egypt*, 23–27. It is in this late-antique discourse of
thusia—from Decius and Valentinian through Julian—that the practice and interpretations
of public animal-slaughter rituals became enmeshed, complicating the model Stanley Stowers develops in his chapter in this volume.

48. Cf. Price, *Rituals and Power*, 230; Smith, "Domestication of Sacrifice," 179. Even
feasting and meat consumption in the Roman world had an inconsistent relationship with
public ritual animal slaughter; see Nicole Belayche, "Religion et consummation de la viande
dans le monde romaine: des réalités voilées," *Food and History* 5.1 (2007): 29–43.

49. Gordon, "Veil of Power," 206. See also Roger S. Bagnall and James B. Rives, "A
Prefect's Edict Mentioning Sacrifice," *Archiv für Religionsgeschichte* 2.1 (2000): 77–86, esp.
85–86. Bradbury, "Julian's Pagan Revival," shows that *thusia* was fundamentally an opportunity for displaying euergetism.

50. Paulinus of Nola, *Carmen* 20, with Dennis Trout, "Christianizing the Nolan
Countryside: Animal Sacrifice at the Tomb of St. Felix," *JECS* 3 (1995): 281–98, and
Cristiano Grottanelli, "Tuer des animaux pour la fête de Saint Félix," in Georgoudi,
Koch Piettre, and Schmidt, *La cuisine et l'autel*, 387–407. Cf. Stella Georgoudi, "Sancti-
fied Slaughter in Modern Greece: The 'Kourbáni' of the Saints," *The Cuisine of Sacrifice
among the Greeks*, edited by Marcel Détienne and Jean-Pierre Vernant, translated by

Paula Wissing (Chicago: University of Chicago Press, 1989), 183–203, 259–68, on similar problems in interpreting animal dedication, killing, and communal feasting in modern Greek Christianity.

51. Marcel Détienne, "Culinary Practices and the Spirit of Sacrifice," in Détienne and Vernant, *Cuisine of Sacrifice*, 20.

4

Jewish Sacrifice

ITS NATURE AND FUNCTION (ACCORDING TO PHILO)

William K. Gilders

In its Second Temple era (ca. 520 BCE–70 CE), Judaism was a religion of sacrifice. As such, it was not in the least out-of-place in the ancient Mediterranean world, where most national cults, in one form or another, were centered on sacrifice. A study of ancient Jewish sacrifice must locate the practice within its larger cultural context. Therefore, this chapter is oriented toward understanding Jewish sacrifice as a practice that *made sense* in its historical-cultural context and considering the ways in which ancient Jewish texts about sacrifice reflected and engaged that context.

Many readers will recognize that the chapter's title evokes the classic essay by Henri Hubert and Marcel Mauss, *Sacrifice: Its Nature and Function*, which sought, through a detailed comparative discussion of Jewish and Vedic sacrifice, to elucidate the nature and function of sacrifice as a cultural practice.[1] My goal is more modest—to elucidate what Jewish sacrifice meant to some ancient Jews and to explore their understanding of its nature and function. As an exercise in what I will term "literary ethnography," I will relate to literate-specialist producers of ancient Jewish texts—to use Stanley Stowers' taxonomy from chapter 1 in this volume—as cultural informants, seeking to make sense of what those informants tell me.

As a specific example, I focus on the writings of the Hellenistic Jewish scholar Philo of Alexandria (ca. 20 BCE–ca. 50 CE). Unique amongst ancient Jewish writers on sacrifice, Philo offers what can be termed an explicit theory of sacrifice (more correctly, to use Philo's own Greek term, a theory of *thysia*). I will discuss Philo's theory of sacrifice as a system of symbolic actions in relation to its historical-cultural context. I will then place Philo's ancient Jewish thinking about sacrifice into dialogue with modern ritual theory, engaging with debates about the "meaning" of sacrifice as a type of ritual activity. In doing so, I will locate Philo within the history of the interpretation of sacrifice.

Philo wrote in Greek in a context—the cosmopolitan city of Alexandria in Egypt—in which sacrifice was a living reality. While he and many of his Alexandrian Jewish readers might, conceivably, never have seen, let alone participated directly in sacrificial rites at the Jewish temple in Jerusalem, they could easily have encountered the sacrificial rituals of their non-Jewish neighbors, and Philo's non-Jewish readers almost certainly would have had some kind of involvement with sacrificial practice. Thus, before turning to my focus on Philo's ideas about sacrifice, it will be helpful to discuss ancient Jewish sacrifice more generally, and its relationship with non-Jewish sacrifice.

Sacrifice was something Jews and non-Jews in the ancient Mediterranean world had in common. Jewish sacrifice fit its larger cultural world, in which most cults were sacrificial—that is, they involved the ritualized processing of animal (and sometimes human) bodies, along with vegetal materials, liquids such as oil and wine, and incense, in relation to supernatural forces, usually "gods." For most adherents of a Hellenistic cult, and particularly for those who participated in the Greek and Roman sacrificial cults, Jewish sacrifice would have been recognizably the same ritual phenomenon as their own. They would have been able to place Jewish practices into the same ritual category as their own. The same would have been true, reciprocally, for Jews. Jewish and Greco-Roman sacrificial practices were indeed very similar in basic form. They involved the slaughter of animal victims at designated cult places and the manipulation of their bodies in various ways. Notable points of commonality were application of blood to an altar, the burning of select body portions in an altar fire as an offering to the deity or deities, and the cooking and consumption of parts of the animals by the sacrificers.[2]

Thus, when Jewish writers (including Philo) produced texts in Greek, they employed the same word, *thysia*, for Jewish sacrifice as was used for Greco-Roman sacrifice. Moreover, those Greek-language texts that seem to assume that non-Jews will be part of their readership may explain the distinctive elements of Jewish sacrifice, but they give no indication that sacrifice itself requires explanation. They also assume many of the basic ideas about sacrifice that non-Jewish readers would have assumed. For example, the pseudepigraphic author of the Letter of Aristeas quotes a letter from the Jewish high priest in Jerusalem, stating that he had offered sacrifices for the Ptolemaic king and his family (§45), evoking a common practice in this cultural context—sacrifice as a means of seeking blessing and benefit for rulers.

Philo's Theory of Sacrifice

Philo is unique amongst ancient Jewish writers on sacrifice in giving focused attention to elucidating the *meaning* of sacrificial ritual in conceptual terms. Indeed, he not only seeks to explain what is signified by the various distinct sacrificial complexes and the ritual actions that compose them, he also offers general observations about the origin and meaning of sacrifice as a religious practice. Philo offers an explicit "theory" of sacrifice as a system of symbolic actions. This theory is set out in considerable detail in Philo's work *On the Special Laws*, his apologia for and elucidation of Jewish cultural practices based on biblical legislation.[3]

Fundamental to Philo's theory is his conviction that the practice of sacrifice stems from and meets a basic human desire, an aspiration to relationship with the Divine, a dual aspiration to seek positive blessing and to compensate for failures of virtue that might inhibit the relationship. At the beginning of his discussion of the Jewish temple (*Spec. Laws* 1.66), Philo asserts that the whole universe is truly God's temple (ἱερόν), with heaven as the sanctuary (νεώς) and the angels as priests.[4] There is, however, also a temple made with hands (χειρόκμητον),

> for it was right [ἔδει γὰρ] that no check should be given to the forwardness [ὁρμή, or "effort," "impulse," "eager desire"] of those who pay their tribute to piety and desire by means of sacrifices either to give thanks for the blessings that befall them or to ask for pardon and forgiveness for their sins. (1.67)

Philo's characterization of the motivation for sacrifice here is strongly positive, as is his characterization of the temple and its cult. Sacrifice exists to meet a fundamental human need and aspiration. Philo develops this point when he begins his discussion of the distinct types of sacrifices set out by Moses and insists that these various sacrifices perfectly meet the fundamental aspirations of human beings:

> For if anyone cares to examine closely the motives [τὰς αἰτίας] which led men of the earliest times to resort to sacrifices as a medium of prayer and thanksgiving, he will find that two hold highest place. One is the rendering of honor to God for the sake of Him only and with no other motive, a thing both necessary and excellent. The other is the signal benefit which the worshipper receives, and this is twofold, on the one side directed to obtaining a share in blessings, on the other to release from evils. (1.195)

This is a rich theoretical statement about sacrifice, which merits close consideration. Philo refers in general terms to human *motivations* for sacrifice, apparently treating the creation of this practice as inherent to human nature at its best. He makes a claim about the antiquity of sacrifice as a basic human religious act, and he identifies what led to the performance of the act—namely, that the motivation is God-directed. Sacrifice was created to serve as a medium of prayer and thanksgiving through which two goals could be achieved: rendering honor *to* God and seeking benefits *from* God.

Of particular note is that Philo does not treat sacrifice as a uniquely Jewish activity. He attributes it to humankind as a whole. What distinguishes Jewish from non-Jewish sacrifice, according to Philo, is the former's perfection: it serves perfectly the goal for which sacrifice was created. It is not surprising that Philo treats sacrifice this way, since it was the religious norm in his cultural world. Philo's goal is to establish the worth of the specifically Jewish version of this religious norm. As Jutta Leonhardt puts it in her detailed study of Philo's view of Jewish ritual, "Philo's Judaism is the ultimate Hellenistic cult."[5]

Why is *sacrifice*, rather than some other practice, such a positive and fundamental expression of human religious aspirations? Philo does not answer this question explicitly. However, his view is strongly implicit in his elaborate presentation of the meaning of the sacrificial acts. For Philo, it is the analogical character of human and animal bodies that makes sacrifice the appropriate vehicle of religious aspirations, since an animal can be used as a symbolic surrogate for a human being, and the various rites can function to represent a human aspiration for complete devotion to Deity.

To understand this view of sacrifice, we must engage with Philo's basic conception of the symbolic nature of ritual elements and actions. According to Philo, symbols are vehicles of mystical realities, since "words in their plain sense are symbols of things latent and obscure" (*Spec. Laws* 1.200). Symbolic interpretation is crucial for Philo; material objects and actions in ritual all refer to a higher, spiritual reality. *In this sense* we can speak of Philo's "spiritualization" of the cult—that its material, "external" aspects refer to inner and spiritual *realities.*[6] For Philo, the meaning of sacrifice (indeed, of all ritual activity) is *conceptual.* Actions are given to be interpreted in symbolic terms and contemplated. The elements of sacrifice, especially the parts of the animal, *symbolize* inner dispositions of the sacrificer: the mind, soul, will.

Philo's approach to sacrifice is premised on the relationship between animals and humans: animal bodies stand for human inner realities. Thus, the offering of animals represents human devotion to God, and to be valid it must come from and enhance this motivation. A few examples will suffice to illustrate this approach to sacrifice. First, there is Philo's discussion of the need to inspect the sacrificial animal for blemishes. According to Philo, the careful examination of the animal is really about the inner disposition of the sacrificer:

> The examination is carried out with this excessive minuteness in consideration not of the victims offered but of the innocence of those who offer them. For it would teach them through symbols [διὰ συμβόλων] that when they approach the altar to offer either prayers or thanks they must come with no infirmity or ailment or evil affection in the soul [τῇ ψυχῇ], but must endeavor to have it sanctified and free throughout from defilement, that God when He beholds it may not turn His face from the sight. (*Spec. Laws* 1.167)[7]

In short, the sacrificial animal symbolizes the soul (ψυχή). Likewise, the blood of the animal offered as a whole burnt offering refers to the mind, the intelligence, the faculty of thought (διάνοια) of the sacrificer:

> The blood is poured in a circle round the altar because the circle is the most perfect of figures, and in order that no part should be left destitute of the vital oblation [ψυχικῆς σπονδῆς]. For the blood may truly be called a libation of the life-principle [ψυχῆς]. So, then, he teaches symbolically [συμβολικῶς οὖν ἀναδιδάσκει] that the mind [διάνοια], whole and complete, should as it moves with measured tread passing circle-wise through every phase of word and intention and deed, show its willingness to do God's service. (*Spec. Laws* 1.205)

The blood manipulation, for Philo, is a symbol that evokes devotion of one's highest faculties to God. The blood of the animal, identified with its ψυχή (soul), is a symbolic referent of the human mind. As F. H. Colson puts it, for Philo "the ψυχή in its lower sense . . . is an apposite symbol of the higher ψυχή, 'the mind.'"[8] This passage also makes it clear that Philo sees ritual symbols as conveying concepts; they are pedagogical in character.

Philo exemplifies the fact that sacrifice is always interpreted within a larger worldview and religious framework. Its meaning as religious practice is determined by the value-system into which one places and "reads" it. For Philo, sacrifice is a subsystem of a larger system of contemplative cultivation and asceticism directed, always and ultimately, to what he identifies as the higher and truer human faculty, the soul (ψυχή) (frequently equated with the intellect or mind, διάνοια), "which we are told was fashioned after the image of the Self-existent [τοῦ ὄντος]. And the image of God is the Word [λογός] through whom the whole universe was framed" (*Spec. Laws* 1.81).[9] The cultivation of the soul, the rational (logical) part of the human being is, then, the cultivation of that which is Godlike, and the goal of such cultivation is the bringing of the Godlike part of humankind into communion with God, its source and model. Thus, according to Philo, sacrifice of an animal (or any other offerings) represents *self*-sacrifice, the giving of one's true being over to God: "He, then, who is adorned with these [virtues] may come with boldness to the sanctuary [τὸν νεών] as his true home . . . there to present himself as victim [ἱερεῖον ἐπιδειξόμενος αὐτόν]" (*Spec. Laws* 1.270).[10]

In this respect, Philo radically relativizes sacrifice: it is not an end in itself, and he can urge that a preoccupation with the material facts of sacrifice carries the danger of missing its real point (*Spec. Laws* 1.270–72). Furthermore, he can insist that inward motivation inevitably trumps material offerings, so that a small grain of incense offered by one whose soul is perfected is far superior to huge numbers of animals offered by the unworthy. Indeed, because incense smoke is a superior symbol of the nonmaterial soul, it is superior to sacrificial blood (*Spec. Laws* 1.275). Nevertheless, Philo's relativization of sacrifice should not be misunderstood or exaggerated. While he insists that it is not an end in itself, his overall treatment of sacrifice—the context in which he relativizes it—is vigorously positive.[11] While only a means to an end, given the supreme value of the end, this means is of immense significance for Philo. Furthermore, Philo insists that the symbolic significances of Jewish practices cannot be separated from the practices themselves, and he criticizes those who argue that one can abandon obedience to Jewish law once one has grasped the inner, spiritual meanings of the practices.[12]

What has remained unclear to me as I have engaged with Philo's theory on sacrifice is whether he believed that the sacrifices "worked" only if their conceptual significance was recognized. That is, did one need to be able to fully decode the symbols in order to benefit from the performance of the act? A partial answer to this question comes through attention to Philo's basic explanation of the source and goal of sacrifice. Philo sees sacrifice as a medium of human aspiration for God.

Thus, to the extent that sacrifice is performed with that motive in mind—with that intentionality—certainly it would be effective, apart from any exegesis of its symbolic elements. Furthermore, as I have suggested, Philo seems to take the identification between sacrificer and sacrificial animal as inherent to sacrifice. Thus, I would suggest that he regarded some level of the identification of this foundational symbolic key as available to all rightly disposed sacrificers—not only to those who were of Philo's enlightened status. Still, it appears that Philo believed that most Jews failed to grasp the full symbolic meaning of their activity, and it is clear that he saw serious potential danger in this failure, to judge from his critique of sacrificial practice inspired by incorrect motives.[13]

A fact that is clear about Philo's approach to sacrifice is that he *does not* treat it fundamentally as cuisine. He has very little to say about food-related symbolism, reserving such comments for nonblood offerings; in fact, he distinguishes animals from food gifts (see, e.g., *Spec. Laws* 1.179). This should come as no surprise, given his emphasis on the symbolic identification of the sacrificer with the sacrificial animal: it would have been problematic to equate the aspiration to union with God in terms of either human or divine preparation and consumption of food. Rather, Philo keeps his focus on the ways in which sacrificial acts can be "read" symbolically as referring to the soul's relationship to God. The fact that Philo avoids speaking of sacrifice in terms of cuisine highlights the distinctiveness of different approaches to sacrifice even within a common cultural environment, and it should caution us against applying conclusions drawn from one contiguous culture to another.[14]

Philo's Theory and Modern Ritual Theory

Philo's notion of sacrifice as a primarily symbolic activity has striking echoes in the dominant discourses about sacrifice found in the works of modern social-cultural anthropologists. For example, Philo's insistence that ritual activity works on the senses to shape attitudes and dispositions (see, e.g., *Spec. Laws* 1.191, 193, 203) anticipates Clifford Geertz's classic definition of religion as "a system of symbols which acts to establish powerful, pervasive, and long-lasting moods and motivations in men."[15]

Most immediately, Philo's conception that ritual is a vehicle for symbolic communication finds strong echoes in modern anthropological approaches to activity identified as "ritual." "Ritual" has frequently been defined so that *symbolism* is essential to its identity. Ritual, in this approach, is *inherently* symbolic activity. As Talal Asad explains in his critical assessment of the modern anthropological study of ritual, "Modern anthropologists writing on ritual tended to see it as the domain of the symbolic in contrast to the instrumental."[16] The dominance of this approach is exemplified by the definition of ritual that appears in the new (2008) edition of the *International Encyclopedia of the Social Sciences*: "a patterned, repetitive, and symbolic enactment of a cultural belief or value."[17] Robbie Davis-Floyd, the author of the reference work's articles on "Rites of Passage" and "Ritual," elaborates on the definition by explaining that "a belief system is enacted through ritual," highlights as a major characteristic of ritual "the symbolic nature of ritual's messages," and asserts that "rituals work through symbols."[18] This understanding of ritual has recently been energetically defended and applied by Jonathan Klawans in his work on ancient Israelite and early Jewish sacrifice.[19]

The argument that communicative symbolism is an essential element of ritual has been challenged in various ways by a number of interpreters of culture. Most notorious, and frequently most misunderstood, is Frits Staal's assertion of the "meaninglessness of ritual."[20] Staal's argument, generalizing from his work on Vedic ritual, is that symbolism is not an inherent and primary characteristic of ritual activity and that pure performance is the real concern of ritual actors, even when symbolic or other interpretations are provided. The problem with this argument, however, is that it rests on a too-sharp dichotomy between thought and action and therefore ignores the very real cognitive dimensions of ritual activity.[21] A more nuanced approach is offered by Roy Rappaport, whose definition of ritual lacks reference to symbolism, but whose discussion of ritual deals in detail with the symbolic *dimensions* of ritual activity.[22] As Rappaport ably demonstrates, ritual often functions communicatively, especially through its symbolic dimensions, but much else is also involved in such communication, and symbolism is often fraught with tensions and difficulties stemming from the inherent weaknesses in symbolic communication—as Rappaport puts it: "the embarrassments of symbolic communication (notably the two vices of language, lie and the confusions of Babel)."[23] In other words, ritual symbols may be used to communicate falsely, and they may be misinterpreted even when the intention is to communicate effectively.

In this connection, it is also worth noting that there are problems involved in defining and characterizing what *symbols* are and how they relate to their referents. While there has been discussion of "natural symbols,"[24] it has come to be widely understood that "symbols are without specific meanings aside from the connotations assigned to them."[25] What this means is that the symbolic meanings that might be attached to ritual acts within a particular cultural context can only be decoded using the cultural lexicon of that context.

The argument that ritual is not *inherently* symbolic activity does not amount to an assertion that ritual actions should *never* be interpreted symbolically or that rituals are never devised or performed with symbolic significances in view. Rather, I would emphasize three distinct but related points: First, symbolism is *conventional* rather than natural and obvious. Second, rituals do not *only* signify symbolically. To use the terminology of the semiotician Charles Sanders Peirce, ritual actions may signify as "icons," as "indices," or as symbols.[26] Third, not all cultures, nor all individuals within cultures, understand their own rituals symbolically. A focus on Staal's particular position misses the fact that many critiques of classic symbolic anthropology have not denied that ritual actions are meaningful; rather, they have questioned the nature of the meaning, where it comes from, and how it is developed.

For example, the French anthropologist Dan Sperber has argued against what he terms a "cryptological view of symbolism" and "the semiological illusion according to which it is symbols that constitute the *significant*, the interpreted message."[27] Rather than being interpreted or "decoded," symbols are often experienced and related to emotionally or engaged cognitively to *evoke* particular attitudes, ideas, and memories; thus, a ritual symbol may be more like a smell or a sound than like a word. As Sperber emphasizes, "The attribution of sense is an essential aspect of symbolic development in *our* culture," but is not a universal phenomenon.[28] Similarly, Talal Asad emphasizes the need for attention to the historical contingency of modern approaches to ritual as symbolic activity. Symbolic interpretation has a history.[29] Philo, it turns out, is part of this history.

In the case of Philo, we certainly *are* dealing with an exponent of a view that ritual is symbolic activity and that its true value lies in its symbolic quality. We can, therefore, delve deeply into Philo's explication of sacrificial ritual and seek to grasp the meanings he, as a cultural informant, attaches to it. From Philo we have what Victor Turner identifies as "the level of indigenous interpretation (or, briefly, the exegetical meaning)."[30] It may be that Philo represents a dominant view amongst a certain type of intellectual elite in Diaspora Judaism.[31] However, evidence from other textual corpora, such as the Dead Sea Scrolls, suggests that other Jewish thinkers approached sacrifice with very different interests, particularly interests in the definition and elaboration of correct practice. A signal example of this approach is the Qumran Temple Scroll, which has a great deal to say about the details of sacrificial performance, but almost nothing to say about the meanings of such performances. Put another way, performance itself seems to be the meaning of sacrifice for the authors of the Temple Scroll.

With this in view, I would agree with Jonathan Klawans's programmatic statement about the study of ancient Jewish sacrifice: "A full understanding of the meanings of sacrifice in the Second Temple period . . . must be based not on an anthropologically informed reading of the Hebrew Bible but on careful analysis of symbolic meanings ascribed to sacrifice in ancient Jewish literature such as Josephus and Philo."[32] However, I would put forth two significant caveats: First, while it is indeed problematic to try to understand Second Temple Jewish sacrifice based on "an anthropologically informed reading *of the Hebrew Bible*," it is certainly not inappropriate to bring anthropological ideas to bear on the data of Second Temple Judaism to produce "an anthropologically informed reading." Second, and more seriously, while I have myself given careful attention to the symbolic meanings Philo attributes to sacrifice, I do not believe that we should seek *only* or primarily symbolic meanings in ancient Jewish texts. We must also be open to nonsymbolic approaches to meaning—for example, to instrumental-effective understanding and to attitudes toward sacrifice that seem to eschew concern for conceptual meaning in favor of attention to proper practice as an end in itself. Otherwise, we run the risk of privileging some "native" voices over others and failing to grasp the rich complexity of ancient conceptions of sacrifice. Philo's is one compelling ancient Jewish voice explaining sacrifice; it is certainly not the only one. Thus, I would add to my caution about applying conclusions from one contiguous culture to another. We must also be very cautious about generalizing the ideas of one representative of a culture to the whole of that culture.

I would emphasize at this juncture that I am not arguing that ancient Jews (and before them, ancient Israelites) were incapable of symbolic thought. Clearly, they did think symbolically, as Philo exemplifies. However, the fact that a culture necessarily includes some forms of symbolic thought does not require that every cultural action will be symbolic in nature or interpreted symbolically. It is noteworthy, I believe, that while we have explicit symbolic activity on the part of Israelite prophets, with attendant exegesis of these symbolic actions, we do not find corresponding symbolic exegesis in the case of cultic ritual. In short, the fact that some prophets drew on metaphor and symbolism to communicate their messages does not require us to conclude that ritual experts did.[33]

On a related note, I believe it is important to distinguish the symbolic and instrumental interpretations of ritual actions offered by native informants from the symbolic and functional explanations offered by ethnographic interpreters. One of the severe problems with modern anthropological approaches to ritual has been a failure to distinguish clearly between these categories. The result has been that ethnographers' symbolic interpretations have too often been presented as if they represented indigenous meanings. The same problem exists in the study of ancient Jewish sacrifice. Therefore, in my view, the key issue is not the distinction between symbolic meaning and social function—indeed, the social function of a ritual *may* very well lie in its symbolic signifying—but the distinction between native categories of interpretation and those of nonnative scholarly interpreters.[34] Thus, while we may confidently explore Philo's indigenous Jewish symbolic interpretation of sacrifice, we should exercise caution in injecting symbolic interpretations where our textual witnesses are silent. We should be equally cautious about proposing social-functional explanations for ritual activity where our witnesses are silent. Such explanations should be clearly marked as being more or different than what native informants themselves assert about the efficacy of their ritual activities.

This leads to a final caution concerning the nature of our evidence. At the outset of this chapter, I referred to literate-specialist producers. It is important to keep in mind that we are dealing with the textual production—and interpretive activity—of a minority elite. It really is impossible to know how the majority of Jews in ancient times related to their ritual activities. A comparison with the case of native informants in modern ethnography is helpful in this regard. Sperber notes that much of the detailed information Victor Turner received on the "meaning" of Zambian Ndembu ritual came from one enthusiastic informant, "marginal in his own society," and that this information had an impact on Turner's overall approach to the information he received from other informants.[35] By way of comparison, Sperber notes how little "exegetic" explanation he received from informants among the Ethiopian Dorze people with whom he worked.[36] Sperber's examples indicate that ritual as "symbolic" activity is approached differently within and between different cultural groups and that particular informants can have distinctive viewpoints about meaning. In the case of ancient Judaism, we are dealing with a widely dispersed people, living in different cultural contexts, and drawing on and relating to different influences. Philo is clearly influenced by Hellenistic philosophical constructions, and it is not surprising, in my view, to find him treating sacrificial ritual symbolically. Symbolic interpretation of ritual—such as Philo's—is culturally and historically contingent rather than universal. In short, and in sum, it must be kept in mind that not all practitioners of ritual engage in symbolic exegesis of their practice.

Notes

1. Henri Hubert and Marcel Mauss, *Sacrifice: Its Nature and Function*, translated by W. D. Halls (Chicago: University of Chicago Press, 1964); originally published as "Essai sur la nature et le fonction du sacrifice," *L'Annee Sociologique* 2 (1897–99): 29–139.

2. For detailed explorations of Greek sacrifice, see Marcel Detienne and Jean-Pierre Vernanteds., *The Cuisine of Sacrifice among the Greeks*, translated by Paula Wissing (Chicago: University of Chicago Press, 1989).

3. Throughout this chapter, I cite the Greek text of Philo's *On the Special Laws* (*Spec. Laws*) and F. H. Colson's English translation from the Loeb Classical Library (LCL) edition: *Philo*, vol. 7, LCL (Cambridge: Harvard University Press, 1937).

4. On the historical-cultural context of this identification of the whole cosmos as temple with heaven as sanctuary, see Harold W. Attridge, *The Epistle to the Hebrews, Hermeneia: A Critical and Historical Commentary on the Bible* (Philadelphia: Fortress, 1989), 222. He references various ancient non-Jewish and Jewish sources. See, esp., Joseph., *Ant.* 3.63 §123; 3.7.7 §180–81.

5. Jutta Leonhardt, *Jewish Worship in Philo of Alexandria*, Texts and Studies in Ancient Judaism 84 (Tübingen: Mohr Siebeck, 2001), 294.

6. For a somewhat different approach to "spiritualization" of sacrifice in Philo, see Valentin Nikiprowetzky, "La spiritualisation des sacrifices et le culte sacrificiel au Temple de Jérusalem chez Philon d'Alexandrie," *Semitica* 17 (1967): 97–116.

7. See also *Spec. Laws* 1.260: "For you will find that all this careful scrutiny of the animal is a symbol representing in a figure the reformation of your own conduct, for the law does not prescribe for unreasoning creatures, but for those who have mind and reason. It is anxious not that the victims should be without flaws but that those who offer them should not suffer from any corroding passion."

8. Colson, in *Philo* (216),

9. See also, for example, *Spec. Laws* 1.96, on the high priest's *contemplation* of his vestments.

10. See also *Spec. Laws* 1.272: "And indeed though the worshippers bring nothing else, in bringing themselves they offer the best of sacrifices [τὴν ἀρίστην. . .θυσίαν]."

11. See the similar judgment by Nikiprowetzky, "Spiritualisation," 100.

12. See Philo, *Philonis Alexandrini opera quae supersunt* (*On the Migration of Abraham*), edited by P. Wendland, vol. 2 (Berlin: Reimer, 1897; repr., De Gruyter, 1962), 89–93, and Nikiprowetzky's discussion, "Spiritualisation," 114–16.

13. See, for example, *Spec. Laws* 1.270–71, 283–84.

14. On this point, see also Jonathan Klawans's critique of Bruce Chilton in *Purity, Sacrifice, and the Temple: Symbolism and Supersessionism in the Study of Ancient Judaism* (New York: Oxford University Press, 2006), 44–45.

15. Clifford Geertz, *The Interpretation of Cultures: Selected Essays* (New York: Basic Books, 1973), 90. Note, also, Godfrey Lienhardt's statement: "What the symbolic action is intended to control is primarily a set of mental and moral dispositions." From *Divinity and Experience: The Religion of the Dinka* (1961), quoted by Talal Asad, "Toward a Genealogy of the Concept of Ritual," in *Genealogies of Religion: Discipline and Reasons of Power in Christianity and Islam* (Baltimore: Johns Hopkins University Press, 1993), 55.

16. Talal Asad, "On Discipline and Humility in Medieval Christian Monasticism," in Asad, *Genealogies of Religion*, 126; see also Talal Asad, "Concept of Ritual," 55–79.

17. Robbie Davis-Floyd, "Rituals," *International Encyclopedia of the Social Sciences,* 2nd ed., edited by William A. Darity, Jr. (New York: Thomson Gale, 2008), 7: 259.

18. Robbie Davis-Floyd, "Rituals," 259, 260.

19. Jonathan Klawans, *Purity, Sacrifice, and the Temple*, (esp. 3, 66–68); Jonathan Klawans, "Methodology and Ideology in the Study of Priestly Ritual," in *Perspectives on Purity and Purification in the Bible*, edited by Baruch J. Schwartz et al., Library of Hebrew Bible/Old Testament Studies 474 (New York: T. & T. Clark, 2008), 84–95.

20. Frits Staal, "The Meaninglessness of Ritual," *Numen* 26.1 (1975): 2–22.

21. See Catherine Bell's concise and cogent critique of Staal in *Ritual Theory, Ritual Practice* (New York: Oxford University Press, 1992), 59–60 n. 48; see also Roy E. Gane, *Cult and Character: Purification Offerings, Day of Atonement, and Theodicy* (Winona Lake, Ind.: Eisenbrauns, 2005), 4–7. Gane (a former student of Staal) highlights what is valuable in Staal's critique of the view of ritual as inherently symbolic activity, while also pointing to its limitations.

22. Roy A. Rappaport, *Ritual and Religion in the Making of Humanity*, Cambridge Studies in Social and Cultural Anthropology 110 (Cambridge: Cambridge University Press, 1999), 24–68, esp. 26 and 50–68. See also Nancy Jay, *Throughout Your Generations Forever: Sacrifice, Religion, and Paternity* (Chicago: University of Chicago Press, 1992), 6–7; Bell, *Ritual Theory*, 30–46, 182–87.

23. Rappaport, *Ritual and Religion*, 26.

24. The most sophisticated and productive treatment is Mary Douglas's collection of essays, *Natural Symbols: Explorations in Cosmology* (New York: Routledge, 2003), originally published in 1970.

25. Jerome M. Levi, "Symbols," *International Encyclopedia of the Social Sciences*, 2nd ed. 8: 250.

26. For a helpful entry to Peirce's theory of signs, see Justus Buchler, ed., *Philosophical Writings of Peirce* (New York: Dover, 1955), 98–119. On the relevance for the study of ritual of Peirce's distinction between symbols, icons, and indices as three types of signs, see Rappaport, *Ritual and Religion*, 54–68. For an example of the application of Peirce's semiotics to the interpretation of biblical ritual, see William K. Gilders, "Why Does Eleazar Sprinkle the Red Cow Blood? Making Sense of a Biblical Ritual," *Journal of Hebrew Scriptures* 6 (2006), online: http://www.arts.ualberta.ca/JHS/Articles/article_59.htm.

27. Dan Sperber, *Rethinking Symbolism,* translated by Alice L. Morton, Cambridge Studies in Social Anthropology (Cambridge: Cambridge University Press, 1975), 22, 49.

28. Sperber, *Rethinking Symbolism*, 83.

29. Asad, "Concept of Ritual."

30. Victor Turner, *The Forest of Symbols: Aspects of Ndembu Ritual* (Ithaca: Cornell University Press, 1967), 50.

31. On this issue, see Klawans's useful discussion and the scholarship cited there, in *Purity, Sacrifice, and the Temple*, 117–18.

32. Klawans, *Purity, Sacrifice, and the Temple*, 45.

33. In my view, therefore, the argument for ancient Israelite symbolic understanding of sacrificial ritual on the basis of the existence of prophetic symbolic action is a significant weakness in Klawans's essay "Methodology and Ideology."

34. I must disagree, therefore, with the thrust of Jonathan Klawans's contribution to this collection. My critique of his approach to ancient Israelite and ancient Jewish ritual is not that it focuses on symbol over function (*pace* his interpretation of my review of his book). Rather, my concern is that his approach involves treating symbolism as an inherent and defining dimension of ritual and that he constructs symbolic meanings for Israelite and Jewish rituals on the basis of indigenous evidence that is often quite weak.

35. Sperber, *Rethinking Symbolism*, 18–19.

36. Sperber, *Rethinking Symbolism*, 17–18.

5

Symbol, Function, Theology, and Morality in the Study of Priestly Ritual
Jonathan Klawans

The pairing of symbol with function is rather commonplace in the study of ritual, and a good number of well-regarded theorists—Edmund Leach, Mary Douglas, and Victor Turner among them—modeled ways of balancing symbolic meanings with social functions.[1] With regard to the study of ancient Israelite ritual in particular, some scholars seem more inclined to favor symbol over function, while other writers argue against what they perceive to be an undue emphasis on symbolism.[2] This chapter will revisit the relative values of symbol and function for an understanding of ancient Israelite ritual, and it will argue that, *with regard to the rituals of ancient Israel*, the emphasis indeed ought to be on symbol over function.

It will also emerge that greater clarity is needed with regard to what scholars mean when speaking of functions; with that goal in mind, some clarifications will be offered below. Moreover, it will be emphasized that function should not be overlooked, downplayed, or denied. Indeed—and notably—scholars working on ancient Israelite ritual rarely deny the rituals' functionality outright. Curiously, while symbolism is denied by some of those who are interested in functions, the reverse does not appear to pertain. Symbolism is what scholars tend to deny; if symbolic interpreters put the emphasis on symbol over function, the reason may be more to counter this denial than to assert that ritual has no function. Be that as it may, the present argument that symbol ought to preside over function—*with regard to ancient Israel*—will proceed in conversation with theoretical and comparative arguments, but will be grounded primarily, as it must, in evidence drawn from biblical texts themselves.

Symbol and Theology

For heuristic purposes, three very general approaches to the question of symbolism in Israelite ritual can be identified: ubiquitous symbolism, selective symbolism, and antisymbolic (the denial of symbolism).[3] "Ubiquitous symbolism" refers to those approaches inspired by the theoretical works of Mary Douglas[4] and Victor Turner[5] that are inclined to find symbolism in many if not all rituals. "Selective symbolism" refers to works such as Jacob Milgrom's in the present day[6] and William Robertson Smith's a century ago,[7] which set out to study some rituals symbolically, while viewing others as fossilized vestiges. "Antisymbolic" refers to writers such as Ithamar Gruenwald who vociferously deny that biblical rituals can be understood symbolically at all. Before presenting arguments in defense of the first of these options, I would like to consider the other two approaches briefly.

The problem with the second option, selective symbolism, is that all too often the singling out of certain disliked rituals (purity in the Victorian era, sacrifice in our own) as nonsymbolic fossilized vestiges aligns too easily with identifiable contemporary cultural or religious priorities.[8] Equally problematic is the common tendency to find symbolism in some (usually favored) cultural contexts (e.g., ancient Israel) while denying its place in others (e.g., Babylon).[9] And although this argument has not yet been developed fully with regard to ancient Israel, I would also deem problematic the newer tendency (evident in some essays in this volume) to confine symbolism to literate elites, asserting that illiterate nonelites were engaged primarily in rites that were literal, personal, and practical, as if the poor have no religious yearnings beyond their personal material needs and no communal commitments beyond what can be exchanged for their personal benefit. Ubiquitous symbolism is therefore a safer route—methodological consistency may well be an antidote to the selective application of disparate methods that characterizes much of the recent work on ancient Israelite ritual systems.[10]

We must admit, however, that the need for methodological consistency could also be met by approaches that deny symbolism while advocating a consistently *unsympathetic* approach. Why not take a consistently *unsympathetic* view?[11] Granted, if a consistently unsympathetic reading could prove valuable for understanding ancient Israel, then that too would be methodologically valid. But unsympathetic treatments of biblical ritual—such as that of René Girard—have proven more detrimental than beneficial to the field.[12] The present atmosphere, alas, calls for both consistency and sympathy.

We must also admit that there is nothing inherently wrong with a selective approach to symbolism: why, after all, should symbolism be found everywhere? Perhaps, as Robertson Smith maintained with regard to "taboos," some rituals survive as vestiges bereft of their earlier symbolic meanings. And perhaps—as some contributors of the present volume maintain—symbolism is to be limited to certain skilled, advantaged groups or classes. The famed Sabbath practices of Crypto-Jews *may* be an example of the former, and perhaps Greek sacrifice is an example of the latter. The problem with selective symbolism—as applied to ancient Israel—is twofold. In the first instance, some scholars deny symbolism to disliked rituals, such as purity (in the case of Robertson Smith) or sacrifice (in the case of Girard and Milgrom, albeit in vastly different ways). In the second instance, scholars deny symbolism to underprivileged groups, perhaps thinking that the disadvantaged would remain focused exclusively on what is to their personal advantage. In either case, the lack of symbolic value to ritual is not positively demonstrated; it is simply asserted. If selective symbolism is to emerge as a viable approach, criteria must be established for determining which rituals are symbolic and for whom. Ideally, these criteria would emerge from analysis of evidence in context(s), not aligned simply with presuppositions about which rituals are valuable or which classes are symbolically skilled.

The third approach to biblical rituals denies altogether that biblical rituals are symbolic. This type of approach has been taken most recently by Ithamar Gruenwald in *Rituals and Ritual Theory in Ancient Israel* (2003), who defends his view in part by noting that advocates of ubiquitous symbolism may be engaged in an apologetic activity.[13] In his view, symbolic approaches to symbolism are theological ones. Gruenwald may be correct in his diagnosis here. Mary Douglas's passionate efforts at countering Protestant antiritualist biases can be (and has been) accused of aligning all too neatly with her own Catholic background and sympathies.[14] Moreover, Gruenwald has allies in the field of religious studies, such as Jonathan Z. Smith (who asserts the arbitrary nature of Israelite cultic practices in particular)[15] and Frits Staal (who speaks of the "meaninglessness of ritual" in general).[16]

Douglas's arguments in *Purity and Danger* (1966) were addressed, of course, against a very specific target: the long history of Protestant antiritualism, as evidenced especially (but not exclusively) in the works of James Frazer and William Robertson Smith.[17] The Protestant biases of these and other classic works on religion in general and biblical ritual in particular have been sufficiently established (not only by Douglas, but notably also by Jonathan Z. Smith[18]) that we need not argue her case against the late-nineteenth-century giants once again. But it must be said that *Purity and Danger* is not an unaligned critique. It is an apologetic defense of ritual systems, one that is explicitly sympathetic with Jewish, Catholic, and Hindu ritual practices.[19] Indeed, as far as the broader field of ritual studies is concerned, the jury is still out on Douglas's ubiquitous symbolism. Her critics' arsenal includes the charges of inadequate evidence[20] and (as mentioned above) her predisposition toward a Catholic (that is, pro-ritual) viewpoint.[21] Clifford Geertz's symbolic anthropology is similarly criticized in the field as being both apologetic and insufficiently analytic.[22] Anyone who has ever used the third chapter of *Purity and Danger* in an undergraduate Hebrew Bible class in the service of defending the meaning of biblical dietary laws would have to admit that the charge of pro-ritualist apology is one that cannot be dismissed lightly.

The problem for Gruenwald's position is that denying that ritual is symbolic can also be a theologically aligned move. Indeed, all our problems here result from the fact that there is not *a* theological or religious approach to symbolism. For centuries—indeed, for millennia—the question of whether one can take a symbolic (or allegorical) approach to ritual has been questioned by some and defended by others. Figures like Philo, Josephus, and Pseudo-Aristeas *defended* ritual practices against various calumnies by asserting their symbolic significance.[23] But others have feared that symbolic understandings would lead to the abandonment of the letter in favor of the spirit. That is why later religious figures such as Moses Maimonides and Moses Mendelssohn—with certain rabbinic traditions behind them—argued in favor of the arbitrary nature of practices such as the dietary laws.[24] Denying symbolism can be as much of a theological move as asserting it. For this reason, we scholars may be well served to step aside from the binary debate about symbol and meaning. Symbolic explanations are neither inherently nor uniquely tied to theology in such a way as to render them invalid ipso facto. Nor ought we to side with the theological rejection of symbolism, to the effect that such explanations pose a threat to the practice or meaning of ritual.[25] Finally, we ought not restrict our discussions of symbolism to those sources (e.g., Philo) that explicitly offer symbolic explanations. Perhaps Sigmund Freud's single, lasting contribution to the field of ritual studies is precisely this point: that symbols (and not just phallic ones) can operate subconsciously.[26] This may well be the case irrespective of whether the symbolism in question is discussed publicly or written up in educated, elite treatises.

Another problem here is that the general conversation is just that: all too general. Staal's examples come primarily (if not exclusively) from the rituals of India. Assuming for a moment that we accept Staal's interpretation of Hindu rites, does that mean that biblical rites are necessarily similar in their essential nonsymbolic nature? The case for the symbolic or nonsymbolic nature of rituals needs to be made on a case-by-case basis. After all, if what Catherine Bell calls "ritual density" can vary from culture to culture, shouldn't we assume that what we could call "symbolic density" would similarly vary from culture to culture?[27] Moreover, the claim that rituals are nonsymbolic in essence is a claim pertaining to origins—it cannot be denied that, at the very least, some rituals are infused with symbolic meanings in certain religious traditions, at least according to some religious authorities (e.g., Philo). Even if some cultures' rituals remain free of symbolic explanation, that fact does not eliminate the possibility that symbolism looms large in others. Even if it could be established that rituals were *originally* arbitrary, that does not preclude the possibility that developed ritual systems infuse rituals with symbolism. Since we are interested here in a developed ritual system, it matters little that symbolism may be secondary; it matters even less that symbolism may be absent elsewhere.

We can begin to find a better way out of this impasse if we put the general questions of origins and comparison aside and try to determine what we can with regard to the role of symbolism in ancient Israelite culture.[28] Perhaps the strongest argument in favor of the symbolic nature of ancient Israel's cultic rituals comes from a rather unlikely place: the biblical prophets.[29] Progress on the question of the symbolic nature of ancient Israel's cult requires that we recognize the problematic and biased nature of some of the scholarly terminology frequently used with reference to our themes. Of course, many thematic discussions of prophecy in biblical Israel point out that the prophets were wont to perform "symbolic acts" in order to dramatize and illustrate their message to the Israelite people.[30] It suffices for our concerns to note only a few of the more famous actions: Hosea's marrying a prostitute to symbolize Israel's infidelity (Hos 1:2); Isaiah's walking barefoot and naked to symbolize Egypt's impending doom (Isa 20:1–6); and Jeremiah's wearing a yoke to symbolize God's desire for the nations to submit to Babylon (Jer 27:1–15). What is seldom appreciated in the context of the present theme is that the very existence of this performative phenomenon proves that the prophets were aware of and sympathetic to symbolic behavior. By referring to the prophets' behavior as "symbolic action," while dryly describing cultic behavior as "ritual," scholars force a divide between—and prevent a comparison of—two phenomena that are not altogether different and ought in truth to be mutually informative.

But surely, Max Weber might object, there is a difference between a passionate, spontaneous, individual, symbolic act and a communal, cultic ritual.[31] To that argument one must remember not only that Hosea married a prostitute (Hos 1:2)—and possibly two (Hos 3:1–3)—but that he remained so married for some time. Isaiah, it is said, walked naked and barefoot *for three years* (Isa 20:3). Jeremiah must have worn that yoke for some time as well (Jer 27:1–2; 28:1, 10). The historicity of such claims is not our concern; we simply call attention to the fact that one can safely wonder whether all prophetic "symbolic actions" were conceived as fully spontaneous or free of regulation.[32] A repeated, patterned, symbolic action is hardly all that different from a ritual.

The suggestion—still made in some quarters[33]—that the prophets opposed sacrifice because they denied the value of ritual really makes them out to be the hypocrites that the priests are commonly assumed to have been: how could the prophets believe in the communicative value of their own symbolic behavior but deny such to ritual? Indeed, the phenomenon of prophetic symbolic action demonstrates the *fact* that symbolic behavior was part of the culture of ancient Israel. This, perhaps, is the most compelling argument that various aspects of the priestly cult (sacrifice included) ought to be understood as symbolic. Indeed, if biblical and ritual studies emerged in a non-Protestant context, I highly doubt we would even have two different terms here at all. We would, rather, be accustomed to speaking of either the symbolic actions of Israel's priests or the ritual actions of Israel's prophets.

The more recent suggestion—offered by some contributors to this volume—that symbolism ought to be limited to certain literate elites can also now be questioned more directly, at least with regard to ancient Israel. It is not just the priests who were interested in symbolism, but the prophets as well. And both were interested not only in communicating symbolically, but also in explicitly unpacking that symbolism from time to time (see the following section for explicit symbolism in the priestly tradition). Of course, this still will not tell us what the masses were interested in. But two lines of evidence converge to suggest that we ought not assert that the Israelite masses lived symbolically impoverished lives. First, the fact that the prophets and priests both produced competing literatures engaged in symbolic interpretations of ritualized behavior suggests that their audience—namely, nonelite Israelites—were receptive to such things. A second line of argument comes from archaeology: what little we know about the religious lives of regular Israelites suggests that they too engaged in symbolic behavior, albeit of a non-Yahwistic sort.[34]

Symbols and Functions

A successful argument in defense of the prioritization of symbol over function in ancient Israel must not only argue in favor of the value of symbolism, but must in some respects argue against the relative merit of functional arguments. Of course, there are diverse kinds of functionalist arguments; therefore, different kinds of critiques can be offered. The classic Durkheimian "society-maintenance" arguments are largely (but not entirely) out of fashion and for good reason: it is indeed very difficult to believe any more that religion, on the general level, successfully creates or even maintains social orders.[35] And as far as ancient Israel is concerned, there's very little evidence that any particular social order was successfully maintained, by any mechanism, for any significant length of time.

As for other arguments in defense of the pragmatic accomplishments of ritual, Geertz's classic critique of Bronislaw Malinowski's work on religion and ritual comes to mind:

> [T]here is little doubt that a thoroughgoing instrumentalist view of such phenomena reduces them to caricatures of themselves by leaving out of account that which most sets them apart as distinctive forms of life. When Malinowski concludes that religion has an immense biological value because it enhances "practical mental attitudes" because it reveals to man "truth in the wider, *pragmatic* sense of the word," one doesn't, remembering Aztec human sacrifices or the self-immolation of Indian widows, know whether to laugh or to cry.[36]

Forty years later—in the age of suicide bombers who ritually purify themselves before engaging in slaughter[37]—perhaps we should be more inclined to cry than laugh.

Of course these arguments are general ones, and therefore by our own standards they do no more than just set the stage. The question of symbol versus function *in ancient Israel* must be played out with reference to evidence from ancient Israel. Perhaps we do well, then, to look again at recent efforts to explain Israelite ritual from such a perspective. With regard to ritual in general and sacrifice in particular, Gruenwald maintains in *Rituals and Ritual Theory* that

rituals create, or establish, their own meaning in the very act of doing and in
the logic that constitutes the processual manner in which they are done. . . .
Let me repeat that, to say that there is meaning in rituals is not tantamount—
as many scholars think—to saying they are symbolic expressions of ideas.
The meaning is contained in the performed essence of the rituals.[38]

Put more briefly, Gruenwald states elsewhere in the same book that rituals "should
be understood by what they aim to accomplish, rather than by what they stand
for."[39] In the course of his study, Gruenwald defends his approach in reference to
particular rituals from the Hebrew Bible and the New Testament.

While Gruenwald's approach has an empirical aura about it—enhanced in part
by overstated attacks on the symbolic approach—the fact is that it is very difficult
to establish empirically that ancient Israelite rituals accomplish very much at all.
Let us take, for example, the scapegoat ritual (Lev 16:1–28) that figures prominently
in Gruenwald's own analysis. The assorted purifications and expiations serve, in
Gruenwald's analysis, to help the Israelites avert dangers.[40] In a sense, of course,
this is correct: ancient Israelites did believe that dangers awaited those who failed
to purify or atone, and they worried that the community would suffer if unexpiated
sin or unexpurgated defilements accumulated in their midst. But of what use is it
for scholars to assert that sacrifices served these purposes and achieved these goals?
These are not measurable goals, for these are not empirical problems. Neither sin
nor defilement exists as such in any empirical, measurable way. Purification and
atonement are not therefore real accomplishments of Israelite ritual at all. They
are *perceived* accomplishments: the rituals in question are mechanisms of pretense
for dealing with problems that exist only in the realm of ideas. An important recent
collaborative work suggests, quite provocatively, that ritual creates and operates in
a "subjunctive," or "as-if" universe.[41] In light of this suggestion, one needs to ask:
do rituals *really* do what practitioners *perceive* or *believe* them to do?

It is not clear to me that ritual studies has yet developed an adequate vocabulary
to express this distinction, and therefore confusions persist in the works of biblical
scholars struggling with the matter. Robert Merton's classic distinction between
"latent" and "manifest" functions[42]—used recently by William Gilders[43]—will not
do, because "manifest functions" is a strange way to refer to stated motivations for
behavior that have no empirically measurable correlation with reality.[44] The literal-
metaphor distinction is not going to help here either.[45] In his important discussion
of the matter, Roy Rappaport distinguishes the "physical" from the "formal," the
"actual" from the "putative," and the "patent" from the "occult."[46] And, indeed,
his focus is clearly on the latter of each of these pairs; the former—what he also
calls "material efficacy"—may not always be absent, but is certainly not necessarily present either.[47] Whether rituals in general accomplish "physical," "patent,"
or "actual" goals—especially ones where the there is some intrinsic connection
between the means and the ends[48]—will continue to be asserted by some and denied
by others. Moreover, this binary opposition—the importance of which should be

more broadly recognized—does not exhaust the possibilities, for ritual also has communicative roles, above and beyond what believers claim it achieves and alongside whatever it may or may not measurably accomplish.[49]

At the risk of reaching too far—and fearful that I have overlooked some better attempt to clarify the matter—I wish to suggest that we characterize the assorted functions of ritual in light of the following distinctions:

1. *Putative* versus *actual.* By "actual" functions we mean material effects of ritual that are empirically measurable (e.g., the killing of an animal, the manipulation of blood, the transfer of property). By "putative" we mean the ritual practitioners' own goals (such as purification and atonement), effects that are not apparently or intrinsically related to the actual effects that can be measured.

2. *Practical* versus *communicative.* This distinction recognizes that while many rituals do things on the practical level (either putatively or actually) other rituals serve more to communicate messages.

These two distinctions, as many readers can infer, are based closely on the work of Roy Rappaport.[50] To these distinctions I propose adding the following:

3. *Stated* versus *unstated.* These terms allow us to distinguish between those goals that are explicitly stated in ritual texts or by ritual practitioners, and those goals that are inferred by the interpreter.

4. *Primary* versus *secondary.* These terms allow us to distinguish between effects that are intended as main goals, and those effects (whether stated or unstated, practical or communicative, putative or actual) that are either secondary or merely side effects of the ritual performance in question.

Let us see if these terms help clarify some of the questions we face, and perhaps even allow us to express more clearly the roles that symbols play in biblical rituals.

If ancient Israelite rituals do accomplish things, they do so primarily in a "putative" sense: the rituals act out Israelite hopes, performing actions that imitate, emulate, symbolize, and otherwise represent the immeasurable goals they wish to accomplish.[51] Of course, various actions performed along the way have measurable and "actual" consequences (bodies are bathed, animals are killed, blood is manipulated, fires are fed, and smoke is produced). But there is no intrinsic relationship between these actions and the primary goals—atonement from sin, purification from defilement, attracting the divine presence—that ancient Israelites wished for. To be sure, various secondary goals are also achieved: pilgrimages may well help bring the community together; periodic festivals mark off the passage of time; and, as in virtually all cultic rituals, social hierarchies are acted out.[52] But again, these are not necessarily the primary or stated goals of the rituals in question.

Importantly, there is one explicitly stated, primary goal of ancient Israelite ritual that can be understood as a goal that was likely an achieved one as well. A number of Israelite rituals were explicitly intended to function in a communicative way, to act as public reinforcements of communal memory: the Passover ritual recalls the Exodus (Exod 12:27, 13:3–8), the Sukkot festival recalls the wandering in the wilderness (Lev 23:43), and the Sabbath recalls both the slavery in Egypt (Deut 5:15) and the creation of the world (Exod 20:11). Sending messages in order to reinforce memory is also the stated function of the fringes on Israelite garments (Num 15:37–41), the phylacteries on their arms and head (Exod 13:9, 16; Deut 6:8, 11:18),[53] and the lazuli stones bearing the names of the tribes on the priestly Ephod (Exod 28:12, 29). And if etymological evidence is allowed, remembrance may well be the purpose of the "token portion" (*azkarata*) of the meal offering (Lev 2:2, 9, 16, etc.). It is in these passages that we may find the clearest evidence of the symbolic nature of many Israelite rituals.

We could, of course, quibble about whether the English term *symbol* should be used here. While there is value in this discussion, there is also a limit to its significance: If one defines *symbol* so narrowly as to exclude it, one has not necessarily convincingly denied the role or place of symbolism; one has simply redefined it out of existence. And if one turns to semiotics in order to displace the term *symbol* with *index*,[54] one has not really countered the views of those who use *symbol* in its more common, inclusive sense.

If we take our cues from the biblical texts themselves, we easily see that a number of rituals that are meant to foster memory are also explicitly described by the biblical writers themselves as "signs" (*otot*): This is true of circumcision (Gen 17:11), the Sabbath (Exod 31:17; Ezek 20:12, 20), the phylacteries (Exod 13:9, 16),[55] and the twelve uncut stones of Joshua's altar by the Jordan (Josh 4:1–9)—and these are just the rituals that are *explicitly* termed "signs." If a good number of rituals have clearly stated, primary, communicative functions—some of which are then explicitly identified as "signs"—are we really on safe ground to downplay the role that symbol plays in the communicative dimension of ancient Israelite ritual?

As we have seen, many of the primary, stated, practical purposes of Israelite ritual—to purify, to atone, to please God, and so on—can be understood as "putative" or "perceived" functions (or goals): there is nothing empirically measurable that is achieved, nothing tangible that is exchanged, and there is no intrinsic connection between the means and the ends. Thus studying these rituals by means of what they do, without clearer qualification, will prove to be of limited use. One primary, stated function of Israelite ritual is not putative at all, and that is the communicative function, which Israelites themselves may well have understood to operate symbolically, with visible signs serving as reminders and representations of past events and present obligations.

The explicit evidence that ancient Israelites' communicative behavior included ritual signs goes hand-in-hand with the evidence mentioned above concerning prophetic "signs" (Isa 20:3), adding further weight to the general argument being presented here: that symbolic action was an undeniably central feature of ancient Israelite culture.

Function and Morality

Having introduced distinctions between perceived and empirical results of ritual, there is benefit in taking a fresh look, one last time, at Israel's prophets. The prophetic critique of Israel's cult is often understood as denying, at least at some level, the efficacy of sacrifice, particularly sacrificial atonement (cf. Heb 10:4, 11). I have argued elsewhere, however, that a fuller understanding of the prophetic critique requires that we recognize not so much what sacrifice fails to do, but what turns out to be its all-too-frequent unintended practical consequence—the misappropriation of property, or even theft.[56] We can see this by looking first at David's startling assertion that he can sacrifice only what he properly owns (2 Sam 24:24). We then contrast that with Saul's faulty assertion that he meant to sacrifice to God the Amalekite goods he should never have taken to begin with (1 Sam 15:15). When we then turn to reread Amos's critique of Israelite sacrifice, we better understand that the prophet views Israelite sacrifice as problematic precisely because the offerings of the wealthy are inherently—we could say, functionally—tainted by the mistreatment of the poor:

> They lay themselves down beside every altar
> on garments taken in pledge
> and in the house of their God they drink
> wine bought with fines they imposed. (Am 2:8)

The power of the image conjured by Amos is the irony of the wealthy Israelites worshiping God with goods stolen from the poor. The objection to sacrifice rests on the assumption that God detests not what sacrifice represents or what Israelites hope it will achieve, but rather, the facts of the situation at hand. One who has taken unjustly from the poor cannot properly *give* anything; therefore, the "sacrifice" offered by such a person is anathema.

The significance of Amos's critique for our concerns is this: what we have here is, in a sense, a functionalist critique of sacrifice, one that can be better understood when we distinguish between "putative" and "actual" functions, and between "primary" and "secondary" effects, all the while recognizing that the communicative level operates independently of these. The prophets, as we have already seen, fully understand the communicative value of symbolic behavior, so their critique unlikely operates on that level. Moreover, the prophets very likely believed that proper sacrifice would produce the perceived ("putative") results that Israelites in general believed—that is why the prophets almost unanimously imagine Israelites sacrificing once again in the temple in the future (e.g. Isa 2:1–4; Mic 4:1–5; Jer 17:26, 33:17–18). The problem with sacrifice for the prophets, rather, rests on its actual (but secondary) results, especially when performed by wealthy Israelites who themselves have (in the prophets' minds) misappropriated property from the poor. That is why the prophets contrast sacrifice with obedience, justice, and mercy: for the putative, primary benefits of sacrifice to occur—which the prophets also hoped would come about—the actual, practical (and secondary) moral injustices in Israel's economic life had to be corrected. But that can only come about by means of practical behaviors, aimed at achieving empirical results.

Conclusion

A number of reflections have been presented here, all pointing toward the goal of justifying the prioritization of symbol over function, *for the purpose of understanding ancient Israelite ritual.* Ancient Israel's awareness of and fondness for symbols can be documented in both prophetic symbolic acts as well as the various ritual practices explicitly referred to as "signs." Those who deny that rituals had symbolic meaning need to address head-on the prophetic symbolic acts and the priestly ritual signs and explain better how ostensibly nonsymbolic rituals interfaced with these other documented examples of meaningful and representative patterned behavior in Israelite society. Theoretical and definitional concerns—as important as these may be—cannot on their own justify the claim that Israelite rituals were nonsymbolic.

That said, theoretical and definitional concerns are hardly to be shunted aside. Indeed, we need more clarity here, not less. We need to do a better job of selecting among the available theoretical models and methods, choosing to apply those theories that we can demonstrate hold promise for illuminating the evidence before us. We also need to seek those terminological clarifications that will work well to solve our particular problems. This includes, as suggested above, distinguishing carefully between ancient Israelite aspirations for their behavior and our own understandings of its achievements. In the final analysis, it is extremely difficult to maintain that there is any calculable or causal connection between the empirical consequences of Israelite ritual behavior and the seemingly practical goals (such as atonement, purification, and attracting the divine presence) that Israelites hoped would be the ultimate ramifications of their ritual behavior. We can and should continue to speak of the functions of ancient Israelite rituals, but we must do a better job of distinguishing empirical functions from perceived ones and primary stated goals from secondary, less consciously intended achievements. We must also be willing to recognize that some functions of Israelite ritual—especially as they pertain to fostering memory and transmitting messages—are functions entirely interwoven into the rituals' symbolism. Indeed, a very good case can be made that entire realms of ritual behavior were understood by ancient Israelites in just that way, as "eternal signs" (Exod 31:17) recalling salvations past (Exod 13:16) and pointing toward covenantal obligations pertaining in the present and future (Num 15:39).

This is not to say that symbolism will be discovered in every detail of biblical ritual or that varied symbolisms will necessarily all operate together as some single symbolic system.[57] Surely many details of biblical ritual simply serve, as J. Z. Smith claimed many years ago, to signify sheer difference.[58] And even complex, interrelated structures—such as defilement in ancient Israel—may well operate in overlapping, confusing, but still disparate ways.[59] So we ought not insist on symbolic unity or systemic consistency, and we must recognize that the rituals we study, just like the texts we now have, changed and developed over time, incorporating newer elements in older structures. And perhaps some elements or groups in ancient Israel would have been less inclined toward symbolism than others. Still, as argued above, symbolism was a prominent element of ancient Israelite culture—something Israelite prophets and priests, despite their differences, were consciously aware of. Precisely because Israelite culture exhibited "symbolic density," we must remain open to the possibility that there are layers of symbolism beyond those prophetic acts and ritual signs that have explicitly been identified as such or explained for us in our texts. If some ritual texts appear to focus exclusively on rules and procedures, that may well tell us more about the genre of such texts than it does about the meaning of rituals for the societies that produced and preserved them.

Finally, we also need to be more deliberate in the ways we make use of the evidence beyond ritual texts, especially from the prophets. Far from only indicating examples of what was wrong with ancient Israelite ritual, the prophets illustrate both the degree to which symbolic activity was part and parcel of ancient Israelite life and the importance of differentiating between actual results and the ideological ambitions of ancient Israelite ritual. To be sure, some writers believe we need to restrict ourselves to ritual texts—or, more narrowly, to P—in order to understand the meaning of Israelite rituals.[60] But those who set out to study biblical rituals in light of ritual studies should remember that the anthropological tools at the heart of ritual studies are intended, in the final analysis, not to analyze texts or rituals, but societies. One way to ensure that the analysis is focused on ancient Israelite society as a whole is to expand the scope beyond Leviticus and its priests to include Amos, Hosea, and the prophetic narratives of the Deuteronomistic history. When we clarify our terms, put evidence in front of theory, and consider not only the priests but the prophets as well, the prioritization of symbol over function *for the understanding of ancient Israelite ritual* emerges, if not as a settled matter, at least as a very safe bet.

Notes

Although this chapter was not presented as a paper at the Boston University conference, it was germinated there and developed in its wake. I am grateful to the editors for their willingness to include it here. This essay was delivered in Helsinki, August 2009, at the Workshop on Ritual in Early Judaism and Early Christianity, organized and sponsored by the Helsinki Collegium for Advanced Studies and the Network for the Study of Early Christianity in Its Greco-Roman Context. I am grateful to the organizers and participants of that conference for the stimulating conversation and helpful responses. I also thank Adam B. Seligman for helpful advice and encouragement when I began to write this essay.

1. See, for example, Edmund Leach, *Culture and Communication: The Logic by Which Symbols Are Connected; An Introduction to the Use of Structuralist Analysis in Social Anthropology* (Cambridge: Cambridge University Press, 1976); Mary Douglas, *Purity and Danger: An Analysis of the Concepts of Pollution and Taboo* (London: Routledge and Kegan Paul, 1966); and Victor Turner, *The Forest of Symbols: Aspects of Ndembu Ritual* (Ithaca: Cornell University Press, 1967).

2. For an example of the former, see Klawans, *Purity, Sacrifice and the Temple: Symbolism and Supersessionism in the Study of Ancient Judaism* (New York: Oxford University Press, 2005); for a counter-voice, see William K. Gilders, review of *Purity, Sacrifice, and the Temple*, in *Catholic Biblical Quarterly* 69 (2007): 784–85.

3. The following paragraphs summarize points more fully developed in Klawans, "Methodology and Ideology in the Study of Priestly Ritual," in *Perspectives on Purity and Purification in the Bible*, edited by Baruch J. Schwartz, David P. Wright, Jeffrey Stackert, and Naphtali S. Meshel (London: T. & T. Clark International, 2008), 84–95.

4. Douglas, *Purity and Danger*, 29–57 (chaps. 2–3), 114–28 (chap. 7); cf., more recently, the broad thrust of *Leviticus as Literature* (Oxford: Oxford University Press, 1999). On these works, see Klawans, *Purity, Sacrifice, and the Temple*, esp. 17–20, 45–46, and also Klawans, "Rethinking Leviticus and Rereading *Purity and Danger*: A Review Essay," *AJS Review* 27 (2003): 89–101.

5. See, for example, Turner, *The Forest of Symbols*, and *Dramas, Fields, and Metaphors: Symbolic Action in Human Society* (Ithaca: Cornell University Press, 1974).

6. In Milgrom's case, a sympathetic and symbolic interpretation of rituals concerning purity and diet is balanced by a rather dismissive approach to matters sacrificial, one that sees various integral aspects of priestly practice (including the shew bread and the sacrificial act itself) as fossilized vestiges. See Jacob Milgrom, *Leviticus 1–16: A New Translation with Introduction and Commentary*, Anchor Bible 3 (New York: Doubleday, 1992), esp. 440, 1003; see also Milgrom, *Leviticus 23–27: A New Translation with Introduction and Commentary*, The Anchor Bible 3b (New York: Doubleday, 2001), 2091–93. Compare the comments of Menahem Haran, *Temples and Temple-Service in Ancient Israel: An Inquiry into Biblical Cult Phenomena and the Historical Setting of the Priestly School* (Winona Lake, Ind.: Eisenbrauns, 1985), 17, 221–25, and Roland de Vaux, *Studies in Old Testament Sacrifice* (Cardiff: University of Wales Press, 1964), 38–42. Hyam Maccoby also speaks of various sacrificial practices (including the red-cow and scapegoat rituals) as vestiges throughout his *Ritual and Morality: The Ritual Purity System and Its Place in Judaism* (Cambridge: Cambridge University Press, 1999), esp. ix, 93, 102, 114, 123, 125, 139–40. For a fuller discussion and critique, see Klawans, "Ritual Purity, Moral Purity, and Sacrifice in Jacob Milgrom's *Leviticus*," *Religious Studies Review* 29 (2003): 19–28, and Klawans, *Purity, Sacrifice, and the Temple*, 27–32. Milgrom has recently reiterated his view that various elements of Israel's cult are indeed vestiges; see "Systemic Differences in the Priestly Corpus: A Response to Jonathan Klawans," *Revue Biblique* 112.3 (2005): 321–29, esp. 322–24.

7. In Robertson Smith's case, by contrast with Milgrom, the disdain was directed toward purity rites ("taboos" in his parlance), which were seen as meaningless survivals from primitive times. At the same time, Robertson Smith respected sacrifice: for him it was social, symbolic, and appropriate; it even possessed a "sacramental efficacy." See Robertson Smith, *Lectures on the Religion of the Semites: The Fundamental Institutions*, 3rd ed., with an introduction and additional notes by Stanley A. Cook (New York: Macmillan, 1927), esp.

269 and 312; for his very different take on purity (taboos), see 446–54. For a fuller discussion of Robertson Smith's selective approach, see Klawans, *Purity, Sacrifice, and the Temple*, 18–19, 32–34.

8. Robertson Smith's conservative Protestantism combines with Victorian prudery and yields a disdain for taboo and a valorization of sacrifice. Milgrom's work is sympathetic to practices concerning diet and purity that are still maintained by traditional and modern Jews; it is less sympathetic—but by no means hostile—to those aspects of the cult that are seemingly unethical or outdated, such as animal sacrifice. See Klawans, *Purity, Sacrifice, and the Temple*, esp. 28–34.

9. See Frank Gorman, "Pagans and Priests: Critical Reflections on Method," in Schwartz et al., *Perspectives on Purification*, 96–110, esp. 98–99, where Gorman takes Milgrom to task for this kind of selectivity.

10. See Klawans, "Ritual Purity, Moral Purity, and Sacrifice."

11. See T. M. Lemos, "The Universal and the Particular: Mary Douglas and the Politics of Impurity," *Journal of Religion* 89.2 (2009): 236–51 (esp. 249–50).

12. On Girard, see Klawans, *Purity, Sacrifice, and the Temple*, 17–48, and "Religion, Violence, and the Bible," in *Religion and Violence: The Biblical Heritage*, edited by David A. Bernat and Jonathan Klawans (Sheffield: Sheffield Phoenix Press, 2007), 1–15.

13. Ithamar Gruenwald, *Rituals and Ritual Theory in Ancient Israel* (Leiden: Brill, 2003), esp. 1, 5–6, 34–35, 200–201. See also my review of this book in *AJS Review* 29 (2005): 163–65.

14. See, for example, Edmund Leach, "Mythical Inequalities," review of Mary Douglas, *Natural Symbols*, in *New York Review of Books*, January 28, 1971, 44–45. For a fuller discussion of Mary Douglas's life and work—including the impact of her Catholic upbringing—see Richard Fardon, *Mary Douglas: An Intellectual Biography* (London: Routledge, 1999), esp. 75–101 (on *Purity and Danger*) and 102–24 (on *Natural Symbols*).

15. Jonathan Z. Smith, *To Take Place: Toward Theory in Ritual* (Chicago: University of Chicago Press, 1987), 83–86, 96–117.

16. Frits Staal, "The Meaninglessness of Ritual," *Numen* 26.1 (1979): 2–22; Gruenwald rightly steps back from Staal's extreme position in this regard (*Rituals and Ritual Theory*, 198). For a general discussion on ritual and symbolism, see Catherine Bell, *Ritual: Perspectives and Dimensions* (New York: Oxford University Press, 1997), 61–89.

17. See, for example, Douglas, *Purity and Danger*, 7–28 (chap. 1), 58–72 (chap. 4), and esp. 18–19, 62–63; see also Douglas, *Natural Symbols: Explorations in Cosmology*, Routledge Classics edition, with a new introduction (London: Routledge, 2003), esp. 1–38 (chaps. 1–2) and 152–67 (chap. 9).

18. Jonathan Z. Smith, *Drudgery Divine: On the Comparison of Early Christians and the Religions of Late Antiquity* (Chicago: University of Chicago Press, 1990), 1–34.

19. See, for example, Douglas's comments regarding the ritual observances of M. N. Srinivas and Franz Steiner in the acknowledgments (vii) to *Purity and Danger*.

20. See, for example, Melford E. Spiro, review of *Purity and Danger*, in *American Anthropologist*, New Series 70 (1968): 391–93.

21. For a discussion of anti- and pro-ritual biases in modern scholarship, see Bell, *Ritual*, esp. 3–22, 253–67.

22. Nancy K. Frankenberry and Hans H. Penner, "Clifford Geertz's Long-Lasting Moods, Motivations, and Metaphysical Conceptions," *Journal of Religion* 79 (1999): 617–40.

23. On symbolic approaches to cultic rituals among Second Temple–era Jews, see Klawans, *Purity, Sacrifice, and the Temple*, 111–44.

24. Maimonides, *Guide of the Perplexed*, translated with an introduction and notes by Shlomo Pines, 2 vols. (Chicago: University of Chicago Press, 1963), 2:502–10, 612–13 (= *Guide* III:25–26, 49); Mendelssohn, *Jerusalem: Or On Religious Power and Judaism*, translated by Alan Arkush, with introduction and commentary by Alexander Altmann (Waltham: Brandeis University Press, 1983), 117–18, 133–34. See discussion on rabbinic sources in Ephraim E. Urbach, *The Sages: Their Concepts and Beliefs*, translated by Israel Abrahams (Cambridge: Harvard University Press, 1987), 365–99. One rather famous tradition attributes to the late-first-century sage Yohanan Ben Zakkai the view that the red heifer ritual of Numbers 19 has no known symbolic or rational basis (*Pesikta de Rav Kahana, Parah* 7). On the latter source, see Bernard Mandelbaum, ed., *Pesikta de Rav Kahana: According to an Oxford Manuscript, with Variants from All Known Manuscripts and Genizoth Fragments and Parallel Passages, with Commentary and Introduction*, 2 vols. (New York: Jewish Theological Seminary, 1987), 1:74.

25. See, for example, Gorman, "Pagans and Priests," 100–101, who expresses such a concern.

26. See Freud, *The Interpretation of Dreams* (1900).

27. On "ritual density" and its social or cultural variables, see Bell, *Ritual*, 173–209.

28. In this regard, compare the first item in Bell's list of methodological advice in *Ritual*, 81–82.

29. For a fuller treatment of the relationship between priests and prophets (as well as ritual and ethics), see Klawans, *Purity, Sacrifice, and the Temple*, 75–100.

30. For example, Joseph Blenkinsopp, *A History of Prophecy in Israel*, rev. and enlarged ed. (Louisville: Westminster John Knox, 1996), 146, 157, 167; J. Lindblom, *Prophecy in Ancient Israel* (Oxford: Blackwell, 1962), 165–73; Helmer Ringgren, *Israelite Religion* (Philadelphia: Fortress, 1966), 214–15, 256–57, and 284; Alexander Rofé, *Introduction to the Prophetic Literature*, translated by Judith H. Seeligmann (Sheffield: Sheffield Academic Press, 1997), 71–73; Marvin A. Sweeney, *Isaiah 1–39: With an Introduction to Prophetic Literature*, vol. 16, *The Forms of Old Testament Literature* (Grand Rapids: William B. Eerdmans, 1996), 19–20.

31. For the classic articulation of Max Weber's contrasting "ideal types" of the priest and prophet, see his *The Sociology of Religion*, translated by Ephraim Fischoff (Boston: Beacon, 1963), 20–31, 46–59.

32. For a recent assertion of the difference between symbolic acts and rituals, see Ronald S. Hendel, "Prophets, Priests, and the Efficacy of Ritual," in *Pomegranates and Golden Bells: Studies in Biblical, Jewish, and Near Eastern Ritual, Law, and Literature in Honor of Jacob Milgrom*, edited by David P. Wright, David Noel Freedman, and Avi Hurvitz (Winona Lake, Ind.: Eisenbrauns, 1995), 185–98, esp. 188–89.

33. For example, Hendel, "Prophets, Priests."

34. For a nontechnical review of this evidence (especially cult figurines) and recent scholarship on it, see William G. Dever, *Did God Have a Wife? Archaeology and Folk Religion in Ancient Israel* (Grand Rapids: William B. Eerdmans, 2005), esp. 176–208.

35. For a general critique, see Hans H. Penner, "The Poverty of Functionalism," *History of Religions* 11.1 (1971): 91–97.

36. Clifford Geertz, *Islam Observed: Religious Development in Morocco and Indonesia* (Chicago: University of Chicago Press, 1968), 92–93.

37. See Bruce Lincoln, *Holy Terrors: Thinking about Religion after September 11*, 2nd ed. (Chicago: University of Chicago Press, 2006), esp. 1–18, 97–102, where Lincoln discusses and reproduces the Mohamed Atta's final instructions to the 9/11 hijackers.

38. Gruenwald, *Rituals and Ritual Theory*, 198–99.

39. Gruenwald, *Rituals and Ritual Theory*, 69.

40. Gruenwald, *Rituals and Ritual Theory*, 202–30.

41. Adam B. Seligman, Robert P. Weller, Michael J. Puett, and Bennett Simon, *Ritual and Its Consequences: An Essay on the Limits of Sincerity* (New York: Oxford University Press, 2008).

42. Robert K. Merton, *Social Theory and Social Structure* (Glencoe, Ill.: Free Press, 1957), esp. 60–69.

43. William Gilders, *Blood Ritual in the Hebrew Bible: Meaning and Power* (Baltimore: Johns Hopkins University Press, 2004), esp. 182–89.

44. As John Holmwood has pointed out, the stated purpose isn't a function at all—it's a motive. See "Functionalism and Its Critics," in *Modern Social Theory: An Introduction*, edited by A. Harrington (Oxford: Oxford University Press, 2005), 87–109. The ambiguities inherent in Merton's terms (and evident in his use of them) have rightly prevented this distinction from gaining wider usage. See, for example, Paul Helm, "Manifest and Latent Functions," *Philosophical Quarterly* 21.82 (1971): 51–60, and Colin Campbell, "A Dubious Distinction? An Inquiry into the Value and Use of Merton's Concepts of Manifest and Latent Function," *American Sociological Review* 47.1 (1982): 29–44.

45. See Klawans, *Impurity and Sin in Ancient Judaism* (New York: Oxford University Press, 2000), 32–34 (cf. vii).

46. Roy A. Rappaport, *Ritual and Religion in the Making of Humanity* (Cambridge: Cambridge University Press, 1999), 45–50.

47. Rappaport, *Ritual and Religion*, 471 n. 10.

48. See Jack Goody, "Religion and Ritual: The Definitional Problem," *British Journal of Sociology* 12.2 (1961): 142–64. Goody defines ritual as a "category of standardized behaviour (custom) in which the relationship between the means and the end is not 'intrinsic', i.e. is either irrational or non-rational" (159).

49. Rappaport, *Ritual and Religion*, 50–138.

50. Rappaport, *Ritual and Religion*, 45–50.

51. So, for example, performing Israelite sacrifice in order to attract and maintain the divine presence is a *putative* function, but not an actual one. See Klawans, *Purity, Sacrifice, and the Temple*, 68–72.

52. See Gerald Klingbeil, *Bridging the Gap: Ritual and Ritual Texts in the Bible* (Winona Lake, Ind.: Eisenbrauns, 2007), 205–25, for further examples of these sorts of functions of biblical rituals.

53. Curiously, the fringes and phylacteries are not listed in Klingbeil's appendix (245–52), perhaps because they are more personal than communal. On the "self-informative" nature of many ritual practices (whether communal or individual), see Rappaport, *Ritual and Religion*, 104–106.

54. As, for example, Gilders does in *Blood Ritual*, esp. 78–82.

55. Note Exod 13:9: "a sign [*ot*] on your arm and a remembrance [*zikaron*] between your eyes."

56. What follows summarizes, in part, *Purity, Sacrifice, and the Temple*, 75–100, esp. 84–89, with a few statements reformulated in light of the terminological distinctions introduced above.

57. For a recent caution against the analytic drive for symbolic consistency (evident, for example, in Milgrom's works), see Gorman, "Pagan and Priest," esp. 101–107.

58. Smith, *To Take Place*, 108.

59. See, for example, Klawans, *Impurity and Sin*, which argues for distinctions between ritual and moral defilements in the Hebrew Bible and ancient Judaism.

60. See, for example, Gilders, "Blood as Purificant in Priestly Torah: What Do We Know and How Do We Know It?" in Schwartz et al., *Perspectives on Purity*, 77–83, esp. 82–83.

PART II

Negotiating Power through Sacrifice

{ 6 }

Political Murder and Sacrifice
FROM ROMAN REPUBLIC TO EMPIRE

Zsuzsanna Várhelyi

Homo Sacer?

As the time for the tribunal election approached in Rome in 133 BCE, an irreconcilable political conflict emerged between the popular movement of the tribune, Tiberius Gracchus, and a number of conservative senators who opposed his unusual candidacy for a second term as tribune of the people. To the extent we can reconstruct what ensued,[1] it seems clear that the senate was called to meet at the temple of Fides, where the conservative senator P. Scipio Nasica then urged the consul to decide against the candidacy of Tiberius. He also suggested that they declare Tiberius an enemy of the state for aiming at tyranny. The consul P. Mucius Scaevola, also a famous jurist, had advised Tiberius on his land-distribution legislation previously and was reluctant to support actions against him now; it was even less likely that he would authorize an action that could likely lead to the tribune's death, which the declaration as an enemy of the state entailed. Nasica, seeing his preferred course of action failing, took the lead and called upon his fellow senators to take arms: "Those of you wishing to save the *res publica*, follow me!" At this dramatic height of events, Tiberius was addressing a large group of his supporters outdoors, in front of the temple of Jupiter. It was here, on the podium of the temple, that Nasica appeared, approaching the tribune from behind. To be veiled like Roman priests, Nasica had his purple-edged toga pulled up around his head, which was especially suggestive given that Nasica was the pontifex maximus at this time. Thus implying pontifical authority, Nasica pronounced a few select phrases, and, upon his words, Tiberius and hundreds of his followers were slain. The victims offered surprisingly little resistance against the conservative forces of Nasica, which has been difficult to explain. A recent study by Jerzy Linderski, however, has conclusively identified the key feature of these events: Nasica engaged in a religious intervention—in Roman terms, a *consecratio*, that is, a curse that made Tiberius *sacer*—which allowed the pontifex to kill him in a ritually understood act.[2]

The notion of *homo sacer*, a man turned "sacred," has been widely discussed among philosophers, theologians, and political scientists in the past decade, particularly since the appearance of a 1995 monograph of the same title by the Italian thinker Giorgio Agamben.[3] Leaving aside the possible modern implications of this work, I want to highlight here the specification Agamben offers for the Roman concept of *homo sacer*, namely that it exists in "a zone of indistinction between sacrifice and homicide."[4] This notion is less revolutionary within ancient studies, where, as Carlin Barton insightfully observed, scholars of both early Roman law and of Roman religion have long been seeking a shared origin for both executions and sacrifice.[5] Yet as Barton also rightly points out, part of the problem is that we cannot presume a separation of religious and political life (the like of which we are accustomed to in the modern era) in ancient Rome in general, even if it is also clear that the late republic, starting at the time of Tiberius's tribunate, saw the development of a distinct religious discourse and therefore some differentiation of the religious sphere for the first time in Roman history.[6] My argument here is that the tribunate of Tiberius Gracchus not only opened up, as we know, a new and violent period of Roman political history, the late republic, but that it also started a new period in which this newly thematized sacrificial imagery appeared in the depiction of politically high-stake murders. In other words, the ritualized murder of Tiberius marked the beginning of a new era in which the increasingly factious debates concerning politically contentious murders started to include similarly contentious arguments that referenced sacrifice as the right or wrong association of these killings. My interest is thus not strictly in the legal definitions of sacrifice, or in the generic Roman condemnation of regularly practiced ritual murder, but in the wider, symbolic references to actions similar to sacrificial ritual.[7] This was not simply a rhetorical matter, however. As I unfold the various elements that went into the public discussions about the circumstances of Tiberius's death and about a number of further deaths that were to take place in the first century BCE, I intend to show how closely discourses about proper political and religious conduct—the proper execution of power and of sacrifice—touched upon each other. Ultimately, I hope to demonstrate that these debates—concerning whether such killings were acceptable in political and religious terms—shaped how, at the end of this period, the first emperor, Augustus, combined political and religious authority into one, including the prime role that Roman emperors claimed in performing sacrifice.

Debating the Killing of Tiberius Gracchus in the Late Republic

The surviving accounts of Tiberius's death range in their perspective widely, from the early first-century BCE *Rhetorica ad Herennium*, which exclusively favored the tribune, to a slightly later account, written by Diodorus Siculus, which clearly favored Nasica, the pontifex. In the middle of these two extremes are the accounts of Appian and Plutarch, which are both more favorable to Tiberius, and those of Velleius and Valerius, which emphasize the exemplary aspects of Nasica's conduct.[8]

This wide range in the characterization of events attests to how contested Tiberius's death remained throughout the late republic; it also suggests that an analysis seeking to explore the notions of sacrifice in these debates can offer insights into the particular mix of religious and political arguments in this period.

Let us start with a depiction highly favorable to Tiberius in the earliest of our sources, the *Rhetorica ad Herennium*, dated to the 90s BCE. The bias for Tiberius is especially clear in the highly negative representation of Nasica, the pontifex:

Nasica in the meantime ran out of the temple of Jupiter, abounding in criminal and evil thoughts: sweating, with his eyes burning, his hair upheaved, his toga twisted.

Employing the tropes of Latin invective, the *Rhetorica* represents Nasica differently from the ideal Roman man, which gets even more specific as he is further described, approaching Tiberius Gracchus from behind:

foaming crime from his mouth, breathing cruelty from the depth of his breast; he flung his arm and struck Gracchus on the temple of his head.[9]

This characterization is typical, in part, of mad rage as this trope appears in other Latin literature, but it also shows mad rage acted out, turning into violence. The depiction of Tiberius offers a stark contrast: he is shown as beginning a prayer to the gods when Nasica appears behind him, and, upon the strike of the pontifex, he "falls silently, not betraying his innate *virtus* with any sound."[10] The silent manliness of Tiberius contrasts to the foaming madness of Nasica, and their contradistinction is built on the opposing images of calm masculinity and mad rush. In fact, the almost feminine loss of control on the part of Nasica makes him comparable to the religious excesses said to be characteristic among female worshipers—like the frenzied women worshipping Dionysus, who were mad with both rage and lust and served as key examples of female sexual licentiousness and religious excess in Latin literature.[11] In other words, in offering a view on the circumstances of his death, Tiberius's posthumous supporters preferred an emphasis on the religious interpretation of events that was, on their reading, not a perfectly performed ritual but comparable to the excessive, mad outbursts of unacceptable religion.

The apparent anger of Nasica during the incident remained the subject of discussion in the first century BCE. Even such a favorable source as Diodorus Siculus, who suggested that Nasica's actions had primarily a constitutional motivation, described the pontifex as angry.[12] Cicero, similarly favorable to Nasica, identified here by his family name, Scipio, tried to argue away the by then well-known rage of his hero. As he put it in his *Tusculan Disputations*:

I don't think even Scipio—I mean the *pontifex maximus*, who demonstrated the truth of the saying of the Stoics that the wise man is never a private citizen—was angry with Tiberius Gracchus at the time when Scipio abandoned the feeble consul, and as if he, a private citizen, were consul himself, ordered those who wished the republic safe to follow him.[13]

Cicero sublimated the emotional arousal of Nasica into a righteous motive that allowed the senator to take on a larger role than allowed by his actual public office—essentially turning him into a quasi-consul and thereby claiming that the act of killing was primarily a constitutional obligation, rather than the performance of a religious ritual.

Such a variety of interpretations, vacillating between religious and political emphases, became quite usual in Rome in the first century BCE. What seems remarkable in this debate is the openness it suggests in the interpretation of these (and similar) killings that individual statesmen could rely upon in order to justify their acts. While already in the mid-republican era the religious evaluation of politicians could be part of their praise or blame, it seems that, around the time of Tiberius Gracchus's death, new types of actions, not part of the tradition of religious praise, could be added to the praise or the criticism of ambitious members of the elite referencing varied notions of sacrifice.

Another contemporary debate with both political and religious dimensions further confirms this openness in interpretations. The complicated religious representations in the case of the defeated Roman commander C. Hostilius Mancinus, who negotiated the surrender of his troops to the victorious Spaniards in 137 BCE, offer a prominent example of how such praise or blame could play out in Rome. It is likely that soon after the news of his surrender reached Rome, rumors started to circulate in the city about various prodigies that Mancinus had supposedly disregarded before going to battle: at his Lavinium sacrifice, the sacred chickens ran away; at the port of Hercules (Monaco), an eerie voice called on him to wait rather than go on his campaign; and when he finally boarded ship in Genoa, a snake of unusual size was spotted.[14] Valerius Maximus later observed that the prodigies corresponded in number to Mancinus's debacles: first, the battle was lost; second, he made a humiliating peace treaty, which Rome refused to accept; third, the Roman *fetiales* priests carried out the appropriate ritual to invalidate the treaty—namely, they handed over Mancinus, naked and bound, to the enemy. So far, the case appears to follow Roman tradition: the inappropriate religious actions of Mancinus are rectified by the priests' actions. But the most striking feature of the debate that must have surrounded this case in Rome, for the purposes of my argument, is that Cicero claims that Mancinus proposed this ritual solution himself to show his *honestas*.[15] That Mancinus saw the potential for enhancing his image in this act is clear from the fact that, after the Spaniards returned the disgraced general home to Rome—instead of retiring from public life—he had a statue of himself set up in Rome, bound and practically naked, to represent his own initiative in offering his life for the benefit of the state.[16] In this first almost nude heroic self-portrait in Rome, Mancinus tried to create and exploit a nontraditional religious claim to righteous behavior. If the Tiberian Velleius Paterculus is to be trusted, taking his imagery depicting Mancinus's acts from sallust, then the Numantine rejection of Mancinus was understood, at least by some Romans, in religious terms as a measure of them "saying that that the public violation of good faith should not be expiated by the blood of one."[17]

If this argument is historical, it would have likely emerged from circles trying to save face for Mancinus and benefit from a metaphorical notion of self-sacrifice in order to make up for his complex political, military, and religious infamy. This innovative application of sacrificial imagery confirms that arguments referencing sacrifice, whether in the case Tiberius Gracchus or Mancinus, were available for Roman statesmen to pursue for political purposes.

Responses to the *Consecratio* of Tiberius

The aftermath of Tiberius's murder had multiple religious resonances in Rome—most importantly, the plebeian goddess Ceres needed to be propitiated. On the advice of the Sybilline books, the "oldest" Ceres, the one in Henna, Sicily, was offered sacrifices. This conveniently coincided with the religious pacification of that city after the bloody siege of slaves who had gathered there earlier in the same year.[18] The individuals who had participated in the murder of Tiberius lived on with a mixed legacy: Nasica, highly unusually for a pontifex maximus, left Rome on an embassy to Asia, only to die in Pergamum in the next year, 132 BCE. The aedile of the plebs, Lucretius, under whose leadership the corpses of Tiberius and his followers were thrown into the river Tiber, acquired the cognomen Vespillo, referencing the slave undertakers responsible for disposing of unburied bodies in Rome.[19]

More significant for my purposes, however, was the introduction of some new measures that clearly responded to the mixed political and religious interpretations of Nasica's actions. The first of these was the newly established ultimate decree, the so-called *senatus consultum ultimum*, a constitutional measure that created a legal tool allowing the Senate to declare a state of emergency and authorizing the consuls to use any tools necessary "lest the state suffer a detriment."[20] The first instance when this measure was applied came just after Tiberius's younger brother, Gaius Gracchus, completed his first year of the tribunate in 123 BCE. After Gaius's failed attempt for a second tribunate, not dissimilar to Tiberius's actions, his forces and those of the consul L. Opimius faced off each other on the Aventine hill of Rome. This conflict was described primarily in legal terms: Gaius tried to avoid meeting his brother's fate through the enactment of a law during his tribunate, the *lex Sempronia de capite civis*, which protected citizens from magistrate-ordered execution; in response, the senate issued the ultimate decree (*senatus consultum ultimum*) that authorized Opimius to attack. Gaius and, according to Plutarch, up to three thousand of his supporters were incarcerated and then killed in prison.

The modern notion of a legal process, an ultimate decree, may, again, suggest a clean-cut distinction between political and religious procedures. But, in reality, every subsequent application of the *senatus consultum ultimum* was contested. Killing a Roman citizen, usually a member of the elite, was not only a potential challenge to the political notion of freedom, *libertas*, but also a challenge to Roman notions of the sacred status of the city and its citizens. It is a measure of this contestable boundary that, based on the republican evidence, Roberto Fiori could convincingly argue for a direct connection between the declaration of a *senatus consultum ultimum* and the declaration of someone as enemy (*hostis*), comparable to the archaic call to make one's enemy *sacer*.[21]

Leaving aside for now those later instances, in 121 no one could deny the religious significance of what had happened. A religious resolution was sought for Gaius's murder. Opimius, the consul responsible for the killings, performed a ritual purification of the city; then, adjacent to his *basilica Opimia*, he dedicated a temple to Concord, emphasizing the reestablishment of civic harmony. On the opposing side, and in an interesting alternative development, the Gracchi gained an emerging popular cult—likely with worship at the sites of their deaths.[22] The memory of the two brothers clearly remained alive—possibly, as Harriet Flower suggested, not only at the location of their deaths, but also at alternative sites in the neighborhoods of Rome.[23]

The ban on human sacrifices in 97 BCE may also be understood, in part, as a response to Nasica's actions.[24] Our knowledge of this ban is drawn from literary sources written 150 years after the fact; however, if it is historical, as likely, it would fit well with our discussion so far. The *immolatio* of humans in a religious contest would have been much criticized in circles familiar with Greek philosophy, and the Gracchi were famous for their interest in Stoic thought.[25] We know that Posidonius, the most influential Greek historian writing about this period, was also a Stoic philosopher, and, as expected, he criticized the barbarian custom of bloody human sacrifice among the Germans. The interpretation of the death of Tiberius as a religious ritual gone wrong is therefore consonant with the Stoic background of the Gracchi and their supporters; they, like other contemporary Stoics, tried to set an ethical limit to the flexibility of Roman religion, and did so, at least here, by standing by the cause of one of their own.

What these discussions make clear—shifting between religious and nonreligious emphases and claims for divinely sanctioned ritual action—is that there was an increased interest in exploring new religious ideas and new extensions of old ideas; it was as part of this reconsideration that notions related to the ritual world of sacrifice emerged in discussions concerning violent action in late republican culture. In the following section I will turn to a few incidents that I see as key examples of how notions of sacrifice played into the interpretations of the increasingly violent strife in Rome.

Beyond Tiberius: Religion and Violence in Late Republican Rome

In the 80s BCE civic infighting enveloped Rome more violently than ever before, as two charismatic political leaders, Marius and Sulla, fought for power. The control of the city started to pass back and forth between the partisans of these two leaders, often leading to a change in the city's officials. It was among such circumstances that in 87 BCE one of the Marian consuls, L. Cornelius Cinna, was deposed and in his place the *flamen Dialis*, L. Cornelius Merula, was appointed to serve as the consul for the rest of the year. But even before the year came to an end, Marius returned to Rome, and his supporters started to seek out Sulla's supporters in the city. Recognizing the change in the general situation and seeing the danger of his own position, Merula chose to resign from his consulship in the hope of saving his life. He was put on trial nevertheless for his illegal exercise of the consular office; the outcome of the trial seemed a foregone conclusion, and the fate of Merula, his imminent murder, appeared sealed.

What actually happened afterwards we know from the Augustan Livy and the Tiberian Velleius Paterculus. Florus, excerpting from Livy, writes:

> Merula, the priest of Jupiter in the Capitol, bespattered the visage of the god himself with the blood from his veins. (Florus, *Epitome* 3.21.16)[26]

Velleius Paterculus offers more details

> However, Merula, who had abdicated his consulship before the arrival of Cinna, cut his veins open and his blood flowed over the very same altars, at which he had frequently prayed as *flamen Dialis* for the well-being of the state to the gods, whom he now called to curse Cinna and his party and thus he gave up his life so worthy to the state. (Vell. Pat., 2.22.2)[27]

Both of these sources suggest a sacrificial logic, in which Merula is acting both as a sacrificing priest at his accustomed altar of Jupiter, the god whom he as *flamen Dialis* was supposed to worship, and, at the same time, as the sacrificial victim whose blood spatters the altar. The regular ritual in which Merula used to partake was meant for the well-being of the state—but now Merula called upon the same Jupiter at the same altar to curse his enemies. This latter ritual might remind us of *devotio*, in which a Roman commander supposedly cursed himself together with the enemy in order to "devote" both to the gods of underworld. The technical term Velleius employs to describe this religious procedure, however, is *execratio*; although this term also had the general meaning of "curse" in popular usage, a deeper religious sense is implied when the ritual is carried out by a priest, at an altar.[28]

As a religious term, *execratio* is best known from a passage of Livy, in which he gives the words that the *pater patratus*, a special priest, pronounced at the oath accompanying the treaty of the Romans and the Albans:

> If the Romans first abandon this treaty in their common council with false and evil intent, then Jupiter himself will thus strike the Roman people as I shall strike this pig here today; and he will strike them all the more as you are more powerful and strong. (*AUC* 1.24)[29]

The religious logic of this *execratio* works through exposing the oath-breaking party to the wrath of Jupiter. It is analogous to the *consecratio* we have seen in the case of Tiberius Gracchus, except that *execratio* is traditionally applied to enemy nations. While a *consecratio* dedicates someone or something to the god, thus removing him or it from the human order of life, the *execratio* places a bind on a person or thing, with the threat that regular divine protection will be withdrawn, rendering the person outside of the rules of normal order. The logic of these two procedures, however, is very similar, as is evident in the words of Pliny the Younger, who quotes the words of an *execratio*: the person breaking the curse "*consecrates* his head and his house to the anger of the gods" (my emphasis). [30]

Of course, it is a rather unusual situation to have Merula act both as priest and as victim at the same ritual. Appian offers an interesting detail in this respect:

> But Merula had opened his veins, and a tablet lying at his side showed that when he cut his veins he had removed his *flamen*'s cap, for it was accounted a sin for the priest to wear it at his death. (App., *BC* 1.8.74)[31]

This extreme attention to the proper execution of the religious action confirms that, as Merula performed his suicide, he took special care to observe the applicable religious rules, thereby leaving the ritual logic unharmed; in other words, he wanted to make sure his *execratio* would work and Marius and his bloodthirsty supporters would become *sacer*.

The particular details of Merula's death must have been known in Rome. Even if we cannot securely assign a fragment of Sallust to the case of Merula, it clearly depicts to what extent religion and violence were now intertwined. As Sallust puts it: "the altars and other things set aside for the service of the gods were being defiled by the blood of suppliants."[32] These words would have resonated in Rome for the rest of the 80s, which was dominated by violent clashes between the partisans of Marius and of Sulla. As Cicero liked to recount, another important statesman, Q. Mucius Scaevola, pontifex and consul of 95 BCE, was murdered by Marians while he sought safety at the altar of Vesta in 82 BCE; the visual depiction of his blood spattering the image of the goddess represented to late republican writers the apparent limits of divine protection in the face of the political violence.[33]

A number of our imperial Greek sources, including Plutarch in his *Life of Sulla* and Cassius Dio in his history of Rome, offer a similar description, in which neither sacred nor profane locations remained free from murders as a new form of violence emerged when, upon taking Rome by force again in 82 BCE, Sulla planned to get rid of his political enemies for good. The particular way he pursued this goal was through a new method, the so-called proscriptions, borrowing from criminal law the punishment of those declared enemies of the state (*hostes*), in which their property was "proscribed," or put on a list for sale. While technically the proscriptions were later recognized as a legal edict of the (later) dictator Sulla, we need to distinguish a particular new element in the proscriptions, namely that those "proscribed" by Sulla and his partisans could not only lose their property but could also be summarily killed by anyone—an element that is not identical, yet clearly similar to, the logic in declaring someone *sacer*.

Caesar, Pompey, Octavian: Towards the Augustan Compromise

The history of the first century BCE in Rome was filled with practically nonstop emergencies and follow-up actions that were consequently subject to debate and, in some cases, even to litigation. Numerous emergencies were declared and ultimate decrees of the senate were passed, yet the murders authorized by these decrees were almost always subject to serious debate. Famously, the legality of killing the tribune Saturninus, which took place in 100 BCE, was the topic of a legal case of Cicero, thirty-seven years later, in 63 BCE.

In the rest of this chapter I want to turn to what I see as the resolution of this seemingly indefatigable debate about who had the right to claim religiously sanctioned power, including the prerogative to declare a person *sacer*. The final resolution was to come from Octavian, who emerged in the political scene starting in 44 BCE as the adoptive son of his uncle, Julius Caesar. It is useful, nevertheless, to start this discussion by analyzing the religious claims of his adoptive father, Julius Caesar himself. These included both traditional and innovative religious powers: he was pontifex maximus, the highest priesthood in Rome, and he also sought unusual privileges, among them a cult for himself, with plans for Mark Antony to become the first priest—plans that came to a halt in 44 BCE when Caesar was murdered.

Most importantly for my argument, Caesar was also involved in a strange ritual that negotiated the boundaries of acceptable and unacceptable sacrifice. Cassius Dio reports that, when in 46 BCE Caesar faced numerous popular protests in Rome, including some mutinous behavior among his own soldiers, he ordered one soldier killed, and

> [t]wo other soldiers were executed in some ritual [*hierourgia*]. The cause for this I cannot say, because neither the Sibyl offered an utterance, nor was there any other such oracle, yet the two men were sacrificed [*etuthesan*] on the Campus Martius in the presence of the *pontifices* and the *flamen* of Mars, and their heads were put up on display on the Regia. (43.24.4)[34]

Given that Dio, who wrote more than 250 years later, is our only source for this event, his sacrificial interpretation of this ritual has been challenged by modern interpreters. Bennett Pascal characterized Dio's depiction as an example of "sarcastic wit" and argued that "the involvement of priests of the republic in an open, hardly legal beheading of Roman citizens is not an imitation of a regular sacrifice but a scandal."[35] But it seems to me a mistake to disregard Dio's interpretation too soon; the sacrificial imagery that he uses may have been relevant to the interpretation of the incident in Caesar's time.

It is useful to compare Dio's language depicting this sacrificial act of Caesar with the language he used to describe another strange ritual, which was performed a few years later, in 37 BCE, by the youngest son of Caesar's archenemy, Pompey. This son, Sextus Pompey, fought and defeated Caesar's adoptive son, Octavian, off the coast of Sicily, and celebrated his victory in the following manner:

[B]ut Sextus was still more elated, believing himself in very truth to be the son of Neptune, and he put on a dark blue robe and cast alive into the strait not only horses but also, as some relate, men as well. (48.48.5–6)[36]

In this case Dio clearly identifies Sextus Pompey as acting as a priest, both in terms of his special robe and his agency in a ritual that may have included human sacrifice. This is quite a contrast to the ritual murders by Julius Caesar in Dio's narrative; there, employing the passive voice, Dio underplays the role Julius Caesar must have taken on, as pontifex maximus, in the ritual performance.

How should we explain this difference in the depiction of these ritual acts? Why is Caesar shown as passive, only partially present while men are killed in an apparently ritual action? Why is Pompey shown so active, acting as the chief priest of what must be some strange religion that includes the killing of men and horses? To my mind, the reason for the difference between Dio's two depictions may result less from differences in the religious nature of these actions than from differences in the actors themselves, and also from the later tradition about Sextus Pompey's interest in unusual forms of ritual. In the mid–first century, Lucan famously depicted Sextus Pompey as initiating a necromancy—that is, a magic ritual in which a dead person was brought back to life through the agency of a witch—in order to communicate with his infamous, long-dead father (*Pharsalia* 6.413–830). That there was a general rhetorical interest in perverted forms of religion in the first century CE, under the rule of Nero, is obvious, among others, from Senecan tragedy. But specifically concerning the strange religious interests of Sextus Pompey, an epigram survives, mistakenly attributed to Seneca, which opens with the following words:

The impious chief of an unspeakable religion, accustomed to learning the fates in advance through human entrails, laid the spasming guts of a free born breast in the flames and broke the ground with a magical incantation. (*Anth. Lat.* 402)[37]

Although the focus of this epigram is on necromancy rather than on human sacrifice, it depicts Sextus again as taking a *leading religious role* himself. He is also identified with the by-name "impious" (*impius*); a subversive use of the word in the case of Sextus Pompey, since he used the name "Pius" to refer to his father's battle cry against Julius Caesar in 45 BCE and to emphasize his own familial obligation to his now-dead father, Pompey the Great.[38] From the point of view of Augustus's later victory, it is easy to forget about the potential of the young Sextus Pompey's religious propaganda in this period, as Augustan representations successfully replaced any positive image of the Pompeys' religious claims with accusations of practicing magical ritual by the early empire.[39] But Sextus Pompey's association with Neptune and his claim to be the descendant of the god was widely known in Rome from the late 40s on.[40] As early as 42 BCE, Sextus had coins minted with Neptune's image, and in 40 BCE a statue of the god entering the Circus in a procession caused enough of an association with Sextus's claim to the god's support that Octavian had it removed from among the other divine images present.[41]

There was thus likely quite a strong connection between Sextus Pompey and Neptune, and also a sense of Pompey's religious agency on behalf of the god, acting as a priest of sorts of either good or bad religion, depending on the perspective of the one describing his religious activities. His sacrifice of horses and possibly also of men then offers an interesting twist on the ways in which we have seen Roman politicians exploit the notion of sacrifice so far: his role in the ritual was not justified through a membership in any one of Rome's priestly colleges, but rather through the direct, personal connection he claimed to have to the god. While the difference is subtle, since priests also acted as agents of a god or gods, it nevertheless suggests that there was a new openness when it came to leaders setting the parameters of ritual. Whether or not one is willing to classify Sextus Pompey's ritual as a proper sacrifice, the validity of the ritual was reinforced and connected to the appreciation of Neptune, the god.

This innovation, namely that Sextus claimed religious authority not through performing the rituals associated with the duties of a Roman priesthood, but rather as a descendant or agent of a god, is similar to rituals performed by Octavian, the adoptive son of Julius Caesar, during his early career, before he became the famously pious emperor we know by the name of Augustus. It is well known that in the aftermath of Caesar's murder in 44 BCE, Octavian was very much looking to gain power by taking revenge against the killers of his adoptive father; details regarding how he joined up with Caesar's former ally, Mark Antony, abound. There were many examples of murder with potentially religious connotations: in 43 BCE the two, together with Lepidus, instituted a new instance of proscriptions; then, in 42, they tracked down and killed Brutus and Cassius, Caesar's murderers, in revenge, at Philippi.

What I am interested in pursuing here, however, is a slightly different religious interpretation of and response to Caesar's death, i. e. that Caesar's murder not only was a wrongful act and thus deserved to be avenged by his dutiful son, but was also a sacrilege, a case of "bad" religion. Our best evidence for the presence of this view is the poetic depiction by Ovid, in his *Fasti*, written during the later years of Augustan rule. In discussing the Ides of March, Ovid hesitantly commemorated the assassination of Julius Caesar, having the goddess Vesta herself speak these words : "[Julius Caesar] was my priest, the sacrilegious hands [*sacrilegae manus*] attacked me with their weapons" (*Fast.* 3.699–700).[42] Understood as a sacrilege, Caesar's murder called for religious revenge—a context that I believe is crucial to understand not only the proscriptions and murders but also some other unusual aspects of Octavian's actions against his enemies.

After the killing of Brutus and Cassius in 42 BCE, the alliance of Octavian and Antony had accomplished its original mission of revenge, and conflicts started to arise between the two. At a particular juncture of this struggle, in late 41 BCE, Octavian faced off against Antony's wife, Fulvia, and his brother, Lucius, at Perusia, to which the two had withdrawn with their legions. A long siege ensued until the surrender of Fulvia and Lucius in 40 BCE, and it is from this siege that fifty-five lead sling-bullets survive that were fired both from inside the city and from the external fortifications, respectively, according to their inscriptions. Many of these sling-bullets carried representations common to such lead bullets, such as thunder-bolts; more unusual, however, were the sexual references that some of these sling-bullets bore in both images and words. As Judith Hallett convincingly suggested, the young Octavian likely used these bullets to parade his masculine prowess in this fight, especially against Antony's wife.[43] There is a rich context against which we can read these sling-bullets, including a later quotation of an epigram attributed to Octavian-Augustus himself, emphasizing his own manliness against Fulvia: they are likely the earliest elements in what later became Augustus's full-blown self-representation as a highly masculine military leader.

What I want to pursue here is another one of these sling-bullets with an inscription that offers insight into the religious aspect of how Octavian represented the conflict. The text reads "*L(egio) XI / Divom / Julium*," or "the 11th Legion for the Divine Julius Caesar"; it must have been intended to be shot into Perusia from Octavian's side.[44] While the notion of a sacrifice is not completely spelled out when a sling-bullet inscribed with the name of the Divine Julius Caesar is fired to kill the enemies of his adoptive son, this bullet nevertheless suggests that the young Octavian may have referred to his campaign against Perusia as a religious mission.

Such a religious reading of the events in Perusia may be the best context in which to examine a gruesome ritual Octavian performed upon the surrender of his enemies in which as many as three hundred members of Perusia's elite perished.[45] As a number of later sources reference it, the altars of Perusia, *arae Perusinae*, included the following, as Suetonius describes:

> After Perusia had been seized, Octavian punished many, and responded to those trying to beg forgiveness or to make excuses with the same retort: "you must die." Some write that three hundred men from among those surrendered were selected, from both orders of senators and knights in Perusia, and sacrificed [*mactatos*], like captured enemies, at an altar raised for Divus Julius on the Ides of March. (Suet., *Aug.* 15)[46]

The language Suetonius employs is clearly sacrificial: the men are slaughtered (*mactatos*), using the same verb describing the killing of sacrificial animals; the scene takes place at an altar. Another description, by Cassius Dio, references this sacrificial interpretation as widely known:

> The leader and some others obtained pardon, but most of the senators and knights were put to death. And the story goes that they did not merely suffer death in an ordinary form, but were led to the altar consecrated to the former Caesar and were there sacrificed—three hundred knights and many senators. (Cass. Dio, 48.14.3–4)[47]

Suetonius and Dio both offer this explanation of the deaths as sacrifice at an altar consecrated to the Divinized Julius Caesar, at an altar inscribed with the same name as the sling-bullet above, namely "Divus Julius." Syme thought that these were primarily judicial murders, which the anti-Augustan propaganda enlarged into a sacrificial scene.[48] While that judicial aspect was likely present as a possible interpretation of events, to my mind the parallel between these post-siege murders and the divine reference inscribed on the sling-bullet suggests that a religious interpretation of the conflict should also be considered as a context in which to read this horrible event. In fact, the perspective of Seneca the Younger may be closer to a change in tone that occurred when Octavian became Augustus, the first emperor— Seneca specifically refers to the altars of Perusia, when he contrasts Octavian-Augustus's early cruelty with his later propaganda of *clementia*:

> Suppose [Augustus] to have shown restraint and clemency—but this was only after the sea at Actium had been stained with Roman blood, only after both his own and his enemy's fleets had been shattered off Sicily, only after the sacrifices at Perusia and the proscriptions.[49]

What connects the altars of Perusia and the sacrifice performed by Sextus Pompey honoring Neptune is that neither leader acts as a traditional Roman priest, but rather as a human who has a direct, personal connection to a god. In the quest to gain exclusive powers, Octavian fully engaged the late republic's openness in terms of pushing the notion of sacrifice to its limits, in Octavian's case by acting as a priestly figure of his divinized adoptive father, Julius Caesar.

Conclusions

As we have seen, political murder was regularly depicted and discussed in sacrificial terms during the late republican period. Thus, the "sacrifice" at the altars of Perusia could well have been perceived as sacrifice indeed, a sacrifice that divided the community into factions on the basis of how this sacrifice/murder was perceived. "Sacrifice" in each of these instances served to divide a community and to distinguish right and wrong by invoking religion. Thus, in my early examples, Nasica and Merula tried to claim divine legitimation for their actions through an emphasis on their traditional priestly roles. Later, Sextus Pompey and Octavian sought to gain a new kind of religious power by emphasizing not a traditional, collegial priestly role, but a direct personal connection between themselves and a divine power. By the end of the late republic, leaders such as Caesar, Sextus, and Octavian had much to gain when they pushed the traditional notion of "good sacrifice" to its limits, thereby proving the vast reach of their own power.

Clearly such competition in sacrificial power as we can see between Sextus and Octavian could not be sustained in a pacified setting. As Octavian reached sole power in 31 BCE and became Augustus, the first emperor of Rome, the representations of sacrifice underwent changes, leaving behind the kind of competitive association with and claim to divine power we have observed above. The end result is the well-known image of the emperor as the prime sacrificer—with his religious power above all those that were attributed to individual priestly colleges in the

Roman tradition.[50] As Andrew Feldherr has shown in his study of the imagery of sacrifice in Livy, the historian forged a strong link between sacrifice and *imperium* (power).[51] As far as we can tell, the story about the ritual at Perusia was left out of Livy's extant works, as it seems to be missing also from Appian's otherwise complete narrative in his *Bellum civile*, written about two hundred years after the Perusia incident, which is especially interesting given that Appian claimed to rely on Augustus's own historical memoirs in writing a history of Augustan Rome. Could Augustus have wished to remove the altars of Perusia from common memory and to depict his sacrificial activities in a different light later on? Quite so. While Appian mentions the deaths of some Perusians as killings (*BC* 5.48), he connects Octavian-Augustus's to a different kind of sacrifice, one that also takes place right after the surrender of the city, yet does not challenge the traditional practice of sacrifice, unlike what we saw in other sources concerning the aftermath of the fall of Perusia:

> the next morning Octavian offered sacrifice, and Lucius sent his soldiers to him bearing their arms, but prepared for marching. They saluted Octavian as imperator while still at some distance, and each legion took its separate position as Octavian had directed, the colonist veterans apart from the new levies. When Octavian had accomplished the sacrifice he took his seat in front of the tribunal, crowned with laurel, the symbol of victory, and ordered them all to lay down their arms where they stood. (*BC* 5.46)

Here the sacrifice is the animal sacrifice of old Roman tradition and is presented as being emphatically under the power of Octavian, who is saluted as *imperator*.[52] We should also note how its end result is different: rather than avenging his father by pursuing his enemies, Octavian reunites the soldiers who have served on opposing sides.

Appian's depiction of Octavian-Augustus offers a notion of sacrifice in which a very powerful, singular leader uses a traditional ritual to reunite groups separated from each other by civil strife. Sacrifice is thus associated with the new message of Augustan rule: the bringing of concord and peace and the practice of *clementia*, which was dependent on the religiously understood capacity of the emperor to provide a resolution to the crisis. To my mind, the model of the emperor as the prime sacrificer grew out of a traditional notion of sacrifice that was, however, expanded in the political struggles of the late republic to allow the prime sacrificer to claim a personal connection to the divine. Thus, the emperor was not only the one who carried out the majority of traditional sacrifices in the name of the Roman people, but also the one who claimed a personal connection to the divine.

Notes

1. I discuss the sources in detail below, but in general our main evidence comes from Plut., *Tib. Gracchus*; App., *BC* 1.35–70; Diod., 34/5.24–27, Vell. Pat., 2.2–3; Livy, *Per.* 58; Val. Max. 1.4.2, 3.2.17. All translations of ancient texts are mine unless identified otherwise.

2. Jerzy Linderski, "The Pontiff and the Tribune: The Death of *Tiberius Gracchus*," *Athenaeum* 90 (2002): 339–66.

3. Giorgio Agamben, *Homo sacer: Il potere sovrano e la nuda vita* (Turin: G. Einaudi, 1995). English translation by Daniel Heller-Roazen, *Homo Sacer: Sovereign Power and Bare Life* (Stanford: Stanford University Press, 1998).

4. Agamben, *Homo sacer,* 83.

5. Carlin Barton, "The Emotional Economy of Sacrifice and Execution in Ancient Rome," *Historical Reflections* 29 (2003): 341–60, 343.

6. J. A. North, "Religion and Politics, from Republic to Principate," *JRS* 76 (1986): 251–58.

7. On the distinctions between what ritual murders the Romans accepted and what they saw as unacceptable, see Celia E. Schultz, "The Romans and Ritual Murder," *JAAR* 78 (2010): 1–26, with earlier literature.

8. A. J. Clark, "Nasica and *Fides*," *CQ* 57 (2007): 125–31, esp. 129; and R. Fiori, *Homo Sacer: dinamica politico-costitutzionale di una sanzione giuridico-religiosa* (Naples: Jovene, 1996), 413–14.

9. 4.68.5: iste interea scelere et malis cogitationibus redundans evolat e templo Iovis: sudans, oculis ardentibus, erecto capillo, contorta toga. [. . .] spumans ex ore scelus, anhelans ex infimo pectore crudelitatem, contorquet brachium et Gracco [. . .] percutit tempus.

10. 4.68.5: *Cum Graccus deos inciperet precari [. . .]. Ille, nulla voce delabans insitam virtutem, concidit tacitus.*

11. Albert Henrichs, "Greek Maenadism from Olympias to Messalina," HSCP 82 (1978): 121–60, at 134–36, usefully contrasts maenadic cult with the image of female religious and sexual excess in Latin literature.

12. Diod. 34/35.7.2.

13. 4.51: *Mihi ne Scipio quidem ille pontifex maximus, qui hoc Stoicorum verum esse declaravit, numquam privatum esse sapientem, iratus videtur fuisse Ti. Graccho tum, cum consulem languentem reliquit atque ipse privatus, ut si consul esset, qui rem publicam salvam esse vellent, se sequi iussit.*

14. Val. Max., 1.6.7.

15. Cic., *De off.* 3.109.

16. Nathan Stewart Rosenstein, "*Imperatores Victi*: The Case of C. Hostilius Mancinus," *CA* 5 (1986): 230–52; Cristopher H. Hallett, *The Roman Nude: Heroic Portrait Statuary 200 B.C.–A.D. 300* (Oxford: Oxford University Press, 2005), 94–96.

17. Vell. Pat., 2.1.5: *dicentes publicam violationem fidei non debere unius lui sanguine.*

18. Barbette Stanley Spaeth, *The Roman Goddess Ceres* (Austin: University of Texas Press, 1996), 73–79.

19. Sextus Aurelius Victor, 64.8; Lea Beness, "The Punishment of the Gracchani and the Execution of C. Villius in 133/132," *Antichthon* 34 (2000): 1–17, at 1.

20. Caesar, *B. Civ.* 1,5,3 and Livy, *AUC* 3,4,9: *ne quid detrimenti res publica capiat.*

21. Fiori, *Homo Sacer,* 441–45.

22. Plut., *G. Gracchus* 17.4.5 (murders) 18.3 (worship).

23. Harriet I. Flower, *The Art of Forgetting: Disgrace and Oblivion in Roman Political Culture* (Chapel Hill: University of North Carolina Press, 2006), 79.

24. Plin. (E), *NH* 30.1.12.

25. Plut., *Tib. Gracchus* 8.6. Note Suzanne Dixon, *Cornelia: Mother of the Gracchi* (London: Routledge, 2007), 33–48, describing these conflict as "culture wars." cf.

26. *Merula flamen Dialis in Capitolio Iovis ipsius oculos venarum cruore respersit.*

27. *Merula autem, qui se sub adventum Cinnae consulatu abdicaverat, incisis venis superfusoque altaribus sanguine, quos saepe pro salute rei publicae flamen dialis precatus erat deos, eos in execrationem Cinnae partiumque eius tum precatus optime de re publica meritum spiritum reddidit.*

28. By the time of Cicero, *execratio* could be used in a generic sense to mean a regular curse without any significant religious implications, but this case is clearly different.

29. *Si prior defexit publico consilio dolo malo, tum ille Diespiter populum Romanum sic ferito ut ego hunc porcum hic hodie feriam; tantoque magis ferito quanto magis potes pollesque.*

30. Plin. (Y), *Pan.* 64: *explanavit verba quibus caput suum, domum suam, si sciens fefellisset, deorum irae consecraret.*

31. Μερόλας μὲν τὰς φλέβας ἐνέτεμεν ἑαυτοῦ, καὶ πινάκιον αὐτῷ παρακείμενον ἐδήλου, ὅτι κόπτων τὰς φλέβας τὸν πῖλον ἀποθοῖτο (οὐ γὰρ ἦν θεμιτὸν ἱερέα περικείμενον τελευτᾶν.

32. (*Quum*) *area et alia dis sacrata supplicum sanguine foedarentur.* Translated by McGushin. Frg. 1.38 (McGushin, *Historiae*) = frg. 26 (Kritz, *Fragmenta*) = Servius, *Comm. Ad Aen.* 2.502. Kritz connected the fragment to Merula's death, although whether Merula was a suppliant is of course debatable. McGushin placed the fragment after Sulla's victory at the Colline Gate in 82 BCE.

33. Cic., *Nat. D.* 3.32.8; *De oratore* 3.3.10. Cf. Ovid's claim that there was no statue of Vesta in the sanctuary (*Fast.* 6.295–98). The murder of Scaevola was also discussed by Augustine as a sacrilege (*De civ. D.* 3.28); this view, however, is more relevant in terms of Scaevola's scholarly achievements in religious law. See also Livy, *Per.* 86.

34. ἄλλοι δὲ δύο ἄνδρες ἐν τρόπῳ τινὶ ἱερουργίας ἐσφάγησαν. καὶ τὸ μὲν αἴτιον οὐκ ἔχω εἰπεῖν οὔτε γὰρ ἡ Σίβυλλα ἔχρησεν, οὔτ' ἄλλο τι τοιοῦτο λόγιον ἐγένετο, ἐν δ' οὖν τῷ Ἀρείῳ πεδίῳ πρός τε τῶν ποντιφίκων καὶ πρὸς τοῦ ἱερέως τοῦ Ἄρεως ἐτύθησαν, καὶ αἵ γε κεφαλαὶ αὐτῶν πρὸς τὸ βασίλειον ἀνετέθησαν.

35. Cecil Bennett Pascal, "October Horse," *HSCP* 85 (1981): 261–91, at 263.

36. καὶ διὰ τοῦτο ὅ τε Καῖσαρ τῆς μὲν Σικελίας ἀπέγνω, τῆς δ' ἠπεί-ρου τῆς παραθαλασσίας φυλακὴν ἀγαπητῶς ἐποιήσατο, καὶ ὁ Σέξτος ἔτι καὶ μᾶλλον ἤρθη, καὶ τοῦ τε Ποσειδῶνος υἱὸς ὄντως ἐπίστευεν εἶναι, καὶ στολὴν κυανοειδῆ ἐνεδύσατο, ἵππους τε, καὶ ὥς γέ τινές φασι, καὶ ἄνδρας ἐς τὸν πορθμὸν ζῶντας ἐνέβαλε.

37. *Fatas per humanas solitus praenoscere fibras / impius infandae religionis apex / pectoris ingenui salientia viscera flammis / imposuit, magico carmine rupit humum.* Translated by Daniel Ogden in *Magic, Witchcraft and Ghosts in the Greek and Roman Worlds: A Sourcebook* (London: Oxford University Press, 2007), number 147.

38. On Pompey the Great's call for *pietas,* see App., *BC* 2.104.430. For Pompey's *pietas* coins, see *RRC* 477.

39. Cf. the report in Pliny the Elder (*NH* 7.178–79) on a soldier returning from death to prophesize Sextus Pompey's success in the Sicilian War (38–36 BCE). R. Grenade, "Le mythe de Pompée et les pompéians sou les Césars," *REA* 52 (1950): 28–63, 32, referencing Tac., *Ann.* 3.22–23, 16.31. See the useful comments by Mary Beagon, *The Elder Pliny on the Human Animal,* Natural History Book 7 (Oxford: Clarendon, 2005), 400–401.

40. Hor., *Epodes* 9.7–8: *Neptunius dux.*

41. On Pompey's Neptune coins, see *RRC* 511, ca. 42–40 BCE. On the Neptune statue incident, see Suet., *Aug.* 16, and Cass.Dio 48.31.

42. *"meus fuit ille sacerdos; / sacrilegae telis me petiere manus."* Cf. the later consensus that Caesar's murderers all met their ends through the revenge of Augustus. Geraldine Herbert-Brown, *Ovid and the Fasti: An Historical Study* (Oxford: Oxford University Press, 1994), 125–26.

43. Judith P. Hallett, *"Perusinae glandes* and the Changing Image of Augustus," *AJAH* 2 (1977): 151–71.

44. John Osgood, *Caesar's Legacy: Civil War and the Emergence of the Roman Empire* (Cambridge: Cambridge University Press, 2006), 166–67. The sling-bullet cited is CIL XI 6721, nr. 26 = *EE* 6.77.

45. Alison Futrell, *Blood in the Arena. The Spectacle of Roman Power* (Austin: University of Texas Press, 1997), 196.

46. *Perusia capta in plurimos animadvertit, orare veniam vel excusare se conantibus una voce occurrens "moriendum esse." Scribunt quidam trecentos ex dediticiis electos utriusque ordinis ad aram Divo Iulio exstructam Idibus Martiis hostiarum more mactatos.*

47. καὶ αὐτὸς μὲν ἄλλοι τέ τινες ἄδειαν εὕροντο, οἱ δὲ δὴ πλείους τῶν τε βουλευτῶν καὶ τῶν ἱππέων ἐφθάρησαν. καὶ λόγος γε ἔχει ὅτι οὐδ᾽ ἁπλῶς τοῦτο ἔπαθον, ἀλλ᾽ ἐπὶ τὸν βωμὸν τὸν τῷ Καίσαρι τῷ προτέρῳ ὡσιω- μένον ἀχθέντες ἱππῆς τε τριακόσιοι καὶ βουλευταὶ ἄλλοι τε καὶ ὁ Καννούτιος ὁ Τιβέριος, ὅς ποτε ἐν τῇ δημαρχίᾳ τὸ πλῆθος τῷ Καίσαρι τῷ Ὀκταουιανῷ ἤθροισεν, ἐτύθησαν.

48. Ronald Syme, *The Roman Revolution* (Oxford: Clarendon, 1939), 212.

49. Sen., *Clem.* 1.11.1: *fuerit moderatus et clemens, nempe post mare Actiacum Romano cruore infectum, nempe post fractas in Sicilia classes et suas et alienas, nempe post Perusinas aras et proscriptiones.* Text and English translation from Susanna Braund, *De clementia* (Oxford: Oxford University Press, 2009).

50. Richard Gordon, "The Veil of Power: Emperors, Sacrificers, and Benefactors," in *Pagan Priests: Religion and Power in the Ancient World*, edited by Mary Beard and John North. (Ithaca: Cornell University Press, 1990), 199–231, at 202–206.

51. Andrew Feldherr, *Spectacle and Society in Livy's History* (Berkeley: University of California Press 1998), 155–64.

52. See Feldherr, *Spectacle and Society*, 153–54.

7

The Embarrassment of Blood

EARLY CHRISTIANS AND OTHERS ON SACRIFICE, WAR, AND RATIONAL WORSHIP

Laura Nasrallah

The Column of Trajan was dedicated by the Senate and people of Rome in 113 CE, paid for by the booty from the Dacian wars of 101–2 and 105–6 CE.[1] It stands in the center of the library of the Forum of Trajan in Rome and rises over 40 meters (131 feet) to celebrate Trajan's victory over Dacia. As the images wind upwards, scenes of sacrifice function visually as a peaceful pause in the midst of the bloodiness of war; and within scenes of sacrifice, as is typical of depictions of the Roman period, there is little violence, no blood. As Inez Ryberg and Richard Gordon have argued, in such reliefs the pious emperor becomes the focus of the sacrifice, rather than the straining animal.[2]

In several scenes from the column, we find this juxtaposition of quiet and chaos and see how the emperor is usually distanced from blood of two sorts: blood in war and blood in sacrifice. In one scene, for example, the emperor, a flute player, and military officials—shields tucked under arms, standards high—stand within a walled enclosure (fig. 7.1). The scene-within-a-scene is visually controlled, a quiet *pietas* surrounded by pious busyness. Immediately outside the walls, flute players lead in the victims of the *suovetaurilia;* the ox turns its head away, its horn grasped by the strong right arm of a public slave. Behind are the *victimarii,* carrying axes high.

Two themes emerge from this representation of sacrifice that will echo throughout this chapter. First, the relief brings together a sliding scale of beings that range from the animal to the divine: animals for sacrifice, slaves (who were considered less rational than citizen men and dwelt in the in-between space as both things and people), the emperor, and the hint of the emperor-as-god, since the Column of Trajan was to house the ashes of Trajan and within the forum was a temple of the deified Trajan. The column thus prepares us for texts we shall encounter later in this chapter—texts that state that humans are the highest form of sacrifice to the gods, and texts that argue that the gods must be like humans if they need the food of sacrifice. Second, on the column, the sacrifice and its attendant blood and killing are only

FIGURE 7.1 *The emperor offers a lustration in a secure camp.*
Source: Column of Trajan, Rome. DAIR 89.714.

potential: that is to be expected from iconographic conventions for sacrifice scenes and given the reality that elite males when sacrificing had others to perform the dirty work. But even the potential for blood is walled off from the emperor who, *capite velato,* enclosed in the circular drape of the toga's heavy fabric, piously pours wine or offers mcens on the altar.[3] How is the blood (or the lack of it) in animal sacrifice part of a larger rhetoric of piety?

This clean scene of sacrifice—and others like it on the column—contrasts with the more frequently recurring scenes of the busy, banal, muscular activity of war's preparations and aftermaths, as well as war itself. They also contrast with the jumble of shields and bodies in war (fig. 7.2). In one scene, a helmeted Roman soldier catches the long hair of a Dacian soldier to pull his head back; another raises his right arm likely to spear a kneeling Dacian. Another Dacian has tumbled head first on the ground, and, further, a Dacian sinks down, straining to push up his torso as his head droops. Above all this, an inverted triangle of space separates the

FIGURE 7.2 *Combat scene.*
Source: Column of Trajan, Rome. DAIR 89.660.

emperor and some of his men from the chaos and brutality of the scene. Yet, elsewhere on the column, Roman soldiers thrust the severed heads of Dacians toward
the emperor, who is wearing military garb, as their comrades in the next scene turn
to another slaughter (fig. 7.3).[4] This is an exception to Natalie Boymel Kampen's
otherwise apt analysis of the "emperor's remove from violence." In the visual rhetoric of the column, Trajan is usually an exemplar of *moderatio, humanitas,* and
manly reserve.[5] Such iconographic choices are common in the early empire; in fact,
the visual rhetoric of the Column of Trajan draws in part from scenes like those
on the Altar of Peace (*Ara Pacis*), where military struggle is celebrated and yet not
depicted, and the imperial family piously processes forward to sacrifice.

Yet, amid this widespread imperial rhetoric of piety and quiet control even in
war, on the Column of Trajan there is the disquieting scene of Dacians' decapita-
tions and the proffering of their heads to the emperor Trajan. The tension between
this bloody scene and the quiet, "unbloody" piety of sacrifice inspired this chapter
and its purpose: to trace several participants, Christian and not, in ancient discussions about human sacrifice to the gods.

In the first and second centuries CE, there were at least four discourses on human
sacrifice. First, as expected, we find accusations of human sacrifice that function
polemically to distinguish one cult (a barbarous, wrong-headed one) or time period
(an ancient, primitive one) from one's own cult or ongoing religious practices. Second, we find discussion of humans as appropriate, living, rational sacrifices to the
gods, if the humans are properly formed by philosophical or theological practices.

FIGURE 7.3 *Roman soldiers proffer severed heads of Dacians to the Emperor Trajan.*
Source: Relief from Column of Trajan, Rome. Column of Trajan, Rome. DAIR 41.1455.

Third, we find Christ's death or Christians' deaths in martyrdom described as a form of sacrifice.

This chapter explores the fourth discussion, which lies at the intersection of theological and political debate. A work like the Column of Trajan both asserts and denies the connection between war and sacrifice. Sacrifice is necessary for pious war, but the reliefs on the column distance the death of the human in war from the clean and organized deaths of animals in sacrifice. On the one hand, this chapter explores some ancient literature and imagery that juxtapose warfare and human sacrifice to the gods, often in order to critique both war *and* sacrifice. In the Roman period, there is an elite philosophical-theological embarrassment at the idea of human sacrifice, and indeed sometimes at the idea of animal sacrifice. Polemic against sacrificial practices is often intertwined with a concern about violence and the possibility that the human animal could be considered a legitimate sacrifice offered to the gods. On the other hand, this chapter investigates another ancient discourse, one that celebrates war and presents the death of the enemy as a kind of pious sacrifice, and thus subtly reclaims human sacrifice in a visual rhetoric of martial threat and pride. As we shall see, the idea of war as human sacrifice is intertwined with a theological debate about the economy of sacrifice and what might be the most costly sacrifice one could offer to God or the gods: the human animal.

Christian Critiques of Sacrifice

JEWISH AND GREEK SACRIFICE AND CHRISTIAN SELF-DEFINITION

Before moving to texts of human sacrifice, we should understand the broader context of the term; we should recognize the problem of the modern term *sacrifice,* and we should see how ancient Christians use sacrifice as a means of self-definition. Scholars of religion and classics have sometimes rejected the term *sacrifice* as a modern, Christianizing imposition on antiquity. Is *ritual killing* a better term—or, in the case of human death for the gods, *ritual murder?*[26] Or should one rename sacrifice as tasty barbeque with a "comedy of innocence," to use Karl Meuli's phrase, to keep everyone from feeling badly about the death of an animal? Such debates about terminology are important. In the sources used in this chapter, however, it makes sense to use the term *sacrifice* because so-called Christian apologists, among other writers, lump together various ethnoreligious rituals and critique them under the rubric of "sacrifice," often using the Greek term *thusia* and its cognates. Christians write in the midst of a range of sacrificial practices: the pouring of libations, the burning of incense, the slaughter of animals. They engage this world critically, taking back the term *sacrifice* (perhaps broadly, carelessly, and often polemically) and even use it to define Christian piety and identity. This strategy is not unique to Christians; other educated elites questioned the need for sacrifice, especially bloody animal sacrifice, even if they and their Christian co-philosophers were a minority voice. *Sacrifice* is a term we can legitimately trace not because it signifies one precise thing or the apex of "pagan" ritual, but because it is a polemical category used by ancient authors.[7]

"Sacrifice" is an unsubtle knife by which Christians, among others, differentiate themselves from others on two fronts as they philosophically debate (and deliberately misinterpret) the sacrificial practices of their proximate others. On the one hand, Christians insist that cults of the Greco-Roman world are so intellectually boorish as to believe that their insensate, material, statuary gods need material food. The *Epistle to Diognetus* provides a good example, famously distinguishing Christians as a "new race" in relation to Greeks' consideration of the gods (and Jews' *deisidaimonia,* or superstition) (*Diog* 1). Christian *theosebeia,* or piety, the author argues, rejects Greek sacrificial practices. These practices are laughable because the dumb gods—that is, their statuary images—cannot even open their mouths to swallow the sacrifices of blood and fat (*Diog* 2).[8]

On the other hand, Christians insist that they also differ from Jews because of sacrificial practice. The *Epistle to Diognetus* postdates the destruction of the temple in Jerusalem in 70 CE, yet cites Jewish sacrificial practices in order to articulate Christian difference.[9] According to the epistle, Jews abstain from "the aforementioned *latreia*" (*Diog* 3)—that is, Greek sacrifices—and worship one God, yet fail in their sacrifices. Both Jews and Greeks misapprehend the Divine; and the ignorance of both groups is precisely exposed in their sacrificial rites:

> But those who suppose they are performing the sacrifices of blood and fat and whole burnt offerings, and thereby to be bestowing honor on him by these displays of reverence, seem no different to me from those who show the same honor to the gods who are deaf—one group giving to gods who cannot receive the honor, the other thinking that it can provide something to the one who needs nothing. (*Diog* 3)[10]

SACRIFICE AS PHILOSOPHICAL CONFUSION

Christians thus use animal sacrifice to define who they are in contrast to religious others. Justin Martyr, writing in the mid–second century CE, exemplifies another early Christian rhetoric of sacrifice, in which sacrifice reveals non-Christians' antiphilosophical stance and inability to set a sensible boundary between the animal and the Divine. "This is the only thing of which you accuse us: that we do not worship the same gods as you, nor do we bring to those who are dead drink-offerings and fat cauls and crowns and sacrifices, in their graves," complains Justin. But he then points to the illogic of such an accusation: "For you know that the same things are considered precisely by some to be gods, by some wild animals, by some sacrificial victims" (*1 Apol.* 24.3).[11] Writing just after Justin, the Christian Tatian makes the point with more vigor: "Why have you stolen away my God? Why are you dishonoring God's creation? You sacrifice a sheep, and you worship the same. There is a bull in heaven, and you slaughter its image" (*Ad Gr.* 10.2).[12] How can a religious system have any coherence if a god is an animal (that is, is represented by one), and yet an animal is slaughtered for the god?[13]

First- and second-century discussions of sacrifice sometimes become a moment for theological reflection upon the varied worth of human and animal life. Such discussions open the possibility that animal, human, and god are not divided by ontological chasms, but belong on a sliding scale of being.[14] In the last quarter of the third century, for instance, Porphyry argues that the first sacrifices to the gods were crops; then, neglecting holiness and in a state of famine, people ate each other and offered human sacrifices to the gods. Eventually, other animals became substitute sacrifices for human sacrifice (*Abst.* 2.27). The crop, the human, and the animal are all placed upon the altar in Porphyry's history, but his larger argument is that the true God does not require such sacrifices. Animal sacrifice was for Porphyry a devolution from truly pious practice, in part because it represents a misunderstanding of the kinship between human and animal.[15] Appropriate sacrifice should instead occur through pure thoughts and "our own uplifting as a holy sacrifice to god [τὴν αὐτῶν ἀναγωγὴν θυσίαν ἱερὰν προσάγειν τῷ θεῷ] (*Abst.* 2.34): he suggests a very different form of human sacrifice. Where does the human belong in the social and ontological order, and how may s/he be a fit sacrifice?

HUMAN SACRIFICE AS RATIONAL WORSHIP

The ancient world was busy with philosophical arguments of this type, but it was even more clogged with the accoutrements and architecture that supported sacrifice—large altars that themselves were architectural phenomena, such as the great altar at Pergamon; small-scale *bōmoi;* pedestals that served as altars; shovels for incense; tiny votive altars with equally tiny inscriptions and reliefs; and the like.[16] Christians in the midst of this environment used sacrifice (a particular kind of sacrifice and a particular characterization of it) to sharpen Christian self-definition: Christians were those who did not sacrifice.

Yet Christians also used the terminology of sacrifice, even of human sacrifice, in positive ways for Christian self-definition. Paul, that Jew-in-Christ, had offered in the mid–first century an image of a sort of human sacrifice:

> Therefore I entreat you, brothers and sisters, by the mercies of God, to present your bodies a sacrifice, living, holy, well-pleasing to God—your rational worship. [Παρακαλῶ οὖν ὑμᾶς, ἀδελφοί, διὰ τῶν οἰκτιρμῶν τοῦ θεοῦ παραστῆσαι τὰ σώματα ὑμῶν θυσίαν ζῶσαν ἁγίαν εὐάρεστον τῷ θεῷ, τὴν λογικὴν λατρείαν ὑμῶν.] (Rom 12:1)[17]

Paul enjoins the Romans whom he addresses to crawl onto the altar to become one sacrifice, but one that is rational worship or service to the gods. In ca. 176 CE, the Christian apologist Athenagoras takes up Paul's writing in Romans 12:1 in his defense of Christianity against charges of atheism, charges launched because Christians refused to sacrifice. His opponents "don't know—even dimly—what God is, and are unlearned and unable to perceive natural or theological reason, measuring piety in terms of sacrifices [μετροῦντες τὴν εὐσέβειαν θυσιῶν νόμῳ]" (*Leg.* 13.1).[18] You can nearly picture the heaped bodies of animals. Christians instead know that:

> The creator and father of all does not need blood or fat or the fragrance of flowers and incense. . . . but the best sacrifice to him is if we know who spread out the heavens and made them spheres. . . . We lift holy hands to him; of what kind of hecatomb does he have need?! "And with sacrifices and pleasing vows people move them [the gods], with libation and savory smoke, beseeching, when someone transgresses and sins" [Hom., *Il.* 9.499–501]. But what do I have to do with whole burnt offerings, which God has no need of? And what do I have to do with making offerings? What is necessary is bloodless sacrifice: to move towards rational worship [δέον ἀναίμακτον θυσίαν τὴν λογικὴν προσάγειν λατρείαν]. (*Leg.* 13.2–4)

For Athenagoras, via Paul, a truly pious human has nothing to do with sacrifice as traditionally construed, because God has no needs (see Rom 11:35–36). Sacrifice to this needless deity takes the form of human knowledge of God as creator who stretched out the heavens, on the one hand, and human rational worship, on the other. In making this argument, of course, Athenagoras draws on a long tradition within Judaism and Greek thought, especially as represented later in the Hermetic tradition, of understanding ethically and theologically correct human behavior to *be* sacrifice.[19] Porphyry himself moved from the image of impious, bloody human sacrifice to the idea that humans become sacrifices to God if they direct their thoughts purely and philosophically.

SACRIFICE AND CHEATING THE GODS

Christians are not the only ones to reform ideas about sacrifice. They participate in a broader satire of religion and, more specifically, a satire of the economics of sacrifice. Among others, they ask: How do humans, even as they enact pious gestures, seek to cheat the gods? What kind of sacrifice is it that the gods most desire? Could the gods desire the human animal for sacrifice?

There is, of course, the story of Prometheus duping Zeus, offering him the choice of sacrifice: glistening fat (but wrapped around hard thigh bones) or the stinking guts of an animal (into which was stuffed nutritious meat). The Christian writer Clement of Alexandria alludes to this episode when writing about God's anatomy. God does not need "sacrifice" (*thusia*) because God has no hunger or creaturely needs:

> To bring food to one who is not nourished is stupid. And that comic poet Pherecrates, in *The Fugitives,* wittily represents the gods themselves as finding fault with humans because of their offerings [τῶν ἱερῶν]: "When you sacrifice to the gods, you first of all set apart what is esteemed among the sacrifices for yourselves—it is a shame to say—well and with care stripping off all meat around both thighs until the groins, and the beloved loins, you distribute what remains—the vertebrae, which you scraped with a file—to us as if we were dogs." (*Strom.* 7.6.30)[20]

Clement goes on to contrast the cleanliness and purity of Christian sacrifice:

> For the sacrifice of the Church is the word rising as smoke [ἀναθυμιώμενος] from holy souls, while at the same time the entire mind [διανοίας] is unveiled in sacrifice to God. But they have babbled about the most ancient, pure altar in Delos, to which they say indeed even Pythagoras alone approached, since it was not polluted by murder and death, but they do not believe us when we say that a just soul is a truly holy altar, and sacred prayer is its [the soul's] incense. But I think that sacrifices are an excuse, contrived by humans, for eating flesh [σαρκοφαγιῶν]. (*Strom.* 7.6.32)

Clement does not even need to invent his own invective against sacrifice; he merely borrows from the traditional pagan stand-up comedy and its philosophical roots. The idea that animal sacrifice was linked to humans' unfortunate gluttony for meat is famously found in Porphyry.[21] Clement frames such ideas with Christian insights, where the human becomes an altar and prayer becomes incense ascending.[22]

Clement said that sacrifice cheated the gods, who received only scraped bones. According to the mid-second-century satirist Lucian, also discussed by Fritz Graf in this volume, the gods have in fact noticed the problem and feel cheated. *On Sacrifices* depicts the gods peering over the edge of heaven; they "gaze about in every direction, leaning down to see if they can see fire being lighted anywhere, or steam drifting up to them 'about the smoke entwined.' If anybody sacrifices, they all have a feast, opening their mouths for the smoke and drinking the blood that is spilt at the altars, just like flies; but if they dine at home, their meal is nectar and ambrosia" (*De sacr.* 9).[23] Elsewhere Lucian offers a picture of religion in crisis: humans have figured out that the gods too are ruled by Fate (*Heimarmenē*) (*Iupp. conf.* 11), and thus are turning away from the gods and from sacrificial rites, leaving the gods in danger of loneliness and hunger (*Iupp. trag.* 14). Zeus himself reflects upon the decline of sacrifice—and the economy of sacrifice—when he mentions the sacrificially stingy ship captain Mnesitheus: "To feast sixteen gods he had sacrificed only a cock, and a wheezy old cock at that, and four little cakes of frankincense that were thoroughly well mildewed . . . and yet he had promised whole herds of cattle while the ship was drifting on the rock and was inside the ledges" (*Iupp. trag.* 15).[24] Lucian satirizes the symbolics of sacrifice, as well as the whining gods who depend upon humans for their dinners.

Lucian implies that there is an economy of sacrifices: one either cheats the gods, as did Mnesitheus, or, alternatively, offers what one can afford. Lucian says that "the poor man . . . propitiates the god by just kissing his own hand" (*De sacr.* 12).[25] The farmer offers an ox; the shepherd, a lamb; the goatherd, a goat; someone else, incense or a cake. Lucian's description of the pan-Mediterranean diversity of sacrifice accelerates: "The Scythian, in fact, rejecting all sacrifices and considering them too humble, offers humans to Artemis, and thus pleases the goddess" (*De sacr.* 13).[26] Lucian gleefully crescendos from the quiet of kissing one's hand to the extreme of human sacrifice: perhaps, the Scythian ascends to the height of piety by offering the richest animal sacrifice of all— the human.[27]

A sliding scale of sacrifices reaches its apex at human sacrifice. Together Clement and Lucian, Christian and non-Christian, reveal some of the broader questions about sacrifice at their time: What is a proper sacrifice, in the midst of the diversity of contemporaneous practices and ancient traditions of sacrifice? What is a sacrifice worth? How much do you have to pay to compensate the gods, to feed their hunger, to receive their efficacious attentions? Might the gods even desire human sacrifice—the best animal, the most expensive of all? Christians thus shared in a mockery of human sacrifice, but this was a risky rhetorical move for them, given that Christians sometimes embraced the rhetoric of human-as-sacrifice.

Human Sacrifice

Christians indulge their own rhetoric of human sacrifice, for example, using the imagery of sacrifice to talk about Jesus: "Christ our *pascha* has been sacrificed [τὸ πάσχα ἡμῶν ἐτύθη Χριστός] (1 Cor 5:7).[28] Hebrews depicts Christ as both high priest and sacrifice (e.g., Heb 7:27). Christians sometimes equate persecution in the arena with sacrifice. Ignatius of Antioch begs: "Rather, coax the wild beasts, so that they may become my grave and leave behind nothing of my body, lest I in my death should become a burden to anyone. . . . Entreat Christ on my behalf, that I may be found a sacrifice to god through these instruments" (*Rom.* 4.2). In the *Martyrdom of Polycarp,* Polycarp will not sacrifice on behalf of Caesar (8.2), and thus he becomes a sacrifice: "He was like a remarkable ram from a great herd for an offering, prepared as a whole burnt offering acceptable to God" (14.1).

Thus some first- and second-century Christians, amid political and religious pressure and in the context of a foundational narrative of violent death, employ a rhetoric of human sacrifice positively. But many other Christian texts do not understand their Christ or themselves (in *imitatio Christi* or, in the case of Ignatius, *imitatio Pauli*) to be sacrificial victims. They engage another, different rhetorical deployment of the image of human sacrifice, participating in a larger trend where accusations of human sacrifice functioned to mark civilized and barbarian, as James Rives has shown. This rhetoric could be employed against distant peoples; it could also be employed within one's own community to make the proximate distant, as in Cicero's hints regarding Catiline: one's opponent is vilified as the sort of person who would guzzle human blood.[29] Even if Pliny declares proudly that the Roman senate officially outlawed human sacrifice in 97 BCE (*NH* 30.13),[30] Christians adopt the rhetoric of human sacrifice and even accuse the Romans of it in order to define "pagan" religion as depraved. In doing so, Christians may respond to similar accusations directed at themselves, as has long been suggested of the Roman governor Pliny's report to Trajan: he investigated Christians only to find that they engaged in a common and innocent meal (*cibum promiscuum tamen et innoxium,* Plin. [Y], *Ep.* 10.96.7). Christians grasp the rhetoric of human sacrifice at the hilt, turning the blade outwards.

In speaking of Romans as human-sacrificers, Christians question Roman piety. Tatian, who takes back the term *barbarian* for Christian identity and works to destabilize claims to civilization and high culture everywhere,[31] calumnies practices of human sacrifice: "I discovered that, among the Romans, their own Zeus Latiaris was delighted by human gore and blood from human slaughter [*androktasiōn*], and Artemis, not far from the great city, receives another form of the same things" (*Ad Gr.* 29). Minucius Felix's *Octavius,* which dates to the late second century or early third and is set in Ostia, treats the accusation that Christians engage in a form of human sacrifice, covering infants with dough, ripping their limbs, and sipping up the blood (*Oct.* 9.5). In response, he presses the same charge against other cults.

As Rives has shown, Minucius Felix quickly links present-day practices of infant exposure and abortion to sacrificial practices, and then offers a rhetorical climax:

> In some parts of Africa, infants are sacrificed to him [Saturn] by their parents, who stifle their squalling by caresses and kisses to prevent the sacrifice of a tearful victim. Moreover, it was a custom among the Taurians on the Black Sea and for the Egyptian king Busiris to sacrifice strangers, as it was with the Gauls to slay human, or rather inhuman, victims. It was a sacrifice peculiar to the Romans to bury alive a Greek man and woman, and a Gallic man and woman. Even today, their worship of Jupiter Latiaris includes a human sacrifice, and, as befits the son of Saturn, he gorges upon the blood of a scoundrel and evil-doer. (*Oct.* 30.3–4)[32]

Minucius Felix draws together diverse evidence of human sacrifice.[33] He also links explicitly barbarian practices—who had not heard of, or mocked, Carthaginian child sacrifice (?!)—with Roman practices. This hodgepodge of *exempla* links what some would claim was the center of civilization, Rome, with its margins, and challenges claims of Roman piety.

Such rhetoric is not a Christian invention. Plutarch especially works through the issues of sacrifice and superstition, even addressing questions of the Romans and human sacrifice. He writes that the Romans critique the Blentonesii as "barbarians" for their "sacrificing a person to the gods [ἄνθρωπον τεθυκέναι θεοῖς]," and yet the Romans themselves "not many years before, had buried alive two men and two women, two of them Greeks, two Gauls, in the place called the Forum Boarium" (*Quaest. Rom.* 83; *Mor.* 283F).[34] Indeed, as Zsuzsanna Várhelyi points out with regard to the 97 BCE legislation forbidding the *immolatio* of humans: "this official disclaimer on the part of the Roman elite through legislation unmistakably marked how Hellenized Romans had grown uncomfortable with the involvement of human victims as part of a legitimate religious ritual by the early first century B.C.E."[35] First-century sources writing about the burial of Greeks and Gauls—a burial to which Plutarch affixes the verb *thuein*, "to sacrifice"—disavow the practice even as they retain traces that such a republican-period ritual may have been a way of dealing with threats, past or future, from enemies external to Rome.[36] As Várhelyi shows, Roman authors record with some fascination the ritual killing of enemies: Plutarch mentions the stoning of enemy victims of the general Philopoemen (182 B.C.E.) at his burial (*Phil.* 21); Strabo, the Cimbri priestesses who cut the throats of prisoners of war in religious ritual (*Geog.* 7.3); Servius's later commentary on Vergil's *Aeneid* claims to record the precise moment when the Romans shifted from the killing of captives at the funerals of great men to the presentation of gladiatorial games instead (Verg. *Aen.* 3.67).[37] And there is, of course, the practice of the general in war sacrificing himself in the ritual of *devotio*.[38]

Elsewhere in Plutarch we find another convergence of war and sacrifice. One speaker compares festivals and sacrifices of the mysteries to unlucky and sad days, during which there are eatings of raw flesh and tearing apart [of victims]. . . . I should say that [such] gentling and persuasive [measures] are fulfilled for none of the gods, but for averting evil *daimones*. And it is not plausible that the gods demand or welcome the ancient deeds of human sacrifice [ἀνθρωποθυσίας], nor would kings and generals have offered up their children for no reason, giving them over and beginning the sacrificial ceremonies and cutting their throats, except for the purpose of making atonement to and appeasing the anger and sullenness of difficult and peevish avenging spirits. . . . Powerful and violent *daimones,* in demanding a human soul surrounded by a body, bring plagues upon a state and sterility upon the earth, and stir up wars and discords, until they obtain and take what they desire [καὶ πολέμους καὶ σ τάσεις ταράττουσιν, ἄχρι οὗ λάβωσι καὶ τύχωσιν οὗ ἐρῶσιν]. (*Mor.* 417 D–E [*De def. or.*])

Non-Christian writers made it easy for Christians to argue about the depravity of sacrifice. The Christian Athenagoras uses a rhetoric that approaches the non-Christian Plutarch's in its goriness. He argues that some sacred images are efficacious and have healing powers, but that this is because they are inhabited by *daimones* hungry for sacrifice: "These *daimones* that we have been discussing are also those who drag people to the images; they stick close to the blood of the sacrificial animals and lick these up" (*Leg.* 26.1).[39] The non-Christian Porphyry would echo this viewpoint a century later.[40]

Warfare as Human Sacrifice

Thus not only a Christian, but also "pagans"—and a priest of Apollo, no less—say that religion and sacrifice have gone wrong because of evil daimonic forces. In the last quotation from Plutarch, we see that he certainly juxtaposes human sacrifice to war and discord, both with his use of the term *anthrōpothusia* (human sacrifice) to talk about kings and generals sacrificing their children (presumably before war, as with Iphigenia) and with his statement that "powerful and violent *daimones,* in demanding a human soul surrounded by a body, . . . stir up wars and discords, until they obtain and take what they desire" (*Mor.* 417E). Does Plutarch suggest that war is another instance of human sacrifice, even if it is different from the Roman republican-period ritual murder in the Forum Boarum, or different from the human-as-"living, holy sacrifice, well-pleasing to God" in Romans 12:1?

We find Plutarch's link between human sacrifice and some forms of violence, including the violence of war, more explicitly articulated in Christian apologetic sources. Tatian polemically implies that human death—not in war, but in the arena, for sport—is a form of depraved pagan sacrifice:

Some are so abandoned as to make a profession of idleness and actually sell themselves to be murdered; the hungry person sells him or herself and the

rich person buys the murders-to-be. . . . You sacrifice animals in order to eat
meat[41] and you buy humans to provide human slaughter for the soul, feeding
it with bloodshed of the most ungodly kind [θύετε ζῷα διὰ τὴν κρεωφαγίαν
καὶ ἀνθρώπους ὠνεῖσθε τῇ ψυχῇ [διὰ] τὴν ἀνθρωποσφαγίαν παρεχόμανοι,
τρέφοντες αὐτὴν αἱμαιτεκχυσίαις ἀθεωτάταις]. The bandit murders for
the sake of what s/he can get, but the rich man buys gladiators for the sake
of murder. (*Ad Gr.* 23.2)

We recall that some of the writers we have investigated—especially Lucian—satirize
the economics of sacrifice, which range from the poor man's kiss of his own hand
to the highest gift: human sacrifice. Tatian too looks at the economics of sacrifice, observing how the poor man sells himself as a murderer-to-be. But the poor
person—the bought slave, trained as combatant in the arena—is also placed in parallel construction with the animal sacrificed for meat eating. Even if non-Christian
contemporaries would not necessarily have made the same link between violence
in war and violence in the amphitheater, the Christian juxtaposition of the arena
performer and the war victim is not surprising for two reasons. First, the *munus,* or
gladiatorial game, is sometimes interpreted as a substitution for the killing of war
captives, as we have seen. Second, Christians regularly and polemicallyelide various
forms of Roman spectacular violence.[42]

Tatian's equation of the poor arena combatant with animal meat is also not surprising in view of ancient philosophical writings against eating meat. Plutarch connects the gluttony of human carnivores with acts of war: "And so when our murderous
instincts had tasted blood and grew practised on wild animals, they advanced to the
labouring ox and the well-behaved sheep and the housewarding cock; thus, little by
little giving a hard edge to our insatiable appetite, we have advanced to wars and the
slaughter and murder of human beings."[43] Porphyry blames Ares and war for animal
sacrifice and human misunderstanding of their ontological connection with animals:

These practices [of the sacrifice of myrrh, frankincense, and honey] are still
preserved among some peoples, like traces of the truth: "the altar was not
soaked by violent deaths of bulls." I think that when friendship and perception
of kinship ruled everything, no one killed any creature, because people
thought the other animals were related to them. But when Ares and Battle-
noise and all kinds of conflict and source of war were in control, then for the
first time no one spared any related creature at all. (*Abst.* 2.21–22)[44]

In Tatian's argument, the spectacle in the arena and the spilling of blood feeds
the ravenous soul, presumably of the watching audience. In this economy, the poor
man and the sacrificial animal are both devoured. Clement of Alexandria uses a
similar concept to bolster his argument against sacrifice:

Come now, then, and let us add this: that your gods are inhuman and human-
hating *daimones,* not only rejoicing in madness, but also enjoying human

slaughter [ἀνθρωποκτονίας]. Now in the armed rivalries in stadiums, now by countless ambitious displays in wars, they provide for themselves occasions of pleasure, in order, doubtless, that they might violently be able to take their fill of human bloodshed. (*Protr.* III 42.1)

Clement then goes on to provide all sorts of examples of such depravity, including some from Euripidean tragedy.[45] He continues:

Certainly, while they are aiming to sacrifice with good omens to them [the *daimones*], they let themselves forget that they are slaughtering humans [καλλιερεῖν γοῦν τοπάζοντες αὐτοῖς σφᾶς αὐτοὺς λελήθασιν ἀποσφάττοντες ἀνθρώπους]. For murder [*phonos*] does not therefore become an animal sacrifice [*hierion*] on account of place, not even, in truth, if someone, having pledged an animal sacrifice, should cut a person's throat for Artemis and Zeus in a sacred area rather than in anger or love of money—[or] for other similar *daimones*—upon altars [*bōmois*] rather than in roads. But such a sacrifice is murder and human slaughter [*androktasia*]. (*Protr.* III 42.8–9)[46]

The arena and war are the occasion for the gods—that is, *daimones*[47]—to glut themselves on sacrificial blood, but sacrificial blood that is human. For Clement and Tatian, sacrifice and homicide are sometimes hard to distinguish.

Weapons and the Sacrificial Altar

Thus in the first to the third centuries people questioned the theology of sacrifice, as they had for centuries before. The immaterial gods have no material needs, argued Christians and non-Christians alike, and the bloodiness of animal sacrifice led to an embarrassment that produced talk of "unbloody," "pure," and "rational" sacrifice.[48] Yet this theological-philosophical conversation—which turns both outward, to critique practices of sacrifice, and inward, to see the ethical self as a sacrifice to the god—coexists with robust practices of sacrifice. There was a rich funding of old-time religion and its concomitant sacrifices that flourished, for example, in the reign of Hadrian. Religious sites made up "his most frequent single type" of benefaction; one-third of all known Hadrianic architectural and engineering donations were to temples, shrines, or (cult-associated) tombs; at least eleven temples or shrines associated with the imperial cult also received Hadrian's benefactions.[49] Hadrian and other emperors are often depicted as sacrificants, as enacting *pietas* toward the gods and thereby holding together the empire,[50] at the same time as sacrifices to and on behalf of the emperors as gods were being conducted.[51] These images "publish" an important message about the centrality of sacrifice to the role of the emperor. Yet images of the emperor as sacrificing priest, as Inez Scott Ryberg and Richard Gordon have argued, depict remarkably clean and ungory scenes and focus the ceremony not on the act of animal sacrifice itself, but on the emperor,[52] as we have already seen on the Column of Trajan.

Various second-century writers questioned the piety and economy of sacrificial practices, and even suggested that human sacrifice is the logical end of sacrifice, the height of transactions with bloodthirsty divinities. Such discussions of human sacrifice are, obviously, theological satires and critiques. But we also find hints of what such writers might oppose in an altar that brings together visually the act of sacrifice and the rhetoric of human warfare.

In 1930 an altar was found in Ephesos in the middle of the east end of the precinct of what we now know is a temple to the Flavian Sebastoi, or the Flavian imperial family (fig. 7.4). The U-shaped platform for the altar measured approximately 9 m². Its east-west axis aligns with the temple and its north-south axis with the monumental entrance on the north side of the precinct.[53] Not all of the orthostats that formed the face of the altar have survived. Those that do probably do not belong to the late-first-century building phase, but to the second or third century.[54]

Temple of the Sebastoi

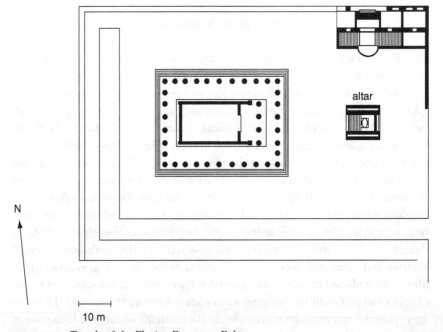

N

10 m

FIGURE 7.4 *Temple of the Flavian Emperors. Ephesos.*
Source: Courtesy of Koester, *Cities of Paul* and Fortress Press.

FIGURE 7.5 *Relief of bull tethered to altar. Altar of the Temple of the Flavian Emperors, Ephesos.*

Source: Selçuk Museum. Author's photograph.

On one of the short ends of this altar from Ephesos, a bull is depicted, its head low and its back tensed, tethered to an iron ring at the base of an altar, under the garlands and the *boukranion* that repeats the results of sacrifice (fig. 7.5). Another small relief from the short side of the altar depicted two crossed shields and swords.[55] It was not unusual in the first century and beyond to depict on an altar the instruments and objects of sacrifice.[56] Altars can be self-referential, depicting the very thing that occurs upon and around them.

The friezes that decorated the long southern end of the altar (those on the north side have been lost) are low, and scholars usually characterize them as of poor workmanship (fig. 7.6). To my eye, they evoke war abstractly and flatly, like Picasso's *Guernica*. These war implements on the Ephesian altar echo similar, older depictions in friezes of weaponry that likely served as intercolumniar parapets in the second story of the propylon of the temenos of the Temple of Athena on the Pergamene acropolis or, later, of military gear, depicted in relief, heaped high in one scene on the Column of Trajan in Rome. There, Victory, in a form echoing the

FIGURE 7.6 *Relief of weapons and captive. Altar of the Temple of the Flavian Emperors, Ephesos.*

Source: Selçuk Museum. Author's photograph.

FIGURE 7.7 *Victory writing on a shield among the spoils of war.*
Source: Column of Trajan, Rome. DAIR 89.752.

Venus of Capua, writes upon a shield. She props her foot upon an empty helmet. Stacked behind her and in front of her are shields and helmets and axes; surmounting these are two trophies, wearing armor and holding in their ghostly scarecrow arms more shields, arrows, and an ax (fig. 7.7). This stack is echoed in the column's base, made from tons (literally) of Luna marble, which is decorated with a jumble of weaponry typical of the Dacians and their allies the Roxolani.[57] Shields with delicate scrollwork and varied designs lie under fine mail armor; axes tumble near the helmets of the defeated. On the front facade they are tucked under an inscription honoring Trajan, carried by two winged Victories; the inscription refers to the emperor as the "son of the deified."[58] On the Column of Trajan we see sacrifice, the piety of the emperor, the divinity of the emperor, and human death as four themes interwoven into a harmonious counterpoint, even if the column's visual rhetoric tries to deny the emperor's proximity to blood of war and blood of sacrifice.

It is not unusual in antiquity to have an altar that depicts warfare. The Hellenistic altar at Pergamon is perhaps the most famous and monumental example; such altars usually depict mythical warfare or scenes from the distant past, involving giants and gods, centaurs, Amazons, and the like. In second-century CE Ephesos, there was the so-called Parthian Monument, probably a monumental altar celebrating the warfare and life of Lucius Verus and depicting battles between Parthians and Romans. On the altar associated with the Temple of the Flavian Emperors in Ephesos, however, we see a more strident message, especially as it is launched in the midst of a

FIGURE 7.8 *Detail, relief of weapons and captive. Altar of the Temple of the Flavian Emperors, Ephesos.*
Source: Selçuk Museum. Author's photograph.

philosophical-theological discussion about the worth of blood sacrifice, tinged by memories of human sacrifice and fears that the human might be the most valuable animal to the gods. The altar is covered with reliefs of a bound barbarian (fig. 7.8), military implements, and ghostly trophies, like human forms. The barbarian in his helplessness and bound state echoes the relief of the bull. These reliefs literally surround and support animal sacrifice. In this precinct dedicated to imperial cult, we find interwoven the themes of imperial piety, imperial divinity, sacrifice, and human death.

Conclusion

Scholars have long been familiar with the invective of human sacrifice, or ritual killing, nearly the worst one could say about the twisted (im)piety of another. We have known about the language of Christ or Christians going to their death as sacrifices; we have understood that there was a broad, long-standing theological discussion across cults about the human properly attuned to god and neighbor as him- or herself a pleasing sacrifice to god.

Among the discourses regarding human sacrifice in the ancient world, this chapter has delineated another discussion of human sacrifice, less prominent but politically and theologically significant. In Tatian's comment about the enslaved arena combatant as producing or becoming human sacrifice; in Plutarch's reference to war and sacrifice; in Clement's association of the killing of humans and war with sacrifice, we see literature that brings together the image of the blood of animals with that of humans. In Lucian, we find the idea that on the scale of cheap-to-expensive sacrifices, human sacrifice is the priciest and the most likely to win the waiting gods' attention. This is satirically expressed, but nonetheless offers a pointed theological critique amid the ongoing wars and occupations of the Roman empire. We find a different depiction of such wars and human death in two monuments: the Column of Trajan and the altar at the Temple of the Flavian Sebastoi in Ephesos. In the Column of Trajan we see human bloodshed in war separated from peaceful scenes of imperial sacrifice, yet inevitably juxtaposed as well, since scene follows scene and literally stacks upwards in a spiral. Finally, in the altar in Ephesos, we can imagine the bull tethered next to the altar, echoing the depiction on one of its sides, and the blood of animals running near the depictions of empty armor and weapons, trophies of war, and even near the form of a kneeling captive. These sources engage one strand of debate on sacrifice; and, in the midst of the frequent wars of the second century, these sources assert—some critically, some acceptingly—that warfare is a form of human sacrifice. This discourse has implications for how we might understand those Christian texts that adopt a rhetoric of war and sacrifice, like Revelation, as well as for study of conceptualizations and practices of war and sacrifice in the Roman empire.

Notes

I thank Jennifer Knust and Zsuzsanna Várhelyi for the invitation to contribute to their engaging and well-organized conference at Boston University and to this volume, as well as for their suggestions for this essay. I have also appreciated comments and suggestions from Celia Schultz, Joan Branham, David Frankfurter, and Lawrence Wills, as well as discussions with Katherine Shaner on the issues of representations of slaves at sacrifice, a topic she treats in her dissertation, "Religion and the Civic Life of the Enslaved: A Case Study in Roman Ephesos" (in progress at Harvard University: The Divinity School).

1. James Packer, *The Forum of Trajan in Rome: A Study of the Monuments in Brief* (Berkeley: University of California Press, 2001); Filippo Coarelli, *The Column of Trajan*, translated by Cynthia Rockwell (Rome: Editore Colombo in collaboration with the German Archaeological Institute, 2000), 26–27.

2. Inez Scott Ryberg, *Rites of the State Religion in Roman Art*, Memoirs of the American Academy in Rome 22 (Rome: American Academy in Rome, 1955). My reading of sacrificial reliefs is indebted to Richard Gordon, "The Veil of Power," in *Pagan Priests: Religion and Power*

in the Ancient World, edited by Mary Beard and John North (Ithaca: Cornell University Press, 1990), 199–231. See also his two other excellent essays in that volume. On the relative control and lack of violence in the Column of Trajan, compared to the Column of Marcus Aurelius, see Sheila Dillon, "Women on the Columns of Trajan and Marcus Aurelius and the Visual Language of Roman Victory," in *Representation of War in Ancient Rome,* edited by Sheila Dillon and Katherine E. Welch (Cambridge: Cambridge University Press, 2006), esp. 252–57.

3. Coarelli, *Column of Trajan,* 99; Frank Lepper and Sheppard Frere, *Trajan's Column: A New Edition of the Cichorius Plates* (Gloucester, U.K.: Alan Sutton, 1988), 100. See also Richard Brilliant, *Visual Narratives: Storytelling in Etruscan and Roman Art* (Ithaca: Cornell University Press, 1984), chap. 3.

4. See also the scene on the Column of Marcus Aurelius where a Roman soldier carries by his teeth the severed head of an enemy combatant; and, on the Column of Trajan, the scene of the Dacian leader Decabalus's death. See also Sheila Dillon's theory that the relative lack of violence on the Column of Trajan is a deliberate visual rhetoric to reassure those in Rome that the Roman army was not to be feared ("Women on the Columns of Trajan and Marcus," 260).

5. Natalie Boymel Kampen, "Looking at Gender: The Column of Trajan and Roman Historical Relief," in *Feminisms in the Academy,* edited by Donna Stanton and Abigail Stewart (Ann Arbor: University of Michigan Press, 1995), 60, passim, shows that the emperor is usually "at least one compositional unit away from the actual bloodshed," by means of walls, trees, and the reversal of the emperor's direction of movement in relation to the battle. See also Brilliant, *Visual Narratives,* 97–99; Coarelli, *Column of Trajan,* 27; Dillon, "Women on the Columns of Trajan and Marcus," 261.

6. See Celia Schultz, "The Romans and Ritual Murder," *JAAR* 78.2 (2010): 516–41.

7. We can tell as much from Porphyry, *Abst.* 2.5.3, since he calls it an error to understand *thusia* as worship that uses animals, and demonstrates a richer semantic field (which by the late third century, presumably, had narrowed). David Frankfurter, "Egyptian Religion and the Problem of the Category 'Sacrifice'" (chapter 3, this volume), rightly criticizes modern scholars for unsubtle and uncritical use of the term *sacrifice,* and our inattention to the details of a complex ritual act. For a treatment of key texts of this time period, see George Heyman, *The Power of Sacrifice: Roman and Christian Discourses in Conflict* (Washington, D.C.: Catholic University of America Press, 2007).

8. On Christians' refusal to sacrifice, see Stanley K. Stowers, "Greeks Who Sacrifice and Those Who Do Not: Toward an Anthropology of Greek Religion," in *The Social World of the First Christians: Essays in Honor of Wayne A. Meeks,* edited by L. Michael White and O. Larry Yarbrough (Minneapolis: Fortress, 1995), 293–332.

9. See also, for example, *Barn* 2:4–10. An ongoing discussion of sacrificial practice, as if sacrifice were still occurring or about to occur, characterizes Jewish writing as well.

10. The English translation is *The Apostolic Fathers,* 2 vols., LCL, translated by Bart D. Ehrman (Cambridge: Harvard University Press, 2003), 2.137.

11. The Greek edition is Miroslav Marcovich, ed., *Iustini Martyris Apologiae Pro Christianis* (New York: De Gruyter, 1994). If no translator is noted in this chapter, the translation is mine.

12. The edition is Eduard Schwartz, ed., *Tatiani Oratio Ad Graecos* (Leipzig: J. C. Hinrichs Buchhandlung, 1888). See *Ad Gr.* 21, where Tatian shows one direction in which his argument drives: a justification of the idea that God could come to be in human form.

13. Christian and other literature deliberately blurred the line between representation and the thing, especially with regard to statuary of the gods; see my *Christian Responses to Roman Art and Architecture: The Second-Century Church Amid the Spaces of Empire* (New York: Cambridge University Press, 2010), chaps. 5, 7.

14. See Porph., *Abst.* 3.25.3–4, and discussion by Philippa Townsend in chapter 11 of this volume. On this topic more broadly, see Ingvild Gilhus, *Animals, Gods and Humans: Changing Attitudes to Animals in Greek, Roman and Early Christian Ideas* (New York: Routledge, 2006).

15. Porphyry argues that even if certain gods demand animal sacrifice, humans need not eat that sacrifice. One strand of the human-sacrifice discourse of antiquity partcipated in discussions of why one should not eat flesh; the thin line between human animals and others, as well as the nerve-wracking question of the transmigration of the soul, fed such debates. See Porphyry, *Abst.* 1.7, and esp. book 2, including 2.26 on Jews as a pious, philosophical model because they did not eat animal sacrifices; Plut., *De esu carnium* I–II.

16. See, for example, J. J. Coulton, "Pedestals as 'Altars' in Roman Asia Minor," *Anatolian Studies* 55 (2005): 127–57.

17. The Greek edition is Nestle-Aland 26.

18. The edition is Athenagoras, *Legatio and De Resurrectione*, edited and translated by William Schoedel (Oxford: Clarendon, 1972); Schoedel's translations aided my own.

19. Athenagoras takes the phrase "lift holy hands" from Ps 141:2 (see also 1 Tim 2:8): "Let my prayer be counted as incense before thee, and the lifting up of my hands as an evening sacrifice." On broader conversations about spiritual sacrifice, see Everett Ferguson, "Spiritual Sacrifice in Early Christianity and Its Environment," *ANRW* II.2 (1980): 1152–89; Katell Berthelot, "Jewish Views of Human Sacrifice in the Hellenistic and Roman Period," in *Human Sacrifice in Jewish and Christian Tradition*, edited by Karin Finsterbusch et al. (Leiden: Brill, 2007), 151–74; Robert Jewett, *Romans: A Commentary,* Hermeneia (Minneapolis: Fortress, 2007), 724–35.

20. The Greek edition is *Clemens Alexandrinus*, edited by Ludwig Früchtel, Otto Stählin, and Ursula Treu, reprinted GCS (Berlin: Akademie Verlag, 1960–1984).

21. Porph., *Abst.* 2.28; see also Plut., *De esu carnium* I–II esp. at *Mor.* 994A–E.

22. "Certainly, the earthly altar [θυσιαστήριον] that is with us here is the gathering of those devoted to prayer, just as if they had one common voice and one mind [γνώμην]" (*Strom.* 7.6.31). Here and elsewhere in the passage Clement may allude to Rom 12:1 in his image of human sacrifice and to Phil 4:18 and Eph 5:2, among other texts, in his idea of Christ or the people of God as fragrant incense, and thus sacrifice to God. Also referring to the economy of sacrifice and in the context of criticizing practices of reinscribing honorary statues with someone else's name, Dio of Prusa's *Rhodian Oration* describes human benefactors as more demanding than the gods in seeking honors; the gods will accept incense if it is offered with a right spirit (*Or.* 14–15). Dio says that in the economics of sacrifice, people may even cheat the gods (*Or.* 31.10–12). On imagery of Christian women as altars in early Christian literature, and the arrangement of early church structures, see Joan Branham, "Women as Objects of Sacrifice? An Early Christian 'Chancel of the Virgins,'" in *La cuisine et l'autel: Les sacrifices en questions dans les sociétés de la Méditerranée ancienne,* edited by S. Georgoudi, R. Koch Piettre, and F. Schmidt (Turnhout: Brepols, 2006), 371–86, and Joan Branham, "Mapping Sacrifice on Bodies and Spaces in Ancient Judaism and Early Christianity," in *Constructions of Sanctity: Ritual and Sacred Space in Mediterranean*

Architecture from Classical Greece to Byzantium, edited by Bonna Wescoat and Robert Ousterhout (New York: Cambridge University Press, forthcoming).

23. Translation from Lucian, *Works*, LCL, translated by A. M. Harmon, 8 vols. (Cambridge: Harvard University Press, 1960), 3.165.

24. Translation from Lucian, *Works*, 2.115; see also *Iupp. conf.* 5–6.

25. Translation from Lucian, *Works*, 3.167. We know, too, from the Latin work of Minucius Felix the gesture of kissing one's hand when one passes an image of a god (*Oct.* 2.4).

26. In his *Peri deisidaimonias* (*On superstition*), Plutarch had argued that the superstitious person, overcome by fear, trembled to engage in sacrificial rites instead of enjoying the "pleasantest" events of festal days and temple banquets (*Mor.* 169D–E). According to Plutarch, superstition is far worse than atheism, and it is far better to be an atheist than to carry superstition to its trembling extreme, the sacrifice of humans. Gauls, Scythians, and Carthaginians come under discussion (*Mor.* 171B–C).

27. Elsewhere, too, Lucian says that "they [the gods] sell people their blessings, and it is possible to buy from them health, if possible, for a calf, or wealth for four cows, a kingship for a hecatomb, a safe return from Troy to Pylos for nine bulls, and a passage from Aulis to Troy for a royal virgin" (*De sacr.* 2). In the last example, Lucian links war and human sacrifice. On the idea of animals as hard to get and expensive, and on the idea that the gods take more pleasure in consistent piety than in expensive offerings, see Porph., *Abst.* 2.14–16.

28. Some witnesses add "on your behalf" or "for you." Peter Lampe concludes that Paul and Pauline communities did not understand the Eucharist to be a sacrifice, as we find in later Christian texts. See his discussion of 1 Cor 5:7 and other relevant passages in "Human Sacrifice and Pauline Christology," in *Human Sacrifice in Jewish and Christian Tradition*, edited by Karin Finsterbusch et al. (Leiden: Brill, 2007), 191–209. See also Clement, *Strom.* 5.10–11, on the connection of this passage with Socrates' death.

29. James Rives, "Human Sacrifice among Pagans and Christians," *JRS* 85 (1995): 65–85. See also Heliodorus's *Ethiopika* 10.

30. See discussion in Schultz, "The Romans and Ritual Murder," esp. 527; Zsuzsanna Várhelyi, "The Specters of Roman Imperialism: The Live Burials of Gauls and Greeks at Rome," *Classical Antiquity* 26 (2007): esp. 284.

31. Laura Nasrallah, "Mapping the World: Justin, Tatian, Lucian, and the Second Sophistic," *HTR* 98.3 (2005): 283–314.

32. The translation is Rudolph Arbesmann's in *Tertullian Apologetical Works and Minucius Felix Octavius* (Washington, D.C.: Catholic University of America Press, 1950), 385–86.

33. Celia Schultz ("The Romans and Ritual Murder") has shown that Romans themselves did not or did not want to understand *as sacrifice* their odd traditions of burying alive a Greek man and woman and a man and woman from Gaul; see also her "Containment or Sacrifice: The Proper Disposal of a Polluting Presence," Papers of the British School at Rome (forthcoming). I thank the author for advance copies of her work.

34. The English translation is Plutarch, *Moralia*, LCL, vol. 4, translated by Frank Cole Babbitt, (1939; repr., Cambridge: Harvard University Press, 1999), 125; see also Várhelyi, "The Specters of Roman Imperialism," 298–99, for other sources.

35. Várhelyi, "Specters of Roman Imperialism," 284.

36. Várhelyi, "Specters of Roman Imperialism," 300.

37. Várhelyi, "Specters of Roman Imperialism," esp. 287, 289, 290.

38. See for example, Livy, *Ab urbe condita libri* 10.28–30 regarding Decius's *devotio*. There was also an old tradition of *devotio hostium*, the killing of captives. Várhelyi, "Specters of Roman Imperialism," 293–94.

39. On ritual for dealing with avenging spirits, and the possibility that the burial of Gauls and Greeks is such a ritual, see Várhelyi, "Specters of Roman Imperialism," 295–96.

40. *Abst.* 2.37–43; see discussion in Townsend, chapter 11, this volume.

41. See prior discussion of Clem. Al., *Strom.* 7.6.

42. See also, for example, Dio of Prusa, *Or.* 31.121, regarding the Athenians using their theater for human slaughter on the seats of the hierophant and priests of Dionysos, and Philostr., *VA* 4.22, on the impurity of the Athenian assembly because it was also the location of human sacrifice in spectacle combat. Both passages are discussed in Cavan Concannon, "*Ecclesia Laus Corinthiensis*: Negotiating Ethnicity under Empire," Ph.D. diss., Harvard University, 2010.

43. Plut., *On Eating Meat* II.4, *Mor.* 998 B–C, in *Plutarch's Moralia*, translated by Franck Cole Babbitt, LCL, vol. 6.1 (Cambridge: Harvard University Press, 1999): 105–12. (Greek accessed online through TLG.)

44. Translated by Gillian Clark in *On Abstinence from Killing Animals* (Ithaca: Cornell University Press, 2000).

45. See Rives, "Human Sacrifice," 67ff.

46. Note that what follows is the story of Apollo leading Croesus to his death (in warfare, it is implied). S.v. LSJ ἀνδροκτασία "*slaughter of men* in battle."

47. Porphyry, *Abst.* 2.37–43, on the nature of *daimones*, good and bad, and how the bad ones create theological confusion.

48. See, for example, Plut., *De superst.*; Varro, *Ant. div.*, which no longer exists but Augustine discusses it in *De civ. D.*; Cic., *Nat. D.*; Porph., *Abst.* 2.37. Some texts argue that stories of the gods are better understood as allegories for the forces of nature, and that one true God rules over all things, but one should still practice ancestral religions. See Harold W. Attridge, "The Philosophical Critique of Religion under the Early Empire," *ANRW* 2.1 (1978): 45–78; Robert Grant, *Gods and the One God* (Philadelphia: Westminster, 1986), 75–83; and esp. Polymnia Athanassiadi and Michael Frede, "Introduction," in *Pagan Monotheism in Late Antiquity*, edited by Polymnia Athanassiadi and Michael Frede (Oxford: Clarendon, 1999), 7–10; and, in the same volume, Michael Frede, "Monotheism and Pagan Philosophy in Later Antiquity," 46–57. Regarding prohibitions on or substitutions for bloody sacrifice in the fourth and fifth centuries CE, see Michele Salzman's chapter in this volume.

49. Mary Boatwright, *Hadrian and the Cities of the Roman Empire* (Princeton: Princeton University Press, 2000), 127–40, at 28. See also Laura Nasrallah, "The Acts of the Apostles, Greek Cities, and Hadrian's Panhellenion," *JBL* 127.3 (2008): 533–66.

50. See, for example, Min. Fel., *Oct.* 6.2.

51. S.R.F. Price, *Rituals and Power: The Roman Imperial Cult in Asia Minor* (Cambridge: Cambridge University Press, 1984), chap 8.

52. Ryberg, *Rites of the State Religion in Roman Art*; Gordon, "The Veil of Power," 199–231.

53. On the terrace at the Temple of the Flavian Emperors see H. Vetters, "Domitianterrasse und Domitiangasse (Grabungen 1960–61)," *JÖAI* 50 (1972–73): Beiblatt 311–30; on the colossal statue associated with the complex (probably of Titus), see Recep Meriç, "Rekonstruktionsversuch der Kolossalstatue des Domitian in Ephesos," in *Pro Arte Anti-*

qua: Festschrift für Hewig Kenner, edited by Wilhelm Alzinger and Gudrun Neeb (Vienna: A. F. Koska, 1985), 239–41, pl. XX–XXIV.

54. Steve Friesen, *Twice Neokoros: Ephesus, Asia and the Cult of the Flavian Imperial Family* (Leiden: Brill, 1993), 64–75. Josef Keil, "XVI. Vorläufiger Bericht über die Ausgrabungen in Ephesos," *JÖAI* 28 (1932): Beiblatt 5–72, esp. 57, dates the reliefs to early third century CE; W. Alzinger notes that style of ornamentation cannot be earlier than mid–second century CE; W. Alzinger and Dieter Knibbe, "Ephesos vom Beginn der römischen Herrschaft in Kleinasien bis zum Ende der Principatszeit," *ANRW* 2.76.2 (1980): 820.

55. Helmut Koester et al., *The Cities of Paul: Images and Interpretations from the Harvard New Testament Archaeology Project*, CD-ROM (Minneapolis: Fortress, 2005), Ephesos: "Temple of the Flavian Sebastoi" and "Altar with Weapon Relief."

56. So, too, we find on the altar in the Temple of Vespasian at Pompeii not only sacrificial instruments on two sides but also a sacrificial scene with a bull (Ryberg, *Rites of the State Religion in Roman Art*, 81).

57. James Packer, *The Forum of Trajan in Rome: A Study of the Monuments*, 2 vols. (Berkeley: University of California Press, 1997), 1.4–5, regarding the column base, including plans, see 1.113–120; see also Coarelli, *Column of Trajan*, 21, 25–26. For a full analysis of building materials and construction of the column, see Lynne Lancaster, "Building Trajan's Column," *AJA* 103.3 (July 1999): 419–39. For a discussion of warfare and offerings to God, see also C. Batsch, "Le herem de guerre dans le judaïsme du deuxième temple," in *La cuisine et l'autel: Les sacrifices en questions dans les sociétés de la méditerranée ancienne*, edited by Stella Georgoudi, Renée Koch Piettre, and Francis Schmidt, Bibliothèque de l'École des Hautes Études Sciences Religieuses 124 (Turnhout: Brepols, 2005).

58. Packer, *Forum of Trajan*, 1.117. For further analysis of the column in relation to Christian apologetic materials, see Nasrallah, *Christian Responses to Roman Art and Architecture*, chap. 4.

8

The End of Public Sacrifice

CHANGING DEFINITIONS OF SACRIFICE IN POST-CONSTANTINIAN ROME AND ITALY

Michele Renee Salzman

To many in the post-Constantinian world, the end of public animal sacrifice would signal the triumph of Christianity.[1] Given Christian hostility and increasing imperial opposition to this rite, it is not surprising that some defenders of traditional religion felt compelled to justify animal sacrifice. Certain advocates, like Julian's contemporary Sallustius, sought to articulate the significance of animal sacrifice in accord with the Neo-Platonic philosopher Iamblichus's idea that animal sacrifice was a good and entirely appropriate offering.[2] Many scholars who examine animal sacrifice in the post-Constantinian period focus on Julian and his circle of intellectual Hellenists because of the extant textual evidence and because of Julian's very open and polarizing efforts at using public animal sacrifice to advance his notion of paganism.[3] After Julian's death, Christian leaders redoubled their efforts to undermine traditional religion by attacking public animal sacrifice in particular. Nonetheless, traditional cult continued and so too did public animal sacrifice, though it remained the focus of imperial legislation into the late fifth century.[4]

Among those who defended traditional religion in the decades after Julian's demise was the pagan senator Quintus Aurelius Symmachus; unlike members of Julian's circle, however, Symmachus took a different path to validate traditional cult. Symmachus's *Letters* as well as his *Third State Paper,* from the 370s and early 380s, offer not just a justification, but a redefinition of the nature and validity of traditional public cult and its rituals, including animal sacrifice.

As I will show, Symmachus's efforts were based on two, more broadly based sociocultural and religious developments in late antiquity. First, Symmachus turned to prominent private individuals, instead of cult officials or magistrates, to perform state cult rites like sacrifice even in civic spaces. Of course, individuals had performed rites in honor of the gods of the state cults in private spaces for centuries, and this was increasingly the case in the fifth century, as we will see. But Symmachus advocated something unusual insofar as he proposed a move toward greater local autonomy and what I would call "privatization" of what had previously been considered the public sphere. His ideas reflect the reemergence of the local elites and their willingness to assert their traditional role as *euergetes* in the post-Constantinian period, especially in Rome and Italy where the reduced presence of the emperor had opened up new opportunities for public displays of beneficence. Second, Symmachus's writings reveal a willingness to focus on a range of religious rituals other than animal killing as valid ways of maintaining the state cults; indeed, animal sacrifice had always consisted of a series of ritual actions in which the slaughter of the animal was accompanied by oaths, prayers, vegetable or incense offerings, banquets, purificatory rites, and ceremonial processions.[5] Unlike the killing and communal consumption of the sacrificial animal, these latter activities were less repugnant to Christians. Symmachus's willingness to focus on these other elements of state cult as well as his reticence in mentioning animal killing were viable strategies for a traditional religionist in the late fourth century.

In this chapter I am interested primarily in examining "normative" public religion in the Western empire in the late fourth century. I will focus on the West since its culture and institutions were different enough from the Eastern empire to matter in regard to religion, especially in the fourth century and especially after Julian. Moreover, Symmachus is a good and underappreciated source not just for understanding the interpretive strategies that traditional religionists employed to justify the survival of Roman cult and rituals, like animal sacrifice, but also for assessing what happened on the ground, as the evidence of contemporary texts and material remains suggest.[6] The performance of rituals by private individuals, not necessarily as magistrates or even priests, in the public civic space—with or without animal sacrifice—could satisfy the key aim of state cult as Symmachus and many of his contemporaries viewed it, namely the maintenance of the *pax deorum*. Thus Symmachus's writings reveal the flexibility and innovation inherent in traditional religiosity that had enabled it to survive, even without what Christians and intellectual Hellenists saw as its quintessential cult act of animal killing.

Public Cult by Private Individuals: A Form of Privatization

According to Roman scholars like the second-century grammarian Festus and to politicians and jurists in the Roman world, a public cult rite, like animal sacrifice, required state funding and had to be performed on behalf of the people; a public religious space was one that was consecrated to the gods according to the customs and institutions of the state.[7] From a legal perspective, everything that fell outside this narrow range of ritual action was left to the category of "private cult"—*sacra privata*. This would include such well-known cults as the cult of the Lares and the household gods, but also neighborhood shrines dedicated to the *genius* of the emperor in Rome (not funded by the state) and Eastern cults like that of Mithras. This was the normative Roman legal distinction as well as practice.

Symmachus describes one instance of public animal sacrifice in expiation of some undetermined prodigy at ancient Spoletum, modern Spoleto, in the decade after Julian's death, between 375 and 384 CE. What is noteworthy here is how Symmachus's narrative elides the boundary between public and private cult, as he tells of the rites undertaken at Spoletum in a letter to his friend and coreligionist, the eminent senator Vettius Agorius Praetextatus:

> I am intensely distressed, because, despite numerous sacrifices [*sacrificiis multiplicibus*], and these often repeated by each of the authorities [*per singulas potestates*], the prodigy [*ostentum*] of Spoleto, has not yet has been expiated in the public name. For the eighth sacrificial victim [*mactatio*] scarcely appeased Jove and for the eleventh time honor was paid to Public Fortune with multiple sacrificial victims [*multiiugis hostiis*] in vain.[8] You know now where we are. The decision now is to call the college to a meeting. I will make sure you know if the divine remedies make any progress. Farewell.[9]

Since the civic leaders had failed to propitiate this prodigy by animal sacrifice, Symmachus states that there will be a meeting with his colleagues, meaning here either the members of the priestly college at Rome devoted to Vesta to which he belonged as *pontifex maior,* or his colleagues in the senate, many of whom also belonged to the same priestly college.[10]

This narrative would not be problematic if we found it in a text before the rule of Constantine's sons, Constantius and Constans; as I have argued elsewhere, it was only in a law of 341 directed to Madalianus, vicarius of Italy, that emperors prohibited animal sacrifice in Italy; this 341 law stipulated that "[s]uperstition shall cease; the madness of sacrifices shall be abolished."[11] However, even this 341 law could have been interpreted by those enforcing it as aimed at divinatory, not public cult sacrifices. Much would depend on the magistrate's understanding of the term *superstitio* and his willingness to enforce prohibitions. Indeed, although a series of imperial laws after 341 and continuing into the fifth century prohibited animal sacrifice, the unwillingness or inability of officials to enforce these restrictions, as well as the high status of pagan elites in Rome and Italy help to explain why public animal sacrifice continued in the West at least into the late fourth century.[12] In that city, as Libanius remarked in his *Oratio* 30.33–34, dated to 386 CE, "they [the officials] have not yet dared rob Rome of its sacrifices."[13]

But what I want to focus on at ancient Spoletum is Symmachus's description of the performed ritual. Symmachus states that sacrifices by each of the authorities (*per singulas potestates*) were not successful and that "the prodigy had not yet been propitiated in the public name [*necdum publico nomine Spoletinum piatur ostentum*]." Symmachus's language leaves open two possible interpretations of what happened. The most likely interpretation is that these public cult sacrifices had not yet been successful in placating the gods. But there is a second possibility; the omen had not yet been propitiated because the sacrifices had not yet been performed *in the name of the public*—that is, they were not carried out with public monies; or by the correct public official; or in a public, sacred space. This is a second alternative that we cannot rule out. If so, it would underscore Symmachus's concern for the public nature of this cult act of animal sacrifice.

Because the sacrifices had failed to propitiate the omen, Praetextatus—whom Symmachus described at the beginning of this letter as a man "born for the common good"—was concerned. Hence Symmachus tells Praetextatus of a meeting of his colleagues at Rome to consult about what to do next. More or different rites in the public name—sacrifices with or without public funding, with or without cult priests—may have been recommended. We simply do not know what happened next, but it was the traditional role of the urban elite as priests and as magistrates— be it at Spoletum or in Rome—to correct the imbalance in the city's relationship with the Divine.

Concern about maintaining the *pax deorum* through the correct public cult ritual was also the issue at the heart of Symmachus's *Third State Paper*. Symmachus, then urban prefect of Rome, presented a request of the Roman senate to the Christian emperor Valentinian II for the return of the Altar of Victory to the senate; it had been removed (we think) by Constantius II as a sign of imperial hostility toward animal sacrifice. The altar was likely returned under Julian, but it was removed again as of the time of this request in 384.[14]

It is no doubt a sign of the force of Christian sentiment and imperial hostility that Symmachus's request for the return of the Altar of Victory makes no mention of its role in animal sacrifice or even incense offerings. Rather, Symmachus focuses on the altar as the traditional locus for oaths of allegiance to the emperor:

> Where else are we to take the oath of allegiance to your laws? What religious sanction is going to deter the treacherous from giving false evidence? That altar holds together the harmony of all as a group and that same altar makes its appeal to the good faith of each separately, and nothing gives more authority to the proceedings of the senate than the feeling that all its measures are passed by a body of men acting, as it were, on oath.[15]

Individuals can only be united for the public good when these swear an oath in public on this altar. In Symmachus's narrative, the oath Roman senators share takes the place of the animal sacrifice or incense offering in winning over the gods in support of the emperor and the state. I will return to Symmachus's willingness to focus on alternatives to animal sacrifice in the second part of this chapter, but here I want to underscore how notions of the public/civic good and the individual/ private are merged; at the altar the individual joins in a public ritual of oath taking to benefit the emperor and the state.

Another key issue that elides the public and the private in Symmachus's *Third State Paper* is the status of public funding for the state cults, or what we might call the economy of sacrifice. The emperor Gratian had just recently, likely in 382, prohibited individuals from bequeathing private monies to the traditional state cults.[16] In making his case for maintaining public funding, Symmachus advanced an argument that, like the situation at Spoletum, obscured the distinction between public and private rites:

> But someone will say that public money was refused to meet the cost of religion which was not that of the state. I hope good emperors will not entertain the view that what was in time past granted to individuals from public funds should be regarded still in the jurisdiction of the exchequer. The state is composed of individuals and once a thing leaves the state it becomes the property of individuals once again.[17]

That the Vestals and the traditional state cults should continue to receive state funding because these now belonged to the priests of the state cults on analogy with gifts made by the state to private individuals is indeed an argument of questionable logic. Symmachus did not, in the end, win his case. The altar was not returned. But this "privatization" of public funds is very much in keeping with Symmachus's broader attempts to find ways to validate public cult, here in an innovative definition of the right of the state cults to continue to receive public monies that had been given to them in the past and hence in the future.

Similarly, and with more compelling logic, Symmachus defends the right of the individual to contribute to the public cults. So Symmachus argues in his *Third State Paper*:

> [I]t was the wishes of dying men that bequeathed to virgins and servants of religion the lands which the exchequer now retains. I beg you who are the priest of justice that the right to benefit from private bequests should be restored to the religious institutions of your city. Let men dictate their wills in peace of mind. [...] Are we to take it that Roman religious institutions are outside Roman law?[18]

If the emperor can prevent private individuals from leaving monies for the state cults in their wills, this would undermine a long-standing source of prestige for urban elites, not just those of Rome whom Symmachus is here referencing. Private funding for the public good—traditional euergetism in the civic context—has to be defended, a tie between the two spheres that had been in existence for centuries. What is not valid, claims Symmachus, is the emperor's attempt at seizing the monies of private individuals; imperial "privatization" of public cults has to be resisted.

Symmachus's ingenuity in obscuring the boundaries of the public and the private in defense of Roman state cult and its rituals recurs in other of his writings that are not so obviously intended to persuade as was his *Third State Paper*. So, for example, in one of his letters, again from the period 375–84 CE, sent to the same friend and coreligionist, Vettius Agorius Praetextatus:

> The public priests [*publicos sacerdotes*] agreed that we should hand over care of the gods to the guardianship of the citizens [*in custodiam civium*] for an act of public observance [*publico obsequio*].[19] Without a doubt, the goodwill of the gods is lost, unless cult ritual maintains it. Therefore, honor to the gods was carried out more splendidly than was customary.[20]

This letter, like so many by Symmachus, omits precise details including the key information about what precipitated this change; the particular act of public worship that was involved; and how it was made "more splendid [*ornatior*] than was customary." It is possible that this last phrase was a reference to a costly rite, like an animal sacrifice. The second part of this letter does, however, mention an unspecified imperial edict that, it has been argued, was aimed at restoring statues to temples; if so, it is possible that Symmachus is here referring to some sort of ritual involving statues—that is, a public procession with a cult statue, with or without animal sacrifice.[21]

What I wish to highlight here is Symmachus's willingness for the public priests to hand over this rite to citizens to perform. A public cult ritual was then performed, but not by the public priests—nor are any magistrates noted as being involved, nor is it noted that public monies were used for this rite, all of which are components of the traditional legal definition of a public cult rite. Rather, according to Symmachus, all that was necessary to satisfy the gods was for powerful private citizens to perform the rite for the benefit of the state. So, in a real sense, the public cult has been handed over to private citizens; this, I would propose, is a new form of privatization, which, lacking official priests or magistrates, and possibly also lacking state funding, was now being proposed as a viable act of "public" worship.

Symmachus's acknowledgment of the role of prominent individuals performing rituals in public, without the aid of priests—what I have termed the "privatization" of public cult—fits well with what we know happened in the case of another of the public cults in Rome, namely that of the Magna Mater and Attis, as evidenced by a series of inscriptions from the Phrygianum precinct in the Vatican area of Rome. This cult provides a particularly apt comparison since the extant inscriptions which continue through 391 CE show direct evidence for the rituals practiced by traditional religionists who belonged to the senatorial elite in the city of Rome in the fourth century. Among those who are attested as having performed a ritual bull sacrifice, or *taurobolium,* was Symmachus's correspondent, the Roman senator Praetextatus, and Praetextatus's wife, Paulina.[22]

Admittedly, the fourth-century rite of the *taurobolium* had changed from how it had been practiced in the second and third centuries. Earlier, the rite had entailed a conventional animal sacrifice, most often of a bull, and the consecration of the animal's testicles *(vires),* which were "handed over" by the officiant to the dedicator to obtain good fortune from the Magna Mater.[23] This rite could be performed in public by the priests of the cult (the Galli) "on behalf of the safety of the emperor [*pro salute imperatoris*]" and in the presence of local civic officials and elites. Individuals could, however, consecrate the testicles of the publicly sacrificed bulls for their own benefit. Alternatively, the *taurobolium* could also be entirely "private" (i.e., for the well-being of the individual dedicator); if so, the sacrifice and consecration of testicles were performed without the members of the priestly colleges and without the local civic officials.[24]

This public/private distinction seems to have changed in fourth-century Rome. The bull sacrifice remained part of the ritual, but it was "privatized" insofar as now—as the inscriptions show—it was only performed for the benefit of the dedicant, not the Christian emperor.[25] Moreover, as Neil McLynn has argued convincingly, the dedicants, who now claimed explicit and intimate bonds with Magna Mater and Attis, were at the center of the ceremony; these gods served as the individual's, not the emperor's, "saviours," "preservers," and "guardians."[26] This focus accompanied an important change in the presentation of the rite itself: "The supporting cast of priests, *collegia* and flautists disappear from the record entirely."[27] With the loss of the cult's institutional representatives, the Galli, there is room for individuals to take on a more prominent role in the rite itself. Indeed, Praetextatus's claim that he "honored" his wife with the *taurobolium* (*CIL* 6.1779: *teletis honoras taureis*) suggests that he not only paid for this rite, but also orchestrated the ceremony of her initiation, since he had already been officially initiated. This does not mean that he killed the animal; ritualized animal slaughter was traditionally carried out by slaves or assistants.

These changes combined with two other developments in the cult, as suggested by inscriptions. First, the dedicants of the *taurobolia* altars were drawn from the same social elite, made up of the most prominent members of the late-Roman aristocracy; in essence, the sacrificial bull killing and communal meal, once associated with the emperor or held in his honor, had now become the privilege of the city's elite. Second, although the *taurobolia* inscriptions mention the dedicant's priesthoods, the emphasis is on the priests "as individuals, not as members of the college"; moreover, the inscriptions focus on the person's "purified condition."[28]

These developments in the fourth century cult of the Magna Mater and Attis suggest that the *taurobolium* had taken on a more personal import; this rite was valued for the benefits it bestowed on the individual. This changed focus is, on the one hand, an appropriate response to contemporary Christian and Jewish emphases on the self and the salvation of the individual.[29] On the other hand, this emphasis on the individual is also consonant with Symmachus's views on how to merge the public and the private in matters of traditional religion; as we saw in Symmachus's *Letter* 1.6, prominent citizens could take over public cult rites if they were of sufficiently high status in the community and were acting for the benefit of the people. Similarly, a private person could perform the correct rite and reap the personal benefits of the *taurobolium* even without the presence of an official priest of the Magna Mater cult or a magistrate. Indeed, this focus on the individual and not the office of priesthood seems a good adaptive strategy since it allowed traditional religionists to continue to perform their rituals without risking their career opportunities. Indeed, this was a world which, as Symmachus complained, some men turned away from the traditional state priesthoods "out of ambition," fearful of jeopardizing their advancement in an increasingly Christian empire.[30]

If we connect the cult rituals practiced in the Vatican precinct with Symmachus's interpretive strategies for validating civic cult (discussed earlier), it becomes clear that one key to the continuing importance of traditional religion remained its ability to engage and augment the status of Rome's elite in the public eye. Indeed, the bull sacrifice and accompanying rituals performed at the Vatican precinct were in no sense secretive. On the contrary, the fourth-century *taurobolium* was a significant public event, proclaimed by large, expensive altars dedicated in commemoration of the sacrifice in a ceremony that was followed by a feast, all of which would have drawn large, enthusiastic crowds. Such a costly ritual as a bull sacrifice that was paid for by private funds might not meet Festus's legal definition of public cult; but, more importantly for those involved, it provided the opportunity for Rome's elites to practice traditional euergetism in a public setting. It is perhaps not accidental that these expensive rituals took place in the Vatican precinct that stood directly adjacent to St. Peter's, where Christian aristocrats practiced different forms of public euergetism, such as Pammachius's lavish funerary banquet in 396 CE.[31] No wonder, then, that Symmachus remarked with approval the expense that accompanied the rites described in *Letter* 1.46.

The growing presence of senatorial elites in fourth-century public cult in Rome is an outgrowth of the vacuum left in the city by the departure of the emperor. In the early empire, it was the emperor as pontifex *maximus* who was head of the priestly colleges; as sacrificant, the figure of the emperor provided the paradigmatic model for citizens to follow.[32] But in the late third and fourth centuries, emperors rarely resided in Rome or even in their provincial capitals. Hence, the urban elite was increasingly left in charge of public cult in the cities of the West. This development helps explain Symmachus's advocacy of a greater role for citizens—what I have termed "privatization"—in Rome's public cults; it was a natural way for the elites to continue as civic leaders, especially as the fourth-century emperors embraced Christianity and increasingly distanced themselves from traditional state cult. This was a gradual process, but following Constantine, Christian emperors did not participate in public sacrifices, even if they still held the title of head priest of the state cults.[33]

This "privatization" of traditional cult—be it by prominent people in public (as Symmachus described in Rome in *Letter* 1.46) or in the open on privately owned land (as was likely the case of the Magna Mater and Attis at the Phrygianum), or on private land and in secret—shows the flexibility that had allowed traditional religion to survive for so many centuries. The civic elites were critical in this process. They orchestrated the rites and once the funds were withdrawn from the public cults, they could underwrite the costs of the ritual activities deemed essential. But elite willingness to fulfill the role of *euergetes* and to act as leaders in cult ritual was not predicated on the killing and eating of the sacrificed animal; there was a range of activities that traditionally accompanied animal slaughter, and these continued to offer opportunities for individuals to attain status and prestige as they sought to direct the traditional religions of their cities.

The New Normal: Public Pagan Cult with or without Animal Sacrifice

Unfortunately, Symmachus's writing says little explicitly about the precise ways in which religious cult, public or private, was practiced. Indeed, in the over nine hundred

Letters of Symmachus's corpus, there are few references to actual rituals; only the public sacrifices noted above are mentioned. But in keeping with his focus on public cult, Symmachus does often refer to the meetings of the public priesthoods to discuss controversial issues, like the immorality of a Vestal, or the state festivals that he or his correspondents must attend.[34] As noted above, in his *Third State Paper*, this reticence to narrate ritual per se appeared as part of Symmachus's rhetorical strategy; he omitted references to animal sacrifice and focused instead on the offering of an oath in an effort to convince Valentinian II of the desirability of returning the allegedly inoffensive Altar of Victory (Relatio 3.5). Nor does Symmachus mention the practice, which was normative in the third century if not the fourth, of accompanying an oath with an animal sacrifice.[35]

Not surprisingly, the bishop Ambrose, who wrote to the emperor in response to Symmachus's *Third State Paper*, did not accept Symmachus's attempt to shift the focus away from animal sacrifice. Ambrose graphically describes the "impious sacrifice" that was so offensive to Christians: "ash from the altar, cinders from the sacrilege, smoke from the pyre, would fill the breath and mouths of the [Christian] faithful [senators]."[36] Ambrose follows a long line of Christian thinkers who contrasted the false pagan "superstition" about bloody animal sacrifice with the correct Christian understanding of the powerful "blood spilt by the martyrs."[37] In contrast to Christian virtue attained through the martyr's or Christ's sacrifice, the traditional religionists are concerned only with cult ritual and the cost of maintaining it.[38] Nonetheless, Ambrose also asserts that sacrifices were still possible all over Rome in 384: "There are altars in all the temples, an altar even in the temple of Victories. Since they take pleasure in numbers, they [pagan senators] perform their sacrifices everywhere."[39] Ambrose focuses on the sacrilege of smoke-filled public spaces and the altars on which the sacrifice and/or incense offerings took place as of these were current practices.[40]

If this is not purely for rhetorical effect, then Ambrose is claiming that public sacrifices *could* take place all over Rome. The problem, from Ambrose's perspective, was not merely the animal killing, but the whole host of attending rituals that had traditionally accompanied and been part of the sacrifice ritual performed in public cult for centuries. Many of these other rites are also attested archaeologically. In an important study, Christophe Goddard surveyed the material evidence for the continued use of temples and sanctuaries in Rome and Italy between the fourth and sixth centuries. In at least three excavations from late-fourth-century Italy, lamps were discovered that had been systematically buried in front of altars; we know, from Theodosius's 392 law, that offering lamps to divinities was a common cult act, one that certainly accompanied the public holiday of the Lychnapsia in connection with the cult of Isis.[41] In seven sites identified with cult buildings, Goddard reported coins that he associated with a *stips*, an act of worship that consisted in throwing a coin to a god's statue; Lactantius mentions this rite along with sacrifice.[42] Two of the sites with evidence of coins that are possibly identified as *stipes* were tied to public cults that Goddard dated to the late fourth or early fifth century CE.[43]

Perhaps the best-attested public ritual that we know accompanied animal sacrifice was the offering of incense; this rite, thurification, could also take place without animal sacrifice. Indeed, through the early fifth century, Christians called traditional cult worshippers "incense offerers" to denigrate this rite.[44] In the fourth century, however, incense offering seems to have become the visual representation of public cult rites.[45] The illustrated *Codex-Calendar of 354,* for one, depicts the January rituals of the *Compitalia* with a consul taking his vows by pouring incense, not offering an animal sacrifice.[46] Similarly, on the *contorniates* as well as on other Roman mosaics, sacrifices were represented with thurification and not with animal slaughter.[47] In a private context, this rite seems to have been increasingly preferred; a well-known dyptich that celebrated a marriage between the house of the Symmachi and that of the Nichomachi commemorated the event by depicting a rite of incense offering.[48] We do not have any evidence that animal sacrifice was still performed for non-Christian marriages in the late fourth century when this dyptich was made, but clearly it was more desirable to announce this marriage in a mixed religious world with this far less problematic visual image of incense offering.[49]

This reticence in representing animal sacrifice in late-fourth-century art fits well with the archaeological evidence from Rome and Italy after 400; Goddard's study reported no evidence for the continuation of animal sacrifice after this date, although he noted that many archaeologists ignore late-antique phases of occupation in excavating pagan temples and sanctuaries.[50] Moreover, animal killing does not leave much in the way of material evidence; unless there are vast quantities of bones left on the site, it is hard to document this ritual on the ground. Goddard proposed that pagans substituted other rites—coins, incense, lamps, processions—for animal slaughter; unfortunately, he fails to see that these rites had been associated with animal sacrifice for centuries.[51] Given the continuity of these practices, I would suggest, instead, that what we have in the late fourth and fifth centuries is the persistence of traditional rites, sometimes in public sacred spaces, sometimes in private ones, rather than a straightforward act of ritual substitution of animal sacrifice by new rituals.

That many of these rituals—incense burning, processions, ritualized donations and burial of cultic objects such as lamps—continued into the fifth century can be documented; in addition to the instances noted above, the discovery of cult statues and eggs in a private shrine to Osiris, dated to the late fourth or fifth century on the Janiculum hill in Rome lends further support for this phenomenon, though here it is clearly in a private house.[52] However, the degree to which the participants understood these rituals in public or private as part of traditional cult is open to interpretation; in my view, the participants likely varied then, as now, as to how "religious" or "neutral" such rituals were. That animal sacrifice continued alongside these rites, in public or private, is harder to document.

Many historians have assumed that public animal sacrifice ended in Rome and Italy as a direct response to the emperor Theodosius's markedly harsher financial penalties for this ritual enshrined in a law of 391 CE; this law was specifically directed to the urban prefect of the city of Rome—and hence at the civic elites (*C. Th.* 16.10.10). Indeed, there are no extant *taurobolia* altars from Rome after this date.[53] An even harsher law directed at a full range of traditional cult rites (*C. Th.* 16.10.12) followed in 392 CE, though this later law was directed to Rufinus, praetorian prefect in the East, hence not directed at Rome or even Italy. Moreover, the 391 imperial initiative did not have an immediate impact in the West; implementation was delayed because the emperor Theodosius was by 392 CE negotiating with the usurpers Eugenius and Arbogastes before going to war; in the course of this civil war, the ecclesiastical historian Rufinus claimed that the pagans performed animal sacrifice in public.[54]

After Theodosius's victory in 394 and his death soon after, his sons, Arcadius and Honorius, again reiterated harsh restrictions on traditional cult rites, again singling out animal sacrifice.[55] Moreover, the fact that emperors felt the need to continue to pass similar laws into the fifth century, specifying a range of cult rites including animal sacrifice, prohibited not only on public properties but also on private estates, suggests that such rites were thought to be continuing.[56] Such injunctions, especially directed at rituals or animal sacrifice on private lands or in private homes, were hard to enforce, as demonstrated by the reiteration of such prohibitions as late as 472 CE.[57]

Although Symmachus's attempt to "privatize" animal sacrifice in the public sphere was ultimately ineffective, his second strategy—focusing on the elites' continuation of elements of public cult that traditionally accompanied animal killing—was more successful. Certainly, many of the public rituals and festivals survived into the fifth century. Perhaps best known from Rome are the rituals attendant on the festival of the *Lupercalia,* where naked men dressed in animal skins, the *luperci,* ran through the streets of the city; this rite continued in Rome at least until Pope Gelasius in 494 CE argued strenuously against it. Gelasius decried the rites of the Lupercalia as idolatry, but even as he did, he faced the resistance of civic elites, now Christian, who defended such activities as part of their Roman identity and viewed them as necessary to placate the "demons."[58] Such traditional rites, like those that accompanied the Lupercalia, along with processions, incense offering, and the giving of *stipes,* continued in public even though by the fifth century they were likely undertaken by individuals at private expense; we know that the imperial government diverted temple and cult funds to other ends.[59]

Conclusion

Symmachus's strategies for privatizing state cult and shifting its focus to allow for the survival of certain public rites enabled some traditional cults to survive into the fifth century. Indeed, other religions had continued to thrive after radically changing their central cult rituals, including even the loss of animal sacrifice; ancient Judaism, for one, had successfully negotiated just such a transition after the destruction of the Second Temple in 70 CE ended the central role that animal sacrifice had traditionally played.[60]

But unlike the Jews, traditional religionists in the late fourth and fifth centuries lost not only the ability to perform public animal sacrifice, but more importantly over time they lost the right to meet in public to share in religious ritual. According to the fifth-century Church historian Sozomen, this was the critical factor in converting pagans to Christianity; once they could no longer meet together in communal sacred places, pagans came to the Christian basilicas.[61] Over time, bloodless ritual offerings in large Christian basilicas replaced not just animal sacrifice, but most importantly altered the foci for public communal ritual activity. Although some traditional rites tied to animal sacrifice continued in public—processions, oaths, offerings—these were, over time, redefined so as to lose their traditional religious meanings. This was a long and complicated process, but the loss of a communal venue for their rituals gradually undermined the long-standing religious vitality of the state cults over the course of the fourth and fifth centuries.

Despite his failure, Symmachus's attempts at preserving public cult at the end of the fourth century represent creative solutions to the problem of how to preserve traditional rites, with or without animal sacrifice, as part of elite civic identity. Symmachus would have likely agreed with Sozomen as to why the public cults ultimately died; it was not the demise of animal sacrifice per se that brought about their end. Rather, the lack of a communal venue to perform shared cult acts of all kinds undermined the viability of these rites for the very civic elites whose traditional religious roles Symmachus had tried so hard to preserve.

Notes

I am indebted to the comments of David Frankfurter and to the chapter by James Rives in this volume for shaping my current views. Particular thanks are owed to Jennifer Wright Knust and Zsuzsanna Várhelyi for inviting me to participate in the conference at Boston University.

1. On the role of sacrifice in Greek and Roman religion until the age of Constantine, I am in agreement with Robin Lane Fox, *Pagans and Christians in the Mediterranean World from the Second Century AD to the Conversion of Constantine* (New York: Knopf, 1987), 69–72, at 71: "The bloodless alternative to sacrifice owed something to ease and economy, but nothing to growing scruples about shedding animals' blood. When pagans could pay for it, they did, and other scruples of a few philosophers made no impact." For Greek religion, see too Maria-Zoe Petropoulou, *Animal Sacrifice in Ancient Greek, Religion, Judaism and Christianity, 100 BC–AD 200* (Oxford: Oxford University Press, 2009), 32–111. For the argument for a decline in animal sacrifice in the fourth century, see Scott Bradbury, "Julian's Pagan Revival and the Decline of Blood Sacrifice," *Phoenix* 49 (1995): 331–56, but his analysis is based mostly on philosophical discourse and practice in the Greek East.

2. See the chapter by James Rives in this volume, and Iambl., *Myst.* 5, esp. 5.4.

3. Bradbury, "Julian's Pagan Revival," 331–56. See, too, on Julian and his philosophical teachers, John F. Matthews, *The Roman Empire of Ammianus* (Baltimore: Johns Hopkins

University Press, 1989), 115–29, and Alessandro Saggioro, "Il sacrificio pagano nella reazione al cristianesimo: Guiliano e Macrobio," *Annali di Storia dell'Esegesi* 19.1 (2002): 237–54.

4. The last law against sacrifice in the *Theodosian Code* is dated to 435 CE: see *C. Th.* 16.10.25. See n. 56 below for late-fifth-century legislation against sacrifice preserved in the *Justinianic Code*.

5. For the view that the main modern interpretations of sacrifice tend to overlook the many steps involved and for the notion that the offerings to the gods could take various forms, see the chapter by David Frankfurter in this volume.

6. The distinction between a discourse of sacrifice and the practice of sacrifice is worth maintaining; see the chapters of Stanley Stowers and David Ullucci in this volume.

7. Festus 248L: *publica sacra, quae publico sumptu pro populo fiunt.* For sacred space, see Festus 414L: *Gallus Aelius ait sacrum esse quocumque modo atque instituto civitatis consecratum sit . . .* Cf. Macrob., *Sat.* 1.16.4–8.

8. Symmachus's reference to the Public Fortune suggests a specific cult at Spoleto to this goddess.

9. Symmachus, *Letter* 1.49: *Sed mihi opinonum talium quae sine auctore prodeunt nulla curatio est. Inpendio angor animi, quod sacrificiis multiplicibus et per singulas potestates saepe repetitis necdum publico nomine Spoletinum piatur ostentum. Nam et Iovem vix propitiavit octava mactatio et Fortunae publica multiiugis hostiis nequiquam undecimus honor factus est. Quo loci simus, intellegis. Nunc sententia est in coetum vocare collegas. Curabo ut scias, si quid remedia divina promoverint. Vale.* All translations of Symmachus's *Letters* are by the author; see *The Letters of Symmachus, Book 1*, introduction, text, and commentary by M. R. Salzman; translation with M. Roberts (forthcoming 2011).

10. Symmachus's priesthoods are attested epigraphically. For discussion, see *PLRE* 1, s.v. *Symmachus* 4, 865–70. The senate was the authority that dealt initially with all prodigies, but they sought the guidance of specialists. The priests collected lists of prodigies in Rome and in other cities in Italy; information and recommendations concerning alarming prodigies could be passed directly from the priests to the magistrates and the senate; see John Scheid, *An Introduction to Roman Religion*, translated by Janet Lloyd (Bloomington: Indiana University Press, 2003), 116–18, for a clear discussion of how Romans traditionally dealt with prodigies. For the continuity of augurs and priests into the fifth century, see the arguments of Rita Lizzi Testa, "Augures et pontifices: Public Sacral Law in Late Antique Rome (Fourth-Fifth Centuries AD)," *The Power of Religion in Late Antiquity*, edited by Andrew Cain and Noel Lenski (Aldershot, U.K.: Ashgate, 2009), 251–78.

11. *C. Th.* 16.10.2. See M. R. Salzman, "*Superstitio* in the *Codex Theodosianus* and the Persecution of Pagans," *Vigiliae Christianae* 41 (1987): 172–88. For an opposing view arguing for the restrictions on pagan sacrifice beginning as early as the reign of Constantine, see Scott Bradbury, "Constantine and the Problem of Anti-Pagan Legislation in the Fourth Century," *CP* 89 (1994): 120–39; and Timothy Barnes, "Was There a Constantinian Revolution?" (review article), *Journal of Late Antiquity* 2.2 (2009): 375–76. However, even those who propose Constantinian legislation against pagan sacrifice (based largely on the literal acceptance of Eusebius's *Life of Constantine* 2.45.2) acknowledge that this was aimed only at the Eastern empire in 324 CE; hence, there was a need for a 341 law to extend provisions to the Western empire.

12. M. R. Salzman, *On Roman Time: The Codex Calendar of 354 and the Rhythms of Urban Life in Late Antiquity* (Berkeley: University of California Press, 1990), 205–209. Traditional

cult rituals continued later than the late fourth century, but the evidence for public animal sacrifice is hard to uncover; see the discussion following and in nn. 42, 55–58.

13. Lib., *Oration* 30.33–34, ed. R. Foerster: *hoi tan Roman tou thuein ou tolmasantes apheletesthai.*

14. The importance of the Altar of Victory controversy in analysis of the demise of paganism cannot be underestimated. The general outlines of it are well set forth by J.W.H.G. Liebeschuetz with the assistance of Carole Hill, *Ambrose of Milan: Political Letters and Speeches* (Liverpool: Liverpool University Press, 2005), 13–14, and 61. For a thorough discussion of the issues with full bibliography, see Rita Lizzi Testa, "Christian Emperor, Vestal Virgins and Priestly Colleges: Reconsidering the End of Roman Paganism," *AnTard* 15 (2007): 251–62.

15. Symmachus, *Relatio* 3.5: *Ubi in leges vestras et verba iurabimus? Qua religione mens falsa terrebitur, ne in testimonies mentiatur? omnia quidem deo plena sunt nec ullus perfidis tutus est locus, sed plurimum valet ad metum delinquendi etiam praesentia numinis urgueri. Illa ara concordiam tenet omnium, illa ara fidem convenit singulorum, neque aliud magis auctoritatem facit sententiis nostris, quam quod omnia quasi iuratus ordo decernit.* Translation here by R. H. Barrow, *Prefect and Emperor*, 37.

16. I do not agree with the argument advanced by Lizzi Testa, "Christian Emperor, Vestal Virgins and Priestly Colleges," 251–62, that Gratian's actions were aimed only at the cult of Vesta. For a fuller rebuttal, see Alan Cameron, *The Last Pagans of Rome* (New York: Oxford University Press, 2010).

17. Symmachus, *Relatio* 3.18: *dicet aliquis sumptum publicum denegatum alienae religionis inpendiis. Absit a bonis principibus ista sententia, ut quod olim de communi quibusdam tributum est, in iure fisci esse fideatur. Nam cum res publica de singulis constet, quod ab ea proficiscitur, fit rursus proprium singulorum.*

18. Symmachus, *Relatio* 3.13–14: *Agros etiam virginibus et ministris deficientium voluntate legatos fiscus retentat. Oro vos, iustitiae sacerdotes, ut urbis vestrae sacris reddatur privata successio. Dictent testamenta securi [. . .] ergo Romanae religiones ad Romana iura non pertinent?*

19. For discussion of the possible interpretations of this passage, see Jean-Pierre Callu's commentary in his French edition and translation of Symmachus's letters, *Symmaque* (Paris: Les Belles Lettres, 1972), 1.109.

20. Symmachus, *Letter* 1.46.2: *Convenit inter publicos sacerdotes, ut in custodiam civium publico obsequio traderemus curam deorum. Benignitas enim superiorum, nisi cultu teneatur, amittitur. Ergo multo tanto ornatior quam solebat caelestis factus est honor.*

21. Symmachus, *Letter* 1.46.2: *Edictum principum, nisi iam notum est, idem tibi adsertor expediet. Et iam statuas receptistis iisdem paene populi adclamationibus quibus amiseratis.* Callu, *Symmaque,* 1.109 n. 4, associates this imperial edict with temple property and statuary.

22. For Paulina and Praetextatus, see *CIL* 6.1779. For the Taurobolium in general, see J. B. Rutter, "Three Phases of the *Taurobolium*," *Phoenix* 22 (1968): 236–37.

23. Neil McLynn, "The Fourth Century *Taurobolium*," *Phoenix* 50 (1996): 321.

24. Rutter, "Three Phases," 236–37.

25. The description of the bull sacrifice with the blood dripping over the dedicant as described by Prudentius's *Peristephanon* 10 is a lurid account that, McLynn has rightfully observed, is more valuable as poetry than as an accurate description of a cult rite There is, however, evidence of bloodshed and ritual slaughter in the inscriptions: see McLynn, "*Taurobolium*," 312–30.

26. McLynn, "*Taurobolium*," 323.

27. McLynn, "*Taurobolium*," 322–23.

28. McLynn, "*Taurobolium*," 325.

29. See Guy G. Stroumsa, *The End of Sacrifice: Religious Transformations in Late Antiquity*, translated by Susan Emanuel (Chicago: University of Chicago Press, 2009), chap. 1, esp. 8–9, in which Stroumsa sets out his notion of the new importance of individual eschatology as a profound psychological but also social transformation in the later Roman empire.

30. Symmachus, *Letter* 1. 51 notes this trend in explaining why it was difficult to find a priest to substitute for him at a festival.

31. For Pammachius's banquet for his wife Paulina, see the documents in *PLRE* 1.663–64.

32. On this point, see esp. Richard Gordon, "The Veil of Power: Emperors, Sacrificers, and Benefactors," in *Pagan Priests: Religion and Power in the Ancient World*, edited by Mary Beard and John North (Ithaca: Cornell University Press, 1990), 201–31.

33. For Constantine's likely refusal to perform public acts of sacrifice and his increasingly negative public stance on sacrifice, see Raymond Van Dam, *The Roman Revolution of Constantine* (Cambridge: Cambridge University Press, 2007), 30–31. Scholars have generally argued that Gratian (ca. 382) refused the title of *pontifex maximus*, based on a passage in Zosimus, *Historia nova* 4.36.1–5; see Zosimus, *Histoire nouvelle par Zosime*, edited with French translation by François Paschoud, 3 vols. Collection des universités de France (Paris: Les Belles Lettres, 1971–1989), 301–302. However, Alan Cameron, "The Imperial Pontifex," *HSCP* 103 (2007): 341–85, has demonstrated that no fourth-century emperor gave up the pontificate; they only changed the adjective describing the priesthood from *maximus* to *inclitus*.

34. For references to pontifical duties, see, for example, Symmachus's *Letters* 1.47, 1.51, 2.36 (about Praetextatus's statue), 9.108–109, 9.147–48 (on the Vestal Virgins). For references to public festivals, see, for example, *Letters* 2.34, 2.53, 2.59, and 6.40.

35. Petropoulou, *Animal Sacrifice*, 36–37, makes this point on the basis of Tert., *De idol.* 17.3. Tertullian stated that Christians could not hold public office because they could not swear oaths; that this changed in the fourth century seems likely, and Symmachus certainly does not reference it.

36. Ambrose, *Letter* 72 (Maur 17.9).

37. Ambrose, *Letter* 73 (Maur 18.11). As Stroumsa, *End of Sacrifice*, remarked, "Christianity defined itself precisely as a religion centered on sacrifice, even if it was a reinterpreted sacrifice" (72). See also George Heyman, *The Power of Sacrifice: Roman and Christian Discourses in Conflict* (Washington, D.C.: Catholic University of America Press, 2007).

38. Ambrose, *Letter* 73.11 (Maur 18.11).

39. Ambrose, *Letter* 73.31 (Maur 18.31).

40. While Ambrose mentions sacrifice several times, his rhetoric focuses on the smoke and ashes, not the animal killed; see Ambrose, *Letter* 72.9–10; .16 (Maur 27.9–10, 16); and *Letter* 73.31 (Maur 18.31).

41. *C. Th.* 16.10.2. Christophe Goddard, "The Evolution of Pagan Sanctuaries in Late Antique Italy (Fourth-Sixth Centuries A.D.): A New Administrative and Legal Framework: A Paradox," in *Les cités de l'Italie tardo-antique (IVe-Vie siècle)*, edited by Massimiliano Ghilardi, Cristophe J Goddard, and Pierfrancesco Porena, Collection de l'École

Française de Rome 369 (Rome: École Française de Rome, 2006), 281–308, at 296. For the Lychnapsia, see Salzman, *On Roman Time,* 175.

42. Lactantius, *Div. inst.* 2.2.14–15: "to them [the statues of idols] they [pagans] throw a coin or kill a victim [illis stipem iaciunt, victimas caedunt]." Translation by author.

43. Goddard, "Evolution of Pagan Sanctuaries," 296–97. The two sites are the Jovian Sanctuary on the Grans S. Bernard and the Temple of Minerva in Akragas, Sicily.

44. See, for example, Prudentius's view of idolaters as an "incense-bearing crowd" (*"de grege turifero,"* in Prudent., *Apoth.* 292); and Cyprian calls a Christian apostate an incense offerer *("turificatus,"* in *Ep.* 55.2).

45. Martin P. Nilsson, "Pagan Divine Service in Late Antiquity," *HTR* 38 (1945): 63–69. See also Martin P. Nilsson, "Lampen und Kerzen im Kult der Antike," *Opuscula Archaeologica VI,* edited by Insitutum Romanum Regni Sueciae (Lund: C.W.K. Gleerup 1950), 96–111.

46. Salzman, *On Roman Time,* 79–83.

47. Salzman, *On Roman Time,* 226 and nn. 149–50.

48. On the circumstances of the diptych, see Alan Cameron, "Pagan Ivories," in *Colloque genevois sur Symmaque à l'occasion du mille six centième anniversaire du conflit de l'autel de la Victoire,* edited by G. W. Bowerstock, published by François Paschoud in collaboration with G. Fry and Y. Rütsche (Paris: Les Belles Lettres, 1986), 41–72.

49. Petropoulou, *Animal Sacrifice,* 97, citing among other texts, Plut., *Arist.* 20.6.

50. Goddard, "Evolution of Pagan Sanctuaries," 281–308.

51. I thank David Frankfurter for raising this objection to the notion of substitution and for pointing out the continuity of these rites.

52. Christophe J. Goddard, "Nuove osservazioni sul Santuario cosidetto 'Siriaco' al Gianicolo," in *Culti Orientali tra Scavo e Collezionismo,* edited by Beatrice Palma Venetucci (Rome: Artemide Press, 2008), 165–73.

53. Goddard, "Evolution of Pagan Sanctuaries," 297.

54. Eugenius was proclaimed Augustus by Arbogastes in August 392, as noted in *Cons. Const.* s.a. 392 and Socrates *Historia ecclesiastica* 5.25. For sacrifices alleged on the part of Nicomachus Flavianus and the pagans under Arbogastes, see Rufinus, *Historia ecclesiastica* 11.33 (GCS n.f. 6.2:1037–38). Augustine, *De civ. D.* 5.26, does not specifically cite sacrifices when he tells of the statues of Jupiter that were set up by the usurpers in the Alps and consecrated in some way against Theodosius. On the evidence for this usurpation, see M. R. Salzman, "Ambrose and the Usupation of Arbogastes and Eugenius: Reflections on Pagan-Christian Conflict Narratives," *JECS* 18.1 (2010): 191–223.

55. *C. Th.* 16.10.19:407/408. For more on these laws, see also Rita Lizzi Testa, "Legislazione imperiale e reazione pagana. I limiti del conflitto," *Cristianesimo nella storia* 31 (2009): 131–56.

56. *C. Th.* 16.10.19–.25. For more on the worship on private estates in the West, see Kim Bowes, *Private Worship, Public Values and Religious Change in late Antiquity* (Cambridge: Cambridge University Press, 2008), 18–60.

57. *Cod. Iust.* I.11.8, to Disocurus, praetorian prefect, possibly of the East. See *PLRE* II, Dioscorus 5, 367–68.

58. On the Lupercalia, see Neil McLynn, "Crying Wolf: The Pope and the Lupercalia," *JRS* 98 (2008): 176–81. For Gelasius's representation of his opposition, see Gelasius, *Epistle* 100.3: *"Quomodo autem non in hanc partem recidit qui cum se Christianum videri*

velit, et profiteatur, et dicat, palam tamen publiceque praedicare non horreat, non refutiat, non pavescat, ideo morbos gigni, quia daemonia non colantur, et deo Februario non litetur?"

59. See, for example, *C. Th.* 16.10.19 that diverts income from taxes in kind from the temples to benefit the *annonae* of the soldiers in 407/408.

60. This is a complex topic, but on this point see Stroumsa, *End of Sacrifice.*

61. Sozomen, *Hist. eccl.* 7.20.1–2: "As a result of not having houses of prayer, in the course of time they [pagans] accustomed themselves to attend the churches." Translation by C. D. Hartranft, *NPNF*, series 2, vol. 2 (Grand Rapids: Eerdmans, 1976). Sozomen's views on Theodosius's legislation which he thinks had little effect are brilliantly analyzed by R. Malcolm Errington, "Christian Accounts of the Religious Legislation of Theodosius I," *Klio* 79 (1997): 410–35.

PART III

Toward a Theology of Sacrifice

9

The Theology of Animal Sacrifice in the Ancient Greek World

ORIGINS AND DEVELOPMENTS

James B. Rives

That animal sacrifice held a central place in the Greek religious tradition through-out its history has long been accepted as a given, and this has in recent decades been reinforced by the work of some of the most prominent scholars of ancient Greek religion.[1] The ritual slaughter of an animal, followed by the communal consumption of its flesh, has been widely regarded as a defining feature of Greek culture, embodying and likewise reinforcing many of its core assumptions.[2] But the mono-lithic place of animal sacrifice in accounts of ancient religion is now starting to be called into question. Recent scholars have pointed out that rituals involving the slaughter of an animal varied widely in terms of their goals and constituent ele-ments and so do not constitute a single coherent category; they have stressed that sacrificial rituals comprised a number of steps and that the main interpretations of sacrifice tend to overemphasize some and neglect others; and they have emphasized that offerings to the gods took a whole range of forms, of which those involving the slaughter of animals were only one group—and perhaps not the most important. Some scholars have even raised the question whether "sacrifice" remains a useful category of analysis at all.[3]

In this chapter I hope to contribute in a small way to this discussion by con-sidering the cultural significance of animal sacrifice in its diachronic dimension. An important corollary of its assumed centrality to Greek religion is that its cul-tural meaning remained constant over time. I would argue instead that its meaning changed in tandem with other social, political, and cultural developments. Here I will focus on only one particular facet of these shifts of meaning and trace changes in philosophical reactions to animal sacrifice. The core of my argument is that phi-losophers of the imperial period took animal sacrifice much more seriously than did earlier philosophers and that only in this period did they develop a real theology of sacrifice—that is, a philosophical analysis that focused on the role of sacrifice as a cult act meant to establish connections between humans and the divine and that located it within a large-scale and coherent understanding of the cosmos.

I take as my starting point Porphyry of Tyre's treatise *On Abstinence from Killing Animals*, which he wrote sometime in the last decades of the third century CE.[4] Porphyry devotes the second book of this treatise, a quarter of the whole, to a discussion of the problem that the practice of animal sacrifice poses for those who wish to avoid eating meat. After a brief introduction, he provides in the first half of the book (*Abst.* 2.5–32) an exposition of Theophrastus's arguments against animal sacrifice, taken from that philosopher's now-lost treatise *On Piety*. (I will return to Theophrastus later in this chapter.) Porphyry then presents a theology of sacrifice, according to which different types of sacrifice are appropriate to different levels of deity (*Abst.* 2.33–43); lastly, he makes the argument that even if at times it is necessary to sacrifice animals, it does not necessarily follow that we must also eat them (*Abst.* 2.44–57). The last two arguments are closely linked to one of the main elements of Porphyry's philosophical agenda, the idea that the true philosopher must do everything he can to dissociate himself from the corruption and passions of the sensible world and to assimilate himself to the divine realm of the intelligible, from which the soul originally derives.

Porphyry's theology of sacrifice involves some interesting ideas, and it is worth considering it more closely. First of all, he is careful to point out that he is not "trying to destroy the customs which prevail among each people: the state," he says, "is not my present subject" (*Abst.* 2.33.1).[5] That is, a rejection of animal sacrifice does not mean a rejection of sacrifice altogether. On the contrary, he says, philosophers will also sacrifice;

> but we shall make, as is fitting, different sacrifices to different powers. To the god who rules over all, as a wise man said, we shall offer nothing perceived by the senses, either by burning or in words. For there is nothing material which is not at once impure to the immaterial. So not even *logos* expressed in speech is appropriate for him, nor yet internal *logos* when it has been contaminated by the passion of the soul. But we shall worship him in pure silence and with pure thoughts about him. (*Abst.* 2.34.1–2)

> For his offspring, [however,] the intelligible gods, hymn-singing in words should be added. For sacrifice is an offering to each god from what he has given, with which he sustains us and maintains our essence in being. (*Abst.* 2.34.4)

> [Lastly,] for the gods within the heaven, the wandering and the fixed [. . .], we should kindle fire which is already kin to them, and we shall do what the theologian says. He says that not a single animate creature should be sacrificed, but offerings should not go beyond barley-grains and honey and the fruits of the earth. (*Abst.* 2.36.3–4)

The basic principle behind this theology is obvious. Porphyry has taken the Platonic notion of a divine hierarchy and has correlated it with a hierarchy of sacrifices, so that the offering corresponds in nature to the deity being honored. In doing so, he seems to have taken the principle of correspondence that informed much traditional sacrificial practice (e.g., male animals to male deities) and to have translated it into a Platonic framework. But if the gods at the bottom of the hierarchy, the visible gods, are to receive inanimate offerings, what place is there in this schema for animal sacrifice?

The answer, of course, is that the visible gods are not the bottom of the hierarchy: "there remains the multitude of invisible gods, whom Plato called *daimones*" (*Abst.* 2.37.4). Porphyry makes a sharp distinction between two classes of daimones: those that subject their material part, their *pneuma*, to reason and act as the beneficent rulers of the material world, and those that do not control their *pneuma* but are instead controlled by it, with the result that they are subject to the appetites and passions of the material world; the latter, he says, "may reasonably be called maleficent" (*Abst.* 2.38.4). These maleficent daimones are responsible for many of the physical evils of human life, but they fool people into thinking that they are the beneficent daimones. "It is they who rejoice in the 'drink-offerings and smoking meat' [Hom., *Il.* 9.500] on which their pneumatic part grows fat, for it lives on vapors and exhalations, in a complex fashion and from complex sources, and it draws power from the smoke that rises from blood and flesh" (*Abst.* 2.42.3). Accordingly, "an intelligent, temperate man will be wary of making sacrifices through which he will draw such beings to himself. He will work to purify his soul in every way, for they do not attack a pure soul, because it is unlike them" (*Abst.* 2.43.1).

Porphyry's analysis is striking in a number of ways, but the particular aspect to which I want to call attention here is the extent to which he takes sacrifice seriously as a ritual that establishes a connection between the human and superhuman spheres.[6] Porphyry assumes a correspondence between sacrificial ritual and the structure of the cosmos; his objection to animal sacrifice is that by its very nature it establishes a connection between the person who performs it and a particular segment of the cosmos, namely, the maleficent daimones. These daimones work against the proper goal of the philosopher, which is to ascend upward into the realm of the intelligible, by involving us more deeply in the world of matter and the passions. Animal sacrifice, therefore, has serious consequences that ought to concern philosophers deeply and that they can appreciate only by understanding the relationship between sacrificial ritual and the structure of the cosmos. Porphyry's theology of sacrifice arises from the serious philosophical consequences that he attributes to sacrificial ritual, and it is this, I would argue, that represents something not found in earlier Greek tradition.

This argument may seem problematic, however, because it is widely accepted that many earlier thinkers also paid serious attention to the practice of animal sacrifice: the followers of Orpheus and of Pythagoras, most famously, as well as Empedocles and Theophrastus. Yet there is no good evidence that any of these earlier figures developed a theology of sacrifice; in my view, none of them did so because none of them was actually much interested in sacrifice as a ritual meant to establish a connection between the human and divine spheres.[7]

We may first consider the followers of Orpheus. That they refused to eat meat is fairly certain, although the evidence is more meager than many people might assume. The earliest piece of evidence, which we can date quite precisely to the year 428 BCE, is a passage from Euripides' *Hippolytus*. In it, Theseus derides his son as one who ostentatiously eats only inanimate food (δι' ἀψύχου βορᾶς), has Orpheus for his lord, and reveres a smoke of writings (*Hipp.* 952–54 = 627 Bernabé, *PEG*).[8] From two or three generations later we have a passage in Plato's *Laws* (*Leg.* 782c–d = 625 Bernabé, *PEG*), in which the Athenian is discussing how people's customs with respect to eating and drinking have changed over time. He says that

> the custom of men sacrificing one another is, in fact, one that survives even now among many peoples; whereas amongst others we hear of how the opposite custom existed, when they were forbidden so much as to eat an ox, and their offerings to the gods consisted, not of animals, but of cakes of meal and grain steeped in honey, and other such bloodless sacrifices, and from flesh they abstained as though it were unholy to eat it or to stain with blood the altars of the gods; instead of that, those of us men who then existed lived what is called an "Orphic life," keeping wholly to inanimate food and, contrariwise, abstaining wholly from things animate.[9]

These two passages constitute the only clear evidence prior to the imperial period for the Orphic refusal to eat meat.[10] Nevertheless, the casualness of the references suggest that both Euripides and Plato expected their audiences to be familiar with people who claimed to follow Orpheus and refused to eat animal flesh. It is important to note three particular aspects of these passages, two negative and one positive. First, in neither passage is there any explicit indication of why followers of Orpheus abstained from eating animal flesh. Second, a key term in both passages is *psyche*: followers of Orpheus must eat food that is *apsychos* and avoid that which is *empsychos*. Third, and for our purposes the most important point, in neither passage does animal sacrifice per se seem to have been a focus of Orphic attention. Euripides does not mention sacrifice at all, and Plato, who does, does not associate the Orphic life with any particular doctrine about sacrifice, but only with abstention from animate food.

For the Pythagoreans, we have evidence that is both more abundant and more inconsistent. Since the Pythagorean avoidance of meat is so familiar, it is first of all worth noting that some early and weighty evidence points in the opposite direction. Aristotle, it seems, claimed that Pythagoras "abstained from the womb, the heart, the *akalēphē*, and some other things of that sort, but made use of the rest."[11] Likewise, Aristoxenus asserted that Pythagoras enjoined abstention only from the plow-ox and the ram, but allowed the eating of all other animate things; he evidently went so far as to claim that Pythagoras had a particular fondness for little piglets and tender young goats.[12] Scholars have been uncertain what to do with these finicky yet carnivorous Pythagoreans, but we should at least keep in mind the existence of this early, alternative tradition.[13]

The more familiar tradition, that Pythagoras and his followers completely abstained from animate food, is one that we can also trace back relatively early, to the first half of the fourth century BCE. According to Porphyry, Eudoxus said that Pythagoras so avoided contact with slaughter that he not only abstained from animals (ἐμψύχων ἀπέχεσθαι), but never even came near butchers and hunters.[14] Similarly, the comic poets of the fourth century BCE made much of Pythagorean vegetarianism, which they apparently regarded as something that could always evoke a laugh from their audience; we have references to it in Mnesimachus, Antiphanes, and Alexis, all of whom employ almost the identical phrase ἐσθίειν οὐδὲν ἔμψυχον, "to eat nothing animate."[15] Lastly, Strabo quotes a passage from Alexander's steersman Onesicritus in which he claims to have explained to an Indian Brahman, who inquired whether doctrines similar to his own were taught among the Greeks, that Pythagoras had taught people to abstain from animate beings, ἐμψύχων ἀπέχεσθαι.[16]

We can make virtually the same observations about the evidence concerning Pythagoreans as we did about that concerning followers of Orpheus. First, none of it specifies the reasons why Pythagoreans abstained from meat. Second, those writers who do attribute to Pythagoras and his followers a total abstinence from meat consistently use the same terminology that was applied to the followers of Orpheus: abstinence from that which is *empsychos*, animate or "ensouled." Finally, in virtually none of these quotations is there any reference to the ritual of animal sacrifice. The only exception is a couplet of Mnesimachus preserved by Diogenes Laertius: "To Loxias we sacrifice: Pythagoras his rite / of nothing that is animate we ever take a bite."[17] And even here the emphasis is on the consumption of meat, not on the ritual of sacrifice per se.

Given this evidence, I would propose the thesis that these groups were not concerned with the ritual of animal sacrifice at all, but instead simply with the consumption of food from "ensouled" sources. Now there are two strong arguments against this thesis, one derived from reason and the other from authority. The argument from reason is that it denies or at least downplays the crucial and integral connection that existed in ancient Greek culture between normal sacrificial practice and the consumption of meat. The argument from authority is that Marcel Detienne has forcefully and repeatedly explained that the Orphic and Pythagorean rejection of meat is really all about the rejection of normative Greek sacrifice and, consequently, of the normative Greek politico-religious system of the polis embodied therein.[18] I will deal first with the argument from authority before turning to the argument from reason.

Detienne's analysis is elegant and persuasive, but his project is of a very particular kind. His focus on structure leads him to subsume the diachronic dimension within the synchronic; according to Detienne, historical change is simply one kind of variation and can accordingly be treated atemporally.[19] As a result, he tends to downplay or even disregard questions about the date and provenance of his evidence. When dealing with teachings attributed to Orpheus and Pythagoras, this seems to me highly problematic. These are traditions that extended over some eight centuries or more, with by far our fullest evidence coming from the third and fourth centuries CE or, in the case of the Orphic poems, even later. Since Greek culture in general changed drastically over this long span of time, it is not unreasonable to assume that the Orphic and Pythagorean traditions also changed. Moreover, there was no structure of authority within these traditions, no fixed body of texts that could lend them a measure of stability and coherence. On the contrary, the names "Orpheus" and "Pythagoras" seem to some extent simply to have functioned as hooks on which people could hang a variety of ideas and practices.[20] For all these reasons, Detienne's atemporal and associative use of evidence makes me deeply uncomfortable. In my own project, accordingly, I want to insist on the diachronic dimension and be as scrupulous as possible about the date and source of the evidence. It is true that sources for the Orphic and Pythagorean traditions from the imperial period have more to say about animal sacrifice; it is likewise true that some of this later material may derive from earlier sources.[21] Yet in the absence of other evidence, it is generally difficult to date a particular statement or tradition without becoming involved in a *petitio principii*. If we confine ourselves to evidence that can be firmly linked to pre-Hellenistic sources, we get a fairly consistent picture that contemporary observers did not particularly associate Orphic and Pythagorean doctrine with the ritual of animal sacrifice.

But, of course, the foundation of Detienne's analysis is the argument from reason that I have already mentioned.[22] It does seem to have been true that in ancient Greek culture there was an integral connection between animal sacrifice and the consumption of meat, insofar as anyone who refused to eat meat ipso facto had to reject animal sacrifice; the connection is explicit in the passages of Mnesimachus and especially Plato that I have already discussed. To that extent Detienne is surely right: the conscious decision to avoid eating meat must inevitably have meant the rejection of Greek animal sacrifice. Nevertheless, two things are worth stressing. First, a refusal to eat meat did not mean the rejection of the entire Greek sacrificial system, much of which took the form of nonblood offerings. We may in fact be reasonably certain that contemporary observers did not perceive any rejection of the sacrificial system on the part of Pythagoreans; if they had, the comic poets who so mercilessly mocked the social deviance of the Pythagorean diet would surely also have fastened on their impiety in refusing to offer sacrifice. Second, we should not arbitrarily reverse the logic of the practice as the sources present it: the problem for the followers of Orpheus and Pythagoras was not, it seems, that people were attempting to establish a connection with the divine by killing animals and roasting their flesh, but rather that people were consuming food from animate sources. The actual ritual of animal sacrifice seems to have been of concern only by implication, simply because eating meat typically took place in that context.[23]

If the followers of Orpheus and Pythagoras were not concerned with animal sacrifice, why were they so concerned with abstaining from meat? The usual assumption is that this followed from their belief in the transmigration of souls, the doctrine that *psychai* can pass after death from the body of a human to that of an animal; to eat animals, therefore, is tantamount to cannibalism.[24] Although the earliest extant author to make an explicit connection between abstinence from animate food and the doctrine of reincarnation is Ovid (*Met.* 15.453–78), that explanation is surely correct. Not only is it consistent with the regular emphasis that we have noted on the terminology of food that is *apsychos* or *empsychos*, it also receives corroboration from what we know of the teachings of Empedocles.

Extant citations of his work allow us to be fairly certain that for Empedocles, at least, the reason for abstaining from killing and eating animals was indeed a belief in the transmigration of souls between humans and animals.[25] A particularly celebrated passage, quoted at varying length by Plutarch, Origen, and Sextus Empiricus, seems to make this quite clear:

A father lifts up his dear son, who has changed his form,
and prays and slaughters him, in great folly, and they are at a loss
as they sacrifice the suppliant. But he, on the other hand, deaf to the rebukes,
sacrificed him in his halls, and prepared himself an evil meal.
In the same way, a son seizes his father and the children their mother,
and tearing out their life-breath devour their own dear flesh.[26]

As in Plato, we have here reference to sacrifice as the specific context for the slaughter and consumption of animals; I would again argue, however, that the underlying concern is with the sheer consumption of animate food and not so much with its ritual context. This is suggested by a couplet quoted by Porphyry and preserved in slightly different form in the Strasbourg papyrus: "Woe is me! That the pitiless day did not destroy me / before I devised with my claws terrible deeds for the sake of food."[27] In my view, Empedocles uses sacrificial imagery primarily as a means of heightening the emotional impact of his teachings, employing a literary strategy very similar to that used by the tragic poets who were his contemporaries.[28]

Whatever the precise nature of Empedocles' relationships to the Pythagorean tradition, the evidence for his ideas provides corroboration for the interpretation of Orphic and Pythagorean views that I have already advanced. That is, the thinkers of the late archaic and classical period who are commonly said to have rejected animal sacrifice were in fact not concerned with animal sacrifice as a cultic practice intended to establish a connection between the human and divine spheres; their concern was instead with the practice of eating meat, which they regarded as problematic because of their belief in the transmigration of souls between humans and animals.

Now, when we turn to Theophrastus, writing in the latter part of the fourth century BCE, we find something very different. It is quite clear from the passages quoted by Porphyry that Theophrastus was indeed interested specifically in animal sacrifice and how it relates to the gods, and not more generally in the practice of eating meat. Porphyry first gives us Theophrastus's cultural history of sacrifice, in which primitive offerings of grasses were succeeded by offerings of progressively more sophisticated agricultural products; war and famine, however, brought about human sacrifices, for which animal sacrifices were eventually substituted (*Abst.* 2.5.1–9.1). This historical sketch is followed by a series of arguments against animal sacrifice as an appropriate way to honor the gods. The main thrust of Theophrastus's arguments is that it is not right to honor the gods by acting unjustly, which is what we do when we deprive an innocent animal of its life. In one particularly striking extract, Theophrastus develops this argument in the form of a logical dilemma. On the one hand, since there is agreement that it is right to kill people who are evil-doers, "[p]erhaps, then, it is also right to exterminate those of the irrational animals that are [. . .] evil-doers" (*Abst.* 2.22.2). But it would not be proper to offer animals like this to the gods, any more than it would be to offer them defective animals. On the other hand, "we agreed that those of the other animals which do us no wrong should not be killed, so they too should not be sacrificed to the gods. If, then, neither these nor the evil-doers should be sacrificed, is it not obvious that we should in all cases abstain, and that none of the other animals should be sacrificed?" (*Abst.* 2.23.2).

Unlike the followers of Orpheus and Pythagoras, then, Theophrastus was interested specifically in the ritual of sacrifice: he provides a fully developed history of the ritual and presents a case against it that makes much of the fact that it is directed toward the gods. Nevertheless, I would argue that Theophrastus's real concern was not with the effects of the ritual or its relation to the structure of the cosmos, but with a problem of ethics. The reason that he puts so much stress on the gods as the recipients of sacrifices is that it allows him to focus on the ethical question of whether it is just to kill animals; the underlying assumption throughout is that the gods are concerned above all with "the quality of the sacrificers [rather] than the quantity of the sacrifice" (*Abst.* 2.15.3; cf. 2.19.4–5). Although Porphyry himself never mentions the title of the work from which he took these extracts, a comparison of one of them with a brief citation in a scholium to Aristophanes proves that it was Theophrastus's treatise *On Piety*, Περὶ Εὐσεβείας.[29] Even though we have no other certain evidence about the arguments of this work, it is likely that Theophrastus regarded piety as an ethical virtue, akin to or perhaps even a species of justice; this is certainly a view that is attested in later Peripatetic sources.[30] For all that Theophrastus emphasized the gods as the recipient of animal sacrifices, then, his real interest lay not in the way that sacrifice established a connection between humans and gods, but rather in the way that it expressed the internal disposition of the sacrificer, that is, the ethical virtue of piety or, more precisely, its lack.[31]

I hope that this discussion of earlier philosophical responses to animal sacrifice helps to bring out the distinctive features of Porphyry's treatment. It is of course true that Porphyry was deeply indebted to these earlier thinkers. The overarching subject of his treatise after all is specifically abstinence from eating animal flesh, something that he quite explicitly characterizes from the start as "the philosophy of Pythagoras and Empedocles" (*Abst.* 1.3.3); throughout he uses what we have seen is the characteristic vocabulary of food that is *empsychos* or *apsychos*. Yet despite the fact that Porphyry's main focus is not animal sacrifice but rather the practice of eating meat, his critique of animal sacrifice is logically independent of this particular context and derives instead from his wider philosophical program. He devotes much of Book 2 to developing a specific argument why animal sacrifice is bad in and of itself, regardless of whether we should or should not eat the animals that are sacrificed; moreover, as we have seen, he advances a fully developed theology of sacrifice, something in which the early Pythagoreans and Orphics apparently had no interest. Seen in this context, Porphyry's focus on the materiality of animal sacrifice as a cult act that brings people into association with maleficent daimones appears radically different from the concern of the early Pythagoreans and Orphics that eating animate food is tantamount to cannibalism.

Similarly, Porphyry makes great use of Theophrastus. The question that seems to lie at the center of Theophrastus's analysis, whether or not it is just to kill animals, is one that occupies Porphyry's attention for large parts of his treatise: not only in the extracts from Theophrastus himself in Book 2, but also in the first half of Book 1 (*Abst.* 1.4–26) and in the whole of Book 3. Yet it is striking that Porphyry's discussion of justice is framed entirely in terms of refuting the arguments of earlier philosophers; it is an issue that he addresses because it is central to the preexisting debate, not to his own philosophical concerns. When he comes to present his own arguments for abstaining from animate food, he grounds them not in the demands of justice but in the overarching need to free the soul from the sensible world in which it is enmeshed and restore it to the realm of the intelligible from which it has fallen (*Abst.* 1.27–57). It is within this same framework that he advances his theology of sacrifice. Sacrifice for Porphyry, as we have already seen, was a ritual that corresponded to the structure of the cosmos and thus had serious consequences for the attainment or nonattainment of the central goal of philosophy; it was not, as it seems to have been for Theophrastus, important simply because of the ethical problems involved in killing animals.

I have used Porphyry as an example of the new philosophical interest in sacrifice that we can observe in the imperial period largely because his treatment is both full and also relatively straightforward. But Porphyry was hardly the only philosopher to show this kind of interest in sacrifice. His younger contemporary, Iamblichus, presents a theology of sacrifice that in its fundamentals is very similar to the one we find in Porphyry's *On Abstinence*, although more complex and subtly developed. The main difference between their ideas is that Iamblichus did not regard animal sacrifice in a negative light, as Porphyry did, but as a ritual that was good and entirely appropriate in its proper place.[32] Moreover, the idea of a hierarchy of offerings correlated with a hierarchy of divinities was by their day apparently already an old one. We find traces of it, for example, in the systematic attack on Christianity that the philosopher Celsus wrote about a century before Porphyry. Celsus reproved Christians for refusing to offer animal sacrifice by invoking a similar theology. Like Porphyry, Celsus evidently believed that animal sacrifices were offered not to gods but to daimones; unlike Porphyry, however, he saw these daimones not as maleficent, but as the legitimate rulers of the material world, to whom the supreme god has assigned the various provinces of nature (Origen,

C. Cels. 8.24–36). Like Iamblichus, then, Celsus was able to justify animal sacrifice by claiming that it was the appropriate offering for a particular level of divinity.

Can we say anything about the origin of this theology of sacrifice? I would suggest that we can find some hints in Porphyry's own account. Porphyry in fact presents two slightly different accounts of the various levels of divinity with which offerings must be correlated. In the first, he begins with the supreme god, proceeds first to the intelligible gods and then to the visible, celestial gods, and ends with the daimones (*Abst.* 2.34–36). In the second, he again begins with the supreme god, but then proceeds to the world soul before continuing to the visible, celestial gods and the invisible gods, here identified with daimones, without mentioning the intelligible gods at all (*Abst.* 2.37). This second account, which leads into his detailed discussion of good and bad daimones, he explicitly attributes to "certain Platonists" (*Abst.* 2.36.6), by which he seems to have meant various philosophers of the second century CE.[33] The first account, by contrast, he does not explicitly attribute to any named individual or group, although at one point he refers to the Pythagoreans.[34] He does, however, cite two unnamed authorities: at the beginning of his exposition, he attributes the idea of worshipping the supreme god with pure thought alone to "a wise man," τις ἀνὴρ σοφός (*Abst.* 2.34.2); and at the end, he refers to the teaching of "the theologian," ὁ θεολόγος, that nothing animate should be sacrificed to the visible gods (*Abst.* 2.36.3–4). He seems to be continuing with the teaching of this theologian in what follows, when he asserts that anyone who gives thought to piety knows that animate offerings are not made to any gods, but only to daimones. He then concludes by invoking holy silence as a reason for not proceeding further with the exposition of the first account; it is in fact the obligation not to reveal a mystery that causes him to turn instead to the second account, the one that he attributes to the Platonists (*Abst.* 2.36.5–6).

What was Porphyry's source for the first account? His explicit reference to Pythagoreans and his use of the language of mysteries at the end of it has led some commentators to suppose a Neo-Pythagorean source; some have identified "the theologian" as Pythagoras himself.[35] I think that we can be more specific. It has long been recognized that the "wise man" to whom Porphyry attributes his ideas about the worship of the supreme god at the beginning of this section is Apollonius of Tyana. We know this thanks to Eusebius, who, after discussing this passage of Porphyry, goes on to quote a passage from Apollonius's treatise *On Sacrifices*, Περὶ Θυσίων, that is quite obviously Porphyry's source.[36] Now it seems to me entirely plausible that not only the particular idea about the supreme god but the account as a whole derives from this same source. Apollonius was in Porphyry's day certainly regarded as an authority on the Pythagorean tradition; Porphyry in fact used Apollonius's biography of Pythagoras as one of the sources for his own *Life of Pythagoras*.[37] The *theologos* whom he cites at the end of this section could just as well be Apollonius as Pythagoras—or, even more probably, Apollonius's "Pythagoras."[38] Moreover, the account that Porphyry presents fits perfectly well with what we know of Apollonius's treatise, which Philostratus describes as explaining "how to sacrifice to each of the gods appropriately and acceptably" (*VA* 3.41.2; cf. 4.19). It is true that Philostratus's claim to have found Apollonius's treatise "in many sanctuaries, many cities, and the homes of many wise men" (*VA* 3.41.2) does not fit too well with Porphyry's elaborate refusal to reveal a mystery, but the latter seems much more appropriate when we consider that the alternative title of Apollonius's treatise, according to the *Suda* (A 3420), was Τελεταί, *Initiations*. There is thus some reason to think that Porphyry's first account of the correlation of offerings with the divine hierarchy derives from this treatise of Apollonius.[39]

Given the enormous uncertainties about the historical Apollonius, I would not want to press this argument too far. Yet the combined evidence of Eusebius and the *Suda* indicates that a treatise on sacrifices circulated under Apollonius's name, and the similarity of the idea that Porphyry attributes to his "wise man" and the passage from this treatise quoted by Eusebius suggests that Porphyry was familiar with it, at least indirectly, and was to some extent influenced by it. The treatise itself may well have been pseudonymous, and thus later than the historical Apollonius; by the same token, the idea of a divine hierarchy correlated with a hierarchy of offerings may well antedate him. Nevertheless, I would suggest that the Neo-Pythagorean circles of the first century CE, of which we may take Apollonius as emblematic, is the most likely context for the origin of this kind of theology of sacrifice.

Since it is not possible here to develop this suggestion at any length, I will limit myself to two suggestions. First, the revival of the Pythagorean way of life, with its emphasis on abstention from animate food, provided a context in which its adherents would have reason to reconsider the purpose and effects of sacrifice and to develop a theology of sacrifice that would justify their own particular practice. As we have seen, Detienne was right to point out that a refusal to eat meat would also entail a refusal to take part in the most common forms of animal sacrifice, and such a refusal might well invite comment or explanation. [40] But abstinence from eating animate food is on its own clearly not enough to account for the appearance of a theology of sacrifice; as we have seen, the Pythagoreans of the archaic and classical periods seem to have rejected the practice of eating meat without feeling a need to develop such a theology. I would thus also suggest that in the early imperial period the practice of animal sacrifice was becoming invested with greater cultural significance than it had in earlier times. We might consider, among other things, the spread of large-scale civic animal sacrifices as a form of euergetism and the role played by animal sacrifice in defining the relationship between the Roman emperor and the inhabitants of the empire. As a result of developments like these, the particular ritual of animal sacrifice came to acquire a more prominent role within the larger sacrificial system, so that there were consequently greater pressures to justify its rejection.

Regardless of the date and reasons for this new theology of sacrifice, however, the development that I have traced here should at least call into question the assumption that the cultural meaning of animal sacrifice remained stable throughout Graeco-Roman antiquity. I am of course dealing here primarily with a discourse about sacrifice, the product of what Stanley Stowers and Daniel Ullucci in their contributions to this volume characterize as literate-cultural producers, and not to any significant extent with the practice itself. Yet in the fundamental transformation of religion that took place with the development and spread of Christianity, it was precisely this philosophical discourse, the theology of animal sacrifice, that came to be central to debates over its cultural role.

Notes

Earlier versions of this paper were presented at King's College London and the University of North Carolina at Chapel Hill; I owe thanks to the audiences on those occasions for comments and suggestions. I am also indebted to my colleague Fred Naiden for much thoughtful discussion on the topic of sacrifice, as well as some specific suggestions. Particular thanks are due to Jennifer Wright Knust and Zsuzsanna Várhelyi for their invitation to take part in the conference on sacrifice at Boston University, and to my fellow participants for their stimulating papers and comments. All translations are my own, unless otherwise noted.

1. Most notably Walter Burkert, *Homo Necans: The Anthropology of Ancient Greek Sacrificial Ritual and Myth*, translated by Peter Bing (Berkeley: University of California Press, 1983), and Marcel Detienne and Jean-Pierre Vernant, *La cuisine du sacrifice en pays grec* (Paris: Gallimard, 1979).

2. For a particularly thorough and elegant development of this approach, see Stanley Stowers, "Greeks Who Sacrifice and Those Who Do Not: Toward an Anthropology of Greek Religion," in *The Social World of Early Christianity: Essays in Honor of Wayne A. Meeks,* edited by L. M. White and O. L. Yarbrough (Minneapolis: Fortress, 1995), 293–333.

3. See David Frankfurter's contribution in this volume. For other work, see, for example, Kathryn McClymond, *Beyond Sacred Violence: A Comparative Study of Sacrifice* (Baltimore: Johns Hopkins University Press, 2008); F. S. Naiden, "Rejected Sacrifice in Greek and Hebrew Religion," *Journal of Ancient Near Eastern Religions* 6 (2006): 189–223; Naiden, "The Fallacy of the Willing Victim," *Journal of Hellenic Studies* 117 (2007): 61–73; Naiden, "Sacrifice and Self-Interest," in *Violent Commensality: Animal Sacrifice and Its Discourses in Antiquity,* edited by Ian C. Rutherford and Sarah Hitch (Cambridge: Cambridge University Press, forthcoming).

4. *Porphyre: De l'abstinence, Tome I: Introduction, Livre I*, edited with French translation and notes by J. Bouffartigue and M. Patillon (Paris: Les Belles Lettres, 1977), xviii–xix. The treatise is certainly later than 268 CE, when Porphyry left Rome, and probably later than the death of Plotinus in 270, but it is impossible to be more precise.

5. Quotations from *On Abstinence* (*De Abstinentia*) are taken from the translation of Gillian Clark, *Porphyry: On Abstinence from Killing Animals* (Ithaca: Cornell University Press, 2000).

6. Philippa Townsend, in her contribution to this volume, addresses another aspect of Porphyry's complex and multifaceted critique of animal sacrifice; whereas I concentrate on the role of sacrifice in linking the human and superhuman spheres, she focuses on its role in constructing relationships among humans. I share her doubts concerning Porphyry's participation in Diocletian's scheme of enforcing animal sacrifice.

7. As should be clear from my arguments, I am fully in agreement with Daniel Ullucci's insistence (see chapter 2, this volume) that we must analyze ancient statements about sacrifice

within the specific context of the individual writer's program, and not as examples of a generalized critique of animal sacrifice. I differ from him, however, in arguing that the ritual of animal sacrifice becomes a distinct focus of discursive interpretation, as opposed to being incidental to discussions whose primary focus lay elsewhere, only in the imperial period. I am not convinced that Plato, for example, paid serious philosophical attention to traditional ideas about the gods and traditional practices for establishing contact with them, since he makes little attempt to explain their relation to the central concepts of his metaphysics (strikingly unlike his later interpreters in the imperial period); the same is obviously true of Epicurus and also, I suspect, of the Stoics. I hope to develop this argument more fully in later publications.

8. Earlier editors regarded the text here as problematic—see I. M. Linforth, *The Arts of Orpheus* (Berkeley: University of California Press, 1941), 50–53, and W. S. Barrett's notes in his edition of Euripides' *Hippolytus* (Oxford: Clarendon, 1964), 342–44—but recent editors accept it as transmitted.

9. ἀψύχων μὲν ἐχόμενοι πάντων, ἐμψύχων δὲ τοὐναντίον πάντων. Plato, *Laws,* Greek text with English translation by Robert G. Bury, 2 vols. (1926; rev. ed., Cambridge: Harvard University Press, 2000).

10. Some scholars also cite Ar., *Ran.* 103 (= 626 Bernabé, *PEG*: Orpheus taught men φόνων ἀπέχεσθαι), but others rightly point out that the context strongly suggests that the reference here is to murder or possibly cannibalism (Linforth, *The Arts of Orpheus*, 68–70; Barrett, *Hippolytus*, 344). The chorus in a fragment of Euripides' *Cretans* (ap. Porph., *Abst.* 4.19.2 = 567 Bernabé, *PEG*) claims to avoid the eating of animate food, but the lack of any reference to Orpheus makes its relevance uncertain at best. The next definite reference to Orphic abstinence from animal food is in Plutarch (*Conv. sept. sap.* 16, 159C = 629 Bernabé, *PEG*).

11. We have this on the authority of Plutarch, as quoted by Aulus Gellius, who also helpfully explains that the *akalêphê* is a kind of marine animal (*NA* 4.11.11 = Arist. F 194 Rose); cf. Diog. Laert., 8.19, who cites the authority of Aristotle for the womb and the red mullet (*triglê*), and the list given by Porphyry (*Vit. Pyth.* 45), who does not cite Aristotle but names the womb, the red mullet, the *akalêphê*, "and practically all other sea creatures."

12. Diog. Laert., 8.20; according to Aulus Gellius (*NA* 4.11.6–7), he got his information from a Pythagorean friend of his named Xenophilus.

13. Marcel Detienne, *Les jardins d'Adonis* (Paris: Gallimard, 1972), 78–88, assumed that the conflicting accounts concern two different groups of Pythagoreans: the *theoretikoi* rejected meat entirely, the *akousmatikoi* or *politikoi* ate it selectively; Christoph Riedweg, *Pythagoras: His Life, Teaching, and Influence*, translated by Susan Rendall (Ithaca: Cornell University Press, 2005), 69, suggests a similar solution. Walter Burkert, *Lore and Science in Ancient Pythagoreanism*, translated by E. L. Minar, Jr. (Cambridge: Harvard University Press, 1972), 180–83, however, had already proposed that the muddle in the sources reflects the fact that the Pythagorean life "developed from living custom, with all its complexity and paradox, rather than from clearly articulated doctrine," and that the attribution of total abstinence to the *theoretikoi* and selective meat-eating to the *akousmatikoi* was merely an attempt by Nicomachus of Gerasa, writing in the second century CE, to resolve the contradiction that he found in his own sources. C. H. Kahn, *Pythagoras and the Pythagoreans: A Brief History* (Indianapolis: Hackett, 2001), 9, tentatively suggests that strict vegetarianism became the rule only after the collapse of the Pythagoreans as an organized political power.

14. Porph., *Vit. Pyth.* 7 = Eudoxus F 325 Lasserre.

15. Mnesimachus F 1 Kassel-Austin = Diog. Laert. 8.37; Antiphanes F 133 Kassel-Austin = Ath. 4.161a; Alexis F 223 Kassel-Austin = Ath. 4.161b.

16. *FGrHist* 134 F 17 = Strabo, *Geog.* 15.1.63–65, C 715–16.

17. Mnesimachus F 1 Kassel-Austin = Diog. Laert. 8.37; English translation, *Diogenes Laertius: Lives, Teachings and Sayings of Famous Philosophers*, translated by R. D. Hicks, 2 vols. (Cambridge: Harvard University Press, 1925).

18. Pythagoreans: Detienne, *Les jardins d'Adonis*, 71–114; Orphics: Detienne, *Dionysos mis à mort* (Paris: Gallimard, 1977), 161–217; summed up in Detienne, *Dionysos mis à mort*, 138–57, and more briefly in Detienne and Vernant, *La cuisine du sacrifice en pays grec*, 7–16.

19. See, for example, Detienne, *Dionysos mis à mort*, 43.

20. Orpheus: Linforth, *Arts of Orpheus*, esp. 291–306, and M. L. West, *The Orphic Poems* (Oxford: Oxford University Press, 1983), esp. 2–3. For followers of Pythagoras, see, for example, the brief survey of Kahn, *Pythagoras and the Pythagoreans*.

21. There are in fact few explicit statements about sacrificial practice in the Orphic tradition; Detienne relies instead on the myth of the Titan's dismemberment and cooking of Dionysus, which he reads as a critique of the practice of animal sacrifice. Although Detienne dates this myth to the sixth century BCE (*Dionysos mis à mort*, 165), there is no evidence for its existence prior to the third or at most the fourth century BCE (Linforth, *Arts of Orpheus*, 307–64; West, *Orphic Poems*, 140–75). The earliest explicit statements about sacrificial practice in the Pythagorean tradition appear in sources of the third century CE (e.g., Diog. Laert., 8.33; Porph., *Vit. Pyth.* 36; and Iambl., *Vit. Pyth.* 85, 150, and 152–53).

22. "Dans une société où la consommation de la nourriture carnée est inséparable de la pratique du sacrifice sanglant, qui constitue l'acte rituel le plus important de la religion politique, refuser de manger de la viande ne peut être une forme d'originalité purement individuelle ou simplement gastronomique: c'est rejeter d'un coup tout un système de valeurs véhiculé par un certain mode de communication entre les dieux et le monde des hommes" (Detienne, *Les jardins d'Adonis*, 86).

23. It is also worth noting that a refusal to eat food from "ensouled" sources had much broader implications than a refusal to participate in animal sacrifice, since not all animals that were eaten were slaughtered in sacrificial rituals; fish and game, for example, virtually never figured as sacrificial victims; J. N. Davidson, *Courtesans and Fishcakes: The Consuming Passions of Classical Athens* (New York: HarperCollins, 1997), 12–16; I owe this reference to Fred Naiden. Nevertheless, these were presumably also avoided by Orphics and Pythagoreans.

24. See, for example, Burkert, *Homo Necans*, 180; Riedweg, *Pythagoras*, 36–37.

25. For example, G. S. Kirk, J. E. Raven, and M. Schofield, *The Presocratic Philosophers*, 2nd ed. (Cambridge: Cambridge University Press, 1983), 318–20; B. Inwood, *The Poem of Empedocles: A Text and Translation with an Introduction*, rev. ed. (Toronto: University of Toronto Press, 2001), 64.

26. DK 31 B 137 = F 128 Inwood, *Poem of Empedocles*, translated by Inwood.

27. DK 31 B 139 = F 124 Inwood, *Poem of Empedocles*, translated by Inwood; cf. Porph., *Abst.* 2.31.5.

28. Sacrificial imagery is used to great dramatic effect, especially by Aeschylus; see, for example, Froma Zeitlin, "The Motif of Corrupted Sacrifice in Aeschylus' *Oresteia*," *TAPA*

96 (1965): 463–508. It was also used very effectively by Euripides; see, for example, David Sansone, "The Sacrifice Motif in Euripides' *IT*," *TAPA* 105 (1975): 283–95; Robin Mitchell-Boyask, "Sacrifice and Revenge in Euripides' *Hecuba*," *Ramus* 22 (1993): 116–34; and Albert Henrichs, "Drama and Dromena: Bloodshed, Violence, and Sacrificial Metaphor in Euripides," *HSCP* 100 (2000): 173–88.

29. Σ Ar., *Av.* 1354: Κύρβεις [. . .] ἀπὸ τῶν Κορυβάντων, ἐκείνων γὰρ εὕρημα, ὥς Θεόφραστος ἐν τῷ Περὶ Εὐσεβείας. Cf. Porph., *Abst.* 21.1: ὑπὸ τῶν κύρβεων, αἳ τῶν Κρήτηθέν εἰσι Κορυβαντικῶν ἱερῶν οἷον ἀντίγραφα.

30. For example, in the summary of Arius Didymus preserved by Stobaeus 2.7.25, and in the ps.-Aristotelian treatise *On Virtues and Vices* 5.2–3, 1250b22–4; see William W. Fortenbaugh, "Theophrastus: Piety, Justice and Animals," in *Theophrastean Studies*, Philosophie der Antike 17 (Stuttgart: Franz Steiner, 2003), 190.

31. See Dirk Obbink, "The Origin of Greek Sacrifice: Theophrastus on Religion and Cultural History," in *Theophrastean Studies on Natural Science, Physics and Metaphyscics, Ethics, Religion and Rhetoric,* edited by W. W. Fortenbaugh and R. W. Sharples (New Brunswick, N.J.: Transaction Books, 1988), 282–83, and, more generally, Fortenbaugh, "Theophrastus."

32. Iambl., *Myst.* 5, esp. 5.14; for discussion, see Gregory Shaw, *Theurgy and the Soul: The Neoplatonism of Iamblichus* (University Park: Pennsylvania State University Press, 1995), 146–52, and Emma C. Clarke, *Iamblichus' De Mysteriis: A Manifesto of the Miraculous* (Aldershot: Ashgate, 2001), 39–57.

33. See further *Porphyre: De l'abstinence, Tome II: Livres I et II*, edited with French translation and notes by J. Bouffartigue and M. Patillon (Paris: Les Belles Lettres, 1979), 35–36, who discuss various proposals for identifying these Platonists more precisely.

34. *Abst.* 2.36.1–2; the context is his discussion of the proper offerings to make to the intelligible gods. The general principle is that people should offer to the gods that which the gods have given them, and thus hymns in words and contemplation are appropriate for the intelligible gods. The Pythagoreans, who regard the gods as numbers, consequently make offerings of numbers to them.

35. See the discussion in Bouffartigue and Patillon, *Porphyre*, 10–11 and 35.

36. Euseb., *Praep. evang.* 4.13.1: "One might best therefore, so I think, pay the fitting attention to the divine, and in consequence more than any human by comparison find him favorable and kindly, if he was not to sacrifice in any way to God (to Him whom we so name), who is one and superior to all, second to whom we must necessarily suppose the other gods, nor address any perceptible thing to him at all, for he needs nothing even from those who are superior to us, nor is there any plant or animal at all that the earth grows or that the air nourishes to which no pollution is attached. One should always use with Him the superior kind of discourse, I mean that which does not issue through the mouth, but ask for His blessing with the noblest element in us, and this is Mind, which needs no instrument. For these reasons one should in no way sacrifice to the great God who is above all". (*Philostratus, Apollonius of Tyana: Letters of Apollonius, Ancient Testimonia, Eusebius' Reply to Hierocles,* translated by C. P. Jones (Cambridge: Harvard University Press, 2006), T 22. See further Bouffartigue and Patillon, *Porphyre,* 30–34, and Clark, *Porphyry,*152–53, for comparisons of this passage with that of Porphyry.

37. Porph., *Vit. Pyth.* 2. Apollonius's biography of Pythagoras was used more extensively by Iamblichus: I. Lévy, *Recherches sur les sources de la légende de Pythagore* (Paris: Ernest Leroux, 1926), 104–10.

38. Bouffartigue and Patillon, *Porphyre*, 11, note that precepts similar to those attributed to this *theologos* are elsewhere explicitly attributed to Pythagoras both by Porphyry himself (*Vit. Pyth.* 36) and by Diogenes Laertius (8.20 and 8.22). Porphyry elsewhere in this work uses the term *theologos* in the singular only once, at *Abst.* 2.55.1, of a certain "Seleucus the *theologos*"; when he uses it in the plural, which he does much more frequently, he seems to have in mind the Chaldean Oracles (Bouffartigue and Patillon, *Porphyre*, 39–46).

39. For a very different view of this treatise's possible contents, see the chapter by Fritz Graf in this volume; given the lack of evidence, certainty is impossible. Our two suggestions are not necessarily incompatible, however, since the broad theology of sacrifice that I propose might well have been sketched out as a sort of preface to a more detailed manual of rituals.

40. We may note, for whatever it is worth, that these are the circumstances in which Philostratus depicts Apollonius as expounding on sacrifice (*VA* 1.31–32 and 5.25).

10

A Satirist's Sacrifices

LUCIAN'S *ON SACRIFICES* AND THE CONTESTATION OF RELIGIOUS TRADITIONS

Fritz Graf

The story has been often told how the Greeks, almost as soon as they started to think about their ritual tradition, were bothered by animal sacrifice and rationalized its strange form or even replaced it with other rituals.[1] In this scholarly discussion, a short text buried in the body of texts ascribed to Lucian of Samosata, the satirist of the second century CE, has been curiously overlooked. In the manuscripts, it has the title Περὶ θυσιῶν, *On Sacrifices*. Few scholars have worked on it, despite the recent interest on Lucian; fewer still have taken it seriously as a theological text.[2] There is thus some room at least for a footnote on this curious text. I will also use it as a springboard for a wider thesis: at least in pagan discourse, there was never a contestation of sacrifice alone, but always as part of a larger rethinking and contesting of religious tradition in its mythical and ritual expression and against the backdrop of a theology, as old as (or older than) Plato, that insists on the essential goodness of divinity.[3]

I

Lucian's text is a diatribe, a polemical address to philosophically untrained people, a form for which the itinerant philosophers of the Hellenistic and imperial epoch were famous. From the start, its author sets a harsh tone:

> When I see what empty-headed people do in sacrifices, festivals and other encounters with the gods, what they ask and pray for, and what they are thinking about the gods, then I am not certain whether anyone is so sad and full of sorrow that he would not laugh out loud at the silliness of what they are doing.[4]

It is not just animal sacrifice, it is the entire ritual sequence that forms any Greek festival with its prayers and its underlying assumptions about the gods that provokes this rejection by the speaker.

Citing several well-known myths, the speaker then makes it clear that the general assumption in Greek religion is that "the gods do nothing without remuneration, and that they sell their goods to the humans"[5]—health costs a small ox; wealth, four oxen; a kingdom, a hecatomb; and the safe return from the campaign to conquer Troy, the life of the general's daughter. But these stories fit into what we have always known about poets such as Homer and Hesiod: they tell lies and spread defamations about the gods. In the central part of his diatribe, Lucian presents some of these defamatory myths, from Kronos castrating his father to old hag Rhea seducing the boy Attis, and he ends with the image of the hungry Olympians nervously looking out for sacrificial fire with its rising smoke; "and when someone sacrifices, they inhale the smoke with gaping mouths and like flies they drink the blood that is poured over the altar."

But the blame does not rest with the poets alone. All Greek worship is local, and in every place the locals assume that the gods reside in their town: the local temples are their residences; the statues in the temples, made in human form by artists such as Phidias and Polycletus, do not just represent them, but are the gods themselves.[6] Under the eyes of these gods, the local worshippers perform the sacrifices, from the fat bull offered by the wealthy farmer to the kiss that the very poor press on the god's right hand.

Still, animal sacrifice is the worst for Lucian:

> They put garlands on the animal that they first had carefully examined lest they kill something useless; they lead it to the altar and murder it under the god's eyes while it lows lamentably, presumably uttering blissful sounds and already being half suffocated sounding the flute to the sacrifice. [. . .] And the priest himself stands by, spattered with blood and just like that infamous Cyclops carving up the bodies, pulling out the entrails, cutting out the heart, pouring the blood over the altar and performing all these pious acts.[7]

This text resonates deeply with what Walter Burkert famously has seen as happening in Greek animal sacrifice, and what he understood as deep-seated remnants of our hunting past that preceded the neolithic agricultural revolution. A sacrifice is an act of bloody butchering, the victim is murdered, not just slaughtered ($\phi o \nu \epsilon \acute{u} o \upsilon \sigma \iota \nu$), despite its lament; the ritual plays out a comedy of innocence (in the words of Karl Meuli), with the participants simply pretending that everything is okay, that the animal agrees and even rejoices in the act, and that in the end it can be put together again. Far from being a commonplace act of preparing meat for consumption (as Jean-Pierre Vernant and his students have understood animal sacrifice), sacrifice for Burkert is an act of gruesome, albeit necessary violence, made palpable by acts of make-believe.[8]

In another paper on sacrifice, I have analyzed the merits and deficiencies of both Burkert's and Vernant's theories.[9] Here, it suffices to underline that Lucian's text is a public satirical condemnation of sacrifice. As such, it makes sense only if its sensibility is not that of the ordinary Greek who sacrifices—good satire does not state the obvious. In this reading, Lucian contradicts Burkert—ordinary Greeks did not think of grisly violence when performing a sacrifice; at the same time, this reading also shows that such an evaluation as Burkert's was not impossible in the framework of Greek religious thought in the same way as the make-believe reconstitution of the victim was not impossible in Greek sacrificial practice. Burkert himself highlights the sacrifice at the Athenian Diipoleia, the so-called Bouphonia, "Ox-Murder," at whose end the skin of the sacrificial bull was stuffed with straw and the blame for killing was shifted from the butcher to his knife.[10] Less well known is an ancedote about king Ptolemy IV Philopator that is told by Plutarch: when the king sacrificed four elephants and was then censured in his dreams by the gods for killing a sacred and god-fearing animal, he got back his sleep by having four bronze elephants dedicated instead.[11]

Back to Lucian: The Greeks, Lucian continues, are by no means the worst religious transgressors; non-Greeks offend in two directions. The Scythians sacrifice humans to Artemis (in all ancient thought on sacrifice, human sacrifice is in disquieting proximity to animal sacrifice, either preceding a less noxious rite or being the natural continuation of animal sacrifice on a spectrum that reaches from honey and fruit to living beings). The Egyptians, on the other hand, prefer animal-headed gods to divine anthropomorphism. Both are worse than Greek animal sacrifices, the one because it so utterly disregards human life, the other because it short-circuits the basic hierarchy that leads down from gods to humans to animals.

To a logical mind, the argument might seem somewhat strange: after all, Lucian just had discredited animal sacrifice by humanizing the animal victim. But this lack of logic underlines the fact that Lucian's main emphasis is not on ritual, but rather on what we could call theology, and what he and his contemporaries call philosophy, as the conceptual basis of ritual practice; in good Platonic tradition, he and his contemporaries construct philosophy in opposition and as a reaction to poetry. But since this is a satire and diatribe, Lucian's text is aggressively negative and depicts everything that he thinks is wrong with Greek ritual. The Cynic preacher castigates human foolishness; he does not educate through positive teaching. Positive theology has to be learned from elsewhere.

Despite this satirical, Cynic stance, Lucian is not always as negative as this. In the much longer and more elaborate *Icaromenippus* (the story of a philosopher flying up to heaven where he meets the gods), which derives from a different intellectual tradition, there is a passage that comes close to *On Sacrifices* in its overall intentions, but is less negative. Zeus shows his human visitor around Olympus, and they come to the Olympian Communications Center—a room with four interfaces, structures that look like wellheads with lids, with a gold throne next to each. Zeus seats himself on the first throne and lifts the lid of the adjoining well: up come the prayers of humans, most of them foolish or even criminal; Zeus deals with them in a very long scene that demonstrates how wrong human prayers are. Lucian is much shorter with the other three wells—the wells of oaths, of omina, and of sacrifices. This Zeus, however, is different from the gods as the humans assume them to be in

On Sacrifices: he thinks hard about answering the different prayers, and he carefully weighs the moral merits of each prayer.[12]

II

None of the arguments used by Lucian against anthropomorphism, images, prayers, and sacrifices is entirely new or isolated in the second century CE. I will try to assess the place and role of Lucian's diatribe in this contemporary debate.[13]

Besides Lucian's short text, *On Sacrifices,* the pagan contestation of sacrifice during the high empire appears mainly in two texts, Philostratus's *Life of Apollonius of Tyana* and Porphyry's *On Abstinence*, whereas the defense of sacrifice is important in Celsus's attack on Christianity, as reported by Origen. Other texts rarely add new points of view.[14] The works of Porphyry and Philostratus share a common interest in Pythagoreanism, and they agree in their assessment of how vegetarianism and sacrificial practice correlate: they both accept animal sacrifice as a religious practice of most people, but reject it for the philosopher; and they do so for different reasons, none connected with the Pythagorean insistence on vegetarianism.

This confirms that even for some philosophers of the imperial epoch vegetarianism did not necessarily lead to the rejection of sacrificial practice, unlike the extreme view advocated by radical Pythagoreans of the classical epoch: but even with them, as we know, full rejection of animal sacrifice came with a price, the loss of civic communality, or it led to all sorts of compromises, ranging from the token sacrifice of an animal made of dough to the prohibition of certain body parts such as the heart only.[15] Both young Seneca and, following a reasonable guess, young Plutarch advocated vegetarianism, but they both confined the argument to a question of diet and did not, as far as we know at least, renounce participation in sacrifices. Seneca later changed his mind because the nonconformism of being a vegetarian threatened his career; Plutarch is thought to have moved to mainstream Middle Platonism because this seemed to suit his overall personality better.[16] The theoretical stance in this question has been formulated by Porphyry: he makes a distinction between animal sacrifice and meat diet and concedes that it might be necessary even for a vegetarian to sacrifice an animal (for example, in a purification rite), but he insists that there is no necessity even then for eating its meat.[17] Thus, a philosopher has to have better reasons to reject sacrifices than his personal lifestyle.

Porphyry's first reason to reject animal sacrifice for the philosopher comes straight out of his fourth-century BCE source, the Aristotelian Theophrastus and his history of sacrifice.[18] Historically, animal sacrifice is a recent development, introduced after a long period during which humans offered only fumigations and libations—water and honey, grass, flowers, fruit and vegetables. Tradition thus is no argument in favor of animal sacrifice and could well argue for its rejection. (It is somewhat unclear what Theophrastus's position was; most likely, he argued for a scarce use of animal sacrifice, at least in private ritual practice. Polis cult, however, was unthinkable without animal sacrifice.) Porphyry's second reason is Platonic and theological: animal sacrifices address the daimones only who revel on blood, and a true philosopher does not want to converse with daimones; neither does he need purificatory sacrifices, being pure himself.

Philostratus shows us the same doctrine in action, through his work on the Pythagorean and vegetarian Apollonius of Tyana.[19] Like Pythagoras, whom Philostratus introduces in the prologue of this work,[20] Apollonius personally abstained from eating meat and shedding blood in sacrifice, but he did not advocate a general prohibition of it. During the time he spent in the sanctuary of Asclepius in Cilician Aegae, Apollonius observed the daily practice of sacrifice; when he censured it, he censured extravagant ritual killing, not ritual killing as such.[21] This is a topic that was already important to Theophrastus and through him to Porphyry, although Porphyry used it to bolster his arguments against animal sacrifice: the gods rejoice in simple offerings; fruits, vegetables, or even cakes are much more easily obtained than animals.[22] Even when discussing the practice of animal sacrifice with an Egyptian priest, Apollonius is ambivalent: he defends his own sacrifice, the burning of a statuette of a bull made of incense or some other pure resin, with the argument that the gods, being pure themselves, prefer to feed on the smell of pure substances and that a fire fed by pure resin communicates much better divine signs than any fire fed by wood (and, one has to add, animal fat). But even here, he refuses to turn this into a program of general ritual reform, and the same is true in other instances.[23]

According to Philostratus, when he was in India Apollonius also wrote a book "on sacrifices and the way to offer sacrifice to each god in a suitable and pleasing way."[24] If we can take Philostratus's description seriously, the book recalls the oracle cited by Porphyry in *On the Philosophy From Oracles* in which Apollo prescribed sacrifices to single categories of gods. The one fragment of this book that we possess does not contradict this description: it emphasizes wordless, noetic prayer as the most powerful sacrifice to the first and supreme god, but intimates that there are other gods below him;[25] but even so, it would address not a general audience, but mainly philosophers. Given the little we know about it, it is also possible that the book was more specialized than Porphyry's treatise *On Abstinence*: In the entry on Apollonius of Tyana, the *Suda* lexicon lists a book with the title *Initiations or On Sacrifices,* which might well be the same work. Rather than to a philosophical treatise, the double title points to a manual of rituals for a Neo-Pythagorean community—in the same way as the equally shadowy *Teletai* of Orpheus must address a Bacchic group, and the sacrifices to the many individual gods might be nothing more spectacular than the different fumigations that accompany each divinity in the book of *Orphic Hymns,* dated somewhere in the imperial epoch. Again, however this might be, there is no indication of a program to reform ancient sacrificial practice as a whole. This fits Apollonius's claim that he makes during his defense before Domitian, that his vegetarianism does not make him attack the eating habits of other people: nor did his Pythagoreanism make him prohibit animal sacrifice, except when he had to defend himself against an Egyptian specialist who should know better, given the Egyptian fame of theological wisdom.[26] Even the Ethiopian high priest in Heliodorus's *Ethiopian Tales* knows better: when his king is preparing a human sacrifice, he retires to his temple, because

> we do not condone with such a lawless sacrifice nor do we think that the divine attends to it, given that it prohibits sacrifices from other living beings and is, in our opinion, content with sacrifices of prayers and perfumes.[27]

Like Lucian, Apollonius directs other general criticism against other manifestations of ancient religion. When lecturing on religion in Athens, he talked not only about sacrifice, but also about libations and prayer, and he explained that he was praying only that the gods would give him what he deserved—a prayer recommended already by Socrates.[28] When preaching to the Smyrnaeans, he made a point by using a comparison between Phidias's Olympian statue of Zeus and Zeus in heaven: the latter is the real god, the former is an image that is confined to Earth. This makes the same point Lucian makes about statues: statues are not identical with the divinity. Nor are they indifferent objects, however: a merchant of statues is heavily censured when he refuses to carry Apollonius and his friends across the Aegean under the pretense that they might defile the divine images: philosophers are pure people; what is reprehensible, however, is to peddle divine images; the great artists of old exported their skills and tools and made the images on the very spot of their worship.[29] It comes as no surprise that Apollonius also rejects traditional mythology:

> The myths about the heroes, of which all poetry is full, corrupt their audience: the poets inform about outlandish passions, marriage between siblings, slander about the gods, the eating of children, mean crimes and punishments.

The only acceptable myths are the moralistic stories told in Aesop's animal fables.[30]

In many respects, Apollonius acts like an itinerant sophist, teaching in front of large crowds in cities such as Athens or Smyrna. It is tempting to compare a body of actual sophistic teaching, the thirty-five *Discourses* (Διαλέξεις) that, according to the manuscript title, the Platonic philosopher Maximus of Tyre performed during his first stay in Rome; Maximus is more or less a contemporary of Lucian. The main theme of the *Discourses* is popular ethics, but the correct religious behavior is also important: according to most ethicists of the time, incorrect religious behavior damages one's soul in the same way as unethical behavior towards fellow humans does, be it superstition (δεισιδαιμονία), an excess of religion that leads humans to be afraid of the gods, or atheism, the lack of due respect and reverence for the gods.

Three discourses address topics we already know. The *Fourth Discourse* compares poetry and philosophy and comes to the conclusion that both are about the same thing, human improvement. The corollary, however, is that crude anthropomorphism is rejected without hesitation or discussion: mythical narratives are allegories, not historical facts (which is a common stance in philosophical thinking about mythology).[31] The *Second Discourse* deals with a question of divine images, "[w]hether one should erect statues to the gods." The question is answered in the affirmative since to create an image of one's gods is an anthropological constant, as Maximus shows in a lengthy history that is echoed in Lucian: mountaintops, rivers, and trees were the first images of the gods, statues came later. But divine images are just this, images; they are signs (σημεῖα) that remind one to worship the Divine. Thus, forms and materials for divine images are not essential to the gods, but are culturally determined; as signs, the images are unable to express the radical otherness of the Divine. But in a somewhat inconsistent view Maximus still prefers anthropomorphic images, since the human body is very beautiful, and like Lucian he rejects the animal-headed statues of the Egyptians.

The *Fifth Discourse* answers a question about "[w]hether one should pray." The answer is again affirmative; but like Apollonius, Maximus rejects the prayer for specific things. The gods cannot be influenced by our requests, but this does not mean that prayer is useless, as already understood by Socrates and Plato, who simply prayed to the gods to give them what they deserved. Such a prayer is a way of reflecting with the gods about oneself and one's virtue. As Maximus himself phrased it:

> You think that a philosopher's prayer is a demand for what one does not
> have; I however that it is a conversation and discussion with the gods about
> what one has, and a demonstration of one's virtue.[32]

Sacrifice is only once mentioned in this context, in a list of strategies tried by humans to escape destiny: the assumption of sacrifice as a gift to sway the gods is as mistaken as the prayer for material goods. Maximus does not clarify how the correct sacrifice would look like, but there is no indication that he objected to animal sacrifice.[33] Much later, under Julian, the Neo-Platonist philosopher Salustius will include animal sacrifice without hesitation in his allegorical reading of the different types of sacrifice—"we offer first fruits of our possession in the form of votive offerings, of our bodies in the form of hair, of our life in the form of animals."[34]

In other words: There is a consistency in the religious discussion in the imperial epoch insofar as it addresses the same arguments over and over: anthropomorphic myths, statues as images of the gods, prayer, and sacrifice. And there is a consistency in the way these arguments are addressed. Anthropomorphic myths are rejected as morally and theologically wrong; but there is always the possibility of reading the poetical narratives as moral allegories. Statues are accepted if one takes them not as representations of the gods in the crude sense that they are the gods themselves, but as culturally determined signs of the gods. This agrees also with Porphyry's treatise *On Divine Images,* where he explains divine images as representations of invisible things that should be read as one reads a book, although as a Neo-Platonist he has to reject any attempt of defining these signs as random;[35] anthropomorphic images are better than theriomorphic ones. Prayer is accepted only if it does not ask for material things, since the gods know much better than we do what we should receive from them—although at least Maximus seems to imply that a philosopher is more apt to offer a disinterested prayer than a commoner would be. Sacrifice finally is accepted, even if it is animal sacrifice: bloodless sacrifice is possible in private only and mostly for the philosopher.

Two things result from all this. First, the pagan contestation of animal sacrifice was never meant for everybody; it was not intended as a mass conversion to a purer form of worship, but was addressed to small groups on the margin of society.[36] Given the centrality of animal sacrifice in public religious action (Lucian's festivals), it could not have been otherwise. Second, there was another discussion, aimed at the public at large, in which sacrifice was inserted into a larger debate about ritual behavior (offering prayers, erecting statues, telling myths) that was not meant to undermine and subvert traditional practice but to adapt the practice to the higher standards of philosophical theology. It was only the Christians who were seen as subverting traditional practice: Celsus, another contemporary of Lucian, censures them for rejecting to erect altars, images, and temples as if they were a mystery association, and he urges them to participate in the public festivals of the ancient city.[37] The subtext must be that the Christians are the only mystery association radically to stay away, whereas Neo-Pythagoreans such as Apollonius and Neo-Platonists such as Porphyry were able to combine their private religious beliefs and actions with the different demands of their overall community.

III

How does Lucian's diatribe fit into all this? As a diatribe, it is addressed not to the small community of esoteric philosophers, but to the public at large, to the crowds on the marketplace that itinerant sophists used to address. Thus, it should not subvert sacrificial practice, but only criticize its excesses that were not compatible with a refined theology.

It is possible to read the diatribe in this way. The one condition is to move away from what the title suggests, that it is a diatribe against sacrifice, and to regard it as a diatribe against the absurdities of traditional religion as expressed in daily practice. If read in this way, neither are the attacks on traditional mythology and the rejection of Egyptian images somewhat loose excurses anymore, as earlier interpreters had thought, nor is the remark on the statues (that they should not be seen as identical with divinity) a mere afterthought. And, more importantly, the words with which the treatise opens gain a much better sense: when the speaker attacks "what empty-headed people do in sacrifices, festivals and other encounters with the gods, what they ask and pray for, and what they are thinking about the gods," he censures everything that happens in a public festival, of which the animal sacrifice is only a part. It remains an important part, to judge from the vivid and gruesome picture of the blood-spattered priest, but only a part nevertheless, together with the stories about the partiality and venality of the gods, the idea that gods live in statues, and the theriomorphic absurdities of Egyptian religion. It might well be that the title

On Sacrifices is not Lucian's title at all, but the addition of a Christian monk in Byzantium whose fancy was caught, as is ours, by the image of the bloodied priest.

Notes

1. See, most recently, Stella Georgoudi, Renée Koch Piettre, and François Schmidt, eds., *La cuisine et l'autel: Les sacrifices en questions dans les sociétés de la Méditerrannée ancienne*, Bibliothèque de l'École des Hautes Études Sciences Religieuses 124 (Turnhout: Brepols, 2005); Véronique Mehl and Pierre Brulé, *Le sacrifice antique: Vestiges, procédures et stratégies* (Rennes: Presses Universitaires de Rennes, 2008); and Maria-Zoe Petropoulou, *Animal Sacrifice in Ancient Greek Religion, Judaism, and Christianity, 100 BC–AD 200* (Oxford: Oxford University Press, 2009); in a much wider perspective, also Kathryn McClymond, *Beyond Sacred Violence: A Comparative Study of Sacrifice* (Baltimore: Johns Hopkins University Press, 2008).

2. Rudolf Helm, *Lucian und Menipp* (Leipzig: Teubner, 1906); Klaas Johan Popma, *Luciani De Sacrificiis* (Amsterdam: Becht, 1931); Marcel Caster, *Lucien et la pensée religieuse de son temps* (Paris: Les Belles Lettres, 1937); Hans-Dieter Betz, *Lukian von Samosata und das Neue Testament* (Berlin: Akademie-Verlag, 1961).

3. Already Hesiod's story of Prometheus's instauration of sacrifice, *Th.* 535–57, tries to deal with its theological awkwardness in the light of Zeus's justice (but see the contribution of James Rives to this volume).

4. Lucian, *De sacr.* 1: Ἃ μὲν γὰρ ἐν ταῖς θυσίαις οἱ μάταιοι πράττουσι καὶ ταῖς ἑορταῖς καὶ προσόδοις τῶν θεῶν καὶ ἃ αἰτοῦσι καὶ ἃ εὔχονται καὶ ἃ γιγνώσκουσι περὶ αὐτῶν, οὐκ οἶδα εἴ τις οὕτως κατηφής ἐστι καὶ λελυπημένος ὅστις οὐ γελάσεται τὴν ἀβελτερίαν ἐπιβλέψας τῶν δρωμένων. Translations of Lucian are adapted from the Loeb edition; all other translations are mine.

5. Lucian, *De. sacr.* 2: Οὕτως οὐδέν, ὡς ἔοικεν, ἀμισθὶ ποιοῦσιν ὧν ποιοῦσιν, ἀλλὰ πωλοῦσιν τοῖς ἀνθρώποις τἀγαθά.

6. This is a correct observation; see, for example, the often-noted habit of Pausanias to use a god's name to designate the statue, or the Laconian inscriptions where the person carrying the statue in a procession is "he who carries the god," τὸν σιὸν φέρων (*IG* V:1.210–11, first century BCE).

7. Lucian, *De. sacr.* 12–13: στεφανώσαντες τὸ ζῷον καὶ πολύ γε πρότερον ἐξετάσαντες εἰ ἐντελὲς εἴη, ἵνα μηδὲ τῶν ἀχρήστων τι κατασφάττωσιν, προσάγουσι τῷ βωμῷ καὶ φονεύουσιν ἐν ὀφθαλμοῖς τοῦ θεοῦ γοερόν τι μυκώμενον καὶ ὡς τὸ εἰκὸς εὐφημοῦν καὶ ἡμίφωνον ἤδη τῇ θυσίᾳ ἐπαυλοῦν. . .ὁ δὲ ἱερεὺς αὐτὸς ἕστηκεν ἡμαγμένος καὶ ὥσπερ ὁ Κύκλωψ ἐκεῖνος ἀνατέμνων καὶ τὰ ἔγκατα ἐξαιρῶν καὶ καρδιουλκῶν καὶ τὸ αἷμα τῷ βωμῷ περιχέων καὶ τί γὰρ οὐκ εὐσεβὲς ἐπιτελῶν;

8. Walter Burkert, *Homo Necans: Interpretationen altgriechischer Opferriten und Mythen*, Religionsgeschichtliche Versuche und Vorarbeiten 32 (Berlin: De Gruyter, 1972); Walter Burkert, *Homo Necans: The Anthropology of Ancient Greek Sacrificial Ritual and Myth*, translated by Peter Bing (Berkeley: University of California Press, 1983); Marcel Detienne and Jean-Pierre Vernant, *La cuisine du sacrifice en pays grec* (Paris: Editions Gallimard, 1979). See also Burkert's and Vernant's contributions in *Le sacrifice dans l'antiquité*, edited by Olivier Reverdin and Bernard Grange, Entretiens sur l'antiquité classique (Geneva: Fondation Hardt, 1981), with their ensuing debate.

9. "One Generation after Burkert and Girard: Where Are the Great Theories?" conference paper, Chicago, Spring 2008, to be published in *Ancient Victims, Modern Obervers: Reflections on Greek and Roman Animal Sacrifice*, edited by Christopher A. Faraone and F. S. Naiden (Cambridge: Cambridge University Press, forthcoming).

10. Main passage: Porph., *Abst.* 2.29–30.

11. Plut., *De soll. an.* 17 (972 BCE).

12. Lucian, *Icar.* 25–26.

13. See now Petropoulou, *Animal Sacrifice*.

14. In a way, the most important theoretical statement is Sal., *De Diis* 15–16.

15. See the overview in Walter Burkert, *Weisheit und Wissenschaft: Studien zu Pythagoras, Philolaos und Platon* (Nuremberg: Hans Carl, 1962), 167–69; translated by E. L. Minar, Jr. as *Lore and Science in Ancient Pythagoreanism* (Cambridge: Harvard University Press, 1972), 180–83.

16. Sen., *Ep.* 108.17–19. Plutarch: the two fragmentary speeches collected in *On Eating Flesh* (*De Esu Carnium*) advocate vegetarianism but are generally regarded as drafted in his youth, see Harold Cherniss in his introduction to the text in the LCL edition (Cambridge: Harvard University Press, 1957), 537.

17. Porph., *Abst.* 2.2. See also Philostr., *VA* 1.1 who tells us that Pythagoras "abstained from all meat eating and from sacrifice"; this implies that the two could be disconnected.

18. An extensive reconstruction of Theophrastus's treatise is given by Walter Pötscher, ed., *Theophrastos.* Περὶ Εὐσεβείας. *Griechischer Text herausgegeben, übersetzt und eingeleitet* (Leiden: Brill, 1964).

19. Philostratus's *Life of Apollonius of Tyana* is curiously absent in Petropoulou, *Animal Sacrifice*.

20. Philostr., *VA* 1.1.

21. Philostr., *VA* 1.10. See also his bloodless sacrifice to the heroes in Troy, Philostr., *VA* 4.11.

22. Porph., *Abst.* 2.15–20, adding a story from Theopompus in 2.16, on which see Pötscher, *Theophrastos*, 44.

23. Philostr., *VA* 5.25.

24. Philostr., *VA* 3.41, 4.19; the *Suda* cites a title Τελεταὶ ἢ περὶ θυσιῶν, Α 3420.

25. Euseb., *Praep. evang.* 4.14.

26. Philostr., *VA* 8.7.4.

27. Heliod., *Aeth.* 10.9.6: Ἀλλ' ἡμεῖς μὲν εἰς τὸν νεὼν μεταστησόμεθα, θυσίαν οὕτως ἔκθεσμον τὴν δι' ἀνθρώπων οὔτε αὐτοὶ δοκιμάζοντες οὔτε προσίεσθαι τὸ θεῖον νομίζοντες ὡς εἴθε γε ἦν καὶ τὰς διὰ τῶν ἄλλων ζῴων θυσίας κεκωλῦσθαι μόναις ταῖς δι' εὐχῶν καὶ ἀρωμάτων καθ' ἡμέτερον νόον ἀρκουμένους.

28. Philostr., *VA* 4.40.

29. Philostr., *VA* 5.20.

30. Philostr., *VA* 5.14.

31. The most important treatment is Ilaria Ramelli and Giulio Lucchetta, *Allegoria. 1: L'età classica* (Milan: Vita e Pensiero, 2004); see also still Jean Pépin, *Mythe et allégorie: Les origines grecques et les contestations judéo-chrétiennes*, 2nd ed. (Paris: Études Augustiniennes, 1976); Jean Pépin, *La tradition d'allégorie: De Philon d'Alexandrie à Dante*, Études Augustiniennes 120 (Paris: Études Augustiniennes, 1987).

32. Maximus of Tyre, *Dialexeis* 5.8: ἀλλὰ σὺ μὲν ἡγεῖ τὴν τοῦ φιλοσόφου εὐχὴν αἴτησιν εἶναι τῶν οὐ παρόντων, ἐγὼ δὲ ὁμιλίαν καὶ διάλεκτον πρὸς τοὺς θεοὺς περὶ τῶν παρόντων καὶ ἐπίδειξιν τῆς ἀρετῆς.

33. Maximus of Tyre, *Dialexeis* 5.5.

34. Sal., *De diis* 16: χρημάτων μὲν δι' ἀναθημάτων, σωμάτων δὲ διὰ κόμης, ζωῆς δὲ διὰ θυσιῶν ἀπαρχόμεθα.

35. Porphyry, frg. 351.

36. The association for which the *Orphic Hymns* were written did not perform animal sacrifice, at least in the initiation ritual that is outlined by the hymn book, on which see Anne-France Morand, *Études sur les hymnes orphiques*, Religions in the Graeco-Roman World 143 (Leiden: Brill, 2001), and my "Serious Singing: The Orphic Hymns as Religious Texts," *Kernos* 22 (2009): 169–82. The lengthy rules of a late Hellenistic private association in Philadelphia (Lydia) are silent about sacrifices, whereas the Dionysiac community reflected in an inscription from second-century CE Smyrna accepts animal sacrifices and prohibits only to eat the heart; Frantisek Sokolowski, *Lois sacrées de l'Asie Mineure* (Paris: Boccard, 1958), nos. 20, 84. The same prohibition appears in a short law from Rhodes;František Sokolowski, *Lois sacrées des cités grecques. Supplément* (Paris: Boccard, 1962), no. 108.

37. In Orig., *C. Cels.* 8.17 and 8.21.

11

Bonds of Flesh and Blood

PORPHYRY, ANIMAL SACRIFICE, AND EMPIRE

Philippa Townsend

Despite its prevalence, sacrifice was the subject of much controversy, innovation, and analytical attention in the first few centuries CE. Christian texts provide some of the clearest examples of the complexity of sacrificial discourses in this period, with their polemics against animal sacrifice and their simultaneous development of sacrificial interpretations of Jesus' death; but non-Christians were also debating how sacrifice should properly be performed and understood.[1] One way to understand this proliferation of sacrificial discourses is by considering the role that sacrifice played in ordering social relations—particularly kinship relations—in the ancient Mediterranean. In her influential work *Throughout Your Generations Forever*, Nancy Jay argued that sacrifice has been tied to the establishment of patrilineal descent in various cultures, providing a ritual initiation into kin groups that "transcends birth," and thus subordinates the reproductive role of women.[2] Building on Jay's work, Stanley Stowers has explored in depth the connections between sacrifice and kinship in Greek society from classical times to the early Roman empire. He has shown that sacrificial practices functioned to regulate membership of varying types of descent groups' and furthermore that the association between sacrifice and childbirth emerged explicitly in Greek literary and medical texts.[3] According to Stowers, "Intuiting 'obvious' similarities between the birth of a child and the sacrifice of an animal was a reflex of a sacrificially constructed habitus."[4] It is important to note, however, that identifying a persistent discursive association between sacrifice and descent is not the same as claiming that sacrifice has an inherent "meaning," even within a particular culture.[5] Nor does it imply that there was only one way in which people interpreted sacrifice.[6] It is simply to suggest that sacrifice was commonly (not universally) understood to have a connection to descent and kinship within ancient Greek society. This association was not static, however, and it could be deployed in myriad ways.[7]

While Jay was particularly interested in the gendered implications of sacrificial and kinship practices, Stowers pointed out that in Hellenistic and Roman times "sacrifice seems to have increasingly worked to establish and maintain many types of social relations beyond gender."[8] Indeed, the work of Jay and Stowers provides rich resources for thinking about how *ethnic* groups were shaped and perpetuated in the ancient world, since kinship is constitutive of ethnicity.[9] The expansion and consolidation of the Roman empire necessitated new means of producing knowledge and perpetuating control: accordingly, imperial authorities used ethnic classifications to order and hierarchize their subjects, regulate their behavior, extract taxes, extend or withhold privileges, impose punishments, and even relocate people geographically. Categorizations that were created or exploited for the deployment of imperial power, however, could also be challenged, sidestepped, disrupted, or co-opted by subject people.[10] Because of the discursive connection between sacrifice and kinship in the Roman empire, reformulating sacrifice simultaneously provided ways to intervene in, or critique, established practices of kinship and ethnic organization within a colonial context. Accordingly, sacrifice emerged in this period as a key discursive site across communities for the negotiation of ethnic identity within empire. I have argued elsewhere that the early Christians' reformulation of sacrifice was inextricable from their transformation of the relationship between ethnicity and religion.[11] In this chapter, I focus on the Neo-Platonist philosopher Porphyry, arguing that his theories on sacrifice similarly illuminate his vision of the religious functions of ethnic tradition and imperial rule.

Porphyry on Sacrifice, Kinship, and Community

Porphyry's treatise *On Abstinence from Killing Animals*, written in the mid- to late third century CE, is perhaps the most famous non-Christian text to criticize blood sacrifice. Porphyry does not object to sacrifice in total, but he argues that different sacrifices should be made to different powers. No material sacrifices should be made to the highest god, he claims, but only "pure silence and pure thoughts"; then, "for his offspring, the intelligible gods, hymn-singing in words should be added" (*Abst.* 2.34).[12] To the celestial gods, however, we should offer fire (*Abst.* 2.37). As for animals, they can never be offered up to the higher gods, only to good or bad *daimones* (*Abst.* 2.36), which, Porphyry explains, are souls that have been generated from the world soul, but administer only the regions below the celestial sphere and are animated by *pneuma,* which is partly corporeal. It is bad *daimones* in particular who relish the smoke and vapors of blood sacrifices and are nourished by them (*Abst.* 2.42). For this reason, the person who wishes to pursue the philosophical life will avoid such sacrifices, so as not to draw these beings into proximity with himself (*Abst.* 2.43).[13]

Porphyry identifies *daimones*, both good and bad, with some of the divinities worshiped through local tradition: "People have given some of them names, and they receive from everyone honors equal to the gods and other forms of worship. Others have no name at all in most places, but acquire a name or a cult inconspicuously from a few people in villages or cities" (*Abst.* 2.37). Since civic or community cult often involves the worship of bad *daimones*, Porphyry advises that the wise should participate only at a minimal level, offering nonblood sacrifices: "If it is necessary for cities to appease even these beings, that is nothing to do with us. In cities, external and corporeal things are thought to be good and their opposites bad, and the soul is the least of their concerns" (*Abst.* 2.43; cf. *Abst.* 2.33). In a series of moves, then, Porphyry not only associates blood sacrifices particularly with malevolent powers that rank lowest on the supernatural scale, but also associates the worship of these *daimones* with community or civic cult. This is not to say that he believes that civic cult is *exclusively* aimed at *daimones*, but that the worship of gods and daimones is mixed together in it, so that participating is potentially dangerous for the philosopher.[14] In fact, Porphyry makes it clear that the path to the highest god does not run through community cult at all, and he emphasizes instead the individualistic nature of this journey: "The philosopher, priest of the god who rules all, reasonably abstains from all animate food, working to approach the god, alone to the alone, by his own effort, without disruption from an entourage" (*Abst.* 2.49). So Porphyry's disparagement of animal sacrifice in this text corresponds to a downgrading of kinship and community affiliation as firmly located in the lower realm of experience.

However, there is an aspect of Porphyry's treatise that reveals an even closer connection between his views on sacrifice and on kinship. In Book 3, he challenges the idea that because animals are different from us we do not owe them just treatment, arguing that, not only do animals indeed possess souls and reason, but the fact that they consist of the same natural elements as humans means that they are our kin:[15]

> Thus also we say, I think, that Greek is related and kin [οἰκείους τε καὶ συγγενεῖς] to Greek, barbarian to barbarian, all human beings to each other, for one of two reasons: either they have the same ancestors, or they have food, customs and race [γένους] in common. Thus also we posit that all human beings are kin [συγγενεῖς] to one another, and moreover to all the animals, for the principles of their bodies are naturally the same. I say this not with reference to the primal elements, for plants too are composed of these; I mean, for instance, skin, flesh and the kinds of fluids that are natural to animals. . . . The race [γένος] of other animals would then be related and kin to us in all respects, for all of them have the same foods and breath, as Euripides says, and the same "blood-red flows" [φοινίους . . . ῥοάς], and show that the common parents of all are heaven and earth. (*Abst.* 3.25)[16]

Porphyry's opposition to animal sacrifice is not due to an abandonment of the association of sacrificial blood with kinship then, but rather to a shift in the significance of that association. The blood of animals and the blood of human procreation are not analogous or homologous,[17] but essentially *identical* ("the same blood-red flows"). Animal blood cannot function as a map on which human groups mark out their own consanguinity, because animals and humans are actually part of the same territory. Therefore, from Porphyry's perspective, the construction of kinship communities through animal sacrifice both relies on, and creates, false distinctions.

Porphyry's extension of shared kinship, not only to all of humanity but to nonhuman animals as well, attenuates boundaries based on birth or race, employing ideas of blood and flesh to stress the commonality of all animate creatures, rather than to mark differences between groups. Conventional distinctions (Greek/barbarian, human/nonhuman) remain, but their significance is diminished by his emphasis on an underlying uniformity. This does not mean that Porphyry viewed everyone as equal—he makes it clear that he considers the philosopher to be superior to the masses, and he also distinguishes between savage and tame animals. But he argues that hierarchical distinctions should not be made on the basis of blood, but on the extent to which we have "perfected" ($\dot{\alpha}\pi\eta\kappa\rho\iota\beta\omega\mu\acute{\epsilon}\nu\alpha\varsigma$) the characteristics of the soul that we all share—appetite, anger, reason, and perception (*Abst.* 3.25).

This extreme universalism emerges again in a cultic context in Porphyry's *Letter to Anebo*, in which he challenges the veneration of Egyptian wisdom, asking skeptically why barbarian sacred names alone are used in religious rituals:

> Why of meaningful names do we prefer the barbarian to our own? . . . For a listener looks to the meaning, so surely all that matters is that the conception remains the same, whatever the kind of words used. . . . For he who is invoked is not Egyptian; nor does he use Egyptian language. (*Letter to Anebo*, quoted by Iambl., *Myst.* 7.4–5)[18]

Once again, Porphyry downplays the importance of ethnic differences by emphasizing a deeper homogeneity: common blood should unite, not divide, and particular ethnic traditions are valuable only as interchangeable instantiations of universal truth.

Universalism and Imperialism

Clearly, Porphyry's philosophical universalism has political implications. Universalism, according to postcolonial writers, has played a fundamental role in the establishment and propagation of modern imperialism:

> The question of universality has emerged perhaps most critically in those Left discourses which have noted the use of the doctrine of universality in the service of colonialism and imperialism. The fear, of course, is that what is named as universal is the parochial property of dominant culture, and that "universalizability" is indissociable from imperial expansion.[19]

Historians of the ancient world have applied this insight to Greco-Roman universalistic discourses, particularly those of Platonism.[20] Accordingly, Porphyry's devaluation of cultural particularity has been interpreted as an implicit defense of Greek cultural hegemony and imperial power. Peter Struck, for example, points out that Porphyry's rhetoric of universalism "fits all too well the needs and imagination of an imperial culture, where the local is always the parochial, and the universal is the common good."[21] Similarly, Jeremy Schott characterizes Porphyry's position as a defense of a "staunchly polarized world" and a "carefully constructed dichotomy between Greeks and others," which places him firmly on the side of Roman imperial power: "Porphyry is immersed in foreign wisdom, but nothing from Egypt, Syria, or any other province is valuable unless it can be filtered through a Greek lens."[22]

This view of Porphyry as "chauvinistically Greek"[23] has been developed to some extent in reaction to older scholarship that tended to characterize Porphyry, and the Neo-Platonists in general, as "Oriental," and sometimes even as contributors to the supposed degeneration of Greek culture under Eastern influence. In an important article, Fergus Millar both summarized and challenged this older view, pointing out that Porphyry consistently self-identifies as Greek, and demonstrating how sparse the evidence is for the continuity of native Phoenician culture into the period of the Roman empire in any case.[24] Scholars since Millar have generally maintained that Porphyry can best be described as Greek, rather than Eastern or Phoenician.[25]

Identities are always multifaceted however, and the recent emphasis on Porphyry's Greekness elides other important aspects of his identity. The question of what it meant to be Greek in the Roman empire was in general highly charged:[26] while the acquisition of *paideia* enabled people of different ethnic backgrounds to lay claim to a Hellenic identity, that identity had to be continually reenacted and confirmed.[27] Furthermore, the idea that Greekness could be achieved by anyone with the right education was challenged by some who insisted instead on the importance of purity of descent and language.[28] One way to read Porphyry's dismissiveness of ethnic differences then is in the context of a cultural competition in which Greekness was highly prized and his own Greek identity was neither an obvious nor an unassailable fact. While we have no way of knowing for sure how securely and exclusively "Greek" Porphyry felt himself to be, we can identify occasional moments in his writings where he seems to call Greek cultural superiority into question. One, also noted by Gillian Clark, is in the course of his argument in *De Abstinentia* that animals possess *logos*:[29]

> How then can it not be ignorant to call only human language *logos*, because we understand it, and dismiss the language of other animals? It is as if ravens claimed that theirs was the only language, and we lack *logos*, because we say things which are not meaningful to them, or the people of Attica said that Attic is the only language, and thought that others who do not share the Attic way of speaking lack *logos*. (*Abst.* 3.5)

This passage provides a mocking rebuke to Greek stereotypes about the irrationality of barbarians, thus illustrating how the depreciation of hierarchical ethnic distinctions can function to undermine the chauvinistic assumptions of the hegemonic culture.

Furthermore, even if we could securely label Porphyry as Greek, this identification would not in itself enable us to determine his position with respect to Roman imperial rule. As many scholars have pointed out, the relationship between Hellenism and Roman power was complex: Greek culture often inspired veneration among Romans, but it could also be seen as alien, threatening, or emasculating.[30] In turn, Greek texts display a range of stances towards the empire, sometimes praising Rome, sometimes ignoring it altogether, continuing to construct the world in terms that leave no place for its prominence.[31] Porphyry reveals little explicitly about his attitude towards Rome, and he acknowledges no familiarity with Latin language or culture;[32] nevertheless, he has been seen as an ally of Roman imperial power, his stance exemplified by his apparent collaboration with the anti-Christian policies of Diocletian.[33] It is instructive, however, to consider how Porphyry's views on sacrifice would have informed his relationship with the imperial center. Roman rule was deeply bound up with the practice of animal sacrifice—the imperial cult offering only one obvious example—and from the time of Augustus onwards, the emperor was consistently and conspicuously depicted as a priest officiating at blood sacrifices, as befitted his role as pontifex maximus.[34] On the other hand, Porphyry, as we have seen, argued that participation in blood sacrifice exposed one to demonic contamination and that such civic ceremonies were at best a sign of the disorientation of political priorities (*Abst.* 2.43). His dismissal of those who involve themselves with animal sacrifice while claiming to be concerned with philosophy is scathing (*Abst.* 2.35).

An exploration of Porphyry's positions on sacrificial cult helps to unravel the full complexity of his relationships to Hellenism, "barbarian" cultures, and Roman rule. While Porphyry did indeed embrace Greek philosophical universalism, his relationship with Greco-Roman culture and imperial power was more ambiguous than has sometimes been acknowledged. Universalism is not *inherently* imperialistic, and furthermore, ancient Platonists' attitudes towards "particularity" were neither monolithic nor straightforwardly negative. Like the discourses of Enlightenment humanism, Platonism actually provided rich resources for the subtle negotiation of the particular and the universal in an imperial context.[35]

Sacrifice, Ancestral Tradition, and Empire

In his writings, Porphyry frequently deploys the figure of the barbarian to disturb the self-satisfaction of Greeks and Romans who believe their sacrificial customs to be superior. For example, in a fragment of *Philosophy from Oracles*, preserved by Eusebius, Porphyry invokes Greco-Roman reverence for "barbarian wisdom" while disparaging the Greeks for being ignorant of the path to the Divine. The oracle in question, according to Eusebius, is specifically on the subject of sacrifices, and claims that divine wisdom has appeared in many barbarian cultures. Porphyry comments on it as follows:

For the road to the gods is bound with brass, and both steep and rough; the barbarians discovered many paths thereof, but the Greeks went astray, and those who already held it even perverted it. The discovery was ascribed by the god to Egyptians, Phoenicians, Chaldeans (for these are the Assyrians), Lydians, and Hebrews. (Euseb., *Praep. evang.* 9.10.3)[36]

On other occasions, Porphyry uses the *negative* associations of "barbarism" to undermine Greco-Roman religious practices. To a hypothetical defender of divination from animal entrails, which held a particularly important place in Roman religion, he retorts: "This person should destroy people too, for they say that the future is more apparent in human entrails; indeed many barbarians use humans for divination by entrails" (*Abst.* 2.51); and to refute the argument that eating sacrificed animals is justifiable because animals are irrational, he cites the Scythians—the paradigmatic savages—who, he claims, could use the same excuse to justify eating their own fathers (*Abst.* 3.17). In both these passages, Porphyry invokes a stereotypical association of human sacrifice with barbarism, but turns it back on the Greeks and Romans, equating their practices with those of the barbarians they despise.[37]

Porphyry's accusation that animal sacrifice is equivalent to human sacrifice is based on the idea, discussed previously, that we should recognize the kinship of all animate beings rather than using the blood of animals to mark out group boundaries among ourselves (*Abst.* 3.13). Yet the Roman imperial authorities used blood sacrifice in precisely this way, reordering group boundaries by means of sacrificial cult. Decius's edict mandating empire-wide participation in sacrifice in 250 CE, at which time Porphyry would have been about eighteen years old, offers one significant example. Papyri certificates surviving from that time explicitly include the phrase: "in accordance with the edict's decree, I have poured a libation, sacrificed, and tasted of the sacred victims." This phrasing suggests that the sacrifice and consumption of *animals* were necessary to fulfill the terms of the edict.[38] James Rives has argued that Decius's decree was an important step in creating an imperial religion:

> Decius' decree in effect established a requirement that all Romans, i.e. all those living in the Roman Empire, had to sacrifice to their local gods in a manner approved by the imperial authorities. It thus created a religious obligation between the individual and the Empire; the city merely functioned as the religious agent of the imperial administration, just as in taxation it functioned as its financial agent. Consequently, Decius' decree helped to weaken the old tradition of collective local cults that linked the individual with his or her city, and put an increased emphasis on the ties between the individual and the Roman Empire.[39]

Rives connects Decius's edict to Caracalla's extension of Roman citizenship, the *Constitutio Antoniniana*, promulgated in 212, and the consequent centralization of power.

If we take into account the traditional role of sacrifice in kinship construction in the Greco-Roman world, we can further understand the decree as an attempt to bind citizens with the common ties traditionally associated with kinship.[40] Indeed, the idea of the Roman empire as a "race" had already been voiced explicitly by Aelius Aristides in the second century, who wrote that Rome was no longer a city but a *genos*.[41] In the aftermath of this shift towards the establishment of an empire-wide Roman "kinship" through animal sacrifice, Porphyry's views would have placed him at the very least in an ambivalent position with respect to the religious perpetuation of imperial rule.

In fact, far from seeing blood sacrifice as conducive to the proper ordering of kinship within empire, Porphyry understood it to be a result of the *disordering* of kinship relations:

> I think that when friendship [φιλίας] and perception of kinship [συγγενὲς] ruled everything, no one killed any creature because people thought that other animals were related [οἰκεῖα] to them. But when Ares and Battle-noise and all kinds of conflict and source of war were in control, then for the first time no one spared any related creature [τῶν οικείων] at all. (*Abst.* 2.22)[42]

Porphyry believed that the contemporaneous practices of Greco-Roman (and much barbarian) religion transgressed the natural laws of kinship: they resulted from, and perpetuated, disruptions in people's relationships with one another and with the gods. He argues that those who endorse animal sacrifice fail to understand how humans, animals, and gods are related, and should "learn from the Egyptians, who were so far from killing any other animal that they made likenesses of them as images of the gods. This is how closely related and kin [οἰκεῖα καὶ συγγενῆ] they thought animals are to the gods, and to humans" (*Abst.* 2.26).

Porphyry's views on the disruptive nature of animal sacrifice cast doubt on the proposal, defended vigorously in recent scholarship, that Porphyry was involved in the Great Persecution.[43] Sacrifice, particularly blood sacrifice, played a central role in Diocletian's attempt to bolster Roman religious tradition, and refusal to participate in it became a mark of deviance.[44] While Porphyry's antipathy towards Christians is well-attested, and he may well have strategically supported any measures against them, it is hard to imagine that he would have allied himself with Diocletian's mission without some ambivalence.[45] Scholars have recently argued that Porphyry shared Diocletian's desire to restore the "old ways."[46] Nevertheless, his conception of what those "old ways" were did not conform to the established practices of the Roman imperial cult, to which animal sacrifice was central. Indeed, the discourse of tradition was commonly invoked in the Roman world to legitimize a huge range of— sometimes conflicting—positions. Novel religious practices were often justified by combining this reverence for the past with another common trope: the degeneration of cultures. Thus, apparent innovations were presented as restorations of authentic ancestral practice, which had become corrupted through time.[47] The question was not so much *whether* one should follow the "old ways," as *what* those "old ways" were.

To get behind the common rhetoric of tradition and figure out what exactly Porphyry was advocating, we need to look carefully at the places where he discusses ancestral custom explicitly. The passage most frequently quoted to demonstrate that Porphyry promoted established cult practices, including sacrifice, comes from the letter he wrote to his wife (*Ad Marcellam*): "For this is the principle fruit of piety: to honor the divine according to ancestral tradition" (*Ad Marcellam* 18).[48] However, Porphyry makes this statement in the course of a larger argument that cult practice is useless if not accompanied by inner virtue. The context is important, and I therefore quote it at some length:

> For a wise man in his silence honors God, but a foolish man, even when he is praying and offering sacrifices, defiles the divine. . . . And the man who practices wisdom practices the knowledge of God, not by continually praying and offering sacrifices, but by practicing piety toward God through his deeds. . . . The impious man is not so much the one who does not treat the statues of the gods with respect as the one who is united to the opinions of the masses regarding God. May you never adopt any thought that is unworthy of God or of his blessedness and immortality. For this is the principle fruit of piety: to honor the divine according to ancestral tradition [κατὰ τὰ πάτρια], *not because he needs it but because he summons us by his venerable and blessed dignity to worship him*. (*Ad Marcellam* 16–18)

Quoted out of context, and without the phrase that completes the sentence, Porphyry's statement about *ta patria* can be taken to suggest that he thinks cult practices are of the utmost importance; but when put into context, we see that it is not the ritual performance *in itself* that is the "fruit of piety," but the ability to perform it with true understanding. The point he is emphasizing is that cult practice should grow out of inner virtue (as its "fruit," καρπὸς), otherwise it is at best useless, at worst blasphemous:

> God's altars, if they are consecrated do not harm us; if they are neglected they do not help us. But whatever man honors God as though he needs it, this man has failed to recognize he has formed a false opinion that he is better than god. . . . Tears and supplications do not move God, sacrifices do not honor God; numerous votive offerings do not adorn God. . . . The sacrifice of the ignorant is fuel for fire, and their votive offerings are public contributions of the intemperate to temple-robbers. (*Ad Marcellam* 18–19)

Porphyry's views here hardly seem compatible with Diocletian's policy of forcing people to sacrifice, whatever their inner beliefs: since God himself gains nothing from the act of sacrifice, forcing an impious man to make an offering against his will would presumably be of no benefit to anybody. Porphyry's point is that sacrificial acts *in themselves* are a matter of indifference, so that their worth for the virtuous is simply that they offer a way to convey outwardly a deep human reverence for, and connection to, the Divine.

Even more importantly, nothing in *Ad Marcellam* suggests that Porphyry meant *animal* sacrifice when he referred to *ta patria*. Gillian Clark points out, "In *On Abstinence* he argues . . . that the true ancestral tradition is bloodless sacrifice, in so far as any material sacrifice is appropriate."[49] Animal sacrifice was itself a corruption of authentic ancestral tradition, a point that Porphyry reiterates in *De Abstinentia*: "The sacrifice of animals, then, is later than other forms, indeed the most recent, and it is not a benefit, as for the sacrifice of crops, but a problem arising from famine or some other misfortune" (*Abst.* 2.9; cf. 2.20, 2.27); therefore, "when Apollo advises sacrifice according to ancestral tradition [θύειν κατὰ τὰ πάτρια]" he means cakes and crops, not animals (*Abst.* 2.59).[50] We cannot assume then that Porphyry's mention of *ta patria* in *Ad Marcellam* refers to the customs that prevailed in his own time, certainly not to the laws of the Roman empire. Indeed, it is telling that on one of the few occasions when Porphyry mentions the Romans in his writings, it is as the *destroyers* of ancestral tradition:

> Among those known to us, the Jews—before they suffered intolerable outrage to their traditions [τὰ ἀνήκεστα παθεῖν εἰς τὰ νόμιμα τὰ ἑαυτῶν] first from Antiochus and then from the Romans, when the temple in Jerusalem was captured and became open to all to whom it had been forbidden, and the city itself was destroyed—consistently abstained from many animals and in particular, even now, from the meat of pigs. (*Abst.* 4.11)

So when empire (in both its Roman and its Hellenistic instantiations) does make an explicit appearance in Porphyry's arguments, it is as the annihilator of pious customs, rather than as their guarantor. Animal sacrifice here is emblematic for Porphyry not of ancestral tradition, but of its obliteration by imperial violence. Porphyry's overall argument in *De Abstinentia* actually uses universalism *against* empire, in that he argues that all ancient ethnic cultures started out without blood sacrifice and gradually fell away into diverse and corrupt sacrificial practices. Imperialism is seen here as an agent of this degeneration.

None of this is to claim that Porphyry would have been in as antagonistic a position with respect to the empire as were Christians, for whom any sacrifice to non-Christian gods was anathema. Unlike a committed Christian, Porphyry could probably have complied with Diocletian's edicts by sacrificing grain or incense. As he writes in *De Abstinentia*:

> For myself, I am not trying to destroy the customs which prevail among each people: the state is not my present subject. But the laws by which we are governed allow the divine power to be honored even by very simple and inanimate things, so by choosing the simplest we shall sacrifice in accordance with the law of the city, and will ourselves strive to offer a fitting sacrifice, pure in all respects when we approach the gods. (*Abst.* 2.33)

Here Porphyry advises virtuous people to comply with the sacrificial laws of the state, but at the most minimal level; this is a strategy of accommodation rather than of wholehearted endorsement.[51]

So while Porphyry did not see the state and the divine order as fundamentally opposed (as did many Christians) neither did he see them as identical. In fact, in many ways, Porphyry's views on sacrifice were more similar to those of the Christians than to those of the imperial authorities, and the similarities, as well as the differences, are instructive. Just as in the case of the Christians, Porphyry's devaluation of established ethnic divisions was accompanied by a denigration of animal sacrifice, which had traditionally played such a central role in marking out kinship and ethnic boundaries. Christians did not attempt to transcend kinship boundaries, so much as to reconfigure them radically, establishing a "new race" through sacrificial participation in the blood and flesh of Christ.[52] But for Porphyry, blood ties were at best insignificant and at worst detrimental, because they bound one more securely to the material order; the philosopher should strive to rise above them in full recognition that the most important criterion of kinship to others and to God was that were those of inner virtue.

Conclusions

When Nancy Jay referred to sacrifice as "birth done better,"[53] she was characterizing its role in the assertion of male control over procreation. But in the changing context of the Roman empire, another meaning seems to have come to the fore: sacrifice as a means of contesting social structures that had traditionally been discursively aligned with birth and descent. The association of sacrifice with kinship construction in the Greco-Roman world rendered it a rich discursive site for working through the complex social transformations effected by empire.

Porphyry's writings are marked by the perception that there is a disjunction between one's true self and one's contingent identity. This belief raised questions about how the particularity of our physical bodies, of the languages we speak and the places we know, relate to our authentic identity. If the tension between universal and particular, one and many, was a longstanding "cultural problematic" of Greek thought,[54] it gained ever more urgency and complexity within the social context of the Roman empire. Porphyry and his contemporaries struggled with such issues as: How do we find our place within the multiplicity of communal structures—familial, ethnic, civic, imperial—within which we move? What is the significance of bonds forged through flesh and blood, whether in birth or in sacrifice? And (how) can kinship or ethnic groups, formed through material processes (whether "naturally" or "ritually") help us in our quest for God? Sacrificial discourse—encompassing, as it did, connotations of blood and seed and flesh, of kinship formation, and of mediation between human and divine—provided a shared medium within which they worked out their answers to these questions.

Notes

I would like to thank Jennifer Knust, Zsuzsanna Várhelyi, and all the participants in the colloquium, especially my respondent Lawrence Wills. Thanks too to Daniel Barbu, Peter Brown, and Kevin Wolfe for many fruitful discussions and helpful comments. I am also grateful to the Hebrew University of Jerusalem, the Albright Institute for Archaeological Research, and the National Endowment for the Humanities for fellowships that have given me valuable time for research. Most of all, I thank Guy and Sarah Stroumsa for their intellectual support, hospitality, and friendship during my time in Jerusalem. This article is adapted from parts of chapter 5 of my dissertation, "Another Race? Ethnicity, Universalism, and the Emergence of Christianity," Princeton University, 2009.

1. Ingvild Gilhus, *Animals, Gods and Humans: Changing Attitudes to Animals in Greek, Roman and Early Christian Ideas* (London: Routledge, 2006), 114ff.; Guy Stroumsa, *La fin du sacrifice: Les mutations religeuses de l'antiquité tardive* (Paris: Odile Jacob, 2005), 105ff.

2. Nancy Jay, *Throughout Your Generations Forever: Sacrifice, Religion, and Paternity* (Chicago: University of Chicago Press, 1992). She writes: "Sacrificially constituted descent, incorporating women's mortal children into an 'eternal' (enduring through generations) kin group, in which membership is recognized by participation in sacrificial ritual, not merely by birth, enables a patrilineal group to transcend mortality in the same process in which it transcends birth. In this sense, sacrifice is doubly a remedy for having been born of woman" (40). See chapter 4, "Creating Descent through Fathers and Sons," for her main discussion of Greek and Roman sacrifice.

3. Stanley Stowers, "Greeks Who Sacrifice and Those Who Do Not," in *The Social World of the First Christians: Essays in Honor of Wayne A. Meeks,* edited by L. Michael White and O. Larry Yarbrough (Minneapolis: Fortress, 1995). See 312–25 for Stowers's discussion of the role sacrifice played in ordering kinship structures, and 300–306 for various examples of analogies between sacrifice and childbirth from medical and literary writers, including Sophocles, Aristotle, and Artemidorus. See also Helen King, "Sacrificial Blood: The Role of Amnion in Greek Gynecology," *Helios* 13 (1987): 117–26 (cited by Stowers in "Greeks Who Sacrifice," 302), for a discussion of the analogy in medical writers between the fetal sack and the vessel that collected the blood of a sacrificed animal.

4. Stowers, "Greeks Who Sacrifice," 309.

5. On the futility of attempts to identify a single essential "meaning" of sacrifice across cultures, see the discussion by Daniel Ullucci in this volume. As he argues, we should not ask what the meaning of sacrifice is, but rather what interpretations are given to it. While participants can bring any number of understandings to a ritual, however, certain interpretations can, over time, become particularly associated with a specific ritual within a culture.

6. Stowers, drawing particularly on the work of Catherine Bell and Pierre Bourdieu, offers a nuanced approach to the methodological issues: see "Greeks Who Sacrifice," especially 307–309 and 330–32. He cautions against privileging one aspect of sacrifice over all others, as many theorists have tended to do—even, he suggests, Jay herself (Stowers, "Greeks Who Sacrifice," 299 n. 26).

7. In emphasizing the persistence of this association, I do not consider my argument to be incompatible with that of James Rives in this volume. Indeed, I agree with Rives's skepticism regarding "the assumption that the cultural meaning of animal sacrifice remained stable throughout Graeco-Roman antiquity." Rives argues convincingly that philosophers

in the Roman empire developed innovative theological justifications for particular forms of sacrifice, in part as a consequence of the "greater cultural significance" that animal sacrifice acquired in "defining the relationship between the emperor and the inhabitants of the empire." My argument in this chapter is that Porphyry (among others) developed his sacrificial theories precisely in the context of this heightened imperial significance of sacrifice, but that he did so by simultaneously deploying and contesting well-established aspects of sacrificial discourse.

8. Stowers, "Greeks Who Sacrifice," 331.

9. I take the perception of common kinship and descent to be a fundamental criterion of ethnic identity, in the ancient world as today. There has been much scholarly debate over the definition of ethnicity, which I cannot enter into in any depth here, but for the purposes of my analysis, I find Jonathan Hall's definition, developed in his work on Greek ethnicity, most useful: "Ultimately, the definitional criteria or 'core elements' which determine membership in an ethnic group—and distinguish the ethnic group from other social collectivities—are a putative subscription to a myth of common descent and kinship, an association with a specific territory and a sense of shared history"; *Hellenicity: Between Ethnicity and Culture* (Chicago: University of Chicago Press, 2002), 9–10. Hall discusses the attempts by many scholars to downplay the elements of descent and birth in definitions of ethnicity; however, as he points out, if we employ only cultural criteria in our definition, we have to include the Chicago Bulls and the Freemasons as ethnic groups, too, and the category loses specificity (*Hellenicity,* 10ff.). On the political importance of kinship in the ancient world, see Christopher Jones, *Kinship Diplomacy in the Ancient World* (Cambridge: Harvard University Press, 1999).

10. In his discussion of colonial ethnic identities, Thomas Eriksen argued that "ethnic labels . . . function in a recursive way, since the labels used by colonizers, missionaries and foreign scholars were returned to and appropriated by the people in question"; *Ethnicity and Nationalism* (London: Pluto Press, 1993), 89. More generally on the "ambivalence of colonial discourse," see the now classic works of Homi Bhabha, especially his discussion of colonial mimicry as a "process by which the look of surveillance returns as the displacing gaze of the disciplined"; *The Location of Culture* (London: Routledge, 1994), 121, 127.

11. See chapter 5 of my dissertation, "Another Race? Ethnicity, Universalism, and the Emergence of Christianity" (Princeton University, 2009), and also Philippa Townsend, "Sacrifice and Race in the *Gospel of Judas*," in *Judasevangelium und Codex Tchacos: Studien zur religionsgeschichtlichen Verortung einer gnostischen Schriftensammlung,* edited by Gregor Wurst and Enno Popkes, WUNT (Tübingen: Mohr Siebeck, forthcoming 2011). For a sophisticated treatment of early Christian ethnic self-understanding, see Denise Kimber Buell, *Why This New Race: Ethnic Reasoning in Early Christianity* (New York: Columbia University Press, 2005). Buell's overall thesis is that far from abandoning ethnic self-identification, Christians used similar strategies of "ethnic reasoning" as other ethnic groups in the ancient world. While I agree that Christians did use "ethnic reasoning," I would argue that they nevertheless participated in a transformation of the discursive relationship between ethnic and religious identity in the Roman empire.

12. Quotations in English from *On Abstinence* (*De Abstinentia*) are taken from the translation of Gillian Clark, *Porphyry: On Abstinence from Killing Animals,* Ancient Commentators on Aristotle (Ithaca: Cornell University Press, 2000), unless otherwise noted. Quotations in Greek are from *Porphyre, De l'Abstinence,* Vol. I edited and translated by

Jean Bouffartigue (Paris: Les Belles Lettres, 1977); Vol. II edited and translated by Jean Bouffartigue and Michel Patillon (Paris: Les Belles Lettres, 1979); Vol. III edited and translated by Michel Patillon and Alain Ph. Segonds (Paris: Les Belles Lettres, 1995).

13. It is difficult to reconcile Porphyry's rejection of animal sacrifice throughout this treatise with his commentary on an oracle of Apollo that designates the correct sacrifice to be offered to each god (preserved by Euseb., *Praep. evang.* 4.9; Eusebius delighted in pointing out the inconsistency). While some scholars argue that the two are reconcilable if one interprets the gods in the oracle as daimones, it is still strange that Porphyry would give divinely sanctioned advice on how to perform blood sacrifice when he produces so many sustained arguments against participation in any kind of animal sacrifice in *Abst.* Elizabeth DePalma Digeser argues that Porphyry "saw no contradiction in asserting the necessity of animal sacrifice," citing *Abst.* 2.33–34 as evidence; *The Making of a Christian Empire: Lactantius and Rome* (Ithaca: Cornell University Press, 2000), 99. However, Porphyry only defends *nonblood* sacrifice in this passage, while reiterating his opposition to animal sacrifice. Of course, we do not have any context for the fragment from *Philosophy from Oracles*, and perhaps the two views would look less contradictory if we did; it was Eusebius's whole purpose to make Porphyry appear inconsistent, after all, as Jeremy Schott argues in *Christianity, Empire, and the Making of Religion* (Philadelphia: University of Pennsylvania Press, 2008), 136ff., esp. 146–49 on this particular fragment. It is also quite possible that Porphyry changed his mind about the issue. If this is the case, it seems likely that *Abst.* represents the later, more considered position, since it is obviously the product of much thought and elaborate study of philosophical views on sacrifice; however, it is difficult to be sure of the chronological sequence of Porphyry's works: see Clark, *On Abstinence*, 5–6; Mark Edwards, *Culture and Philosophy in the Age of Plotinus* (London: Duckworth, 2006), 37.

14. Porphyry's idea that the gods of civic cult are actually lowly daimones draws on a philosophical tradition of interpreting the gods of particular cities or peoples as subordinate deities, subject to the universal god. The tradition has roots in Plato's *Crit.* (109B), in which Critias explains that the gods divided the earth up by lots and each established and settled his or her own country. The idea provided a rich resource for later Platonists to theorize the relationship of the universal God to particular ethnic traditions: for examples, see Celsus as quoted in Origen, *C. Cels.* 5.25; Iambl., *Myst.* 5.25; Julian, *Contra Galilaeos* 100C.

15. On common blood (*homaimon*)as a frequently invoked criterion for kinship in the world, see Hall, *Hellenicity*, 18.

16. Here Porphyry is quoting Theophrastus (frequently his preferred authority for criticisms of animal sacrifice).

17. I refer here to Stowers's formulation: "Greek discussions of procreation and the blood of men and women illuminate the logic of the analogy or homology between men's sacrifice and women's procreation" ("Greeks Who Sacrifice," 302).

18. Translation from *Iamblichus On the Mysteries, Translated with an Introduction and Notes,* translated by Emma C. Clarke, John M. Dillon, and Jackson P. Hershbell, Writings from the Greco-Roman World 4 (Atlanta: Society of Biblical Literature, 2003).

19. Judith Butler, "Restaging the Universal: Hegemony and the Limits of Formalism," in *Contingency, Hegemony, Universality: Contemporary Dialogues on the Left*, edited by J. Butler, E. Laclau, and S. Žižek (London: Verso, 2000), 15.

20. Examples include Daniel Boyarin, *A Radical Jew: Paul and the Politics of Identity* (Berkeley: University of California Press, 1994), for example, 7–10, 13ff.; Daniel Boyarin, *Carnal Israel: Reading Sex in Talmudic Culture* (Berkeley: University of California Press, 1993), for example, 231; Schott, *Christianity, Empire*, 8.

21. Peter Struck, "Speech Acts and the Stakes of Hellenism in Late Antiquity," in *Magic and Ritual in the Ancient World*, edited by Paul Mirecki and Marvin Meyer (Leiden: Brill, 2002), 393.

22. Schott, *Christianity, Empire*, 73, 61. Schott's focus is on the reasons for Porphyry's opposition to Christianity, and he argues that "Porphyry and the emperors perceived the Christians as a threat to imperial order, an order that depended on sharp contrasts between ruler and ruled, metropolis and provinces" (77); cf. his article, "Porphyry on Christians and Others: 'Barbarian Wisdom,' Identity Politics, and Anti-Christian Polemics on the Eve of the Great Persecution," *JECS* 13 (2005): 280.

23. Struck, "Speech Acts," 398.

24. "Porphyry, Ethnicity, Language and Alien Wisdom," in *Philosophia Togata II: Plato and Aristotle at Rome*, edited by Jonathan Barnes and Miriam Griffin (Oxford: Clarendon, 1999); cf. Fergus Millar, *The Roman Near East 31 B.C.–A.D. 337* (Cambridge: Harvard University Press, 1993), 264–309.

25. For a strong statement of this position, see Mark Edwards, who defends the Neo-Platonists as actually having "a coherent, rational and (as we might style it) Greek view of the world," and describes them as "Greeks in spirit," *Culture and Philosophy*, 127, 39. Cf. Struck, "Speech Acts," 402; Schott, *Christianity, Empire*, 67. Gillian Clark, on the other hand, emphasizes the complexity of Porphyry's identity: "Translate into Greek," in *Constructing Identities in Late Antiquity*, edited by Richard Miles (London: Routledge, 1999), passim.

26. There has been a great deal written about Greek identities in the Roman empire, especially in terms of the phenomenon of the "Second Sophistic." For sophisticated app-roaches to this scholarship and its problems, see Tim Whitmarsh, *Greek Literature and the Roman Empire: The Politics of Imitation* (Oxford: Oxford University Press, 2001), esp. the introduction (1–38); and the volume edited by Simon Goldhill, *Being Greek under Rome: The Second Sophistic, Cultural Identity, and the Development of the Roman Empire* (Cambridge: Cambridge University Press, 2001).

27. Tim Whitmarsh, "'Greece Is the World': Exile and Identity in the Second Sophistic," in Goldhill, *Being Greek under Rome*, 304. So, for example, texts from the period reveal provincials' anxieties over using Attic Greek perfectly and avoiding "barbarisms" of speech: Simon Swain, *Hellenism and Empire: Language, Classicism and Power in the Greek World, AD 50–250* (Oxford: Oxford University Press, 1996), 48; cf. Whitmarsh, "Greece Is the World," 294. G. Clark makes the intriguing suggestion that Plotinus's mistakes in Greek, as reported by Porphyry in *Plot.* 13, 20, may have been just these sorts of "barbarisms." See Clark, "Translate into Greek," 120.

28. Emma Dench, *Romulus' Asylum: Roman Identities from the Age of Alexander to the Age of Hadrian* (Oxford: Oxford University Press, 2005), 262–63.

29. See Clark, "Translate into Greek," 120–21; cf. her note to this passage in her trans-lation of this text (*On Abstinence*, 167).

30. On Roman anxiety about Greek and Eastern foreignness, see, for example, Goldhill, *Being Greek under Rome*, 10–11. The Greek/barbarian binary that they inherited also posed

a problem for Romans. On this issue, see Suzanne Saïd, "The Discourse of Identity in Greek Rhetoric," in *Ancient Perceptions of Greek Ethnicity*, edited by Irad Malkin (Washington, D.C.: Center for Hellenic Studies / Cambridge: Harvard University Press, 2001): "Therefore the old Greek/barbarian dichotomy is often transformed by the addition of the Romans as a tertium quid. . . . But this rather simple division is immediately complicated" (288). It should be noted that Hellenic identity never depended solely on a straightforward Greek/barbarian binary: even in the fifth century BCE, Jonathan Hall has argued, "barbarians were more commonly situated at the other end of a linear continuum which did in fact permit category crossing" (*Hellenicity*, 8).

31. On the complexity of Greek attitudes to Rome, see Christopher Jones, "Multiple Identities in the Second Sophistic," in *Paideia: The World of the Second Sophistic*, edited by Barbara Borg (Berlin: De Gruyter, 2004), 14.

32. Millar, "Porphyry: Ethnicity," 246; Clark, "Translate into Greek," 115.

33. For this view, see, for example, Digeser, *Making of a Christian Empire*, esp. 5–7, 108, 113–14; Schott, *Christianity, Empire*, 73, 77–8.

34. "A distinctive symbol of the Augustan restructuring of religion was the image of the emperor officiating at sacrifices. . . . The links between emperor and sacrifice were so emphasized that from the reign of Augustus onwards almost no-one other that the emperor (and his immediate family) was depicted at sacrifice in public images"; Mary Beard, John North, and Simon Price, *Religions of Rome* (Cambridge: Cambridge University Press, 1998), 1: 350.

35. Many postcolonial thinkers, while acknowledging the dangers of Enlightenment universalism, simultaneously recognize the potential of—even the necessity for—universalistic discourses in anti-imperialist struggles. For example, see Dipesh Chakrabarty, *Provincializing Europe: Postcolonial Thought and Historical Difference* (Princeton: Princeton University Press, 2000), 5; Butler, "Restaging the Universal," 40; Ernesto Laclau, "Constructing Universality," in Butler, Laclau, and Žižek, *Contingency, Hegemony, and Universality*, 306; Partha Chatterjee, *Nationalist Thought and the Colonial World: A Derivative Discourse* (Minneapolis: University of Minnesota Press, 1993), 170; Etienne Balibar, "Race as Universalism," in *Masses, Classes, Ideas: Studies on Politics and Philosophy before and after Marx* (New York: Routledge, 1994), 204. Daniel Boyarin also recognizes the ambiguous power of universalism, arguing that "the claims of difference and the desire for universality are both—contradictorily—necessary; both are also equally problematic" (*Radical Jew*, 10).

36. Translated by Edwin Gifford, *Eusebius of Caesarea: Preparation for the Gospel* (Oxford: Clarendon Press, 1903).

37. James Rives has identified several functions that the idea of human sacrifice recurrently served in ancient discourse: as a boundary marker between barbarians and Greeks (or Romans); as the hallmark of bad religion; and as a symptom of the influence of wicked demons on religious practice: "Human Sacrifice among Pagans and Christians," *JRS* 85 (1995): 65–85. Porphyry employs all these connotations, equating animal sacrifice with demonic influence, then associating it with human sacrifice, then showing how it is barbaric and bad religious practice. In doing so, he employs a strategy that Rives has identified in Christian and other "nonhegemonic" texts, of turning the accusation of human sacrifice, and thus barbarism, back on the Greeks and Romans themselves (Rives, "Human Sacrifice," 74ff.)

38. The formula, with little variation, states: κατὰ τὰ προσταχθέντα ἔσπισα καὶ ἔθυσα καὶ τῶν ἱερείων ἐγευσάμην. See John R. Knipfing, "The *Libelli* of the Decian Persecu-

tion," *HTR* 16.4 (1923): 345–90, for discussion, texts, and translations of the extant certificates. Rives notes that "Cyprian at one point mentions *thurificati* (Ep. 55.2.I), presumably people who had only offered incense; whether this was a special dispensation for the poor or simply a local variation is unknown"; James Rives, "The Decree of Decius," *JRS* 89 (1999): 135–54; 137 n. 13. Even if there were some exceptions, however, it is clear that the standard requirement was to taste of sacrificial meat, as Rives acknowledges.

39. Rives, "Decree of Decius," 152.

40. The idea of Rome employing strategies of kinship (rather than just civic) self-definition may seem unlikely, but as Emma Dench has recently shown, Roman identity was often constructed through appeals to blood and descent. See Dench, *Romulus' Asylum*, esp. chap. 4. The dichotomy between "civic" and "ethnic" should perhaps not be drawn too sharply, although Aelius Aristides employs something similar (see my n. 41, following). On the difficulty of disentangling civic and ethnic identity, see Hall, *Hellenicity*, 4.

41. Aelius Aristides, *To Rome*, 63. See Dench's remarks, *Romulus' Asylum*, 262: "Emphasis on the purity of Athenian descent in [Aristides'] panegyric of Athens makes it most unlikely that this is a mere figure of speech."

42. This passage seems to be a quotation from Theophrastus. In *Abst.* 2.32, Porphyry tells us that he has "added or summarized a few things" in his recounting of Theophrastus's arguments, so it is not always clear where quotations end or to what extent Porphyry has changed them: see Clark, *On Abstinence*, 144 n. 209.

43. There has been a great deal of scholarly debate about whether, and to what extent, Porphyry was involved with the Great Persecution. Some scholars have claimed that Porphyry was the unnamed philosopher mentioned by Lactantius in *Div. inst.* 5.2, who was stirring up anti-Christian feeling in Nicomedia before the persecution was launched. This view was cautiously suggested by Henry Chadwick, who proposed that Porphyry may have been "invited to attend the confidential deliberations which preceded the launching of the persecution of the Church under Diocletian in 303"; *The Sentences of Sextus: A Contribution to the History of Early Christian Ethics,* Texts and Studies 5 (Cambridge: Cambridge University Press, 1959), 142–43. Recent supporters of this idea include Digeser, *Making of a Christian Empire*, 93ff., and Schott, *Christianity, Empire*, 52 and 179–85. Others have been more skeptical, including Timothy Barnes, who pointed out that "there was no lack of intellectuals and philosophers in the Greek East, some of whom doubtless came to Nicomedia when Diocletian took up residence there"; "Scholarship or Propaganda? Porphyry against the Christians and Its Historical Setting," *BICS* 39 (1994): 59.

44. Rives, "Decree," 153. J. L. Creed notes that "pagan authors recognized in Diocletian a special addiction to divinatory practices"[*Lactantius De Mortibus Persecutorum,* edited and translated by J. L. Creed (Oxford: Clarendon, 1984), 91. According to Lactantius, the first purge was initiated when a sacrifice of cattle was ruined by Christians who made the sign of the cross and caused the demons to flee (*De Mortibus Persecutorum* 10). Later, the "sacrifice test" (as Ste. Croix termed it) was applied to suspected Christians, and finally the fourth edict required universal participation in sacrifice: for discussion, see the classic article of G.E.M. de Ste. Croix, "Aspects of the Great Persecution," in *Christian Persecution, Martyrdom and Orthodoxy*, edited by Michael Whitby and Joseph Streeter (Oxford: Oxford University Press, 2006). However, we have no evidence of *libelli* specifying that participants taste of the sacrificial animals (as we do for the Decian persecution), and the evidence of the martyr acts suggests that it was possible to fulfill the requirement by simply

offering incense, rather than making a blood sacrifice, as Ste. Croix points out ("Aspects," 61; 38 n.15).

45. Norman Baynes points out how unsuitable Porphyry's views would have been as a basis for what he describes as "a fundamentalism which admitted of no doubts, which reaffirmed the whole portentous inheritance—gods and statues, bloody sacrifices and libations, magic and theurgy," "The Great Persecution," *CAH* 12 (1939): 651.

46. Scholars who have pointed to Diocletian's and Porphyry's shared concern for tradition include Digeser, *Making of a Christian Empire*, and Schott, *Christianity, Empire*, 52 and 179–85.

47. See, for example, Beard, North, and Price on how the "discovery" of an ancient Sibylline oracle served to legitimate Augustan religious innovations (*Religions of Rome*, 205). Even Christians often argued that they were restoring the ancient traditions of the Hebrews, from which the Jews had strayed (see, for example, Justin's *Dialogue with Trypho*, 19–23). As Armstrong remarks: "The Christians, as is well known, were very conscious of the apologetic advantage which their claim to possess an immemorial Oriental wisdom gave in their world, and asserted and exploited it to the full": A. H. Armstrong, "Pagan and Christian Traditionalism," *Studia Patristica* 15 (1984): 422.

48. See, for example, Digeser, *Making of a Christian Empire*, 7. Translations of *Ad Marcellam* are taken or modified from *Porphyry the Philosopher To Marcella*, text and translation with introduction and notes by Kathleen O'Brien Wicker, Texts and Translations 28, Graeco-Roman Religion Series 10 (Atlanta: Scholars Press, 1987). Greek quotations are taken from the same source.

49. Gillian Clark, "Augustine's Porphyry," in *Studies on Porphyry*, edited by G. Karamanolis and A. Sheppard, BICS Supplement 98 (London: Institute of Classical Studies, School of Advanced Study, University of London, 2007), 140.

50. See Gillian Clark's note on this passage: "'Sacrifice according to ancestral tradition' was a standard response of the Delphic oracle, usually interpreted as 'according to local practice'" (*On Abstinence*, 161). Porphyry, however, is arguing that local practice, when it involves animal sacrifice, is actually a corruption of ancestral tradition, so he is *challenging* this common interpretation.

51. Porphyry distinguishes in *Ad Marcellam* 25–27 between divine law, natural law, and the contingent law of states and states that the philosopher should be concerned primarily with the former two types of law.

52. See Buell, *Why This New Race.*

53. Jay, *Throughout Your Generations*, xxiv.

54. Boyarin, *Radical Jew*, 16.

{ PART IV }

Imaginary Sacrifice

12

Don't Cry Over Spilled Blood

Kathryn McClymond

As a comparative historian of religions working primarily in the Jewish and Hindu traditions, I am mainly interested here in "rituals gone wrong"—that is, rituals in which certain errors occur in the course of a ritual. The reality of ritual mistakes raises several questions about the nature of individual ritual systems. What kinds of ritual mistakes can arise? What are the consequences of these mistakes? How can these mistakes be corrected? In what contexts do ritual communities discuss these mistakes? Which mistakes cannot be corrected, and what is the fallout from this? The ways in which religious communities incorporate (or ignore) ritual mistakes reveal their understandings of the nature of ritual and the cosmos more broadly.

I am also interested in what we can learn about the nature of ritual *in general* by studying ritual errors and their remedies. Historically, the discipline of religious studies has tended to focus on specific ritual mistakes that occur in the context of individual performances outlined in ethnographic or sociological studies. Mistakes are treated as aberrations and marginalized from general discussions of ritual systems. Scholars have largely ignored the fact that discussions of ritual mistakes make up a significant portion of many indigenous traditions' religious literature, and the obvious fact that mistakes occur has largely been ignored in broader theorizing about ritual. As far as I have been able to determine, while the possibility of ritual error has been noted, no ritual theorist has incorporated ritual error systematically into scholarship about any specific ritual tradition or the nature of ritual broadly speaking.[1] This chapter is the beginning of a larger effort to address this gap in ritual studies literature.

The following pages will initiate this larger discussion by concentrating on a very narrow topic. This essay will focus on a section of the Mishnah (ca. 220 CE), the first codification of rabbinic discussions of Jewish law. A substantial part of the Mishnah involves discussions of ritual errors. We will examine Mishnah tractate Zevachim (M. Zev.), the first tractate of seder Kodashim. M. Zevachim focuses on "slain offerings," that is, animal offerings that were killed, dismembered, and then presented to the Israelite god YHWH via the altar in the Temple in Jerusalem. More specifically, we will focus on discussions of the manipulation of blood during the Temple rites. While various parts of animals were offered to YHWH in the context of sacrifice, I have argued elsewhere that blood manipulation was a key element in the work of sacrifice, as indicated in part by the fact that the handling of blood was restricted to the priests.[2] Thus it is appropriate to focus on blood manipulation when examining Temple sacrifice, since errors in its handling would have significant impact on the ritual. However, it should be emphasized that many different types of errors can occur in a sacrificial ritual, not simply blood manipulation.

M. Zevachim describes numerous possible situations involving the mishandling of blood, so we will restrict our discussion largely to this tractate. At this point it is important to note that we will not, in fact, be studying ritual; rather, we will be examining a rigorously constructed discourse about ritual behavior. Thus our data is literary data, not the ritual activity itself. In fact, much of the work done in the field of ritual studies does not actually examine ritual, but rather its representations in historical records, literary projects, and archeological artifacts. It is important to keep this in mind as we proceed, because arguments about and guidelines for ritual practice are decidedly distinct from ritual practice itself. For my present purpose, the Mishnah's representations of the discussions regarding how to handle mistakes in blood manipulation are useful, because they reveal the socioreligious system developed by the rabbis.

Two other complications should be kept in mind. First, the Mishnah is an edited compilation of early rabbinic (tannaitic) opinions, roughly prior to 200 CE. The collection is traditionally said to have been crafted by Rabbi Judah ha-Nasi not merely to present information, but rather as an entire system of organizing, transmitting, and evaluating distinct opinions and trains of thought. It is the expression of the development of an authoritative process constructed to resolve disputes regarding the interpretation of Torah. As such, the Mishnah is not simply an anthology of rabbinic opinions. It is a heavily redacted document, organized to present an authoritative framework for further thought and debate.

Finally, the Mishnah's discussions of Temple sacrifice, including blood manipulation, are completely anachronistic. Temple sacrifice was not performed, for all intents and purposes, after 70 CE, when the Jerusalem Temple was razed by the Romans. At the beginning of the third century, when Judah ha-Nasi was editing the Mishnah, there was nothing to suggest that the Temple would be rebuilt anytime soon. As a result, the debates recorded in the Mishnah regarding blood manipulation as part of Temple sacrifice had no practical application whatsoever. Given this situation, we must ask ourselves what the rabbinic debate concerning possible errors in blood manipulation is really about.

In the following pages I will review the tannaitic material discussing ritual error connected to the mishandling of sacrificial blood. As a result of that review, I will propose two conclusions regarding what ritual error signifies: First, the characterization of the nature of ritual error and the remedies offered for specific errors tell us something significant about the nature of the Jewish sacrificial ritual system as presented in the Mishnah. That is, by noting what can go wrong in blood manipulation, we learn something about underlying concerns driving the discussions of blood manipulation as one element in a complex ritual system that, in itself, was out-of-date but still informed an active community. Ritual errors and the corrections prescribed to address ritual errors are thus instructive regarding the social and intellectual worlds of the *tannaim*.

More specifically, what emerges in the mishnaic discussion of sacrificial ritual is *not* primarily a guidebook as to what *should* occur in Temple sacrifice, but an elaborate argument for the priests' ability to identify and correct errors and, more indirectly but just as significantly, a demonstration of the rabbis' ritual expertise. Consequently, discussions that appear on the surface to be about what God demands are really primarily a display of rabbinic ritual mastery in the face of countless challenges to ritual perfection.

Second, M. Zevachim raises a number of issues for the general study of ritual. As noted above, the tractate does not, strictly speaking, present ritual. Rather, it presents a complex discourse regarding ritual, involving extensive speculation. Consequently, much of our contemporary scholarship on ritual theory cannot apply directly or should be used with great caution. We will see, for example, how Jonathan Z. Smith's oft-cited arguments characterizing ritual as the "ought" to reality's "is" are somewhat complicated when the object of study is not ritual per se, but discourse about ritual—particularly when that discourse focuses on ritual *not* proceeding as it "ought" to proceed. In addition, in discussing Temple sacrifice, the M. Zevachim focuses on ritual activity that no longer occurs, without ever mentioning its absence. How do we apply ritual theory to ritual discourse about ritual that no longer occurs? Finally, how do we approach ritual discourse by one group of religious elite (the rabbis) that purports to focus on another ritual elite (the priests) who no longer exist and therefore cannot speak for themselves? We will need to explore how ritual theory applies to discourse about ritual, discourse that, in and of itself, has been ritualized.

Blood Manipulation

Let me begin with a general overview of blood manipulation within the Jewish sacrificial system. For the purposes of this chapter, I will focus primarily on the discussions of blood manipulation in the Torah and their subsequent development in M. Zevachim, with a few brief references to M. Parah as well. Such a summary will require over-simplification, particularly regarding differences between the sacrificial systems of the Bible and the Mishnah, but it will be adequate for our present discussion.

General guidelines regarding blood handling are presented in the Bible, and they explicitly prohibit the consumption of blood. Instead, the blood of sacrificial animals is to be drained from the animal's body and applied to the altar.[3] The biblical material provides the bare outlines of the correct procedures for handling the blood, although one should note that the biblical material makes many assumptions about the reader's familiarity with sacrificial practice, and should not be thought of as a comprehensive ritual manual.[4] There continue to be lively debates about the purpose of the blood manipulation among scholars today, whether it effected purification of the altar itself (e.g., Jacob Milgrom) or fulfilled some other purpose (e.g., Baruch Levine). In general, the application of blood seems to bring about some ritual purification, although the relevant passages are by no means clear. For our purposes, the actual meaning of the ritual is not crucial; rather, the guidelines for and parameters of ritual activity are key.

The manipulation of an animal victim's blood is a key element of animal sacrifice. In general, the sacrificial animal is slaughtered by having its throat cut. The blood is captured in basins as it pours out from the throat, and then it is applied by a priest in prescribed ways to the altar, an elevated structure about fifteen feet high, accessible by a ramp. Blood may be applied in four ways: (1) daubed (Hebr. *ntn*) on the horns of the altar; (2) tossed (Hebr. *zrq*) against the sides of the altar; (3) sprinkled (Hebr. *nzh*) on the priests during their ordination and toward the veil of the sanctuary; and (4) poured out (Hebr. *špk*) at the base of the altar. Each of these verbs indicates a specific type of blood manipulation appropriate to the rite in which it is performed.

The specific blood manipulation employed is determined by several factors. First, certain logistical concerns related to the nature of the offering govern its handling. Thus, in the *'ōlâ* (whole burnt offering) ritual, an unblemished animal is chosen (bull, sheep, or goat) and then killed by having its throat cut. Next, "Aaron's sons, the priests, shall offer the blood, tossing the blood against the altar, round about" (Lev 1:5).[5] The priests take the basins containing the freshly collected blood and splash it against all four sides of the altar. As William Gilders notes, the process largely involves "a priestly circumambulation of the altar accompanied by the dashing of blood from a vessel one time on each side of the altar."[6] By contrast, if the *'ōlâ* offering is a bird, the priest pinches off the bird's head, then drains its blood by pressing the bird's throat immediately against the altar; its blood "shall be drained out against the side of the altar" (Lev 1:15). Thus, bird blood is handled differently than other animal blood, presumably for logistical reasons.

In addition, blood manipulation varies according to the type of sacrifice being performed. For example, in the first-fruits offering, the blood is tossed against the altar (Num 18:17). Blood is also tossed against the altar in the *'ōlâ, šĕlāmîm*, and *'āšām* sacrifices.[7] In the Yom Kippur sacrifice, by contrast, some blood is daubed on the "horns" of the altar and the rest of the blood is tossed against the altar seven times. Blood is sprinkled and daubed on the horns of the altar in certain *ḥaṭṭā't* rites as well, and the blood remaining after these "sprinkling" and "daubing" activities is poured out at the base of the altar.[8] Different rites, then, incorporate different blood manipulations; conversely, the distinctive manipulation of blood is one of the identifying characteristics of each individual sacrificial rite. Thus blood manipulation can act as a "marker," along with other elements (such as the type of animal offered and its gender), distinguishing one sacrifice from another.

In addition, in certain contexts, blood is manipulated in multiple ways depending upon the intended result. In the *ḥaṭṭāʾt* sacrifice, for example, the manipulation is somewhat complex: "The priest shall dip his finger in the blood and sprinkle [Hebr. *nzh*] the blood seven times before the Lord, in front of the veil of the sanctuary. The priest shall daub [Hebr. *ntn*] some of the blood on the horns of the altar of incense, which is in the Tent of Meeting, before YHWH, and the rest of the bull's blood he shall pour out [Hebr. *špk*] at the base of the altar of the burnt offering, which is at the entrance to the tent of meeting" (Lev 4:6–7). Note that the blood in this ritual is manipulated in at least three distinct ways.

In addition, blood is handled differently depending upon whose ritual contamination is being addressed. For example, the passage quoted above describes the *ḥaṭṭāʾt*, or purification, ritual performed on behalf of an anointed priest. If a priest brings impurity into the sanctuary, he might bring "guilt on the people [of Israel]" (Lev 4:3). The *ḥaṭṭāʾt* ritual described above purges the sanctuary and allows the priest to act ritually on behalf of the people.[9] The same procedure occurs when a *ḥaṭṭāʾt* needs to be performed on behalf of the whole congregation to cleanse them of their ritual impurity. A *ḥaṭṭāʾt* performed on behalf of a tribal ruler, however, does not require that the blood be tossed "seven times before YHWH in front of the veil." Neither is this required if the same ritual is performed for a common person. Thus the socio-cultic rank of the individual is sometimes reflected in the manipulation of the blood.

It should be apparent from these few examples that the blood manipulation outlined in the biblical texts is extremely complex. The priests would have been responsible for performing the rituals correctly, based on logistical concerns driven by the offering itself, the type of ritual being performed, the intended purpose of the sacrifice, and the person benefiting from the ritual activity. From even this brief overview one can imagine how easily someone could make mistakes while performing these complicated rituals. Let us turn now to a discussion of the possibilities for mishandling blood.

Ritual Errors

The ritual system laid out in the Bible is meant to address actions that occur largely in everyday life and that violate standards of purity and holiness. Numerous studies have been published that address these issues, and I shall not repeat those arguments here.[10] One key point to emphasize is that many actions that generate impurity are not mistakes or moral transgressions. They include natural bodily functions (nocturnal emissions, menstruation, childbirth) as well as normal social activities (care for a dead body) that are not morally wrong. These activities, however, generate ritual problems of impurity, many of which are addressed by ritual. The ritual system laid out in the Torah is meant to address impurity and sin, but in so doing the ritual system itself opens the doors for a second order of problems: sacrificial errors.

As a largely *halakhic* document, the Mishnah is focused on correct and incorrect behavior. As a result, much of the document outlines what may and may not occur in ritual behavior, and what to do when mistakes occur. Compared with the Bible, the Mishnah contains relatively little narrative material. As such, the Mishnah comes across as a practical document, grounded in the "real world," where mistakes occur on a daily basis. In terms of blood manipulation, the biblical material lays out general guidelines but spends almost no time discussing the errors that can occur while handling the blood. M. Zevachim, by contrast, provides extensive detail regarding blood handling, concentrating almost entirely on sacrificial mistakes. A careful review indicates that blood-manipulation errors tend to fall into one of the following categories. First, errors occur when blood for one specific offering is offered accidentally as if it were a different type of offering. The Hebrew literally describes this as a sacrifice being offered "not under its own name" (M. Zev. 1:3; Hebr. *šelo' lišmô*). For example, if "a Passover offering or a sin offering were slaughtered not under its own name, or if the blood were received, conveyed, or sprinkled not under its own name, or under its own name and subsequently under a different name, or under a different name and then subsequently under its own name, the sacrifice is invalid" (M. Zev. 1:4; see also M. Parah 4:1). This passage is describing a situation in which the *initial* procedures were performed as if the offering were one type of sacrifice (fulfilling one ritual purpose), but somewhere along the line the procedures changed, and the ritual continued as if it were another type of sacrifice (thus fulfilling a different ritual purpose). Thus, the error occurs in that an offering that was originally intended to fulfill one ritual purpose became confused with another type of offering. In such a situation, the offering is invalid.

In addition, ritual errors can occur related to the priest, the ritual participant who manipulates the blood. While the Mishnah seems to permit lay members of the community to slaughter sacrificial animals, only a priest may manipulate the blood. M. Zevachim explains that a sacrifice can be invalidated if blood is received by a nonpriest, if it is received incorrectly by the designated priest (e.g., in his left hand), if the priest who acts is ritually ineligible to perform the ritual, (e.g., he is uncircumcised, unclean), or if the priest receives the blood while sitting (2:1). M. Parah 4:1 declares a red heifer invalid if the heifer were slaughtered by a priest with unwashed feet and hands or if the priest were not dressed in the required white garments.[11] Thus, the blood can be invalidated by the ritual unfitness of its handler.

Further, an error occurs if the blood is mishandled. For example, an offering is invalidated if the blood is spilled on the ramp leading to the top of the altar, or if it is sprinkled somewhere that it should not have been (e.g., M. Zev. 3:2; 8:9–10). The blood also becomes invalid if it is carried outside the Temple Court (M. Zev. 8:12). M. Parah states that the rite of the red heifer is invalidated if the priests perform any other work during the ritual (M. Parah 4:4). In addition, there are various ways in which "valid" blood can become mingled with "invalid" blood. In most cases, the dominant view is that all of the blood must be disposed of when this occurs (M. Zev. 8:7–8).

Finally, intention also plays a role in blood manipulation. Here the Mishnah is distinct from the biblical material, which never discusses priestly intention. The Mishnah, by contrast, is very concerned with a priest's intentions while performing ritual activity. According to the Mishnah, a ritual is invalidated when the priest intends to perform an act "outside its proper time or place." That is, certain actions must be performed within a limited period of time following the slaughter of a sacrificial victim and in a designated place. Usually discussions regarding intention focus on when and where a priest may eat his allotted portion of a sacrifice. For example, M. Zevachim 2:2–3 explains that a sacrifice becomes "abomination" (Hebr. *pgl*) if the priest intends to eat sacrificial meat after the two days following slaughter (the period designated for consumption) have passed. Similarly, the tractate discusses priests who intend to leave the blood to be manipulated on a later day (e.g., M. Zev. 3:6). Such an offering is an abomination; it is invalid and may involve severe penalties.

Ritual errors, no matter what their form, can have four consequences. First, they may simply be corrected, with no harmful result. For example, M. Zevachim 3:2 lists a series of mistakes that may be corrected "on the spot" and the blood manipulation remains valid (*kšr*). Second, ritual errors may render an offering invalid (Hebr. *psl*), meaning that its performance has no expiatory effect, but no ritual penalty is required. A quick review of the tractate reveals that this is the most common result when ritual error occurs. For example, M. Zevachim 4:2 explains that if a priest fails to perform all of the prescribed acts of blood sprinkling (Hebr. *nzh*), the ritual is invalid, but no additional penalty is required. M. Parah 4:2 states, "If [the priest] tossed [the blood] not in the direction of the entrance of the shrine, [the offering] is invalid," but again no penalty is incurred.

Third, an error may require an individual to present an additional offering, even if his original, flawed offering is valid. For example, M. Zevachim 1:1 argues that all sacrifices that have not been slaughtered under their correct name or designation are valid, but they do not fulfill the offering party's ritual obligation. Similarly, M. Zevachim 6:7 states that the *ʿōlâ* of a bird not correctly offered under its own name "remains valid, but is not credited to its owner [so he must bring another offering to fulfill his obligation]." The texts convey no concern regarding this—the ritual must simply be performed again, correctly, to fulfill the ritual requirement.[12]

Finally, however, some errors are more serious; here is where we find ritual "angst." Rituals involving these kinds of errors are punished by *kārēt*, usually translated "cut off" or "extirpation," which has been understood in the following ways: (1) the offending individual dies prematurely (at YHWH's hand, not the community's); (2) the individual will not be "gathered with his forefathers" after his death; (3) the individual is cut off from social and cultic contact with the community; or (4) the individual will not have children, effectively cutting him off in the long run from any share with the rest of the Israelites in YHWH's blessings on His people.[13] M. Zevachim 2:2 describes a situation involving blood manipulation that warrants *kārēt*:

> [If the priest intended] to sprinkle its blood the next day, or [if he intended to sprinkle] some of its blood the next day, or [if he intended] to burn its sacrificial portions the next day or some of its sacrificial portions the next day or [if he intended] to eat some of its flesh the next day or an olive's bulk of its flesh the next day or an olive's bulk of the skin of the fat-tail the next day, [the sacrifice] becomes abomination, and *kārēt* [is warranted] thereby. (M. Zev. 2:2)

The Mishnah takes pains to clarify which of the penalties apply in specific cases. When someone unintentionally commits an error, the sacrifice is generally judged valid or invalid, but no further penalty is applied. By contrast, the punishment of "cutting off" is generally reserved for those who intentionally act against YHWH's commands. In the Mishnah, the intention specifically involves eating the portion of an offering designated for consumption at an inappropriate time.

It is interesting to note that the first half of M. Zevachim 2:2 describes a similar situation in which the person slaughters the sacrifice "intending to sprinkle its blood outside [the Temple Court] or [intending to sprinkle] some of its blood outside, or [with the intention of] burning its sacrificial portions outside," continuing with a list of variations on eating a portion of the offering in an inappropriate *place*.[14] In this case, the Mishnah concludes that the sacrifice is invalid, but that the more severe punishment of *kārēt* is not required. The Mishnah next lays out the general rule clearly: the intention to consume an offering outside of its proper *place* renders an offering invalid, but a wrongful intention to consume an offering outside of its proper *time* renders an offering invalid *and* warrants the penalty of *kārēt* (M. Zev. 2:3).[15] For example, blood that is accidentally sprinkled against the altar in the Temple court when it should have been sprinkled within the veil shielding the inner sanctum renders an offering invalid, but does not incur *kārēt* (M. Zev. 2:1). However, as mentioned previously, M. Zevachim 2:2 states that if the priest intends to sprinkle an animal's blood the day after he is supposed to sprinkle it, the sacrifice "becomes abomination, and *kārēt* [is warranted] thereby."

Note that in the Bible only one form of mishandling blood warrants punishment by *kārēt*: the consumption of blood (Lev 7:27; 17:10, 14). The Torah expressly forbids anyone from consuming blood (see Gen 9:4; Deut 12:16, 23–25; Lev 3:17; 7:26–27; 17:10–12, 14). In the Mishnah, however, *kārēt* is applied in response to very different circumstances. M. Parah 4:3 states, "If he [the priest] slaughtered [the red heifer] intending to eat from its flesh *or to drink from its blood*, it is valid." Thus the intention to consume blood does not invalidate the offering, let alone incur *kārēt*. However, as seen above, if the priest intends to sprinkle an animal's blood the day after he is supposed to sprinkle it, the sacrifice "becomes abomination, and *kārēt* [is warranted] thereby" (M. Zev. 2:2). The priest knowingly intends to perform the ritual outside its proper (or designated) time. Thus, the intention to consume blood does not warrant *kārēt* (as it did in the Torah), but the intention to consume the flesh of an offering in an inappropriate place (or, more frequently, at an inappropriate time) does.

M. Zevachim records different opinions regarding the relative importance of eating outside of the proper time and place. *Kārēt* is more frequently applied as a penalty when a ritual actor intends to eat outside the designated time, not outside the designated place. For example, if a priest intends to eat a bird sin-offering "outside its appointed place, it is invalid, but the penalty of *excision* is not incurred," but if the priest intended to eat "outside its proper time, it becomes *refuse*, and punishment by *excision* is incurred thereby" (M. Zev. 6:7). Thus the most serious penalty (*kārēt*) is invoked largely in situations involving inappropriate intentions regarding time. There may be a straightforward reason for this. The Mishnah was redacted when there was no access to the Temple, but the sacred time of Temple sacrifice continued to be pertinent, as it provided a prototype for the developing liturgical calendar. Carl Perkins notes that the opening passage of the Mishnah (M. Ber. 1:1f) establishes a link between the appropriate times to recite the *shema* and Temple ritual. Thus, from its very opening, the Mishnah emphasizes linking specific time-bound liturgical activities to Temple sacrifice. "Hence the recitation of the *shema* becomes like a (lay, rather than priestly) Temple offering which must be offered (or completed) *b'zmanah* (in its required time)."[16] One could imagine that, in the late second/early third centuries, it would be in the Jewish community's interest to emphasize penalties that reinforced the importance of sacred time more than penalties regarding location that, quite frankly, no longer applied in any real sense. Thus the rules governing the ritual manipulation of blood protect the liturgical calendar, if not for sacrifice, then for its replacement, prayer. Broadly speaking, then, the ritual penalties outlined in the Mishnah protect sacred time more seriously than sacred space. This seems consistent with what we see developing in Judaism in the tannaitic period, and it gives us a general thread to follow throughout additional complex treatments of sacrifice in other tractates.

Errors in Blood Manipulation and the Jewish Sacrificial System

We have seen that the most serious offenses in sacrificial blood manipulation are related to priestly intentions regarding time and place. At the most superficial level, this seems an obvious reference to the centrality of Temple ritual and an attempt to link developing liturgical practices to the authoritative sacrificial system. On a deeper level, however, I would argue that M. Zevachim's discussions regarding ritual error are part of a much broader tannaitic enterprise. As noted earlier, the Mishnah is generally attributed to Rabbi Judah ha-Nasi (referred to as simply "Rabbi" in the pages of the Mishnah itself). Within the Jewish tradition, the Mishnah's authority arises simultaneously with its inception, based on its organization, clarity, and precision. However, it is clear that the compilation of the Mishnah was a long-term, complicated activity, and Judah ha-Nasi drew on frameworks developed by Rabbi Akiva and Rabbi Meir as he organized material that had been generated over hundreds of years.[17] More importantly, it is easy to think of the Mishnah as a written literary document, one with a fixed form and recognized authority since its inception. Current research, however, challenges this notion. I tend to agree with Elizabeth Shanks Alexander, who makes a strong case for thinking of the Mishnah primarily as an oral tradition and, hence, as a fluid tradition. The conclusions summarized in the Mishnah are condensed opinions arrived at after complicated debate involving sages and students in the context of the rabbinic academy. As Alexander states, the oral traditions of the rabbis, including the Mishnah, "unfolded in an ongoing manner through debate, dialogue, and argumentation."[18] As such, the written document we have now is simply a snapshot of a constantly evolving tradition. Alexander is primarily concerned with demonstrating that

> these traditions and formulations were not always uniquely privileged within the rabbinic corpus. . . . [I]n the earliest phases of composition and transmission, notions of textual continuity existed that did not depend on fixed linear sequences of words. In such circumstances, it is difficult to imagine that any single formulation or arrangement of tradition stood out definitively among the others as original, authentic, or privileged.[19]

What is more accurate, she argues, is that the mishnaic authors were more concerned with "an appreciation of the multiplicity of fluidity of textual forms. Rather than seeing texts as fixed and stable and labeling variants as deviants from an original, the oral view recognizes the inherent fluidity of texts in oral settings."[20]

How does this relate to our discussion of blood manipulation? Most significantly, it should draw our attention away from the details of ritual-error correction (which apparently were not fixed for a period of time) to the system underlying those details, the developing rabbinic system of argumentation. What were the *tannaim* concerned with as they engaged in these fluid debates concerning blood manipulation? Along with Alexander, I would argue that the transmission of the Mishnah involved "the crafting of their [rabbinic] authority and the cultivation of intellectual habits through which to analyze and interpret them."[21]

The key point here is that the Mishnah is more than a commentary on the Torah or an explication of the implications of the Torah's instruction. Rather, it establishes a new intellectual system, one that replaces priestly authority and ritual practice with rabbinic authority and ritual argument. Through the shift from instruction regarding priestly ritual practice to debates concerning the correction of priestly error via rabbinic discourse, the axis of Jewish ritual life shifts, reorienting the community to new agents and structures of authority.

As a reminder, since we are dealing with a text, we are not actually observing or analyzing a world of actual ritual sacrifice, but rather a textual—and purely speculative—representation of a ritual world. In this complicated fabrication of ritual reality, I wish to draw attention to one point in particular: In the ritual world constructed in the Mishnah, the choice was not to minimize the discussion of error, thus presenting some idealistic representation of past priestly action. In fact, we find quite the opposite; the Mishnah highlights ritual error. In these texts we have a portrayal of ritual activity constantly on the verge of failing. Why? I would argue that this is because the real "masters" on display here are not the priests, but the rabbis themselves, demonstrating their command of the technical knowledge involved in Temple sacrifice. Where priestly activity fails to achieve perfection, the rabbis demonstrate complete control. The rabbinic conversation is most impressive precisely because it demonstrates knowledge of intricate details, both in terms of what can go wrong and in terms of how to identify and then correct what has gone wrong. The rabbis master a world that, in actual performance, could never be mastered. In so doing they actually surpass the priests, and the rabbinic tradition is established as superior to the cultic one.

I noted earlier that the Mishnah seems to ignore seismic events in Jewish history in the period immediately prior to its redaction (the first Jewish Revolt, the destruction of the Temple, and the Bar Kochba Revolt, for example). Given the social, political, and theological magnitude of these events, the Mishnah's silence is almost unfathomable. As Jacob Neusner comments,

> [I]t is unthinkable that anything done in the aftermath of the destruction of the Temple in 70 C.E. and the failed revolt of 135 CE should ignore these events. So in our [scholarly] interpretation of the Mishnah as a whole, as a system in itself, we have to invoke these events. On the other hand, when we turn to the system of Mishnah and examine as best we can its history in detail, the picture is quite different. . . . Mishnah is a profoundly anti-historical, anti-contextual document.[22]

In terms of the *content* of the Mishnah, this is certainly the case. However, Neusner concludes from this that the rabbis were simply trying to protect their peers from shifting to a different religio-cultic tradition: "They [the rabbis] repeat and augment the Scriptural laws and apply their logic. They also make certain that, for the time being, there will be no other cult and sacrificial system."[23] The mishnaic authors, Neusner seems to imply, take the ongoing continuity of the past tradition to heart: "Mishnah's system is a transitional one. It preserves interests and themes important to the priests, doing so through the methods and literary and cultural preferences of the scribes."[24]

I take a somewhat more cynical view of the Mishnah's complete silence regarding the destruction of the Temple. As Robert Alter notes, "'The *not saying* of something (or the pretending not to say it) is an ancient rhetorical device. . . . Often enough the reticence is intended to increase the impact of what it purports to conceal while making it inevitable that a properly informed reader will at once, and with the added emotion attendant on discovery, recognize what is really meant.' Irony persuades by misdirecting in a complex way."[25] It has frequently been noted that the Bible includes ironic material, particularly in its narrative (and even in its prophetic) material. But can we not find irony in legal material as well? It seems to me quite ironic that significant attention in the Mishnah is directed toward ritual activities that had been impossible to perform for over a hundred years. The "properly informed readers" to whom the Mishnah was addressed were largely the sages themselves and their students. The absent Temple would be the elephant in the rabbinic academy classroom, particularly during discourses focused on Temple practices.

Carolyn Sharp, in her discussion of irony in the Hebrew Bible, references Linda Hutcheon and notes:

> [I]rony functions in a relational and additive way much as metaphor does, with an important distinction: where metaphor signifies and establishes connection chiefly through the construction of similarity, irony signifies and establishes connection chiefly through the construction of difference. The dialectical relationship between the said and the unsaid creates a "third" meaning; it is this third meaning, which is not simply the implied opposite of the false literal meaning, that is properly understood as the ironic meaning.[26]

The unspoken absence of the Temple actually creates the possibility of a discourse that seems, on the surface, to establish continuity while, in actuality, it draws attention to a new reality based inexorably on distinction.

To sum up, the detailed discussions of penalties attending errant blood manipulation, at the surface or conscious level, link prayer to Temple sacrifice, particularly in emphasizing ritual time more than ritual place. At a more fundamental (but less obvious) level, the discussions of ritual error reinforce an axial shift from a priestly cultic matrix to a rabbinic-textual matrix. In this new system ritual errors are simultaneously addressed and nullified by a master rabbinic class. While appearing to looking backward, the *tannaim* shape how the community will move forward. The Mishnah trains its readers to think like rabbis rather than like priests, and thus to imagine the world in a discursive rather than cultic way. As Alexander notes in the concluding words of her book, "[T]hose who transmitted Mishnah played an active role in shaping not only the vagaries of its concrete formulation but also, and equally importantly, the intellectual environs within which it was received."[27]

Errors in Blood Manipulation and Ritual Theory

M. Zevachim's discussions of blood manipulation also have something to contribute to broader theorizing about ritual in general. Specifically, the data presented in the Mishnah's treatment of "blood manipulation gone wrong" draws our attention to layers of ritual discourse, and in so doing complicates any theoretical approach that fails to distinguish between ritual practice and ritual discourses. While we could apply this distinction to any one of a number of theoretical approaches, let me play this out with respect to some of Jonathan Z. Smith's well-known statements concerning ritual. First, Smith has tended to privilege space, focusing on "the role of place as a fundamental component of ritual: place directs attention."[28] But we have seen that both time and space are organized in the construction of ritual in the rabbinic presentation of the Temple ritual world. In fact, the ritual correction and penalty system presented in the Mishnah suggests that time had replaced space as the more significant ritual medium in the tannaitic period.

In addition, the Mishnah complicates the characterization of ritual as the "ought" to reality's "is." As you will recall, Smith rejects the classic myth/ritual divide (myth has content, ritual is "empty," devoid of content), characterizing ritual instead as "a mode of paying attention."[29] In an oft-cited passage Smith states, "Ritual is a means of performing the way things ought to be in conscious tension to the way things are."[30] Such a characterization suggests a dualism between that which is left as mundane and that which is designated as sacred via ritual activity. But the Mishnah complicates this, presenting a constant deferral of "making sacred" by the necessary interpolation of ritual correctives whenever mistakes occur. The ritual world of sacrifice as portrayed in the Mishnah is not a clean shift from "is" to "ought," but rather the constant striving after "ought," including an endless dance of action, error, correction, and action again. Mishnaic ritual, rather than clearly designating the ordinary from the sacred, presents the constant jockeying between the sacred and the mundane, as mistakes and their corrections open up sacrificial ritual to more and more possibilities. As a result, there is a constant renegotiation of what actually constitutes the ritual, as infelicitous actions prompt corrective actions, and so on.

In addition, the Mishnah complicates the social relations constructed by ritual. Ritual studies have tended to note how ritual activity marks "us" (the community) as distinct from "them" (those outside the community). In addition, ritual activity tends to distinguish between ritual elite and laity. In discussing the biblical sacrificial world, Gilders notes that "the manipulation of blood marks, defines, enacts, and reinforces relationships and status within the context of the cult as it is represented in the textual corpus."[31] The Mishnah takes this one step further: the *discourse* regarding blood constructs a new "us" relative to a new "them"—the rabbinic, textual world, in conversation with but distinguished from the priestly, cultic world—through conversations about sacrifice. Just as the "burnt offering blood manipulation functions as an index of relationships in the cultic sphere,"[32] the rabbinic debates concerning the repair of errant blood manipulations function as an index of relationships in the discursive, post-cultic sphere, limiting the priestly community even while validating their past role.

Over the course of the extended rabbinic debates regarding ritual practice, the text unseats the priest as the central agent (by focusing on his errors and keeping his voice out of the conversation) and replaces him with the rabbi. The priest repeatedly fails to fulfill his role as ritual agent by failing to manipulate the blood successfully. He dis-authorizes himself. Ultimately, this ritual discourse reorients the reader. Over the course of a review of the mishnaic material the reader is repositioned within a tannaitic system, rather than a cultic one, and the sacred of the Temple is replaced with the sacred of the rabbinic academy.

Conclusions

This essay, along with the others in this volume, demonstrates that sacrifice is much richer and complex in its ancient religious contexts than the dominant theories of sacrifice have suggested. No single, monothetic definition of sacrifice encompasses the range of sacrificial phenomena referenced in ancient texts. More significantly, no single-minded approach to sacrifice takes fully into account the problems inherent in examining textual *representations* of sacrifice. Such representations, as we have seen here, cannot be treated as accurate or unbiased descriptions of actual ritual activity. Rather, textual discussions of sacrifice are distinct (and complex) phenomena that require their own analysis. As I have suggested above, these texts are often written in response to historical events and cultural situations that inform the texts without ever being directly referenced. As such, these representations tell us virtually nothing about "actual" sacrifice, but they can contribute a great deal to our understanding of how sacrifice was deployed as an authoritative religious category by specific communities.

As I stated at the beginning of this essay, my interest in "ritual gone wrong" extends beyond the material in the Mishnah to a broader comparative project. I am interested in what we can learn about the nature of ritual in general by examining ritual mistakes, and asking questions about them. Do ritual communities discuss mistakes? In what contexts do they discuss these mistakes? Up until now, the cluster of issues related to ritual mistakes has been drawn from ethnographic or anthropological studies. This data has been treated as marginal, and thus insignificant with regard to general theoretical discussions regarding ritual. However, the data we have reviewed in this essay clearly indicates that textual representations of ritual mistakes have much to contribute to ritual theory. For example, the tannaitic discussions of errors in blood manipulation complicate the notion of ritual as the construction of an "ought" in contradistinction to an "is." Ritual activity, because of its constant need for self-correction, is continually deferred through a dynamic interplay between what the ritual player should do, what actually occurs, and the ritual correction of errors. One's attention is not simply directed to a specific object, action, or place; the ritual actor's attention is constantly shifted from the "is" to the "ought," back to the "is-but-should-not-be," and on to the "ought, revised." In so doing, ritual does not simply shift attention in a monolithic way; rather, ritual involves constant reflection, constant shifting of attention, and constant renegotiation.

What emerges from the Mishnah's authoritative discussion of ritual, then, is *not* a clear articulation of what *should* occur in a ritual performance, but an elaborate display of the ritual system's ability to deal with human error. More indirectly but just as significantly, the intricate conversations about ritual error and correction provide a flamboyant demonstration of the rabbis' ritual expertise. To explain a phenomenon is to claim to stand outside of it, to encompass it within one's own, presumably broader, scope of knowledge and understanding. By deliberating about priestly activity, and rendering authoritative opinions on the basis of that deliberation, the rabbis assert their comprehension of (and therefore superiority to) the sacrificial system. Consequently, discussions that appear on the surface to be about what God demands in sacrifice are really displays of rabbinic ritual knowledge. Discussions of ritual remedy in general de-center the apparent intended recipient of the ritual (YHWH) and the ritual technicians (the priests), highlighting instead the new ritual elite's ability to contend with ritual error. Ultimately, the most important question is not what the gods demand, but how the religious system responds when those demands cannot be met.

Notes

1. I would be remiss not to mention Clifford Geertz's essay "Ritual and Social Change: A Javanese Example," in *The Interpretation of Cultures* (New York: Basic Books, 1973), and Jonathan Z. Smith's "The Bare Facts of Ritual," in *Imagining Religion: From Babylon to Jonestown* (Chicago: University of Chicago Press, 1982), both of which mention ritual errors. Despite the wide-ranging impact these essays have had on the study of ritual, however, neither author used his data regarding ritual mistakes as part of the foundation for broad theorizing about ritual that included ritual mistakes.

2. Kathryn McClymond, *Beyond Sacred Violence: A Comparative Study of Sacrifice* (Baltimore: Johns Hopkins University Press, 2008).

3. If the blood cannot be applied to the altar, it is to be poured out on the ground. For the purposes of this essay, I will focus on the blood manipulation at the Temple, which is the focus of the tractate.

4. For details, see the work of Jacob Milgrom and Baruch Levine, who have both written extensively on this topic. See, for example, Jacob Milgrom, *Leviticus 1–16*, Anchor Bible 3 (New York: Doubleday, 1991), and Baruch Levine, *The JPS Torah Commentary: Leviticus* (Philadelphia: Jewish Publication Society, 1989). I also recommend William Gilders, *Blood Ritual in the Hebrew Bible* (Baltimore: Johns Hopkins University Press, 2004).

5. All translations are my own unless indicated otherwise.

6. Gilders, *Blood Ritual*, 67. See Gilders's detailed discussion of various points of view on the application of animal blood throughout this book. I am indebted to William Gilders for this work and for many extended personal conversations regarding the Jewish sacrificial system that have contributed to my thinking over the years.

7. McClymond, *Beyond Sacred Violence*, 56–58.

8. Lev 4:7, 4:18, 4:25, 4:30, 4:34.

9. Here I follow Jacob Milgrom's understanding of the verb *ḥaṭṭā't*. See "The Function of the Hatta't Sacrifice," *Tarbiz* 40 (1970):1–8.

10. Note that purity and holiness are distinct from one another. See Jonathan Klawans, *Impurity and Sin in Ancient Judaism* (Oxford: Oxford University Press, 2000).

11. M. Parah is the tractate concerned with ritual purification brought about by water mingled with the ashes of the red heifer.

12. See also M. Zev. 7:2.

13. Based on M. Meg. 1:5, Elizabeth Shanks Alexander notes that the rabbis understood *kārēt* to refer to "death at the hands of heaven." *Transmitting Mishnah: The Shaping Influence of Oral Tradition* (Cambridge: Cambridge University Press, 2006), 153. While this essay focuses on blood manipulation that warrants *kārēt*, other actions do as well. For example, Jonathan Klawans notes that a man who has sexual relations with his wife while she is menstruating is liable for *kārēt* (M. Ker 1:1). In addition, M. Shab. 2:6 suggests that one possible explanation for a woman dying in childbirth is that she was not careful with regard to menstruation. See Klawans, *Impurity and Sin*, 106.

14. Philip Blackman, trans. and ed., *Mishnayoth* (Gateshead, U.K.: Judaica Press, 1990).

15. The relationship between intentions regarding time and place are discussed repeatedly in the tractate, and differing opinions are presented. For example, M. Zev. 2:5 records a debate in which Rabbi Judah asserts that intentions regarding time are more significant than intentions regarding place. However, the Sages disagree, arguing, "In both cases [the *offering*] becomes invalid, but punishment by *kārēt* is not incurred."

16. Carl M. Perkins, "The Evening *Shema*: A Study in Rabbinic Consolation," *Judaism* 43.1 (Winter 1994): 3. By contrast, Perkins argues that the Tosefta does not open the same way; the later rabbinic material moves gradually toward acknowledging the destruction of the Temple explicitly.

17. See B. Metzi'a. 86a, which links Judah ha-Nasi with the "end of mishnaic instruction."

18. Alexander, *Transmitting Mishnah*, 3.

19. Alexander, *Transmitting Mishnah*, 77.

20. Alexander, *Transmitting Mishnah*, 6.

21. Alexander, *Transmitting Mishnah*, 8.

22. Jacob Neusner, "Halakhah and History," *Judaism* 29.1 (Winter 1980): 53.

23. Neusner, "Halakhah and History," 55.

24. Neusner, "Halakhah and History," 55–56.

25. Robert Alter, quoted in Carolyn J. Sharp, *Irony and Meaning in the Hebrew Bible*, Indiana Studies in Biblical Literature, edited by Herbert Marks (Bloomington: Indiana University Press, 2009), 1.

26. Sharp, *Irony and Meaning*, 20.

27. Alexander, *Transmitting Mishnah*, 223.

28. Jonathan Z. Smith, *To Take Place: Toward Theory in Ritual* (Chicago: University of Chicago Press, 1987), 103.

29. Smith, *To Take Place*, 103.

30. Smith, *To Take Place*, 109.

31. Gilders, *Blood Ritual*, 61.

32. Gilders, *Blood Ritual*, 79.

13

Passing

JESUS' CIRCUMCISION AND STRATEGIC SELF-SACRIFICE

Andrew S. Jacobs

Small Sacrifices

In a refutation of Christians who denied Christ's fleshly reality, Tertullian luxuriated in the incarnational impossibilities of God's death: "The son of God was crucified; it is no shame, since it must be shameful. And the son of God died: it is believable, since it is absurd. And having been buried, he rose again: it is certain, since it is impossible."[1] Not only the indignities of death, but those of birth attracted Tertullian: "What's more unworthy of God? What is more blushworthy [*erubescendum*]: to be born, or to die? To bear flesh, or the cross? To be circumcised, or crucified [*suffigi*]? To be in a cradle, or a coffin? To be laid down in a manger, or laid to rest in a tomb?"[2] At the beginning of his life as at the end, Christ sacrifices the power of his divinity to the sorrows of the flesh.

As Virginia Burrus has noted, "Tertullian's christological aesthetics links nativity tightly to mortality."[3] Indeed, as Tertullian writes, "there is no flesh without nativity,"[4] and therefore Christ's self-sacrifice must acquire a certain specificity: he possesses not just generic "flesh," but flesh formed in a particular time and place. So, in the list of blush-worthy sorrows suffered by Christ, we find paired together circumcision and crucifixion: the shedding of blood at the beginning of life and the end. Circumcision, of course, was not a universal or random moment of childhood suffering: it marks Jesus' life of human travail as a *Jewish* life, and his blush-worthy travails as particularly Jewish.

That Tertullian should signal this self-sacrificing Jewishness through circumcision is not, I think, incidental or driven by the rhetorical need to find a suitably surgical counterpart to the crucifixion.[5] The hard reality and substantiality of this mark, combined with what it does (and does not) signify, afford us a unique vantage point on the early Christian understanding of precisely what (and why) Jesus gave up in the incarnation. That Christianity internalized and reimagined the concept of sacrifice in the *crucifixion* of Jesus is clear enough: "Christianity defined itself precisely as a religion centered on sacrifice," Guy Stroumsa has written, "even if it was a reinterpreted sacrifice. The Christian *anamnēsis* was the reactivation of the sacrifice of the Son of God, performed by the priests."[6] It is my suggestion here that, in crucial ways, early Christians could look upon the entire incarnation itself as a kind of sacrifice, drawing not simply on discourses of religious ritual but on broader images of power and personhood in the ancient world. My use of the term *sacrifice,* then, differs in many ways from that of the other contributors to this volume (as became clear during the conference at Boston University during which I first presented this work). My scope widens out from the focus on "ritual slaughter" that animates the fine contributions herein to consider the sacrifice of Jesus visible not only on the cross but in his particular human body.

The cultural context in which Christians imagined Jesus sacrificing his divinity and descending into a demeaning and impossible carnality—literally marked as Jewish by his circumcision—was one in which identities emerged out of and were contested in the crucible of discipline and mastery, of self and others. The power of Rome itself was created out of the use—and, often, abuse—of others' bodies: slaves, provincials, women, soldiers, and so on, without which sacrifice Rome could not function. But this sacrifice of other persons was also internalized, engendering a sense of slippery *self*-discipline and *self*-mastery: Roman gentlemen had to train their bodies rigorously to appear naturally masculine;[7] Roman nobles had to sacrifice leisure—negate *otium*—to take up the duties of public life.[8] It would make sense to an ancient Roman audience, then, to envision Jesus as part of what Carlin Barton has called Rome's "emotional economy of sacrifice":[9] "an elaborate physics of binding, capturing, taming, and domesticating energy with the purpose of enhancing and concentrating it," a physics which included all manner of self-sacrifice as well.[10] Not only the bodies of victims made visible this cultural dynamism, but all bodies located in and operating along the pathways of this "emotional economy" felt the sting of sacrifice, of ceding, of "giving up" of oneself. So we must imagine the sacrifice of Jesus not only on the cross, but in his particular material existence as well.

We can see this view of Jesus' incarnation as a daily sacrifice, the dymanic pull of this "emotional economy," in the ways Christians imagined his Judaized, circumcised body. Jesus' Jewish circumcision was demeaning: a mark of opprobrium that Jesus took upon himself willingly, like the shameful marks of crucifixion. Justin Martyr, in his *Dialogue with Trypho*, admits to his Jewish interlocutor that Christ was circumcised, and immediately adds this context: "Likewise I confess that he underwent fatal crucifixion and that he became a human being and that he suffered as many things as those members of your people arranged for him."[11] Crucifixion and circumcision alike were moments that located Jesus squarely, even sacrificially, among the Jews.

Yet on Christ's body, the divine suffering of circumcision—like that of crucifixion— underwent a strange transformation, from *skandalon* to *sotēria*. Orthodox Christians were clear on three points: (1) Jesus was truly, physically, *Jewishly* circumcised; (2) this circumcision played a particular role in his condescension to human form, particularly among Jews; (3) finally, as a consequence of this specific birth and life among Jews, followers of Christ are utterly and absolutely distinct from Jews and Judaism. The logical shift from the first two points to the third point are only possible because the Christians I'm discussing viewed Christ's human existence—his Jewish existence—in a particular way. Although these early Christians viewed Jesus' earthly existence—his suffering, his self-sacrifice, his condescension to Judaism—as inescapably *real*, they also understood it to be ultimately strategic, even misleading. I suggest we might describe Jesus' self-sacrificing Jewish life on earth (as it was understood by early Christians) using the language of *passing*.

Passing emerged as a distinct narrative of racial camouflage in U.S. literature of the nineteenth century, when "race" as a category acquired its patina of scientific inevitability.[12] Accounts of passing primarily portrayed a black individual "passing" for white, reinforcing the binary nature of U.S. racial politics;[13] but "passing" has been read into a diverse array of deceptive identities, encompassing race, class, gender, religion, and sexuality.[14] Narratives of passing destabilize an existing "optical economy of identity."[15] That is, passing both undermines and necessitates the recognition of stable, mutually exclusive categories of personhood (categories of race, gender, sexuality, and so on). Passing emerges in social settings that rely on what Amy Robinson and others have called "specular identification":[16] the interior qualities of a person must be, in some way, legible on the body's surface, conveying deeper, more ingrained and essential aspects of identity.

To "pass" from one category to another, therefore, calls that link between exterior surface and interior essence into question. How meaningful can "white" be as an essential category if a black person can mimic it so perfectly as to "pass"? How meaningful can "black" be as an essential category if a black woman—as philosopher and artist Adrian Piper recounted in a 1992 essay—has to remind or even insist to friends and colleagues that she is not "really" white?[17] The pass over the racial boundary calls that boundary—and the essential categories it supposedly divides—into question. Yet in the logic of passing, those essences are also paradoxically affirmed: the notion of interior essence is never evaporated, it is temporarily dissociated from the surface of the passer's skin. To successfully pass *as* white, the "real person" (underneath? within?) must—somehow, in some fashion—remain *not* white, or else they are not "passing."[18] As Elaine Ginsberg writes in her introduction to a collection of essays on the subject, "One cannot pass for something one *is not* unless there is some other, prepassing identity that one *is*."[19] Valerie Rohy in the same collection concurs, "[P]assing insists on the 'truth' of racial identity . . . framing its resistance to essentialism in the very rhetoric of essence and origin."[20] Passing creates a situation in which the building blocks of identity are revealed to be a fantasy: constantly under invention, but still powerful and even "real" in their way.[21]

In many ways, Jesus is obviously a figure who "passes." In several varieties of early Christianity, he is a divine figure "passing" for human. Those Christians,

labeled "docetists" by their opponents, even believed that all of Jesus' material existence was a deception, a mirage that perfectly fooled all but the elect.[22] In this they
both destabilized the boundary between human and divine—allowing those elect
to cross over—and yet locked it firmly into place. Those Christians who eventually
became the triumphant "orthodox" also believed that Christ "who was in the form
of God" nonetheless "took the form of a servant" and was "born in the likeness
of humanity" (Phil 2:6–7). Jesus' human passing here too reaffirms the essential
natures of "humanity" and "divinity" even as it confounds them.

Arguably, Jesus is unique in his ability to be God and "pass" for human in early
Christian thought. Nonetheless, Jesus' unique ability to be *both-and* and *neither-nor*
expanded outward in antiquity to provide a template for the increasingly complex
production of interlocking, contradictory identities known as "Christianity." Jesus'
sacrifice of self—literal, physical, cultural, and even ethnic—creates for Christians
the opportunity to rethink the power politics of their culture, to appropriate the
power of a self that is created, fractured, even sacrificed, but never lost or power-
less. When Christians contemplated Jesus circumcised, they identified with this impossible personhood, straddling essential, unchangeable identities that could shift,
mutate, and incorporate their "other" opposites.

Christians understood that Christ's circumcision must have been deliberate—
even as an infant, after all, Jesus was still God—and it must be meaningful. Its
meaning, however, could *not* be precisely the same meaning that attached to rou-
tine, non-Jesus-related Jewish circumcision. Not precisely the same meaning, but
necessarily related: there was no question that his circumcision took place "under
the Law"—that is, because of the Jewish covenant—and yet did not *make* Jesus
Jewish. What did that circumcision accomplish? It functioned, I suggest, as the
surface sign that allowed Jesus to *pass* as Jewish: it was his white skin, his American
accent, his macho swagger, his visible—yet deceptive—Jewishness.

Jesus' docetic Jewishness is a feature of this larger project on the circumcision of
Christ that I often have to explain to people who don't work in ancient Christianity,
especially—interestingly—to contemporary Christians. Surely, I am told, Jesus was
circumcised because he was Jewish! Bart Ehrman even said so, in his popular 1999
book on the historical Jesus:

> There's probably no reason to belabor the point that all of our sources portray
> Jesus as Jewish—he came from a Jewish home, he was circumcised as a Jew,
> he worshiped the Jewish God, he kept Jewish customs, followed the Jewish
> Law, interpreted the Jewish Scriptures, and so on. . . . [T]he tradition of Jesus'
> Jewish origin and upbringing is firmly entrenched in all of our traditions at
> every level.[23]

This assertion relies on modern notions of historical reconstruction, on a "historical Jesus" who did not exist in this way for ancient Christians. For these Christians,
Jesus was God, incarnate *among* Jews. He passed as human, and he did so in a
perfect Jewish disguise.

Jesus Passing

Let's return to Tertullian, whose treatise on Christ's flesh so memorably linked nativity, carnality, mortality, and self-sacrifice. "How could he be admitted to the synagogue," Tertullian asked in the early third century, "so out-of-nowhere, and entirely unknown?"[24] Tertullian was writing against what he perceived as the extremist position of Marcion, whose followers did not think Christ had anything to do with Jews and Judaism other than geographic coincidence: Christ simply appeared one day from heaven in the middle of Galilee.[25] Tertullian finds laughable the idea that Jesus could walk unmolested among the Jews without appropriate cover: "No one knowing his tribe, his people, his house [. . .]? Certainly they would have remembered, if they did not know that he was circumcised, that he should not be admitted into the holiest places [*sancta sanctorum*]!"[26] For Tertullian, Jesus' circumcision functions like his genealogy, which also appears in the Gospel of Luke and also is not quite what a proper, Jewish genealogy should be (it does not, of course, actually recount *Jesus'* physical descent, but his stepfather's). These pieces of camouflage enable Jesus' admission into the Jewish "holiest places"; they guarantee him a seat at the table in the synagogue. And what does Jesus do in the synagogue according to Tertullian? "He offers first to the Israelites the bread of his own teaching."[27]

We often find Christ "passing" as Jewish for this reason: to bring his teaching to the Jews. And, frequently, his circumcision is explained as enabling this Jewish mission. In his commentary on the Gospel of Luke, Ambrose of Milan claimed (borrowing a line from the apostle Paul): "He was fashioned [*factus est*] under the Law so that he might win those who were under the Law" (cf. Gal 4:4).[28] That this "fashioning" was more fashion than fact Ambrose makes clear later in his commentary. Once again he borrows from Paul, this time reassigning—and reimagining—Paul's missionary self-description:

> For those who are under the Law, as if he himself were under the Law (although he is not under the Law), he was circumcised, so that he might acquire those who are under the Law. But for those who were apart from the Law, he dined in fellowship with them, so that he might acquire those who lived apart from the Law. He was made weak for the weak through bodily suffering, so that he might acquire them. Afterwards he was made all things for all people: poor for the poor, rich for the rich, weeping for the weeping, hungry for the hungry, thirsty for the thirsty, flowing forth with abundance [*profluus abundantibus*].[29]

Jesus, like Paul (1 Cor 9:20–22), came "as if under the Law, although not under the Law," and the circumcision was—apparently—part of this Jewish disguise by which he could give up a part of himself in order to win those "under the Law." (The strategy for winning gentiles involved the less physically challenging "dining in fellowship.")

Jesus was (again, like Paul) "all things for all people"; or, more precisely, he *seemed* to be all things for all people. Ambrose understands that Jesus came to initiate a particular and specific economy of salvation that would ultimately exclude those Jews he sacrificed so much to "win."[30] A century later, Maximus of Turin imagines the same rationale for the circumcision: "so that the Jewish people, brought up in circumcision [*alumna circumcisionis plebs Iudaïca*] would not reject him as a foreigner."[31] Circumcision enables a disguise, one designed to dupe the Jews into hearing Jesus out.

To understand the trickiness of Christ's disguise, we must realize that it was predominantly anti-Jewish Christians who conceived of Jesus "passing" as Jewish in this manner; that is, an undercurrent of these protestations that Jesus came to "win" the Jews was the understanding that these Jews were not to be won.[32] There were, to be sure, Christians who celebrated Jesus' circumcision and viewed it as a model for their own behavior. The so-called orthodox referred to these Christians as "Ebionites," and modern scholarship has dubbed them "Jewish-Christians."[33] According to their fourth-century detractor Epiphanius of Salamis, they claimed the precedent of both the patriarchs of the Old Testament and Christ in the New Testament as warrant for their continued practice of circumcision. "Christ," we are told they claimed, "was circumcised, so you should be circumcised!"[34] From the orthodox perspective, however, the Ebionites have been duped: they are successfully fooled by Christ's Jewish passing, to the point where they emulate his disguise and think it is real.

Epiphanius, however, is not so fooled: he knows that Christ's circumcision gave him a Jewish appearance, but meant something else. It was, he insists, entirely real: "he set things up," Epiphanius writes, "so that he would be truly circumcised, and not merely in appearance, on the eighth day." His disguise, in order words, was perfect. But in Epiphanius's refutation of the Ebionites we begin to see why this disguise was perpetrated at all. Ambrose had said that Jesus came "like" a Jew to win the Jews. Epiphanius is a bit more precise:

> [He was circumcised] in order to affirm that the circumcision which had been given in ancient times was justly ordained until his own arrival, and so that the Jews would not have any defense [ἀπολογίαν]. For if he were not circumcised, they would have been able to say, "We cannot accept an uncircumcised messiah."[35]

Epiphanius repeats a little further on: "Having perfect humanity, he was circumcised, arranging everything truly, so that the Jews, as I said before, would be defenseless [ἀναπολόγητοι]."[36] Epiphanius makes explicit what is only implicit in Tertullian, Ambrose, or Maximus: Jesus may have come to "win" the Jews and fashioned the perfect disguise to get the job done, but the Jews *still* rejected him (and continue to do so). The division between Jew and Christian, even when muddled on Christ's own body, ultimately reasserts itself.

Part of the paradoxical logic of passing in modern accounts is the affirmation of essentialism: "black" and "white" are destabilized by racial passing, but affirmed as "real" categories of race (to and from which one can pass). The Jewish passing of Jesus engineers the same confusion and reaffirmation of categories: "as if under the Law, but not under the Law," Ambrose wrote. "In the circumcision justly given until his own arrival," Epiphanius affirmed. Jesus' circumcision is unquestionably Jewish—so Jewish even the Jews are fooled!—and in this way his act both recognizes and affirms the category of "Jew," as distinct from Christian. And yet his disguise is *so* perfect, *so* admirable that our Christian authors must take care to point out what every good Christian should already recognize: it is a ruse.

After all, some *Christians* are being fooled as well, thinking that Jesus came not just to "fulfill the Law"—which, for orthodox Christians contemplating the circumcision, means he "paid it in full," rendering its actual practice unnecessary.[37] These "heretical" Christians have themselves become "dupes," believing they can maintain the strange admixture of essences they believe to be present on Jesus' earthly body: faithful to the Law and members of the Christian community. Of course, our evidence for these Ebionites in antiquity is slim, almost entirely reliant on the obsessive, persistent detractions of their enemies. We might even posit that the Ebionite Christian *desire* for "the other" is really a projection of orthodox desires: it is, after all, Epiphanius who elaborates in such detail the perfect Jewishness of Jesus' circumcision "under the Law."[38] Epiphanius uses his refutation of the too-Jewish Ebionites to work out his own desire for and fear of the Jewish other: Christ's "passing" then provides a model for Epiphanius as well, who can get inside and understand Judaism even as he repudiates it.[39] Christ's circumcised body allows Epiphanius to gauge the narrow (and illusory) distance between self and other, Jew and Christian, to locate himself, like Christ, momentarily in that "in-between" space where the fantasy of Christian identity is, for a second, unveiled.

By the fifth century, most Christians seemed comfortable with understanding Jesus' self-sacrifice as a strategy, part of his economy of salvation (and condemnation). Cyril of Alexandria, the great Christological theologian of the early fifth century—who also deployed violence against the Jews and pagans of his city—makes clear in an early treatise that Jesus was not, in fact, quite Jewish:

> You might rightly be amazed at this: that he [Christ] of necessity came down from above into the land of Judea, among those by whom he was mocked impiously; there he was born according to the flesh. But, in truth, he wasn't a Jew, insofar as he was the Word [καίτοι κατὰ ἀλήθειαν Ἰουδαῖος οὐκ ὢν ὁ Λόγος], but rather from both heaven and his father.[40]

Cyril comments in a later *Commentary on Luke*:

> He is circumcised on the eighth day along with Jews [μετὰ Ἰουδαίων], so that he may confirm his kinship [τὴν συγγένειαν]. For the messiah [Christ] was expected from the seed of David, and he offered the proof of his kinship. For if even though he was circumcised they said, "We do not know where he comes

from" [John 9:29], had he not been circumcised according to the flesh, and
kept the Law, their denial would have had just cause [πρόφασιν εὔλογον].[41]

Here the logic of Jesus' passing—essential, yet illusory—is fully articulated: Christ
was circumcised in "kinship" with the Jews, but his submission to their Law was a
strategy, a means of defusing future Jewish critique. Cyril and his audience know
that, in fact, the Jews—Christ's own "kin"—*did* proclaim (unjustly, we now learn)
that they did not know "where he comes from" (cf. Matt 13:55 and parallels). The
Jews are fooled—they think Christ is their kin—but only to their detriment: their
rejection forever severs a kinship that only existed contingently, temporarily, pass-
ingly, on Jesus' body.

"Seen and Unseen"

Passing narratives are compelling because of the triangular tension they create:
between the passer, the "dupe," and the knowing gaze of a third viewer (the reader,
the narrator, or a character within the narrative) who can see through the pass.
Ebionites and Jews are both "dupes," responding inappropriately to Jesus' seeming
Jewishness: Ebionites embrace his disguise, Jews reject him despite it. Christians
like Ambrose, Epiphanius, or Cyril, on the other hand, see through the disguise to
the deeper truth.

In this, Christians were arrogating to themselves a particularly Roman power
and playing with a peculiarly Roman danger. The Roman empire was a deliberate
mosaic of cultures and populations only lightly assimilated into any common
language or system of values. Romans had long distinguished themselves from
the Greeks—rightly or wrongly—because their power emerged out of the absorp-
tion of diverse "other" peoples into the Roman state. As a consequence of that
power, Romans delighted in the danger of the exotic, imported into the city and
made legible by a cultural economy of signs. By gazing upon the others whom
they had conquered, whom they now knew so perfectly, Romans were looking at
their own power and authority.[42] Even when Romans imagined the failure of legible
identities—as in an ancient novel like the *Aithiopika,* in which an Ethiopian prin-
cess is born with inexplicably white skin—they also imagine the ways in which false
identities are ultimately pierced by knowing and authoritative viewers.[43] Roman
elites did not construe themselves as dupes, but rather as master-gazers, ensuring
that the optical economy of power remained intact.

Of course, this very certainty of the gaze necessitates its opposite: the fear of
deception, the unrecognized pass, the undermining of the political economy. Elaine
Ginsberg writes that

passing is about identities: their creation or imposition, their adoption or
rejection, their accompanying rewards or penalties. Passing is also about the

boundaries established between identity categories and about the individual
and cultural anxieties induced by boundary crossing. Finally, passing is about
specularity: the visible and the invisible, the seen and the unseen.[44]

So, too, Christians, gazing upon Christ's body, seeing its Jewishness, and seeing
through its Jewishness, are operating from within a precarious political economy,
fraught with anxiety.

I do not mean to reduce Christology to politics but, rather, to remind us that in
this ancient context politics and the sacred cannot be disentangled. Sacrifice, too,
was a political act, mapping mundane human relations of power and affection into
the celestial sphere.[45] Sacrifice was also in many ways about specularity, boundaries,
and "things seen and unseen." And, like the Roman politics of identity, sacrifice
engendered a well-defined—and therefore precarious—political economy.

Christianity relied on this sacrificial economy, even as it challenged its workings.
The crucifixion was a *skandalon* because it rearranged sacrificial politics: the subject of sacrifice (God) was also the sacrificial victim. Christians taught that Jesus
conquered death by dying: the crucifixion both reifies the boundary between life
and death and perforates it. This is the narrative logic of passing, of boundaries
established and crossed. So, too, Jesus sacrificed himself (in these Christians' eyes)
to Judaism, thereby reifying Judaism as a thing to be ultimately conquered and
repudiated.

Ambrose, like Tertullian centuries earlier, paired these two sacrificial moments—
circumcision and crucifixion—in a letter concerning Christ's circumcision:

> [Christ] was circumcised first according to the Law, in order not to dissolve
> the Law [*ne legem solveret*]; afterward [he was circumcised] through the cross,
> so that he might fulfill the Law [see Matt 5:17]. Therefore that which was
> partial ceased, since perfection has come; for in Christ the cross has
> circumcised not one member, but the superfluous desires of the whole body.[46]

Ambrose's circumcising cross is a powerful image of Christian theological and
political superiority, and anxiety. It is a supercircumcision: the mark of Judaism
now covers the whole body (*totius corporis*), and not only Jesus' contingently Jewish body, but the resolutely non-Jewish bodies of his followers. Both circumcision
and crucifixion invert meaning: Just as Jesus' crucifixion brings life, and not
death, so his circumcision brings Christianity ("perfection"), not Judaism. The
power of these sacrifices is to pass through death to life, and through Judaism
to Christianity.

Of all the various Christians who contemplated Jesus' passing, only one pushed
back against this specular play on the body of Christ. For Augustine, bishop of
Hippo Regius, the surface of Christ's body and its interior must reveal the same
person no matter what the consequences. In his protracted debates with Jerome,
with bitter accusations of "judaizing" flying across the Mediterranean, Augustine
held a strict line on the Jewish observance of the apostles and Jesus:

Nor, moreover, do I think that the Lord himself was insincerely [*fallaciter*] circumcised by his parents. Perhaps someone might object on account of his age. Well, I don't think that he insincerely [*fallaciter*] said to the leper [. . .]: "Go and offer for yourself a sacrifice because Moses commanded it as a covenant for them" [Mark 1:44]. Nor did he go up insincerely [*fallaciter*] on the festival day, since he wasn't showing off for other people: rather, he went up secretly, not openly [John 7:10].[47]

Augustine refuses to imagine Jesus acting *fallaciter*, "falsely" or "insincerely." Jesus' circumcision cannot be a ruse to pass among Jews, it must rather be a sincere gesture of faith in the Jewish covenant.[48] Of course, Augustine asserts here and elsewhere that Jesus rendered the Jewish sacraments moot;[49] but in his time, in his life, on his body, they were real, and they signified an interior state that matched the exterior appearance. Augustine displays, throughout his life, an acute anxiety over signs and their meanings, seeking stability and fixity where others enjoyed variety and diversity.[50] He also famously mistrusts human perception, making popular the innovative idea that the human will has been so twisted by sin that it can never, on its own, correctly perceive God.[51]

For late-ancient Christians, Jesus' passing models sovereign power over the categories of Jew and Christian, orthodox and heretic, living and dead. To traverse those boundaries is an act of *bravura*, a sacrifice that leads to impossible triumph; moreover, passing does not merely sacrifice a piece of the self, some drops of blood and pieces of flesh, but rather risks sacrificing the very idea of selfhood. Literary critic Marion Rust comments, in a psychoanalytic vein, "passing is merely one more indication that subjectivity involves fracture—that no true self exists apart from its multiple, simultaneous enactments."[52] Augustine, writing on the edge of an empire, on the hinge of history as the barbarians truly began to break in and Roman and orthodox Christian power disintegrated, feared precisely such a loss of self. He points us away from the early Christian era, to the foreclosing of horizons that we will call the middle ages.

Notes

Many thanks to the participants of the Boston University conference at which this chapter was first presented as a paper: particular thanks to the organizers, Zsuzsanna Várhelyi and Jennifer Wright Knust, and the respondent to my paper, Ross Shepard Kraemer.

1. Tert., *De carne Christi* 5.4 (SC 216:228). All translations throughout this essay are my own.

2. Tert., *De carne Christi* 5.1 (SC 216:226). See now Jennifer Glancy, "The Law of the Opened Body: Tertullian on the Nativity," *Henoch* 30 (2008): 45–66, who perceptively demonstrates that Tertullian adopts an almost Marcionite disgust for the body in order elevate the significance of Christ's incarnation.

3. Virginia Burrus, *Saving Shame: Martyrs, Saints, and Other Abject Subjects*, Divinations (Philadelphia: University of Pennsylvania, 2008), 55.

4. Tert., *De carne Christi* 1.3 (SC 216:212): *nec caro sine nativitate.*

5. See the salutary warnings of Willamien Otten, "Christ's Birth of a Virgin Who Became a Wife: Flesh and Speech in Tertullian's *De Carne Christi*," *Vigiliae Christianae* 51 (1997): 247–60, concerning the prior failures of rhetorical analysis to adequately address Tertullian's theology; but see also the rhetorico-theological analyses of Geoffrey Dunn, "Mary's Virginity *in partu* and Tertullian's Anti-Docetism in *De carne Christi* Reconsidered," *Journal of Theological Studies* n.s. 58 (2007): 467–84, and Dunn's direct response to Otten's criticisms of rhetorical analysis in his "Rhetoric and Tertullian's *de virginibus velandis*," *Vigiliae Christianae* 59 (2005): 1–30.

6. Guy G. Stroumsa, *The End of Sacrifice: Religious Transformations in Late Antiquity*, translated by Susan Emanuel (Chicago: University of Chicago Press, 2009), 72.

7. Maud Gleason, *Making Men: Sophists and Self-Presentation in Ancient Rome* (Princeton: Princeton University Press, 1995).

8. Raymond Van Dam, *Leadership and Community in Late Antique Gaul* (Berkeley: University of California Press, 1985).

9. Carlin Barton, "The Emotional Economy of Sacrifice and Execution in Ancient Rome," *Historical Reflections/Réflexions Historiques* 29 (2003): 341–60.

10. We can think of persistent figures such as Lucretia, whose memory creates a bright thread through this "emotional economy" from Livy to Augustine: see Dennis Trout, "Re-Textualizing Lucretia: Cultural Subversion in the *City of God*," *Réflexions JECS* 2 (1994): 53–70.

11. Justin Martyr, *Dial.* 67.7; text in *Iustini Martyris Dialogus cum Tryphone*, edited by Miroslav Marcovich, Patristische Texte und Studien 47 (Berlin: De Gruter, 1997), 186. On this passage, see my "Dialogical Differences: (De-)Judaizing Jesus' Circumcision," *JECS* 15 (2007): 291–335, at 298–304.

12. As a literary phenomenon, "passing" already appears in the 1853 novel by William Wells Brown (a former slave) entitled *Clotel, or the President's Daughter*, and other midcentury fiction (as well as ambiguous memoirs). Sometimes "the pass" is central to the plot, sometimes one of many complicating factors, as the passing of the slave Eliza as a white man in *Uncle Tom's Cabin*; see Julia Stern, "Spanish Masquerade and the Drama of Racial Identity in *Uncle Tom's Cabin*," in *Passing and the Fiction of Identity*, edited by Elaine K. Ginsberg (Durham: Duke University Press, 1996), 103–30. Most recent studies of passing in novels focus on the twentieth century, especially Nella Larsen's 1929 novel *Passing*; see Catherine Rottenberg, "*Passing*: Race, Identification, and Desire," *Criticism* 45 (2003): 435–52.

13. One famous account of "passing" was of a white man as black: John Howard Griffin, *Black Like Me* (New York: Houghton Mifflin, 1961). See also the recent account of the late-nineteenth-century geologist (and inaugural head of the U.S. Geological Survey) Clarence King in Martha A. Sandweiss, *Passing Strange: A Gilded Age Tale of Love and Deception across the Color Line* (New York: Penguin, 2009).

14. Elaine K. Ginsberg, "Introduction: The Politics of Passing," in Ginsburg, *Passing*, 1–18: "By extension, 'passing' has been applied discursively to disguises of other elements of an individual's presumed 'natural' or 'essential' identity, including class, ethnicity, and sexuality, as well as gender, the latter usually effected by deliberate alterations of physical appearance and behavior, including cross-dressing" (3). See also Valerie Rohy, "Displacing Desire: Passing, Nostalgia, and *Giovanni's Room*," in Ginsberg, *Passing*, 218–33, who

discusses passing on the "axis of sexuality"; and Gayle Freda Wald, *Crossing the Line: Racial Passing in Twentieth-Century U.S. Literature and Culture* (Durham: Duke University Press, 2000).

15. One of many felicitous phrases from Amy Robinson, "It Takes One to Know One: Passing and Communities of Common Interest," *Critical Inquiry* 20 (1994): 715–36, at 719.

16. Robinson, "It Takes One," 720.

17. Adrian Piper, "Passing for White, Passing for Black," *Transition* 58 (1992): 4–32; this essay has been reprinted multiple times, including in Piper's own collected works: *Out of Order, Out of Sight*, vol. 1, *Selected Writings in Meta-Art, 1968–1992* (Cambridge: MIT Press, 1996), 275–307.

18. I'm speaking here of narrative accounts of passing, in which the audience at some point (and often characters within the story) pierce the disguise of the passing character. It is true, though, that even in real-world accounts of "passing," in which a person *consciously* "passes," there is a sense of essential identities at play even as they are disrupted.

19. Ginsberg, "Introduction: The Politics of Passing," 4.

20. Rohy, "Displacing Desire," 226.

21. It is worth noting recent, postmodern attempts to appropriate the concept of "passing" as a positive mode of performativity that works to undermine all essentialism: see, for example, Pamela L. Caughie, *Passing and Pedagogy: The Dynamics of Responsibility* (Urbana: University of Illinois Press, 1999).

22. On "docetism," see Guy G. Stroumsa, "Christ's Laughter: Docetic Origins Reconsidered," *JECS* 12 (2004): 267–88, and Ronnie Goldstein and Guy G. Stroumsa, "The Greek and Jewish Origins of Docetism: A New Proposal," *Zeitschrift für Antikes Christentum* 10 (2007): 423–41.

23. Bart D. Ehrman, *Jesus: Apocalyptic Prophet of the New Millennium* (New York: Oxford University Press, 1999), 98.

24. Tert., *Adv. Marcionem* 4.7. Text in *Tertullian: Adversus Marcionem*, edited and translated by Ernest Evans, Oxford Early Christian Texts, 2 vols. (Oxford: Clarendon, 1972), 2: 278.

25. One of our difficulties reconstructing Marcion's beliefs, and "Marcionite Christianity," is our reliance on his detractors to reconstruct his texts and beliefs. Tertullian, especially, has been employed to reconstruct Marcion's "Bible." Among others, see the recent overviews (and references) of Harry Y. Gamble, "Marcion and the 'Canon,'" in *The Cambridge History of Christianity*, vol. 1: *Origins to Constantine*, edited by Margaret M. Mitchell and Frances M. Young (Cambridge: Cambridge University Press, 2006), 195–213; Peter Lampe, *From Paul to Valentinus: Christians at Rome in the First Two Centuries*, translated by Michael Steinhauser, edited by Marshall Johnson (Minneapolis: Fortress, 2003), 241–56; and the essays in *Marcion und seine kirchengeschichtliche Wirkung*, edited by Gerhard May and Katharina Greschat, Texte und Untersuchungen zur Geschichte der altchristlichen Literatur, 150 (Berlin: De Gruyter, 2002).

26. Tert., *Adv. Marcionem* 4.7 = Evans, *Tertullian*, 2:278.

27. Tert., *Adv. Marcionem* 4.7 = Evans, *Tertullian*, 2:278.

28. Ambrose, *Expositio evangeli secundam Lucam* 2.55 (CCL 14:54).

29. Ambrose, *Expositio evangeli secundam Lucam* 4.6 (CCL 14:107).

30. On Ambrose's literary production of orthodoxy, see the original thoughts of Virginia Burrus, *"Begotten, Not Made": Conceiving Manhood in Late Antiquity*, Figurae:

Reading Medieval Culture (Stanford: Stanford University Press, 2000), 134–83. On Ambrose's anti-Judaism, particularly his forceful social division of Jews and Christians in the later fourth century, see n. 32 below.

31. Maximus of Turin, *Homilia* 35 (= *homilia 7 de baptismo Christi*) (PL 57:299). See also the earlier hymnography of Ephrem in Syriac, who proposes similar rationales for Jesus' circumcision in his hymns *On the Lord* and *On the Crucifixion*, on which see Christine Shepardson, *Anti-Judaism and Christian Orthodoxy: Ephrem's Hymns in Fourth-Century Syria*, Patristic Monograph Series (Washington, D.C.: Catholic University Press, 2008), 102–103.

32. Ambrose famously decried the public rights of Jews in his confrontation over the destruction of the synagogue in Callinicum; for discussion, see Neil McLynn, *Ambrose of Milan: Church and Court in a Christian Capital*, Transformation of the Classical Heritage 22 (Berkeley: University of California Press, 1994), 298–308. Tertullian, of course, wrote a treatise *Adversus Iudaeos* which, interestingly, used much of the same material found in sections of his *Adversus Marcionem*; see brief discussion in Geoffrey D. Dunn, *Tertullian*, Early Church Fathers (London: Routledge, 2004), 47–51 and 63–68. A partial treatise by Maximus of Turin *adversus Iudaeos* survives, as well (PL 57:739–806).

33. On the heuristic problems with this term, see now Daniel Boyarin, "Rethinking Jewish Christianity: An Argument for Dismantling a Dubious Category (to Which Is Appended a Correction of My *Border Lines*)," *Jewish Quarterly Review* 99 (2009): 7–36.

34. Epiph., *Panarion* 30.26 (GCS 25:368).

35. Epiph., *Panarion* 30.28 (GCS 25:371).

36. Epiph., *Panarion* 30.28 (GCS 25:372).

37. See, for example, Ambrose, *Ep.* 72.23 (PL 16:1249); Cyril of Alexandria, *Commentarii in Lucam (homilia 3 = Homiliae 12 diversae)* (PG 77:1041).

38. On the discursive reflexiveness of late ancient and Byzantine heresiologists (including, and preeminently, Epiphanius), see Averil Cameron, "Jews and Heretics—A Category Error?" in *The Ways That Never Parted: Jews and Christians in Late Antiquity and the Early Middle Ages*, edited by Annette Yoshiko Reed and Adam H. Becker, Texts and Studies in Ancient Judaism 96 (Tübingen: Mohr Siebeck, 2003), 345–60; and Averil Cameron, "How to Read Heresiology," in *The Cultural Turn in Late Ancient Studies: Gender, Asceticism, and Historiography*, edited by Dale B. Martin and Patricia Cox Miller (Durham: Duke University Press, 2005), 193–212.

39. For a similar reading of Epiphanius, repressing theological desires through description of a heresy, see the analysis of Mary veneration by Stephen J. Shoemaker, "Epiphanius of Salamis, the Kollyridians, and the Early Dormition Narratives: The Cult of the Virgin in the Fourth Century," *JECS* 16 (2008): 371–401.

40. Cyril of Alexandria, *Glaphyra in Exodum* 1.7 (PG 69:404–5). The *Glaphyra*, a commentary on the Pentateuch, comes from early in Cyril's career; the *Commentarius in Lucam* probably originated later in his episcopate as homilies, and was edited together.

41. Cyril, *Commentarius in Lucam (in catena)* (PG 72:499–500).

42. See, among other recent studies, Catharine Edwards and Greg Woolf, "Cosmopolis: Rome as World City," in *Rome the Cosmopolis*, edited by Catharine Edwards and Greg Woolf (Cambridge: Cambridge University Press, 2006), 1–20, and Christopher Frilingos, *Spectacles of Empire: Monsters, Martyrs, and the Book of Revelation*, Divinations (Philadelphia: University of Pennsylvania Press, 2004).

43. Previous studies that have used the concept of "passing" to decode the logics of late Roman texts also suggest this. See Judith Perkins, "An Ancient 'Passing' Novel: Heliodorus' *Aithiopika*," *Arethusa* 32 (1999): 197–214, on the *Aithiopika*; Virginia Burrus, "Mimicking Virgins: Colonial Ambivalence and the Ancient Romance," *Arethusa* 38 (2005): 49–88, at 82–83; and Rebecca Lyman, "The Politics of Passing: Justin Martyr's Conversion as a Problem of 'Hellenization,'" in *Conversion in Late Antiquity and the Early Middle Ages: Seeing and Believing*, edited by Kenneth Mills and Anthony Grafton, Studies in Comparative History (Rochester: University of Rochester Press, 2003), 36–60.

44. Ginsberg, "Introduction: The Politics of Passing," 2.

45. See the thoughtful overview of Roman sacrifice in Jörg Rüpke, *Religion of the Romans*, translated by Richard Gordon (Cambridge: Polity, 2007), 137–53, as well as the many chapters in this volume.

46. Ambrose, *Ep.* 78.2 (PL 16:1268).

47. Augustine, *Ep.* 82.18 (PL 33:283).

48. On Augustine's perhaps idiosyncratic (but nonetheless influential) view of Judaism and Jewish practice, see Paula Fredriksen, *Augustine and the Jews: A Christian Defense of Jews and Judaism* (New York: Doubleday, 2008).

49. See, for example, his discussion in Augustine, *Ep.* 23.4 (PL 33:97). The context is a discussion of baptism in response to Donatist purists; interestingly, Augustine notes that, just as after Jesus' first coming the *sacramentum* of circumcision was "set aside," so too will baptism be "set aside" after his second coming.

50. See Brian Stock, *Augustine the Reader: Meditation, Self-Knowledge, and the Ethics of Interpretation* (Cambridge: Harvard University Press, 1996).

51. James J. O'Donnell describes original sin as Augustine's "most original and nearly single-handed creation": *Augustine: A New Biography* (San Francisco: HarperCollins, 2005), 296.

52. Marion Rust, "The Subaltern as Imperialist: Speaking of Olaudah Equiano," in Ginsberg, *Passing*, 21–36, at 35.

{ 14 }

Confounding Blood

JEWISH NARRATIVES OF SACRIFICE AND VIOLENCE IN LATE ANTIQUITY

Ra'anan S. Boustan

Late antiquity saw a profound transformation in the organization of religious life as societies throughout the ancient Mediterranean world ceased, albeit only gradually, to engage in animal sacrifice. As Peter Brown and Jonathan Z. Smith have famously argued, the far-reaching process whereby a mobile class of exceptional persons eclipsed the traditional Temple cults as the locus of the holy played an instrumental role in the emergence of new forms of religious community and identity in the Hellenistic and especially Roman periods.[1] It would be misleading, however, to characterize the so-called end of sacrifice as the progressive spiritualization of religion.[2] Indeed, sacrificial cult continued to serve throughout late antiquity as the dominant paradigm for ritual action and religious piety, even in the "post-sacrificial" forms of Judaism, Christianity, and indeed paganism that emerged in this period.[3] If anything, sacrifice—and specifically, the symbolic function of sacrificial blood—provided an increasingly charged domain of contact and competition across the full spectrum of religious groups in the Mediterranean world.[4] More specifically, the language of sacrifice was reinvigorated within both Jewish and Christian discourses of martyrdom, which figured the executions of privileged human beings as purificatory or atoning sacrifice.[5]

Animal sacrifice represented a vexed ideological and religious problem for Jewish communities in the Roman empire in the wake of the destruction of the Jerusalem Temple and its cult in 70 CE, which Roman and early Christian writers framed (albeit in different ways) as a sign of the Jews' loss of divine favor.[6] Indeed, Jewish sources from late antiquity attest the gradual internalization of this view of the calamitous end of the Jewish cult.[7] Yet, as Jonathan Klawans has argued, we need not adopt the modern scholarly predilection for reading the negative views of the Jerusalem Temple in the ancient sources—Roman, Christian, and indeed Jewish—as evidence that the cult had become moribund or even corrupt well before its destruction.[8] Klawans instead advises scholars to focus attention on how Jewish (and Christian) authors "channeled the sanctity of the temple" into novel forms of religious practice and discourse.[9]

This chapter contributes to the renewed interest in the "resignification" of sacrificial language and concepts within post-Temple Judaism by comparing two contemporaneous narratives from late antiquity that explore the complex relationship between animal sacrifice and human violence.[10] The first is the widely disseminated martyrology known as *The Story of the Ten Martyrs*, which gathers together within a single narrative framework various earlier traditions regarding the rabbinic martyrs executed by the Romans during the Jewish revolts of the first and second centuries.[11] I contrast this martyrological cycle with the rabbinic retelling of the cryptic biblical account of the murder of Zechariah ben Yehoyada (2 Chr 24:17–22), which appears in multiple forms in both Palestinian and Babylonian rabbinic compilations.[12] In their narrative expansion of this biblical episode, the rabbinic authors trace a causal link between Zechariah's unrequited blood and the destruction of the Jerusalem Temple by the Babylonians 250 years later. I argue that the radically distinct approaches to sacrifice in these two narratives demonstrate that the late-antique Jewish discourse of sacrifice was far from univocal; rather, biblical sacrifice and the narratives associated with it emerged as a charged site of contestation, both among Jews and between Jews and Christians.

Specifically, I show that, while the two narratives at the heart of this chapter were both produced in Roman-Byzantine Palestine in the late fourth to sixth centuries, they differ fundamentally in their application of the language of biblical sacrifice to contemporary Jewish piety and practice. *The Story of the Ten Martyrs* puts forward an elaborate theology of vicarious atonement in which the suffering and death of the righteous martyrs serve as sacrificial expiation for the ancestral sin of the Jewish people and are seen to guarantee their ultimate redemption from the wicked powers of this world, namely, the Roman empire. By contrast, the rabbinic renarration of Zechariah's murder refuses the application of sacrificial logic to the ancestral act of collective violence that it situates at the heart of biblical history. The creators of this narrative tradition left no place in this history of violence for martyrdom, understood as a ritually efficacious offering that purifies the cultic shrine, atones for sin, or ensures redemption. Rather, the murder of Zechariah represents a dramatic breach of cultic protocol, and no subsequent sacrificial bloodletting—either animal or human—can mitigate the consequences of this defiling act. This narrative thus insists on a sharp distinction between illicit violence and proper animal sacrifice.

The significant differences between the approaches to sacrifice and martyrdom present in these two works, while emphasizing the diversity of late-ancient Jewish thought, also call into question recent attempts to formulate a universal theory of sacrifice. Most notably, René Girard's writings on sacrifice, which posit that all sacrificial practice has its origins in the common human impulse to murderous violence (more on this below), could find support in *The Story of the Ten Martyrs* even as the Zechariah story would resist a Girardian point of view. Like Girard, *The Story of the Ten Martyrs* presents the institution of (one specific type of) blood sacrifice as the product of internecine murder *and* as the provisional resolution to the crisis this murder engenders. That is, the martyrology builds upon an etiological explanation rooted in Second Temple Judaism for the sacrifices of the Day of Atonement (Yom Kippur), which according to this tradition commemorates the day that Jacob's sons mislead their father concerning the "apparent death" of Joseph their brother (Gen 37:29–35). The sacrificial practices of Yom Kippur are thus directly linked to the competition among the progenitors of the tribes of Israel for the affections of their father. Finally, as Girard himself might postulate, this explicitly sacrificial narrative both constructs martyrdom as an act of sacrifice and presents it as the sole means for resolving the cycle of violence that forms the inner scaffolding of human history.

By contrast, a Girardian reading of the Zechariah story, as retold in the fourth-century Palestinian Talmud and the fifth- to sixth-century midrashic collection known as *Lamentations Rabbati*, would significantly distort its message. Girard's interpretation of the "murder of the prophets" motif in the New Testament might suggest that this narrative seeks to demystify blood sacrifice as a "sacred cult of violence," thereby offering a blueprint for a more advanced and indeed universal form of religious piety that would transcend the sacrificial complex and the mythic and magical thinking upon which it depends.[13] In my view, however, this rabbinic tale provides a graphic accounting—tallied in the monstrously and futilely spilled blood of the people of Jerusalem and their leaders—of the ethical *and* ritual failings of ancient Israel that lead to the destruction of their Temple. The events leading to the destruction do not disclose the awful "truth" about the violent nature of the sacrificial system: both Zechariah and those who are later killed in the temple precincts to expiate his blood are precisely not "sacrificial victims"—their deaths are murders and not sacrifices, in the sense that they serve no ritual or redemptive function. As such, especially within the context of *Lamentations Rabbati*, the Zechariah narrative reflects the larger hesitation, even discomfort, about the theology of martyrdom being formulated in other contemporary Jewish sources from Palestine, as evidenced by *The Story of the Ten Martyrs*.

When taken together, these narratives undermine Girard's homogenizing view of sacrifice, with its transhistorical and transcultural sweep. A single, overarching theory of sacrificial practice and, more importantly, of sacrificial narrative produces a set of reading practices that occlude rather than explain the varied and contested conceptions of sacrifice operative in late antiquity among both Jews and their neighbors. Indeed, Girard's impulse to create a universally valid theory has its genealogy in the totalizing Christian theologies of sacrificial killing to which the two Jewish narratives that I analyze are themselves responding, albeit in distinct ways. We shall see that in the contemporary Euro-American context—no less than the ancient Mediterranean one—the discourse of sacrifice can serve as a strategy of religious or ideological contestation.

In addition to these theoretical considerations, the specific narratives analyzed in this chapter suggest a corrective to the dominant scholarly account of the history of the Jewish acclimatization to a post-Temple reality. According to this historical narrative, the rabbis and liturgists of late antiquity self-consciously crafted novel forms of piety, such as Torah study and prayer, to serve as direct replacements for the less ethically and spiritually nourishing sacrificial cult of the Temple.[14] Thus, in a recent analysis of rabbinic tales concerning the destruction of the Temple, Paul Mandel has argued that the "chronological and geographic distance from the Temple caused the centrality of the Temple, and the memories of the rituals of sacrifice so central in its day, to recede, so to be replaced by the more immediate concerns of the populace and its leaders."[15] As such, the sacred center gave way to rabbinic narrative and exegesis, which "sustained the Jewish people through generations of retold tales."[16] This familiar narrative of the transformation of Judaism from a "cultic" into a "textual" community may well fit some trajectories within late-antique Judaism, such as those reflected in the sources analyzed by Mandel. But time and distance from the Jerusalem Temple did not work in a uniform or linear way. Jews did not conceptualize the Temple cult in any one way, nor was the "problem of sacrifice" (if it was a problem at all) ever finally and definitively resolved.

Indeed, the rise of Christianity to dominance in the fourth to sixth century and, in particular, the hegemony of Christian claims to the legacy of biblical sacrifice provoked Jews to invest renewed energy in grappling with the loss of their cultic center. The application of sacrificial logic to rabbinic martyrdom and the liturgical recitation of *The Story of the Ten Martyrs* on Yom Kippur demonstrate that the model of the sacrificial cult was not only salient within Jewish culture long after the destruction of the Jerusalem Temple, but in fact enjoyed conspicuous revitalization in fifth- and sixth-century Palestine, with a lasting impact on medieval Jewish conceptions of martyrdom.[17]

René Girard on Sacrificial Practice and Sacrificial Narrative

This section reviews and assesses Girard's bold account of the historical origins of sacrificial practice in a primordial act of collective violence. In the process, I consider the charge lodged by Jonathan Z. Smith, Ivan Strenski, and others that Girard has in fact produced a culturally specific, even polemical view of sacrifice masquerading as an academic theory with universal validity. While I share this critical assessment of Girard's project, I nevertheless find his theory helpful in classifying the specific strategies deployed in ancient Jewish sources to contest the meaning of the biblical sacrificial cult and thus to assert control over its legacy. The question of whether or not blood sacrifice is a substitute for violence—Girard's central problematic—is indeed a recurrent theme in Jewish narratives from late antiquity that address the loss of the Temple cult. How a given text answered this question had direct implications for its particular conception of Judaism in the post-Temple order.

Girard's theory of sacrifice stands at the heart of his voluminous writings on the place of religion in human history and society.[18] Girard marshals countless narratives—from ancient Mediterranean and Near Eastern myths to the narratives of so-called primitive societies and the modern novel—in order to show that animal sacrifice arises from and brings at least provisional resolution to the murderous dynamics of social conflict and cohesion that characterize all human collectivities. This generative process binds together violence, sacrifice, and the act of narration into a single, mutually constituting sacrificial complex. Girard's universalizing move has been widely criticized. Nevertheless, his engagement with sacrificial atonement theology, though provoked by his own historically situated context, is rooted in the very Christian theological conceptions first developed in late antiquity that were also engaged by Jewish writers in that formative period of Jewish–Christian relations.

The centrality that Girard's theory accords sacrifice in social and historical processes might suggest to students of ancient Mediterranean religions avenues for understanding why shifts in sacrificial practice had such profound and far-reaching consequences for social organization and religious life in antiquity. Yet, many historians of religion would argue, instead, that the analytical tools Girard uses are so compromised by his patently theological insistence on the uniqueness and even superiority of the biblical tradition as refracted by Christian lenses that we are better off sidestepping his project entirely. Many have been particularly critical of Girard for his "reductive" and "evolutionist" account of animal sacrifice, which fails to situate the practice properly within its specific social, historical, and discursive contexts.[19]

Perhaps most potent among these critiques is Jonathan Z. Smith's contention that sacrifice is not an act of transmuted and barely contained violence rooted in so-called primitive societies, but rather is distinctive to stratified agrarian or pastoralist societies in which, he suggests, sacrifice might serve as a sustained and ritualized form of meditation on the process of "domestication."[20] Likewise, Smith's thoroughgoing historiographic critique of the Protestant roots of the study of late-antique religions should be enough to call into question Girard's Christian exceptionalism—his apparent insistence on the uniqueness of the Christ-event.[21] Indeed, Girard's blanket rejection of sacrificial understandings of Jesus' death—often articulated in conjunction with a powerful distaste for mimetic conceptions of Eucharistic practice—has also failed to persuade most scholars of early Christianity on either internal literary or historical-contextual grounds.[22]

Ivan Strenski's study of Girard's thought within its specific intellectual and cultural context adds an important historical dimension to these theoretical and methodological criticisms.[23] According to Strenski, Girard should be read as a Christian theologian and moralist, rather than as a historian of religion. As a historian or ethnographer, he is merely wrong—though wrong in a particularly pernicious way. But, as a contributor to modern theological or ethical debates about religious practice and its relationship to political agency, Girard is significant in his own right. According to Strenski, "Girard's theory of sacrifice should be seen as a rejection of a view of sacrifice originally developed in the seventeenth-century eucharistic theology of the Roman Catholic reaction to the Reformation in France."[24] Girard's theory is thus heir to the legacy of post-Reformation French debates regarding the notion of sacrifice and its political and religious meanings.

Moreover, Strenski points to the ironic, if predictable, similarities between Girard's theory and the "conservative" and "authoritarian" French Catholic tradition in which he was raised and against which he reacts so vehemently. Most notable is his understanding of sacrifice as an act of foundational violence that both delineates and fosters human community. In addition, in line with his religious upbringing, Girard likewise accords centrality to the Christ-event in the teleological unfolding of human history. At the same time, there are significant differences. For Girard, the Eucharist is not a mimetic reenactment of the violent self-sacrifice of Jesus, but an act of remembrance that marks a revolutionary advance over the pre-Calvary human condition. In the post-Calvary world, wherever sacrificial thought or practice have not been fully purged, Girard diagnoses the lingering and destructive hold of the primitive dynamics of the scapegoat mechanism—the very mechanism that he believes set in motion the violent institution of sacrifice in the first place. Seen from this perspective, Girardian thought advocates a reformist tradition centered upon the ideal of an individually oriented religious conscience, which he believes has superseded the collectivist ethos and politics of clerically oriented sacramental theology—be it Catholic, Jewish, or otherwise. For Strenski, this is all well and good, provided that we strenuously resist Girard's attempt to formulate a universalizing theory of religion and human culture in the historically contingent—not to say parochial—terms of modern theological debates regarding Christian "sacrifice."

As problematic as Girard's project has been shown to be, his provocative equation of sacrifice and violence nevertheless echoes narrative traditions from late antiquity. Indeed, Girard was hardly the first to explore the complex relationship between these concepts; many Christians and Jews in late antiquity shared Girard's interpretation of sacrifice as a substitute for murderous violence and, in turn, the deaths of the innocent righteous as a means for transcending the sacrificial process. Even more, it would seem that they likewise invested great energy in exploring just how the liturgical reenactment and narrative recitation of the sacrificial drama relates to the actual act of sacrifice. The impressive thematic correlations between Girard's theory of sacrifice and the representation of sacrifice in the literature of late antiquity, both Jewish and Christian, suggests that, rather than explaining sacrifice, Girard's theory has replicated and naturalized a highly particular conception of sacrifice with a specifically late-antique genealogy.

The Story of the Ten Martyrs and Girard's Christian Exceptionalism

The rabbinic martyrological cycle known as The Story of the Ten Martyrs is perhaps the most striking example of Jewish narrative from late antiquity that thematizes the relationship between ancestral murder and the power of human sacrifice.[25] This martyrology, in its poetic forms, has been an integral part of the Yom Kippur liturgy since late antiquity.[26] Although set during the "Hadrianic persecutions" of the second century CE, the martyrology developed as a literary composition in Palestine between the fifth and early seventh centuries.[27] The martyrology relates in gruesome detail the sequential executions of ten rabbinic sages at the hands of the Romans. According to the narrative's overarching conceptual framework, the deaths of the ten martyred sages are not caused by the immediate political circumstances, but rather are the direct consequence of the crime committed by Joseph's twelve brothers when they sold him into slavery (Gen 37:18–28). The scriptural logic works in the following fashion: based on the authority of Exodus 21:16 ("He who kidnaps a man—whether he has sold him or is still holding him—shall be put to death"), the narrative considers the sale of Joseph to be a capital crime. The deaths of these rabbinic martyrs are thus vicarious atonement for the original national sin committed by the progenitors of the tribes of Israel.

As Solomon Zeitlin suggested more than fifty years ago, the association between the sin of Joseph's brothers and Israel's need for communal atonement on Yom Kippur entered rabbinic martyrology from early Jewish sources of the Second Temple period.[28] The clearest statement of this etiology for the holiday is found in the second-century text *Jubilees* (34:12–19).[29] Although this passage does not explicitly refer to Yom Kippur, the date indicated for the commemorative mourning of Joseph's "apparent death"—the tenth day of the seventh month—unequivocally denotes this holiday. Zeitlin rightly explains that the authors of *Jubilees* "held that the sin of the ten sons of Jacob, who sold Joseph into slavery, had not been atoned, and that hence the Jews must afflict themselves annually on the day on which Joseph was sold, in order to attain atonement for this sin which their forefathers committed."[30]

The association of the sale of Joseph into slavery with Yom Kippur is well attested in rabbinic literature. This etiological motif always appears in conjunction with rabbinic traditions concerning the expiatory function of the special vestments worn by the high priest when officiating over the sacrifices prescribed for the Day of Atonement.[31] It should be noted that the emphasis in this case is explicitly on the blood sacrifices for the Day of Atonement and not on the famous scapegoat ritual, which does not involve blood sacrifice at all (a distinction wholly lost on Girard in his writings).[32] These traditions were subsequently embellished in the Yom Kippur liturgy that developed in the late fourth and fifth centuries.[33] And, once embedded in the synagogue liturgy, the motif played a generative role in the production of novel literary compositions that were associated with the Day of Atonement, including *The Story of the Ten Martyrs*.

The ideology of vicarious atonement through martyrological self-sacrifice that is at the heart of *The Story of the Ten Martyrs* centers on the image of the heavenly altar upon which the angelic high priest Metatron (or Michael) sacrifices the souls of the righteous martyrs who offer their lives on behalf of the Jewish people (*Ten Martyrs*, I–IX.20.1–5). We learn about this awful truth when the central martyr in the story, Rabbi Ishmael ben Elisha, ascends to heaven in order to learn whether it is in fact the will of God that the group of ten sages should embrace their deaths as martyrs. There, Rabbi Ishmael, who is himself of high priestly lineage, is met by the angelic high priest Metatron.[34] It is from his angelic guide that Rabbi Ishmael learns that Israel's ultimate redemption depends on the willingness of the martyrs to lay down their lives in order to atone for the nation's ancestral sin.

The narrative makes absolutely clear that the spilling of the martyrs' blood will affect atonement for the blood-guilt of the Jewish people. After having learned from the angelic high priest Metatron that it is the sin of Joseph's brothers that has set in motion the cruel fate he and his colleagues now face, Rabbi Ishmael asks the angel in despair:

> "Has the Holy One, blessed be He, not found someone to redeem the blood of Joseph from the days of Jacob until now throughout all those generations?" He answered: "The Holy One, blessed be He, has not found ten like the sons of Jacob except you."[35]

The atoning function of the martyrs' blood is a leitmotif running through the remainder of the narrative. Following this awful revelation, Rabbi Ishmael is given a guided tour through heaven by Metatron. As they are moving about, the sage and future martyr comes across an object he does not immediately recognize, and he asks the angel,

> "What is this in front of you?" He replied: "An altar." He asked him: "Is there an altar above [in heaven]?" He answered him: "Yes, everything that exists above also exists below, as it is written I have now built for You a stately house [1 Kgs 8:13]." He asked him: "And what do you sacrifice upon it? Do you have bulls, rams, and lambs?" He answered him: "We sacrifice the souls of the righteous upon it." He declared: "Now I have heard something that I have never before heard!"[36]

As this dialogue between martyr and angel makes clear, martyrdom on earth is paralleled in heaven by the sacrifice of the souls of the righteous martyrs, presided over by the angelic high priest Metatron.

Moreover, this sacrifice is essential to the proper maintenance of Israel's relationship with God and, ultimately, to the redemption of Israel from the yoke of Rome. Thus, immediately following Rabbi Ishmael's return to earth to inform his colleagues what he has learned, Rabban Simeon ben Gamaliel declares that they should rejoice because "God will receive our souls as a sacrifice so that He may exact vengeance through them from wicked Rome."[37] The message is quite clear: the human sacrifice entailed in the martyr's death replaces the animal offerings of the earthly Temple. Moreover, the blood of the martyrs is the sole guarantee of ultimate salvation for the Jewish people.[38]

The Story of the Ten Martyrs betrays deep affinities with early Christian conceptions of the heavenly cult of Christ and its role in salvation history, especially as formulated in such texts as the New Testament Epistle to the Hebrews.[39] At the same time, it offers a damning critique of the coercive power of the Roman (or, perhaps better, Roman-Christian) state. The creators of the martyrology painted a graphic portrait of the bleak experience of late-antique Jews under Roman domination. But they did so by deploying a set of highly charged literary motifs that were seemingly at odds with the more conventional scholastic orientation of their rabbinic source material—and seemingly far closer to the religious imagery and attitudes of their Christian neighbors.

Like *The Story of the Ten Martyrs* and the narrative tradition on which it draws, Girard reads the Joseph story in Genesis as a meditation on the origins of sacrifice in fratricidal conflict provoked by jealousy and competition. In his most sustained discussion of the figure of Joseph, Girard argues that the biblical authors self-consciously reject what he calls the "older" or "pre-biblical" mythic tradition (e.g., the Oedipus legend) by "inverting the relationship between the victim and the persecuting community."[40] On this account, classical myth sanctions communal violence against the hero-turned-scapegoat by insisting on his guilt, while Genesis instead stresses Joseph's innocence in each chapter of the narrative, from his conflict with his brothers to the false accusation of adultery he faces in Egypt. For Girard, this inversion has, in turn, significant implications for the biblical conception of sacrifice: "The kid that provided the blood in which Joseph's tunic was dipped in order to prove to his father that he was really dead would have played a directly sacrificial role in the pre-biblical account."[41] The biblical story thus demystifies and desacralizes—in short, humanizes—Joseph; the linkage in the narrative between violence and sacrifice paradoxically aims to break the cycle of killing that fuels and is fueled by the sacrificial complex.

But it is precisely with this final step that Girard parts ways with the interpretation of the story offered in *The Story of the Ten Martyrs*. In sharp contrast to Girard's reading of the "apparent murder" of Joseph as exemplifying the antisacrificial perspective of the biblical authors, the martyrology presents this act as the inauguration of a specific set of sacrificial practices. This sacrificial complex would, in turn, find its ultimate expression in the ritual-liturgical performance of a martyrology in which the foundational act of violence committed by Joseph's brothers is linked through the blood of the sacrifices, first animal and then human, to the eschatological violence to be inflicted by God on Rome. From a Girardian perspective, the creators of the martyrology replicated the sacrificial complex rather than unmaking it; they thus failed to grasp what Girard holds to be the "true" significance of the Joseph narrative in the biblical tradition.

Thus, despite his explicit aim to offer a formal, academic theory of sacrifice, Girard's reading practices do not provide him with the tools he (and we) might need to make historical sense of specific theological formulations or the contestations that surround them, but rather cast him as arbiter of their correctness. We can thus place Girard side by side with the martyrology: both are polemical and totalizing accounts of the biblical message and its place in human history and culture.

Moreover, *The Story of the Ten Martyrs* raises significant problems for Girard's Christian exceptionalism, which bypasses postbiblical sources entirely and traces a linear progression from the prophetic books of the Hebrew Bible to the New

Testament gospels.[42] In his insistence on the uniqueness of the New Testament in unmasking the violence at the heart of the sacrificial process, Girard fails to consider the complex interaction between Jews and Christians as both groups grappled with the problem of the "end of biblical sacrifice." But, in fact, the creators of the rabbinic martyrology—and presumably also those who participated in its liturgical performance on Yom Kippur—shared a sacrificial understanding of martyrdom with their Christian neighbors. There was no stable core of essential differences between late-antique Jews and Christians in matters of religious ideology and practice, even in such highly sensitive issues as collective, vicarious atonement through self-sacrifice. Rather, the martyrology attests the degree to which Jews and Christians continued to occupy a common discursive space, in matters of sacrifice as in many other domains, well after the fourth century.

Reading the Blood of Zechariah with and against Girard

Like *The Story of the Ten Martyrs*, rabbinic retellings of the biblical story concerning the murder of the prophet and priest Zechariah ben Yehoyada (2 Chr 24:17–22) provocatively explore the interrelationship among social conflict, murder, animal sacrifice, and the expiatory value of human blood. The rabbinic versions of the Zechariah story draw a causal link between the murder and the destruction of Jerusalem and its Temple 250 years later by the Babylonian general Nebuzaradan, the head of Nebuchadnezzar's army (2 Kings 25; cf. 2 Chr 36). Both the martyrology and the Zechariah tradition grapple with how the biblical discourse of sacrifice might best be understood and resignified in the wake of the destruction of the Temple cult. But I argue that the Zechariah story, especially as it was deployed within the fifth- or sixth-century midrashic collection known as *Lamentations Rabbati*, does not support the Girardian equation of sacrifice with violence, however tempting such a reading might be. Indeed, the narrative should not be read as a theological statement regarding the replacement of the cult by more ethically and spiritually "advanced" forms of religious piety. Rather, the narrative stresses that Israel's murderous crime is precisely out-of-the-ordinary, an extreme violation of the standard sacrificial system. As a consequence of its insistence on the fundamental difference between sacrifice and violence, the text also rejects a sacrificial conception of martyrdom as a crucial means for effecting atonement or guaranteeing redemption.

Postbiblical Jewish and Christian retellings of the murder of Zechariah and its bloody aftermath build upon the brief report in 2 Chronicles in which King Joash orders the execution of the son of the righteous high priest Jehoiada for his prophecy of doom:

Then the spirit of God took possession of Zechariah son of the priest
Jehoiada; he stood above the people and said to them, "Thus says God: Why

do you transgress the commandments of the Lord, so that you cannot prosper? Because you have forsaken the Lord, he has also forsaken you." But they conspired, and by command of the king they stoned him to death in the court of the house of the Lord. King Joash did not remember the kindness that Jehoiada, Zechariah's father, had shown him, but killed his son. As he [Zechariah] was dying, he said: "May the Lord see and avenge!" (2 Chr 24:20–22 NRSV)

Jewish and Christian sources from late antiquity reflect the common reorientation that this narrative underwent in the course of the Second Temple period as the episode increasingly became a narrative backdrop for in-depth exploration of the curious nature and power of the blood itself. Especially instrumental in this process of narrative expansion were the allusions in the base-text to the precise location of the murder in the Temple and the emphasis on the visible remains of the murder that Zechariah prays will ensure divine retribution ("may the Lord *see* and avenge"). Already in the biblical base-text, the themes of location, divine witness, and future retribution are yoked together, even if only in incipient form.[43]

Scholars of Second Temple and rabbinic Judaism have dedicated a great deal of energy to tracing the literary history of this narrative within Jewish sources.[44] More recently, however, scholars have begun to explore the dynamic interaction between Jewish and Christian versions of this narrative.[45] Most well-known, of course, are the allusion to the blood of Zechariah in the gospels of Matthew and Luke as part of Jesus' final woe to the Pharisees, upon whom will come "all the innocent blood shed on the earth, from the blood of Abel the righteous to the blood of Zechariah, the son of Barachiah, whom you murdered between the sanctuary and the altar."[46] The story seems to have enjoyed such wide currency across a range of genres that numerous ritual artifacts and incantation texts attest the active use of this narrative as a historiola for curing uncontrolled bleeding.[47] And it would seem that this process of interreligious contestation spilled beyond the confines of narrative, assuming a concrete spatial dimension through local traditions of pilgrimage centered on Jerusalem. As Galit Hasan-Rokem has stressed, just as the pilgrim of the *Itinerarium Burdigalense* reports seeing the bloody traces of Zechariah's murder, so, too, *Lamentations Rabbati* anchors its retelling of the story to the apparent status of the locale as a site of healing: "The blind, what would they say? Who will show us Zechariah's blood? And the lame, what would they say? Who will show us the place where Zechariah was killed, and we'll embrace it and kiss it?"[48] In light of this evidence, I fully endorse Jean-Daniel Dubois' persuasive claim that the blood of Zechariah represented one particularly potent site in Jewish-Christian competition over the memory and meaning of the biblical past.[49]

The story concerning the murder of Zechariah and especially the fate of his unjustly shed blood appears in various forms in both Palestinian and Babylonian rabbinic literature and in a range of literary and exegetical contexts.[50] In what follows, I present and analyze the earliest full version of the narrative, found in the Palestinian

Talmud.[51] In addition, I consider how the narrative was subsequently used in later centuries by the creators of *Lamentations Rabbati*, a verse-by-verse exegetical commentary on the book of Lamentations from fifth- or perhaps sixth-century Palestine. While the Zechariah story is by no means unique to *Lamentations Rabbati*, this midrashic collection does repeat the story four separate times and places it within a structured and perhaps even systematic literary framework. It, therefore, provides a broader context for assessing the meaning that this narrative held in this period, at least for some Jews.

The Palestinian Talmud presents a series of semi-independent traditions concerning the murder of Zechariah; this loose, but thematically coherent, collection will culminate in the story of Nebuzaradan's encounter with the blood of Zechariah and his attempt to solve its riddle. But, first, the text begins with briefer discussions of the story.

The passage opens with a statement in the name of R. Yoḥanan that "eighty thousand young priests were slain on account of the blood of Zechariah." This tradition is followed by a dialogue between two rabbis concerning the precise location of the murder: "R. Yudan asked R. Aḥa: 'Where was Zechariah murdered, in the Women's Court or in the Court of the Israelites?' He answered him: 'Neither in the Women's Court nor in the Court of the Israelites, but in the Court of the Priests.'" These statements frame the narrative in such a way that we expect the Temple priesthood, rather than the nation as a whole, to have played a particularly central role in the crime. This expectation is partly realized in the subsequent narrative and partly frustrated: the murder is especially noteworthy because it generates pollution within the Temple, but there is no attempt to limit the culpability for the murder to the priests or to absolve either the king or the people of their responsibility. Moreover, as both priest and prophet, the figure of Zechariah defies facile attempts to pit a supposedly wicked priesthood against the tradition of righteous prophecy.

The talmudic text then presents an exegetical unit intended to emphasize the enormity of the crime. This unit juxtaposes the regulation in Leviticus 17:13, which instructs the Israelite or stranger to cover with earth the blood of a kosher wild animal, with Ezekiel 24:6–8, which chastises the "bloody city" of Jerusalem for placing the blood that it shed "on a bare rock; she did not pour it out on the ground, to cover it with earth" (Ezek 24:7 NRSV). These verses, when taken together, demonstrate that Zechariah's murderers treated his blood differently from the blood of animals: rather than covering his blood with earth, they left it visible and thus ensured that it would provoke God's "fury to take vengeance" (Ezek 24:8 NRSV). I will return to this detail below.

This unit is followed by a tradition that enumerates the seven concurrent sins that were committed at the time of the murder: "Israel committed seven transgressions ['*aveirot*] on the same day: They killed a priest, a prophet, and a judge; they spilled innocent blood; they polluted the Temple Court [*ve-tim'u ha-'azarah*]; and it was both Sabbath and the Day of Atonement."[52] Interestingly, like *The Story of the*

Ten Martyrs, the Zechariah text links the murder that stands as the fountainhead of Israel's guilt to Yom Kippur, though the detail is here primarily intended to emphasize the enormity of the crime.

It is only following this series of preliminary apodictic and exegetical traditions that the Talmud presents the story proper. The narrative moves from the time of King Joash and Zechariah to the conquest of Judea by the Babylonians in the sixth century BCE. The conquering Babylonian general, Nebuzaradan, upon entering the Jerusalem Temple, notices a bizarre phenomenon: a pool of blood in the courtyard of the priests, perhaps near the altar itself, seething restlessly. When he inquires concerning the origins of this blood, the residents of Jerusalem assure him that it is the blood of animal sacrifices.

> When Nebuzaradan ascended here [to the Temple Court], he saw blood seething. He said to them, what is the nature [of this blood]? They said to him, "The blood of bulls, lambs, and rams[53] that we sacrificed upon the altar." He immediately brought bulls, rams, and lambs and slaughtered them upon the blood, but it continued to seethe.

Just as in *The Story of the Martyrs*, the Zechariah narrative here raises the question of whether animal blood and human blood are of the same nature. Indeed, both texts employ an almost identical phrase when formulating the comparison: can the slaughter of the righteous serve the same—or, at least, a ritually comparable—function as the sacrifice of "bulls, rams, and sheep" (*parim 'eilim u-khevasim*).[54] As we have seen, the answer in the martyrology is a resounding "yes," whereas the present narrative rejects the equivalence.

When Nebuzaradan discovers that the blood of sacrificial animals cannot quell the prophet's blood, he suspects murder most foul. The general extracts from the Jerusalemites a confession of their bloodguilt: it is the blood of Zechariah, they explain, who 250 years earlier had been murdered by their ancestors.

> And since they did not confess to him [the crime of their ancestors], he hung them upon the gallows. They said: "[It seethes] because the Holy One, blessed be He, still plans to avenge his blood from us." They continued: "This is, in fact, the blood of the priest, prophet, and judge who prophesied against us [concerning everything you are now doing to us][55] and we rose against him and murdered him."

Having learned the true nature of the seething blood, Nebuzaradan reasons that only human blood can appease it and thus expiate the ancestral guilt. He proceeds to slaughter—or, perhaps better, sacrifice—thousands of the best and brightest from among the Israelite population, eighty thousand priests in the flower of youth.[56] Yet, even this excessive spilling of human blood turns out not produce the desired effect.

At last, having tried to quell Zechariah's blood with both animal and human blood, Nebuzaradan recoils from the bloodletting.

At that moment, he [Nebuzaradan] rebuked him [Zechariah][57] and said to him: "What do you want me to do—destroy your entire people on your account?!?"[58] Immediately the Holy One, blessed be He, was filled with mercy and said: "If this man, who is but flesh and blood and is cruel, is filled with mercy for my children, how much more so should I be [merciful toward them], about whom it is written, 'Because the Lord your God is a merciful God, he will neither abandon you nor destroy you; he will not forget the covenant with your ancestors that he swore to them' [Deut 4:31]"? Immediately he signaled to the blood that it should be swallowed up in its place.[59]

By rejecting the killing of animals and human beings as a mode of expiating the ancestral crime of murder, the Babylonian general succeeds in shaming the God of Israel into subduing Zechariah's demand for vengeance.

What might a Girardian reading of this expansive version of the Zechariah story look like? Girard has himself written about the allusion to the killing of Zechariah in the New Testament as a "revelation of the founding murder" that inaugurated the cycle of human violence to which Jesus has come to put an end.[60] Indeed, the "murder of the prophets" is both structurally and thematically central to the narrative of human ethical progress that Girard views as the core message of the gospels.[61]

The rabbinic treatment of this tradition might, at first glance, seem to conform to Girard's hypothesis concerning the transformative unmasking of the scapegoat mechanism in biblical literature. In Girardian terms, the Zechariah narrative in both its biblical and postbiblical iterations is a sustained meditation on the universal and integral connection between sacrificial cult and violence. The conflict between Joash and Zechariah, the king's own "son-in-law," with whom he is in competition for control over the community and its religious life, ruptures the social fabric.[62] In the biblical base-text, the crisis coincides with an unspecified divine punishment of the Judah and Jerusalem (2 Chr 24:18), perhaps a plague or other generic form of calamity, another theme that Girard links to the social disruption generated by the sacrificial crisis.[63]

Finally, the narrative culminates with the "scapegoating" of Zechariah, which seems to return the Temple community to concord. A Girardian reading would suggest that sacrificial cult has only provisionally masked the guilt of the Israelite community, which clings to a self-delusional and patently ineffective belief in the efficacy of animal sacrifice to atone for guilt. Human blood is no more able to expiate sin than is the blood of the sacrificial animals that has been substituted for it. It is only Nebuzaradan's decision to turn away from the whole sacrificial complex that brings an end to the cycle of killing. His heartfelt prayer provides an antidote to the violent nature of sacrifice and thereby brings an end to the cycle of violence.

Indeed, the version of the story in the Babylonian Talmud goes a step further and has the general convert to Judaism at the culmination of the narrative: "Thereupon he debated with himself whether to repent, saying, 'If such vengeance is exacted for one life, how much more will happen to me for having taken so many lives!' He fled, sent a parting gift to his household, and became a convert to Judaism."[64] According to Girard, the motif of conversion is central to the possibility of transcending the sacrificial complex: "conversion is resurrection" insofar as "awareness of guilt is forgiveness in the Christian sense," he writes.[65] If Girard were to relinquish his Christian exceptionalism, he might argue that this late antique Jewish narrative exemplifies the distinctive and superior perspective of the biblical tradition, which produces a vision of non-sacrificial or even anti-sacrificial dedication of the self that supersedes the sacrificial context out of which it emerges.

But is the rabbinic retelling of the Zechariah narrative, in fact, about sacrificial practice at all? In his recent interpretation of this text, Michael Swartz has persuasively argued that the story goes to great lengths to draw a clear distinction "between any kind of blood of a sacrificial or alimentary animal and the blood of the martyr."[66] As noted above, the text emphasizes that the human blood of the murdered hero is explicitly treated in a manner that departs from the prescription in Leviticus 17:13 for covering with earth the blood of a wild animal that is permitted to be eaten. Along similar lines, Jonathan Klawans has likewise argued that the Zechariah tradition in rabbinic literature does not address the inadequacies of the sacrificial cult per se, but rather belongs to a broader rabbinic discourse concerning the moral and ritual defilement of the Jerusalem Temple caused by acts such as idolatry, sexual sin, and murder.[67] This discourse, Klawans argues, is not an indictment of the regular regime of sacrifice as presented in Leviticus and elsewhere in the Torah, but an indication of Israel's own culpability for the eventual destruction of the Jerusalem Temple.[68]

The redactional use of the Zechariah story within the fifth- or sixth-century *Lamentations Rabbati* confirms this interpretation.[69] Like many midrashic collections, *Lamentations Rabbati* does not form a coherent literary or conceptual whole: the thirty-six proems at the beginning of the work were likely affixed to it at a later time; similarly, the commentary on the first two chapters of the biblical book is considerably more extensive than that on the final three chapters, suggesting an extended and varied compositional history.[70] Nevertheless, as Shaye Cohen has argued, the work does exhibit a general unity of purpose and perspective—namely, an exegesis of the book of Lamentations as a sustained reflection on the causes of the destruction of Second Temple.[71] In particular, Cohen has called attention to the tendency in *Lamentations Rabbati* to minimize the significance of martyrdom in the events of the destruction, despite the obvious potential for highlighting this very theme.[72] The Zechariah narrative, which was incorporated in four separate textual contexts within the work, conforms to this general pattern.[73] Neither Zechariah nor the descendants of his murderers who are themselves killed by a foreign power are treated as *martyrs,* if that term is understood, as we have seen it so often was, to index a person who dies as a ritually efficacious sacrifice. Rather, the bloodshed in the Zechariah narrative stands as a physical indictment of the simultaneous ritual and ethical shortcomings of the Jewish people, which lead ineluctably to the destruction of the Temple. On this point, Jewish and Christian writers converged: the destruction and exile from Jerusalem and Judea were a consequence of Jewish guilt.[74] But only post-Reformation readings of the ancient sources would insist that this shared historico-theological conviction reflects an understanding of sacrifice as nothing other than atavistic violence.

Conclusion

René Girard—or a scholar adopting his conceptual framework—might argue that it is the still unresolved sacrificial complex at the heart of *The Story of the Ten Martyrs* that accounts for its doctrine of divinely sanctioned vengeance. This same scholar might read the rabbinic versions of the Zechariah narrative as a principled rejection of the necessity of sacrifice, whether animal or human, in favor of an ethics of revelatory conversion. Despite the stark difference between the two narratives, the scapegoat mechanism might nevertheless be invoked as the common structural principle governing the very notion of sacrifice operative in the texts.

I have argued, however, that these particular Jewish texts from late antiquity neither bear out Girard's hypothesis of a universal scapegoat mechanism nor encode any putative psychological discomfort with sacrificial violence. Rather, both texts index the pervasive concern among late-antique Jews with the meaning and function of the blood of the murdered righteous, which intensified as the theorization of martyrdom as sacrifice was employed to secure Christian hegemony. On my reading, the Zechariah narrative rejects the equation of sacrifice and murder, thereby deflating the discursive power of martyrdom that had so captivated many Jews and Christians in late antiquity. By contrast, the rabbinic martyrology insists on the abiding power of sacrificial blood to affect salvation, implicitly celebrating the passage from mere animal sacrifice to a heightened form of cult in which human victims are specifically chosen from among the ranks of the heroes of rabbinic tradition.

The two narratives thus reflect the diversity of approaches to the phenomenon of sacrifice among late-antique Jews, a heterogeneity that is likewise attested in early Christian writings.[75] But beneath the diversity of approaches to sacrifice stood a very concrete competition among Jews and between Jews and Christians over the biblical past, as embodied in the physical remains of exemplary figures spread across the sacred geography of the Holy Land.

Notes

I would like to express my heartfelt thanks to Jennifer Wright Knust and Zsuzsanna Várhelyi for inviting me to present an early version of this paper at the Boston University conference and for their generous editorial guidance and support—and, above all, for their patience! I would also like to acknowledge the incisive response to this paper that Jonathan Klawans presented at the conference, which redirected my thinking in crucial ways. I owe a number of key insights into this material to the participants in the UCLA / Ben Gurion University / Open University of Israel workshop on "The Limits of Power" (Zikhron Ya'akov, Israel). Thanks are also due to Lisa Cleath and Alice Mandell, UCLA, for their comments on earlier drafts. And, as always, Leah Boustan provided stimulating reflections and crucial editorial suggestions along the way. Any remaining errors are all my own.

1. Peter Brown, "The Rise and Function of the Holy Man in Late Antiquity," in *Society and the Holy in Late Antiquity* (London: Faber and Faber, 1982), 103–52; and J. Z. Smith, *Map Is Not Territory: Studies in the History of Religion* (Leiden: Brill, 1978), 172–89. For revisions of this perspective that emphasize the continuing vitality of the traditional temple cults and the complexity of their transformation to new modes of religious authority and practice, see David Frankfurter, *Religion in Roman Egypt: Assimilation and Resistance* (Princeton: Princeton University Press, 1998), 30–33, 37–82, and passim.

2. For a thoroughgoing critique of the use of the concept of "spiritualization" in modern scholarship, see Jonathan Klawans, *Purity, Sacrifice, and the Temple: Symbolism and Supersessionism in the Study of Ancient Judaism* (New York: Oxford University Press, 2006), esp. 147–74, 213–54; Jonathan Klawans, "Interpreting the Last Supper: Sacrifice, Spiritualization, and Anti-Sacrifice," *New Testament Studies* 48 (2002): 1–17.

3. Guy G. Stroumsa, *The End of Sacrifice: Religious Transformations in Late Antiquity*, translated by S. Emanuel (Chicago: University of Chicago Press, 2009), esp. 56–83. On the role of sacrifice in the development of postbiblical Judaism in particular, see esp. Michael D. Swartz, "Judaism and the Idea of Ancient Ritual Theory," in *Jewish Studies at the Crossroads of Anthropology and History: Authority, Diaspora, Tradition*, edited by R. S. Boustan, O. Kosansky, and M. Rustow (Philadelphia: University of Pennsylvania Press, 2011), 294–317; Michael D. Swartz, "The Topography of Blood in Mishnah Yoma," in *Jewish Blood: Reality and Metaphor in History, Religion, and Culture*, edited by Mitchell B. Hart (London: Routledge, 2009), 70–82; Michael D. Swartz, *Place and Person in Ancient Judaism: Describing the Yom Kippur Sacrifice*, International Rennert Center Guest Lecture Series 9 (Ramat Gan: Bar-Ilan University, Faculty of Jewish Studies, 2000). On the search for alternative ritual means to fulfill the obligations of sacrifice within late antique paganism, see especially Salzman's essay in this volume.

4. See the introduction and individual contributions in Ra'anan S. Boustan and Annette Yoshiko Reed, eds., *Blood and the Boundaries of Jewish and Christian Identities in Late Antiquity*, special theme-section of *Henoch* 30 (2008): 229–364.

5. On sacrificial language in Christian martyrology, see Elizabeth A. Castelli, *Martyrdom and Memory: Early Christian Culture Making* (New York: Columbia University Press, 2004), 50–61; also George Heyman, *The Power of Sacrifice: Roman and Christian Discourses in Conflict* (Washington, D.C.: Catholic University of America Press, 2007). On sacrificial language in early Jewish martyrology, see Jan Willem van Henten, *The Maccabean Martyrs as Saviours of the Jewish People: A Study of 2 and 4 Maccabees* (Leiden: Brill, 1997), esp. 140–56; Ra'anan S. Boustan, *From Martyr to Mystic: Rabbinic Martyrology and the Making of Merkavah Mysticism*, TSAJ 112 (Tübingen: Mohr Siebeck, 2005), 149–98.

6. On the ideological use to which the Romans put the destruction, see esp. Jodi Magness, "The Arch of Titus at Rome and the Fate of the God of Israel," *Journal of Jewish Studies* 59 (2008): 201–17; Fergus Millar, "Last Year in Jerusalem: Monuments of the Jewish War in Rome," in *Flavius Josephus and Flavian Rome*, edited by J. Edmondson, S. Mason, and J. Rives (Oxford: Oxford University Press, 2005), 101–28.

7. On the Christian interpretation of the destruction as a sign of the transfer of divine favor from the Jewish people to the Christian Church, and the Jewish internalization of this theological construct, see Israel J. Yuval, "The Myth of the Jewish Exile from the Land of Israel: A Demonstration of Irenic Scholarship," *Common Knowledge* 12 (2006): 16–33.

8. Klawans, *Purity, Sacrifice, and the Temple*, 175–211.

9. Klawans, *Purity, Sacrifice, and the Temple*, 106. See also Ishay Rosen-Zvi, "Bodies and Temple: The List of Priestly Bodily Defects in Mishnah *Bekhorot*, Chapter 7" (Hebrew), *Jewish Studies* 43 (2005–2006), 49–87; and Steven D. Fraade, "The Temple as a Marker of Jewish Identity before and after 70 C.E.: The Role of the Holy Vessels in Rabbinic Memory and Imagination," in *Jewish Identities in Antiquity: Studies in Memory of Menahem Stern*, edited by L. I. Levine and D. R. Schwartz (Tübingen: Mohr Siebeck, 2009), 235–63.

10. The term *resignification* is taken from Michael Fishbane's synthetic analysis of how rabbinic Judaism "reinterpreted and reenacted the old Temple sacrifices" in *The Exegetical Imagination: On Jewish Thought and Theology* (Cambridge; Harvard University Press, 1998), 123–35, at 124.

11. A comprehensive critical edition appears in Gottfried Reeg, ed., *Die Geschichte von den Zehn Märtyrern*, TSAJ 10 (Tübingen: Mohr Siebeck, 1985).

12. For a full list of the sources, see my n. 50, following.

13. See esp. René Girard, *Things Hidden since the Foundation of the World*, translated by S. Bann and M. Metteer (Stanford: Stanford University Press, 1987), 158–63; René Girard, *The Scapegoat*, translated by Y. Freccero (Baltimore: Johns Hopkins University Press, 1986), esp. 100–24.

14. For critical discussion of this entrenched view, see Klawans, *Purity, Sacrifice, and the Temple*, 203–11.

15. Paul Mandel, "The Loss of the Center: Changing Attitudes towards the Temple in Aggadic Literature," *HTR* 99 (2006): 17–35, at 34.

16. Mandel, "Loss of the Center," 35.

17. On the seminal place of the Jewish martyrologies of the early Byzantine period in the development of medieval Jewish martyrdom, see Shmuel Shepkaru, *Jewish Martyrs in the Pagan and Christian Worlds* (New York: Cambridge University Press, 2006), esp. 107–40.

18. The theory was most fully articulated in René Girard, *Violence and the Sacred*, translated by Patrick Gregory (Baltimore: Johns Hopkins University Press, 1977); also Girard, *Scapegoat* and *Things Hidden*. See also René Girard, "Generative Scapegoating," in *Violent Origins: Walter Burkert, René Girard, and Jonathan Z. Smith on Ritual Killing and Cultural Formation*, edited by R. G. (R, G.) Hamerton-Kelly (Stanford: Stanford University Press, 1987), 73–105.

19. See esp. Klawans, *Purity, Sacrifice, and the Temple*, 22–26, as well as the previous literature cited there.

20. Jonathan Z. Smith, "The Domestication of Sacrifice," in *Violent Origins: Walter Burkert, René Girard, and Jonathan Z. Smith on Ritual Killing and Cultural Formation*, edited by R. G. Hamerton-Kelly (Stanford: Stanford University Press, 1987), 191–214.

21. Jonathan Z. Smith, "On Comparison," in *Drudgery Divine: On the Comparison of Early Christianities and the Religions of Late Antiquity* (Chicago: University of Chicago Press, 1990), 36–53.

22. See esp. the critical assessment in Heyman, *Power of Sacrifice*, 151–56.

23. Ivan Strenski, "At Home with René Girard: Eucharistic Sacrifice, the 'French School' and Joseph De Maistre," in *Religion in Relation: Method, Application, and Moral*

Location (Columbia: University of South Carolina Press, 1993), 202–16; see also Ivan Strenski, *Contesting Sacrifice: Religion, Nationalism, and Social Thought in France* (Chicago: University of Chicago Press, 1997), esp. 101–11.

24. Strenski, "At Home with René Girard," 204.

25. All citations of the work refer to Reeg, *Geschichte von den Zehn Märtyrern*. All translations of this work below are mine, though I have also consulted David Stern, "Midrash Eleh Ezkerah; or, *The Legend of the Ten Martyrs*," in *Rabbinic Fantasies*, edited by D. Stern and M. J. Mirsky (New Haven: Yale University Press, 1990), 143–65.

26. Shulamit Elizur, *Wherefore Have We Fasted? Megillat Ta'anit Batra and Similar Lists of Fasts* (Hebrew) (Jerusalem: Magnes, 2006), 204–14. The earliest versions of the martyrology number among the anonymous, preclassical *piyyutim* dating to the fifth century and the first half of the sixth century and were likely already used for Yom Kippur. A number of examples of these early poetic versions of the martyrology have been published: Az beshivyeinu appears in A. M. Habermann, "Ancient Piyyutim" [Hebrew], *Tarbiz* 14 (1942): 57–58, and in a slightly different form in S. Speyer, "The Dirge Az be-veit shivyeinu" (Hebrew), *Sinai* 63 (1968): 50–55; see also the *qedushta* entitled *Az be-ma'asi diberot 'asarah*, which may have been composed by the Byzantine-period liturgical poet Yannai, published in M. Zulay, *The Liturgical Poems of Yannai, Collected from Geniza Manuscripts and Other Sources* (Hebrew) (Berlin: Schocken, 1938), 374–75.

27. Boustan, *From Martyr to Mystic*, 51–98. The Byzantine-period dating for the martyrology was already suggested by Leopold Zunz, *Die synagogale Poesie des Mittelalters*, 2nd ed. (Repr., Hildesheim: G. Olms, 1967), 139–44, and P. Bloch, "Rom und die Mystiker der Merkabah," in *Festschrift zum siebzigsten Geburtstage Jakob Guttmanns* (Leipzig: Gustav Fock, 1915), 113–24.

28 Solomon Zeitlin, "The Legend of the Ten Martyrs and Its Apocalyptic Origins," *Jewish Quarterly Review* 36 (1945–1946): 1–16.

29. *Jubilees* 34:12–19. The passage is translated in James C. Vanderkam, trans., *The Book of Jubilees*, CSCO 511 (Leuven: Peeters, 1989), 228–29. For discussion of this passage in the context of the various etiologies for Yom Kippur in Jewish literature of the Second Temple period, see Daniel Stökl Ben Ezra, *The Impact of Yom Kippur on Early Christianity: The Day of Atonement from Second Temple Judaism to the Fifth Century*, WUNT 163 (Tübingen: Mohr Siebeck, 2003), 95–97.

30. Zeitlin, "Legend," 4–7; Urbach, *Sages*, 521–22.

31. For example, *y Yom* 7.5 (44b–c); *LevR* 10.6; *SongR* 4.4.5; *bZev* 88b; *b'Arak* 16a. According to Friedrich Avemarie, trans., *Yoma-Versöhnungstag*, Übersetzung des Talmud Yerushalmi 2.4 (Tübingen: Mohr Siebeck, 1995), 193 n. 92, the different versions share a common source, although they have subsequently developed in distinct directions.

32. This crucial observation is emphasized in Daniel Stökl Ben Ezra, "The Christian Exegesis of the Scapegoat between Jews and Pagans," in *Sacrifice in Religious Experience*, edited by A. I. Baumgarten (Leiden: Brill, 2002), 207–32.

33. Michael D. Swartz, "The Semiotics of the Priestly Vestments in Ancient Judaism," in *Sacrifice in Religious Experience*, edited by A. Baumgarten, SHR 93 (Leiden: Brill, 2002), 57–80, esp. 72–76.

34. This material is found in its fullest form at *Ten Martyrs*, I–X.15.20–28 + 18.1–3. It is also found in what is perhaps its earliest extant formulation in *Midrash Shir ha-Shirim* to Song 1:3; Eliezer Halevi Grünhut, ed., *Midrash Shir ha-Shirim*, 2nd ed. (Jerusalem: Wilhelm Gross, 1971), 4a.

35. *Ten Martyrs*, I–X.18.1–3. See the parallel in *Midrash Shir ha-Shirim* to Song 1:3 (Grünhut, p. 4a).

36. *Ten Martyrs*, I–IX.20.1–5. The translation follows recension VII.

37. *Ten Martyrs*, V–VIII.21.10. Similarly, following Rabbi Ishmael's death, Michael and Gabriel, along with the rest of the angelic host, praise Rabbi Ishmael for joining the rest of the martyred righteous, who are blessed to have been "brought as offerings upon the altar that is in heaven" (*Ten Martyrs*, V–VIII.22.63).

38. The imagery associated with the theme of eschatological vengeance in *The Story of the Ten Martyrs* is not an isolated phenomenon, but appears in many of the individual martyrologies that make up the larger anthology. See the martyrdoms of Rabbi Eleazar ben Shammua' (*Ten Martyrs*, I, VI–VII, IX–X.43.13–15; I, III–V.51.18–19) and of Yeshevav the scribe (*Ten Martyrs*, I.50.6–8).

39. Boustan, *From Martyr to Mystic*, 133–39. On the transformation—and conflation—of the various elements of the biblical Yom Kippur ritual within the cultic theology of Hebrews, see Stökl Ben Ezra, *Impact of Yom Kippur on Early Christianity*, 187–90. On Hebrews and its relationship to the legacy of biblical sacrifice more generally, see now Morna D. Hooker, "Christ, the 'End' of the Cult," in *The Epistle to the Hebrews and Christian Theology*, edited by R. Bauckham et al. (Grand Rapids: Eerdmans, 2009), 189–212, and Christian A. Eberhart, "Characteristics of Sacrificial Metaphors in Hebrews," in *Hebrews: Contemporary Methods—New Insights*, edited by G. Gelardini (Leiden: Brill, 2005), 37–64.

40. Girard, *Things Hidden*, 149–53, at 151. See also Girard's discussion of the story of Cain and Abel at the very opening of *Violence and the Sacred* (4), which he invokes in support of his central contention that sacrifice is a substitution for violence since Cain, as a tiller of the soil rather than shepherd, is cast as a murderer precisely (if paradoxically) because he has no outlet for his violent impulses; the same basic argument is presented again in René Girard, "Satan," in *The Girard Reader*, edited by J. G. Williams (New York: Crossroad, 1996), 203.

41. Girard, *Things Hidden*, 152.

42. This supersessionist progression is apparent throughout Girard's corpus, but is particularly pronounced in the chapter here under discussion (*Things Hidden*, 141–79).

43. See the discussion of this narrative tradition as a series of "accretions" to the biblical text in Sheldon H. Blank, "The Death of Zechariah in Rabbinic Literature," *Hebrew Union College Annual* 12–13 (1937–1938): 327–46.

44. Important studies that focus primarily on the rabbinic versions of this narrative include Betsy Halpern Amaru, "The Killing of the Prophets: Unraveling a Midrash," *Hebrew Union College Annual* 54 (1983): 153–80, and Blank, "Death of Zechariah in Rabbinic Literature," 327–46.

45. On the Christian recontextualization of the Zechariah traditions in *Vitae Prophetarum* 23.1–2, see David Satran, *Biblical Prophets in Byzantine Palestine: Reassessing the Lives of the Prophets*, SVTP 11 (Leiden: Brill, 1995): 22–33, 46–49; also A. M. Schwemer, *Studien zu den frühjüdischen Prophetenlegenden Vitae prophetarum*, 2 vols., TSAJ 49–50 (Tübingen: Mohr Siebeck, 1995–96), 2:283–321.

46. Matt 23:35 // Luke 11:51. Naturally, the scholarly literature on the uses of this narrative in these passages is vast. See esp. Catherine Sider Hamilton, "'His Blood Be upon Us': Innocent Blood and the Death of Jesus in Matthew," *Catholic Biblical Quarterly* 70 (2008):

82–100; H.G.L. Peels, "The Blood 'from Abel to Zechariah' (Matthew 23,35; Luke 11,50f.) and the Canon of the Old Testament," *Zeitschrift für die Alttestamentliche Wissenschaft* 113 (2001): 583–601. For detailed argumentation that the Zechariah in the two Gospels is to be identified with the priest-prophet Zechariah son of Jehoiada of 2 Chr 24:20–22 and not with Zechariah son of Barachiah of the early Second Temple period who authored the prophetic book of Zechariah, see Isaac Kalimi, "The Story about the Murder of the Prophet Zechariah in the Gospels and Its Relations to Chronicles," *Revue Biblique* 116 (2009): 246–61.

47. See the impressive range of sources gathered in A. A. Barb, "St. Zacharias the Prophet and Martyr: A Study in Charms and Incantations," *Journal of the Warburg and Courtauld Institutes* 11 (1948): 35–67.

48. See Galit Hasan-Rokem, *Web of Life: Folklore and Midrash in Rabbinic Literature*, translated by B. Stein (Stanford: Stanford University Press, 2000), 170–71, comparing *Lamentations Rabbati* 4:13, §16, with *Itinerarium Burdigalense* 592.1. For discussion of the motif of Zechariah's blood in *Itinerarium Burdigalense* as well as in later Christian pilgrimage texts, see John Wilkinson, *Jerusalem Pilgrims before the Crusades* (Warminster, U.K.: Aris and Phillips, 1977), 173. Oded Irshai, "Historical Aspects of the Christian-Jewish Polemic Concerning the Church of Jerusalem in the Fourth Century" (Hebrew), 2 vols., Ph.D. diss., Hebrew University of Jerusalem, 1993, 1: 8–12, already noted the significant similarities between these Zechariah traditions and the pilgrimage traditions concerning James, the brother of Jesus, who likewise was said to have been slain in the middle of the temple or even adjacent to the altar.

49. Jean-Daniel Dubois, "La mort de Zacharie: Mémoire juive et mémoire chrétienne," *Revue des Etudes Augustiniennes* 40 (1994): 23–38.

50. Variants of the narrative are found at *yTa'an* 4.8 (69a–b); *Pesiqta de-Rav Kahana* 15, §7; *LamR*, Proems 5 and 23; 2:2, §4; 4:13, §16; *EcclR* 3:16, §1; 10:4, §1; *bGit* 57b; *bSan* 96b. See also the version in the eleventh-century *Midrash Aggadah* to Num 30:15, on which see Halpern Amaru, "Killing of the Prophets."

51. *yTa'an* 4.8 (69a–b). Unless otherwise noted, I follow the readings in MS Leiden as printed by Peter Schäfer and Hans-Jürgen Becker, eds., *Synopse zum Talmud Yerushalmi*, Band II/5–12: *Ordnung Mo'ed*, TSAJ 83 (Tübingen: Mohr Siebeck, 2001), 264. The translation is my own. I have also consulted the translation and textual notes in Michael Swartz, "Bubbling Blood and Rolling Bones: Agency and Teleology in Rabbinic Myth," in *Antike Mythen: Medien, Transformationen und Konstruktionen*, edited by U. Dill and C. Walde (Berlin: De Gruyter, 2009), 224–41, at 229–30.

52. This unit appears at the end of the passage in *LamR* 4:13, §16, rather than before it, as here.

53. The *editio princeps* (Venice, 1523) reads: "bulls, rams, and sheep" (*parim 'eilim u-khevasim*) (Schäfer and Becker, *Synopse zum Talmud Yerushalmi*, Band II/5–12: *Ordnung Mo'ed*, 264).

54. Compare *Ten Martyrs*, I–IX.20.3–5.

55. The phrase in brackets was added by a later scribe to MS Leiden; it appears as part of the text in the Venice edition of the Palestinian Talmud as well as in the parallel versions in the Palestinian midrashim. On the scribal additions in MS Leiden and the relationship of the manuscript to the Venice edition, see Yaacov Sussman, "Introduction," in *Talmud Yerushalmi: According to Ms. Or. 4720 (Scal. 3) of the Leiden University Library with Restorations and Corrections* (Jerusalem: Academy of the Hebrew Language, 2005), 23–29.

56. The versions in *Lamentations Rabbati* and the Babylonian Talmud list in addition to "the eighty thousand young priests" also the men of the Great and Minor Sanhendrin; youths and maidens, and school children.

57. The phrase might also be translated: "he rebuked it [the blood]." But I translate it this way because in some parallels Nebuzaradan here addresses Zechariah by name (e.g., *LamR,* Proem 23 and 2:2, §4; *bGit* 57b).

58. This entire sentence is in Aramaic, after which the text returns to Hebrew.

59. This final unit of the narrative differs considerably in the parallel in *bGit* 57b. For discussion, see the following.

60. Girard, *Things Hidden,* 158–62.

61. Especially Girard, *Scapegoat,* 100–24.

62. The high social status of Zechariah, as "son-in-law of the king, high priest, a prophet, and a judge," conforms to Girard's paradigm, in which the scapegoat is as likely to be the king as the outcast: see especially René Girard, "A Venda Myth Analyzed," appendix to R. J. Golsan, *René Girard and Myth: An Introduction* (New York: Garland, 1993), 151–79.

63. See esp. Girard, *Violence and the Sacred,* 39–67, 75–78, and 95–98.

64. *bGit* 57b. This form of the story also appears in *LamR,* Proem 23.

65. "The Anthropology of the Cross: A Conversation with René Girard," in Williams, *Girard Reader,* 262–94, at 286.

66. Swartz, "Bubbling Blood and Rolling Bones," 227–31.

67. Klawans, *Purity, Sacrifice, and the Temple,* 183–84; Jonathan Klawans, *Impurity and Sin in Ancient Judaism* (New York: Oxford University Press, 2000), 121–22.

68. A similar conclusion concerning the defiling force of Zechariah's murder is drawn by Sider Hamilton in "'His Blood Be upon Us,'" esp. 99–100, which, however, treats the rabbinic story as background to the New Testament gospels rather than as a fourth-century Jewish response to Christian uses of this story, as I do.

69. My discussion addresses the recension of *Lamentations Rabbati* printed in Solomon Buber, *Midrasch Echa Rabbati: Sammlung aggadischer Auslegungen der Klagelieder* (Vilna: Romm, 1899; repr. Hildesheim: Olms, 1967).

70. For discussion of the text, sources, genres, and transmission of *Lamentations Rabbati,* see Paul D. Mandel, "Midrash Lamentations Rabbati: Prolegomenon and a Critical Edition to the Third Parasha" (Hebrew), Ph.D. diss., Hebrew University of Jerusalem, 1997; Paul D. Mandel, "Between Byzantium and Islam: The Transmission of a Jewish Book in the Byzantine and Early Islamic Periods," in *Transmitting Jewish Traditions: Orality, Textuality and Cultural Diffusion,* edited by Y. Elman and I. Gershoni (New Haven: Yale University Press, 2000), 74–106.

71. Shaye J. D. Cohen, "The Destruction: From Scripture to Midrash," *Prooftexts* 2 (1982): 18–39.

72. Cohen, "The Destruction," 24–25.

73. Halpern Amaru, "Killing of the Prophets," argues that the Zechariah story contributes to the martyrological emphasis of Moshe ha-Darshan's eleventh-century *Midrash Aggadah.* But, even if this is so, the narrative should not be understood to carry a single meaning; the redactional context of the narrative there does not have a direct bearing on the meaning of the narrative here within *Lamentations Rabbati.*

74. Yuval, "Myth of the Jewish Exile."

75. See esp. Heyman, *Power of Sacrifice.*

{ BIBLIOGRAPHY }

Ancient Sources

Ambrose. *Epistles*. Edited by Otto Faller, revised by Michaela Zelzer. *Sancti Ambrosii Opera*, Pars X, *Epistulae et acta*. CSEL 82.1, 82.2, 82.3. Vindob: Tempsky, 1968–96. Also see Migne, *PL* 16. Repr., Paris: De Vrayet de Surcy, 1845.

———. *Epistles*, Book X. English translation by J.H.W.G. Liebeschuetz with the assistance of Carol Hill. *Ambrose of Milan: Political Letters and Speeches*. Liverpool: Liverpool University Press, 2005.

———. *Expositio evangelii secundum Lucam*. Edited by Marcus Adriaen, Paolo Angelo Ballerini, and Maurice Testard. *Sancti Ambrosii Mediolanensis Opera*. Vol. 4, *Expositio evangelii secundum Lucam*. CCL 14. Turnhout: Brepols, 1957.

Anthologia Latina. Edited by Alexander Riese, Franz Buecheler, and Ernst Lommatzch. 2 vols. BT. Leipzig: Teubner, 1894–1926.

Appian. *Bellum civile*. Edited by Paul Viereck and A. G. Roos. *Appiani Historia romana*. Vol. 2, *Bellacivilia*. BT. Leipzig: Teubner, 1879–1905. Repr., 1962.

Aristides, Aelius. *Orations*. Edited by Friedrich Walther Lenz and Charles Allison Behr. *P. Aelii Aristidis Opera quae exstant omnia*. 4 vols. Leiden: Brill, 1976–.

Aristophanes. *The Birds*. Greek text edited with French translation by Victor Coulon and Hilaire van Daele, *Aristophane*. Vol. 3, *Aves*. Collection des universités de France. Paris: Les Belles Lettres, 1928. Repr., 1967. English translation by Eugene O'Neill. *The Complete Greek Drama*. New York: Random House, 1938.

———. *Ranae*. Edited by Nigel Guy Wilson. *Aristophanis fabulae*. Vol. 2, *Lysistrata, Thesmophoriazusae, Ranae, Ecclesiazusae, Plutus*. Scriptorum classicorum bibliotheca Oxoniensis. Oxford: Oxford University Press, 2007.

Aristotle. *Fragments*. Edited by Valentinus Rose. *Aristotelis qui ferebantur liborum fragmenta*. BT. Leipzig: Teubner, 1886.

[Aristotle]. *On Virtues and Vices*. Edited with an English translation by Harris Rackham. LCL. Cambridge: Harvard University Press, 1935.

Arnobius. *Against Gentiles*. Book VII. Edited by Concetto Monchesi. *Arnobii Adversus nationes Libri VII*. Corpus scriptorum Latinorum Paravianum 62. Turin: Paraviae, 1934.

Athenagoras. *Legatio*. Edited with English translation by William R. Schoedel. *Athenagoras: Legatio and De Resurrectione*. Oxford: Clarendon, 1972.

Augustine. *City of God*. Edited by Bernhard Dombart and Alfons Kalb. *Sancti Aurelii Augustini episcopi De Civitate Dei*. CCL 47–48. Turnhout: Brepols, 1955.

———. *Epistles*. Migne. *PL* 33. Paris, 1844–1864.

———. *On the Psalms*. English translation by Maria Boulding. *The Works of Saint Augustine: A Translation for the 21st Century*. Vol. 3.15, *Expositions of the Psalms*, 1–32. Hyde Park, N.Y.: New City Press, 2000.

————. *Sermon* 148 [98]. Migne, *PL* 39–39: 799–800. English translation by Edmund Hill. *The Works of Saint Augustine: A Translation for the 21st Century*. Vol. 3.5, *Sermons 148–183*. Edited by John E. Rotelle. New Rochelle, N.Y.: New City Press, 1992.

Aulus Gellius. *Noctes Atticae*. Edited by Peter K. Marshall. 2 vols. Oxford: Clarendon Press, 1990–.

Biblia Hebraica. Edited by K. Elliger and W. Rudolph. Stuttgart: Deutsche Bibelgesellschaft, 1977.

Cassius Dio Cocceianus. *Roman History*. Edited with an English translation by H. B. Foster and E. Carey. LCL. Cambridge: Harvard University Press, 1954–1955.

Cicero, Marcus Tullius. *De natura deorum*. Latin text with English translation by Harris Rackham. *Cicero*. Vol. 19, *De natura deorum; Academica*. LCL. Cambridge: Harvard University Press, 1967.

————. *De officiis*. Latin text with English translation by Walter Miller. *Cicero*. Vol. 21, *De Officiis*. LCL. Cambridge: Harvard University Press, 1913.

————. *De oratore*. Edited by F. Kumaniecki. BT. Stuttgart: Teubner, 1995.

————. *Tusculanae disputationes*. Latin text with English translation by J. E. King. *Cicero*. Vol. 18, *Tusculan Disputations*. LCL. Cambridge: Harvard University Press, 1945.

Clement of Alexandria. *Stromateis*. Edited by Ludwig Früchtel, Otto Stählin, and Ursula Treu, *Clemens Alexandrinus*. Vol. 2, *Stromata. Buch I–VI*. Vol. 3, *Stromata. Buch VII–VIII* Die Griechischen christlichen Schriftsteller der ersten Jahrhunderte 15, 52. Berlin: Akademie Verlag, 1960–1984.

Clement of Rome. *First Letter of Clement to the Corinthians*. (1 Clement). Edited with English translation by Bart D. Ehrman. *The Apostolic Fathers*. Vol. 2, *First Letter of Clement to the Corinthians, Second Letter of Clement to the Corinthians, Letters of Ignatius. Letter of Polycarp to the Philippians. Martyrdom of Polycarp. Didache*. LCL. Cambridge: Harvard University Press, 2003.

Codex Iustinianus. Edited by Paul Kreuger. *Corpus juris civilis*. Vol. 2, *Codex Iustinianus*. Berlin: Weidmann, 1928–1929.

Codex Theodosianus. Edited by Paul Krueger, Theodore Mommsen, and Paul Meyer. *Codex Theodosianus*. 3 vols. Repr., Hildesheim: Weidmann, 1990. English translation by Clyde Pharr. *The Theodosian Code and Novels, and the Sirmondian Constitutions*. Princeton: Princeton University Press, 1952.

Corpus inscriptionum Latinarum. 17 vols. Berlin: Brandenburg Academy of Sciences and Humanities, 1863–.

Cyprian. *Epistles*. Edited by G. F. Diercks. *Sancti Cypriani episcopi opera, pars III, 1–4. Sancti Cypriani Episcopi epistularium*. 4 vols. CCL 3B, 3D, 3D, 3E. Turnhout: Brepols, 1994–. English translation by Ernest Wallis. *Fathers of the Third Century: Hippolytus, Cyprian, Caius, Novation, Appendix*. Edited by A. Cleveland Coxe, 275–409. ANF 5. Christian Literature Publishing, 1886. Repr., Peabody, Mass.: Hendrickson, 1995.

————. *Testimonies*. Latin text edited by Wilhelm August Hartel. *S. Thasci Caecili Cypriani opera omnia*. Vol. 3:143–44. CSEL 3. Vindobonae: C. Geroldi, 1871. English translation by Ernest Wallis. *Fathers of the Third Century: Hippolytus, Cyprian, Caius, Novation, Appendix*. Edited by A. Cleveland Coxe, 530–557. ANF 5. Christian Literature Publishing, 1886. Repr., Peabody, Mass.: Hendrickson, 1995.

Cyril of Alexandria. *Commentarii in Lucam (in catena)*. Migne, *PG* 72, 476–949. Paris, 1857–1866.

———. *Commentarii in Lucam (homilia 3 et 4)* (= *In occursum domini* [*homilia diversa* 12]). Migne, *PG* 77, 1040–49. Paris,1857–1866.

———. *Glaphyra in Pentateuchum.* Migne, *PG* 69, 9–677. Paris, 1857–1866.

Dio Chrysostomus. *Orations.* Edited by Hans Freidrich August von Arnim. *Dionis Prusaensis quem vocant Chrysostomum quae exstant omnia.* Vols. 1–2. 2nd ed. Berlin: Weidmann, 1893, 1896. Repr., 1962.

Diodorus Siculus. *Bibliotheca historica.* Edited by Immanuel Bekker, Ludwig August Dindorf, and Curt Theodor Fischer. 6 vols. BT. Leipzig: Teubner, 1964–1969. Greek text with an English translation by C. H. Oldfather. *Diodorus Siculus. The Library of History.* 6 vols. LCL. Cambridge: Harvard University Press, 1933–1967.

Diogenes Laertius. *Vitae philosophorum.* Greek text edited by H. S. Long, *Diogenis Laertii vitae philosophorum,* 2 vols. Oxford: Clarendon Press, 1964. Repr., 1966. English translation by R. D. Hicks. *Diogenes Laertius: Lives, Teachings and Sayings of Famous Philosophers.* 2 vols. LCL. Cambridge: Harvard University Press, 1925.

Empedocles. *Works.* Edited and translated by Brad Inwood. *The Poem of Empedocles: A Text and Translation with an Introduction.* Rev. ed. Toronto: University of Toronto Press, 2001.

Epictetus. *Enchiridion.* Edited by Henricus Schenkl. *Epicteti dissertationes ab Arriano digestae.* Leipzig: Teubner, 1916. Repr., 1965.

Epiphanius. *Panarion.* Edited by Karl Holl. *Epiphanius. Herausgegeben im Auftrage der Kirchenväter-Commission der Königl. Preussischen Akademie der Wissenshaften.* 4 vols. GCS 13, 25, 31, 37. Leipzig: J. C. Hinrichs, 1915–1933; Berlin: De Gruyter, 2006.

Epistle of Barnabas. Edited with English translation by Bart D. Ehrman. *The Apostolic Fathers.* Vol. 1, *Epistle of Barnabas, Papias and Quadratus, Epistle to Diognetus, The Shepherd of Hermas.* LCL 25. Cambridge: Harvard University Press, 2003.

Eudoxus. *Die Fragmente.* Edited with introduction and commentary by François Lasserre. Texte und Kommentare 4. Berlin: De Gruyter, 1966.

Euripides. *Cretans.* Edited with English translation by Christopher Collard and Martin Cropp. *Euripides. Fragments.* Vol. 1. LCL. Cambridge: Harvard University Press, 2008.

———. *Hippolytus.* Greek text with English translation by W. S. Barrett. Oxford: Clarendon Press, 1964.

Eusebius of Caesarea. *Historia Ecclesiastica.* Edited with French translation by Gustav Bardy. *Eusèbe de Césarée. Histoire ecclésiastique.* 4 vols. SC 31, 41, 55, 73. Paris: Éditions du Cerf, 1952–1971.

———. *Life of Constantine.* Edited by Freidhelm Winkelmann. *Eusebius Werke.* Vol. 1.1, *Über das Leben des Kaisers Konstantin.* Die griechischen christlichen Schriftsteller. Berlin: Akademie Verlag, 1902. Repr., 1975.

———. *Praeparatio evangelica.* Edited by Karl von Mras. *Eusebius Werke.* Vol. 8, *Die Praeparatio evangelica.* 2 vols. Die griechischen christlichen Schriftsteller. Berlin: Akademie Verlag, 1902. English translation by Edwin Gifford. *Eusebius of Caesarea: Preparation for the Gospel.* Oxford: Clarendon Press, 1903.

Festus. *Glossaria.* Edited by W. M. Lindsay. Volume 4. *Glossaria Latina iussu Academiae britannicae edita.* Paris: Société anonyme d'édition "Les Belles Lettres," 1926–1931.

Florus. *Epitome rerum Romanarum.* Latin text with English translation by E. S. Forester. LCL. Cambridge: Harvard University Press, 1929.

Die Fragmente der griechischen Historiker. Edited by Felix Jacoby. Berlin: Weidmann, 1923–1958.

Gelasius. *Epistles.* Edited by Andreas Theil. *Epistolae Romanorum Pontificum Genuinae.* Braunsburg: E. Peter, 1868.

Gregory the Great. *Epistles.* English translation by James Barmby. *The Book of Pastoral Rule and Selected Epistles of Gregory the Great, Bishop of Rome.* NPNF, second series 12: 73–243. Christian Literature Publishing, 1895. Repr., Peabody, Mass.: Hendrickson, 1995.

Heliodorus. *Ethiopika.* Edited by T. W. Lumb, J. Maillon, and R. M. Rattenbury. *Héliodore. Les éthiopiques (Théagène et Chariclée).* 3 vols. 2nd ed. Paris: Les Belles Lettres, 1960.

Heraclitus. Edited and translated by Donald A. Russell and David Konstan. *Heraclitus: Homeric Problems.* Atlanta: Society of Biblical Literature, 2005.

Hesiod. *Theogony.* Edited by Friedrich Solmsen, Reinhold Merkelbach, and Martin L. West. *Theogonia. Opera et dies, Scutum.* Oxford: Clarendon Press; New York: Oxford University Press, 1983.

Horace. *Odes and Epodes.* Edited with English translation by Niall Rudd. LCL. Cambridge: Harvard University Press, 2004.

Iamblichus. *De Mysteriis.* English translation with notes and introduction by Emma C. Clark, John M. Dillon, and Jackson P. Pershbell. *Iamblichus On the Mysteries.* Writings from the Greco-Roman World 4. Leiden: Brill, 2003.

Itinerarium Burdigalense. Edited by Paul Geyer. *Itinera hierosolymitana saeculi IIII–VIII.* CSEL 39. Vindob: Temsky, 1898.

Jerome. *Letters.* English translation by Charles C. Mierow. *The Letters of Jerome.* Vol. 1. ACW 33. Westminster, Md.: Newman Press, 1963.

John Chrysostom. *In acta apostolorum.* Migne, *PG* 60, 13–384. Paris:1857–1866. English translation by J. Walker, J. Sheppard, and H. Browne, with revisions by George B. Stevens. *The Homilies of St. John Chrysostom on the Acts of the Apostles and the Epistle to the Romans.* NPNF, first series 11:1–330. Christian Literature Publishing, 1889. Repr., Peabody, Mass.: Hendrickson, 1995.

Josephus, Flavius. *Antiquitates Judaicae.* Edited by B. Niese. *Flavii Iosephi opera,* vols. 1–4: 1:3–362; 2:3–392; 3:3–409; 4:3–320. Berlin: Weidmann. Repr., 1955.

———. *Contra Apionem.* Edited by B. Niese. *Flavii Iosephi opera,* vol. 5: 3–99. Berlin: Weidmann, 1889. Repr., 1955.

Jubilees. Ethiopic text edited with English translation by James C. Vanderkam. *The Book of Jubilees.* 2 vols. CSCO 510–511, Scriptores Aethiopici 86–87. Leuven: Peeters, 1989.

Julian. *Contra Galilaeos.* Edited by Karl Johannes Neumann and Eberhard Nestle. *Iuliani imperatoris librorum contra Christianos quae supersunt.* Scriptorum graecorum qui Christianam impugnauerunt religionem quae supersunt 3. Leipzig: Teubner, 1880.

Justin Martyr. *Apologiae Pro Christianis.* Edited by Miroslav Marcovich. *Iustini Martyris Apologiae Pro Christianis.* Patristische Texte und Studien 38. Berlin: De Gruyter, 1994.

———. *Dialogue with Trypho.* Edited by Miroslav Marcovich. *Iustini Martyris Dialogus cum Tryphone.* Patristische Texte und Studien 47. Berlin: De Gruyter, 1997.

Lactantius. *Divinae institutiones.* Edited with French translation by Pierre Monat. 6 vols. SC 204, 205, 326, 337, 377, 509. Paris: Éditions du Cerf, 1973. Repr., 2007.

———. *De Mortibus Persecutorum.* Edited with English translation by J. L. Creed. Oxford Early Christian Texts. Oxford: Clarendon Press, 1984.

Lamentations Rabbah. Edited by S. Buber. *Midrasch Echa Rabbati: Sammlung aggadischer Auslegungen der Klagelieder.* Vilna: Romm, 1899. Repr., Hildesheim: Olms, 1967. Translated by A. Cohen. *Lamentations Rabbah.* 3rd ed. London: Soncino, 1983.

Libanius. Edited by Richard Foerster. *Libanii opera.* 12 vols. BT. Leipzig: Teubner, 1903–1927. Repr., Hildesheim: Olms, 1963.

Livy. *Ab urbe condita libri.* Edited with an English translation by B. O. Foster. *Livy. History of Rome.* 14 vols. LCL. Cambridge: Harvard University Press, 1967–1984.

Lucan. *Pharsalia.* Latin text with an English translation by J. D. Duff. *Lucan. The Civil War.* LCL. Cambridge: Harvard University Press, 1943.

Lucian of Samosata. *De sacrificiis.* Edited by Klaas Johan Popma. Amsterdam: Becht, 1931.

———. *Works.* Greek text with English translation by A. M. Harmon. Vol. 6 translated by K. Kilburn, vols. 7–8 by M. D. Macleod. LCL. Cambridge: Harvard University Press, 1960–1967.

Lucretius, Titus. *De rerum natura Liber 5.* Edited with English translation by Monica R. Gale. Oxford: Oxbow Books, 2009.

Macrobius. *Saturnalia.* Edited by Iacobus Willis. 2 vols. BT. Leipzig: Teubner, 1963. English translation by Robert Kaster. *Macrobius. Saturnalia.* 3 vols. LCL. Cambridge: Harvard University Press, 2011.

Martyrdom of Polycarp. Edited with an English translation by Bart D. Ehrman. *The Apostolic Fathers.* Vol. 1, *I Clement, II Clement, Ignatius, Polycarp, Didache*, 367–401. LCL. Cambridge: Harvard University Press, 2003.

Maximus of Turin, *Homilies.* Migne , PL 57. Paris, 1844–1864.

———. *Sermons.* Edited by Almut Mutzenbecher. *Maximi Episcopi Taurinensis: Collectionem Sermonum antiquam nonnullis sermonibus extravagantibus adiectis.* CCL 23. Turnhout: Brepols, 1962.

Maximus of Tyre. *Dialexeis.* Greek text edited by George Leonidas Koniaris. *Maximus Tyrius. Philosophumena-dialexeis.* Texte und Kommentare 17. Berlin: De Gruyter, 1995. English translation by M. B. Trapp. *Maximus of Tyre: The Philosophical Orations.* New York: Oxford University Press, 1997.

Midrash Shir ha-Shirim. Edited by Eliezer Halevi Grünhut. 2nd ed. Jerusalem: Wilhelm Gross, 1971.

Minucius Felix. *Octavius.* Edited with French translation by Jean Beaujeu. Collection des universités de France. Paris: Les Belles Lettres. 1974. English translation by Rudolph Arbesmann. *Tertullian Apologetic Works and Minucius Felix Octavius.* Washington, D.C.: Catholic University of America Press, 1950.

Mishnah. Edited and translated by Philip Blackman. *Mishnayot.* Gateshead: Judaica Press, 1990.

Novum Testamentum Graece. Edited by Eberhard Nestle, Erwin Nestle, and Kurt Aland. 26th rev. ed. Stuttgart: Deutsche Bibelgesellschaft, 1979.

———. Edited by Eberhard Nestle, Erwin Nestle, Kurt Aland, Johannes Karavidopoulos, Carlo Martini, and Bruce Metzger. 27th rev. ed. Stuttgart: Deutsche Bibelgesellschaft, 1993.

Origen. *Contra Celsum.* Edited by Marcel Borret. *Origène. Contre Celse. Introduction, texte critique, traduction et notes.* 5 vols. Rev. ed. SC 132, 136, 147, 150, 227. Paris: Éditions du Cerf, 2005–.

Ovid. *Fasti*. Edited with English translation by James G. Frazer. 2nd ed. Revised by G. P. Goold. LCL. Cambridge: Harvard University Press, 1989.

P. Geneva I.32. In P. Schubert, "Continuité et changement des cultes locaux en Égypte romaine: à travers trois documents de la collection papyrologique de Genève." *Les cultes locaux dans les mondes grec et romain*. Edited by G. Labarre, 295–303. Paris: Boccard, 2004.

Papyri Graecae Magicae: Die griechischen Zauberpapyri. Edited and translated by K. Preisendanz et al. 2 vols. 2nd ed. Munich: K. G. Saur Verlag, 1973–1974.

Paulinus of Nola. *Carmina*. In *S. Pontii Meropii Paulini Nolani Opera*. Vol. 2, *Carmina, Indices et Addenda*. Edited by Wilhelm August Ritter von Hartel and Margit Kamptner. 2nd ed. CSEL 29, 30. Vidobonae: Verlag der österreichischen Akademie der Wissenschaften, 1999.

Philo of Alexandria. *On the Migration of Abraham*. Edited by P. Wendland, *Philonis Alexandrini opera quae supersunt*, vol. 2. Berlin: Reimer, 1897. Repr., De Gruyter, 1962.

———. *On the Special Laws*. Greek text with English translation by F. H. Colson, *Philo*. Vol. 7. LCL. Cambridge: Harvard University Press, 1937.

Philodemus. *On Piety*. Greek text with English translation by Dirk Obbink, *Philodemus. On Piety, Part 1: Critical Text with Commentary*. Oxford: Clarendon Press, 1996.

Philostratus. *Life of Apollonius of Tyana, Letters of Apollonius, Ancient Testimonia, Eusebius' Reply to Hierocles*. 2 vols. Edited and translated by C. P. Jones. LCL. Cambridge: Harvard University Press, 2005–2006.

Plato. *Euthyphro*. Greek text with English translation by Harold North Fowler. *Plato*. Vol. 1, *Euthyphro, Apology, Critic, Phaedra, Phaedrus*. LCL. Cambridge: Harvard University Press, 1914. Repr., 1971.

———. *Leges*. Greek text with English translation by Robert G. Bury. 2 vols. LCL. Cambridge: Harvard University Press, 1926. Repr., 2000.

———. *Republica*. Greek text with English translation by Paul Shorey. *Plato The Republic*. 2 vols. Rev. ed. LCL. Cambridge: Harvard University Press, 1980–1982.

Pliny, the Elder. *Naturalis historia*. Latin text with English translation by H. Rackham. 10 vols. LCL. Cambridge: Harvard University Press, repr. 1967-1976.

Pliny, the Younger. *Letters and Panegyricus*. Edited with English translation by Betty Radice. LCL. Cambridge: Harvard University Press, 1969.

Plutarch. *De Iside et Osiride*. Edited with an introduction, translation and commentary by J. G. Griffiths. Cardiff: University of Wales Press, 1970.

Plutarch. *Moralia*. Edited by C. Hubert. Leipzig: Teubner, 1954. Repr., 1959. Greek text with English translation by Frank Cole Babbitt. *Plutarch's Moralia*. 16 vols. LCL. Repr., Cambridge: Harvard University Press, 1999.

———. *Parallel Lives* (*Vitae Parallelae*). Edited by Claes Lindskog and Konrad Zeigler. 4 vols. BT. Leipzig: Teubner, 1969–1970.

Poetae comici Graeci. Edited by Rudolf Kassel and Colin Austin. 8 vols. Berlin: De Gruyter, 1983–.

Porphyry. *De Abstinentia*. Greek text with French translation by Jean Bouffartigue and Michel Patillon, *Porphyre. De l'abstinence*. 3 vols. Collection des universités de France. Paris: Les Belles Lettres, 1977, 1979. English translation by Gillian Clark. *Porphyry: On Abstinence from Killing Animals*. Ithaca: Cornell University Press, 2000.

———. *Ad Marcellam*. Edited by August Nauck. Opuscula selecta. BT. 1886. Repr., Hildesheim: Olms, 1963. English translation by Kathleen O'Brien Wicker. *Porphyry the Philosopher: To Marcella*. Texts and Translations 28, Graeco-Roman Religion Series 10. Atlanta: Scholars Press, 1987.

Posidonius. Edited by L. Edelstein and I. G. Kidd. 2nd ed. Cambridge class texts and Commentarie 13. Cambridge: Cambridge University Press, 19.

———. *Philosophi fragmenta.* Edited by Andrew Smith. Arabic fragments edited by David Wasserstein. BT. Stuttgart: Teubner, 1993.

Prudentius. *Apotheosis.* Edited by Maurice P. Cunningham. *Aurelii Prudentii Clementis Carmina.* CCL 126. Turnhout: Brepols, 1966.

Rhetorica ad Herennium. Edited with an English translation by Harry Caplan. LCL. Cambridge: Harvard University Press, 1954.

Rufinus. *Historia ecclesiastica.* In *Eusebius Werke.* Vol. 2, *Buch VI–X. Eusebius, über die Märtyrer in Palästina. Rufinus Vorrede und Einlage uber Gregorius Thaumaturgus. Rufinus Buch X–XI.* Edited by Eduard Schwartz and Theodor Mommsen. GCS. Neue Folge 6. Berlin: Akademie Verlag, 1999.

Sallustius. *De diis et mundo.* Edited with French translation by Gabriel Rochefort. *Des dieux et du monde.* Collection des universités de France. Paris: Les Belles Lettres, 1983.

Sallust. *Fragmenta.* Edited by Friedrich Kritz. *Die Fragmente des Sallust.* Erfurt: Carl Villaret, 1857.

———. *Historiae.* English translation by Patrick McGushin. *Sallust: The Histories.* 2 vols. Oxford: Oxford University Press, 1992–1994.

Seneca. *De clementia.* Edited with English translation and commentary by Susanna Braund. Oxford: Oxford University Press, 2009.

———. *Epistles.* Edited with English translation by Richard M. Gummere. *Ad Lucilium Epistulae morales.* LCL. Cambridge: Harvard University Press, 1917. Repr., 1979.

———. *On Superstition* (= Augustine, *On the City of God* 6.10). Edited by Bernhard Dombart and Alfons Kalb. *Sancti Aurelii Augustini episcopi De Civitate Dei.* CCL 47. Turnhout: Brepols, 1955.

Servius. *In Vergilii carmina commentarii* (= *Commentary to the Aeneid*). Edited by Georg Thilo and Hermann Hagen. 3 vols. Leipzig: Teubner, 1881–1902.

Socrates. *Historia ecclesiastica.* English translation by A. C. Zenos. *Socrates, Sozomenus: Church Histories.* Edited by Philip Schaff and Henry Wace. NPNF 2. Second Series. Christian Literature Publishing, 1890. Repr., Peabody, Mass.: Hendrickson, 1995.

Sozomen. *Historia ecclesiastica.* Edited by J. Bidez and G. C. Hansen, *Sozomenus. Kirchengeschichte. Die griechischen christlichen Schriftsteller* 50: 1–408. Berlin: Akademie–Verlag, 1960. English translation by C. D. Hartranft. *Socrates, Sozomenus: Church Histories.* Edited by Philip Schaff and Henry Wace. NPNF 2. Second Series. Christian Literature Publishing, 1890. Repr., Peabody, Mass.: Hendrickson, 1995.

The Story of the Ten Martyrs. Edited by Gottfried Reeg. *Die Geschichte von den Zehn Märtyrern.* TSAJ 10. Tübingen: Mohr Siebeck, 1985. English translation by David Stern, "Midrash Eleh Ezkerah; or, *The Legend of the Ten Martyrs.*" In *Rabbinic Fantasies,* Edited by David Stern and Mark J. Mirsky. New Haven: Yale University Press, 1998.

Strabo. *Geographica.* Edited by A. Meineke, *Strabonis geographica.* 3 vols. Leipzig: Teubner, 1877. Repr., 1969.

Stobaeus. *Anthologion.* Edited by Curtius Wachsmuth and Otto Hense. 5 vols. Berlin: Weidmann, 1884–1912.

Suetonius. *Lives of the Caesars.* Edited with English translation by James C. Rolfe. Revised with an introduction by Keith R. Bradley. LCL. Cambridge: Harvard University Press, 1998.

Suidae Lexicon. Edited by Ada Adler. 5 vols. Leipzig: Teubner, 1928–1938. Also available online with English translation at http://www.stoa.org/sol/.

Symmachus. *Letters.* Edited with French translation by Jean-Pierre Callu. *Symmaque, Lettres Tome I* (livres I–II). Paris: Les Belles Lettres, 1972. English translation by Michele R. Salzman and Michael Roberts. *The Letters of Symmachus. Book 1.* Society of Biblical Literature Series: Writers of Greece and Rome. Atlanta: Society of Biblical Literature, 2011.

———. *Relationes.* Edited with English translation by R. H. Barrow. *Prefect and Emperor: The "Relationes" of Symmacnus A.D. 384.* Oxford: Clarendon Press, 1973.

Talmud Bavli. 20 vols. Jerusalem: Tal-man, 1981.

Talmud Yerushalmi. Edited by Peter Schäfer and Hans-Jürgen Becker. *Synopse zum Talmud Yerushalmi.* 7 vols. Texte und Studien zum antiken Judentum 31, 33, 35, 47, 67, 82–83. Tübingen: Mohr Siebeck, 1991–2001.

Tatian. *Oratio ad Graecos.* Edited with English translation by Molly Whittaker. Oxford Early Christian Texts. Oxford: Oxford University Press, 1982. Greek text edited by Eduard Schwartz. *Tatiani Oratio ad Graecos.* Leipzig: J. C. Hinrichs'sche Buchhandlung, 1888.

Tertullian. *Adversus Marcionem.* Latin text with English translation by Ernest Evans. Oxford Early Christian Texts. 2 vols. Oxford: Clarendon Press, 1972.

———. *Apologia.* English translation by Rudolph Arbesmann. *Tertullian Apologetical Works and Minucius Felix Octavius.* Washington, D.C.: Catholic University of America Press, 1950.

———. *De carne Christi.* Latin text with French translation edited by Jean-Pierre Mahé. *Tertullian. La chair de Christ.* SC 216–217. Paris: Éditions du Cerf, 1975.

———. *De idololatria.* Edited with English translation by J. H. Waszink J.C.M. van Winden and P.G. vander Nat. Supplements to Vigiliae Christianae 1. Leiden: Brill, 1987.

Theophrastus. *De pietate.* Edited by Walter Pötscher. *Theoprastus. Greichisher Text herausgegeben, übersetzt und eingeleitet.* Leiden: Brill, 1964.

Valerius Maximus. *Facta et dicta memorabilia.* Edited by John Briscoe. 2 vols. BT. Stuttgart: Teubner, 1998. Edited with an English translation by D. R. Shackelton Bailey. *Valerius Maximus. Memorable Deeds and Sayings.* 2 vols. LCL. Cambridge: Harvard University Press, 2000.

Varro. *Divine Antiquities.* Edited with German commentary by Burkhart Cardauns. *Ms. Terentius Varro, Antiquitates rerum divinarum.* 2 vols. Mainz: Akademie der Wissenschaften und der Literatur, 1976.

Velleius Paterculus. *Historiae romanae, Libri II.* Edited with French translation by Joseph Hellogoarc'h. 2 vols. *Velleius Paterculus Histoire romaine.* Collection des universités de France. Paris: Les Belles Lettres, 1982.

[Victor, Sextus Aurelius] *Liber de viris illustribus urbis Romae.* Latin text edited by Franciscus Pichlmayr. BT. Leipzig: Teubner, 1911. Revised edition edited by Roland Gruendel, 1966.

Virgil. *Georgica.* Latin text edited with introduction and notes by R. Deryck Williams. *Virgil. The ecologues and Georgics* London: Bristol Classical Press, 1979. Repr., 1996.

Zachariah of Mytilene. *Life of Severus.* Syriac text with English translation edited by Lena Ambjörn. Texts from Christian Late Antiquity 6. Piscataway, N.J.: Gorgias Press, 2008.

Zosimus. *Historia nova.* Edited with French translation by François Paschoud, *Histoire nouvelle par Zosime.* 3 vols. Collection des universités de France. Paris: Les Belles Lettres, 1971–1989.

Modern Sources

Abeysekara, Ananda. *Colors of the Robe: Religion, Identity, and Difference.* Columbia: University of South Carolina Press, 2002.

———. "The Saffron Army, Violence, Terror(ism): Buddhism, Identity, and Difference in Sri Lanka." *Numen* 48.1 (2001): 1–46.

Ackerman, Robert. *Myth and Ritual School: J. G. Frazer and the Cambridge Ritualists.* London: Routledge, 2002.

Agamben, Giorgio. *Homo sacer: Il potere sovrano e la nuda vita.* Turin: G. Einaudi, 1995. English translation by Daniel Heller-Roazen, *Homo Sacer: Sovereign Power and Bare Life.* Stanford: Stanford University Press, 1998.

Aitken, Ellen Bradshaw. "τὰ δρώμενα καὶ τὰ λεγόμενα: The Eucharistic Memory of Jesus' Words in First Corinthians." *HTR* 90.4 (1997): 359–70.

Alexander, Elizabeth Shanks. *Transmitting Mishnah: The Shaping Influence of Oral Tradition.* Cambridge: Cambridge University Press, 2006.

Alexander, Loveday. *Acts in Its Ancient Literary Context.* JSNTSup 298. London: T. & T. Clark, 2006.

Algra, Keimpe. "Stoic Theology." In *The Cambridge Companion to the Stoics.* Edited by Brad Inwood, 153–78. Cambridge: Cambridge University Press, 2003.

Alzinger, William and Dieter Knibbe. "Ephesos vom Beginn der römischen Herrschaft in Kleinasien bis zum Ende der Principatszeit." *ANRW* II.7.2 (1980): 748–830.

Amaru, Betsy Halpern. "The Killing of the Prophets: Unraveling a Midrash." *HUCA* 54 (1983): 153–80.

Ando, Clifford. *The Matter of the Gods: Religion and the Roman Empire.* Berkeley: University of California Press, 2008.

Arafat, Karim. *Classical Zeus: A Study in Art and Literature.* Oxford: Oxford University Press, 1990.

Armstrong, A. H. "Pagan and Christian Traditionalism in the First Three Centuries." *Studia Patristica* 15 (1984): 414–31.

Asad, Talal. *Genealogies of Religion: Discipline and Reasons of Power in Christianity and Islam.* Baltimore: Johns Hopkins University Press, 1993.

———. "Religion, Nation-State, Secularism." In *Nation and Religion: Perspectives on Europe and Asia.* Edited by Peter van der Veer and Hartmut Lehman, 178–96. Princeton: Princeton University Press, 1999.

Ascough, Richard S. "Benefaction Gone Wrong: The 'Sin' of Ananias and Sapphira in Context." In *Text and Artifact in the Religions of Mediterranean Antiquity: Essays in Honour of Peter Richardson.* Edited by Stephen G. Wilson and Michel Desjardins. Studies in Christianity and Judaism 9. Waterloo: Wilfrid Laurier University Press, 2000.

Athanassiadi, Polymnia, and Michael Frede. Introduction to *Pagan Monotheism in Late Antiquity.* Edited by Polymnia Athanassiadi and Michael Frede, 7–10. Oxford: Clarendon, 1999.

Attridge, Harold W. *The Epistle to the Hebrews.* Hermeneia Commentary Series. Philadelphia: Fortress, 1989.

———. "The Philosophical Critique of Religion under the Early Empire." *ANRW* II.16.1 (1978): 45–78.

Avemarie, Friedrich, trans. *Yoma-Versöhnungstag.* Übersetzung des Talmud Yerushalmi 2.4. Tübingen: Mohr Siebeck, 1995.

Bagnall, Roger S., and James B. Rives. "A Prefect's Edict Mentioning Sacrifice." *Archiv für Religionsgeschichte* 2.1 (2000): 77–86.

Balibar, Etienne. "Race as Universalism." In *Masses, Classes, Ideas: Studies on Politics and Philosophy before and after Marx 191–209*. New York: Routledge, 1994.

Barb, A. A. "St. Zacharias the Prophet and Martyr: A Study in Charms and Incantations." *Journal of the Warburg and Courtauld Institutes* 11 (1948): 35–67.

Barnes, Jonathan, and Miriam Griffin, eds. *The Roman Near East 31 B.C.–A.D. 337*. Cambridge: Harvard University Press, 1993.

Barnes, Timothy D. "Porphyry against the Christians: Date and Attribution of the Fragments." *Journal of Theological Studies* 24 (1973): 424–42.

———. "Was There a Constantinian Revolution?" Review article. *Journal of Late Antiquity* 2.2 (2009): 375–76.

———. "Scholarship or Propaganda? Porphyry against the Christians and Its Historical Setting." *BICS* 39 (1994): 53–65.

Barrett, C. K. *A Critical and Exegetical Commentary on the Acts of the Apostles*. Vol. 1: Preliminary Introduction and Commentary on Acts I–XIV. NICC 34. Edinburgh: T. & T. Clark, 1994.

Barrett, Justin. "Gods." In *Religion, Anthropology, and Cognitive Science*. Edited by Harvey Whitehouse and James Laidlaw, 179–207. Durham: Carolina Academic Press, 2007.

Barton, Carlin. "The Emotional Economy of Sacrifice and Execution in Ancient Rome." *Historical Reflections/Reflexions Historiques* 29 (2003): 341–60.

———. "Honor and Sacredness in the Roman and Christian Worlds." In *Sacrificing the Self: Perspectives on Martyrdom and Religion*. Edited by Margaret Cormack, 23–38. New York: Oxford University Press, 2001.

———. *Roman Honor: The Fire in the Bones*. Berkeley: University of California Press, 2001.

Barton, Tamsyn. *Ancient Astrology*. Sciences of Antiquity. London: Routledge, 1994.

Batsch, Christophe. "Le herem de guerre dans le judaïsme du deuxième temple." In *La Cuisine et l'autel: Les sacrifices en questions dans les sociétés de la méditerranée ancienne*. Edited by Stella Georgoudi, Renée Koch Piettre, and Francis Schmidt 101–11. BEHE SR 124. Turnhout: Brepols, 2005.

Baynes, Norman. "The Great Persecution." *Cambridge Ancient History*. Vol. 12, *The Imperial Crisis and Recovery*. Edited by S. A. Cook, F. E. Adcock, Mp. P. Charlesworth, and Norman H. Baynes, 646–77. Cambridge: Cambridge University Press, 1939.

Beagon, Mary. *The Elder Pliny on the Human Animal*. Natural History Book 7. Oxford: Clarendon, 2005.

Beard, Mary, John North, and Simon Price. *Religions of Rome, 1: A History*. Cambridge: Cambridge University Press, 1998.

Belayche, Nicole. "Religion et consummation de la viande dans le monde romaine: Des réalités voiles." *Food and History* 5.1 (2007): 29–43.

———. "Sacrifice and Theory of Sacrifice during the 'Pagan Reaction': Julian the Emperor." In *Sacrifice in Religious Experience*. Numen Supplements 93. Edited by Albert I. Baumgarten. Leiden: Brill, 2002.

Bell, Catherine. *Ritual: Perspectives and Dimensions*. New York: Oxford University Press, 1997.

———. *Ritual Theory, Ritual Practice*. New York: Oxford University Press, 1992.

Bendlin, Andreas. "Looking beyond the Civic Compromise: Religious Pluralism in Late Republican Rome." In *Religion in Archaic and Republican Rome and Italy: Evidence and*

Experience. Edited by Edward Bispham and Christopher Smith, 115–35. Edinburgh: University of Edinburgh, 2000.

Bengtson, Herman. *Die Verträge der griechisch-römischen Welt von 700 bis 338 v. Chr.* Vol. 2 of *Des Staatsverträge des Altertums.* Edited by Hermann Bengtson. Munich: C. H. Beck 1962.

Beness, Lea. "The Punishment of the Gracchani and the Execution of C. Villius in 133/132." *Antichthon* 34 (2000): 1–17.

Berger, Peter L. "Charisma and Religious Innovation: The Social Location of Israelite Prophecy." *American Sociological Review* 28.6 (1963): 940–50.

Bernabé, Albert, ed. *Poetarum epicorum Graecorum: Testimonia et fragmenta.* 2 vols. BT. Leipzig: Teubner, 1987–2000.

Bernard, Wolfgang. *Spätantike Dichtung-theorien Untersuchungen zu Proklos, Herakleitos und Plutarch.* Stuttgart: Teubner, 1990.

Berthelot, Katell. "Jewish Views of Human Sacrifice in the Hellenistic and Roman Period." In *Human Sacrifice in Jewish and Christian Tradition.* Edited by Karin Finsterbusch et al. Leiden: Brill, 2007.

Betz, Hans Dieter. *Lukian von Samosata und das Neue Testament: Religionsgeschichtliche und Paränetische Parallelen.* TU 76. Berlin: Akademie-Verlag, 1961.

Bhabha, Homi. *The Location of Culture.* London: Routledge, 1994.

Biale, David. *Blood and Belief: The Circulation of a Symbol between Jews and Christians.* Berkeley: University of California Press, 2007.

Blank, Sheldon H. "The Curse, Blasphemy, the Spell, and the Oath." *HUCA* 23 (1950–1951): 73–95.

———. "The Death of Zechariah in Rabbinic Literature." *HUCA* 12–13 (1937–1938): 327–46.

Blenkinsopp, Joseph. *A History of Prophecy in Israel.* Rev. and enlarged ed. Louisville: Westminster John Knox, 1996.

Bloch, Philipp von. "Rom und die Mystiker der Merkabah." In *Festschrift zum siebzigsten Geburtstage Jakob Guttmanns,* 113–32. Leipzig: Gustav Fock, 1915.

Boatwright, Mary. *Hadrian and the Cities of the Roman Empire.* Princeton: Princeton University Press, 2000.

Boedeker, Deborah. "Domestic Religion in Classical Greece." In *Household and Family Religion in Antiquity.* Edited by John Bodel and Saul M. Olyan, 29–47. London: Blackwell, 2008.

Bouanich, Catherine. "Mise à mort rituelle de l'animal. Offrande carnée dans le temple égyptien." In *La Cuisine et l'autel: Les sacrifices en questions dans les sociétés de la méditerranée ancienne.* Edited by Stella Georgoudi, Renée Koch Piettre, and Francis Schmidt 149–62. BEHE SR124. Turnhout: Brepols, 2005.

Bourdieu, Pierre. *The Field of Cultural Production.* New York: Columbia University Press, 1993.

———. "Genesis and Structure of the Religious Field." *Comparative Social Research.* Edited by C. Calhoun. 13 (1991): 1–44.

———. "Legitimation and Structured Interests in Weber's Sociology of Religion." In *Max Weber: Rationality and Modernity.* Edited by Scott Lash and Sam Whimster, 119–36. London: Allen and Unwin, 1987.

———. *Outline of a Theory of Practice.* Cambridge: Cambridge University Press, 1977.

———. *The Rules of Art: Genesis and Structure of the Literary Field.* Cambridge: Polity, 1996.

Boustan, Ra'anan S. *From Martyr to Mystic: Rabbinic Martyrology and the Making of Merkavah Mysticism.* TSAJ 112. Tübingen: Mohr, 2005.

————. "Immolating Emperors: Spectacles of Imperial Suffering and the Making of a Jewish Minority Culture in Late Antiquity." *Biblical Interpretation* 17 (2009): 207–38.

Boustan, Ra'anan S., and Annette Yoshiko Read, eds. "Blood and the Boundaries of Jewish and Christian Identities in Late Antiquity." *Henoch* 30 (2008): 229–364.

Bowerstock, Glen. *Martyrdom and Rome.* Cambridge: Cambridge University Press, 1995.

Bowes, Kim. *Private Worship, Public Values and Religious Change in Late Antiquity.* Cambridge: Cambridge University Press, 2008.

Boyarin, Daniel. *Carnal Israel: Reading Sex in Talmudic Culture.* Berkeley: University of California Press, 1993.

————. *Dying for God: Martyrdom and the Making of Christianity and Judaism.* Figurae: Reading Medieval Culture. Stanford: Stanford University Press, 1999.

————. *A Radical Jew: Paul and the Politics of Identity.* Berkeley: University of California Press, 1994.

————. "Rethinking Jewish Christianity: An Argument for Dismantling a Dubious Category (to Which Is Appended a Correction of My *Border Lines*)." *JQR* 99 (2009): 7–36.

Boyer, Pascal. *Religion Explained: The Evolutionary Origins of Religious Thought.* New York: Basic Books, 2001.

————. "Why Do Gods and Spirits Matter at All?" In *Current Approaches in the Cognitive Science of Religion.* Edited by Ilkka Pyyiäinen and Veikko Anttonen, 68–92. London: Contiuum, 2002.

Boys-Stones, G. R. *Metaphor Allegory and the Classical Tradition.* Oxford: Oxford University Press, 2003.

Bradbury, Scott. "Constantine and the Problem of Anti-Pagan Legislation in the Fourth Century." *Classical Philology* 89 (1994): 120–39.

————. "Julian's Pagan Revival and the Decline of Blood Sacrifice." *Phoenix* 49 (1995): 331–56.

Branham, Joan. "Mapping Sacrifice on Bodies and Spaces in Ancient Judaism and Early Christianity." In *Constructions of Sanctity: Ritual and Sacred Space in Mediterranean Architecture from Classical Greece to Byzantium.* Edited by Bonna Wescoat and Robert Ousterhout. New York: Cambridge University Press, forthcoming.

————. "Women as Objects of Sacrifice? An Early Christian 'Chancel of the Virgins.'" In *La cuisine et l'autel: Les sacrifices en questions dans les sociétés de la Méditerranée ancienne.* Edited by Stella Georgoudi, Renée Piettre, and Francis Schmidt 371–86. BEHE SR124. Turnhout: Brepols, 2006.

Bremmer, Jan. *Greek Religion.* Greece and Rome: New Surveys in the Classics 24. Oxford: Oxford University Press, 2003.

————. "Human Sacrifice: A Brief Introduction." In *The Strange World of Human Sacrifice.* Edited by Jan N. Bremmer. Leuven, Belgium: Peeters, 2007.

————, ed. *The Strange World of Human Sacrifice.* Leuven Belgium: Peeters, 2007.

Brilliant, Richard. *Visual Narrative: Storytelling in Etruscan and Roman Art.* Ithaca: Cornell University Press, 1984.

Brown, Paul B. "The Meaning and Function of Acts 5:1–11 in the Purpose of Luke–Acts." Ph.D. diss., Boston University, 1969.

Brown, Peter. "Christianization and Religious Conflict." *Cambridge Ancient History*. Vol. 13, *The Late Empire A.D. 337–425*. Edited by Averil Cameron and Peter Garnsey, 632–64. Cambridge: Cambridge University Press, 1998.

———. "The Rise and Function of the Holy Man in Late Antiquity." In Brown, *Society and the Holy in Late Antiquity*, 103–52. London: Faber and Faber, 1982.

Brunt, P. A. "Philosophy and Religion in the Late Republic." In *Philosophia Togata: Essays on Philosophy and Roman Society*. Edited by Miriam Griffin and Jonathan Barnes, 174–98. New York: Clarendon, 1989.

Buchler, Justus, ed. *Philosophical Writings of Pierce.* New York: Dover, 1955.

Buell, Denise Kimber. *Why This New Race: Ethnic Reasoning in Early Christianity*. New York: Columbia University Press, 2005.

Burkert, Walter. *Ancient Mystery Cults.* Cambridge: Harvard University Press, 1987.

———. Interpretationen altgriechischer geschichtliche *Greek Religion*. Translated by John Raffan. Cambridge: Harvard University Press, 1985.

———. *Homo Necans: Interpretationen altgriechischer Opferriten und Mythen*. Religions -geschictliche Versuche und Vorarbeiten 32. Berlin: De Gruyter, 1972. English translation by Peter Bing. *Homo Necans: The Anthropology of Ancient Greek Sacrificial Ritual and Myth*. Berkeley: University of California Press, 1983.

———. *Lore and Science in Ancient Pythagoreanism*. Translated by E. L. Minar, Jr. Cambridge: Harvard University Press, 1972. First published as *Weisheit und Wissenschaft: Studien zu Pythagoras, Philolaos und Platon*. Nuremberg: Hans Carl, 1962.

Burnett, Anne Pippin. *Revenge in Attic and Later Tragedy*. Berkeley: University of California Press, 1998.

Burrus, Virginia. *"Begotten, Not Made": Conceiving Manhood in Late Antiquity.* Figurae: Reading Medieval Culture. Stanford: Stanford University Press, 2000.

———. "Mimicking Virgins: Colonial Ambivalence and the Ancient Romance." *Arethusa* 38 (2005): 49–88.

———. *Saving Shame: Martyrs, Saints, and Other Abject Subjects*. Divinations. Philadelphia: University of Pennsylvania Press, 2008.

Butler, Judith. "Restaging the Universal: Hegemony and the Limits of Formalism." In *Contingency, Hegemony, Universality: Contemporary Dialogues on the Left*. Edited by Judith Butler, Ernesto Laclau, and Slavoj Žižek. London: Verso, 2000.

Cameron, Alan. "The Imperial Pontifex." *HSCP* 103 (2007): 341–85.

———. *The Last Pagans of Rome.* New York: Oxford University Press, 2010.

———. "Pagan Ivories." In *Colloque genevois sur Symmaque à l'occasion du mille six centième anniversaire du conflit de l'autel de la Victoire*. Edited by G. W. Bowerstock. Published by François Paschoud in collaboration with G. Fry and Y. Rütsche. Paris: Les Belles Lettres, 1986.

Cameron, Averil. "Byzantines and Jews: Some Recent Work on Early Byzantium." *Byzantine and Modern Greek Studies* 26 (1996): 249–74.

———. "Disputations, Polemical Literature, and the Formation of Opinion in Early Byzantine Literature." In *Dispute Poems and Dialogues in the Ancient and Medieval Near East*. Edited by G. J. Reinink and H.J.L. Vanstiphout, 91–108. Orientalia Lovaniensia Analecta 42. Leuven, Belgium: Peeters, 1991.

———. "How to Read Heresiology." In *The Cultural Turn in Late Ancient Studies: Gender, Asceticism, and Historiography*. Edited by Dale B. Martin and Patricia Cox Miller. Durham: Duke University Press, 2005.

————. "Jews and Heretics—A Category Error?" In *The Ways That Never Parted: Jews and Christians in Late Antiquity and the Early Middle Ages*. Edited by Annette Yoshiko Reed and Adam H. Becker. Texts and Studies in Ancient Judaism 96. Tübingen: Mohr Siebeck, 2003.

Campbell, Colin. "A Dubious Distinction? An Inquiry into the Value and Use of Merton's Concepts of Manifest and Latent Function." *American Sociological Review* 47.1 (1982): 29–44.

Capper, Brian J. "The Interpretation of Acts 5.4." *JSNT* 19 (1983): 117–31.

Carter, Jeffrey, ed. *Understanding Religious Sacrifice: A Reader*. New York: Continuum, 2003.

Cartledge, Tony W. *Vows in the Hebrew Bible and the Ancient Near East*. JSOTSup 147. Sheffield: Sheffield Academic Press, 1992.

Castelli, Elizabeth A. *Martyrdom and Memory: Early Christian Culture Making.* Gender, Theory, Religion. New York: Columbia University Press, 2004.

Caster, Marcel. *Lucien et la pensée religieuse de son temps.* Collection d'études anciennes. Paris: Les Belles Lettres, 1937.

Castiglione, Ladislas. "Greichisch-ägyptische Studien: Beitrag zu dem griechisch-ägyptischen Privatkult." *Acta antiqua hungaricae* 5 (1957): 220–27.

Caughie, Pamela L. *Passing and Pedagogy: The Dynamics of Responsibility*. Urbana: University of Illinois Press, 1999.

Chadwick, Henry. *The Sentences of Sextus: A Contribution to the History of Early Christian Ethics*. Texts and Studies 5. Cambridge: Cambridge University Press, 1959.

Chakrabarty, Dipesh. *Provincializing Europe: Postcolonial Thought and Historical Difference*. Princeton: Princeton University Press, 2000.

Charron, Alain. "Massacres d'animaux à la Basse Époque." *Revue d'Égyptologie* 41 (1990): 209–13.

Chatterjee, Partha. *Nationalist Thought and the Colonial World: A Derivative Discourse*. Minneapolis: University of Minnesota Press, 1993.

Chepey, Stuart. *Nazirites in Late Second Temple Judaism*. Ancient Judaism and Early Christianity 60. Leiden: Brill, 2005.

Chilton, Bruce. *Rabbi Jesus: An Intimate Biography*. New York: Doubleday, 2000.

Choat, Malcolm. *Belief and Cult in Fourth-Century Papyri*. Turnhout: Brepols, 2006.

Clark, A. J. "Nasica and Fides." *Classical Quarterly* 57 (2007): 125–31.

Clark, Gillian. "Augustine's Porphyry." In *Studies on Porphyry*. Edited by George Karamanolis and Anne Sheppard 127–40. BICS Supplement 98. London: Institute of Classical Studies, School of Advanced Study, University of London, 2007.

————. "Translate into Greek." In *Constructing Identities in Late Antiquity*. 112–32 Edited by Richard Miles. London: Routledge, 1999.

Coarelli, Filippo. *The Column of Trajan*. Translated by Cynthia Rockwell. Rome: Editore Colombo in collaboration with the German Archaeological Institute, 2000.

Cohen, Shaye J. D. "A Brief History of Jewish Circumcision Blood." In *The Covenant of Circumcision: New Perspectives on an Ancient Jewish Rite.* Edited by E. W. Mark, 30–42. Hanover: Brandeis University Press, 2003.

————. "The Destruction: From Scripture to Midrash." *Prooftexts* 2 (1982): 18–39.

————. *Why Aren't Jewish Women Circumcised? Gender and Covenant in Judaism.* Berkeley: University of California Press, 2005.

Cole, Susan Guettel. *Landscapes, Gender, and Ritual Space: The Ancient Greek Experience.* Berkeley: University of California Press, 2004.

―――. *Placing the Gods: Sanctuaries and Sacred Space in Ancient Greece.* Oxford: Clarendon, 1994.

Collins, Billie Jean. "The First Soldiers' Oath (1.66)" and "The Second Soldiers' Oath (1.67)." In *The Context of Scripture.* Vol. 1. Canonical Compositions from the Biblical World. Edited by William W. Hallo. Leiden: Brill, 1997.

Concannon, Cavan. "*Ecclesia Laus Corinthiensis Conntiensis*: Negotiating Ethnicity under Empire." Ph.D. diss., Committee on the Study of Religion, Harvard University, 2010.

Conzelmann, Hans. *Acts of the Apostles: A Commentary on the Acts of the Apostles.* Translated by James Limburg, A. Thomas Kraabel, and Donald H. Juel. Hermeneia Commentary Series. Philadelphia: Fortress, 1987.

Cook, John Granger. *The Interpretation of the New Testament in Greco-Roman Paganism.* Tübingen: Mohr Siebeck, 2000. Repr., Peabody, Mass.: Hendrickson, 2002.

Coulton, J. J. "Pedestals as 'Altars' in Roman Asia Minor." *Anatolian Studies* 55 (2005): 127–57.

Crawford, Michael H. *Roman Republican Coinage.* 2 vols. Rev. and corrected ed. London: Cambridge University Press, 2001.

Dagron, G., and V. Déroche. "Juifs et Chrétiens dans l'Orient du VIIe siècle." *Travaux et Mémoires* 11 (1991): 17–273.

Davidson, J. N. *Courtesans and Fishcakes: The Consuming Passions of Classical Athens.* New York: HarperCollins, 1997.

Davis-Floyd, Robbie. "Rituals." In *International Encyclopedia of the Social Sciences.* 2nd ed. Edited by William A. Dantry, Jr. (editor in chief) et al. New York: Thomson Gale, 2008.

De Ste. Croix, G.E.M. "Aspects of the Great Persecution." In *Christian Persecution, Martyrdom and Orthodoxy.* Edited by Michael Whitby and Joseph Streeter. Oxford: Oxford University Press, 2006.

De Vaux, Roland. *Studies in Old Testament Sacrifice.* Cardiff: University of Wales Press, 1964.

Dench, Emma. *Romulus' Asylum: Roman Identities from the Age of Alexander to the Age of Hadrian.* Oxford: Oxford University Press, 2005.

Derchain, Philippe. "De l'holocauste au barbecue: Les avatars d'un sacrifice." Göttinger Miszellen 213 (2007): 19–22.

Déroche, V. "Polémique anti-judaïque et émergence de l'Islam (7e–8e siècles)." *Revue des Études Byzantines* 57 (1999): 141–61.

―――. "La polémique anti-judaïque au VIe et au VIIe siècle, un mémento inédit, les Kephalaia." *Travaux et Mémoires* 11 (1991): 275–311.

Detienne, Marcel. *Dionysos mis à mort.* Paris: Gallimard, 1977.

―――. *Les jardins d'Adonis.* Paris: Gallimard, 1972.

Detienne, Marcel, and Jean-Pierre Vernant, eds. *Le cuisine du sacrifice en pays grec.* Paris: Gallimard, 1979. English translation by Paula Wissing. *The Cuisine of Sacrifice among the Greeks.* Chicago: University of Chicago Press, 1989.

Dever, William G. *Did God Have a Wife? Archaeology and Folk Religion in Ancient Israel.* Grand Rapids: William B. Eedrmans, 2005.

Digeser, Elizabeth DePalma. *The Making of a Christian Empire: Lactantius and Rome.* Ithaca: Cornell University Press, 2000.

Dillon, J. T. "Iamblichus' Defence of Theurgy: Some Reflections." *International Journal of the Platonic Tradition* 1 (2007): 30–41.

Dillon, M.P.J. "'Xenophon Sacrificed on Account of an Expedition': Divination and the *sphagia* before Ancient Greek Battles." In *Le sacrifice antique: Vestiges, procédures, et stratégies.* Edited by Véronique Mehl and Pierre Brulé, 235–51. Rennes: Presses Universitaires de Rennes, 2008.

Dillon, Sheila. "Women on the Columns of Trajan and Marcus Aurelius and the Visual Language of Roman Victory." In *Representation of War in Ancient Rome.* Edited by Sheila Dillon and Katherine E. Welch. Cambridge: Cambridge University Press, 2006.

Douglas, Mary. "Atonement in Leviticus." *Jewish Studies Quarterly* 1.2 (1993–1994): 109–30.

———. *Leviticus as Literature.* Oxford: Oxford University Press, 1999.

———. *Natural Symbols: Explorations in Cosmology.* Routledge Classics edition, with a new introduction. London: Routledge, 2003.

———. *Purity and Danger: An Analysis of the Concepts of Pollution and Taboo.* London: Routledge and Kegan Paul, 1966.

Drake, H. A. "Lambs into Lions: Explaining Early Christian Intolerance." *Past and Present* 153 (1996): 33–36.

Dubois, Jean-Daniel. "La mort de Zacharie: Mémoire juive et mémoire chrétienne." *Revue des Études Augustiniennes* 40 (1994): 23–38.

Dunand, Françoise. *Religion populaire en Égypte romaine.* Études preliminaries aux religions orientales dans l'empire 77. Leiden: Brill, 1979.

Dunand, Françoise, and Roger Lichtenberg. "Des chiens momifiés à El-Deir Oasis de Kharga." *BIFAO* 105 (2005): 75–87.

Dunn, Geoffrey. "Mary's Virginity *in partu* and Tertullian's Anti-Docetism in *De carne Christi* Reconsidered." *Journal of Theological Studies* n.s. 58 (2007): 467–84.

———. "Rhetoric and Tertullian's *de virginibus velandis.*" *Vigiliae Christianae* 59 (2005): 1–30.

———. *Tertullian.* Early Church Fathers. London: Routledge, 2004.

Dunn, James D. G. "Paul's Understanding of the Death of Jesus as Sacrifice." In *Sacrifice and Redemption: Durham Essays in Theology.* Edited by S. Sykes, 35–56. Cambridge: Cambridge University Press, 1991.

Durand, Jean-Louis. "Greek Animals: Toward a Topology of Edible Bodies." In *Le cuisine du sacrifice en pays grec.* Paris: Gallimard, 1979. English translation by Paula Wissing, 87–118. In *The Cuisine of Sacrifice among the Greeks.* Chicago: University of Chicago Press, 1989.

Durkheim, Émile. *Les formes élémentaires de la vie religieuse, le système totémique en Australie.* Paris: Presses Universitaires de France, 1912. English translation by Joseph Ward Swain. *The Elementary Forms of Religious Life.* New York: Free Press, 1965.

Eaton, Katherine. "Types of Cult-Image Carried in Divine Barques and the Logistics of Performing Temple Ritual in the New Kingdom." *Zeitschrift für ägyptische Sprache und Altertumskunde* 134 (2007): 15–25.

Eberhart, Christian A. "Characteristics of Sacrificial Metaphors in Hebrews." In *Hebrews: Contemporary Methods–New Insights.* Edited by G. Gerlardini, 37–64. Leiden: Brill, 2005.

Edelstein, Ludwig. *Ancient Medicine.* Edited by Owsei Temkin and C. Lilian Temkin. Baltimore: Johns Hopkins University Press, 1987.

Edwards, Catharine, and Greg Woolf. "Cosmopolis: Rome as World City." In *Rome the Cosmopolis*. Edited by Catharine Edwards and Greg Woolf 1–20. Cambridge: Cambridge University Press, 2006.

Edwards, Mark. *Culture and Philosophy in the Age of Plotinus*. London: Duckworth, 2006.

Ehrman, Bart D. *Jesus: Apocalyptic Prophet of the New Millennium*. New York: Oxford University Press, 1999.

Ekroth, Gunnel. "Burnt, Cooked or Raw? Divine and Human Culinary Desires at Greek Animal Sacrifice." In *Transformations in Sacrificial Practices from Antiquity to Modern Times*. Edited by Eftychia Stavrianopoulou, Axel Michaels, and Claus Ambo, 87–111. Berlin: Lit, 2008.

———. *The Sacrificial Rituals of Greek Hero-Cults in the Archaic to Early Hellenistic Periods*. Liege: Centre International d'Étude de la Religion Grecque Antique, 2002.

El-Nassery, S.A.A., and Guy Wagner. "Nouvelles stèles de Kom Abu Bellou." *BIFAO* 78 (1978): 24–29.

Elizur, S. *Wherefore Have We Fasted? Megillat Ta'anit Batra and Similar Lists of Fasts* (Hebrew). Jerusalem: Magnes, 2006.

Eriksen, Thomas. *Ethnicity and Nationalism*. London: Pluto Press, 1993.

Errington, R. Malcolm. "Christian Accounts of the Religious Legislation of Theodosius I." *Klio* 79 (1997): 410–35.

Esler, Philip F. *Community and Gospel in Luke–Acts: The Social and Political Motivations of Lucan Theology*. SNTSMS 57. Cambridge: Cambridge University Press, 1987.

Evans-Pritchard, E. E. *Theories of Primitive Religion*. Oxford: Clarendon Press, 1965.

Faraone, Christopher A. "Household Religion in Ancient Greece." In *Household and Family Religion in Antiquity*. Edited by John Bodel and Saul M. Olyan, 210–28. London: Blackwell, 2008.

Faraone, Christopher A. "Molten Wax, Spilt Wine and Mutilated Animals: Sympathetic Magic in Near Eastern and Early Greek Ceremonies." *JHS* 113 (1993): 60–80.

Faraone, Christopher A., and F. S. Naiden, eds. *Ancient Victims, Modern Observers: Reflections on Greek and Roman Animal Sacrifice*. Cambridge: Cambridge University Press, forthcoming.

Faraone, Christopher A., and Dirk Obbink, eds. *Magika Hiera: Ancient Greek Magic and Religion*. New York: Oxford University Press, 1991.

Fardon, Richard. *Mary Douglas: An Intellectual Biography*. London: Routledge, 1999.

Feeney, Denis. *Literature and Religion at Rome: Cultures, Contexts and Beliefs*. Cambridge: Cambridge University Press, 1988.

Feldherr, A. *Spectacle and Society in Livy's History*. Berkeley: University of California Press, 1998.

Fensham, Charles. "Malediction and Benediction in Ancient Near Eastern Vassal-Treaties and the Old Testament." *ZAW* 74 (1963): 1–9.

Ferguson, Everett. "Spiritual Sacrifice in Early Christianity and Its Environment." *ANRW* II.2 (1980): 1152–89.

Finlan, Stephen. *The Background and Content of Paul's Cultic Atonement Metaphors*. Academia Biblica 19. Atlanta: Society of Biblical Literature, 2004.

Finnestad, Ragnhild Bjerre. "Temples of the Ptolemaic and Roman Periods: Ancient Traditions in New Contexts." In *Temples of Ancient Egypt*. Edited by Byron E. Shafer, 207–17. Ithaca: Cornell University Press, 1997.

Finsterbusch, Karin, Armin Lange, and K. F. Deithard Römheld, eds. *Human Sacrifice in Jewish and Christian Tradition.* Numen 112. Leiden: Brill, 2007.

Fiori, Roberto. *Homo Sacer: Dinamica politico-costituzionale di una sanzione giuridico-religiosa.* Naples: Jovene, 1996.

Fischel, H. A. "Martyr and Prophet (A Study in Jewish Literature)." *JQR* 37 (1947): 265–80, 363–86.

Fishbane, Michael. *The Exegetical Imagination: On Jewish Thought and Theology.* Cambridge: Cambridge University Press, 1998.

Fitzmyer, Joseph A. *The Acts of the Apostles: A New Translation with Introduction and Commentary.* AB. New York: Doubleday, 1998.

Flower, Harriet I. *The Art of Forgetting: Disgrace and Oblivion in Roman Political Culture.* Chapel Hill: University of North Carolina Press, 2006.

Fortenbaugh, W. W. "Theophrastus: Piety, Justice and Animals." In Fortenbaugh, *Theophrastean Studies.* Philosophie der Antike 7. Stuttgart: Franz Steiner, 2003.

Fraade, Steven D. "The Temple as a Marker of Jewish Identity before and after 70 C.E.: The Role of the Holy Vessels in Rabbinic Memory and Imagination." In *Jewish Identities in Antiquity: Studies in Memory of Menahem Stern.* Edited by L. I. Levine and D. R. Swartz, 235–63. Tübingen: Mohr Siebeck, 2009.

Frankenberry, Nancy K., and Hans H. Penner. "Clifford Geertz's Long-Lasting Moods, Motivations, and Metaphysical Conceptions." *Journal of Religion* 79 (1999): 617–40.

Frankfurter, David. "Illuminating the Cult of Kothos: The Panegryic on Macarius and Local Religion in Fifth-Century Egypt." In *The World of Early Egyptian Christianity: Language, Literature, and Social Context.* Edited by James E. Goehring and Janet A. Timbie 176–88. Washington D.C.: Catholic University of America Press, 2007.

———. "On Sacrifice and Residues: Processing the Potent Body." In *Religion in Cultural Discourse.* Edited by Brigitte Luchesi and Kocku von Stuckrad 511–33. Religionsgeschichtliche Versuche und Vorarbeiten 52. Berlin: De Gruyter, 2004.

———. *Religion in Roman Egypt: Assimilation and Resistance.* Princeton: Princeton University Press, 1998.

———. "Religion, Violence, and the Bible." In *Religion and Violence: The Biblical Heritage.* Edited by David A. Bernat and Jonathan Klawans 114–28. Sheffield: Sheffield Phoenix Press, 2007.

———. "Review of Rituals and Ritual Theory in Ancient Israel." *Association for Jewish Studies Review* 29 (2005): 163–65.

———. "Ritual as Accusation and Atrocity: Satanic Ritual Abuse, Gnostic Libertinism, and Primal Murders." *History of Religions* 40.4 (2001): 352–80.

Frazer, James G. *The Golden Bough.* 2 vols. London: Macmillan, 1890. Revised in 3 vols., London: Macmillan, 1900. Revised in 12 vols., London: Macmillian 1911–1915. Revised and abridged in 1 vol., London: Macmillan, 1927.

Frede, Michael. "Monotheism and Pagan Philosophy in Later Antiquity." In *Pagan Monotheism in Late Antiquity.* Edited by Polymnia Athanassiadi and Michael Frede 41–68. Oxford: Clarendon, 1999.

Fredriksen, Paula. *Augustine and the Jews: A Christian Defense of Jews and Judaism.* New York: Doubleday, 2008.

———. "Did Jesus Oppose the Purity Laws?" *Bible Review* 11.3 (1995): 20–25, 42–47.

———. *From Jesus to Christ: The Origins of the New Testament Images of Jesus.* New Haven: Yale University Press, 1988.

———. *Jesus of Nazareth: King of the Jews.* New York: Vintage, 1999.

———. "Mandatory Retirement: Ideas in the Study of Christian Origins Whose Time Has Come to Go." *Studies in Religion/Sciences Religieuses* 35.2 (2006): 231–46.

Freud, Sigmund. *The Interpretation of Dreams.* Translated by James Strachey. New York: Avon Books, 1965.

———. *Totem und Tabu: Cinige Übereinstimmungen im Seelenleben der Wilden und der Neurotiker.* Leipzig: H. Heller, 1913. English translation by A. A. Brill. *Totem and Taboo: Resemblances between the Psychic Lives of Savages and Neurotics.* London: Routledge, 1919.

Friesen, Steve. *Twice Neokoros: Ephesus, Asia and the Cult of the Flavian Imperial Family.* Leiden: Brill, 1993.

Frilingos, Christopher. *Spectacles of Empire: Monsters, Martyrs, and the Book of Revelation.* Divinations. Philadelphia: University of Pennsylvania Press, 2004.

Gaddis, Michael. *There Is No Crime for Those Who Have Christ: Religious Violence in the Christian Roman Empire.* Berkeley: University of California Press, 2005.

Gager, John. *Curse Tablets and Binding Spells from the Ancient World.* New York: Oxford University Press, 1992.

Gallazzi, Claudio, and Gisèle Hadji-Minaglou. *Tebtynis I: La reprise des fouilles et le quartier de la chapelle d'Isis-Thermouthis.* Cairo: Institut Français d'Archéologie Orientale, 2000.

Gamble, Harry Y. "Marcion and the 'Canon.'" In *The Cambridge History of Christianity.* Vol. 1. *Origins to Constantine.* Edited by Margaret M. Mitchell and Frances M. Young. Cambridge: Cambridge University Press, 2006.

Gane, Roy E. *Cult and Character: Purification Offerings, Day of Atonement, and Theodicy.* Winona Lake, Ind.: Eisenbrauns, 2005.

Geertz, Clifford. *The Interpretation of Cultures: Selected Essays.* New York: Basic Books, 1973.

———. *Islam Observed: Religious Development in Morocco and Indonesia.* Chicago: University of Chicago Press, 1968.

Georgoudi, Stella. "L''Occultation de la violence' dans le sacrifice grec." In *La cuisine et l'autel: Les sacrifices en questions dans les sociétés de la Méditerranée ancienne.* Edited by Stella Georgoudi, Renée Piettre, and Francis Schmidt, 115–41. BEHE SR124. Turnhout: Brepols, 2005.

———. "Sanctified Slaughter in Modern Greece: The 'Kourbáni' of the Saints." In *The Cuisine of Sacrifice among the Greeks.* Edited by Marcel Détienne and Jean-Pierre Vernant. Translated by Paula Wissing 183–203. Chicago: University of Chicago Press, 1989.

Georgoudi, Stella, Renée Piettre, and Francis Schmidt, eds. *La cuisine et l'autel: Les sacrifices en questions dans les sociétés de la Méditerranée ancienne.* BEHE SR124. Turnhout: Brepols, 2005.

Gilders, William K. "Blood and Covenant: Interpretive Elaboration on Genesis 9.4–6 in the Book of Jubilees." *Journal for the Study of the Pseudepigrapha* 15 (2006): 83–118.

———. "Blood as Purificant in Priestly Torah: What Do We Know and How Do We Know It?" In *Perspectives on Purity and Purification in the Bible.* Edited by Baruch J. Schwartz, David P. Wright, Jeffrey Stackert, and Naphtali S. Meshel, 77–83. London: T. & T. Clark International, 2008.

———. *Blood Ritual in the Hebrew Bible: Meaning and Power.* Baltimore: Johns Hopkins University Press, 2004.

———. "Review of Purity, Sacrifice, and the Temple." *Catholic Biblical Quarterly* 69 (2007): 784–85.

———. "Why Does Eleazar Sprinkle the Red Cow Blood? Making Sense of a Biblical Ritual." *Journal of Hebrew Scriptures* 6 (2006), online: http://www.arts.ualberta.ca/JHS/Articles/article_59.htm.

Gilhus, Ingvild. *Animals, Gods and Humans: Changing Attitudes to Animals in Greek, Roman and Early Christian Ideas*. London: Routledge, 2006.

Ginsberg, Elaine K. "Introduction: The Politics of Passing." In *Passing and the Fiction of Identity*. Edited by Elaine K. Ginsberg, 1–18. Durham: Duke University Press, 1996.

———, ed. *Passing and the Fiction of Identity*. Durham: Duke University Press, 1996.

Girard, René. "Generative Scapegoating." In *Violent Origins: Walter Burkert, René Girard and Jonathan Z. Smith on Ritual Killing and Cultural Formation*. Edited by R. Hamerton-Kelly, 73–105. Palo Alto: Stanford University Press, 1987.

Girard, René. "Satan." In *The Girard Reader*. Edited by James G. Williams 194–210. New York: Crossroad, 1996.

———. *The Scapegoat*. Translated by Y. Freccero. Baltimore: Johns Hopkins University Press, 1986.

———. *Things Hidden since the Foundation of the World*. Translated by S. Bann and M. Metteer. Stanford: Stanford University Press, 1987.

———. "A Venda Myth Analyzed." Appendix to *René Girard and Myth: An Introduction*. Edited by R. J. Golsan, 151-79. New York: Garland, 1993.

———. *La violence et le sacré*. Paris: Editions Bernard Grasset, 1972. Translated by Patrick Gregory. *Violence and the Sacred*. Baltimore: Johns Hopkins University Press, 1977.

Girard, René, and James Williams. "The Anthropology of the Cross: A Conversation with René Girard." In *The Girard Reader*. Edited by James Williams, 262–94. New York: Crossroad, 1996.

Glancy, Jennifer. "Flesh, Truth and the Fourth Gospel." *Biblical Interpretation* 13.2 (2005): 107–36.

———. "The Law of the Opened Body: Tertullian on the Nativity." *Henoch* 30 (2008): 45–66.

Gleason, Maud. *Making Men: Sophists and Self-Presentation in Ancient Rome*. Princeton: Princeton University Press, 1995.

Goldhill, Simon, ed. *Being Greek under Rome: The Second Sophistic, Cultural Identity, and the Development of the Roman Empire*. Cambridge: Cambridge University Press, 2001.

Goddard, Christophe J. "The Evolution of Pagan Sanctuaries in Late Antique Italy (Fourth-Sixth Centuries A.D.): A New Administrative and Legal Framework: A Paradox." In *Les cités de l'Italie tardo-antique (IVe–Vie siècle)*. Edited by Massimiliano Ghilardi, Cristophe J. Goddard, and Pierfrancesco Porena, 281–308. Collection de l'École Française de Rome 369. Rome: École Française de Rome, 2006.

———. "Nuove osservazioni sul Santuario cosidetto 'Siraco' al Gianicolo." In *Culti Orientali tra Scavo e Collezionismo*. Edited by Beatrice Palma Venetucci, 165–73. Rome: Artemide, 2008.

Goody, Jack. "Religion and Ritual: The Definitional Problem." *British Journal of Sociology* 12.2 (1961): 142–64.

Gordon, Richard. "The Veil of Power: Emperors, Sacrificers, and Benefactors." In *Pagan Priests: Religion and Power in the Ancient World*. Edited by Mary Beard and John North, 199–231. Ithaca: Cornell University Press, 1990.

Gorman, Frank. "Pagans and Priests: Critical Reflections on Method." In *Perspectives on Purity and Purification in the Bible*. Edited by Baruch J. Schwartz, David P. Wright, Jeffrey Stackert, and Naphtali S. Meshel, 96–110. London: T. & T. Clark International, 2008.

Graf, Fritz. "Eid" and "Fluch und Verwünschung." In *Thesaurus Cultus et Rituum Antiquorum*. Vol. 3, *Divination, Prayer, Veneration, Hikesia, Asylia, Oath, Malediction, Profanation, Magic Rituals*, 247–70. Los Angeles: J. Paul Getty Museum, 2005.

———, ed. *Klassische Antike und neue Wege der Kulturwissenschaften: Symposium Karl Meuli (Bael, 11–13 September 1991)*. Beiträge zur Volkskunde 11. Basel: Schweizerische Gesellschaft für Volkskunde, 1992.

———. *Magic in the Ancient World*. Cambridge: Harvard University Press, 1997.

———. "One Generation after Burkert and Girard: Where Are the Great Theories?" In *Ancient Victims, Modern Observers: Reflections on Greek and Roman Animal Sacrifice*. Edited by Christopher A. Faraone and F. S. Naiden. Cambridge: Cambridge University Press, forthcoming.

———. "The Power of the Word in the Graeco-Roman World." In *La Potenza della parola: Destinatari, funzioni, bersagli*. Atti del Convegno di studi, Siena, 7–8 maggio 2002. Edited by Simone Beta. Fiesole (Florence): Cadmo, 2004.

———. "Serious Singing: The Orphic Hymns as Religious Texts." *Kernos* 22 (2009): 169–82.

Graf, Fritz. "What Is New about Greek Sacrifice?" In *Kykeon: Studies in Honour of H. S. Versnel*. Religions of the Greco-Roman World 142. Edited by H.F.J. Horstmanshoff, H. W. Singor, F. T. Van Straten, and J.H.M. Strubbe, 113–25. Leiden: Brill, 2002.

Graf, Fritz, and Sarah Iles Johnston. *Ritual Texts for the Afterlife: Orpheus and the Bacchic Gold Tablets*. London: Routledge, 2007.

Graindorge, Catherine. "Le taureau blanc du dieu Min et l'offrande de la gerbe de blé." In *La Cuisine et l'autel: Les sacrifices en questions dans les sociétés de la méditerranée ancienne*. Edited by Stella Georgoudi, Renée Koch Piettre, and Francis Schmidt 47–75. BEHE SR124. Turnhout: Brepols, 2005.

Grant, Robert. *Gods and the One God*. Philadelphia: Westminster, 1986.

Green, C.M.C. *Roman Religion and the Cult of Diana Aricia*. Cambridge: Cambridge University Press, 2007.

Grenade, R. "Le mythe de Pompée et les pompéians sou les Césars." *Revue des Études Anciennes* 52 (1950): 28–63.

Griffin, John Howard. *Black Like Me*. New York: Houghton Mifflin, 1961.

Grottanelli, Cristiano. "Tuer des animaux pour la fête de Saint Félix." In *La cuisine et l'autel: Les sacrifices en questions dans les sociétés de la méditerranée ancienne*. Edited by Stella Georgoudi, Renée Koch Piettre, and Francis Schmidt, 387–407. BEHE SR124. Turnhout: Brepols, 2005.

Gruenwald, Ithamar. *Rituals and Ritual Theory in Ancient Israel*. Leiden: Brill, 2003.

Guthrie, Stewart. *Faces in the Clouds*. New York: Oxford University Press, 1993.

Habermann, A. M. "Ancient Piyyutim" (Hebrew). *Tarbiz* 14 (1942): 57–58.

Habinek, T. N. "Sacrifice, Society, and Vergil's Ox-Born Bees." In *Cabinet of the Muses: Essays on Classical and Comparative Literature in Honor of Thomas G. Rosenmeyer*. Edited by M. Griffith and D. J. Mastronarde, 209–23. Atlanta: Scholars Press, 1990.

Hall, Jonathan. *Hellenicity: Between Ethnicity and Culture*. Chicago: University of Chicago Press, 2002.

Hallett, Cristopher H. *The Roman Nude: Heroic Portrait Statuary 200 B.C.–A.D. 300.* Oxford: Oxford University Press 2005.

Hallett, Judith P. "*Perusinae glandes* and the Changing Image of Augustus." *American Journal of Ancient History* 2 (1977): 151–71.

Hamilton, Catherine Sider. "'His Blood Be upon Us': Innocent Blood and the Death of Jesus in Matthew." *CBQ* 70 (2008): 82–100.

Hammerton-Kelly, Robert G., ed. *Violent Origins: Walter Burkert, René Girard and Jonathan Z. Smith on Ritual Killing and Cultural Formation.* Stanford: Stanford University Press, 1987.

Haran, Menahem. *Temples and Temple-Service in Ancient Israel: An Inquiry into Biblical Cult Phenomena and the Historical Setting of the Priestly School.* Winona Lake, Ind.: Eisenbrauns, 1985.

Harl, K. W. "Sacrifice and Pagan Belief in Fifth- and Sixth-Century Byzantium." *Past and Present* 128 (1990): 7–27.

Harrill, J. Albert. "The Influence of Roman Contract Law on Early Baptismal Formulae (Tertullian, Ad martyras 3)." *StPatr* 35 (2001): 275–82.

———. *Slaves in the New Testament: Literary, Social, and Moral Dimensions.* Minneapolis: Fortress, 2006.

Hartog, François. "Self-Cooking Beef and the Drinks of Ares." In *Le cuisine du sacrifice en pays grec.* Paris: Gallimard, 1979. English translation by Paula Wissing, 173–82. In *The Cuisine of Sacrifice among the Greeks.* Chicago: University of Chicago Press, 1989.

Hasan-Rokem, Galit. *Web of Life: Folklore and Midrash in Rabbinic Literature.* Translated by B. Stein. Stanford: Stanford University Press, 2000.

Havelaar, Henriette. "Hellenistic Parallels to Acts 5:1–11 and the Problem of Conflicting Interpretations." *JSNT* 67 (1997): 63–82.

Hayes, Christine E. *Gentile Impurities and Jewish Identities: Intermarriage and Conversion from the Bible to the Talmud.* New York: Oxford University Press, 2002.

Heil, J. P. "The Blood of Jesus in Matthew: A Narrative-Critical Perspective." *Perspectives in Religious Studies* 18 (1991): 117–24.

Helm, Paul. "Manifest and Latent Functions." *Philosophical Quarterly* 21.82 (1971): 51–60.

Helm, Rudolf. *Lucian und Menipp.* Leipzig: Teubner, 1906.

Hendel, Ronald S. "Prophets, Priests, and the Efficacy of Ritual." In *Pomegranates and Golden Bells: Studies in Biblical, Jewish, and Near Eastern Ritual, Law, and Literature in Honor of Jacob Milgrom.* Edited by David P. Wright, David Noel Freedman, and Avi Hurvitz, 185–98. Winona Lake, Ind.: Eisenbrauns, 1995.

Henrichs, Albert. "Drama and Dromena: Bloodshed, Violence, and Sacrificial Metaphor in Euripides." *HSCP* 100 (2000): 173–88.

———. "Greek Maenadism from Olympias to Messalina." *HSCP* 82 (1978): 121–60.

Herbert-Brown, Geraldine. *Ovid and the Fasti: An Historical Study.* Oxford: Oxford University Press, 1994.

Heyman, George. *The Power of Sacrifice: Roman and Christian Discourses in Conflict.* Washington, D.C.: Catholic University of America Press, 2007.

Hickson Hahm, Frances. "Performing the Sacred: Prayers and Hymns." In *A Companion to Roman Religion.* Edited by Jörg Rüpke 235–40. Blackwell Companions to the Ancient World. Malden, Mass.: Blackwell, 2007.

Himmelfarb, Martha. *A Kingdom of Priests: Ancestry and Merit in Ancient Judaism.* Philadelphia: University of Pennsylvania Press, 2006.

Hirsch, S. "Spätantike Brotstempel mit der Maske des ägyptischen Gottes Bes." In *Coptic Studies on the Threshold of a New Millennium.* Edited by M. Immerzeel and J. van der Vliet 1259–72. Orientalia lovaniensia analecta 133. Leuven: Peeters, 2004.

Hirzel, Rudolf. *Der Eid: Ein Beitrag zu seiner Geschichte.* Leipzig: Hirzel, 1902.

Hitch, Sarah, and Ian C. Rutherford, eds. *Animal Sacrifice in the Ancient Greek World.* Cambridge: Cambridge University Press, forthcoming.

Hoffman, L. A. *Covenant of Blood: Circumcision and Gender in Rabbinic Judaism.* Chicago: University of Chicago Press, 1996.

Hoffmann, R. Joseph. *Porphyry's "Against the Christians": The Literary Remains.* Amherst, N.Y.: Prometheus Books, 1994.

Holmwood, John. "Functionalism and Its Critics." In *Modern Social Theory: An Introduction.* Edited by A. Harrington 87–109. Oxford: Oxford University Press, 2005.

Hooker, Morna D. "Christ, the 'End' of the Cult." In *The Epistle to the Hebrews and Christian Theology.* Edited by Richard Bauckham et. al., 189–212. Grand Rapids: William B. Eerdmans, 2009.

Horbury, William. "The Aaronic Priesthood in the Epistle to the Hebrews." *JSNT* 19 (1983): 43–71.

Horowitz, Elliot S. *Reckless Rites: Purim and the Legacy of Jewish Violence.* Princeton: Princeton University Press, 2006.

Horton, Robin. *Patterns of Thought in Africa and the West.* New York: Cambridge University Press, 1993.

Hubert, Henri, and Marcel Mauss. *Sacrifice: Its Nature and Function.* Translated by W. D. Halls. Chicago: University of Chicago Press, 1964. Originally published as "Essai sur la nature et le fonction du sacrifice." *L'Année Sociologique* 2 (1897–1899): 29–138.

Humphrey, Caroline, and James Laidlaw. "Sacrifice and Ritualization." In *The Archaeology of Ritual.* Edited by Evangelos Kyriakidis. Los Angeles: Cotsen Institute of Archaeology, 2007.

Ikram, Salima. "Divine Creatures: Animal Mummies." In *Divine Creatures: Animal Mummies in Ancient Egypt.* Edited by Salima Ikram 1–15. Cairo: American University in Cairo Press, 2005.

Ikram, Salima, ed. *Divine Creatures: Animal Mummies in Ancient Egypt.* Cairo: American University in Cairo Press, 2005.

Irshai, Oded. "Historical Aspects of the Christian-Jewish Polemic Concerning the Church of Jerusalem in the Fourth Century" (Hebrew), 2 vols. Ph.D. diss., Hebrew University of Jerusalem, 1993.

Jacobs, Andrew. "Dialogical Differences: (De-)Judaizing Jesus' Circumcision." *JECS* 15 (2007): 291–335.

Jacoby, Felix. *Die Fragmente der griechischen Historiker.* Neudruck vermehrt um addenda zum Text, Nachträge zum Kommentar, Corrigenda und Konkordanz. 3 vols. Leiden: Brill, 1957–.

Jay, Nancy. *Throughout Your Generations Forever: Sacrifice, Religion, and Paternity.* Chicago: University of Chicago Press, 1992.

Jewett, Robert. *Romans: A Commentary.* Hermeneia Commentary Series. Minneapolis: Fortress, 2007.

Johnson, A. P. "Identity, Descent, and Polemic: Ethnic Argumentation in Eusebius' Praepa-
    ratio Evangelica." *JECS* 12 (2004): 23–56.
Johnson, Luke Timothy. *The Literary Function of Possessions in Luke–Acts.* SBLDS 39.
    Missoula, Mont.: Society of Biblical Literature, 1977.
Johnston, Sarah Iles. *Ancient Greek Divination.* Malden: Wiley-Blackwell, 2008.
———. "Sacrifice in the Greek Magical Papyri." In *Magic and Ritual in the Ancient World.*
    Edited by Paul Mirecki and Marvin Meyer 344–58. Religions of the Greco-Roman
    World 141. Leiden: Brill, 2002.
Jones, A.H.M., J. R. Martindale, and J. Morris. *The Prosopography of the Later Roman
    Empire.* 3 vols. Cambridge: Cambridge University Press, 1971–1992.
Jones, Christopher P. "Multiple Identities in the Second Sophistic." In *Paideia: The World
    of the Second Sophistic.* Edited by Barbara Borg 13–22. Berlin: De Gruyter, 2004.
———. *Kinship Diplomacy in the Ancient World.* Cambridge: Harvard University Press, 1999.
Juergensmeyer, Mark. *Terror in the Mind of God: The Global Rise of Religious Violence.*
    Berkeley: University of California Press, 2000.
Kahn, C. H. *Pythagoras and the Pythagoreans: A Brief History.* Indianapolis: Hackett,
    2001.
Kalimi, Isaac. "The Story about the Murder of the Prophet Zechariah in the Gospels and
    Its Relations to Chronicles." *Revue Biblique* 116 (2009): 246–61.
Kampen, Natalie Boymel. "Looking at Gender: The Column of Trajan and Roman Histor-
    ical Relief." In *Feminisms in the Academy.* Edited by Donna Stanton and Abigail Stew-
    art 46–73. Ann Arbor: University of Michigan Press, 1995.
Keil, Josef. "XVI. Vorläufiger Bericht über die Ausgrabungen in Ephesos." *Jahreshefte des
    Österreichischen archäologischen Instituts* 28 (1932): Beiblatt 5–72.
Kessler, Dieter, and Abdel Halim Nur el-Din. "Tuna al-Gebel: Millions of Ibises and Other
    Animals." In *Divine Creatures: Animal Mummies in Ancient Egypt.* Edited by Salima
    Ikram 120–63. Cairo: American University in Cairo Press, 2005.
King, Helen. "Sacrificial Blood: The Role of Amnion in Greek Gynecology." *Helios* 13
    (1987): 117–26.
Kingsley, Peter. *Ancient Philosophy, Mystery, and Magic: Empedocles and the Pythagorean
    Tradition.* Oxford: Clarendon, 1995.
Kirk, G. S., J. E. Raven, and M. Schofield. *The Presocratic Philosophers.* 2nd ed. Cam-
    bridge: Cambridge University Press, 1983.
Klauck, H.-J. *The Religious Context of Early Christianity.* Edinburgh: T. & T. Clark, 2000.
Klawans, Jonathan. *Impurity and Sin in Ancient Judaism.* New York: Oxford University
    Press, 2000.
———. "Interpreting the Last Supper: Sacrifice, Spiritualization, and Anti-Sacrifice." *New
    Testament Studies* 48 (2002): 1–17.
———. "Methodology and Ideology in the Study of Priestly Ritual." In *Perspectives on
    Purity and Purification in the Bible.* Edited by Baruch J. Schwartz, David P. Wright, Jeffrey
    Stackert, and Naphtali S. Meshel, 84–95. London: T. & T. Clark International, 2008.
———. *Purity, Sacrifice and the Temple: Symbolism and Supersessionism in the Study of
    Ancient Judaism.* New York: Oxford University Press, 2006.
———. "Religion, Violence, and the Bible." In *Religion and Violence: The Biblical Heritage.*
    Edited by David A. Bernat and Jonathan Klawans, 1–15. Sheffield: Sheffield Phoenix,
    2007.

———. "Rethinking Leviticus and Rereading Purity and Danger: A Review Essay." *Association of Jewish Studies Review* 27 (2003): 89–101.

———. "Review of *Rituals and Ritual Theory in Ancient Israel* by Ithamar Gruenwald." *Association of Jewish Studies Review* 29 (2005): 163–65.

———. "Ritual Purity, Moral Purity, and Sacrifice in Jacob Milgrom's Leviticus." *Religious Studies Review* 29 (2003): 19–28.

Klingbeil, Gerald. *Bridging the Gap: Ritual and Ritual Texts in the Bible.* Winona Lake, Ind.: Eisenbrauns, 2007.

Knipfing, John R. "The Libelli of the Decian Persecution." *HTR* 16.4 (1923): 345–90.

Knust, Jennifer Wright. "Roasting the Lamb: Sacrifice and Sacred Test in Justin's *Dialogue with Trypho.*" In *Religion and Violence: The Biblical Heritage.* Edited by David A. Bernat and Jonathan Klawans, 100–13. Sheffield: Sheffield Phoenix, 2007.

Koester, Helmut, et al. *The Cities of Paul: Images and Interpretations from the Harvard New Testament Archaeology Project.* Minneapolis: Fortress, 2005.

Konstan, David. "The Active Reader and the Ancient Novel." In *Readers and Writers in the Ancient Novel.* Edited by Nichael Paschalis, Stelios Panayotakis, and Gareth Schmeling, 1–17. Ancient Narrative Supplementum 12. Gronigen: Barkhuis Publishing and Gronigen University Library, 2009.

Laclau, Ernesto. "Constructing Universality." In *Contingency, Hegemony, and Universality.* Edited by Judith Butler, Ernesto Laclau, and Slavoj Žižek. London: Verso, 2000.

Łajtar, Adam. *Deir el-Bahari in the Hellenistic and Roman Periods: A Study of an Egyptian Temple based on Greek Sources.* Journal of Juristic Papyrology Supplement 4. Warsaw: Institute of Archaeology, 2006.

Laks, André, and Glenn Most. *Studies in the Derveni Papyrus.* New York: Oxford University Press, 1997.

Lampe, Peter. *From Paul to Valentinus: Christians at Rome in the First Two Centuries.* Translated by Michael Steinhauser. Edited by Marshall Johnson. Minneapolis: Fortress, 2003.

———. "Human Sacrifice and Pauline Christology." In *Human Sacrifice in Jewish and Christian Tradition.* Numen Supplements 112. Edited by Karin Finsterbusch, Armin Lange, and K. F. Deithard Römheld, 191–209. Leiden: Brill, 2007.

Lancaster, Lynne. "Building Trajan's Column." *American Journal of Archaeology* 103.3 (July 1999): 419–39.

Lane Fox, Robin. *Pagans and Christians in the Mediterranean World from the Second Century AD to the Conversion of Constantine.* New York: Knopf, 1987.

Lanzilotta, Lautaro Roig. "The Early Christians and Human Sacrifice." In *The Strange World of Human Sacrifice.* Edited by Jan N. Bremmer, 81–102. Leuven: Peeters, 2007.

Latte, Kurt. "Meineid." In *Kleine Schriften zu Religion, Recht, Literatur und Sprache der Griechen und Römer.* Edited by Olof Gigon, Wolfgang Buchwald, and Wolfgang Kunkel 367–79. Munich: C. H. Beck, 1968.

Leach, Edmund. *Culture and Communication: The Logic by Which Symbols Are Connected; An Introduction to the Use of Structuralist Analysis in Social Anthropology.* Cambridge: Cambridge University Press, 1976.

———. "Mythical Inequalities: Review of *Natural Symbols* by Mary Douglas." *New York Review of Books* 16 (January 28, 1971): 44–45.

Leadbetter, W. L. "A Libellus of the Decian Persecution." *New Documents Illustrating Early Christianity* 2 (1982): 180–85.

Lemos, T. M. "The Universal and the Particular: Mary Douglas and the Politics of Impurity." *Journal of Religion* 89.2 (2009): 236–51.

Leonhardt, Jutta. *Jewish Worship in Philo of Alexandria.* Texts and Studies in Ancient Judaism 84. Tübingen: Mohr Siebeck, 2001.

Lepper, Frank, and Sheppard Frere. *Trajan's Column: A New Edition of the Cichorius Plates.* Glouchester, U.K.: Alan Sutton, 1988.

Levi, Jerome M. "Symbols." In *International Encyclopedia of the Social Sciences.* 2nd ed. vd. B, 249–53.Detroit: Macmillan Reference, 2008.

Levine, Baruch. *The JPS Torah Commentary: Leviticus.* Philadelphia: Jewish Publication Society, 1989.

Lévy, I. *Recherches sur les sources de la légende de Pythagore.* Paris: Ernest Leroux, 1926.

Lieberman, Saul. *Greek in Jewish Palestine: Studies in the Life and Manners of Jewish Palestine in the II–IV Centuries C.E.* New York: Jewish Theological Seminary of America, 1942.

Liebeschuetz, J.W.H.G., with the assistance of Carole Hill. *Ambrose of Milan: Political Letters and Speeches.* Liverpool: Liverpool University Press, 2005.

Lienhardt, Godfrey. *Divinity and Experience: The Religion of the Dinka.* Oxford: Clarendon, 1961.

Lincoln, Bruce. *Holy Terrors: Thinking about Religion after September 11.* 2nd ed. Chicago: University of Chicago Press, 2006.

Lindblom, J. *Prophecy in Ancient Israel.* Oxford: Blackwell, 1962.

Linderski, Jerzy. "The Pontiff and the Tribune: The Death of Tiberius Gracchus." *Athenaeum* 90 (2002): 339–66.

Linforth, I. M. *The Arts of Orpheus.* Berkeley: University of California Press, 1941.

Lizzi Testa, Rita. "Augures et pontifices: Public Sacral Law in Late Antique Rome (Fourth-Fifth Centuries AD)." In *The Power of Religion in Late Antiquity.* Edited by Andrew Cain and Noel Lenski, 251–78. Aldershot, U.K.:Ashgate, 2009.

———. "Christian Emperor, Vestal Virgins and Priestly Colleges: Reconsidering the End of Roman Paganism." *AnTard* 15 (2007): 251–62.

———. "Legislazione imperiale e reazione pagana. I limiti del conflitto." *Cristianesimo nella storia* 31 (2009): 131–56.

Long, A. A., and D. N. Sedley. *The Hellenistic Philosophers.* 2 vols. Cambridge: Cambridge University Press, 1987.

Lyman, Rebecca. "The Politics of Passing: Justin Martyr's Conversion as a Problem of 'Hellenization.'" In *Conversion in Late Antiquity and the Early Middle Ages: Seeing and Believing.* Edited by Kenneth Mills and Anthony Grafton 36–60. Studies in Comparative History. Rochester: University of Rochester Press, 2003.

Maccoby, Hyam. *Ritual and Morality: The Ritual Purity System and Its Place in Judaism.* Cambridge: Cambridge University Press, 1999.

Mack, Burton. *Who Wrote the New Testament?* New York: HarperOne, 1995.

Maclean, Jennifer. "Barrabas, the Scapegoat Ritual, and the Development of the Passion Narrative." *HTR* 100.3 (2007): 309–34.

———. "Jesus as Cult Hero in the Fourth Gospel." In *Philostratus's Heroikos: Religion and Cultural Identity in the Third Century C.E.* Edited by Ellen Aitken and Jennifer Maclean, 195–218. Atlanta: Society of Biblical Literature, 2004.

Macmullen, Ramsay. *The Second Church: Popular Christianity A.D. 200–400.* Atlanta: Society of Biblical Literature, 2009.

Magness, Jodi. "The Arch of Titus at Rome and the Fate of the God of Israel." *Journal of Jewish Studies* 59 (2008): 201–17.

Maier, Franz G. *Griechische Mauerbauinschriften.* Heidelberg: Quelle & Meyer 1959.

Maimonides, Moses. *Guide of the Perplexed.* Translated with an introduction and notes by Shlomo Pines. 2 vols. Chicago: University of Chicago Press, 1963.

Mandel, Paul D. "Between Byzantium and Islam: The Transmission of a Jewish Book in the Byzantine and Early Islamic Periods." In *Transmitting Jewish Traditions: Orality, Textuality and Cultural Diffusion.* Edited by Y. Elman and I. Gershoni 74–106. New Haven: Yale University Press, 2000.

———. "The Loss of the Center: Changing Attitudes towards the Temple in Aggadic Literature." *HTR* 99 (2006): 17–35.

———. "Midrash Lamentations Rabbati: Prolegomenon and a Critical Edition to the Third Parasha." (Hebrew) Ph.D. diss., Hebrew University of Jerusalem, 1997.

Mandelbaum, Bernard, ed. *Pesikta de Rav Kahana: According to an Oxford Manuscript, with Variants from All Known Manuscripts and Genizoth Fragments and Parallel Passages, with Commentary and Introduction.* 2 vols. New York: Jewish Theological Seminary, 1987.

Manning, Charles. "Seneca and Roman Religious Practice." In *Religion in the Ancient: New Themes and Approache World.* Edited by Matthew Dillon 311–19. Amsterdam: Adolph M. Hakkert, 1996.

Marguerat, Daniel. *The First Christian Historian: Writing the "Acts of the Apostles."* Translated by Ken McKinney, Gregory J. Laughery, and Richard Bauckham. SNTSMS 121. Cambridge: Cambridge University Press, 2002.

Matthews, John F. *The Roman Empire of Ammianus.* Baltimore: Johns Hopkins University Press, 1989.

Matthews, Shelly. "The Need for the Stoning of Stephen." In *Violence in the New Testament*, Edited by E. L. Gibson and S. Matthews, 124–39. New York: T. & T. Clark International, 2005.

May, Gerhard, and Katharina Greschat, eds. *Marcion und seine kirchengeschichtliche Wirkung. Texte und Untersuchungen zur Geschichte der altchristlichen Literatur 150.* Berlin: De Gruyter, 2002.

McClymond, Kathryn. *Beyond Sacred Violence: A Comparative Study of Sacrifice.* Baltimore: Johns Hopkins University Press, 2008.

———. "The Nature and Elements of Sacrificial Ritual." *Method and Theory in the Study of Religion* 16 (2004): 337–66.

McGowan, Andrew. *Ascetic Eucharists: Food and Drink in Early Christian Ritual Meals.* New York: Oxford University Press, 1999.

———. "Eating People: Accusations of Cannibalism against Christians in the Second Century." *JECS* 2.3 (1994): 413–42.

———. "'Is There a Liturgical Text in This Gospel?' The Institution Narratives and Their Early Interpretive Communities." *JBL* 118.1 (1999): 73–87.

McLynn, Neil. *Ambrose of Milan: Church and Court in a Christian Capital.* Transformation of the Classical Heritage 22. Berkeley: University of California Press, 1994.

———. "Crying Wolf: The Pope and the Lupercalia." *JRS* 98 (2008): 176–81.

———. "The Fourth Century *Taurobolium.*" *Phoenix* 50 (1996): 312–30.

Mehl, Véronique, and Pierre Brulé, eds. *Le sacrifice antique: Vestiges, procedures et strat-egies*. Collection "Histoire." Rennes: Presses Universitaires de Rennes, 2008.

Mendelssohn, Moses. *Jerusalem: Or On Religious Power and Judaism*. Translated by Alan Arkush. With introduction and commentary by Alexander Altmann. Waltham: Brandeis University Press, 1983.

Meriç, Recep. "Rekonstruktionsversuch der Kolossalstatue des Domitian in Ephesos." In *Pro Arte Antiqua: Festschrift für Hedwig Kenneri*. Edited by Wilhelm Alzinger and Gud-run Neeb vol. 2, 239–41, pl. xx–xx 111, and fig. 17. Vienna: A. F. Koska, 1985.

Merton, Robert K. *Social Theory and Social Structure*. Glencoe, Ill.: Free Press, 1957.

Meschel, Naphtali S. "Pure, Impure, Permitted, Prohibited: A Study of Classification Systems in P." In *Perspectives on Purity and Purification in the Bible*. Edited by Baruch Schwartz and David P. Wright, 32–42. London: T. & T. Clark International, 2008.

Meuli, Karl. "Griechische Opferbräuche." In *Phyllobolia, für Peter von Muhll zum 60. Geburstag am 1 August 1945*. Edited by Olaf Gigon, 185–288. Basel: Schwabe, 1946. Reprinted in *Gesammelte Shriften*. Edited by Thomas Gelzer, 2:907–1021. Basel: Schwabe, 1975.

Migne, Jacques-Paul. *Patrologiae cursus completus: series Graeca*. 161 volumes in 166. Paris: Migne, 1857–1866.

———. *Patrologiae cursus completus: series Latina*. 221 vols. Paris: Migne, 1844–1864.

Mikalson, Jon D. *Athenian Popular Religion*. Chapel Hill: University of North Carolina Press, 1983.

———. *Honor Thy Gods: Popular Religion in Greek Tragedy*. Chapel Hill: University of North Carolina Press, 1991.

Milgrom, Jacob. "The Function of the Hatta't Sacrifice." *Tarbiz* 40 (1970): 1–8.

———. *Leviticus 1–16: A New Translation with Introduction and Commentary*. Anchor Bible 3. New York: Doubleday, 1992.

———. *Leviticus 17–22: A New Translation with Introduction and Commentary*. Anchor Bible 3a. New York: Doubleday, 2000.

———. *Leviticus 23–27: A New Translation with Introduction and Commentary*. Anchor Bible 3b. New York: Doubleday, 2001.

———. "Systemic Differences in the Priestly Corpus: A Response to Jonathan Klawans." *Revue Biblique* 112 (2005): 321–29.

Millar, Fergus. "Last Year in Jerusalem: Monuments of the Jewish War in Rome." In *Fla-vius Josephus and Flavian Rome*. Edited by J. Edmondson, S. Mason, and J. Rives, 101–28. Oxford: Oxford University Press, 2005.

———. "Porphyry, Ethnicity, Language and Alien Wisdom." In *Philosophia Togata II: Plato and Aristotle at Rome*. Edited by Jonathan Barnes and Miriam Griffin, 241–62. Oxford: Clarendon, 1999.

Mitchell-Boyask, Robin. "Sacrifice and Revenge in Euripides' Hecuba." *Ramus* 22 (1993): 116–34.

Mizruchi, Susan Laura. *The Science of Sacrifice: American Literature and Modern Social Theory*. Princeton: Princeton University Press, 1998.

Morand, Anne-France. *Études sur les hymnes orphiques*. Religions in the Graeco-Roman World 143. Leiden: Brill, 2001.

Moxnes, Halvor. *The Economy of the Kingdom: Social Conflict and Economy Relations in Luke's Gospel*. OBT. Philadelphia: Fortress, 1988.

Nachtergael, Georges. "Un sacrifice en l'honneur de 'Baubo': Scènes figurées sur un moule cubique de l'Égypte romaine." In *Egyptian Religion: The Last Thousand Years*. Edited by Willy Clarysse, Antoon Schoors, and Harco Willems 159–78. OLA 84. Leuven: Peeters, 1998.

Nagy, Gregory. *The Best of the Achaeans: Concepts of the Hero in Archaic Greek Poetry*. Rev. ed. Baltimore: Johns Hopkins University Press, 1999.

Naiden, F. S. "The Fallacy of the Willing Victim." *Journal of Hellenic Studies* 117 (2007): 61–73.

———. "Rejected Sacrifice in Greek and Hebrew Religion." *Journal of Ancient Near Eastern Religions* 6 (2006): 189–223.

———. "Sacrifice and Self-Interest." In *Animal Sacrifice in the Ancient Greek World*. Edited by Sarah Hitch and Ian C. Rutherford. Cambridge: Cambridge University Press, forthcoming.

Nardin, Terry. Review of *Terror in the Mind of God: The Global Rise of Religious Violence*. *Journal of Politics* 63.2 (2001): 683–84.

Nasrallah, Laura. "The Acts of the Apostles, Greek Cities, and Hadrian's Panhellenion." *JBL* 127.3 (2008): 533–66.

———. *Christian Responses to Roman Art and Architecture: The Second-Century Church amid the Spaces of Empire*. New York: Cambridge University Press, 2010.

———. "Mapping the World: Justin, Tatian, Lucian, and the Second Sophistic." *HTR* 98.3 (2005): 283–314.

Neusner, Jacob. "Halakhah and History." *Judaism* 29.1 (Winter 1980): 52–56.

Nikiprowetzky, Valentin. "La spiritualisation des sacrifices et le culte sacrificiel au Temple de Jérusalem chez Philon d'Alexandrie." *Semitica* 17 (1967): 97–116.

Nilsson, Martin P. "Lampen und Kerzen im Kult der Antike." *Opuscula Archaeologica VI*. Edited by Institutum Romanum Regni Sueciae, 96–111. Lund: C.W.K. Gleerup, 1950.

———. "Pagan Divine Service in Late Antiquity." *HTR* 38 (1945): 63–69.

Noort, Ed. "Child Sacrifice in Ancient Israel: The *Status Quaestionis*." In *The Strange World of Human Sacrifice*. Edited by Jan N. Bremmer, 103–25. Leuven: Peeters, 2007.

North, John A. "The Development of Religious Pluralism." In *The Jews among Pagans and Christians in the Roman Empire*. Edited by Judith Lieu, John North, and Tessa Rajak, 174–93. London: Routledge, 1992.

———. "Religion and Politics, from Republic to Principate." *JRS* 76 (1986): 251–58.

Obbink, Dirk. "The Origin of Greek Sacrifice: Theophrastus on Religion and Cultural History." In *Theophrastean Studies: on Natural Science, Physics and Metaphysics, Ethics, Religion and Rhetoric*. Edited by W. W. Fortenbaugh and R. W. Sharples 272–95. New Brunswick, N.J.: Transaction Books, 1988.

O'Donnell, James J. *Augustine: A New Biography*. San Francisco: HarperCollins, 2005.

Ogden, Daniel. *Magic, Witchcraft, and Ghosts in the Greek and Roman Worlds: A Sourcebook*. New York: Oxford University Press, 2009.

Økland, Jorunn. *Women in Their Place: Paul and the Corinthian Discourse of Gender and Sanctuary Space*. JSNTSup 269. Shefflied: T. & T. Clark, 2004.

Osborne, Robyn. "Women and Sacrifice in Classical Greece." *Classical Quarterly* 43 (1993): 392–405.

Osgood, John. *Caesar's Legacy: Civil War and the Emergence of the Roman Empire*. Cambridge: Cambridge University Press, 2006.

Otten, Willamien. "Christ's Birth of a Virgin Who Became a Wife: Flesh and Speech in Tertullian's De Carne Christi." *Vigiliae Christianae* 51 (1997): 247–60.

Packer, James. *The Forum of Trajan in Rome: A Study of the Monuments in Brief*. Berkeley: University of California Press, 2001.

Park, Hyung Dae. *Finding "Herem"? A Study of Luke-Acts in the Light of "Herem."* Library of New Testament Studies 357. London: T. & T. Clark, 2007.

Parker, Robert. *Miasma: Pollution and Purification in Early Greek Religion*. Oxford: Clarendon, 1983.

———. "Pleasing Thighs: Reciprocity in Greek Religion." In *Reciprocity in Ancient Greece*. Edited by Christopher Gill, Norman Postlethwaite, and Richard Seaford, 105–26. New York: Oxford University Press, 1998.

———. *Polytheism and Society at Athens*. Oxford: Oxford University Press, 2005.

Pauly, A. F., G. Wissowa, and W. Kroll. *Real-Encyclopadie der Klassischen Altertums-Wissenschaft*. New Edition G. Wissowa. 49 vols. Stuttgart: J. B. Metzler, 1894–1980.

Peels, H.G.L. "The Blood 'from Abel to Zechariah' (Matthew 23,35; Luke 11, 50f.) and the Canon of the Old Testament." *Zeitschrift für die Alttestamentliche Wissenschaft* 113 (2001): 583–601.

Penner, Hans H. "The Poverty of Functionalism." *History of Religions* 11.1 (1971): 91–97.

Pepin, Jean. Latradition d' allégarie: De Philon d' Alexandie à Dante, Études Augustienne 120 . Daries: Études Augustiennes 1976.

Perkins, Carl M. "The Evening Shema: A Study in Rabbinic Consolation." *Judaism* 43.1 (Winter 1994): 27–36.

Perkins, Judith. "An Ancient 'Passing' Novel: Heliodorus' Aithiopika." *Arethusa* 32 (1999): 197–214.

Perpillou-Thomas, Françoise. *Fêtes d'Égypte ptolémaïque et romaine d'après la documentation papyrologique grecque*. Studia Hellenistica 31. Louvain: Studia Hellenistica, 1993.

Pervo, Richard I. *Acts: A Commentary*. Edited by Harold W. Attridge. Hermeneia Commentary Series. Minneapolis: Fortress, 2008.

———. *Dating Acts: Between the Evangelists and the Apologists*. Santa Rosa, Calif.: Polebridge Press, 2006.

Petropoulou, Maria-Zoe. *Animal Sacrifice in Ancient Greek Religion, Judaism, and Christianity, 100 BC–AD 200*. Oxford: Oxford University Press, 2008.

Pierce, Sarah. "Death, Revelry, and *Thysia*." *Classical Antiquity* 12.2 (1993): 219–60.

Pingree, David. *Vettii Valentis Antiocheni anthologiarum libri novem*. Leipzig: B. G. Teubner, 1986.

Piper, Adrian. "Passing for White, Passing for Black." *Transition* 58 (1992): 4–32. Reprinted in *Out of Order, Out of Sight*. Vol. 1: *Selected Writings in Meta-Art 1968–1992*. Cambridge: MIT Press, 1996.

Plescia, Joseph. *The Oath and Perjury in Ancient Greece*. Tallahassee: Florida State University Press, 1970.

Pongratz-Leisten, Beate. "Ritual Killing and Sacrifice in the Ancient Near East." In *Human Sacrifice in Jewish and Christian Tradition*. Edited by Karin Finsterbusch, Armin Lange, and K. F. Diethard Römheld 3–33. Numen Supplements 112. Leiden: Brill, 2007.

Price, S.R.F. *Rituals and Power: The Roman Imperial Cult in Asia Minor*. Cambridge: Cambridge University Press, 1984.

Quaegebeur, Jan. "L'autel-à-feu et l'abattoir en Égypte tardive." In *Ritual and Sacrifice in the Ancient Near East*. Edited by Jan Quaegebeur. OLA 55. Leuven: Peeters, 1993.

Rajak, Tessa. "Dying for the Law: The Martyr's Portrait in Jewish-Greek Literature." In *The Jewish Dialogue with Greece and Rome: Studies in Cultural and Social Interaction*, 99–133. Leiden: Brill, 2002.

Rappaport, Roy A. *Ritual and Religion in the Making of Humanity*. Cambridge Studies in Social and Cultural Anthropology 110. Cambridge: Cambridge University Press, 1999.

Rauh, Nicholas K. *The Sacred Bonds of Commerce: Religion, Economy, and Trade Society at Hellenistic Roman Delos, 166–87 B.C.* Amsterdam: J. C. Gieben, 1993.

Reeves, J. C. *Trajectories in Near Eastern Apocalypses: A Postrabbinic Jewish Apocalypse Reader*. Atlanta: Society of Biblical Literature, 2005.

Reimer, Ivoni Richter. *Woman in the Acts of the Apostles: A Feminist Liberation Perspective*. Translated by Linda M. Maloney. Minneapolis: Fortress, 1995.

Reverdin, Olivier, and Bernard Grange, eds. *Le sacrifice dans l'antiquité*. Entretiens sur l'antiquité classique. Geneva: Hardt, 1981.

Riedweg, Christoph. *Pythagoras: His Life, Teaching, and Influence*. Translated by Susan Rendall. Ithaca: Cornell University Press, 2005. First published as *Pythagoras: Leben, Lehre, Nachwirkung*. Eine Einführung. Munich: C. H. Beck, 2002.

Ringgren, Helmer. *Israelite Religion*. Philadelphia: Fortress, 1966.

Rives, James B. "The Decree of Decius and the Religion of Empire." *JRS* 89 (1999): 135–54.

———. "Human Sacrifice among Pagans and Christians." *JRS* 85 (1995): 65–85.

———. *Religion in the Roman Empire*. Malden, Mass.: Blackwell 2007.

Robbins, Jill. "Sacrifice." In *Critical Terms for Religious Studies*. Edited by Mark C. Taylor 285–97. Chicago: University of Chicago Press, 1998.

Robinson, Amy. "It Takes One to Know One: Passing and Communities of Common Interest." *Critical Inquiry* 20 (1994): 715–36.

Rofé, Alexander. *Introduction to the Prophetic Literature*. Translated by Judith H. Seeligmann. Sheffield: Sheffield Academic Press, 1997.

Rohy, Valerie. "Displacing Desire: Passing, Nostalgia, and Giovanni's Room." In *Passing and the Fiction of Identity*. Edited by Elaine K. Ginsberg 218–33. Durham: Duke University Press, 1996.

Rosen-Zvi, Ishay. "Bodies and Temple: The List of Priestly Bodily Defects in Mishnah *Bekhorot*, Chapter 7." (Hebrew) *Jewish Studies* 43 (2005–2006):49–87.

Rosenstein, Nathan Stewart. "Imperatores Victi: The Case of C. Hostilius Mancinus." *CA* 5 (1986): 230–52.

Rottenberg, Catherine. "Passing: Race, Identification, and Desire." *Criticism* 45 (2003): 435–52.

Rüpke, Jörg. *Religion of the Romans*. Translated by Richard Gordon. Cambridge: Polity, 2007.

Rust, Marion. "The Subaltern as Imperialist: Speaking of Olaudah Equiano." In *Passing and the Fiction of Identity*. Edited by Elaine K. Ginsberg 21–36. Durham: Duke University Press, 1996.

Rutherford, Ian. "Down-Stream to the Cat-Goddess: Herodotus on Egyptian Pilgrimage." In *Pilgrimage in Graeco-Roman and Early Christian Antiquity: Seeing the Gods*. Edited by Jas Elsner and Ian Rutherford 131–50. Oxford: Oxford University Press, 2008.

Rutter, J. B. "Three Phases of the *Tarobolium.*" *Phoenix* 50 (1996): 226–49.

Ryberg, Inez Scott. *Rites of the State Religion in Roman Art.* Memoirs of the American Academy in Rome 22. Rome: American Academy in Rome, 1955.

Saggioro, Alessandro. "Il sacrificio pagano nella reazione al cristianesimo: Giuliano e Macrobio." *Annali di Storia dell'Esegesi* 19.1 (2002): 237–54.

Saïd, Suzanne. "The Discourse of Identity in Greek Rhetoric." In *Ancient Perceptions of Greek Ethnicity.* Edited by Irad Malkin 275–99. Washington, D.C.: Center for Hellenic Studies; Cambridge: Harvard University Press, 2001.

Salzman, Michele Renee. "Ambrose and the Usurpation of Arbogastes and Eugenius: Reflections on Pagan-Christian Conflict Narratives." *JECS* 18.1 (2010): 191–223.

———. *On Roman Time: The Codex Calendar of 354 and the Rhythms of Urban Life in Late Antiquity.* Berkeley: University of California Press, 1990.

———. "*Superstitio* in the *Codex Theodosianus* and the Persecution of Pagans." *VC* 41 (1987): 172–88.

Sanders, Paul. "So May God Do to Me!" *Bib* 85 (2004): 91–98.

Sandweiss, Martha A. *Passing Strange: A Gilded Age Tale of Love and Deception across the Color Line.* New York: Penguin Press, 2009.

Sansone, David. "The Sacrifice Motif in Euripides' IT." *Transactions of the American Philological Association* 105 (1975): 283–95.

Satran, Daniel. *Biblical Prophets in Byzantine Palestine: Reassessing the Lives of the Prophets,* SVTP 11. Leiden: Brill, 1995.

Sauneron, Serge. *Les fêtes religieuses d'Esna aux derniers siècles du paganisme.* Esna 5. Cairo: Institut Français d'Archéologie Orientale , 1962.

Schatzki, Theodore. *The Site of the Social: A Philosophical Account of the Constitution of Social Life and Social Change.* University Park: Pennsylvania State University Press, 2002.

Scheid, John. *An Introduction to Roman Religion.* Translated by Janet Lloyd. Bloomington: Indiana University Press. 2003.

———. "Roman Sacrifice and the System of Being." In *Ancient Victims, Modern Observers: Reflections on Greek and Roman Animal Sacrifice.* Edited by Christopher A. Faraone and F. S. Naiden. Cambridge: Cambridge University Press, forthcoming.

———. "La spartizione sacrificale a Roma." In *Sacrificio e società nel mondo antico.* Edited by C. Grottanelli and N. Parise, 267–92. Rome: Laterza, 1988.

Schilbrack, Kevin. "Religions: Are There Any?" *Journal of the American Academy of Religion* 78.3 (2010): 1–27.

———. "The Social Construction of 'Religion' and Its Limits: A Critical Reading of Timothy Fitzgerald." In *Method and Theory in the Study of Religion,* forthcoming.

Schmitt, Hatto H. *Die Verträge der griechisch-römischen Welt von 338 bis 200 v. Chr.* Vol. 3: Bengtson, Staatsverträge. Munich: C. H. Beck, 1969.

Schofield, Malcolm. "Cicero For and Against Divination." *Journal of Religious Studies* 76 (1986): 47–65.

Schott, Jeremy. *Christianity, Empire, and the Making of Religion.* Philadelphia: University of Pennsylvania Press, 2008.

———. "Porphyry on Christians and Others: 'Barbarian Wisdom,' Identity Politics, and Anti-Christian Polemics on the Eve of the Great Persecution." *JECS* 13 (2005): 277–314.

Schultz, Celia. "Containment or Sacrifice: The Proper Disposal of a Polluting Presence." Papers of the British School at Rome. Forthcoming.

————. "The Romans and Ritual Murder." *JAAR* 77.2 (2010): 516–41.

Schwabl, Hans, and Erika Simon. "Zeus." *Pauly Wissowa* 10A (1927): 253–376; Supplement 15, 993–1481.

Schwartz, Baruch J., David P. Wright, Jeffrey Stackert, and Naphtali S. Meshel, eds. *Perspectives on Purity and Purification in the Bible*. New York: T. and T. Clark, 2008.

Schwartz, Regina M. *The Curse of Cain: The Violent Legacy of Monotheism*. Chicago: University of Chicago Press, 1997.

Schwemer, A. M. "Prophet, Zeuge und Märtyrer: Zur Entstehung des Märtyrerbegriffs im frühesten Christentum." *Zeitschrift für Theologie und Kirche* 96 (1999): 320–50.

————. *Studien zu den frühjüdischen Prophetenlegenden Vitae prophetarum*. 2 vols. TSAJ 49–50. Tübingen: Mohr Siebeck, 1995–1996.

Seaford, Richard. Introduction to *Reciprocity in Ancient Greece*. Edited by Christopher Gill, Norman Postlethwaite, and Richard Seaford 1–12. New York: Oxford University Press, 1998.

Seligman, Adam B., Robert P. Weller, Michael J. Puett, and Bennett Simon, eds. *Ritual and Its Consequences: An Essay on the Limits of Sincerity*. New York: Oxford University Press, 2008.

Shafer, Byron E., ed. *Temples of Ancient Egypt*. Ithaca: Cornell University Press, 1997.

————. "Temples, Priests, and Rituals: An Overview." In *Temples of Ancient Egypt*. Edited by Byron E. Shafer, 23–25. Ithaca: Cornell University Press, 1997.

Sharp, Carolyn J. *Irony and Meaning in the Hebrew Bible*. Indiana Studies in Biblical Literature. Edited by Herbert Marks. Bloomington: Indiana University Press, 2009.

Shaw, Gregory. *Theurgy and the Soul: The Neoplatonism of Iamblichus*. University Park: Pennsylvania State University Press, 1995.

Shepardson, Christine. *Anti-Judaism and Christian Orthodoxy: Ephrem's Hymns in Fourth-Century Syria*. Patristic Monograph Series. Washington, D.C.: Catholic University Press, 2008.

Shepkaru, Shmuel. *Jewish Martyrs in the Pagan and Christian Worlds*. New York: Cambridge University Press, 2006.

Shoemaker, Stephen J. "Epiphanius of Salamis, the Kollyridians, and the Early Dormition Narratives: The Cult of the Virgin in the Fourth Century." *JECS* 16 (2008): 371–401.

Smith, Brian K. "Monotheism and Its Discontents: Religious Violence and the Bible." *JAAR* 66.2 (1998): 403–11.

Smith, Brian K., and Wendy Doniger. "Sacrifice and Substitution: Ritual Mystification and Mythical Demystification." *Numen* 36.2 (1989): 189–224.

Smith, Jonathan Z. "The Domestication of Sacrifice." In *Violent Origins: Walter Burkert, René Girard, and Jonathan Z. Smith on Ritual Killing and Cultural Formation*. Edited by Robert G. Hammerton-Kelly 191–238. Stanford: Stanford University Press, 1987.

————. *Drudgery Divine: On the Comparison of Early Christians and the Religions of Late Antiquity*. Chicago: University of Chicago Press, 1990.

————. "Here, There, and Anywhere." In *Relating Religion: Essays in the Study of Religion*. Chicago: University of Chicago Press, 2004.

————. *Imagining Religion: From Babylon to Jonestown*. Chicago: University of Chicago Press, 1982.

————. *Map is not Territory: Studies in the History of Religion*. Leiden: Brill, 1978.

————. *Relating Religion: Essays on the Study of Religion*. Chicago: University of Chicago Press, 2004.

———. *To Take Place: Toward Theory in Ritual.* Chicago: University of Chicago Press, 1987.

———. "When the Bough Breaks." *History of Religions* 12.4 (1973): 342–71.

Smith, William Robertson. *Lectures on the Religion of the Semites: The Fundamental Institutions.* 3rd ed., with an introduction and additional notes by Stanley A. Cook. New York: Macmillan, 1927. Also see the 1956 edition: William Robertson Smith, *The Religion of the Semites: The Fundamental Institutions.* New York: Meridian, 1956.

Sommerstein, Alan H., and Judith Fletcher, eds. *Horkos: The Oath in Greek Society.* Exeter, U.K.: Bristol Phoenix, 2007.

Sokolowski, Frantisek. *Lois sacrées de l'Asie Mineure.* Paris: Boccard, 1958.

———. *Lois sacrées des cités grecques. Supplément.* Paris: Boccard, 1962.

Sourvinou-Inwood, Christiane. "Further Aspects of Polis Religion." *Annali Instituto Orientale di Napoli: Archaeologia e Storia* 10 (1988): 259–74.

———. *Tragedy and Athenian Religion.* Lanham, Md.: Lexington Books, 2003.

———. "Tragedy and Religion: Constructs and Readings." In *Greek Tragedy and the Historian.* Edited by Christopher Pelling, 161–85. Oxford: Clarendon, 1997.

———. "What Is Polis Religion?" in *The Greek City from Homer to Alexander.* Edited by Oswyn Murray and S.R.F. Price 295–322. Oxford: Clarendon, 1990.

Spaeth, Barbette Stanley. *The Roman Goddess Ceres.* Austin: University of Texas Press, 1996.

Sperber, Dan. *Rethinking Symbolism.* Translated by Alice L. Morton. Cambridge Studies in Social Anthropology. Cambridge: Cambridge University Press, 1975.

Speyer, S. "The Dirge Az be-veit shivyeinu" (Hebrew) *Sinai* 63 (1968): 50–55.

Spiro, Melford E. "Religion: Some Problems of Definition and Explanation." In *Anthropological Approaches to the Study of Religion.* Edited by Michael Banton, 85–126. New York: Praeger, 1966.

———. "Review of *Purity and Danger* by Mary Douglas." *American Anthropologist, New Series* 70 (1968): 391–93.

Sprague, Rosamond Kent. *The Older Sophists.* Columbia: University of South Carolina Press, 1972.

Staal, Frits. "The Meaninglessness of Ritual." *Numen* 26.1 (1979): 2–22.

Stafford, Emma. "Cocks to Asclepios: Sacrificial Practice and Healing Cult." In *Le Sacrifice antique: Vestiges, procédures, et stratégies.* Edited by Véronique Mehl and Pierre Brulé, 205–21. Rennes: Presses Universitaires de Rennes, 2008.

Stengel, Paul. "Zu den griechischen Schwuropfern." *Hermes* 49 (1914): 90–101.

Stern, Julia. "Spanish Masquerade and the Drama of Racial Identity in Uncle Tom's Cabin." In *Passing and the Fiction of Identity.* Edited by Elaine K. Ginsberg 103–30. Durham: Duke University Press, 1996.

Stewart-Sykes, Alistair. *The Lamb's High Feast: Melito, Peri Pascha, and the Quartodeciman Paschal at Sardis.* Leiden: Brill, 1998.

Stock, Brian. *Augustine the Reader: Meditation, Self-Knowledge, and the Ethics of Interpretation.* Cambridge: Harvard University Press, 1996.

Stökl Ben Ezra, Daniel. "The Christian Exegesis of the Scapegoat between Jews and Pagans." In *Sacrifice in Religious Experience.* Edited by A. A. Baumgarten, 207–32. Leiden: Brill, 2002.

———. *The Impact of Yom Kippur on Early Christianity: The Day of Atonement from Second Temple Judaism to the Fifth Century.* Wissenschaftliche Untersuchungen zum Neuen Testament 163. Tübingen: Mohr, 2003.

Stoops Jr., Robert F. "Riot and Assembly: The Social Context of Acts 19–41." *JBL* 108 (1989): 73–91.

Stowers, Stanley K. "Greeks Who Sacrifice and Those Who Do Not: Toward an Anthropology of Greek Religion." In *The Social World of the First Christians: Essays in Honor of Wayne A. Meeks*. Edited by L. Michael White and O. Larry Yarbrough. Minneapolis: Fortress, 1995.

———. "The Ontology of Religion." In *Introducing Religion: Essays in Honor of Jonathan Z. Smith*. Edited by Willi Braun and Russell T. McCutcheon. London: Equinox, 2008.

———. "Theorizing Religion of the Ancient Household and Family." In *Household and Family Religion in Antiquity*. Edited by Saul Olyan and John Bodel, 5–19. Malden, Mass.: Blackwell, 2008.

———. "Types of Meals, Myths, and Power: Paul and the Corinthians." In *Redescribing Christian Origins*. Vol. 2. Edited by Ron Cameron and Merrill P. Miller. Atlanta: Society of Biblical Literature, forthcoming.

Strelan, Rick. *Strange Acts: Studies in the Cultural World of the Acts of the Apostles*. BZNW 126. Berlin: De Gruyter, 2004.

Strenksi, Ivan. "At Home with René Girard: Eucharistic Sacrifice, the 'French School' and Joseph De Maistre." In Strenski, *Religion in Relation: Method, Application, and Moral Location*. Columbia: University of South Carolina Press, 1993.

———. *Contesting Sacrifice: Religion, Nationalism and Social Thought in France*. Chicago: University of Chicago Press, 1997.

Stroumsa, Guy G. "Christ's Laughter: Docetic Origins Reconsidered." *JECS* 12 (2004): 267–88.

———. "The End of Sacrifice. Religious Mutations of Late Antiquity." In *Empsychoi logoi—religious innovations in antiquity: Studies in honour of Pieter Willem van der Horst*. Edited by Alberdina Houtman, Albert de Jong, and Magda Misset-van de Weg, 30–46. Leiden: Brill, 2008.

———. *La fin du sacrifice: Les mutations religeuses de l'Antiquité Tardive*. Paris: Odile Jacob, 2005. Translated by Susan Emanuel. *The End of Sacrifice: Religious Transformations in Late Antiquity*. Chicago: University of Chicago Press, 2009.

Struck, Peter T. *Birth of the Symbol: Ancient Readers at the Limits of Their Texts*. Princeton: Princeton University Press, 2004.

———. "Speech Acts and the Stakes of Hellenism in Late Antiquity." In *Magic and Ritual in the Ancient World*. Edited by Paul Mirecki and Marvin Meyer. Leiden: Brill, 2002.

Svenbro, Jespter. "La *thusia et le partage*. Remarques sur la 'destruction' par le feu dans le sacrifice grec." In *La cuisine et l'autel: les sacrifices en questions dans les sociétés de la Méditerranée ancienne*. Edited by Stella Georgoudi, Renée Piettre, and Francis Schmidt, 217–25. BEHE SR124. Turnhout: Brepols, 2005.

Swain, Simon. *Hellenism and Empire: Language, Classicism and Power in the Greek World, AD 50–250*. Oxford: Oxford University Press, 1996.

Swartz, David. *Culture and Power: The Sociology of Pierre Bourdieu*. Chicago: University of Chicago Press, 1997.

———. "Bubbling Blood and Rolling Bones: Agency and Teleology in Rabbinic Myth." In *Antike Mythen: Medien, Transformationen und Konstruktionen*. Edited by Ueli Dill and Christine Walde, 432–52. Berlin: De Gruyter, 2009.

———. "Judaism and the Idea of Ancient Ritual Theory." In *Jewish Studies at the Cross-roads of History and Anthropology: Tradition, Authority, Diaspora*. Edited by R. S. Boustan, O. Kosansky, and M. Rustow 194–317. Philadelphia: University of Pennsylvania Press, 2011.

———. *Place and Person in Ancient Judaism: Describing the Yom Kippur Sacrifice*. International Rennert Center Guest Lecture Series 9. Ramat Gan: Bar-Ilan University, Faculty of Jewish Studies, 2001.

———. "The Semiotics of the Priestly Vestments in Ancient Judaism." In *Sacrifice in Religious Experience*. Edited by A. Baumgarten, 57–80. Leiden: Brill, 2002.

———. "The Topography of Blood in Mishnah Yoma." In *Jewish Blood: Metaphor and Reality in Jewish History, Culture and Religion*. Edited by M. Hart, 70–82. London: Routledge, 2009.

Swartz, Michael D., and J. Yahalom, eds. and trans. *Avodah: An Anthology of Ancient Poetry for Yom Kippur*. University Park: Pennsylvania State University Press, 2005.

Sweeney, Marvin A. *Isaiah 1–39: With an Introduction to Prophetic Literature*. Vol. 16: *The Forms of Old Testament Literature*. Grand Rapids: William B. Eerdmans, 1996.

Syme, Ronald. *The Roman Revolution*. Oxford: Clarendon, 1939.

Taylor, Justin. "The Community of Goods among the First Christians and among the Essenes." In *Historical Perspectives: From the Hasmoneans to Bar Kokhba in Light of the Dead Sea Scrolls: Proceedings of the Fourth International Symposium of the Orion Center for the Study of the Dead Sea Scrolls and Associated Literature*. Edited by David Goodblatt, Avital Pinnick, and Daniel R. Schwartz 147–64. STDJ 37. Leiden: Brill, 2001.

Taylor, Mark C. "The Politics of Theo-ry." *JAAR* 59.1 (1991): 1–37.

Thomas, R. F. "The 'Sacrifice' at the End of the Georgics, Aristaeus, and Vergilian Closure." *Classical Philology* 86 (1991): 211–18.

Townsend, Philippa. "Sacrifice and Race in the *Gospel of Judas*." In *Judasevangelium und Codex Tchacos: Studien zur religionsgeschichtlichen Verortung einer gnostischen Schriftensammlung*. Wissenschaftliche Untersuchungen zum Neuen Testament. Edited by Gregor Wurst and Enno Popkes. Tübingen: Mohr Siebeck, forthcoming 2011.

Tremlin, Tod. *Minds and Gods: The Cognitive Foundations of Religion*. Oxford: Oxford University Press, 2006.

Trout, Dennis. "Christianizing the Nolan Countryside: Animal Sacrifice at the Tomb of St. Felix." *JECS* 3 (1995): 281–98.

———. "Re-Textualizing Lucretia: Cultural Subversion in the City Of God." *JECS* 2 (1994): 53–70.

Turner, Victor. *Dramas, Fields, and Metaphors: Symbolic Action in Human Society*. Ithaca: Cornell University Press, 1974.

———. *The Forest of Symbols: Aspects of Ndembu Ritual*. Ithaca: Cornell University Press, 1967.

Tylor, E. G. *Primitive Culture*. 2 vols. London: John Murray; New York: Putnam, 1920.

Ullucci, Daniel. "The End of Animal Sacrifice." Ph.D. diss., Brown University, 2009.

Urbach, Ephraim E. *The Sages: Their Concepts and Beliefs*. Translated by Israel Abrahams. Cambridge: Harvard University Press, 1987.

Van Baal, Jan. "Offering, Sacrifice and Gift." *Numen* 23.3 (December 1976): 161–78.

Van Bekkum, W. J. "Anti-Christian Polemics in Hebrew Liturgical Poetry of the Sixth and Seventh Centuries." In *Early Christian Poetry*. Edited by J. Den Boeft and A. Hilhorst, 297–308. Leiden: Brill, 1993.

Van Dam, Raymond. *Leadership and Community in Late Antique Gaul*. Berkeley: University of California Press, 1985.

————. *The Roman Revolution of Constantine*. Cambridge: Cambridge University Press, 2007.

Van Henten, Jan Willem. *The Maccabean Martyrs as Saviors of the Jewish People: A Study of 2 and 4 Maccabees.* Leiden: Brill, 1997.

Van Straten, Folkert. "Ancient Greek Animal Sacrifice: Gift, Ritual Slaughter, Communion, Food Supply, or What? Some Thoughts on Simple Explanations of a Complex Ritual." In *La cuisine et l'autel: Les sacrifices en questions dans les sociétés de la Méditerranée ancienne.* Edited by Stella Georgoudi, Renée Piettre, and Francis Schmidt, 15–29. BEHE SR124. Turnhout: Brepols, 2005.

Van Wees, Hans. "The Law of Gratitude: Reciprocity in Anthropological Theory." In *Reciprocity in Ancient Greece.* Edited by Christopher Gill, Norman Postlethwaite, and Richard Seaford, 13–50. New York: Oxford University Press, 1998.

Várhelyi, Zsuzsanna. *The Religion of Senators in the Roman Empire.* Cambridge: Cambridge University Press, 2010.

————. "The Specters of Roman Imperialism: The Live Burials of Gauls and Greeks at Rome." *Classical Antiquity* 26 (2007): 277–304.

Vetters, Hermann. "Domitianterrasse und Domitiangasse (Grabungen 1960–61)." *Jahreshefte des Österreichischen archäologischen Instituts* 50 (1972–73): Beiblatt 311–30.

Via, Dan O. *Kerygma and Comedy in the New Testament: A Structuralist Approach to Hermeneutic.* Philadelphia: Fortress, 1975.

Volokhine, Youri. "Les déplacements pieux en Égypte pharaonique: Sites et pratiques cultuelles." In *Pilgrimage and Holy Space in Late Antique Egypt.* Edited by David Frankfurter 51–98. RGRW 134. Leiden: Brill, 1998.

Wald, Gayle Freda. *Crossing the Line: Racial Passing in Twentieth-Century U.S. Literature and Culture.* Durham: Duke University Press, 2000.

Watson, Lindsay. *Arae: The Curse Poetry of Antiquity.* ARCA: Classical and Medieval Texts, Papers, and Monographs 26. Leeds: F. Cairns, 1991.

Watts, James W. "Review of *Beyond Sacred Violence* by Kathryn McClymond." *Religion* 39 (2009): 300–302.

Weber, Max. *The Sociology of Religion.* Translated by Ephraim Fischoff. Boston: Beacon, 1963.

Weinfeld, Moshe. "The Loyalty Oath in the Ancient Near East." *UF* 8 (1976): 379–414.

Weiser, Alfons. *Die Apostelgeschichte: Kapitel 1–12.* Ökumenische Taschenbuch-Kommentar 5/1. Gütersloh: Gerd Mohn; Würzburg: Echter, 1981.

Weiser, Alfons. "Das Gottesurteil über Hananias und Saphira." *TGl* 69 (1979): 150–51.

West, M. L. *The Orphic Poems.* Oxford: Oxford Univerity Press, 1983.

White, Hayden. *The Content of the Form: Narrative Discourse and Historical Representation.* Baltimore: Johns Hopkins University Press, 1987.

Whitehouse, Harvey. *Modes of Religiosity: A Cognitive Theory of Religious Transmission.* Walnut Creek, Calif.: AltaMira, 2004.

Whitehouse, Harvey, and James Laidlaw, eds. *Ritual and Memory: Toward a Comparative Anthropology of Religion.* Walnut Creek, Calif.: AltaMira, 2004.

Whitmarsh, Tim. "'Greece Is the World': Exile and Identity in the Second Sophistic." In *Being Greek under Rome.* Edited by Simon Goldhill 269–305. Cambridge: Cambridge University Press, 2001.

————. *Greek Literature and the Roman Empire: The Politics of Imitation.* Oxford: Oxford University Press, 2001.

Wilkinson, John. *Jerusalem Pilgrims before the Crusades.* Warminster: Aris and Phillips, 1977.

Williams, J. G., ed. *The Girard Reader.* New York: Crossroad, 1996.

Williams, Jonathan. "Religion and Roman Coins." In *A Companion to Roman Religion.* Edited by Jörg Rüpke. Blackwell Companions to the Ancient World. Malden, Mass.: Blackwell, 2007.

Williamson Jr., Lamar. "The Use of the Ananias and Sapphira Story (Acts 5:1–11) in the Patristic Period." Ph.D. diss., Yale University, 1962.

Wills, Lawrence M. "The Death of the Hero and the Violent Death of Jesus." In *Religion and Violence: The Biblical Heritage.* Edited by David A. Bernat and Jonathan Klawans, 79–99. Sheffield: Sheffield Phoenix, 2007.

———. *The Quest of the Historical Gospel: Mark, John and the Origins of the Gospel Genre.* London: Routledge, 1997.

Wipszycka, Ewa. "Considérations sur les persécutions contre les Chrétiens: Qui frappaient-elles?" In *Poikilia: Études offertes à Jean-Pierre Vernant.*Présentation de Marcel Détienne Nicolecoraux Claude mossé, Pierre Vidal-Naguet, 397–405. Paris: Éditions de l'École des Hautes-Études en Sciences Sociales, 1987.

Woolf, Gregory. "*Polis*-Religion and Its Alternatives in the Roman Provinces." In *Römische Reichsreligion und Provinzialreligion.* Edited by Hubert Canick and Jörge Rüpke, 71–84. Tübingen: Mohr Siebeck, 1997.

Yoyotte, Jean. "Héra d'Héliopolis et le sacrifice humain." *Annuaire de l'École Pratique des Hautes-études, 5è Section—Sciences Religieuses* 89 (1980–1981): 31–102.

Yuval, Israel J. "The Myth of Jewish Exile from the Land of Israel: A Demonstration of Irenic Scholarship." *Common Knowledge* 12 (2006): 16–33.

Zecchi, Marco. "On the Offering of Honey in the Graeco-Roman Temples." *Aegyptus* 77 (1997): 71–83.

Zeitlin, Froma. "The Motif of Corrupted Sacrifice in Aeschylus' Oresteia." *Transactions of the American Philosophical Association* 96 (1965): 463–508.

Zeitlin, Solomon. "The Legend of the Ten Martyrs and Its Apocalyptic Origins." *JQR* 36 (1945–1946): 1–16.

Ziegler, Yael. *Promises to Keep: The Oath in Biblical Narrative.* VTSup 120. Leiden: Brill, 2008.

Zivie, Alain, and Roger Lichtenberg. "Les momies d'animaux." *Dossiers d'archéologie* 252 (2000): 52–55.

———. "Les chats du Bubasteion de Saqqâra: État de la question et perspectives." In *Egyptology at the Dawn of the Twenty-First Century: Proceedings of the 8th International Congress of Egyptologists.* Vol. 2. Edited by Zahi Hawass, 605–11. Cairo: American University in Cairo Press, 2003.

———. "The Cats of the Goddess Bastet." In *Divine Creatures: Animal Mummies in Ancient Egypt.* Edited by Salima Ikram 106–19. Cairo: American University in Cairo Press, 2005.

Zivie-Coche, Christiane. "Pharaonic Egypt." In *Gods and Men in Egypt.* Translated by David Lorton. Ithaca: Cornell University Press, 2004.

Zohar, Zvi. "The Yom Kippur 'Avodah Service: Content, Function, and Significance" (Hebrew). *Association of Jewish Studies Review* 14 (1989): 1–28.

Zulay, M. *The Liturgical Poems of Yannai, Collected from Geniza-Manuscripts and Other Sources* (Hebrew). Berlin: Schocken, 1938.

Zunz, Leopold. *Die synagogale Poesie des Mittelalters.* 2nd ed. Repr., Hildesheim: G. Olms, 1967. First ed. Berlin: J. Springer, 1855.

{ INDEX }

abandonment of blood sacrifice, 4
Ackerman, Robert, 24n8
alimentary communion, 6
altars, 148, 155–60
Altar of Victory, 170, 175, 180n14
Ambrose, 175, 259
ancestral tradition, 219–24
animal sacrifices: debates on, 57–74; nonanimal
  versus, 72n35; relationship to agriculture,
  animal husbandry, and land of, 55n43
antisymbolic symbolism, 107
Appollonius of Tyana, 207–8, 210
arena combat, 154, 155
Aristedes, Aelius, 221, 230n41
Aristophanes, 44–45
atheism, 164n26
Athenagoras, 148–49, 153, 163n19
Augustus, 15

Bacis, 44, 45
Beard, Mary, 14
Belayche, Nicole, 14
Biale, David, 13–14
Birds of Aristophanes, 44–45
blood manipulation, 235–50; in application of
  blood, 238; in bird offerings, 238; in Christian
  sacrifice, 17; consequences of ritual errors
  and, 240–41; in consumption of blood
  penalty, 242–43; drained animal's blood in,
  237–38; intended result of, 239; invalidation
  of, 240–42; in Israelite practices, 12–14, 17; in
  Jewish sacrificial systems, 243–46; overview
  of, 237–38; purpose debates of, 238; in
  rabbinic versus cultic tradition, 245; ritual
  errors and, 239–43, 246–48; socio-cultic rank
  in, 239; timeliness of, 241, 242–43; types of,
  238–39. *See also* Mishnah
bonds of flesh and blood, 214–31; ethnic identity
  and sacrifices and, 215; kinship connections
  through sacrifice and, 214, 225n2; "old ways"
  question of, 221–22; Porphyry on sacrifice,
  kinship, and community and, 215–17, 219,
  221; sacrifice, ancestral tradition, and empire
  with, 219–24; universalism and imperialism
  in, 217–19, 229n35
Boustan, Ra'anan S., 22, 23

Boyarin, Daniel, 17
Burkert, Walter, 8–9, 10, 204, 205

Caesar, Julius, 133, 134, 135, 136
Castelli, Elizabeth, 17
cat sacrifice, 88–89n13
Catiline, 15, 151
Celsus, 195–96
Center for Comparative Studies of Ancient
  Societies, 9, 10
centrist Christians and Judaism, 68, 69, 74n53
cereal offerings, 13
cheating the gods, 149–50, 163–64n22
Christian practices, 4, 16–18, 146–50; of
  circumcision, 21–22; condemnation of
  sacrifice in, 22; data reevaluation in, 67–69;
  martyrdom in, 16–18; metaphorical sacrifice
  in, 21–22, 23; Roman piety of sacrifice in,
  151, 154; social/communal role of sacrifice in,
  5–7; substitutionary atonement in, 5
Chrysippus, 46
Cicero: on death of Mucius Scaevola, 132; on
  drinking of human blood, 15; on killing of
  Tiberius Gracchus, 127–28; on Mancinus
  (Hostilus), 128
circumcision of Jesus Christ, 21–22, 251–64
civic religion: Athenians gods of, 43; in classical
  Athens, 42; everyday exchange religion
  versus, 40–41, 43; literacy and, 54n26; literate
  specialist religion versus, 41, 42; particular
  deities and, 55n35; Stowers on, 36, 37. *See
  also* polis religion
Clancy, Jennifer, 17
cognitive science of religion, 53n14, 72n34
Column of Trajan, 142–44, 143f, 144f, 145f, 156,
  157, 159, 159f, 162n4
community. *See* social/communal role of
  sacrifice
consumption of sacrificial food, 9–10, 28n56;
  apportioning of meat in, 9, 13, 14–15; sharing
  by humans and gods in, 14–15
critique model, 58–60, 70n8
crocodiles, 81, 82
Cuisine du sacrifice en pays grec, La (ed.
  Detienne and Vernat), 9
cult of Diana at Aricia, 5, 24–25nn8–9

Printed in the USA/Agawam, MA
December 16, 2016

645165.005